2010 Index of Economic Freedom

2010 Index of Economic Freedom

Ambassador Terry Miller

Kim R. Holmes, Ph.D.

with Anthony B. Kim, Daniella Markheim,
James M. Roberts, and Caroline Walsh

THE WALL STREET JOURNAL.

The Heritage Foundation
214 Massachusetts Avenue, NE
Washington, DC 20002
(202) 546-4400
heritage.org

The Wall Street Journal
Dow Jones & Company, Inc.
200 Liberty Street
New York, NY 10281
(212) 416-2000
www.wsj.com

Cover images by Dreamstime and iStockphoto
ISBN: 978-0-89195-281-7
ISSN: 1095-7308

Table of Contents

Foreword

There's no avoiding the truth: The year 2009 will go down as the worst for global economic freedom since the inflation and wage and price controls of the 1970s, and maybe since the industrial policy and monetary chaos of the 1930s. Many governments and their political agents have used the financial panic and recession as an opportunity to reassert control across the private economy. As I write this in November 2009, the damage is still unfolding, though there are some signs that a backlash on behalf of liberty may be building.

The political assault began with the Panic of '08 that frightened voters and created a clamor for governments to do something. Many have responded around the world with a reflation binge, both monetary and fiscal, among other interventions. The monetary stimulus in particular has helped to stem the financial panic and encouraged an incipient recovery. But the very magnitude of the stimulus, and its eventual cost in higher taxes or perhaps inflation, raises doubts about whether the current recovery can become a durable expansion.

The most striking fact of this year is how many governments are repeating policy mistakes from previous eras. The spending spree is rooted in the so-called Keynesian multiplier, which asserts that one dollar of government outlays stimulates 1.5 times that amount in greater output. Harvard's Robert Barro, among others, demolished this claim a generation ago, but here we go again. Britain's Labour government has little growth to show for its historic reflation campaign, and with a jobless rate of 10.2 percent amid a tepid U.S. recovery, so far Mr. Barro seems more right than the Keynesians.

Meanwhile, the Federal Reserve's extraordinary and continuing monetary stimulus is causing commodity prices to climb and is giving heartburn to world finance ministers who see their currencies rising sharply against the dollar. A whiff of "beggar thy neighbor" competitive devaluation is in the air, the kind of policy the U.S. last tried in the 1970s to destructive effect. The danger is that the entire U.S. establishment, from the Treasury Secretary to

Wall Street, appears to want a weaker dollar in the name of boosting exports. But if a nation could devalue its way to prosperity, Argentina would be paradise. The Fed will eventually have to defend the dollar.

The U.S. is also tempting slower growth with its policies across the microeconomy: a de facto government takeover of health care, a gigantic new tax on carbon energy, the political allocation of capital in energy and autos and so much else, new rules to expand union membership, nationalization of the mortgage market, a hostility to freer trade, and much higher taxes to pay for it all. All of these either had already occurred or were possible at year end, and all impose burdens on private risk-taking and investment that will reduce U.S. prosperity over time.

Amid all of this, it is surprising that the U.S. has fallen only two places in this year's *Index of Economic Freedom*. This reflects the fact that other nations have made similar policy mistakes and perhaps is testimony to the residual strength of U.S. law and institutions. But another lesson of Argentina is that a nation's prosperity must be continually earned and that the rest of the world may not join America if it insists on weakening itself. As columnist Charles Krauthammer has put it, "Decline is a choice."

In this sense, the very global free-market revolution that America did so much to promote over the past 30 years may be a barrier against a repeat of the 1930s or 1970s. The Chi-

nese can't afford stagnation, and they have seen the fruits of greater economic freedom. India continues to shake off its socialist past and wants no part of Western Europe's malaise. The world's investors can move at the flip of an electronic switch. The reality of global competition and instant capital flows means that wise policy decisions will be rewarded faster than ever before.

The larger lesson of this painful year is that old economic lessons must be retaught to a new generation. Milton Friedman must be reread, and Margaret Thatcher's gift for explaining economic liberty to the common man must be relearned by new political leaders. My guess is that this reeducation will become easier as the consequences of the current wave of government intervention become clearer to voters around the world.

Already in the U.S., a populist reaction is forming against the willy-nilly expansion of state power. It is too soon to know how this will play out, but a recurring theme of American history has been resilience and revival. The *Index of Economic Freedom* exists to provide a map for that revival, and its purpose has never been more vital.

Paul A. Gigot
Editorial Page Editor
The Wall Street Journal
November 2009

Preface

In the concluding chapter of their book *Free to Choose*, the late Milton and Rose Friedman were optimistic that freedom would prevail:

> Fortunately, we are waking up. We are again recognizing the dangers of an over-governed society, coming to understand that good objectives can be perverted by bad means, that reliance on the freedom of people to control their own lives in accordance with their own values is the surest way to achieve the full potential of a great society.

Though published in 1980, this observation is astonishingly relevant today.

Over the past year, many have wondered whether the global system of free enterprise could survive what has turned out to be the deepest recession of the post–World War II era. Certainly, anyone looking at the massive stimulus spending undertaken in the United States, coupled with government bailouts or takeovers of financial firms and auto manufacturers, could be forgiven for doubting the future of capitalism in America. Proposals for nationalization of health care and an energy cap-and-trade program put the United States on a path that diverges sharply from its historical leadership in the quest for greater freedom, both economic and political.

It might surprise readers in the United States to know that proposals for greater government control of economic activity have not taken the world by storm. In fact, there has been little global demand for a shift to central planning or extensive state ownership of private businesses in the name of recovery and stability. Too many people in too many countries have lived under such systems too recently. They understand the costs of big government and have no intention of giving up economic freedoms only recently won. The 2010 *Index of Economic Freedom* documents a pattern of countries around the world holding true to the course of economic liberalization. Even in the United States, it was clear by the end of 2009, with opposition to big-government programs in health care and climate change increasing, that the American people were waking up.

Despite the past year's follies in responding to the global economic slowdown, our free-market system and capitalism are not at the edge of catastrophic breakdown. But a revitalized commitment to economic freedom is essential to our well-being in the future. As the late Irving Kristol noted, "once the idea gets around that we are in a profound crisis and that only 'drastic action' by Washington can save us—then it will be time to head for the storm cellars."

The 2010 *Index of Economic Freedom*, our 16th edition, offers a good starting place from which to reflect on the fundamental principles of capitalism and recommit ourselves to economic freedom.

The *Index* began to record the worldwide march of freedom and free exchange shortly after the fall of the Berlin Wall. Over the past 16 years, it has evolved into an essential policy guide that empirically analyzes and demonstrates the link between economic freedom and prosperity in countries around the world. The *Index* has witnessed profound advances as the cause of freedom has swept the globe. Political authorities have found themselves increasingly held accountable by those they govern, and economies with more openness have led the world in a startling burst of innovation and economic growth.

Economies that have risen up the *Index* rankings have achieved levels of prosperity far higher than are found in countries where economic freedoms are constrained by the heavy hand of government. Leaders who have not joined the march of freedom have left their citizens lagging behind and even, in the worst cases, stuck in poverty or destitution. Such failures are inexcusable—and preventable.

In addition to the rankings and analysis of the results, the 2010 *Index* contains three extraordinary chapters that examine facets of economic freedom that are particularly relevant to today's policy debates.

• In chapter 2, former Secretary of Labor Elaine L. Chao, now a Heritage Foundation Distinguished Fellow, highlights the importance of free trade in fostering economic recovery.

• In chapter 3, Dr. Derek Scissors, Senior Economic Research Fellow in The Heritage Foundation's Asian Studies Center, looks into crisis performance among Asian countries and empirically documents that economic freedom, vital to long-term economic stability and growth, also positions a country for a quicker and more positive response to short-term stresses.

• In chapter 4, James Roberts, Research Fellow for Economic Freedom and Growth in The Heritage Foundation's Center for International Trade and Economics, explores the critical relationship between economic freedom and the free flow of information.

Our confidence in economic freedom is being tested. The 2010 *Index of Economic Freedom*, like its predecessors, provides ample evidence of the benefits of economic freedom, both to individuals and to societies. People in economically free societies live longer and healthier lives. They enjoy greater political freedom and can better defend their human rights. Economic freedom reduces poverty, opening the gates of prosperity to ever more people around the world.

Economic freedom is not a dogmatic ideology. It represents instead the rejection of dogma and the embrace of diverse and even competing strategies for economic advancement. It is, however, revolutionary in intent and result. By dispersing economic power and decision-making throughout an economy, economic freedom empowers ordinary people with greater opportunity and more choices.

No other systems that have been tried have come close in terms of providing broad-based prosperity. Experience teaches that even the best efforts of central planners and bureaucrats do not lead to sustainable growth. As the 20th anniversary of the fall of the Berlin Wall reminds all of us, countries that have tried that approach have failed economically as well as politically.

The surer path to prosperity and a greater society is the path of freedom: letting individuals decide for themselves how best to achieve their dreams and aspirations and those of their families. It is that path whose course we map in the *Index of Economic Freedom*.

Edwin J. Feulner, Ph.D., President
The Heritage Foundation
November 2009

Acknowledgments

The *Index of Economic Freedom* is now in its 16th year of publication. Since 1995, countless individuals have contributed to the excellence and vitality of the *Index*, and this 2010 edition, like its predecessors, is the product of collaborative effort and continuing support from people and organizations around the world.

While it is impossible to mention them all, we wish to express our profound gratitude to the many individuals, especially those at The Heritage Foundation, who have made such valuable contributions to this 16th edition of the *Index of Economic Freedom*. Under the vision and leadership of Dr. Edwin J. Feulner, President of The Heritage Foundation, the *Index* has evolved into a key economic policy guide for various readers.

The Heritage Foundation's Center for International Trade and Economics (CITE) produces the *Index*. The CITE team of Anthony Kim, Daniella Markheim, James Roberts, and Caroline Walsh were responsible for grading the 10 components of economic freedom, analyzing the results, and producing the country reports included in this edition. Interns Charlotte Cannon, Elizabeth Hamrick, Stephan Isaac, Peter Neville, Joshua Robbins, Lauren Salz, Jin Sun, and Allison Turbiville also contributed substantial research.

Others at The Heritage Foundation also made valuable contributions to this year's *Index*. In the Kathryn and Shelby Cullom Davis Institute for International Studies, Janice A. Smith, Special Assistant and Policy Coordinator for the Vice President, and Amber Schwartz, Assistant to the Vice President, provided important production assistance. Ariel Cohen, James Phillips, and Ray Walser of the Douglas and Sarah Allison Center for Foreign Policy Studies wrote country background paragraphs and contributed their regional expertise, as did Lisa Curtis, Bruce Klingner, Derek Scissors, and Director Walter Lohman of the Asian Studies Center and Sally McNamara and Brett Schaefer of the Margaret Thatcher Center for Freedom.

The professionalism of Vice President of Information Technology Michael Spiller and his team helped enormously. A particular debt is owed to Director of Online Communications Tim McGovern, Maria Sousa, and Roger Spurzem, Jim Lawruk, Steve Sharman, Joel Smith, and Martha Galante for placing the entire *Index* on the Heritage Web site. This year, armed with valuable Web traffic input from Isabel Isidro, project coordinator of Online Strategy, the Heritage IT staff worked tirelessly to revamp the contents and design of the *Index* Web site and, most important, to increase user access to the raw data behind our assessments through the "Explore the Data" function.

In Creative Services, Director Therese Pennefather, Elizabeth Brewer, Ralph Buglass, and Teresa Matous were responsible for all aspects of the production process, handling design and layout for the *Index* and each subsidiary product. With an emphasis on reader accessibility, they developed and formatted world and country maps, charts, and tables, all of which bring to life the quantitative data underpinning the 2010 *Index* findings.

Once again, we wish to express our deepest appreciation to Senior Editor Richard Odermatt, who is responsible for final review of the completed text, and Senior Copy Editor William T. Poole, who bears the primary responsibility for editing the entire book. Every year, their professionalism, commitment, and attention to detail are essential to maintaining consistency of tone and making the *Index* a reality. We are likewise grateful to Senior Data Graphics Editor John Fleming, who carefully reviewed every one of the many charts and tables included in the book.

The continuing support from Phil Truluck, Executive Vice President of The Heritage Foundation; Becky Norton Dunlop, Vice President, External Relations; Mike Franc, Vice President, Government Relations; and Michael Gonzalez, Vice President, Communications, is sincerely appreciated. We also thank Director of Coalition Relations Bridgett Wagner, Center for Data Analysis Director William Beach, and Deputy Director of Government Relations James Dean for their insightful contributions to the *Index*.

Countless individuals serving with various accounting firms, businesses, research organizations, U.S. government agencies, foreign embassies, and other organizations again cooperated by providing us with the data used in the *Index*. Their assistance is much appreciated. As always, we acknowledge our enduring debt to Heritage Trustee Ambassador J. William Middendorf II, who originally encouraged us to undertake such a study of global economic freedom.

Very special thanks go to Paul Gigot and Mary Anastasia O'Grady at *The Wall Street Journal*, whose partnership and support we truly cherish.

Finally, we would like to express our appreciation to the many people who respond so enthusiastically, year after year, to the *Index of Economic Freedom*. The support and encouragement of people in all parts of the world continue to inspire The Heritage Foundation and *The Wall Street Journal* in their ongoing collaboration on this important work. We hope this year's effort meets the expectations of our supporters as well as the thoughtful critics who so often have provided the insights that enable us to continue to improve the *Index*.

Ambassador Terry Miller
Kim R. Holmes, Ph.D.
November 2009

Executive Highlights

The 2010 *Index of Economic Freedom* covers 183 countries around the world, ranking 179 of them with an economic freedom score based on 10 measures of economic openness, regulatory efficiency, the rule of law, and competitiveness. The basic principles of economic freedom emphasized in the *Index* are individual empowerment, equitable treatment, and the promotion of competition.

The results of the 2010 *Index* include the following:

• **Four Asia–Pacific economies continue to lead the world in economic freedom.** Hong Kong maintains its position as the world's freest economy, a distinction it has enjoyed for 16 consecutive years. Singapore remains close, ranked as the world's second freest economy. Australia and New Zealand, ranked 3rd and 4th this year, have solidified their position at the top of the rankings. As in 2009, a total of seven economies have attained "free" status in the *Index* rankings, although the composition of this group has changed a bit, with Switzerland moving in and the United States dropping out.

• **Every region continues to maintain at least one of the top 20 freest economies**, but there has been noticeable reshuffling within this highly ranked group. With its economic freedom score dropping by 2.2 points, Iceland's ranking slid to near the bottom of the top 20, while Switzerland moved up three places to 6th place. The United Kingdom is now out of the top 10. Nine of the 20 freest economies are European, led by Ireland, Switzerland, and Denmark. Six of the top 20 are from the Asia–Pacific region, and two are from North America. The U.S. dropped two spots in the rankings and now trails Canada. The other regions are represented by one country each: Chile (South and Central America/Caribbean region); Mauritius (Sub-Saharan Africa region); and Bahrain (Middle East/North Africa region). Mauritius recorded impressive progress and is now ranked as the world's 12th freest economy.

• The positive relationship between economic freedom and prosperity is confirmed yet again in the 2010 *Index*. Gross domestic product per capita is much higher in countries that score well in the *Index*. The positive relationship holds true at all levels of economic freedom but becomes even more dramatic as economic freedom increases. Chart 1 shows a strong positive relationship between the level of economic freedom and GDP per capita.

• Economic freedom improves the overall quality of life, promotes political and social progress, and supports environmental protection. The 2010 *Index* provides strong evidence that economic freedom has far-reaching positive impacts on various aspects of human development. Economic freedom correlates with poverty reduction, a variety of desirable social indicators, democratic governance, and environmental sustainability.

With respect to the economic crisis of 2008–2009, the evidence in the *Index* supports several preliminary conclusions:[1]

• Countries diverged sharply in their response to the global crisis: Many continued to promote economic freedom; others did not. Regrettably, attacks on the free market, fueled by the economic slowdown and the political appeal of quick interventionist remedies,

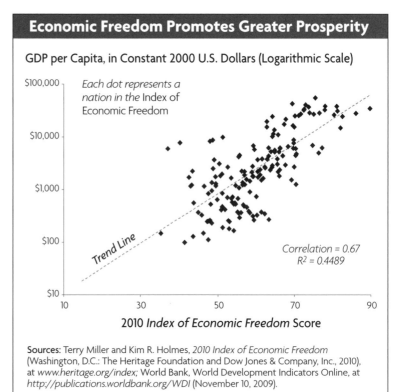

Economic Freedom Promotes Greater Prosperity

GDP per Capita, in Constant 2000 U.S. Dollars (Logarithmic Scale)

Each dot represents a nation in the Index of Economic Freedom

Trend Line

Correlation = 0.67
R^2 = 0.4489

2010 *Index of Economic Freedom* Score

Sources: Terry Miller and Kim R. Holmes, *2010 Index of Economic Freedom* (Washington, D.C.: The Heritage Foundation and Dow Jones & Company, Inc., 2010), at *www.heritage.org/index;* World Bank, World Development Indicators Online, at *http://publications.worldbank.org/WDI* (November 10, 2009).

Chart 1 ☎ heritage.org

gained strong momentum in some countries—and with far-reaching effects. Exactly half of the major economies curtailed economic freedom to some degree through various interventionist measures. Perhaps more significant for the long-term progress of economic freedom, the other half did not.

• As a result of increasing government interference in economic activity in many countries, overall progress toward greater economic freedom has been interrupted. The average economic freedom score for the 2010 *Index* is 59.4, down 0.1 point from 2009. This is only the second time in the history of the *Index* that average scores for countries measured in successive years have declined.[2]

---

1. The 2010 *Index* is based primarily on data covering the period from July 2008 through June 2009. It thus captures only the early effects of the global financial crisis and recession and some of the policy responses by governments. Future editions of the *Index* should provide a more complete picture.

2. The 2009 *Index* expanded its coverage to 183 countries, including for the first time Afghanistan, Bhutan, Comoros, Dominica, Eritrea, Kiribati, Liberia, Liechtenstein, Macau, Maldives, Micronesia, Papua New Guinea, Saint Lucia, Saint Vincent and the Grenadines, Samoa, São Tomé and Príncipe, Seychelles, Timor-Leste, Tonga, and

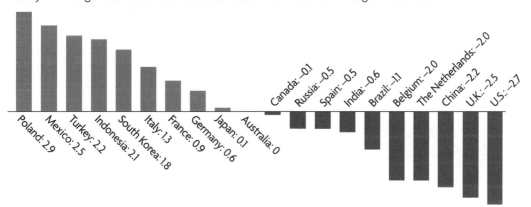

How the Largest Economies Fared

One-year changes in *Index of Economic Freedom* scores for the 20 largest economies

Poland: 2.9 · Mexico: 2.5 · Turkey: 2.2 · Indonesia: 2.1 · South Korea: 1.8 · Italy: 1.3 · France: 0.9 · Germany: 0.6 · Japan: 0.1 · Australia: 0 · Canada: −0.1 · Russia: −0.5 · Spain: −0.5 · India: −0.6 · Brazil: −1.1 · Belgium: −2.0 · The Netherlands: −2.0 · China: −2.2 · U.K.: −2.5 · U.S.: −2.7

Source: Terry Miller and Kim R. Holmes, *2010 Index of Economic Freedom* (Washington, D.C.: The Heritage Foundation and Dow Jones & Company, Inc., 2010), at *www.heritage.org/index*.

Chart 2 ☎ heritage.org

• **Increased government spending did not improve economic crisis performance.** In light of the global financial and economic storm, many advanced economies' governments have stepped up spending to promote growth and employment. The early evidence is that such spending has not worked.

Vanuatu. The expansion of the country coverage resulted in a noticeable decline of the overall economic freedom score for the 2009 *Index*, compared to the 2008 *Index*, which covered 161 countries. For countries covered in both the 2008 and 2009 editions of the *Index*, average scores increased.

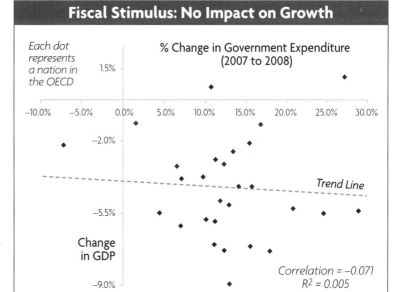

Fiscal Stimulus: No Impact on Growth

Each dot represents a nation in the OECD

% Change in Government Expenditure (2007 to 2008)

Trend Line

Change in GDP

Correlation = −0.071
$R^2 = 0.005$

Notes: GDP changes are from Q2 2008 to Q2 2009; figures are based on the 28 OECD countries for which data are available.

Sources: Terry Miller and Kim R. Holmes, *2010 Index of Economic Freedom* (Washington, D.C.: The Heritage Foundation and Dow Jones & Company, Inc., 2010), at *www.heritage.org/index;* Organisation for Economic Co-operation and Development, OECD.StatExtract, Quarterly National Accounts: Quarterly Growth Rates of GDP, volume, at *http://stats.oecd.org/index.aspx* (November 19, 2009); Organisation for Economic Co-operation and Development, OECD Economic Outlook No. 85 Annex Tables, June 2009, at *http://www.oecd.org/document/61/0,3343,en_2649_34573_2483901_1_1_1_1,00.html* (November 19, 2009); International Monetary Fund, World Economic Outlook Database, at *http://www.imf.org/external/pubs/ft/weo/2009/02/weodata/index.aspx* (November 19, 2009).

Chart 3 ☎ heritage.org

2010 *Index of Economic Freedom* World Rankings

World Rank	Country	Overall Score	Change from 2009	Business Freedom	Trade Freedom	Fiscal Freedom	Government Spending	Monetary Freedom	Investment Freedom	Financial Freedom	Property Rights	Freedom from Corruption	Labor Freedom
1	Hong Kong	89.7	−0.3	98.7	90.0	93.0	93.7	83.1	90.0	90.0	90.0	81.0	87.4
2	Singapore	86.1	−1.0	98.2	90.0	90.7	95.3	80.9	75.0	50.0	90.0	92.0	98.9
3	Australia	82.6	0.0	90.3	85.1	61.4	64.9	82.7	80.0	90.0	90.0	87.0	94.9
4	New Zealand	82.1	0.1	99.9	86.0	63.6	51.3	83.1	80.0	80.0	95.0	93.0	88.8
5	Ireland	81.3	−0.9	92.8	87.5	71.1	61.8	79.0	95.0	80.0	90.0	77.0	79.0
6	Switzerland	81.1	1.7	81.2	90.0	68.2	68.9	81.3	80.0	80.0	90.0	90.0	81.8
7	Canada	80.4	−0.1	96.5	88.1	76.7	54.1	75.4	75.0	80.0	90.0	87.0	81.5
8	United States	78.0	−2.7	91.3	86.9	67.5	58.0	78.1	75.0	70.0	85.0	73.0	94.8
9	Denmark	77.9	−1.7	97.9	87.5	35.9	22.0	79.3	90.0	90.0	90.0	93.0	93.7
10	Chile	77.2	−1.1	64.8	88.0	77.5	89.6	73.0	80.0	70.0	85.0	69.0	75.4
11	United Kingdom	76.5	−2.5	94.9	87.5	61.8	41.9	73.7	90.0	80.0	85.0	77.0	72.8
12	Mauritius	76.3	2.0	82.2	85.6	92.5	83.4	71.2	85.0	70.0	60.0	55.0	78.5
13	Bahrain	76.3	1.5	77.8	82.9	99.9	80.8	73.4	65.0	80.0	60.0	54.0	89.4
14	Luxembourg	75.4	0.2	75.1	87.5	65.9	58.5	78.9	95.0	80.0	90.0	83.0	40.4
15	The Netherlands	75.0	−2.0	82.6	87.5	52.0	38.4	81.0	90.0	80.0	90.0	89.0	59.1
16	Estonia	74.7	−1.7	83.1	87.5	80.2	62.2	71.1	90.0	80.0	80.0	66.0	47.0
17	Finland	73.8	−0.7	95.0	87.5	65.4	32.9	78.9	75.0	80.0	90.0	90.0	43.8
18	Iceland	73.7	−2.2	93.0	87.9	75.4	45.8	69.9	65.0	60.0	90.0	89.0	60.8
19	Japan	72.9	0.1	84.5	82.4	67.2	61.1	88.8	60.0	50.0	80.0	73.0	82.4
20	Macau	72.5	0.5	60.0	90.0	77.8	95.2	77.5	80.0	70.0	60.0	54.0	60.0
21	Sweden	72.4	1.9	95.5	87.5	36.7	17.3	79.5	85.0	80.0	95.0	93.0	54.9
22	Austria	71.6	0.4	73.6	87.5	51.2	28.8	79.3	75.0	70.0	90.0	81.0	79.1
23	Germany	71.1	0.6	89.6	87.5	58.3	41.4	79.9	85.0	60.0	90.0	79.0	39.9
24	Cyprus	70.9	0.1	80.3	82.5	72.7	44.8	82.9	70.0	70.0	80.0	64.0	61.5
25	Saint Lucia	70.5	1.7	88.4	71.9	73.2	71.4	80.1	55.0	40.0	70.0	71.0	84.2
26	Georgia	70.4	0.6	87.9	89.1	89.1	65.3	70.2	70.0	60.0	40.0	39.0	93.7
27	Taiwan	70.4	0.9	83.0	85.8	75.9	90.5	79.3	65.0	50.0	70.0	57.0	47.7
28	Botswana	70.3	0.6	70.5	73.9	74.1	67.1	68.8	80.0	70.0	70.0	58.0	70.8
29	Lithuania	70.3	0.3	82.0	87.5	84.6	63.5	70.8	75.0	80.0	55.0	46.0	58.5
30	Belgium	70.1	−2.0	92.9	87.5	42.2	30.0	77.9	80.0	70.0	80.0	73.0	67.1
31	South Korea	69.9	1.8	91.9	70.8	71.1	74.9	77.4	70.0	70.0	70.0	56.0	47.1
32	El Salvador	69.9	0.1	67.4	83.8	85.7	89.2	74.1	75.0	70.0	50.0	39.0	64.5
33	Uruguay	69.8	0.7	63.1	82.8	81.7	72.6	72.3	75.0	30.0	75.0	69.0	76.2
34	Czech Republic	69.8	0.4	65.5	87.5	80.1	45.6	75.6	70.0	80.0	65.0	52.0	76.4
35	Slovakia	69.7	0.3	72.6	87.5	84.0	64.5	78.2	70.0	70.0	55.0	50.0	65.1
36	Spain	69.6	−0.5	75.8	87.5	58.1	54.8	77.7	80.0	80.0	70.0	65.0	47.3
37	Norway	69.4	−0.8	88.8	89.2	50.5	49.8	74.2	65.0	60.0	90.0	79.0	47.1
38	Armenia	69.2	−0.7	83.4	80.5	89.3	90.9	72.9	75.0	70.0	30.0	29.0	70.6
39	Qatar	69.0	3.2	73.7	82.2	99.9	73.7	65.9	45.0	50.0	65.0	65.0	69.1
40	Barbados	68.3	−3.2	90.0	60.5	70.1	54.6	73.1	45.0	60.0	80.0	70.0	80.0

2010 *Index of Economic Freedom* World Rankings

World Rank	Country	Overall Score	Change from 2009	Business Freedom	Trade Freedom	Fiscal Freedom	Government Spending	Monetary Freedom	Investment Freedom	Financial Freedom	Property Rights	Freedom from Corruption	Labor Freedom
41	Mexico	68.3	2.5	83.0	82.0	83.5	85.2	76.3	65.0	60.0	50.0	36.0	61.9
42	Kuwait	67.7	2.1	65.8	82.5	99.9	76.6	66.4	55.0	50.0	50.0	43.0	88.0
43	Oman	67.7	0.7	66.9	83.4	98.5	57.4	64.8	55.0	60.0	50.0	55.0	86.4
44	Israel	67.7	0.1	66.4	87.8	58.4	35.4	78.2	85.0	70.0	70.0	60.0	65.4
45	Peru	67.6	3.0	65.8	85.0	79.5	92.3	81.6	70.0	60.0	40.0	36.0	66.1
46	United Arab Emirates	67.3	2.6	67.4	82.8	99.9	80.9	68.8	35.0	50.0	50.0	59.0	79.3
47	The Bahamas	67.3	−3.0	73.4	42.2	95.2	83.6	72.7	30.0	70.0	70.0	55.0	81.0
48	Malta	67.2	1.1	70.0	87.5	62.5	45.6	78.1	70.0	60.0	80.0	58.0	60.0
49	Saint Vincent and the Grenadines	66.9	2.6	79.9	73.3	72.5	64.1	71.3	55.0	40.0	70.0	65.0	77.6
50	Latvia	66.2	−0.4	72.9	87.5	82.7	57.4	67.0	80.0	50.0	55.0	50.0	59.1
51	Hungary	66.1	−0.6	76.8	87.5	68.6	25.9	74.1	75.0	70.0	65.0	51.0	67.6
52	Jordan	66.1	0.7	65.6	78.8	83.0	55.1	73.2	65.0	60.0	55.0	51.0	74.2
53	Albania	66.0	2.3	68.0	85.8	92.6	74.2	78.7	70.0	70.0	35.0	34.0	52.1
54	Costa Rica	65.9	−0.5	59.3	82.5	82.4	87.0	67.8	70.0	50.0	50.0	51.0	59.0
55	Trinidad and Tobago	65.7	−2.3	59.0	81.7	80.8	72.3	69.3	60.0	70.0	50.0	36.0	78.0
56	Macedonia	65.7	4.5	65.2	83.3	89.3	65.9	79.0	60.0	60.0	35.0	36.0	83.1
57	Jamaica	65.5	0.3	87.0	72.2	74.8	61.8	68.4	85.0	60.0	45.0	31.0	70.0
58	Colombia	65.5	3.2	83.6	72.5	74.3	74.8	74.0	55.0	60.0	50.0	38.0	72.7
59	Malaysia	64.8	0.2	69.9	78.7	84.3	81.3	76.7	30.0	50.0	55.0	51.0	71.4
60	Panama	64.8	0.1	75.9	75.8	82.6	90.0	73.2	65.0	70.0	40.0	34.0	41.3
61	Slovenia	64.7	1.8	83.3	87.5	64.0	46.1	76.0	70.0	50.0	60.0	67.0	43.5
62	Portugal	64.4	−0.5	80.5	87.5	61.0	37.1	79.7	70.0	60.0	70.0	61.0	37.0
63	Romania	64.2	1.0	72.5	87.5	85.8	59.8	73.3	75.0	50.0	40.0	38.0	60.4
64	France	64.2	0.9	86.3	82.5	51.9	17.9	79.7	50.0	70.0	80.0	69.0	54.7
65	Saudi Arabia	64.1	−0.2	84.6	82.5	99.6	68.1	62.3	45.0	50.0	40.0	35.0	74.4
66	Thailand	64.1	1.1	70.7	75.9	74.7	89.8	66.4	40.0	70.0	45.0	35.0	73.6
67	Turkey	63.8	2.2	68.9	86.4	78.1	82.9	70.0	65.0	50.0	50.0	46.0	41.1
68	Montenegro	63.6	5.4	70.1	83.2	90.0	54.4	73.2	55.0	50.0	40.0	34.0	86.4
69	Madagascar	63.2	1.1	71.9	73.2	87.3	88.8	75.4	60.0	50.0	45.0	34.0	46.9
70	Dominica	63.2	0.6	75.4	74.3	67.7	49.8	80.0	65.0	30.0	65.0	60.0	65.2
71	Poland	63.2	2.9	62.2	87.5	74.9	46.8	78.1	60.0	60.0	55.0	46.0	61.5
72	South Africa	62.8	−1.0	73.0	76.0	69.1	76.8	70.2	45.0	60.0	50.0	49.0	59.0
73	Greece	62.7	1.9	77.4	82.5	65.9	41.9	77.6	60.0	60.0	60.0	47.0	55.1
74	Italy	62.7	1.3	77.9	87.5	55.2	31.2	79.0	75.0	60.0	55.0	48.0	58.2
75	Bulgaria	62.3	−2.3	77.8	87.4	86.3	48.3	69.5	50.0	60.0	30.0	36.0	78.1
76	Uganda	62.2	−1.3	57.0	72.1	80.5	85.5	78.1	45.0	60.0	30.0	26.0	88.1
77	Namibia	62.2	−0.2	73.3	87.8	68.3	69.5	71.0	50.0	40.0	30.0	45.0	87.2
78	Cape Verde	61.8	0.5	63.3	65.5	65.6	65.3	74.5	60.0	60.0	65.0	51.0	48.1
79	Belize	61.5	−1.5	74.1	71.5	68.3	74.9	75.6	50.0	50.0	40.0	29.0	81.7
80	Kyrgyz Republic	61.3	−0.5	76.6	75.9	92.9	80.2	62.2	50.0	50.0	25.0	18.0	82.6

2010 *Index of Economic Freedom* World Rankings

World Rank	Country	Overall Score	Change from 2009	Business Freedom	Trade Freedom	Fiscal Freedom	Government Spending	Monetary Freedom	Investment Freedom	Financial Freedom	Property Rights	Freedom from Corruption	Labor Freedom
81	Paraguay	61.3	0.3	60.9	83.5	96.6	91.7	75.4	65.0	60.0	30.0	24.0	26.1
82	Kazakhstan	61.0	0.9	73.5	85.9	87.9	82.1	65.6	30.0	50.0	30.0	22.0	83.1
83	Guatemala	61.0	1.6	52.5	84.0	79.3	93.9	70.2	60.0	50.0	35.0	31.0	54.3
84	Samoa	60.4	0.9	73.2	70.0	79.6	67.5	73.8	30.0	30.0	55.0	44.0	80.8
85	Fiji	60.3	−0.7	63.5	71.0	75.7	80.6	73.6	25.0	60.0	30.0	40.0	84.0
86	Dominican Republic	60.3	1.1	62.4	80.0	85.3	90.2	70.8	55.0	40.0	30.0	30.0	59.6
87	Ghana	60.2	2.1	56.8	65.3	83.5	58.9	65.9	65.0	60.0	50.0	39.0	57.4
88	Mongolia	60.0	−2.8	69.0	79.8	81.9	56.7	66.5	50.0	60.0	30.0	30.0	75.9
89	Lebanon	59.5	1.4	56.6	80.5	91.6	62.8	71.4	55.0	60.0	30.0	30.0	57.0
90	Burkina Faso	59.4	−0.1	60.0	71.3	80.4	80.0	73.0	50.0	50.0	30.0	35.0	64.4
91	Morocco	59.2	1.5	76.1	71.2	68.5	81.5	78.4	60.0	60.0	40.0	35.0	21.7
92	Croatia	59.2	4.1	61.5	87.8	70.3	47.1	75.8	65.0	60.0	40.0	44.0	40.8
93	Rwanda	59.1	4.9	74.5	67.4	77.1	75.6	66.9	40.0	40.0	30.0	30.0	89.2
94	Egypt	59.0	1.0	65.0	74.0	89.7	73.4	64.2	50.0	50.0	40.0	28.0	55.6
95	Tunisia	58.9	1.0	80.2	53.5	74.4	78.5	76.5	35.0	30.0	50.0	44.0	67.4
96	Azerbaijan	58.8	0.8	74.6	77.1	79.5	77.5	62.7	55.0	40.0	20.0	19.0	82.5
97	Tanzania	58.3	0.0	45.5	70.5	80.3	82.6	70.8	65.0	50.0	30.0	30.0	58.4
98	Nicaragua	58.3	−1.5	55.7	82.8	78.4	78.5	64.1	55.0	50.0	25.0	25.0	68.3
99	Honduras	58.3	−0.4	63.0	83.7	84.7	73.5	70.2	60.0	60.0	30.0	26.0	31.6
100	Zambia	58.0	1.4	66.4	79.9	72.4	82.6	63.3	50.0	50.0	30.0	28.0	57.0
101	Kenya	57.5	−1.2	63.4	67.9	78.1	83.1	72.7	45.0	50.0	30.0	21.0	63.7
102	Swaziland	57.4	−1.7	67.2	74.9	63.1	55.5	68.8	55.0	40.0	45.0	36.0	68.4
103	Bhutan	57.0	−0.7	60.5	52.0	84.1	58.3	73.4	15.0	30.0	60.0	52.0	85.1
104	Serbia	56.9	0.3	58.9	75.2	83.2	41.4	64.5	50.0	50.0	40.0	34.0	72.2
105	Algeria	56.9	0.3	71.2	70.7	83.5	73.4	77.2	45.0	30.0	30.0	32.0	56.4
106	Nigeria	56.8	1.7	53.2	67.2	84.4	64.7	75.4	40.0	40.0	30.0	27.0	85.7
107	Cambodia	56.6	0.0	39.9	70.0	91.0	92.9	70.5	60.0	50.0	30.0	18.0	43.6
108	Vanuatu	56.4	−2.0	68.7	55.1	94.9	84.3	76.8	20.0	40.0	40.0	29.0	55.0
109	The Philippines	56.3	−0.4	48.1	77.8	78.8	91.2	72.7	40.0	50.0	30.0	23.0	51.9
110	Bosnia and Herzegovina	56.2	3.1	61.3	80.8	83.2	28.8	74.7	70.0	60.0	10.0	32.0	61.2
111	Mozambique	56.0	0.3	58.7	74.5	77.6	76.1	74.9	50.0	50.0	30.0	26.0	42.0
112	Mali	55.6	0.0	47.5	69.6	60.2	81.1	73.8	50.0	40.0	35.0	31.0	67.9
113	Brazil	55.6	−1.1	54.5	69.2	68.4	50.3	75.8	45.0	50.0	50.0	35.0	57.5
114	Indonesia	55.5	2.1	53.1	77.9	81.9	89.1	70.8	35.0	40.0	30.0	26.0	50.8
115	Benin	55.4	0.0	42.3	57.0	75.9	85.2	74.6	60.0	50.0	30.0	31.0	47.8
116	Gabon	55.4	0.4	58.8	62.1	61.5	86.4	71.4	45.0	40.0	40.0	31.0	57.4
117	Pakistan	55.2	−1.8	71.7	67.0	80.5	88.8	69.4	30.0	40.0	30.0	25.0	49.8
118	The Gambia	55.1	−0.7	58.5	60.6	71.9	75.3	71.6	55.0	50.0	25.0	19.0	63.8
119	Senegal	54.6	−1.7	63.1	69.7	64.7	77.8	75.2	35.0	40.0	45.0	34.0	41.9
120	Sri Lanka	54.6	−1.4	71.8	62.2	73.5	83.9	56.8	15.0	40.0	40.0	32.0	70.7
121	Yemen	54.4	−2.5	74.4	76.1	83.2	51.3	65.1	45.0	30.0	30.0	23.0	65.4

2010 *Index of Economic Freedom* World Rankings

World Rank	Country	Overall Score	Change from 2009	Business Freedom	Trade Freedom	Fiscal Freedom	Government Spending	Monetary Freedom	Investment Freedom	Financial Freedom	Property Rights	Freedom from Corruption	Labor Freedom
122	Malawi	54.1	0.4	44.8	68.6	78.9	45.8	71.0	50.0	50.0	45.0	28.0	59.3
123	Côte d'Ivoire	54.1	−0.9	43.7	64.3	78.3	87.1	76.0	35.0	50.0	30.0	20.0	56.1
124	India	53.8	−0.6	36.3	67.9	73.4	76.1	67.5	35.0	40.0	50.0	34.0	57.7
125	Moldova	53.7	−1.2	70.2	79.9	85.1	43.0	67.5	30.0	50.0	40.0	29.0	42.7
126	Papua New Guinea	53.5	−1.3	59.1	86.2	65.0	63.3	72.6	35.0	30.0	20.0	20.0	83.3
127	Tonga	53.4	−0.7	78.2	56.2	82.8	70.8	63.5	25.0	20.0	20.0	24.0	93.7
128	Tajikistan	53.0	−1.6	57.4	82.5	88.9	78.0	58.4	25.0	40.0	25.0	20.0	54.4
129	Niger	52.9	−0.9	37.2	75.7	65.1	85.1	77.6	50.0	40.0	30.0	28.0	40.7
130	Nepal	52.7	−0.5	59.4	58.8	86.6	92.3	77.8	15.0	30.0	35.0	27.0	44.7
131	Suriname	52.5	−1.6	41.0	66.4	66.9	77.8	67.8	15.0	30.0	40.0	36.0	84.5
132	Cameroon	52.3	−0.6	37.2	59.7	71.8	92.7	71.9	35.0	50.0	30.0	23.0	52.2
133	Mauritania	52.0	−1.9	48.3	69.9	75.1	73.4	78.0	30.0	40.0	25.0	28.0	52.5
134	Guinea	51.8	0.8	43.7	60.0	69.9	93.1	57.4	40.0	40.0	20.0	16.0	78.0
135	Argentina	51.2	−1.1	62.1	69.5	69.5	75.6	61.2	45.0	30.0	20.0	29.0	50.1
136	Ethiopia	51.2	−1.8	66.3	61.9	77.7	82.9	60.4	25.0	20.0	30.0	26.0	61.5
137	Bangladesh	51.1	3.6	59.4	58.0	72.8	93.9	66.6	45.0	20.0	20.0	21.0	53.8
138	Laos	51.1	0.7	59.4	68.4	80.1	90.3	73.5	25.0	20.0	15.0	20.0	58.9
139	Djibouti	51.0	−0.2	35.7	31.9	78.2	58.9	70.5	60.0	60.0	30.0	30.0	55.3
140	China	51.0	−2.2	49.7	72.2	70.2	88.1	70.6	20.0	30.0	20.0	36.0	53.2
141	Haiti	50.8	0.3	36.0	79.1	81.5	91.3	67.1	30.0	30.0	10.0	14.0	69.2
142	Micronesia	50.6	−1.1	59.1	81.0	97.5	0.0	76.7	20.0	30.0	30.0	30.0	81.8
143	Russia	50.3	−0.5	52.2	68.4	82.3	66.5	62.6	25.0	40.0	25.0	21.0	59.6
144	Vietnam	49.8	−1.2	60.7	68.9	76.1	73.4	58.1	20.0	30.0	15.0	27.0	68.4
145	Syria	49.4	−1.9	59.2	54.0	87.0	80.2	63.3	20.0	20.0	25.0	21.0	64.7
146	Bolivia	49.4	−4.2	57.3	76.9	84.3	67.5	63.2	15.0	50.0	10.0	30.0	39.4
147	Ecuador	49.3	−3.2	52.9	71.8	79.3	77.5	63.9	25.0	40.0	20.0	20.0	42.2
148	Maldives	49.0	−2.3	82.3	44.5	95.5	0.0	69.7	35.0	30.0	30.0	28.0	75.3
149	São Tomé and Príncipe	48.8	5.0	43.5	66.6	87.1	52.5	59.0	45.0	30.0	30.0	27.0	47.6
150	Belarus	48.7	3.7	72.1	80.3	85.2	32.0	62.6	20.0	10.0	20.0	20.0	84.8
151	Equatorial Guinea	48.6	−2.7	44.8	58.9	75.5	83.9	80.9	20.0	40.0	20.0	17.0	44.8
152	Central African Republic	48.4	0.1	37.5	58.1	65.5	94.1	68.3	40.0	30.0	20.0	20.0	50.7
153	Guyana	48.4	0.0	63.4	71.3	55.9	26.2	71.0	30.0	40.0	35.0	26.0	65.2
154	Angola	48.4	1.4	43.4	70.4	85.1	62.8	62.6	35.0	40.0	20.0	19.0	45.2
155	Lesotho	48.1	−1.6	62.0	63.5	52.0	30.0	70.3	25.0	40.0	40.0	32.0	66.1
156	Seychelles	47.9	0.1	64.2	33.4	76.4	9.3	57.9	50.0	30.0	50.0	48.0	59.8
157	Sierra Leone	47.9	0.1	54.6	62.8	80.9	80.5	71.7	40.0	20.0	10.0	19.0	39.0
158	Uzbekistan	47.5	−3.0	67.8	65.1	88.4	72.6	62.4	10.0	10.0	20.0	18.0	61.1
159	Chad	47.5	0.0	32.7	58.4	50.5	89.2	76.7	45.0	40.0	20.0	16.0	46.9
160	Burundi	47.5	−1.3	37.8	68.6	72.2	42.7	62.7	50.0	30.0	25.0	19.0	66.9

2010 *Index of Economic Freedom* World Rankings

World Rank	Country	Overall Score	Change from 2009	Business Freedom	Trade Freedom	Fiscal Freedom	Government Spending	Monetary Freedom	Investment Freedom	Financial Freedom	Property Rights	Freedom from Corruption	Labor Freedom
161	Togo	47.1	−1.5	36.8	62.8	56.2	86.0	74.5	25.0	30.0	30.0	27.0	43.3
162	Ukraine	46.4	−2.4	38.7	82.6	77.9	41.1	61.2	20.0	30.0	30.0	25.0	57.7
163	Liberia	46.2	−1.9	52.8	53.8	67.8	82.3	65.4	20.0	20.0	25.0	24.0	51.3
164	Timor-Leste	45.8	−4.7	46.2	73.0	64.7	54.1	72.5	20.0	20.0	20.0	22.0	65.6
165	Comoros	44.9	1.6	43.7	62.4	65.0	85.1	76.4	10.0	20.0	30.0	25.0	31.4
166	Kiribati	43.7	−2.0	65.6	55.4	42.2	0.0	71.9	25.0	30.0	30.0	31.0	86.1
167	Guinea–Bissau	43.6	−1.8	23.4	58.2	88.6	47.3	67.0	30.0	30.0	20.0	19.0	52.5
168	Iran	43.4	−1.2	69.9	50.2	81.1	79.6	54.7	0.0	10.0	10.0	23.0	55.1
169	Republic of Congo	43.2	−2.2	48.7	61.0	60.3	69.3	70.8	15.0	30.0	10.0	19.0	48.1
170	Solomon Islands	42.9	−3.1	63.2	65.2	67.9	0.0	65.5	10.0	30.0	30.0	29.0	68.4
171	Turkmenistan	42.5	−1.7	30.0	79.2	90.2	94.7	62.8	0.0	10.0	10.0	18.0	30.0
172	Democratic Republic of Congo	41.4	−1.4	33.5	61.7	74.0	90.5	58.7	15.0	20.0	10.0	17.0	33.4
173	Libya	40.2	−3.3	20.0	85.0	81.7	62.8	66.4	10.0	20.0	10.0	26.0	20.0
174	Venezuela	37.1	−2.8	50.3	57.2	74.0	61.8	47.7	5.0	20.0	0.0	19.0	36.2
175	Burma	36.7	−1.0	20.0	72.3	81.9	98.4	46.5	0.0	10.0	5.0	13.0	20.0
176	Eritrea	35.3	−3.2	18.0	69.1	73.0	6.9	59.0	0.0	20.0	10.0	26.0	70.8
177	Cuba	26.7	−1.2	10.0	61.7	45.9	0.0	66.7	0.0	10.0	10.0	43.0	20.0
178	Zimbabwe	21.4	−1.3	30.0	44.8	58.4	0.0	0.0	0.0	10.0	5.0	18.0	48.2
179	North Korea	1.0	−1.0	0.0	0.0	0.0	0.0	0.0	0.0	0.0	5.0	5.0	0.0
n/a	Afghanistan	n/a	n/a	n/a	n/a	n/a	n/a	n/a	n/a	n/a	n/a	n/a	n/a
n/a	Iraq	n/a	n/a	n/a	n/a	n/a	n/a	n/a	n/a	n/a	n/a	n/a	n/a
n/a	Liechtenstein	n/a	n/a	n/a	n/a	n/a	n/a	n/a	n/a	n/a	n/a	n/a	n/a
n/a	Sudan	n/a	n/a	n/a	n/a	n/a	n/a	n/a	n/a	n/a	n/a	n/a	n/a

Chapter 1

Economic Freedom in Uncertain Times

Ambassador Terry Miller

Since the second half of 2008, the world economy has been undergoing a period of uncertainty and slowing economic growth. While some proclaimed the death of capitalism, the free market system has, in fact, demonstrated an impressive level of resilience during 2009 and now shows vital signs of an economic upturn. Policy choices made at this critical juncture of the global recovery will unquestionably shape the growth trajectory for the world economy in the years ahead.

COUNTRIES ON DIVERGING PATHS

The financial crisis and recession that afflicted the world economy in 2008 and 2009 resulted in, and may even have been caused by, significant reductions in economic freedom in a number of countries around the world. At the same time, many other countries have held firm on the path to greater economic freedom and the greater prosperity that it brings. After five years in which economic freedom had shown modest

but steady advances throughout the world, the 2010 *Index* has measured a small decline—one-tenth of a point (0.1 point)—in the world average economic freedom score.[1]

The recession of 2008–2009 was the first major worldwide economic disruption of the age of globalization. Economically free countries are typically more open and engaged with the world economy than their more repressive counterparts. Many of the most economically free were among the first to feel the effects of the crisis, which spread through the financial system. Those that are most open to trade, and particularly those that are most dependent on export-oriented growth, were among the most

---

1. The average score in the *Index* declined from 2008 to 2009 because of the addition in 2009 of a substantial number of countries with below average freedom scores. For countries covered in both the 2008 and 2009 editions, the average overall economic freedom score increased by one-tenth of a point in 2009.

vulnerable to economic downturns in other countries.

On the other hand, the economically free countries, which over the years have grown faster and accumulated more wealth than their repressed counterparts, were in a better position to withstand a temporary downturn. The economically free have more durable and transparent economic institutions, more diversified economies, and more flexibility in responding to a crisis. Thus, we would expect to see less harmful permanent impact from the crisis and recession in the economically free countries. We also would expect to see faster and more pronounced recovery from the negative effects that do occur.

The 2010 *Index of Economic Freedom* is based on data reflecting conditions from July 2008 through June 2009 (and sometimes earlier years when later data are not available). Thus, the effects of the recession and the policies through which governments have tried to respond are not fully captured in the rankings. Indeed, the full effect of some of the policies undertaken by governments, such as the inflationary impact of expansionary monetary policy and various governments' stimulus programs, may not show up for several years.

DIVERGING ECONOMIC FREEDOM SCORES

Many countries, despite the economic difficulties they may be experiencing, have held true to the principles of economic freedom and have continued to adopt measures to liberalize and deregulate economic activity. Eighty-one countries—almost half of all those ranked in the *Index*—showed improvements in their overall economic freedom scores this year. Regrettably, the levels of economic freedom in 90 other countries, as measured in the 2010 *Index*, have declined.

Many of the countries whose scores have dropped have responded to the economic crisis with policy moves that, whether intended or not, add up to a fundamental assault on economic freedom. In the United States, for example, policies or proposals have included

more intrusive regulations, government takeovers of businesses, government subsidies and bailouts of private firms, loose monetary policy, tax increases, and protectionist measures to reduce trade. (See "Can Trade Protectionism Save Jobs?")

Interventionist measures that harm economic freedom are detrimental to economic growth, with effects that in some cases will show up immediately, and sometimes after a delay, but in all cases can endure for years to come. Though bailouts and subsidies may provide short-term relief for some chosen firms, the impact on the overall economy quickly turns negative as governments have to finance spending through increased taxation, borrowing that crowds out private investment, or monetary expansion that fuels inflation.

With countries diverging so strongly in their policy responses to the crisis, more countries than usual show significant movements either up or down in the *Index* rankings. Though the

Biggest Gainers and Losers in 2010

Nations that gained or lost at least 2.5 points in their Index of Economic Freedom *score*

Gainers		Losers	
Montenegro	5.4	Timor-Leste	−4.7
São Tomé and Príncipe	5.0	Bolivia	−4.2
		Libya	−3.3
Rwanda	4.9	Barbados	−3.2
Macedonia	4.5	Ecuador	−3.2
Croatia	4.1	Eritrea	−3.2
Belarus	3.7	Solomon Islands	−3.1
Bangladesh	3.6	The Bahamas	−3.0
Colombia	3.2	Uzbekistan	−3.0
Qatar	3.2	Mongolia	−2.8
Bosnia and Herzegovina	3.1	Venezuela	−2.8
		Equatorial Guinea	−2.7
Peru	3.0	United States	−2.7
Poland	2.9	United Kingdom	−2.5
Saint Vincent and the Grenadines	2.6	Yemen	−2.5
United Arab Emirates	2.6		
Mexico	2.5		

Source: Terry Miller and Kim R. Holmes, *2010 Index of Economic Freedom* (Washington, D.C.: The Heritage Foundation and Dow Jones & Company, Inc., 2010), at *www.heritage.org/index.*

Table 1 ☎ heritage.org

Can Trade Protectionism Save Jobs?

Trade protectionism is simultaneously one of the most popular and least effective measures in response to a recession. Few things in economics are as well established as the idea that trade increases prosperity and that the freer the trade, the greater the benefits to all parties. Sadly, few ideas are also less well understood among members of the general public and even among politicians.

It is easy to focus on those whose jobs are lost when economies grow and develop and harder to see the new jobs that are created in a dynamic environment. For example, Smith Corona's closing of its last U.S. typewriter plant in 1992, costing 875 jobs in Cortland, New York, "fanned concerns in Congress and organized labor about the loss of jobs to foreign competition."[1] No notice was taken of emerging corporate giant Micro-soft, which had introduced the Windows 3.0 operating system in 1990 and had added 2,888 employees to its payroll between 1992 and 1993. By 2009, Microsoft had created over 92,000 jobs, more than 55,000 of which were in the United States.[2]

Those new jobs, which epitomize the value to society of economic freedom that permits and promotes rapid economic evolution and growth, fly below the radar screen in the public and political debates on trade, but they are the lifeblood of our increasing wealth and well-being. We cannot know what would have happened had the protectionists in Congress succeeded in 1992 in protecting Smith Corona's typewriter business, but it is clear that protectionism is always about protecting the status quo, while growing prosperity depends on embracing the new production and commercial possibilities of the future.

1. Keith Bradsher, "Smith Corona Plant Mexico Bound," *The New York Times*, July 22, 1992, at *http://www.nytimes.com/1992/07/22/business/smith-corona-plant-mexico-bound.html?pag* (November 9, 2009).

2. "Facts About Microsoft," at *http://www.microsoft.com/presspass/inside_ms.mspx* (November 9, 2009).

change in the global average economic freedom score in the 2010 *Index* is small, 30 countries gained or lost at least 2.5 points in their economic freedom scores. (See Table 1.)

Montenegro improved the most, gaining 5.4 points on the economic freedom scale. Other European countries that did notably well included Macedonia, Croatia, Belarus, Bosnia and Herzegovina, and Poland. Qatar and the United Arab Emirates made significant gains in the Middle East, as did Colombia, Peru, and Mexico in Latin America. Saint Vincent and the Grenadines was the biggest gainer in the Caribbean. Bangladesh topped the list of gainers in Asia, as did São Tomé and Príncipe and Rwanda in Africa.

There were 15 countries this year whose scores deteriorated by at least 2.5 points.

• Timor-Leste lost the most economic freedom in the 2010 *Index*, down 4.7 points. Mongolia, Uzbekistan, and the Solomon Islands were the only other Asia–Pacific countries to lose so much freedom.

• Five Latin American or Caribbean countries, including Bolivia, Barbados, Ecuador, the Bahamas, and Venezuela, lost significant amounts of economic freedom, as did Eritrea and Equatorial Guinea in Sub-Saharan Africa.

• In the Middle East and North Africa, Libya and Yemen lost significant amounts of economic freedom.

• Finally, and perhaps of most concern, perennial Top 10 performers the United States and the United Kingdom both lost at least 2.5 points in overall economic freedom, with the U.K. dropping out of the Top 10 in the *Index* for the first time ever.

Countries' policy choices in the various areas of economic freedom that are rated in the *Index* diverged significantly.

• 51 countries improved business freedom this year, but 114 increased regulatory pressures on firms.

• 60 countries imposed new levels or types of trade restrictions, but 107 continued the process of opening their economies.

• About 40 percent of countries continued to lower tax rates, yet another 40 percent increased rates or tax collections.

• Over 45 percent of countries—84 in all—reduced government spending as a percentage of GDP. Unfortunately, however, another 84 increased government spending.

Such policy divergence may be understandable in a time of stress, but it represents a slowing of the worldwide momentum toward greater economic freedom and a sharp turn away from freedom in certain countries. Time will tell whether we are seeing the leading edge of a fundamental realignment of countries along the continuum of economic freedom or whether the breaks in progress in some countries are just short-term manifestations of a loss of confidence or even temporary panic.

RESPONDING TO CRISIS: GOVERNMENT INTERVENTION HURTS

In their responses to the financial crisis and recession, many countries have adopted poli-

Progressing and Regressing Nations

A comparison of nations whose economic freedom categories changed since the 2009 Index of Economic Freedom

PROGRESSING

Category Change	Countries			
Mostly Free to Free	Switzerland			
Moderately Free to Mostly Free	Saint Lucia, Georgia, Taiwan, Botswana	**GDP Growth Rate**		
		2007	*2008*	*5 Years*
Mostly Unfree to Moderately Free	Montenegro, Ghana, Guatemala, Samoa, Dominican Republic	**6.3%**	**3.7%**	**5.5%**

REGRESSING

Category Change	Countries			
Free to Mostly Free	United States	**GDP Growth Rate**		
		2007	*2008*	*5 Years*
Mostly Free to Moderately Free	Spain, Norway, Barbados, The Bahamas	**2.2%**	**0.3%**	**2.6%**

Sources: Terry Miller and Kim R. Holmes, *2010 Index of Economic Freedom* (Washington, D.C.: The Heritage Foundation and Dow Jones & Company, Inc., 2010), at *www.heritage.org/index;* International Monetary Fund, at *http://www.imf.org/external/ns/cs.aspx?id=28* (November 9, 2009).

Table 2 ☎ heritage.org

cies that limit economic freedom. The negative effect of these policies on future growth rates is predictable and certain, and it is already beginning to be manifest in the data and in countries' *Index of Economic Freedom* scores.

The recession's impact was muted in countries that moved to a higher category of economic freedom and exacerbated in countries that moved lower. As shown in Table 2, 15 countries moved from a higher to a lower category of economic freedom or vice versa in this year's *Index.* Countries that slipped from one economic freedom category to another (such as from "mostly free" to "moderately free") experienced considerably lower economic growth than did their counterparts that moved up to the next higher category.

The impact of government fiscal stimulus on growth rates will be fully measurable only in future years. However, the early data available for the countries that are members of the Organi-

For OECD member nations

Government Spending as a Percentage of GDP

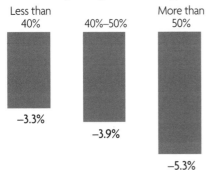

Less than 40%	40%–50%	More than 50%
−3.3%	−3.9%	−5.3%

GDP Growth, Q2 2008 to Q2 2009

Notes: Spending figures are averages from 2008 to 2009; GDP growth data are based on OECD members with 2008 and 2009 data available.

Sources: Terry Miller and Kim R. Holmes, *2010 Index of Economic Freedom* (Washington, D.C.: The Heritage Foundation and Dow Jones & Company, Inc., 2010), at *www.heritage.org/index*; Organisation for Economic Co-operation and Development, OECD.StatExtract, Quarterly National Accounts: Quarterly Growth Rates of GDP, volume, at *http://stats.oecd.org/index.aspx* (November 11, 2009).

Chart 1 ☎ heritage.org

DECLINING MONETARY FREEDOM HURTS AVERAGE SCORES

The average economic freedom score for 2010 is 59.4. This represents a drop of 0.1 point over the past year. The loss of economic freedom was most pronounced in the area of monetary freedom, with inflation rates increasing in most countries around the world in 2008 as a result of increasing commodity prices. Average scores also fell in the areas of government spending, financial freedom, and respect for property rights.

Economic freedom increased on average in the areas of business freedom, trade freedom, fiscal freedom, investment freedom, freedom from corruption, and labor freedom. The largest average gain was in trade freedom, with many countries continuing to resist the protectionist pressure to which a few have succumbed. (See "The 10 Economic Freedoms: A Global Look," next page.)

Of the 179 economies that are numerically graded in the 2010 *Index*,[2] only seven have very

2. Numerical grading was not possible for Afghanistan, Iraq, Liechtenstein, and Sudan due to the limited availability of relevant data.

sation for Economic Co-operation and Development (OECD) show that countries with higher levels of government spending continued to grow more slowly during the crisis. This would seem to confirm the view of many economists that the deadweight loss from government inefficiency, the various burdens associated with financing government deficits, and the crowding-out effects of government spending on private-sector demand and investment combine to make fiscal stimulus a poor policy choice in a recession.

Global Distribution of Economic Freedom

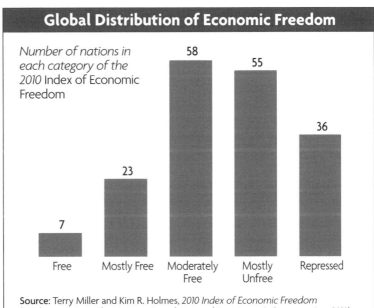

Number of nations in each category of the 2010 Index of Economic Freedom

Free	Mostly Free	Moderately Free	Mostly Unfree	Repressed
7	23	58	55	36

Source: Terry Miller and Kim R. Holmes, *2010 Index of Economic Freedom* (Washington, D.C.: The Heritage Foundation and Dow Jones & Company, Inc., 2010), at *www.heritage.org/index*.

Chart 2 ☎ heritage.org

The 10 Economic Freedoms: A Global Look

BUSINESS FREEDOM — *64.6*

Business freedom improved, sometimes quite significantly, in 52 countries this year. Only India recorded a double-digit drop on this component. The average business freedom score increased slightly by 0.3 point. Globally, starting a business takes an average of 35 days, while getting necessary licenses takes an average of about 218 days. Bankruptcy proceedings take three years on average.

TRADE FREEDOM — *74.2*

For the world as a whole, average tariffs fell by one-half of a percentage point over the past year to 6.8 percent. By contrast, non-tariff barriers increased, reflecting a disturbing trend for countries to resort to more subtle forms of protectionism. The average trade freedom score rose by 1.0 point, with improved scores in 107 countries throughout the world. Only a few of the 60 countries whose scores fell actually increased tariffs. Most resorted instead to a variety of restrictions, quotas, regulations, or subsidies that interfered with the free flow of goods or services.

FISCAL FREEDOM — *75.4*

Overall fiscal freedom improved by 0.5 point in the 2010 *Index*. The average top tax rate on individual income is now 29.3 percent, and the average top tax rate on corporate income is 25.1 percent. The average total tax burden as a percentage of GDP is 23.2 percent. Since July 2008, 32 countries have introduced reforms in direct taxes or have implemented tax cuts as previously planned, despite the challenging economic and political environment caused by the global economic slowdown.

GOVERNMENT SPENDING — *65*

The average score for government spending decreased by 0.1 point in the 2010 *Index*. In response to the global financial and economic turmoil, many governments around the world, particularly in advanced economies, have launched various stimulus measures and have increased spending. This spending is severely worsening deficits and debt levels: The average level of public debt as a percentage of GDP in advanced economies has risen sharply to around 80 percent.[1] The average level of government spending as a portion of GDP is 32.8 percent, a level that is likely to increase in future years.

MONETARY FREEDOM — *70.6*

The 2010 *Index* registered a sharp decline in monetary freedom, with scores off 3.4 points on average as a result of inflationary pressures that began to build in mid-2007 and continued though much of 2008. Much of the acceleration of consumer price inflation in early 2008 was the result of higher energy and commodity prices. Underlying factors included strong demand in emerging economies such as China and India, biofuels policies that restricted food supplies, and price distortions by governments in some key commodity-producing economies.[2]

---

1. Organisation for Economic Co-operation and Development, "OECD in Figures 2009," *OECD Observer 2009/Supplement 1*, p. 80, at *http://browse.oecdbookshop.org/oecd/pdfs/browseit/0109061E.PDF* (November 5, 2009).

2. "Commodity Prices and Global Inflation," remarks by John Lipsky, First Deputy Managing Director, International Monetary Fund, at the Council on Foreign Relations, New York City, May 8, 2008, at *http://www.imf.org/external/np/speeches/2008/050808.htm* (November 5, 2009).

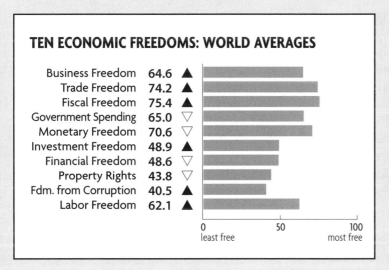

TEN ECONOMIC FREEDOMS: WORLD AVERAGES

Business Freedom	64.6	▲
Trade Freedom	74.2	▲
Fiscal Freedom	75.4	▲
Government Spending	65.0	▽
Monetary Freedom	70.6	▽
Investment Freedom	48.9	▲
Financial Freedom	48.6	▽
Property Rights	43.8	▽
Fdm. from Corruption	40.5	▲
Labor Freedom	62.1	▲

0 least free   50   100 most free

INVESTMENT FREEDOM — *48.9*

The average investment freedom score improved by 0.2 point in the 2010 *Index*. Of the 110 investment-related policy measures initiated in various countries during 2008, 85 encouraged foreign direct investment.[3] Undermining the overall investment environment, government expropriations increased in some countries in Latin America and parts of Central Asia.

FINANCIAL FREEDOM — *48.6*

Only a few countries' financial freedom scores changed in the 2010 *Index*, and most of those changes reflected responses to the global financial crisis. A total of 16 countries, including the United States, the United Kingdom, and Iceland, lost 10 points in the rankings as a result of various interventions, including bailout programs and even nationalizations of financial institutions. Governments that quickly reversed interventionist actions were

not penalized. Six countries continued financial liberalization during the year. Overall, the average financial freedom score dropped 0.6 point in the 2010 *Index*.

PROPERTY RIGHTS — *43.8*

The gradual worldwide improvement in property rights was interrupted this year, and the average score on this component declined 0.2 point in the 2010 *Index*. Some governments sought to justify expropriations and nationalizations on the basis of the global financial turmoil. On the positive side, protection of property rights improved in 27 countries.

FREEDOM FROM CORRUPTION — *40.5*

The average score for freedom from corruption improved by 0.2 point in the 2010 *Index*, but this component still records the lowest average score among the 10 economic freedoms. Only 13 countries score 80 or higher on this component, while 126 countries score below 50. High levels of persistent corruption in many of the less developed countries continue to severely retard economic growth.

LABOR FREEDOM — *62.1*

In light of growing recognition of the importance of labor market flexibility in enhancing productivity and better job growth, many economies have implemented more flexible labor regulations. The overall labor freedom score increased by 0.8 point in the 2010 *Index*, with 44 countries recording gains of 2.5 points or more.

3. United Nations Conference on Trade and Development, *World Development Report 2009: Transnational Corporations*, Agricultural Production and Development, Overview, p. xxii, at *http://www.unctad.org/en/docs/wir2009overview_en.pdf* (November 5, 2009).

high freedom scores of 80 or more, putting them in the "free" category (the highest). The next 23 countries have scores between 70 and 80, placing them in the "mostly free" category.

Thus, a total of only 30 countries, or about one-sixth of all countries graded, have economic systems in which individuals enjoy substantial levels of freedom. The largest portion of the countries graded—113 economies—have freedom scores between 50 and 70. Of those, 58 economies are "moderately free" (scores of 60–70), and 55 economies are "mostly unfree" (scores of 50–60). This year, 36 countries have "repressed economies" with scores below 50.

Countries in every region gained and lost economic freedom. Average freedom went up in Europe and the Middle East and North Africa, bucking the worldwide decline.

ECONOMIC FREEDOM MATTERS

There are clear relationships between economic freedom and numerous other positive economic and social indicators, the most prominent being the strong relationship between the level of economic freedom and the level of prosperity in a given country. (See Chart 3.)

Economies rated "free" or "mostly free" in the 2010 *Index* enjoy incomes that are more than three times the average levels in all other countries and more than 10 times higher than the incomes of "repressed" economies. Economic freedom is also strongly correlated to overall well-being, taking into account other factors such as health, education, security, and political governance.[3] (See Chart 4.)

Previous editions of the *Index* have confirmed the tangible benefits of living in freer societies. Not only are higher levels of economic freedom associated with higher per capita incomes and higher GDP growth rates, but those higher growth rates seem to create a virtuous cycle, triggering faster poverty reduction and further improvements in economic freedom. Over the decade, the countries with greater improvements in economic freedom achieved higher reductions in poverty as measured by the United Nations Human Poverty Index. (See Table 3.)

Economic freedom is a revolutionary concept that promotes rapid change without social unrest or violence. Chart 5 shows the relationship between economic freedom and social unrest as measured by the Economist Intelligence Unit's Political Instability Index.[4]

Economic Freedom and Standard of Living

$28,091 — Free
$23,253 — Mostly Free
$6,819 — Moderately Free
$1,478 — Mostly Unfree
$1,796 — Repressed

GDP per capita for each category of the 2010 Index *of Economic Freedom, in constant 2000 U.S. dollars*

Sources: Terry Miller and Kim R. Holmes, *2010 Index of Economic Freedom* (Washington, D.C.: The Heritage Foundation and Dow Jones & Company, Inc., 2010), at *www.heritage.org/index*; World Bank, World Development Indicators Online, at *http://publications.worldbank.org/WDI* (November 10, 2009).

Chart 3 ☎ heritage.org

3.   For more information on this wealth and well-being measure, see Legatum Institute, *The 2009 Legatum Prosperity Index: An Inquiry into Global Wealth and Wellbeing*, at *http://www.prosperity.com/downloads/2009Legatum ProsperityIndexReport.pdf* (November 9, 2009).

4.   For more information on the EIU Political Instability Index, see "Social Unrest," Views Wire, Economist Intelligence Unit, at *http://viewswire.eiu.com/site_info. asp?info_name=social_unrest_ table&page=noads&rf=0* (November 9, 2009).

Economic Freedom Is Key to Overall Well-Being

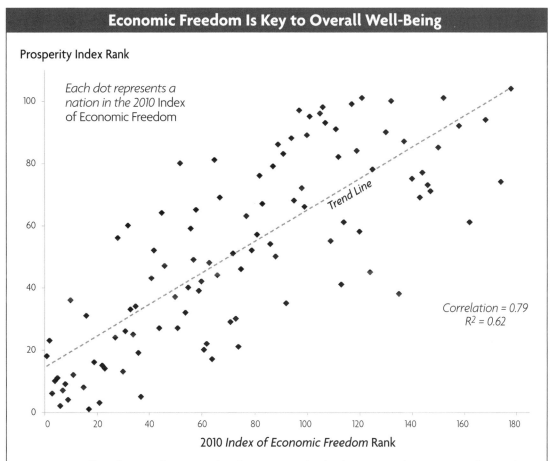

Prosperity Index Rank

Each dot represents a nation in the 2010 Index of Economic Freedom

Trend Line

Correlation = 0.79
$R^2 = 0.62$

2010 *Index of Economic Freedom* Rank

Sources: Terry Miller and Kim R. Holmes, *2010 Index of Economic Freedom* (Washington, D.C.: The Heritage Foundation and Dow Jones & Company, Inc., 2010), at *www.heritage.org/index;* 2009 Legatum Prosperity Index: An Inquiry into Global Wealth and Wellbeing, at *http://www.prosperity.com/downloads/2009LegatumProsperityIndexReport.pdf* (November 9, 2009).

Chart 4 ☎ heritage.org

Economic Freedom and Poverty

The Ten-Year Record

	Change in Poverty Levels
All countries	−4.6
Countries gaining economic freedom	−5.5
Countries losing economic freedom	−3.4

Note: Data from the *Index of Economic Freedom* (2000 to 2010) and the Human Poverty Index (1999 to 2009).

Sources: Terry Miller and Kim R. Holmes, *2010 Index of Economic Freedom* (Washington, D.C.: The Heritage Foundation and Dow Jones & Company, Inc., 2010), at *www.heritage.org/index*, and Human Development Reports, United Nations Human Development Programme, at *http://hdr.undp.org/en/reports* (November 9, 2009).

Table 3 ☎ heritage.org

By empowering people to exercise greater control of their daily lives, economic freedom increases their options for economic progress and lets people decide for themselves how best to improve their lives. Economic freedom ultimately nurtures political reform as well by making it possible for individuals to gain the economic resources necessary to challenge entrenched interests or compete for political power, thereby encouraging the creation of more pluralistic societies.

Greater economic freedom is also strongly correlated with overall human development as measured by the United Nations Human Development Index, which measures life expectancy, literacy, education, and the stan-

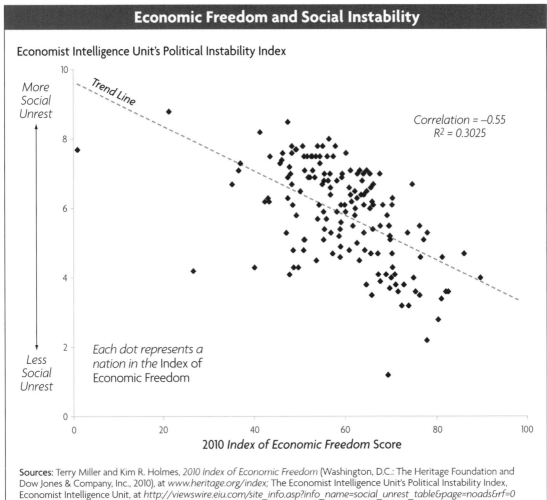

Economic Freedom and Social Instability

Economist Intelligence Unit's Political Instability Index

More Social Unrest

Trend Line

Correlation = −0.55
R² = 0.3025

Less Social Unrest

Each dot represents a nation in the Index of Economic Freedom

2010 *Index of Economic Freedom* Score

Sources: Terry Miller and Kim R. Holmes, *2010 Index of Economic Freedom* (Washington, D.C.: The Heritage Foundation and Dow Jones & Company, Inc., 2010), at *www.heritage.org/index;* The Economist Intelligence Unit's Political Instability Index, Economist Intelligence Unit, at *http://viewswire.eiu.com/site_info.asp?info_name=social_unrest_table&page=noads&rf=0* (November 9, 2009).

Chart 5 ☎ heritage.org

dard of living in countries worldwide.[5] (See Chart 6.)

The prosperity that flows from economic freedom results in greater access to education, reduced illiteracy, increased access to higher-quality health care and food supplies, and longer life expectancy.

In addition, economically free countries do a better job of protecting the environment. In January 2008, the World Economic Forum, the Center for International Earth Science Informa-

tion Network (CIESIN), and the Yale Center for Environmental Law and Policy published an Environmental Performance Index (EPI).[6] The EPI shows a country's performance in coping with environmental challenges, providing "a composite index of current national environmental protection efforts."[7] There is a strong positive relationship between economic freedom scores and the EPI.

The relationship between certain economic

5.   For more information on the United Nations Human Development Index, see United Nations Development Programme, *Human Development Reports*, at *http://hdr.undp.org/en/statistics* (November 9, 2009).

6.   See Daniel C. Esty, M. A. Levy, C. H. Kim, A. de Sherbinin, T. Srebotnjak, and V. Mara, *2008 Environmental Performance Index,* Yale Center for Environmental Law and Policy, 2008, at *http://epi.yale.edu/Framework* (November 9, 2009).

7.   *Ibid.*

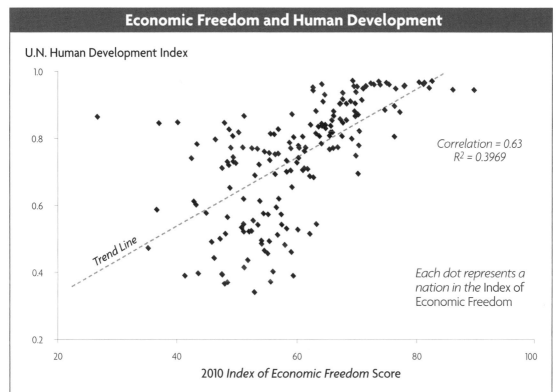

Economic Freedom and Human Development

U.N. Human Development Index

Correlation = 0.63
$R^2 = 0.3969$

Trend Line

Each dot represents a nation in the Index of Economic Freedom

2010 *Index of Economic Freedom* Score

Sources: Terry Miller and Kim R. Holmes, *2010 Index of Economic Freedom* (Washington, D.C.: The Heritage Foundation and Dow Jones & Company, Inc., 2010), at *www.heritage.org/index*; Human Development Reports, United Nations Human Development Programme, at *http://hdr.undp.org/en/statistics* (November 9, 2009).

Chart 6 ☎ heritage.org

---

freedom factors and environmental performance is even stronger.[8] (See Chart 7.) For example, countries with high levels of protection for private property rights and low tolerance for corruption do a much better job of protecting the environment. Environmentalists who see in govern-

8. There are strong positive correlations between the Environmental Performance Index (EPI) and economic freedom. The correlation between the EPI and overall economic freedom is 0.55. The correlations between the EPI and property rights and freedom from corruption are 0.60 and 0.62, respectively.

Trade Freedom and Environmental Performance

Average score of the Environmental Performance Index

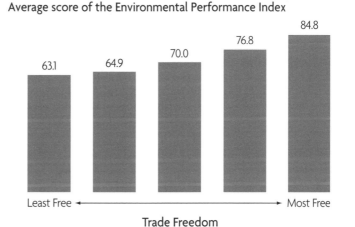

63.1 64.9 70.0 76.8 84.8

Least Free ⟵——————————⟶ Most Free

Trade Freedom

Sources: Terry Miller and Kim R. Holmes, *2010 Index of Economic Freedom* (Washington, D.C.: The Heritage Foundation and Dow Jones & Company, Inc., 2010), at *www.heritage.org/index*; Daniel C. Esty, M. A. Levy, C. H. Kim, A. de Sherbinin, T. Srebotnjak, and V. Mara, *2008 Environmental Performance Index* (New Haven: Yale Center for Environmental Law and Policy, 2008), at *http://epi.yale.edu/Framework* (November 9, 2009).

Chart 7 ☎ heritage.org

ment control of land or resources the panacea for environmental sustainability will find no support in the data. Similarly, countries with more open trade and less protectionism have much better levels of environmental protection or sustainability.

The lesson from the 2010 *Index of Economic Freedom* is clear: Economic freedom is good not only for growth and individual economic advancement, but also for the progressive values and public goods that people seek for society as a whole.

In 2010, more than at any time since the first edition of the *Index of Economic Freedom* appeared in 1995, countries are seriously reexamining the role of economic freedom in fostering economic growth and prosperity. There is a clear divergence in the 2010 *Index* between countries that are hesitating in the promotion of economic freedom, or even turning away, and those that are holding confidently to the path of liberalization.

Governments that turn away from the principles of economic freedom are embarking on an uncertain journey in which their citizens will be guided by government intervention, under increasing state control, along pathways that historically have led to stagnation and societal decline. By contrast, governments that embrace economic freedom for their citizens liberate individuals to find for themselves their most likely paths to greater economic well-being. Such freedom has proven over and over, for generations, to be the best way to encourage entrepreneurship, and a dependable means of dispersing economic power and decision-making throughout an economy so that *all* have a fair and equitable shot at economic gain and prosperity.

The evidence adduced in the 2010 *Index of Economic Freedom* demonstrates clearly that, in general, freer countries grow more surely, recover from setbacks more quickly, and spread prosperity more widely throughout their populations. Those are hallmarks of a society that is healthy and prosperous.

In these uncertain times, that is a result to which we all should aspire.

Chapter 2

Trading for Prosperity

The Honorable Elaine L. Chao

History has proven that trade freedom is the best economic strategy for all of the world's peoples.

History has also shown that we are prone to ignore history.

Since 1979, the value of world exports has risen by an average of 7.1 percent annually. During that same period, world income has skyrocketed. Gross domestic product (GDP) for the world as a whole, measured in constant 2000 U.S. dollars, has risen from $17.5 trillion in 1979 to $40.3 trillion in 2008. Even on a per capita basis, GDP growth has been impressive, jumping from $4,002 to $6,023.

The relationship between trade and economic growth is clear, both in theory and in practice. No single nation has the natural resources, infrastructure, and human capital in sufficient quantity and quality to realize the standard of living to which developed nations have become accustomed and to which developing nations aspire. And so we trade.

SPREADING PROSPERITY TO ALL

The major economic benefits of free trade derive from the differences among trading partners, which allow any country a chance to compete in the global market according to its fundamental economic strengths. Low wage costs, access to cheap capital, a highly skilled workforce, and other fundamental variables all play a role in determining what comparative advantage one country has over another in the global marketplace.

When individuals specialize and trade, the economic advantages of the resulting increased skills and improved allocation of resources are enormous. The baker bakes bread, and the tailor sews shirts; their products are exchanged, and both are better fed and better clothed. In a modern economy, specialization extends much further, both within a nation and across countries. The process of producing bread involves dozens or hundreds of specialists in various tasks related to agriculture, construction, ener-

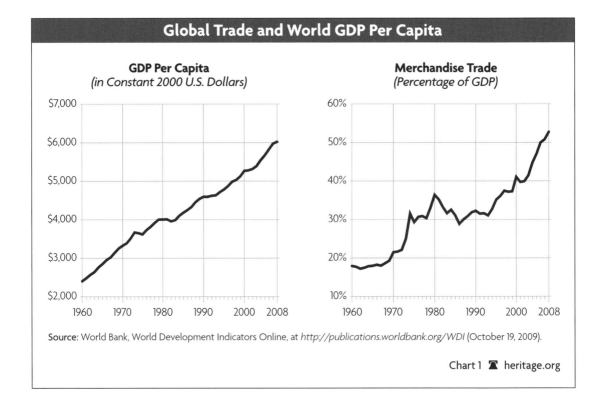

Global Trade and World GDP Per Capita

GDP Per Capita
(in Constant 2000 U.S. Dollars)

Merchandise Trade
(Percentage of GDP)

Source: World Bank, World Development Indicators Online, at *http://publications.worldbank.org/WDI* (October 19, 2009).

Chart 1 ☎ heritage.org

gy, accounting, marketing, transportation, and myriad other skills. The trading process, along with technological advancement that is itself largely spurred by the dynamics of trade, is at the root of all productivity gains—truly the basis for the wealth of nations.

Few would doubt the relationship between increased trade flows and the rapid worldwide economic growth at the end of the 20th century. This growth in trade did not come about by accident; it was the result of visionary political leadership in the United States and other major economies that sustained a 50-year commitment to lowering barriers that separated the peoples of the world, and integrating communities and nations in a global marketplace.

Trade is as old as human civilization. Trade allows individuals and nations to prosper from natural resources, ingenuity, and initiative. Trade increases the standard of living of all nations, rich and poor, developed and developing, and is an added incentive for us to seek a stable world that is safe from upheaval and strife.

From the ruins of World War II, there emerged the basis for the modern international

trading system. With the hard-learned lessons of the Great Depression behind them, countries launched a host of new multilateral institutions dedicated to international economic cooperation, including the World Bank and the International Monetary Fund (IMF).

As a part of that process, more than 50 nations drafted a charter for an International Trade Organization (ITO).[1] However, in 1950, after repeated attempts to gain congressional approval had failed, the United States announced that it would not ratify the charter. This left the ITO without a critical member and effectively killed the nascent organization.

The effects of this failure were eased by promising results under a parallel effort known as the General Agreement on Tariffs and Trade. GATT was a less formal structure than the ITO and offered an easier, more gradual route to reducing tariffs and opening markets among

---

1. Havana Charter for an International Trade Organization, in U.N. Conference on Trade and Employment, *Final Act and Related Documents*, November 21, 1947–March 24, 1948, p. 14, at *http://www.wto.int/english/docs_e/legal_e/havana_e.pdf* (September 23, 2009).

interested member nations. Rather than create an organization that regulated trade and trade-related aspects of the international economy, GATT was a treaty that focused more explicitly on reducing and eliminating specific tariffs, quotas, and subsidies.

The first reductions and rules entered into force in January 1948. Successive negotiating rounds under GATT widened and deepened international trade liberalization. A key concept enshrined under GATT is the most-favored-nation (MFN) principle, which prevents countries from discriminating between different trading partners.

The Uruguay Round, the eighth and final round under GATT, was launched in 1986 in Uruguay. It not only extended GATT rules for the trading system into several new, more difficult negotiating areas, including trade in services, intellectual property rights, and rules governing trade in agriculture and textiles, but also led to the creation of the World Trade Organization in 1995.[2]

GATT provided the context for significant trade liberalization among member countries from 1948 to 1994. During the Uruguay Round, GATT membership increased from 89 countries in 1985 to 128 countries in 1994. The establishment of the WTO continued the rush of new members, demonstrating that the multilateral trading system had been recognized as an anchor for development and an instrument of economic and trade reform. By 2009, the WTO had 153 members, including every major trading nation and most developing countries.

Over the course of several decades, determined negotiators around the world have built a comprehensive structure of trade agreements that promote trade and provide the assurances that trading partners need in terms of transparency and predictability. The mission is to help producers of goods and services, exporters, and importers conduct business. Critical to that mission is ensuring that trade rules are transparent and predictable so that individuals, corporations, and governments can know what they are dealing with and be confident that trade policy will not be subject to sudden changes.

The WTO is a forum for negotiating agreements aimed at reducing obstacles to international trade and ensuring a level playing field for all, thereby contributing to economic growth and development around the world. However, as so clearly illustrated by the current round of trade negotiations, the process can take time. Bilateral and regional free trade agreements allow nations the option of pursuing binding trade arrangements with countries that are willing to liberalize their foreign trade policies more quickly than multilateral negotiations allow.

Free trade agreements between countries can exist in harmony with the WTO. Legally, preferential trade agreements are permitted under the multilateral auspices of the WTO provided (1) that the agreements do not result in higher overall trade barriers for WTO members outside of an agreement,[3] (2) the agreements eliminate duties and other trade barriers on a substantial amount of all trade in products originating in countries participating in an agreement,[4] and (3) the trade barriers are eliminated within a reasonable amount of time.[5] More than 200 trade agreements and customs unions, including NAFTA and the European Union (EU), are currently in force.[6] Some 421 regional trade areas had been notified to the WTO as of December 2008, and 400 agreements could be in force by 2010.[7]

---

3.   General Agreement on Tariffs and Trade 1947, Part III, Article XXIV, Section 4.

4.   *Ibid.*, Section 5.

5.   *Ibid.*, Section 8.

6.   Member countries of a free trade area agree to eliminate tariffs between themselves but maintain independent external tariffs on imports from non-FTA member countries. Member countries of a customs union agree to eliminate tariffs between themselves and set a common external tariff on imports from non-member countries.

7.   World Trade Organization, "Regional Trade Agreements," at *http://www.wto.org/english/tratop_e/ region_e/region_e.htm* (September 23, 2009).

---

2.   World Trade Organization, "The GATT Years: From Havana to Marrakesh," at *http://www.wto.org/ english/thewto_e/whatis_e/tif_e/fact4_e.htm* (September 23, 2009).

THE HARD POLITICS OF TRADE

Visionary leadership and sustained commitment were required to achieve this progress because the concepts that underlie the gains from trade, particularly the economic principle of comparative advantage, are not intuitively obvious. People tend to think in terms of zero sum transactions in which gains for one party imply a loss for the other. The pain of jobs lost to economic restructuring, including that caused by trade, is highly concentrated and thus politically visible, while the gains tend to be diffused throughout society in such a way that while everyone gains, the gains to any individual are not large enough to inspire acute feelings or political action.

Those politics are never harder than when times are hard, and times have been hard during the past two years. 2009 witnessed a dramatic downturn in the world economy and trade. The IMF projects that, overall, world economic activity in 2009 will have subsided by at least 1 percent. The World Bank forecasts a 2.9 percent drop in 2009 in the overall global economy. With so many nations' economies reeling, international trade is inevitably and profoundly affected.

WTO economists estimate that in 2009, exports will have dropped by approximately 9 percent in terms of volume compared to 2008. This would be the largest decline since World War II. Developed countries have seen a larger percentage decline in exports than developing countries, but developing countries are more dependent on trade for economic growth, so the decline could cause even more hardship in those countries.

The precipitous decline in trade prompted WTO Director-General Pascal Lamy to observe on July 13, 2009, that "this crisis is unprecedented in its deepness, wideness and global impact."[8] No country is immune from harm when so many countries are experiencing a severe recession. The WTO has observed that:

Not even China, with its dynamic economy, can insulate itself from global downturn when most of its main trading partners are in recession. China's exports to its top six trading partners (treating the EU as a single partner) represented 70% of the country's total exports in 2007. All of these trading partners are currently experiencing economic contraction or slowdown and are likely to exhibit weak import demand for some time.[9]

In fact, China's exports, in terms of value, were 23.5 percent lower in July 2009 than they were in July 2008. Other major exporting economies had comparable declines.

The automobile industry has been among the more dramatic examples of a sector that is heavily dependent on international trade and has been hit very hard by the worldwide economic crisis. Japan's automobile exports to the United States dropped by 30 percent in the fourth quarter of 2008. In February 2009, Germany's automobile exports were 51 percent lower than a year earlier, and America's automobile sales were 41 percent lower. The European Automobile Manufacturers Association reported that passenger car registrations in Europe in February 2009 dropped 18 percent compared to the previous year. The new EU member states of Eastern Europe experienced a 30 percent drop.

Trade slowed significantly more in the fourth quarter of 2008 and throughout 2009 than it had in previous economic downturns. There are a number of postulations as to why this is the case. In the fall of 2008, the deep and widespread contraction in credit available to finance trade transactions impeded trade globally. Every region slowed nearly simultaneously and in dramatic fashion, which caused the decline in demand for trade to be far more widespread than in the past. Global supply chains are increasingly integrated, with multiple components for a single product often

8. Pascal Lamy, "Third Monitoring Report to the Trade Policy Review Body: Introductory Remarks," World Trade Organization, July 13, 2009, at *http://www.wto.org/english/news_e/news09_e/ tpr_13jul09_e.htm* (October 9, 2009).

9. World Trade Organization, "WTO Sees 9% Global Trade Decline in 2009 as Recession Strikes," March 23, 2009, p. 3, at *http://www.thailandwto.org/ Doc/News/6712.pdf* (October 9, 2009).

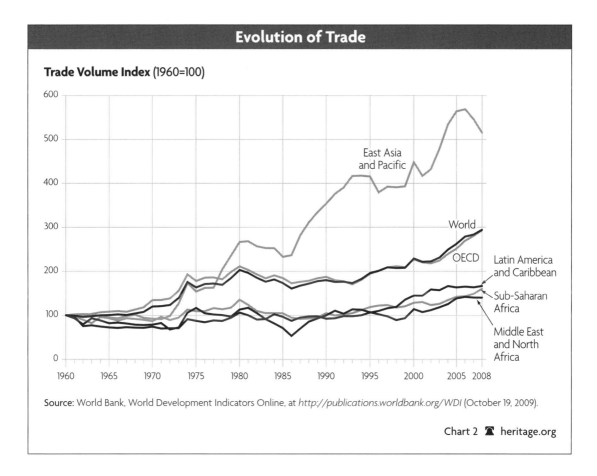

Evolution of Trade

Trade Volume Index (1960=100)

East Asia
and Pacific

World

OECD

Latin America
and Caribbean

Sub-Saharan
Africa

Middle East
and North
Africa

Source: World Bank, World Development Indicators Online, at *http://publications.worldbank.org/WDI* (October 19, 2009).

Chart 2 ☎ heritage.org

sourced in multiple countries. And protectionism has increased.

DIMINISHING TRADE FREEDOM

In the best of times in developed countries, making markets freer and more open requires that political leaders demonstrate courage, foresight, and sustained commitment. Opening a domestic economy to increased competition rarely, if ever, garners widespread popular support, and there are usually near-term costs in terms of the displacement of workers in industries affected by increased competition. In the worst of times, such as many of the world's economies experienced in 2008–2009, it is even more difficult for political leaders to advance trade freedom or even to keep markets as open as they were at the outset of the economic crisis.

History shows that defending and advancing trade freedom is never more important than during an economic downturn. Nations

retreat on trade freedom at their own peril and to the detriment of all trading nations. The most often-cited evidence of the dangers of retreating on trade is the Depression-era enactment in the United States of the Smoot–Hawley Tariff Act of 1930, which raised tariffs on over 20,000 products to an average of 60 percent. Other countries responded accordingly, and there was an escalating pattern of retaliation and counter-retaliation. Along with tariffs, export subsidies were increased, currencies were depreciated, and the toxic stew of protectionism proved devastating to economies around the world.

By 1932, U.S. exports to Europe were just one-third of what they had been in 1929. World trade overall fell two-thirds in the first few years of the Great Depression, and the world learned a painful lesson. That lesson has not been forgotten, but whether it will be sufficiently heeded to avoid protracting and deepening the current economic crisis remains to be seen.

TRYING (AND FAILING) TO HOLD THE LINE

Mindful of the dangers of nations retreating on trade freedom during an economic downturn, on November 15, 2008, finance ministers and central bank governors of the Group of 20 (G-20) nations issued a statement at the Summit on Financial Markets and the World Economy pledging to resist resorting to protectionist measures:

> We underscore the critical importance of rejecting protectionism and not turning inward in times of financial uncertainty. In this regard, within the next 12 months, we will refrain from raising new barriers to investment or to trade in goods and services, imposing new export restrictions, or implementing World Trade Organization (WTO) inconsistent measures to stimulate exports. Further, we shall strive to reach agreement this year on modalities that leads to a successful conclusion to the WTO's Doha Development Agenda with an ambitious and balanced outcome. We instruct our Trade Ministers to achieve this objective and stand ready to assist directly, as necessary. We also agree that our countries have the largest stake in the global trading system and therefore each must make the positive contributions necessary to achieve such an outcome.[10]

The G-20 pledge notwithstanding, on March 17, 2009, the World Bank issued a study showing that these same G-20 nations had implemented 47 measures that restrict trade at the expense of other countries. The study found that since the outset of the financial crisis, policymakers in the G-20 had proposed and/or implemented 78 trade measures, 66 of them containing trade restrictions; 47 trade-

restricting measures took effect.[11]

World Trade Organization Director-General Pascal Lamy stated in that same month that WTO members were exhibiting a "worrying tendency toward increased trade protectionism as a result of the deepening global economic crisis." He said that the WTO had found 85 verified trade measures put forth by 23 countries from September 2008 to March 2009 and that the large majority were trade-restrictive.[12]

The slow rise of protectionism is confirmed by the trade freedom rankings in the *2010 Index of Economic Freedom*. Using tariff data through 2008 and non-tariff barrier data covering the period from July 2008 through June 2009—the period coinciding with the beginning of the worldwide recession in most countries, but generally capturing only the earliest policy responses by governments—the rankings are starting to reflect the impact of rising trade barriers on some countries' scores.

The rankings show that for the world as a whole, average tariffs fell 0.5 percentage point from 7.3 percent in the 2009 *Index* to 6.8 percent in the 2010 *Index*. While average tariff rates fell, the average penalty for non-tariff barriers to trade rose 0.2 point from 11.7 in the 2009 *Index* to 11.9 in the 2010 *Index*. From the 2009 *Index* to the 2010 *Index*, 37 countries experienced a decrease in trade freedom of at least one point, and three countries scored at least 10 points lower.

Approaches to protectionism vary. Blatantly protectionist or "beggar-thy-neighbor" policies by WTO members are subject to limi-

10. Press release, "Declaration of the Summit on Financial Markets and the World Economy," Office of the Press Secretary, The White House, November 15, 2008, at *http://www.iasplus.com/crunch/0811g20declaration.pdf* (October 9, 2009).

11. Elisa Gamberoni and Richard Newfarmer, "Trade Protection: Incipient but Worrisome Trends," World Trade Organization *Trade Note* No. 37, March 2, 2009, p. 1, at *http://siteresources.worldbank.org/NEWS/Resources/Trade_Note_37.pdf* (October 9, 2009).

12. Dick K. Nanto, "The Global Financial Crisis: Foreign and Trade Policy Effects," Congressional Research Service *Report for Congress* R40496, April 7, 2009, p. 22, at *http://74.125.113.132/search?q=cache:m4B58zj-7FEJ:handle.dtic.mil/100.2/ADA497762+wto+worrying+tendency+toward+increased+trade+protectionism+as+a+result+of+the+deepening+global+economic+crisis&cd=1&hl=en&ct=clnk&gl=us* (October 9, 2009).

tation, but WTO rules and obligations do allow for considerable restraints on trade.

• For example, if all WTO members raised tariffs to previously agreed maximum or "bound" rates, tariffs would double worldwide, and the effect on the flow of goods and services between nations would be profound: according to WTO estimates, an 8 percent reduction in world trade.

• WTO rules allow nations to favor domestic industries through relief or subsidy programs, stimulus efforts, currency depreciation, and program stipulations requiring the purchase of domestically produced or sourced goods.

• WTO rules also permit the imposition of countervailing duties on unfairly subsidized imports and other responses against imports that are deemed to be "dumped" (i.e., that cost less than their fair value), thereby unfairly undercutting an importing nation's domestic industry.

The World Bank study found that about one-third of the trade-related actions that it identified involved tariff increases. For instance, Russia raised tariffs on used automobiles, and Ecuador raised tariffs on more than 600 items. Non-tariff protectionism included Argentina's imposition of non-automatic licensing requirements on auto parts, textiles, TVs, toys, shoes, and leather goods and Indonesia's stipulation that five categories of goods (including garments, footwear, toys, electronics, food, and beverages) would be allowed in only a few ports and airports.

Some nations tightened standards to slow import entry. Examples include China's import prohibition on Irish pork and some Belgian chocolate, Italian brandy, British sauce, Dutch eggs, and Spanish dairy products. India banned Chinese toys. The European Union announced that it would be implementing new export subsidies on butter, cheese, and milk powder.

Subsidies can constitute a form of protectionism, and they have proliferated in many countries to benefit domestic auto industries. The World Bank found that by March 2009, these subsidies to auto industries already totaled $48 billion worldwide. The United States, Canada, France, Germany, the United Kingdom, China, Argentina, Brazil, Sweden,

and Italy provided direct or indirect subsidies to avoid layoffs of automobile industry workers. Australia provided support to domestic car dealers, and South Korea and Portugal directed aid to automobile component suppliers. The World Bank study noted that such subsidies skew needed adjustments in an industry that, on a worldwide level, suffers from excess capacity.

The American Recovery and Investment Act of 2009—the so-called stimulus legislation in the U.S., which contains a "Buy American" provision—is emblematic of the historic sensitivities related to protectionism in government procurement. The 1947 General Agreement on Tariffs and Trade excluded government procurement. In the following decades, government spending became an increasingly large factor in many nations' GDP, most notably in countries in which entire sectors of the economy were nationalized, such as steel and airlines. The 1979 Tokyo Round of GATT negotiations resulted in an Agreement on Government Procurement, which members had the option of joining.

The government procurement provision was the only code from the GATT Tokyo Round not to be made a mandatory requirement for membership in the World Trade Organization. The Uruguay Round of the GATT negotiations (1986–1993), which created the WTO, covered government procurement insofar as it relates to antidumping and subsidies in its mandatory agreements, which are binding on WTO members, but members generally may still enter into plurilateral agreements that affect government procurement. China, India, and Brazil have not joined the Agreement on Government Procurement.

Protectionism can also stem from legislation that is apparently entirely unrelated to international trade or the current economic downturn. For instance, efforts to address global warming by implementing government programs that require permits to emit carbon will significantly increase costs for manufacturing and other industry sectors. As a consequence, nations with such carbon-reduction systems will suffer reduced competitiveness compared to countries with few or no restrictions on carbon emissions.

It is inevitable that there will be domestic pressure to impose import tariffs to offset the competitive advantage enjoyed by countries that do not impose such expensive restrictions.

For governments, industries, and labor organizations, protectionism in its various forms always has been and likely always will be appealing in both good and bad times. Protectionism is never more alluring, treacherous, and destructive than it is in the most severe economic crises, such as the one that the world is experiencing today. Moreover, as the experience of the 1930s demonstrates, reversing its harmful effects takes valuable time, thereby allowing the crisis to worsen and delaying recovery.

REASONS FOR OPTIMISM

The current economic downturn is occurring in a worldwide economy and an international system of trade rules that are not entirely analogous to the 1930s, the period of widespread and severe economic distress known as the Great Depression. In the 1930s, nations were able to increase trade barriers without running afoul of international agreements. Today, instead of instantly retaliating, WTO members can utilize WTO dispute resolution mechanisms, and there is wider recognition of the perils of protectionism and the benefits of freer trade.

The world's economies, industries, and corporations are exponentially more reliant on world trade than they were in the 1930s, a tremendously consequential fact that tempers demands for protectionism in the 21st century economy. International diversification and joint ventures with foreign partners lessen the desire for protectionism, as does the increased presence of foreign companies with production facilities in domestic markets.

The current downturn began in a world economy that is far more open than that of the 1930s. Trade tariffs, which averaged about 50 percent in the 1930s and 25 percent in the 1980s, average around 10 percent today. Dramatic tariff increases today would be devastating were they to occur. Meanwhile, there is far more latitude today for freer trade to help lift the world's economies.

There are other contrasts with the Great Depression era. While the automobile industries in Asia, the U.S., and Europe declined precipitously in 2008–2009, it is not nearly as serious as the decline in 1932, when automobile manufacturing dropped 90 percent. The bank failures of 2008–2009, while disturbing, are a fraction of the 10,000 bank failures in the U.S. in 1933, or even the failure of over 3,000 savings and loan institutions in the U.S. in the late 1980s.

The World Bank's March 2009 study found several structural impediments to protectionism that did not exist in the 1930s and that may serve as effective firewalls against destructive anti-trade measures:

Countries are far more interdependent through supply chains, imported inputs, and even services. Export interests are far more powerful than before relative to pure import-competing industries. Producers for the domestic market are more reliant on imported inputs, and production chains link global markets through a web of trade in parts and components. The simple average of trade-to-GDP is today 96 percent compared to 55 percent in 1970—and parts and components trade, an indicator of supply chains, has more than doubled as a proportion of total trade. In addition, successive GATT/WTO agreements have provided much greater legal stability of trading relations. Because of this quite different political economy today, a few proposed restrictions have been rejected or not enacted. In Brazil, for example, the bureaucracy attempted to impose widespread licensing arrangements and import controls reminiscent of the 1970s, only to provoke a response of outrage from the private sector that led to immediate reversal. Similarly, the more egregious forms of the Buy America provision appear to have been circumvented. Moreover, about 10 of the 77 proposed and implemented changes in trade policies involved steps toward greater liberalization, mostly related to free trade agreements.[13]

WTO agreements are binding legal documents that cover a wide range of activities and deal with a range of issues involving agriculture, textiles and clothing, banking, telecommunications, government purchases, industrial standards and product safety, food sanitation regulations, and intellectual property. Overriding principles in the WTO include treating trading partners equally, treating foreigners and locals equally, and negotiating to reduce barriers to trade.

Protectionism is sometimes in the eye of the beholder, and protectionist provisions can be found in the trade agreements of the World Trade Organization, where trade-restraining options are referred to as "contingency" or "defensive" trade measures and may include tariff increases and countervailing and antidumping duties levied on imports. These defensive measures were included in trade agreements to make the costs and risks palatable to signatories. If implemented, they could exacerbate a decline in world merchandise trade that the WTO predicts could total 10 percent.

There is ample reason to hope that the existence of these contingency-defensive provisions will deter some protectionist actions. The WTO recognizes that the contingency measures in trade agreements are not harmless if implemented and that their consequences can be serious. The press release announcing its 2009 World Trade Report observes that:

[C]ontingency measures can be seen as an instrument of adjustment policy, to allow for temporary relief from import competition.... They can also serve to deter certain trade actions employed by trading partners. Moreover, they can act as a means of helping to maintain the rule of law in international trade, in that they channel otherwise arbitrary protectionist actions into prescribed and predictable policy measures.[14]

BOOSTING INTERNATIONAL TRADE AND DOMESTIC CONSUMPTION

In the 1930s, the U.S. was the world's largest current account surplus country. Today, that distinction goes to China. The "current account" measures a nation's international transactions, including trade in goods, services, investments, and transfers. The world's current account surpluses in 2008 were estimated to total about $2 trillion. High-saving countries, including China, Japan, and Germany, have been dependent on exports to generate economic growth. The U.S., being in recent years a non-saving nation in which consumer spending has accounted for 70 percent of the economy, was chief among those nations that were only too happy to oblige through huge amounts of consumption of imported goods and borrowing from overseas.

The collapse of the housing and credit markets, rapidly rising unemployment, the declining stock market, and plunging consumer confidence all contributed to a dramatic contraction in domestic spending and investment in the U.S. and other nations. Americans suddenly became savers, and the U.S. current account deficit dropped to 2 percent or 3 percent of GDP in 2009, down from 6 percent in 2006. To sustain their own economic growth, the current account surplus countries must generate more economic activity within their own borders. This will not be easy for a variety of reasons, some of them rooted in differing national cultures.

- It has been estimated that to offset the decline in U.S. consumption alone, China would have to boost domestic consumption by 40 percent, but that may be beyond the capacity of the Chinese government to do on its own.

13. Press release, "Protectionist Measures Show Worrisome Rise Since Beginning of Financial Crisis: Study Shows 17 of G-20 Countries Have Implemented Trade-Restricting Measures," The World Bank, March 17, 2009, at *http://web.worldbank.org/WBSITE/EXTERNAL/NEWS/0,,contentMDK:22105847~menuPK:34463~pagePK:34370~piPK:34424~theSitePK:4607,00.html* (October 9, 2009).

14. Press release, "World Trade Report: Keeping Trade Open in Times of Crisis," World Trade Organization, July 22, 2009, at *http://www.wto.org/english/news_e/pres09_e/pr565_e.htm* (October 9, 2009).

To spur greatly increased consumer spending by China's households would require changing the behavior of a citizenry accustomed to saving up to 25 percent of their income.

- The Japanese people historically also have saved a higher proportion of their income, and the entire nation—poor in natural resources but rich in productive workers—has been geared toward exporting since the end of World War II.

- Germany has been the world's largest exporter of manufactured goods, is accustomed to export-led growth, and, with post–World War I hyperinflation in mind, got in the habit of stability in its fiscal policy. German citizens are also prodigious savers, especially in this worldwide economic environment.

Changing these behaviors will be difficult, but it must be done both to sustain growth in these countries and to make growth possible in others. Alternatives such as protectionism, which seeks to further insulate domestic markets and unfairly advantage exports to other nations that have their own problems, will surely be met with protectionist backlash. That is why it is so important for WTO member countries to reaffirm their commitment to more open markets for trading.

What became abundantly clear in the 1930s after protectionism exploded and trade collapsed, and is even clearer today, is that no country and no region can go it alone and prosper for long. The post–World War II GATT negotiations and the subsequent creation of the World Trade Organization and numerous regional and bilateral trade agreements are testament to this fundamental truth.

The current economic crisis should underscore the urgency of completing the WTO's Doha Development Agenda of multilateral trade negotiations, which began in 2001 and would achieve important breakthroughs on trade in agricultural products, industrial goods, and services. Success in the Doha Round of WTO negotiations would boost specific trade sectors, provide more deterrence against protectionism, and encourage worldwide confidence in future trade freedom and prosperity. As U.S. Trade Representative Ron-

ald Kirk stated in advance of a meeting of WTO ministers in New Delhi in July of 2009, "Completion of the Doha round can be a key element of helping the world recover from this global economic crisis."[15]

STAYING ON COURSE

World trade is and should be a constantly evolving phenomenon, each trade agreement a segue to the next, with ever greater trade freedom the result. But trade is highly competitive and complex, and never more so than in an economic downturn such as the world has experienced since 2008. Temptations to gain short-term advantages through the protectionist tactics of higher tariffs, subsidies, and other devices abound.

Such tactics, however, are doomed to fail. It is true that they may protect a non-competitive industry or save a few specific jobs, but they will do so only for a short time, and at an extremely high cost. Societies undertaking such protectionist measures impose costs on themselves that include higher prices on goods and services for consumers and producers and lower productivity and wages for workers. The new jobs that would have been created in an open and rapidly evolving economy never materialize, and economic stagnation replaces growth in societies that doom themselves to underdevelopment.

For six decades, the world has reaped the benefits of rapidly expanding trade. That expansion has come to a stop during the recession of 2008–2009. If governments succumb to political pressure or panic, a protectionist response could turn a temporary setback into a long-term change of course that would harm world economic growth for decades. If, instead, leaders remain true to the vision of world integration and interdependence that inspired their predecessors, renewed economic growth and the trade that flows from and underpins it will surely follow.

---

15. Meena Thiruvengadam, "USTR Kirk Expresses Optimism Over Doha Round Potential," Dow Jones Newswires, September 1, 2009, at *http://online.wsj.com/article/BT-CO-20090901-713439.html#articleTabs_article* (October 9, 2009).

Chapter 3

Economic Freedom and Crisis Performance in Asia

Derek Scissors, Ph.D.

Economic freedom has moral and practical dimensions. The moral side—that it is better for people to enjoy liberty in their economic lives—applies in the short term, long term, and every term in between. The practical side is famously more complicated.

There are obvious historical examples where planned economies do well for a time. The classic case, of course, is the Soviet Union. It was initially able to mobilize resources from agriculture to bolster industry, thought to be the sole path to modernization. However, both technological innovation and organizational efficiency stagnated because of misunderstanding and misapplication of incentives.

In Asia, India's socialist experiment started to crumble in the early 1980s with pro-business reforms and ended altogether in 1990 after a balance of payments crisis resulting from central planners being unable to match their price-setting and quantity-setting with actual supply and demand.[1] The pro-market reforms that followed led to sustained, rapid growth.

The practical argument for economic freedom is that the state will inevitably make ugly mistakes, partly because of our incapacity to control systems as complex as national economies. In a crisis, a government regulator or manager may be able to respond quickly and even effectively to a particular problem, but they are likely to do a poor job in adjusting all of the myriad production decisions facing individual firms across an entire economy. A centrally managed economy can thereby actually suffer more from unexpected turbulence. This may even be true when only part of the economy is managed if it turns out to be a pivotal part.

---

1.   Dani Rodrik and Arvind Subramanian, "From 'Hindu Growth' to Productivity Surge: The Mystery of the Indian Growth Transition," International Monetary Fund *Working Paper* No. WP/04/77, May 2004, at *http://www.imf.org/external/pubs/ft/wp/2004/wp0477.pdf*.

The *Index of Economic Freedom* is based on the idea that freer economies perform better over the long run. A wealth of data, both from this *Index* and from independent research, backs the idea that economic freedom promotes long-term prosperity and that advancing economic freedom generates higher economic growth, employment creation, and the reduction of poverty.

In light of the recent global financial and economic turbulence, this chapter examines a different and timely question: whether economic freedom predicts performance in a crisis. Do freer, more flexible economies withstand economic turmoil better? Asian economies provide a good test for this hypothesis. They top the rankings in economic freedom but are also represented at the very bottom. That wide variation should make for a wide variation in crisis performance.

Economic freedom should help predict performance in the present crisis: Holding everything else constant, freer and more flexible economies should survive better. For many Asian economies, however, the *Index* freedom score may be somewhat incomplete on two counts. The first is that some economies were consciously distorted by intervention aimed at building official stockpiles of foreign exchange reserves. The second is that the *Index* scores do not yet fully capture the wide range of policy steps taken in response to the global crisis. Taking into consideration two distinctive policy measures not covered by the *Index*—reserve accumulation and interest rate change—this chapter provides an expanded view of Asian economies' economic freedom and crisis performance.

At this point, there are not enough data on either policy measures or performance in the present crisis for a final assessment. A more complete evaluation will be possible next year at this time. However, partial results tentatively affirm that policies which permit greater economic freedom would have served Asia better in the past, in the present, and into the future.

MEASURING ECONOMIC FREEDOM IN A CRISIS

The Heritage Foundation/Wall Street Journal *Index of Economic Freedom* includes 42 Asian economies. Twelve are too small to chart even

a nominally independent policy course, and there are insurmountable data problems with eight others.[2] The remaining 22 economies offer comparatively credible gross domestic product of nearly $5 billion or more and generate almost all of Asia's GDP, production, investment, and trade by dollar value. These economies are grouped in Chart 1 by *Index* aggregate scores (2009 scores based on data covering July 2007 through June 2008 are used).

In terms of economic freedom, it turns out that these Asian economies appear to represent global patterns well: The same number of countries lies above and below the global mean. The sample also shows wide variation, with multiple economies within each category ranging from free to unfree. The latter is necessary for the sample to be useful.

Measuring crisis performance is somewhat subjective. The chief goal of economic development is sustainable improvement in per capita incomes. Since the duration of the crisis has to this point been short, population will change only slightly. Per capita income can thus be simplified to sustained improvement in national income. GDP is not an ideal measure of national income, but it is universal. In this study, by necessity a short-term analysis, we rate crisis performance by measuring the change in GDP growth rates in 2008 from those in 2005–2007.[3]

---

2. Basic data for this study are not available for Afghanistan, Burma, North Korea, and Turkmenistan. Data for the crisis period are as yet wildly inconsistent for Azerbaijan, the Kyrgyz Republic, Papua New Guinea, and Uzbekistan. The excluded countries range from the middle to the bottom in economic freedom, so the remaining sample is biased toward a higher level of economic freedom. However, the study does not assess the level of economic freedom in Asia, so the bias may be benign.

3. Evaluating performance during the downturn suffers from a standard trade-off: Later is when the evaluation will be clearest, but now is when it is most important. Asian economies were weakening throughout 2008, but weakness became acute in September in some countries and November in others. Unfortunately, GDP data from 2009 are incomplete for all countries and not available for some. An assessment of 2009 cannot be comprehensive. In addition, the crisis did not occur in a vacuum; pre-crisis GDP trend must factor into the

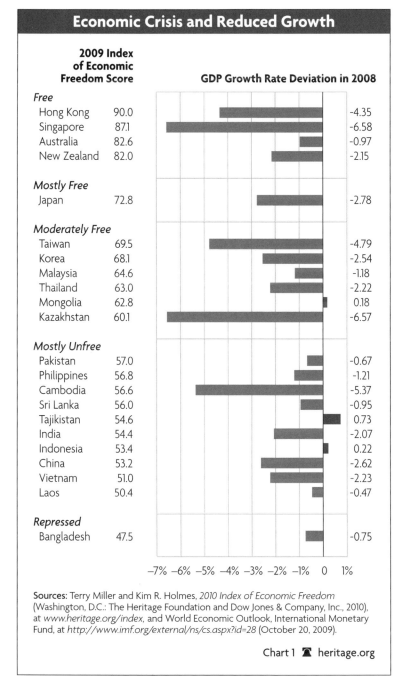

Economic Crisis and Reduced Growth

2009 Index of Economic Freedom Score		GDP Growth Rate Deviation in 2008
Free		
Hong Kong	90.0	-4.35
Singapore	87.1	-6.58
Australia	82.6	-0.97
New Zealand	82.0	-2.15
Mostly Free		
Japan	72.8	-2.78
Moderately Free		
Taiwan	69.5	-4.79
Korea	68.1	-2.54
Malaysia	64.6	-1.18
Thailand	63.0	-2.22
Mongolia	62.8	0.18
Kazakhstan	60.1	-6.57
Mostly Unfree		
Pakistan	57.0	-0.67
Philippines	56.8	-1.21
Cambodia	56.6	-5.37
Sri Lanka	56.0	-0.95
Tajikistan	54.6	0.73
India	54.4	-2.07
Indonesia	53.4	0.22
China	53.2	-2.62
Vietnam	51.0	-2.23
Laos	50.4	-0.47
Repressed		
Bangladesh	47.5	-0.75

−7% −6% −5% −4% −3% −2% −1% 0 1%

Sources: Terry Miller and Kim R. Holmes, *2010 Index of Economic Freedom* (Washington, D.C.: The Heritage Foundation and Dow Jones & Company, Inc., 2010), at *www.heritage.org/index*, and World Economic Outlook, International Monetary Fund, at *http://www.imf.org/external/ns/cs.aspx?id=28* (October 20, 2009).

Chart 1 ☎ heritage.org

These figures are also shown in Chart 1.[4]

With economic freedom scores and a measure of short-term crisis performance in hand, we can ask: Did freer Asian economies respond better in the recent crisis? In Chart 1, the correlation between the level of economic freedom and variations in short-term GDP growth is actually negative. At least among the selected Asian countries, those with less economic freedom suffered a bit less during the 2008 segment of the recent global downturn. This is perhaps not surprising, given the fact that countries with less economic freedom are less engaged with the world economy as a whole.

Obviously, one wants to take into consideration comparative performance before a crisis as well as during a crisis. Since countries with greater economic freedom have, on average, much better long-term growth rates than less free countries, any downturn during a crisis must be evaluated against the higher growth previously achieved.

Equally important is that economic freedom is a dynamic, not static, feature. That is, *changes* in economic freedom also have an important impact on a country's crisis

evaluation. This trend will vary by development stage as well as by level of economic freedom. A smaller base and more unexploited opportunities to enhance either efficiency or resource mobilization make it generally easier for less-developed economies to boast high rates of GDP growth. Here, given the small portion of the crisis captured by 2008 data, a narrower trend measurement better conveys the extent of instability. When 2009 results are available, an extended GDP trend may be appropriate.

4. Because of the comparison to trend, the results may clash with conventional views of the crisis. China does worse than perhaps expected because its still-considerable GDP growth has dropped by a substantial amount. Pakistan's earlier economic struggles, on the other hand, make for only a small decline in growth during the crisis.

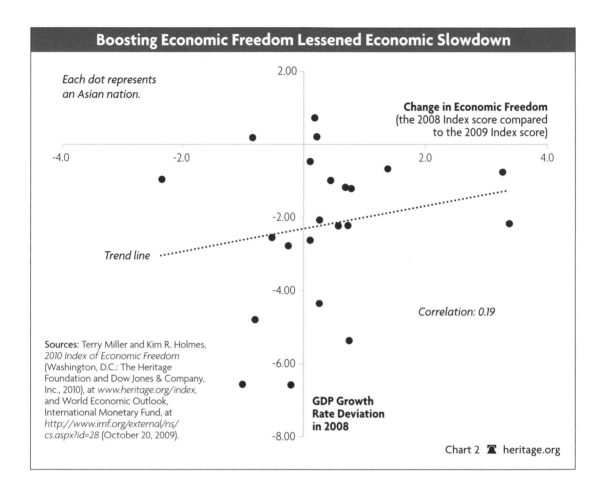

Boosting Economic Freedom Lessened Economic Slowdown

Each dot represents an Asian nation.

Change in Economic Freedom
(the 2008 Index score compared to the 2009 Index score)

Trend line ⋯⋯⋯⋯

Correlation: 0.19

GDP Growth Rate Deviation in 2008

Sources: Terry Miller and Kim R. Holmes, *2010 Index of Economic Freedom* (Washington, D.C.: The Heritage Foundation and Dow Jones & Company, Inc., 2010), at *www.heritage.org/index*, and World Economic Outlook, International Monetary Fund, at *http://www.imf.org/external/ns/ cs.aspx?id=28* (October 20, 2009).

Chart 2 ☎ heritage.org

performance and resilience. As shown in Chart 2, the correlation between changes in economic freedom and the variation of GDP growth rates is positive, indicating that advancing economic freedom has enabled some countries to perform better than others during the recent economic turmoil.

Still, the lack of correlation between the level of economic freedom and short-term crisis performance suggests either that economic freedom does not necessarily promote superior crisis performance or that something important has been missed, at least for Asian countries. It turns out that a strong case can be made for the latter explanation.

The *Index of Economic Freedom* ranks a notably large number of countries from every region of the world. The inclusion of so many countries constrains the number of comparable data sets that can be used to measure economic freedom. The *Index* provides a comprehensive picture of

economic freedom, yet it cannot be claimed that it is measuring every relevant variable, or even necessarily all of the most important variables. It represents a compromise between the ideal and the possible.

Fortunately, in the case of the larger Asian economies, there are available data relevant to economic freedom that enhance understanding of its effects on crisis performance. In determining what information might be most valuable, it is helpful to consider the recent history of government policies and crises in Asia.

THE ASIAN FINANCIAL CRISIS

In the early and mid-1990s, many Asian states intervened in their economies to mobilize capital and other resources. In light of superficially excellent macroeconomic performance, decision-makers dismissed critics of this intervention. They touted an "Asian" path to prosperity that combined private enterprise's pursuit of profit with an activist state's pursuit of national development goals.[5] The invisible hand needed to be guided by an all too visible government brain. More specifically, the state's economic policy was focused on contemporary rapid growth, ignoring the absence of productivity gains that would make growth rates sustainable indefinitely.[6]

This seemed to work until the Asian financial crisis erupted in 1997. It was inefficient resource allocation, largely due to government influence over interest rates and the financial system,[7] that proved to be the main reason for the attacks on regional currencies in 1997. This resource misallocation incorporated, but was not limited to, the concentration of short-term foreign capital flows in specific sectors. The proximate cause of the attacks was even more government intervention, this time in the currency market in the form of incorrect exchange rate valuation and restrictions on foreign currency trading.[8]

The devastating nature of the ensuing shock is well known. For example, in Korea, Indonesia, Malaysia, and Thailand—the four countries hit directly—from 1996 to 1998, GDP fell an average of 8.9 percent, and the average unemployment rate nearly doubled.[9]

An academic debate continues to this day over whether the harshness of the regional crisis was due primarily to fundamental structural problems or to panic and information distortions associated with the currency runs. This debate overlooks the policy lessons actually drawn.

Some financial-sector reform was undertaken to address structural weakness,[10] but the chief reaction among many policymakers was to move to better protect their exchange rates in the future by accumulating foreign reserves. (See Table 1.) This required another flawed round of state action. The conventional wisdom in Asia became not that state intervention contained hidden and painful costs, but that the state should intervene to accumulate foreign exchange reserves and deter currency attacks.

Reserves as a percentage of GDP captures the extent of exchange rate "protection" being purchased by a government. A value of 0, of course, is unnaturally and perilously low. On the other side, as the value moves higher and higher, it begins to seem wasteful and eventually harmful. When excessive reserve accumulation is forced by government action, which inevitably is distorting to some extent, the process is twice inefficient. In this case, reserve accumulation represents a fundamental imbalance caused by the state and, hence, a sharp deviation from economic freedom.

The interventions in Asia may have started as minor distortions in 1998, but they have since pushed foreign reserves in certain economies to unprecedented levels. On some accounts, these reserves are so large as to become the sin-

5.   Nicholas D. Kristof, "Crisis Pushing Asian Capitalism Closer to U.S.-Style Free Market," *The New York Times*, January 17, 1998, at *http://www.nytimes.com/1998/01/17/world/ international-business-crisis-pushing-asian-capitalism-closer-us-style-free.html*.

6.   Paul Krugman, "The Myth of Asia's Miracle," *Foreign Affairs*, November/December 1994, at *http://www.foreignaffairs.com/articles/50550/ paul-krugman/the-myth-of-asias-miracle*.

7.   Beatriz Pont, Liu Lan, Francisco García-Blanch, Clara García, and Iliana Olivié, "The Financial Crisis in East Asia: The Cases of Japan, China, South Korea and Southeast Asia," Compltense Institute for International Studies, Compltense University of Madrid, *Working Paper* No. 11, October 1998, at *http://www.ucm.es/info/eid/pb/ICEIwp11-4.pdf*.

8.   Dick K. Nanto, "The 1997–98 Asian Financial Crisis," Congressional Research Service *Report for Congress*, February 6, 1998, at *http://www.fas.org/ man/crs/crs-asia2.htm*.

9.   Andrew Berg, "The Asia Crisis: Causes, Policy Responses, and Outcomes," International

Monetary Fund *Working Paper* No. WP/99/138, October 1999, at *http://www.imf.org/external/pubs/ft/ wp/1999/wp99138.pdf*; "A Note on Unemployment in the Wake of the Asian Economic crisis and Some Responses," Economic and Social Commission for Asia and the Pacific, *Bulletin on Asia–Pacific Perspectives*, 2002/03, at *http://www.unescap.org/ drpad/publication/bulletin%202002/ch3.pdf*.

10.   "The IMF's Response to the Asian Crisis," International Monetary Fund *Factsheet*, January 1999, at *http://www.imf.org/External/np/exr/facts/asia.htm*.

Foreign Reserves and GDP in Asia

Ratio of Foreign Reserves to GDP

Extremely High		High		Average	
Singapore	1.01	Thailand	0.347	Kazakhstan	0.15
Hong Kong	0.737	Vietnam	0.342	Laos	0.13
Taiwan	0.702	Mongolia	0.304	Indonesia	0.127
		Korea	0.27	*Global Mean*	*0.117*
Very High					
Malaysia	0.541	Above Average		Below Average	
China	0.477	India	0.227	New Zealand	0.127
		Japan	0.217	Sri Lanka	0.109
		Cambodia	0.216	Pakistan	0.098
		Philippines	0.21	Tajikistan	0.081
				Bangladesh	0.076
				Australia	0.03

Sources: Terry Miller and Kim R. Holmes, *2010 Index of Economic Freedom* (Washington, D.C.: The Heritage Foundation and Dow Jones & Company, Inc., 2010), at *www.heritage.org/index*, and individual countries' central banks' Web sites.

Table 1 ☎ heritage.org

Index scores with the lost freedom signified by reserves/GDP provides a more comprehensive version of true economic freedom in the region than is provided by *Index* scores alone.

GOVERNMENT INTERVENTION WITH LASTING CONSEQUENCES

The policies implemented in response to the 1997 crisis did not end with its resolution. They have had an impact during the current crisis as well.

The easiest way to accumulate large quantities of foreign exchange over time is to defend an undervalued currency. This also has the seeming extra advantage of making exports more competitive, thus temporarily boosting employment and GDP. It therefore became standard policy in much of Asia for almost a decade.[13] From the time of their recovery after the regional crisis until the global financial crisis, Asia economies were again praised for their macroeconomic performance, warnings were again raised concerning the unsustainable nature of their policy course, and these warnings were again ignored.[14]

gle most important global economic force.[11]

This dubious accomplishment was made possible by sharply skewing resource allocation toward exports (or supply of exporters) because returns to exporting were artificially enhanced, often by forcefully depressed exchange rates, as the tool for building up reserves. The imbalances caused by the distortion have principally taken the form of unnecessary dependence on foreign demand and corresponding unnecessary weakness in domestic consumption.

Table 1 thus provides an indirect measurement of how much freedom has been lost in Asian economies for the sake of accumulating reserves.[12] If the distortions implied by high reserves/GDP reduce economic freedom, then the sample economies have less freedom than the *Index* would indicate. The Average group lies above the global mean in reserve accumulation. If average levels are taken to be close to ideal, many countries in the sample are far from ideal, having intervened to accumulate seriously excessive reserves. Combining

11. "Remarks by Governor Ben S. Bernanke," Sandridge Lecture, Virginia Association of Economics, Richmond, Virginia, March 10, 2005, at *http://www.federalreserve.gov/boarddocs/speeches/2005/200503102*.

12. See World Bank, *World Development Indicators 2009*, online database.

13. Hans Genberg, Robert N. McCauley, Yung Chul Park, and Avinash Persaud, *Official Reserves and Currency Management in Asia: Myth, Reality and the Future* (Geneva: International Center for Monetary and Banking Studies, 2005).

14. Charles Adams and Donghyun Park, "Causes and Consequences of Global Imbalances: Perspective from Developing Asia," Asian Development Bank, *Asian Development Review*, Vol. 26, No. 1 (2009), at *http://www.adb.org/Documents/Periodicals/ADR/pdf/ADR-Vol26-1-Adams.pdf*; Yilmaz Akyuz, "The Global Financial Turmoil and Asian Developing Countries," paper presented at meeting of Economic and Social Commission for Asia and the Pacific, Bangkok, Thailand, April 29, 2008, at *http://www.twnside.org.sg/title2/finance/twninfofinance20080506.htm*.

As inevitably happens with government intervention, those guiding the state's hands were themselves misguided. One mistake made by Asian policymakers was fighting the last war, believing that the next crisis would look very much like the previous one and foreign reserves would prove decisive.[15] Instead, the mountains of reserves proved irrelevant when the financial system shuddered in September 2008. A year later, the International Monetary Fund found no connection between reserves and economic growth, and IMF chief economist Oliver Blanchard called reserve accumulation "incredibly inefficient" and "very expensive."[16]

The principal mistake, though, was addressing the symptom of currency weakness rather than the disease of structural weakness. Reorientation of economies to accumulate reserves led to greater than necessary dependence on exports and foreign consumption. In particular, undervalued, reserve-accumulating exchange rates fomented Asian dependence on external consumption.

Competitive exports appeared to be the ideal engine for economic expansion when, in fact, this was an artificial construct, reliant primarily on hyperactive American consumers.[17] In protecting against an external blow through currencies, Asian governments engendered vulnerability to an external blow through basic demand and supply. This unnecessary dependence turned intensely harmful when external demand slumped in the fall of 2008.

A very considerable portion of Asia's recovery from its financial crisis was not effective state intervention, as often claimed, but rather playing to the seeds of a similar American financial crisis. Asia's dependence on the U.S. means that it suffered for its own policy mistakes and then for America's. With the collapse of the American financial house of cards and rise in private U.S. saving,[18] Asian economies may now be forced to do what they should have done voluntarily over the past decade: restructure in sustainable fashion.

Alternatively, some Asian governments are again intervening, this time to temporarily boost employment and growth. The argument for economic freedom, twice confirmed already, is that state actions are a double-edged sword and that a third intervention will also have a high price.

THE GLOBAL RECESSION

The financial turmoil that started in the U.S. in 2008 led quickly to a worldwide crisis that saw significant drops in trade, investment, and GDP growth. To respond to the slump, Asian governments have utilized fiscal outlays, trade barriers, financial regulation, and interest rates and money supply. Eventually, all of these should be assessed. Only those actions chosen and implemented very quickly, however, curbed economic freedom in the period covered by this study. For instance, much fiscal expansion promised in late 2008 did not occur until well into 2009.

As in 1997 and its aftermath, crisis-driven state intervention obviously harmed economic freedom across the region, but to a different extent in different countries. To measure the impact of economic freedom on crisis performance accurately, this variance must be assessed.

The assessment presents two timing problems, however. In the crisis, governments chose policies with immediate, positive impacts, accepting or ignoring long-term costs. The superiority of economic freedom is compatible with short-run benefits from state intervention, but these benefits will come with short-run and long-run costs from reduced

15. Wendy Leung, "Hong Kong May Use Foreign Reserves to Prevent Financial Crisis," Bloomberg.com, October 12, 2008, at *http://www.bloomberg.com/apps/news?pid= 20601080&sid=alfYZgGWdOqM&refer=asia.*

16. Dow Jones, "IMF Chief Economist: Ctrl-Bk Reserves Haven't Influenced Growth Rates," *The Wall Street Journal*, September 1, 2009, at *http:// online.wsj.com/article/BT-CO-20090901-704885.html.*

17. "Asian Economies: Troubled Tigers," *The Economist*, January 29, 2009, at *http:// www.economist.com/businessfinance/ displayStory.cfm?story_id=13022067.*

18. "Amid Recession, U.S. Savings Rate Hits Highest Mark Since 1993," Online NewsHour, June 26, 2009, at *http://www.pbs.org/newshour/ updates/business/jan-june09/savingrate_06-26.html.*

competition, higher taxes, and/or financial disintermediation.

At the time of this writing, performance data for the full set of countries are available only through the end of 2008. These data are likely to capture a larger portion of the benefits of state actions, which were chosen for immediate impact, compared to their costs. They will therefore undervalue economic freedom. Since government policy plainly cannot be excluded, there is a pro-intervention bias in this first evaluation of Asian economies in the crisis. It will dissipate in future work.

The second problem is more difficult. Currently, only pre-crisis freedom scores are available. The *Index* is beginning to capture crisis policy in the current volume, but the full extent of government interventions will be revealed only in future years. For this study, therefore, policy stances adopted during the crisis must be identified and measured in some fashion that is independent of the *Index*. Fortunately, data are available for Asian economies that can serve as an adequate proxy for overall policy intervention for 2008.

The policy steps with the fastest effect are monetary. Interest rate changes alter prices immediately, and sharp departures in money supply can influence financial market transactions in just a few days. Further, in many cases, monetary policy is telegraphed and has effects through expectations. In contrast, fiscal or regulatory policies, even if announced or adopted in 2008, are not likely to affect GDP growth in the period under study. Monetary policy is also a proxy for broader government response to the crisis, even in the minority of cases (in-sample) where the central bank is supposed to be independent.

Whatever its perceived or actual value as stimulus, strident government intervention in the money market curbs economic freedom. It unavoidably distorts private financial decisions and typically harms existing asset holders. The extent of interest rate changes made in response to the crisis can thus be used to rank policy as more or less free.

In Table 2, interest rate measures are supplemented by changes in broad money supply to

Policy Intervention in Asia

Change in Interest Rate

Minimal		Considerable	
Bangladesh	0.25	Thailand	3.75
Pakistan	1.00	Australia	4.00
Japan	1.30	India	4.00
		Philippines	4.00
Minor			
Malaysia	1.90	**Heavy**	
Indonesia	2.20	Tajikistan	4.25
Singapore	2.25	Mongolia	4.30
Korea	2.50	China	4.45
New Zealand	2.50	Kazakhstan	4.50
Moderate		**Maximal**	
Cambodia	2.80	Taiwan	4.90
Laos	3.00	Hong Kong	5.00
Sri Lanka	3.10	Vietnam	5.50

Sources: Terry Miller and Kim R. Holmes, *2010 Index of Economic Freedom* (Washington, D.C.: The Heritage Foundation and Dow Jones & Company, Inc., 2010), at *www.heritage.org/index*, and individual countries' central banks' Web sites.

Table 2 ☎ heritage.org

give an overall measure of government policy infringement in the recent crisis.[19] The data are limited but instructive. As with other measures in this study, there is a broad distribution of scores, which is welcome. There are also individual idiosyncrasies. Japanese interest rates were so low at the start of the crisis that Japan's crisis behavior appears responsible almost by default. At the other end, Vietnam does not track money supply and, as a result, uses interest rate changes as a blunt instrument.

SHEDDING NEW LIGHT ON ASIAN ECONOMIC FREEDOM

Crisis performance in Asia can now be measured against an economic freedom score augmented with measures of forced reserve accumulation and monetary easing.

Table 3 represents the GDP growth change from Chart 1 alongside an economic freedom score that is now revised to take into account

19. Monetary variables with the same label are not entirely identical across countries. In all cases, though, interest rates are a price for capital, and all governments have tools available to affect interest rates.

GDP and Economic Freedom		
	GDP Growth Rate Deviation in 2008	Adjusted Economic Freedom Score*
Tajikistan	0.73	57.7
Indonesia	0.22	68.7
Mongolia	0.18	52.8
Laos	-0.47	62.6
Pakistan	-0.67	78.1
Bangladesh	-0.75	79.8
Sri Lanka	-0.95	65.4
Australia	-0.97	70.3
Malaysia	-1.18	60.1
Philippines	-1.21	55.4
India	-2.07	54.2
New Zealand	-2.15	75.3
Thailand	-2.22	54.4
Vietnam	-2.23	39.5
Korea	-2.54	67.1
China	-2.62	42.5
Japan	-2.78	78.0
Hong Kong	-4.35	42.4
Taiwan	-4.79	37.7
Cambodia	-5.37	62.8
Kazakhstan	-6.57	56.0
Singapore	-6.58	49.7

Correlation: 0.39

* With foreign reserves and interest rate changes.

Sources: Terry Miller and Kim R. Holmes, *2010 Index of Economic Freedom* (Washington, D.C.: The Heritage Foundation and Dow Jones & Company, Inc., 2010), at *www.heritage.org/index*, and World Economic Outlook, International Monetary Fund, at *http://www.imf.org/external/ns/cs.aspx?id=28* (October 20, 2009).

Table 3 ☎ heritage.org

crisis performance is now positive and predictive, though at a modest level.[21] It is important to note that the inclusion of policy intervention and currently limited data means that this measure of freedom applies best only from the onset of the crisis late in the summer of 2008 through the end of that year.

The adjusted freedom scores show a natural correlation with the 2009 *Index* results, but there are also notable changes. For example, due to both excess reserve accumulation and sharp monetary intervention, Hong Kong falls far from its lofty perch as freest Asian economy. At the other end, Bangladesh rises noticeably.

These shifts may be more about capacity than intention to preserve economic freedom. Hong Kong has the technical and financial ability to conduct intervention to accumulate reserves or attempt to preserve jobs and acted accordingly. Bangladesh does not have the same ability to distort the economy and reduce economic freedom, whether the government wished to or not.

DID FREEDOM WORK?

While the limitations of the data are stark, they are also temporary. What will not change is the importance of measuring the efficacy of economic freedom with periods of intense economic stress as a crucial measuring stick. For almost two decades, many Asian policymakers have intervened in their economies, confident in the superiority of state action. That superiority was not borne out in the regional downturn of the late 1990s; has it been borne out thus far in this current and broader slump?

The answer, clearly, is no. In the best case, intervention has no predictive power with respect to changes in growth rates. It may have a negative effect on growth. The contortions that many Asian governments have engaged in—the warping of their economies to accumulate foreign exchange reserves and the hundreds of billions of dollars now being spent in response to the financial shock—either have no measurable effect on economic performance or may actually undermine it.

the reserve accumulation data from Table 1 and the policy infringement data from Table 2.[20]

The economic freedom scores that take into account monetary easing and foreign reserve accumulation do a better job than the original scores in predicting crisis performance. The correlation between economic freedom and

---

20. The data from Tables 1 and 2 were converted to a 0–100 scale by the standard maximum-minimum-value–based conversion. These scores were then averaged with the economic freedom score to give the revised and augmented economic freedom score presented in Table 3.

21. The coefficient of correlation is 0.389.

The impact of economic freedom is noticeable and significant in certain countries. Mongolia, singled out in the 2009 *Index* as the Asian economy that has gained the most economic freedom over the life of the *Index*, performed very well in the crisis. Tajikistan, another big gainer of economic freedom, tops the performance rankings. Hong Kong and Singapore, the top performers in the *Index of Economic Freedom*, do much less well when their scores are adjusted for reserve accumulation and interest rate changes, and they wind up near the bottom on our measure of crisis performance. It is worth repeating that the limited period of

China Versus Indonesia

Two important illustrations of the connection between economic performance and freedom are provided by China and Indonesia. Together, these two countries have populations of over 1.5 billion and GDPs of nearly $5 trillion, and were ranked right next to each other at the low end in the 2009 *Index*.

This study, however, reveals striking differences. Indonesia has eschewed the extreme exchange rate manipulations of many of its neighbors, has tolerated current account deficits,[1] and is close to the global average in reserves as a proportion of GDP.

In contrast, China has conducted persistent and powerful monetary intervention to depress its exchange rates, most recently repegging the RMB (renminbi) to the dollar for at least 16 months starting in June 2008.[2] This has led both directly, through purchases by the People's Bank to contain the RMB, and indirectly, by encouraging a larger trade surplus, to by far the world's largest stash of foreign reserves. China has more than four times the global average for reserves as a proportion to GDP.

Due the absence of policy skewing the economy to serving external demand, the global crisis was not as dire threat to Indonesia as it was to some of its neighbors. This made it easier for policymakers to remain restrained, and Indonesian monetary policy loosened only modestly. Also, the original fiscal stimulus proposed was only 1.4 percent of GDP, three quarters of which was tax cuts.[3]

China is again sharply dissimilar. Its announced fiscal program came to about 7 percent of GDP annually,[4] though spending did not commence until mid-November. Monetary stimulus was just as sharp and much faster, among the most powerful in the region in 2008 and intensifying through the first half of 2009 in the form of wildly fast bank lending and money growth.[5]

1. Bank Indonesia, "Indonesia Financial Statistics: Monetary Sector/Government Finance Sector/Real Sector/External Sector," at *http://www.bi.go.id/web/en/Statistik/Statistik+ Ekonomi+dan+Keuangan+Indonesia/Versi+HTML/ Sektor+Eksternal*; Jittima Tongurai and Kazuo Toritani, "Corners Hypothesis and the Proposals on Foreign Exchange System for East Asia: A Perspective from the Incompatible Trinity," paper presented at Asia–Pacific Economic and Business History Conference, Tokyo, Japan, February 18–20, 2009, at *http://www.uow.edu.au/ commerce/econ/ehsanz/Tokyo%20Conference%20 2009/Papers/Tongurai_Toritani.pdf*.

2. "FX History®: Historical Currency Exchange Rates," OANDA Corporation, at *http://www.oanda.com/convert/fxhistory*.

3. Iyanatul Islam and Anis Chowdhury, "Global Economic Crisis and Indonesia," *The Jakarta Post*, May 5, 2009, at *http://www.thejakartapost.com/ news/2009/05/05/global-economic-crisis-and- indonesia.html*. Ostensible stimulus was expanded moderately in 2009, but at the same time, the government budget deficit was rolled back.

4. David Barboza, "China Unveils Sweeping Plan for Economy," *The New York Times*, November 9, 2008, at *http://www.nytimes.com/2008/11/10/world/ asia/10china.html*.

5. People's Bank of China, "Money Supply Continues Rapid Growth," August 14, 2009, at *http://www.pbc.gov.cn/english/detail.asp?col= 6400&id=1413*.

study introduces a performance bias against economic freedom.

It is reasonable to expect that countries that are highly integrated into the world economy might suffer more quickly and profoundly from a global downturn, but it is also reasonable to expect that they might recover more quickly and strongly when conditions improve. The data to demonstrate that latter point are not yet available.

In the data available for this study, economic freedom is only modestly correlated with success in the crisis, but economic freedom is also free, both materially and morally.

Economic freedom correctly predicts Indonesia's superior crisis performance. Indonesia did not distort its economy accumulating foreign exchange and therefore was less harmed by declining global demand. In the future, its muted monetary response and fiscal responses will neither embed serious inflation nor force crushing taxes.

If intense government action was the proper antidote to the crisis, China should have responded better than nearly every other country in the region and far better than most. Instead, it lagged. China's mountain of foreign exchange reserves was of little use. The financial market repression behind the exchange rate controls that accumulated reserves suppressed domestic consumption, leaving China unnecessarily reliant on foreign consumers.[6] The short-term steps taken to try to offset this reliance are savaging the banking system and worsening long-term overcapacity.[7]

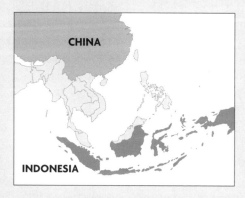

An obvious rejoinder is to point to China's economic success before the crisis as justifying statist policies. While a proper debate on this point is far beyond the scope of this study, economic freedom was completely lacking in China in 1978 and largely lacking in 1991. In both cases, Deng Xiaoping believed—and events proved him to be entirely correct—that more economic freedom was the only solution.

In 1999, then-Premier Zhu Rongji responded to the Asian financial crisis by vigorously adopting reform in order to win accession to the WTO. One of the high points of Zhu's reform was liberalizing urban housing, the same sector now viewed by some as the best hope for leading a sustainable recovery.[8]

When China has moved toward economic freedom, it has succeeded in stunning fashion. When it has moved away, as with reserves and the present crisis, it has wasted resources to no good effect.

6. Nicholas R. Lardy, "Financial Repression in China," Peter G. Peterson Institute for International Economics *Policy Brief* No. PG08-8, September 2008, at *http://www.iie.com/publications/pb/pb08-8.pdf.*

7. "China's Bank Loan Total Exceeds Full-Year Target," *People's Daily Online*, July 9, 2009, at *http://english.peopledaily.com.cn/90001/90778/90857/90859/6696563.html* (originally published by *China Daily*); Zhou Xin and Jason Subler, "UPDATE 1—China Says to Curb Industrial Overcapacity," Reuters, August 26, 2009, at *http://uk.reuters.com/article/idUKPEK16072820090826.*

8. "China's Housing Reform of 10 Years," *World Chinese Weekly*, January 21, 2008, at *http://www.worldchineseweekly.com/weekly_en/article/show.php?itemid=169*; Simon Rabinovitch, "China Goes House Hunting to Rev Up Economy," Reuters, August 18, 2009, at *http://www.reuters.com/article/reutersEdge/idUSTRE57H0Z020090818.*

Governments can permit their citizens freer and less distorted economic choices, including lower taxes and the unrestricted movement of individual savings, and still be no worse off and perhaps slightly better prepared than their interventionist counterparts for the sharp downturns Asia has suffered in each of the past two decades.

THE VALUE OF ECONOMIC FREEDOM

Neither the Asian financial crisis nor the especially sharp downturn in some Asian economies in the global financial crisis a decade later surprised advocates of economic freedom. Both flowed all too predictably from mistaken government intervention to mobilize resources or to orient the economy toward external demand.

The overwhelming reaction to the global crisis has been to call for more government: more spending (implicitly more taxation), more regulation, more trade management. It is widely proclaimed that too much economic freedom caused this crisis or at least made it more severe than it otherwise would have been. This study indicates that, in Asia and through the outset of the present crisis, those who make this claim have it absolutely backward.

A number of Asian governments are accepted to have followed statist paths to disastrous effect before the Asian financial crisis in the late 1990s. Another set of policymakers repeatedly and unapologetically intervened again after the regional crisis to build up foreign reserves and, it was thought, avoid a repeat. These actions distorted many regional economies, leaving them more vulnerable to the global demand slump. In Asia, economic freedom did not lead to this point; avowed statism did.

Nor is statism proving to be any sort of solution to the crisis. While the data are limited, countries that have intervened less have done slightly better than those that have intervened more. The two possible outcomes of public-sector leadership appear to be either accomplishing nothing or actively harming the economy. The crisis interventions are still in category one but were adopted explicitly for short-term benefit, so they may yet move into category two.

Economic freedom is not a panacea. Even undistorted economies with strong internal consumption were hurt by the financial shock. Economic freedom cannot prevent painful slumps, but it does reduce their impact by permitting individuals and firms to make choices that are not warped by misguided state priorities. Freer economies were better situated to survive the crisis. By avoiding mindless economic stimulus, they are also wasting fewer resources and creating fewer long-term problems.

The most important changes in freeing an economy will obviously vary from nation to nation. Identifying the most valuable internal reforms must wait. There must first be an assessment of the comparative efficacy, if any, of the various fiscal and monetary actions taken around the region in 2009. Then, and more ominous, there must a be a longer-term assessment of the inevitable undesired consequences of those actions, such as corruption, asset bubbles, and explicitly higher tax burdens.

On the external side, of particular utility in Asia would be to end the obsession with reserves and the ensuing promotion of undervalued exchange rates and high export growth. The events of the past few years may well make enough of an impression that this will happen—the positive legacy of a difficult time.

Chapter 4

Access to Information: Vital for Efficient Markets and Economic Reform

James M. Roberts

Sometimes it seems to those of us who are fortunate enough to live in the modern economies of the 21st century that our lives have been inundated by a never-ending tsunami of information. The world seems to be drowning in it. E-mails, text messages, Twitter, Facebook, and YouTube videos—each new day brings another advance in communications.

Yet we often forget or take for granted the immense benefits that we receive every day from access to information. The health and growth of the globalized, competitive world economy depend upon the continuing free flow of transparent, timely, inexpensive, and truthful information. Knowledge of domestic and foreign political and economic developments, weather forecasts, and a million other bits of information generated daily around the world allows markets to function more efficiently.

Prices are the purest and most important form of information in any economy. Consumers and producers depend on knowledge of

them to optimize their resource allocations to the highest and best uses. Freely available and unrestricted prices, whether at the wholesale or retail level, or expressed as wages, interest rates, foreign currency cross-rates, quantifiable opportunity costs, or in many other forms, are the single most important signals sent in a healthy economy.

Although it seems obvious to us today, Professor F. A. Hayek created a sensation in 1945 (an era when many put their faith in economies planned centrally by socialist bureaucrats) when he pointed this out in his seminal paper, "The Use of Knowledge in Society." Refuting the central planners, Hayek described the real world where one person or small group, no matter how brilliant, cannot possibly have knowledge of all the relevant facts at any given moment. Since knowledge is dispersed among millions of people in an economy:

> [P]rices can act to coordinate the separate actions of different people. The most

significant fact about this system is the economy of knowledge with which it operates, or how little the individual participants need to know in order to be able to take the right action.[1]

Hayek's paper continues to inspire economists' work on tacit knowledge and dispersed, networked information (e.g., the Internet).

Unfortunately, much of the world still suffers in the dark poverty of ignorance. The scarcity of access to modern information resources in developing countries is a major obstacle to attaining economic freedom, growth, and prosperity. In what may seem a vicious cycle, some obstacles to the free flow of information derive from the low levels of development to which they also contribute. Things like inadequate infrastructure, low education levels, and limited participation of workers in the formal economy can reduce access to and limit the search for information. Improving these factors can be a slow process, though advances in technology, such as the advent of cell phones, can sometimes contribute to leaps ahead.

The process of improving information infrastructure, technology, and access is an integral and understandable part of the development process. What are less understandable (and

1. Friedrich August von Hayek, "The Use of Knowledge in Society," *American Economic Review*, Vol. 35, No. 4 (September 1945), at *http://oll.libertyfund.org/?option=com_staticxt&staticfile=show.php%3Ftitle=92* (October 28, 2009).

Lack of Transparency by Monetary Authorities Hampers Global Economic Recovery

The U.S.-led response by monetary authorities in developed countries to the 2008 financial crash is perhaps the ultimate case study in how the lack of transparency and information flow can harm monetary freedom. The authorities, concerned that "too-big-to-fail" banks would fail, secretly funneled billions in borrowed, taxpayer-backed funds to them in hopes of preventing a run on all banks. The U.S. Federal Reserve blocked "disclosure of companies that participated in and securities covered by a series of emergency funding programs as the global credit crisis began to intensify."[1]

In retrospect, this morally hazardous policy harmed both good and bad banks because the public was not fully informed as to their condition. More than one year later, several U.S. newspapers still had not received details of the secret transactions that they had requested under the federal Freedom of Information Act.[2]

The authorities should have permitted the bad banks to fail (just as U.S. lawmakers later should have permitted the bankruptcy of General Motors and Chrysler). Harvard Professor of Economics Jeffrey Miron asserts that the great bailout was unjustified and reminds us that failure "is an essential aspect of capitalism. It provides information about good and bad investments, and it releases resources from bad projects to more productive ones."[3] As it is, the bad banks have not yet dealt with the bulk of their toxic assets, are still pursuing some dubious business practices, and still represent a large threat to the future health of the U.S. economy.

1. "Federal Reserve Loses Suit Demanding Transparency," Reuters, August 24, 2009, at *http://www.reuters.com/article/wtUSInvestingNews/idUSTRE57O03P20090825* (November 1, 2009).

2. Editorial, "Stop Stalling and Show Us the Bailout Books," *Washington Examiner*, April 16, 2009, at *http://www.washingtonexaminer.com/opinion/Stop-stalling-and-show-us-the-bailout-books-43088037.html* (November 1, 2009).

3. Jeffrey A. Miron, "Bailout or Bankruptcy?" *Cato Journal*, Vol. 29, No. 1 (Winter 2009), at *http://www.cato.org/pubs/journal/cj29n1/cj29n1-1.pdf* (November 1, 2009).

certainly inexcusable) in the midst of today's deluge of data are the increasing attempts by governments around the world to control or even censor information.

MICRO LEVEL: SUCCESSFUL ENTREPRENEURS MUST BE WELL-INFORMED

Economic freedom and prosperity depend on the daily efforts of millions of entrepreneurs who risk their capital and invest their time and energy to supply the high-quality goods and services demanded by the market. Their success hinges not just on their hard work, but also on the public and private institutional frameworks within which they operate. If these entrepreneurs can access reliable information at low cost, markets will function better. Prices will be lower for consumers, price signals will encourage efficient levels of production and innovation, consumer preferences will be better matched, and profits will be higher for the entrepreneur.

In classical liberal economics, the microeconomic theory of the firm rests on the basic assumption that the firm is operating in a competitive marketplace. Free-flowing and accurate information is a core element of that competitive world. In fact, almost any economic analysis has as a starting point the supposition that correct and timely information is available to economic entrepreneurs to enable them to make decisions to maximize the efficient use of all factors of production. That efficient use is the key to productivity growth.

The role of information restrictions in retarding economic growth and development is illustrated in entire disciplines within economics that are dedicated to studying the effects of imperfect knowledge or information. Advancements in the study of information economics were led by Hayek as well as by famed Chicago School economist Dr. George Stigler, a great friend of economic freedom who focused on "search" issues, and fellow Nobel Prize winner Kenneth Arrow. Fields that often focus on the lack of perfect information include economic law, finance, game theory, and public choice.

Information is a vital commodity for every

Intervening in Bankruptcy Proceedings Denies Public Needed Information

The U.S. government's intervention in the bankruptcy of General Motors and Chrysler to benefit the powerful United Auto Workers union in 2009 is another egregious illustration of how artificially imposed constraints on information hurt the cause of economic liberty. Under U.S. law, normal bankruptcy proceedings reveal a great deal of information to the public about the debts, obligations, and managerial missteps of the failed company. This not only helps the market to reprice assets, but also serves as a warning to other companies so that they might take steps to avoid the same fate.

participant in an economy: owners who are manufacturing and selling a product or service as well as consumers considering a purchase. Important information could include the customer's knowledge of the prices of the product produced by the firm and comparable products on the market; the producer's awareness of the costs of inputs needed to produce the product (e.g., labor and materials) from potential suppliers; and the firm owner's comprehensive grasp of the size of market demand for the product so that just the right amount of production is planned, thereby avoiding underinvestment or overinvestment. For maximum efficiency and competitiveness, the information must be available to all participants at minimum cost.

It is especially distressing in times of crisis to see the reflexive use by governments of price controls to provide "stability." What such controls actually do is cut off the flow of accurate market information.

When artificial constraints are imposed on wages and prices, forcing them to fluctuate only within a predetermined band, both the supply of and demand for labor and goods are distorted. The predictable results are shortages and surpluses in markets. When politicians

Methodology of the ICT Development Index

The Information and Communication Technology (ICT) Development Index is broken into three sections—Access, Use, and Skills—each containing several weighted indicators. The Reference Value for each indicator is the ideal value that could be reached.

	Reference Value	Percent of Section's Score	Percent of Total Index Score
Section 1: ICT Access			
Fixed telephone lines per 100 inhabitants	60	20%	
Mobile cellular telephone subscriptions per 100 inhabitants	150	20%	
International Internet bandwith (bits/second) per Internet user	100,000*	20%	40%
Proportion of housholds with a computer	100	20%	
Proportion of households with Internet access at home	100	20%	
Section 2: ICT Use			
Internet users per 100 inhabitants	100	33%	
Fixed broadband Internet subscribers per 100 inhabitants	60	33%	40%
Mobile broadband subscribers per 100 inhabitants	100	33%	
Section 3: ICT Skills			
Adult literacy rate	100	33%	
Secondary gross enrollment ratio	100	33%	20%
Tertiary gross enrollment ratio	100	33%	

* Corresponds to a log value of 5, which was used in the normalization step.

Source: International Telecommunication Union, *Measuring the Information Society: The ICT Development Index*, March, 16, 2009, at *http://www.itu.int/ITU-D/ict/publications/idi/2009/index.html* (November 16, 2009).

Table 1 ☎ heritage.org

legislate minimum wages, impose interest rate caps on private banks, manipulate currency valuations, and use taxpayer subsidies to bail out politically well-connected "too-big-to-fail" companies and powerful labor unions, a comparatively lucky few benefit. The rest of us, however, face the prospect of living with (and paying for) the consequences of these restrictions on information.

MACRO LEVEL: INADEQUATE INFRASTRUCTURE IMPEDES ACCESS TO INFORMATION

Well-functioning markets at the microeconomic level depend on a supportive economic environment at the macroeconomic level. Accurate information about economic variables such as interest rates, credit, the money supply, job creation, and growth rates are fundamental to macroeconomic policymaking. The measurement of such variables and the factors that influence them is a key responsibility of governments and international economic institutions. The *Index of Economic Freedom* is one contribution to this quest for more—and more accurate—information. There are several others, however, that focus more directly on infrastructure or policy questions related to access to information.

The Information and Communication Technology (ICT) Development Index (IDI) prepared by the International Telecommunication Union covers 154 of the 183 countries that are included in the *Index of Economic Freedom*.[2] The building blocks of the IDI (see Table 1) are teledensity (the number of fixed telephone landlines and cellular telephone service subscriptions per 100 inhabitants); access to and

2. See International Telecommunication Union, *Measuring the Information Society: The ICT Development Index*, March 16, 2009, at *http://www.itu.int/ITU-D/ict/publications/idi/2009/index.html* (August 25, 2009).

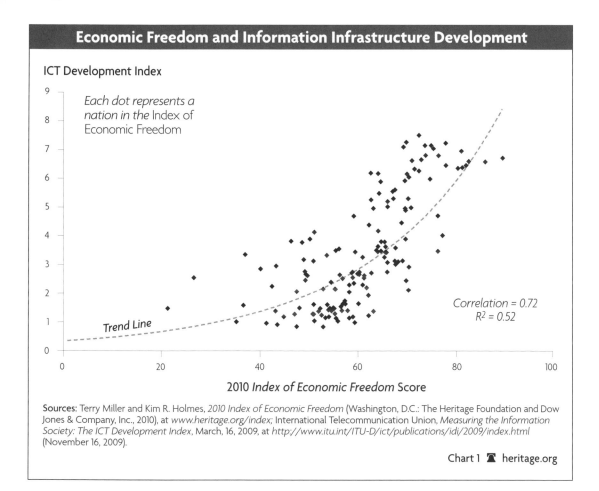

Economic Freedom and Information Infrastructure Development

ICT Development Index

Each dot represents a nation in the Index of Economic Freedom

Trend Line

Correlation = 0.72
$R^2 = 0.52$

2010 *Index of Economic Freedom* Score

Sources: Terry Miller and Kim R. Holmes, *2010 Index of Economic Freedom* (Washington, D.C.: The Heritage Foundation and Dow Jones & Company, Inc., 2010), at *www.heritage.org/index*; International Telecommunication Union, *Measuring the Information Society: The ICT Development Index*, March, 16, 2009, at *http://www.itu.int/ITU-D/ict/publications/idi/2009/index.html* (November 16, 2009).

Chart 1 ☎ heritage.org

usage of the Internet; and literacy rates.

The IDI does not include other data points found in the World Bank's World Development Indicators,[3] such as the percentage of the population and land area in the country covered by cellular telephone service networks or other information measures such as percentage of households with televisions/radios or daily newspapers per 1,000 people. Nor does it include a measure of Internet censorship. Nonetheless, it is the best and most comprehensive measure of the level of information infrastructure development in the countries that it covers.

There is a strong positive correlation between IDI scores and the *Index of Economic Freedom*. (See Chart 1.)

3.   The World Bank, *World Development Indicators 2009*, at *http://web.worldbank.org/WBSITE/ EXTERNAL/DATASTATISTICS/0,,contentMDK: 21725423~pagePK:64133150~piPK:64133175~ theSitePK:239419,00.html* (October 5, 2009).

Although we can theorize from this correlation that higher levels of information infrastructure are associated with ever-greater degrees of economic freedom, we cannot state that more access to information provided by greater development of infrastructure (as reflected by the IDI) causes better scores on the *Index*. There appears to be a strong link between economic freedom and information infrastructure, but we must also consider the relationships between economic freedom and economic development, as well as economic development and information infrastructure. Inevitably, most measures of information infrastructure will be tied to development, and that development is spurred both by the principles of economic freedom and by improvements in information infrastructure.

While the IDI and the *Index of Economic Freedom* are strongly and positively correlated, there is also a strong positive correlation

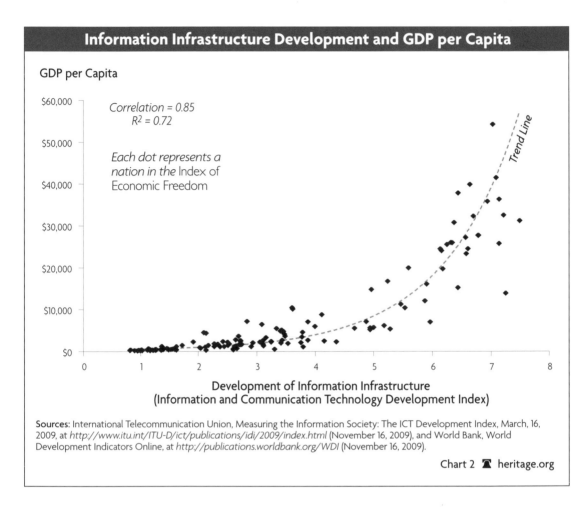

Information Infrastructure Development and GDP per Capita

GDP per Capita

Correlation = 0.85
$R^2 = 0.72$

Each dot represents a nation in the Index of Economic Freedom

Trend Line

$60,000
$50,000
$40,000
$30,000
$20,000
$10,000
$0

0   1   2   3   4   5   6   7   8

Development of Information Infrastructure
(Information and Communication Technology Development Index)

Sources: International Telecommunication Union, Measuring the Information Society: The ICT Development Index, March, 16, 2009, at *http://www.itu.int/ITU-D/ict/publications/idi/2009/index.html* (November 16, 2009), and World Bank, World Development Indicators Online, at *http://publications.worldbank.org/WDI* (November 16, 2009).

Chart 2 ☎ heritage.org

between IDI scores and GDP per capita (0.851), as well as between *Index* scores and GDP per capita (0.702). (See Charts 2 and 3.)

It may well be that it is the higher levels of economic freedom recorded in the *Index* that are causing improvements in information infrastructure, particularly through the mechanism of increased economic growth. The most likely answer may be that there is a feedback loop between information access and economic freedom, with better information contributing to economic freedom and economic freedom providing greater access to information.

Increases in the availability of information are so important to economic functioning that governments historically have treated many improvements in information infrastructure as public goods. For example:

• In South Korea, a state-owned monopoly (Korea Telecom) was allowed to privatize on the condition that it provide broadband to all villages in the country.[4]

• In Sweden, policymaking included deregulation and competition to bring down prices of information access. However, the government owns a significant portion of the high-speed network infrastructure (78 percent as of 2003) and is a large shareholder (45.3 percent) in TeliaSonera, the dominant telecommunications company. The Swedish government also used mandates and subsidies to achieve the highly developed telecommunications infrastructure that its citizens enjoy.[5]

4.   John Borland and Michael Kanellos, "South Korea Leads the Way," CNET News, July 28, 2004, at *http://news.cnet.com/South-Korea-leads-the-way/2009-1034_3-5261393.html* (October 28, 2009).

5.   "Appendix G: Sweden," in Robert D. Atkinson, Daniel K. Correa, and Julie A. Hedlund, *Explaining International Broadband Leadership*, Information Technology & Innovation

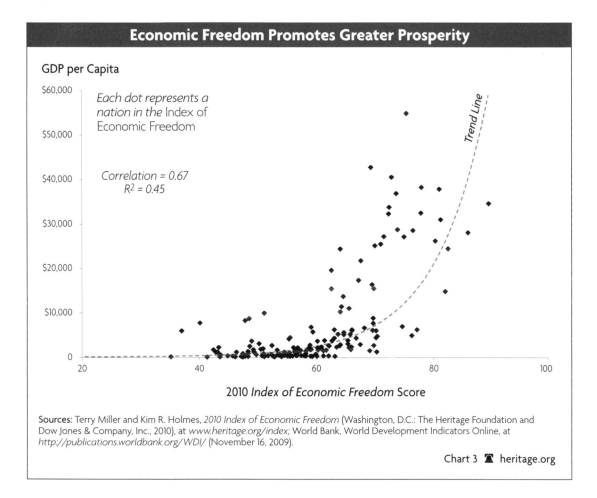

Economic Freedom Promotes Greater Prosperity

GDP per Capita

Each dot represents a nation in the Index of Economic Freedom

Correlation = 0.67
$R^2 = 0.45$

Trend Line

2010 *Index of Economic Freedom* Score

Sources: Terry Miller and Kim R. Holmes, *2010 Index of Economic Freedom* (Washington, D.C.: The Heritage Foundation and Dow Jones & Company, Inc., 2010), at *www.heritage.org/index;* World Bank, World Development Indicators Online, at *http://publications.worldbank.org/WDI/* (November 16, 2009).

Chart 3 ☎ heritage.org

• The government of the Netherlands encouraged competition by lowering barriers to entry in the broadband market, but it has also invested significant amounts of taxpayers' money in research and infrastructure.[6]

In many cases, governments use free-market principles of deregulation and competition to lower costs and provide greater access to information technology. However, these governments also make significant financial investments to develop information infrastructure.

Although more than 70 countries retain state-owned monopolies that control international telecommunications gateway services, many developing countries in Africa (Ghana, Kenya, Nigeria, and Uganda) and South Asia (Bangladesh, Sri Lanka, India, and Pakistan)

have learned that freer and more competitive markets can improve information access and affordability. They have increased the number of telecommunications licenses granted to private operators.[7]

MORE THAN ECONOMIC FREEDOM AT RISK

Information's importance both to the efficiency of the marketplace and to economic freedom is but one aspect of the importance of information in preserving liberty itself. History is replete with examples of deliberate efforts to keep people uninformed about the actions of their governments. It has been said, for exam-

Foundation, May 2008, at *http://www.itif.org/files/2008BBAppendixG.pdf* (October 28, 2009).

6. *Ibid.*

7. Organisation for Economic Co-operation and Development, Directorate for Science, Technology and Industry, *Global Opportunities for Internet Access Developments*, February 4, 2008, pp. 10, 16–19, at *http://www.oecd.org/dataoecd/17/53/40596368.pdf* (October 28, 2009).

ple, that this was the *de facto* official policy in Francisco Franco's Spain and Antonio Salazar's Portugal in the mid-20th century. Salazar reportedly said that keeping people illiterate would ensure a happy and productive peasantry.[8] What he got instead were people who could easily be misled by the Communist Party, which nearly succeeded in taking power in the 1970s.[9] The same scenario had played out in Greece in 1948.[10]

Dictatorial governments' use and misuse of information follows familiar patterns. On the one hand, rulers use control of economic information to enrich themselves. Throughout history, it has not been uncommon to uncover evidence of better, more valuable information being withheld from the people by ruling elites. Access to reliable and useful information is certainly not always treated by governments as an inalienable right. Statistical data may be withheld or altered to encourage support for selected policies or to hide subsidies or other diversions of funds.

In the worst cases, even basic commercial data on commodity supplies or prices may be withheld. Such data are fundamental to the functioning of a market, but producers and consumers require more than just commercial information to compete efficiently. They need wide-ranging knowledge of political and economic developments, both within their own country and around the world. They must be aware of the latest technological innovations, fads that drive consumer choices, music and fashion trends—the list

is endless. If the government attempts to manipulate information to gain political or economic advantage, it will have a negative effect on investor and consumer confidence. More than that, it is a transfer of resources from those who are denied information to those who retain access to it, which usually means the state and its cronies.

Beyond enriching themselves, dictatorial regimes typically exert control over information flows to maintain their political power. Freedom House publishes an index that measures this aspect of information freedom: the annual "Table of Global Press Freedom Rankings."[11] As Freedom House notes:

> A free press plays a key role in sustaining and monitoring a healthy democracy, as well as in contributing to greater accountability, good government, and economic development. Most importantly, restrictions on media are often an early indicator that governments intend to assault other democratic institutions.[12]

The correlation between the Freedom House index scores and those of the *Index of Economic Freedom* is predictably strong, at –0.63, as seen in Chart 4. The trend line slopes down because lower numerical scores from Freedom House indicate *higher* levels of press freedom.

INFORMATION AND THE *INDEX OF ECONOMIC FREEDOM*

The importance of access to information in the maintenance of freedom and the promotion of prosperity is seen clearly in many of the indicators that make up the *Index of Economic Freedom*. Countries that earn the highest scores in the *Index* have benefited from allowing the free flow of labor, capital, goods—and information. Countries that have an information-

8. Erna Paris, "To Mock a Book-Banner," *The Globe and Mail* (Toronto), August 28, 2009, at *http://www.theglobeandmail.com/books/to-mock-a-book-banner/article1268084/* (September 4, 2009).

9. Fernanda Eberstadt, "The Unexpected Fantasist," *The New York Times*, August 26, 2007, at *http://www.nytimes.com/2007/08/26/magazine/26saramago-t.html?pagewanted=all* (September 4, 2009).

10. Press release, "Greek Americans Offer Tribute to Greek Victims of Communism," Victims of Communism Memorial Foundation, November 2, 2008, at *http://www.victimsofcommunism.org/media/article.php?article=4121* (September 4, 2009).

11. See, for example, Freedom House, "Global Press Freedom 2008," at *http://www.freedomhouse.org/uploads/fop08/FOTP2008Tables.pdf* (November 1, 2009).

12. Freedom House, "2008 Freedom of the Press World Ranking," at *http://www.freedomhouse.org/template.cfm?page=442&year=2008* (August 25, 2009).

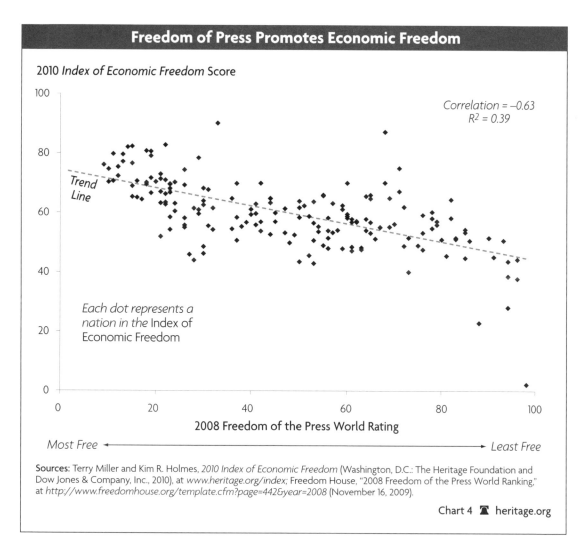

Freedom of Press Promotes Economic Freedom

2010 *Index of Economic Freedom* Score

Correlation = –0.63
$R^2 = 0.39$

Trend
Line

*Each dot represents a
nation in the* Index of
Economic Freedom

2008 Freedom of the Press World Rating

Most Free ← → Least Free

Sources: Terry Miller and Kim R. Holmes, *2010 Index of Economic Freedom* (Washington, D.C.: The Heritage Foundation and Dow Jones & Company, Inc., 2010), at *www.heritage.org/index*; Freedom House, "2008 Freedom of the Press World Ranking," at *http://www.freedomhouse.org/template.cfm?page=442&year=2008* (November 16, 2009).

Chart 4 ☎ heritage.org

poor environment put their entrepreneurs at a disadvantage. Through the prism of the economic freedom indicators, we can see some of the damage that is done when public policy restricts the free flow of information.

Business Freedom

The transparency of the regulatory environment for business is an important element in promoting efficiency and reducing bribery. Entrepreneurs need correct and user-friendly information about compliance and where they are in the regulatory process. Regulations themselves, however, can also impede the flow of information between businesses and consumers.

For example, modern businesses cannot operate successfully without advertising: not just through mass marketing, but also through customized information channels that can target specific markets for products and services. Regulations that interfere with advertising are one way by which governments interfere with the flow of information between buyers and sellers.

Trade Freedom

Knowledge of the marketplace must not be artificially limited only to market conditions within a country's borders. Protectionism cuts off information to producers and consumers alike about competing goods and services made in other countries. Knowledge of the relative prices and quality of those products— of recent innovations, marketing campaigns, safety testing, and an endless list of other factors—could help entrepreneurs in the protectionist country to manufacture and sell better products. Knowledge of available inputs aids domestic manufacturers in planning the most effective production processes to maximize productivity.

While propping up inefficient industries, protectionism reduces consumer choice and exempts producers from the need to adapt and evolve to improve consumer satisfaction. It results in inferior goods and services, as well as higher costs, and causes any country adopting such measures to be industrially crippled and likely to be left in the dust by its more agile, adaptable, and information-rich competitors.

Fiscal Freedom

Countries that lack the institutional infrastructure to collect taxes efficiently usually lack information infrastructure. Perversely, some of the least developed countries in the world receive artificially high scores for fiscal freedom and government spending in the *Index of Economic Freedom*, not because of any particular restraint or virtue by their governments, but rather because they lack the basic information about who is earning income at what levels. Information provides the vital link between taxpayers and tax collectors, both in communicating what government services are needed and in identifying who has the ability and responsibility to pay for them.

Government Spending

Governments that wish to increase spending may resort to restrictions on information or the manipulation of statistics in order to hide their intentions from the public. For example, David Walker, who formerly served as the nation's "Auditor in Chief" as head of the U.S. Government Accountability Office, has warned of a "fiscal cancer" that is threatening America's future economic viability. According to Walker, "off balance sheet obligations associated with Social Security and Medicare put us in a $56 trillion financial hole," and the true costs of the Medicare drug entitlement

benefit adopted in 2003 "were hidden from both Congress and the people."[13]

Countries with large numbers of state-owned enterprises often go even further, exerting tight control of commercial information. This is a hallmark of totalitarian states and one of the principal causes of the economic inefficiency and stagnation that characterize them.

In the Soviet Union, for example, the lack of accurate and timely information conveyed through supply-and-demand price signals contributed to a steady deterioration in product quality. According to Vladimir G. Treml, Professor of Economics at Duke University, the "quality of manufactured goods continued to be inferior by world standards because of the absence of demand pressures on producers isolated from buyers by the centralized supply system."[14] A Library of Congress study notes that because "of the inferior quality of Soviet goods, the Soviet Union was unsuccessful in increasing its exports of manufactured goods. In 1987 only 18 percent of Soviet manufactured goods met world technical standards."[15]

Monetary Freedom

Countries that maintain distortionary price controls of any sort, including controls on the prices of goods, labor (the wage), capital (the

---

13. John Fund, "Warning: The Deficits Are Coming! The Former Head of the Government Accountability Office Is on a Crusade to Alert Taxpayers to Their True Obligations," *The Wall Street Journal*, September 4, 2009, at *http://online.wsj.com/article/SB10001424052970203585004574392620693542630.html* (September 5, 2009).

14. Vladimir G. Treml, "Why Did the Soviet Economic System Collapse? Two Schools of Thought," November 1996, at *http://econ.duke.edu/webfiles/treml/collapse.293* (November 1, 2009). This version specifies as follows: "Originally published in RFE–RL Research Report, Vol. 2, # 43, June 4, 1993, pp. 53–58; reprinted as 'Dve pozitsii,' VOPROSY EKONOMIKI, # 11, 1993, pp. 90–95. Revised and expanded."

15. Raymond E. Zickel, ed., "A Country Study of the Soviet Union," Library of Congress, Federal Research Division, data as of May 1989, at *http://www.country-data.com/cgi-bin/query/r-12794.html* (September 29, 2009).

interest rate), and foreign money (the exchange rate), send incorrect signals to domestic producers and consumers, often creating inflationary pressures they sought to avoid and always harming consumers and putting businesses in their country at a disadvantage. Subsidies have similar effects in warping the information contained in prices.

Opaque Institutions Obstruct Economic Freedom

Another private-sector index measures hazards to investors and traders that are posed by a country's opaque institutions. The Opacity Index looks at risks "associated with the lack of transparency in five areas that can confound global investment and commerce" in 48 countries and the strategies and tactics that foreign firms must use to deal with them successfully. The five areas are:

- Corruption in business and government;
- The legal system—its protection (or lack thereof) of critical rights and its ability to quickly settle disputes;
- The government's economic policy and its impact on business;

- Accounting standards and governance rules; and
- The regulatory structure of the financial system, markets and business in general.[1]

Opacity in these areas obstructs the availability of perfect information. As Opacity Index authors Joel Kurtzman and Glenn Yago point out:

[S]mall-scale, high-frequency risks of operating globally present the real costs to business. These risks interfere with commerce, add to costs, slow growth and make the future even more difficult to predict. They also deter investment. The key to any good investment relationship is clarity—the ability to see and even be in communication with what's really going on.[2]

Not unexpectedly, the Opacity Index and the *Index of Economic Freedom* are strongly correlated.

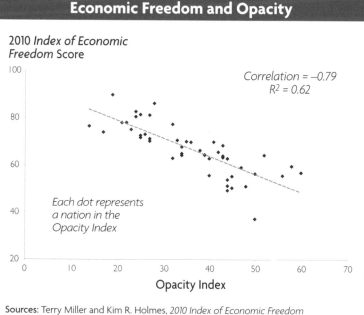

Economic Freedom and Opacity

2010 *Index of Economic Freedom* Score

Correlation = −0.79
$R^2 = 0.62$

Each dot represents a nation in the Opacity Index

Opacity Index

Sources: Terry Miller and Kim R. Holmes, *2010 Index of Economic Freedom* (Washington, D.C.: The Heritage Foundation and Dow Jones & Company, Inc., 2010), at *www.heritage.org/index*; The Kurtzman Group, "Case Studies: The Opacity Index 2009," at *http://www.kurtzmangroup.com/global_edge.php* (November 16, 2009).

Chart 5 ☎ heritage.org

1. The Kurtzman Group, "Case Studies: The Opacity Index 2009," at *http://www. kurtzmangroup.com/ global_edge.php* (August 24, 2009).

2. *Ibid.*

Investment Freedom

Potential foreign investors need information about industry and market conditions in the countries in which they are considering investing. There is an inverse relationship between the level of information available and the level of risk of an investment, and countries in which information is readily available have a large competitive advantage. Regulatory transparency is another vital information-related factor in determining investment levels.

Financial Freedom

Entrepreneurs and investors need timely information about interest rates and credit terms offered by the banking sector. Governments that impose artificial constraints on the private banking sector for political purposes—for example, through subsidized state-owned banks, interest rate caps, currency manipulation, and other burdensome regulations—restrict and distort the price signals vital to firms operating in the economy. At the root of the global financial crisis was the lack of accurate information about the level of risk associated with certain widely traded financial assets, which permitted a bubble in their price that ultimately burst when better information about the risks became known.

Property Rights

Publicly available records of land and real estate transactions provide transparency about market conditions for the entrepreneur or investor—and especially for land and home owners. In his introduction to the 2009 International Property Rights Index, Hernando de Soto champions the protection of both physical and intellectual property. Noting that people in the developing world often lack this protection, de Soto reminds us that:

[A]n environment where both forms of property are safe and legally enforceable contributes to increased levels of stability and encourages the free exchange of goods and ideas. This is done on a daily

basis and often taken for granted by those that are afforded the chance to prosper from their investments.[16]

Without clarity of information, it is impossible to protect property. It is no accident that we speak of having "clear" title to a piece of property. "Clouded" titles end up in courtroom disputes. Countries with transparent rules, procedures, and government institutions to protect both the right to possess property and the right to acquire more of it have more economic freedom.

Freedom from Corruption

This is one of the most important freedoms from the standpoint of access to information, and it lies at the very heart of the definition of transparency. A free press is vital, both to expose political corruption and to guard against bribery, extortion, nepotism, cronyism, patronage, embezzlement, and graft.

Recently, there have been many disturbing acts of censorship, attacks on press freedom, and denials of Internet access around the world. As just one example, according to a recent World Bank report, bloggers in Burma, Iran, Syria, Cuba, Saudi Arabia, Vietnam, Tunisia, China, Turkmenistan, and Egypt are harassed and sometimes imprisoned by government censors who use "regulations and laws that censor bloggers, [as well as] control mechanisms to filter, monitor or limit the access to internet."[17]

---

16. Anne Chandima Dedigama, *International Property Rights Index (IPRI) 2009 Report*, Property Rights Alliance, at *http://www.internationalpropertyrightsindex.org/atr_Final1.pdf* (September 4, 2009).

17. Alfredo Gonzalez Briseno, "When Blogging Becomes an Issue: Worst Places to be a Blogger," Governance Matters, The World Bank, May 19, 2009, at *http://blogs.worldbank.org/governance/when-blogging-becomes-an-issue-worst-places-to-be-a-blogger* (August 26, 2009). See also Freedom House, "Freedom on the Net: A Global Assessment of Internet and Digital Media," March 30, 2009, at *http://www.freedomhouse.org/template.cfm?page=383&report=79* (August 26, 2009).

Labor Freedom

A competitive, merit-based labor market creates a more efficient and prosperous economy. Powerful unions that impose "closed shop" rules on employers cut off information about jobs from potential applicants and information about potential applicants from employers. In Mexico, for example, unions have had a stranglehold on the labor sector since the 1930s. Through rigid labor laws enacted by friendly politicians, they enjoy immense leverage in workplaces, as well as tremendous resources, closed-shop hiring and firing prerogatives, leadership elections by acclamation, and mandatory dues without transparency. Those unions have worked hand-in-glove with state-owned and private corporate monopolies. Of course, this arrangement has been great for those who are on the inside, but the economic stagnation that has resulted from these structural distortions of the economy has forced 40 percent of Mexico's workers into the informal sector.[18]

CONCLUSION

The dark poverty of ignorance, caused by a scarcity of information resources in developing countries and the consequence of government censorship in all countries, is a major obstacle to attaining economic freedom, growth, and prosperity. There is also an increasing tendency by governments around the world to intervene in markets with intrusive regulatory and fiscal measures that restrict the ability of the price system to inform consumers and producers about the most efficient ways to spend or invest their resources. The threats to freedom of information from the lack of infrastructure and from government actions that, intended or not, restrict knowledge vital to economic efficiency are reflected—sometimes bluntly, at other times subtly—in many of the indicators measured in the *Index of Economic Freedom*.

Investments in information infrastructure can pay big dividends in many areas of economic freedom and economic well-being. Gains will be biggest in those countries that are the farthest behind when they begin. Unfortunately, benefits are easily undone when government officials repress information for personal economic or political gain.

One of the primary goals of the *Index of Economic Freedom* is to shed some light on the pathway to prosperity. The greater the availability of information—commercial, macroeconomic, and political—the greater will be the overall illumination of that path, enabling entrepreneurs and policymakers to make the best choices for the future.

---

18. James M. Roberts, "How Reforms in Mexico Could Make the U.S. More Secure," Heritage Foundation *Backgrounder* No. 2135, May 13, 2008, at *http://www.heritage.org/Research/LatinAmerica/bg2135.cfm.*

Chapter 5

Defining Economic Freedom

Ambassador Terry Miller and Anthony B. Kim

Fundamentally, there are only two ways of co-ordinating the economic activities of millions. One is central direction involving the use of coercion—the technique of the army and of the modern totalitarian state. The other is voluntary co-operation of individuals—the technique of the market place.

—Milton Friedman[1]

In an economically free society, each person controls the fruits of his or her own labor and initiative. Individuals are empowered—indeed, entitled—to decide for themselves where to live and work. They have the right to own property and dispose of it as they choose.

In an economically free society, individuals succeed or fail based on their individual effort and ability. The institutions of society do not discriminate against—or in favor of—individuals based on their race, ethnic background, gender, class, family connections, or any other factor unrelated to individual merit. Government decision-making is characterized by transparency and openness, and the light of opportunity replaces the shadows where discrimination can be most insidious.

In an economically free society, the power of economic decision-making is widely dispersed, and the allocation of resources for production and consumption is on the basis of free and open competition so that every individual or firm has a fair chance to succeed.

These three fundamental principles of economic freedom—empowerment of the individual, non-discrimination, and open competition—underpin and inform every measurement in the *Index of Economic Freedom*.

ECONOMIC FREEDOM: AUTONOMY, NOT ANARCHY

The discussion of economic freedom has at its heart consideration of the relationship between the individual and the state. In general, state action or control that interferes with individual autonomy limits economic freedom.

---

1. Milton Friedman, *Capitalism and Freedom* (Chicago: University of Chicago Press, 1982), p. 13.

The *Index of Economic Freedom* is not, however, a call for anarchy. The goal of economic freedom is not simply an absence of government coercion or constraint, but the creation and maintenance of a sense of liberty for all. As individuals enjoy the blessings of economic freedom, they in turn have a responsibility to respect the economic rights and freedoms of others. Governments are instituted to create basic protections against the ravages of nature or the predations of one citizen over another so that positive economic rights such as property and contracts are given societal as well as individual defense against the destructive tendencies of others.

A comprehensive definition of economic freedom should *encompass all liberties and rights of production, distribution, or consumption of goods and services. The highest form of economic freedom should provide an absolute right of property ownership; fully realized freedoms of movement for labor, capital, and goods; and an absolute absence of coercion or constraint of economic liberty beyond the extent necessary for citizens to protect and maintain liberty itself*. In other words, individuals in an economically free society would be free and entitled to work, produce, consume, and invest in any way they choose under a rule of law, with their freedom at once both protected and respected by the state.

Some government action is necessary for the citizens of a community or nation to defend themselves, promote the peaceful evolution of civil society, and enjoy the fruits of their labor. This Lockean idea is embodied in the U.S. Constitution. For example, citizens are taxed to provide revenue for the protection of person and property as well as for the common defense. Most political theorists also accept that certain goods—what economists call "public goods"— can be supplied more efficiently by government than through private means. Some public goods, such as the maintenance of a police force to protect property rights, a monetary authority to maintain a sound currency, and an impartial judiciary to enforce contracts among parties, are themselves vital ingredients of an economically free society. When government action rises beyond the minimal level, however, it can become corrosive to freedom—and the first

freedom affected is often economic freedom.

Throughout history, governments have imposed a wide array of constraints on economic activity. Though often imposed in the name of equality or some other noble societal purpose, such constraints are most often imposed for the benefit of societal elites or special interests, and they come with a high cost to society as a whole. Constraining economic choice distorts and diminishes the production, distribution, and consumption of goods and services (including, of course, labor services).[2] The overall result, inevitably, is reduced growth, declining prosperity, and economic stagnation.

MEASURING ECONOMIC FREEDOM

The measurement of economic freedom in countries as different as Hong Kong and North Korea, Zimbabwe and Singapore, or Australia and Cuba presents formidable challenges. As the number and variety of countries included in the *Index* have increased, it has become ever more difficult to find consistent and reliable data. We are indebted to the various international organizations, both governmental and non-governmental, that have undertaken the arduous task of data collection in their various areas of focus and have shared their data with us.

The *Index of Economic Freedom* is comprehensive in its view of economic freedom as well as in its worldwide coverage of countries. The *Index* looks at economic freedom from 10 different viewpoints. Some aspects of economic freedom are external in nature, measuring the extent of an economy's openness to global investment or trade. Most are internal in nature, assessing the liberty of individuals to use their labor or finances without restraint and government interference. Each is vital to the development of personal and national prosperity. The fundamental right of property, for example, has been recognized for centuries by the great philosophers of liberty, such as

2.   "The property which every man has in his own labor, as it is the original foundation of all other property, so it is the most sacred and inviolable." Adam Smith, *An Inquiry into the Nature and Causes of the Wealth of Nations* (New York: The Modern Library, 1937), pp. 121–122; first published in 1776.

Locke and Montesquieu, as a bulwark of free people.

Over time, scholars and practitioners have recognized many other pillars of economic liberty, including free trade, stable money, the right to work, control of government spending, and lower taxation. Each one illuminates some aspect of the relationship between the individual and the state, and all should be viewed in light of the fundamental principles of economic liberty—individual empowerment, non-discrimination, and open competition—outlined above.

The 10 specific economic freedoms measured in the *Index of Economic Freedom* are discussed below. Each of the freedoms is individually scored on a 0 to 100 scale. A country's overall economic freedom score is a simple average of its scores on the 10 individual freedoms. Detailed information about the methodology used to score each component is contained in the appendix.

FREEDOM #1: BUSINESS FREEDOM

Business freedom is about an individual's right to establish and run an enterprise without interference from the state. Burdensome and redundant regulatory rules are the most common barriers to the free conduct of entrepreneurial activities.

By increasing the costs of production, regulations can make it difficult for entrepreneurs to succeed in the marketplace. Although many regulations hinder business productivity and profitability, the most inhibiting to entrepreneurship are those associated with licensing new businesses.

In some countries, as well as many states in the United States, the procedure for obtaining a business license can be as simple as mailing in a registration form with a minimal fee. In Hong Kong, for example, obtaining a business license requires filling out a single form, and the process can be completed in a few hours. In other economies, such as India and parts of South America, the process of obtaining a business license can take much longer, involving endless trips to government offices and repeated encounters with officious and sometimes corrupt bureaucrats.

Once a business is open, government regulation may interfere with the normal decision-making or price-setting process. Interestingly, two countries with the same set of regulations can impose different regulatory burdens. If one country, for instance, applies its regulations evenly and transparently, it lowers the regulatory burden by enabling businesses to make long-term plans more easily. If the other applies regulations inconsistently, it raises the regulatory burden by creating an unpredictable business environment. Finally, regulations that make bankruptcy procedures onerous are also distortionary, providing disincentives for entrepreneurs to start businesses in the first place.

FREEDOM #2: TRADE FREEDOM

Trade freedom reflects the openness of an economy to imports of goods and services from around the world and the ability of citizens to interact freely as buyers and sellers in the international marketplace.

Trade restrictions can manifest themselves in the form of taxes on imports and exports and quotas or outright bans on trade. However, trade restrictions also appear in more subtle ways, particularly in the form of regulatory barriers. The degree to which government hinders the free flow of foreign commerce has a direct bearing on the ability of individuals to pursue their economic goals and to maximize their productivity and well-being.

Tariffs, for example, directly increase the prices that local consumers pay for foreign imports, but they also distort production incentives for local producers, causing them to produce either a good in which they lack a comparative advantage or more of a protected good than is economically efficient. This impedes overall economic efficiency and growth. In many cases, trade limitations also put advanced-technology products and services beyond the reach of local entrepreneurs, limiting their own productive development.

FREEDOM #3: FISCAL FREEDOM

Fiscal freedom is a direct measure of the extent to which individuals and businesses are permitted by government to keep and control their income and wealth for their own benefit and use. A government can impose fiscal burdens on economic activity through taxation, but it also does so when it incurs debt that ultimately must be paid off through taxation.

The marginal tax rate confronting an individual is, in effect, the government's cut of the profit from his or her next unit of work or engagement in a new entrepreneurial venture; whatever remains after the tax is subtracted is the individual's actual reward for the effort. The higher the government's cut, the lower the individual's reward—and the lower the incentive to undertake the work at all. Higher tax rates interfere with the ability of individuals and firms to pursue their goals in the marketplace and reduce, on average, their willingness to work or invest.

While individual and corporate income tax rates are important to economic freedom, they are not a comprehensive measure of the tax burden. Governments impose many other indirect taxes, including payroll, sales, and excise taxes, tariffs, and the value-added tax (VAT). In the *Index of Economic Freedom*, the burden of these taxes is captured by measuring total government revenues from all forms of taxation as a percentage of total GDP.

FREEDOM #4: GOVERNMENT SPENDING

The burden of excessive government is a central issue in economic freedom, both in terms of generating revenue (see fiscal freedom) and in terms of spending. Some government spending, such as providing infrastructure or funding research or even improvements in human capital, may be thought of as investments. There are public goods whose benefits accrue broadly to society in ways that markets cannot appropriately price. All government spending, however, entails an opportunity cost equal to the value of the private consumption or investment that would have occurred had the resources involved been left in the private sector.

In other words, excessive government spending runs a great risk of crowding out private consumption, thereby thwarting the choices of individuals. Even worse, a government's insulation from market discipline often leads to inefficiency, bureaucracy, lower productivity, and waste.

The government's appetite for private resources affects both economic freedom and economic growth. Even if a state-managed economy achieves fast growth through heavy expenditure, it diminishes economic freedom in the process and can create long-term damage to a country's growth potential.

FREEDOM #5: MONETARY FREEDOM

Monetary freedom, reflected in a stable currency and market-determined prices, is to an economy what free speech is to democracy. Free people need a steady and reliable currency as a medium of exchange, unit of account, and store of value. Without monetary freedom, it is difficult to create long-term value or amass capital.

The value of a country's currency is controlled largely by the monetary policy of its government. With a monetary policy that endeavors to fight inflation, maintain price stability, and preserve the nation's wealth, people can rely on market prices for the foreseeable future. Investments, savings, and other longer-term plans can be made more confidently. An inflationary policy, by contrast, confiscates wealth like an invisible tax and also distorts prices, misallocates resources, and raises the cost of doing business.

There is no single accepted theory of the right monetary policy for a free society. At one time, the gold standard enjoyed widespread support. What characterizes almost all monetary theories today, however, is support for low inflation and an independent central bank. There is also now widespread recognition that price controls corrupt market efficiency and lead to shortages or surpluses.

FREEDOM #6: INVESTMENT FREEDOM

A free and open investment environment provides maximum entrepreneurial opportunities and incentives for expanded economic activity, productivity increases, and job creation. The benefits of such an environment flow not only to the individual companies that take the entrepreneurial risk in expectation of greater return, but also to society as a whole.

An effective investment framework will be characterized by transparency and equity, supporting all types of firms rather than just large or strategically important companies, and will encourage rather than discourage innovation and competition.

Restrictions on the movement of capital, both domestic and international, undermine the efficient allocation of resources and reduce productivity, distorting economic decision-making. Restrictions on cross-border investment can limit both inflows and outflows of capital, shrinking markets and reducing opportunities for growth.

In an environment in which individuals and companies are free to choose where and how to invest, capital will flow to its best use: to the sectors and activities where it is most needed and the returns are greatest. State action to redirect the flow of capital and limit choice is an imposition on the freedom of both the investor and the person seeking capital. The more restrictions a country imposes on investment, the lower its level of entrepreneurial activity.

FREEDOM #7: FINANCIAL FREEDOM

A transparent and open financial system ensures fairness in access to financing and promotes entrepreneurship. An open and free banking environment encourages competition to provide the most efficient financial intermediation between households and firms and between investors and entrepreneurs.

In an efficient banking environment that facilitates open and transparent access to financing, the marketplace is the primary source of protection for all parties involved in a financial transaction. Through a process driven by supply and demand, markets provide real-time information on prices and immediate discipline for those who have made bad decisions. This process depends on transparency in the market and the integrity of the information being made available. An effective regulatory system, through disclosure requirements and independent auditing, ensures both.

Increasingly, the central role played by banks is being complemented by other finan-cial services that offer alternative means for raising capital or diversifying risk. As with the banking system, the useful role for government in regulating these institutions lies in ensuring transparency; disclosure of assets, liabilities, and risks; and ensuring integrity.

Banking and financial regulation by the state that goes beyond the assurance of transparency and honesty in financial markets can impede efficiency, increase the costs of financing entrepreneurial activity, and limit competition. If the government intervenes in the stock market, for instance, it contravenes the choices of millions of individuals by interfering with the pricing of capital—the most critical function of a market economy. Equity markets measure, on a continual basis, the expected profits and losses in publicly held companies. This measurement is essential in allocating capital resources to their highest-valued uses and thereby satisfying consumers' most urgent requirements.

Similarly, government ownership or intervention in the insurance sector undermines the ability of providers to make that service available at prices that are based on risk and market conditions.

FREEDOM #8: PROPERTY RIGHTS

The ability to accumulate private property and wealth is understood to be a central motivating force for workers and investors in a market economy. The recognition of private property rights, with sufficient rule of law to protect them, is a vital feature of a fully functioning market economy. Secure property rights give citizens the confidence to undertake entrepreneurial activities, save their income, and make long-term plans because they know that their income, savings, and property (both real and intellectual) are safe from unfair expropriation or theft.

The protection of private property requires an effective and honest judicial system that is available to all, equally and without discrimination. The independence, transparency, and effectiveness of the judicial system have proven to be key determinants of a country's prospects for long-term economic growth. Such a system is also vital to the maintenance of peace and security and the protection of human rights.

A key aspect of property rights protection is the enforcement of contracts. The voluntary undertaking of contractual obligations is the foundation of the market system and the basis for economic specialization, gains from commercial exchange, and trade among nations. Even-handed government enforcement of private contracts is essential to ensuring equity and integrity in the marketplace.

FREEDOM #9: FREEDOM FROM CORRUPTION

Corruption is defined as dishonesty or decay. In the context of governance, it can be defined as the failure of integrity in the system, a distortion by which individuals are able to gain personally at the expense of the whole. Political corruption manifests itself in many forms such as bribery, extortion, nepotism, cronyism, patronage, embezzlement, and, most commonly, graft, whereby public officials steal or profit illegitimately from public funds.

Corruption can infect all parts of an economy; there is a direct relationship between the extent of government regulation or other government intervention in economic activity and the amount of corruption. Almost any government regulation can provide an opportunity for bribery or graft. In addition, a government regulation or restriction in one area may create an informal market in another. For example, a country with high barriers to trade may have laws that protect its domestic market and prevent the import of foreign goods, but these barriers create incentives for smuggling and a black market for the restricted products.

Transparency is the best weapon against corruption. Openness in regulatory procedures and processes can promote equitable treatment and greater regulatory efficiency and speed.

FREEDOM #10: LABOR FREEDOM

The ability of individuals to work as much as they want and wherever they want is a key component of economic freedom. By the same token, the ability of businesses to contract freely for labor and dismiss redundant workers when they are no longer needed is a vital mechanism for enhancing productivity and sustaining overall economic growth. The core principle of any market is free, voluntary exchange. That is as true in the labor market as it is in the market for goods.

State intervention generates the same problems in the labor market that it produces in any other market. Government regulations take a variety of forms, including wage controls, hiring and firing restrictions, and health and safety restrictions. In many countries, unions play an important role in regulating labor freedom and, depending on the nature of their activity, may be either a force for greater freedom or an impediment to the efficient functioning of labor markets. In general, the greater the degree of labor freedom, the lower the rate of unemployment in an economy.

THE *INDEX*: AN EVOLVING MEASURE OF DURABLE VALUES

Taken together, these 10 economic freedoms provide a comprehensive, albeit imperfect, picture of economic freedom, both in individual countries and in the world as a whole. At present, our understanding of economic freedom has outpaced the availability of data on a worldwide basis.[3] As data become more readily available, we will continue to refine the measures to provide the most complete picture possible.

It may well be also that our understanding of various facets of economic freedom will improve or evolve over time. There is no question, for example, that our understanding of discrimination has broadened in recent decades. Similar advances may occur in our understanding of the ideal relationship between individuals and society and—critically—of the role that government may play in bolstering equitable competition.

What will not change is our commitment to freedom, and particularly economic freedom, as a fundamental and inalienable human right.

---

3. See, for example, Chapter 3 for an augmented view of economic freedom in Asia during the recent crisis.

Chapter 6

Economic Freedom: Regional Patterns

Anthony B. Kim

The diversity of the world's peoples and cultures implies that there will be many paths to economic development and prosperity. Indeed, the whole idea of economic freedom is to empower people with more opportunity to pursue and fulfill their dreams in a manner of their individual choosing, not through a cookie-cutter approach decided by their government or an international organization.

The *Index of Economic Freedom* looks at 10 aspects of economic freedom in which entrepreneurial activity may be amplified or constrained. The country profiles of economic freedom revealed in these pages are unique and diverse. Nonetheless, countries often do share certain characteristics—cultural, geographical, historical, or others—with their regional neighbors that may help shed light on the particular challenges to economic freedom that they face. This brief chapter looks at economic freedom in the six regions covered by the *Index*.

Each of the world's regions has at least one country that is ranked among the top 20 freest

economies in the 2010 *Index of Economic Freedom*. Average levels of economic freedom, however, vary widely among the regions, and there are some stark differences in regional economic performance.

It has been popular to blame lagging economic performance in certain parts of the world on poor endowments of natural resources, geographical disadvantages, a history of colonialism, a lack of foreign aid, or an unfair international economic system. Those who are looking for excuses find in such subjects rich fodder for endless analysis and the shifting of responsibility for failure. The *Index* provides little ammunition for such arguments, finding top performers among countries in all regions, with varied endowments and varied histories. Those who are looking for solutions rather than excuses will find in this *Index* the economic policies and actions that can promote entrepreneurship and long-term economic growth irrespective of history, resources, or level of development.

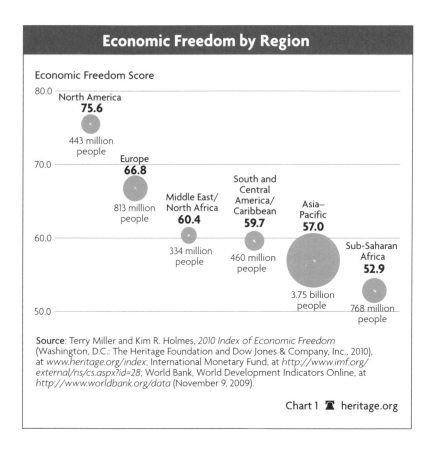

Economic Freedom by Region

Economic Freedom Score

80.0	North America **75.6** 443 million people
70.0	Europe **66.8** 813 million people
	South and Central America/Caribbean **59.7**
	Middle East/ North Africa **60.4**
	Asia–Pacific **57.0**
60.0	334 million people — 460 million people
	Sub-Saharan Africa **52.9**
	3.75 billion people — 768 million people
50.0	

Source: Terry Miller and Kim R. Holmes, *2010 Index of Economic Freedom* (Washington, D.C.: The Heritage Foundation and Dow Jones & Company, Inc., 2010), at *www.heritage.org/index*; International Monetary Fund, at *http://www.imf.org/external/ns/cs.aspx?id=28*; World Bank, World Development Indicators Online, at *http://www.worldbank.org/data* (November 9, 2009).

Chart 1 ☎ heritage.org

As shown in Chart 1, economic freedom varies noticeably across regions, with inhabitants of North America and Europe enjoying far greater levels of economic freedom than are found among those who live in other regions of the world.

Not surprisingly, levels of prosperity are far higher in those two regions than in other areas. (See Table 1.) The world's two freest regions have more than twice the population-weighted average per capita income found in the other four regions. The freest regions also enjoy higher levels of price stability.

Economic Freedom and Performance by Region

	Average Economic Freedom 2010 Score			Population Weighted Average		
	Simple Average	Population Weighted Average	Population	GDP per Capita (PPP)	GDP 5-Year Growth Rate	Inflation
North America	75.6	75.8	443,721,823	$38,222	2.5	4
Europe	66.8	63.3	813,559,596	$24,543	4.1	7.9
Middle East/ North Africa	60.4	55.2	333,819,481	$10,077	5.3	13.5
South and Central America/Caribbean	59.7	56.4	460,716,759	$9,607	5.4	8.9
Asia–Pacific	57.0	53.8	3,752,909,907	$6,084	8.5	8.1
Sub-Saharan Africa	52.9	54.1	768,240,247	$2,122	6.4	12.9*
World	59.4	56.7	6,572,967,813	$10,521	6.9	8.7*

*Excluding Zimbabwe, whose hyperinflation that is estimated at over 10,000 percent would distort the regional and the world average.

Source: Terry Miller and Kim R. Holmes, *2010 Index of Economic Freedom* (Washington, D.C.: The Heritage Foundation and Dow Jones & Company, Inc., 2010), at *www.heritage.org/index*; International Monetary Fund, at *http://www.imf.org/external/ns/cs.aspx?id=28*; World Bank, World Development Indicators Online, at *http://www.worldbank.org/data* (November 9, 2009).

Table 1 ☎ heritage.org

Each Region's Ten Economic Freedoms in Comparison to the World Average

Region	Business Freedom	Trade Freedom	Fiscal Freedom	Government Spending	Monetary Freedom	Investment Freedom	Financial Freedom	Property Rights	Freedom from Corruption	Labor Freedom
North America	+	+	+	+	+	+	+	+	+	+
Europe	+	+	–	–	+	+	+	+	+	–
South and Central America/Caribbean	–	+	+	+	–	+	–	–	–	–
Middle East/North Africa	+	+	+	+	–	–	–	–	–	+
Asia–Pacific	–	–	+	+	–	–	–	–	–	+
Sub-Saharan Africa	–	–	–	+	–	–	–	–	–	–

Source: Terry Miller and Kim R. Holmes, *2010 Index of Economic Freedom* (Washington, D.C.: The Heritage Foundation and Dow Jones & Company, Inc., 2010), at *www.heritage.org/index*.

Table 2 ☏ heritage.org

Table 2 shows components of economic freedom in which regions perform better or worse than the world averages. Only the North America region has scores in every component of economic freedom that exceed the world average. Each of the other regions has one or more components in which the average level of economic freedom falls below the world average. European countries fall over four points below the world average in fiscal freedom and 17 points below the world average in government spending—a reflection of their bloated government budgets that fund high levels of welfare spending that reduce economic dynamism and opportunities for growth. Rigid labor regulations also continue to hamper the region's overall labor freedom, with negative results for job creation and employment growth.

South and Central America/Caribbean countries lag behind world averages in six components of economic freedom, particularly freedom from corruption and property rights. The Middle East/North Africa region has lower than average scores in five economic freedoms, the Asia–Pacific region is behind in seven, and Sub-Saharan Africa lags in nine.

The following analyses provide overviews of economic freedom in each of the six regions covered in the *Index*.

NORTH AMERICA

The North America region has benefited from its openness to international trade and investment. Enjoying the highest degree of economic freedom among the six regions, North America's three countries have been linked by a regional trade agreement, the North American Free Trade Agreement (NAFTA), since 1994. NAFTA has been a positive force, enhancing economic freedom in the North America region and connecting more than 400 million people in an economic area with about one-third of the world's total GDP.

Chart 2 shows North America's overall economic freedom and 10 economic freedoms in comparison to world averages. The region scores at or above the world average in every area of economic freedom. It has high levels of business freedom, trade freedom, monetary freedom, and labor freedom. Weaknesses remain in investment freedom and freedom from corruption, as Mexico lags behind its two

Economic Freedom in North America

Overall Eco. Fdm.	**75.6**	▽
Business Freedom	**90.3**	▲
Trade Freedom	**85.7**	▲
Fiscal Freedom	**75.9**	—
Government Spending	**65.8**	▲
Monetary Freedom	**76.6**	▽
Investment Freedom	**71.7**	▲
Financial Freedom	**70.0**	▽
Property Rights	**75.0**	▽
Fdm. from Corruption	**65.3**	▲
Labor Freedom	**79.4**	▲

0 least free 50 100 most free

| = world average

Source: Terry Miller and Kim R. Holmes, *2010 Index of Economic Freedom* (Washington, D.C.: The Heritage Foundation and Dow Jones & Company, Inc., 2010), at *www.heritage.org/index*.

Chart 2 ☎ heritage.org

northern neighbors in these two areas.

Canada and the U.S. are among the 10 freest economies in the 2010 *Index*, while Mexico remains "moderately free" with a score of 68.3, which is an improvement of 2.5 points from the 2009 *Index*. In many ways, Canada's high level of economic freedom, coupled with its sound and prudent banking sector, has enabled its economy to emerge from the global downturn relatively unscathed. By contrast, the U.S. dropped from the "free" to the "mostly free" category. The U.S. government's policy responses to the crisis and economic slowdown have been far-reaching

and implemented at the cost of curtailing economic freedom.

EUROPE

The Europe region consists of 43 countries and, taken as a whole, is enjoying economic prosperity and stability. The region has continued to maintain a high level of economic freedom in the 2010 *Index*. Despite the recent global financial and economic turmoil, such policy improvements as tax cuts and other structural reforms have resulted in overall score improvements in 24 small but reform-minded economies. By contrast, 18 economies, led by the United Kingdom, Ireland, and Iceland, have recorded significant erosion of their economic freedom.

Overall, extensive and long-established free-market institutions in most countries allow the region to score above the world average in seven of the 10 economic freedoms. It is over 15 points ahead in both property rights and freedom from corruption. The region's business freedom and trade freedom lead world averages by slightly more than 10 points. (See Chart 3.)

Europe's overall economic freedom, however, is still hampered by weak scores in labor freedom, fiscal freedom, and government spending, reflecting the price of welfare states that consume a large percentage of GDP. The burdensome labor regulations that are in place

Economic Freedom in North American Countries

World Rank	Region Rank	Country	Overall Score	Change from 2009	Business Freedom	Trade Freedom	Fiscal Freedom	Government Spending	Monetary Freedom	Investment Freedom	Financial Freedom	Property Rights	Freedom from Corruption	Labor Freedom
7	1	Canada	**80.4**	−0.1	96.5	88.1	76.7	54.1	75.4	75.0	80.0	90.0	87.0	81.5
8	2	United States	**78.0**	−2.7	91.3	86.9	67.5	58.0	78.1	75.0	70.0	85.0	73.0	94.8
41	3	Mexico	**68.3**	2.5	83.0	82.0	83.5	85.2	76.3	65.0	60.0	50.0	36.0	61.9

■ 80%–100% Free
■ 70%–79.9% Mostly Free
□ 60%–69.9% Moderately Free

Table 3 ☎ heritage.org

Economic Freedom in Europe

Overall Eco. Fdm.	**66.8**	▲
Business Freedom	**76.9**	▲
Trade Freedom	**85.5**	▲
Fiscal Freedom	**70.9**	▲
Government Spending	**48.0**	▲
Monetary Freedom	**74.8**	▽
Investment Freedom	**68.3**	▲
Financial Freedom	**63.7**	▽
Property Rights	**61.6**	▲
Fdm. from Corruption	**56.5**	▽
Labor Freedom	**61.8**	▲

0 least free — 50 — 100 most free

| = world average

Source: Terry Miller and Kim R. Holmes, *2010 Index of Economic Freedom* (Washington, D.C.: The Heritage Foundation and Dow Jones & Company, Inc., 2010), at *www.heritage.org/index*.

Chart 3 ☎ heritage.org

United Kingdom now stands at 11th, falling out of the top 10 in the *Index* for the first time. The British economy has undergone far-reaching adjustments in reaction to the global financial and economic turmoil, and a dramatic expansion of state ownership has taken place since late 2008. Luxembourg, the Netherlands, Estonia, Finland, and Iceland all score in the top 20.

Switzerland's overall score is 1.7 points higher than last year. In addition to high transparency and low corruption, the Swiss economy boasts an efficient regulatory regime and an independent judiciary. Impressively for a post-Communist state, Georgia continues to be a leader in labor freedom and fiscal freedom because of a combination of low taxes and a highly flexible labor market. Montenegro enjoyed the biggest gain in economic freedom in the Europe region, improving its score by 5.4 points, followed by Macedonia and Croatia.

to protect traditional sectors are plainly hindering both productivity growth and more dynamic job creation.

Nine of the world's 20 freest countries are in Europe. (See Table 4.) Ireland, whose global ranking has fallen to 5th, is closely followed by Switzerland at 6th and Denmark at 9th. The

Europe has benefited from economic competition over the past decades in the aftermath of the opening of the Berlin Wall. Around 80 percent of the 43 European countries score

Economic Freedom in European Countries

World Rank	Region Rank	Country	Overall Score	Change from 2009	Business Freedom	Trade Freedom	Fiscal Freedom	Government Spending	Monetary Freedom	Investment Freedom	Financial Freedom	Property Rights	Freedom from Corruption	Labor Freedom
5	1	Ireland	*81.3*	−0.9	92.8	87.5	71.1	61.8	79.0	95.0	80.0	90.0	77.0	79.0
6	2	Switzerland	*81.1*	1.7	81.2	90.0	68.2	68.9	81.3	80.0	80.0	90.0	90.0	81.8
9	3	Denmark	*77.9*	−1.7	97.9	87.5	35.9	22.0	79.3	90.0	90.0	90.0	93.0	93.7
11	4	United Kingdom	*76.5*	−2.5	94.9	87.5	61.8	41.9	73.7	90.0	80.0	85.0	77.0	72.8
14	5	Luxembourg	*75.4*	0.2	75.1	87.5	65.9	58.5	78.9	95.0	80.0	90.0	83.0	40.4
15	6	The Netherlands	*75.0*	−2.0	82.6	87.5	52.0	38.4	81.0	90.0	80.0	90.0	89.0	59.1
16	7	Estonia	*74.7*	−1.7	83.1	87.5	80.2	62.2	71.1	90.0	80.0	80.0	66.0	47.0
17	8	Finland	*73.8*	−0.7	95.0	87.5	65.4	32.9	78.9	75.0	80.0	90.0	90.0	43.8
18	9	Iceland	*73.7*	−2.2	93.0	87.9	75.4	45.8	69.9	65.0	60.0	90.0	89.0	60.8

■ 80–100 Free
■ 70–79.9 Mostly Free

(continued on next page)

Table 4 ☎ heritage.org

Economic Freedom in European Countries (continued)

World Rank	Region Rank	Country	Overall Score	Change from 2009	Business Freedom	Trade Freedom	Fiscal Freedom	Government Spending	Monetary Freedom	Investment Freedom	Financial Freedom	Property Rights	Freedom from Corruption	Labor Freedom
21	10	Sweden	72.4	1.9	95.5	87.5	36.7	17.3	79.5	85.0	80.0	95.0	93.0	54.9
22	11	Austria	71.6	0.4	73.6	87.5	51.2	28.8	79.3	75.0	70.0	90.0	81.0	79.1
23	12	Germany	71.1	0.6	89.6	87.5	58.3	41.4	79.9	85.0	60.0	90.0	79.0	39.9
24	13	Cyprus	70.9	0.1	80.3	82.5	72.7	44.8	82.9	70.0	70.0	80.0	64.0	61.5
26	14	Georgia	70.4	0.6	87.9	89.1	89.1	65.3	70.2	70.0	60.0	40.0	39.0	93.7
29	15	Lithuania	70.3	0.3	82.0	87.5	84.6	63.5	70.8	75.0	80.0	55.0	46.0	58.5
30	16	Belgium	70.1	−2.0	92.9	87.5	42.2	30.0	77.9	80.0	70.0	80.0	73.0	67.1
34	17	Czech Republic	69.8	0.4	65.5	87.5	80.1	45.6	75.6	70.0	80.0	65.0	52.0	76.4
35	18	Slovakia	69.7	0.3	72.6	87.5	84.0	64.5	78.2	70.0	70.0	55.0	50.0	65.1
36	19	Spain	69.6	−0.5	75.8	87.5	58.1	54.8	77.7	80.0	80.0	70.0	65.0	47.3
37	20	Norway	69.4	−0.8	88.8	89.2	50.5	49.8	74.2	65.0	60.0	90.0	79.0	47.1
38	21	Armenia	69.2	−0.7	83.4	80.5	89.3	90.9	72.9	75.0	70.0	30.0	29.0	70.6
48	22	Malta	67.2	1.1	70.0	87.5	62.5	45.6	78.1	70.0	60.0	80.0	58.0	60.0
50	23	Latvia	66.2	−0.4	72.9	87.5	82.7	57.4	67.0	80.0	50.0	55.0	50.0	59.1
51	24	Hungary	66.1	−0.6	76.8	87.5	68.6	25.9	74.1	75.0	70.0	65.0	51.0	67.6
53	25	Albania	66.0	2.3	68.0	85.8	92.6	74.2	78.7	70.0	70.0	35.0	34.0	52.1
56	26	Macedonia	65.7	4.5	65.2	83.3	89.3	65.9	79.0	60.0	60.0	35.0	36.0	83.1
61	27	Slovenia	64.7	1.8	83.3	87.5	64.0	46.1	76.0	70.0	50.0	60.0	67.0	43.5
62	28	Portugal	64.4	−0.5	80.5	87.5	61.0	37.1	79.7	70.0	60.0	70.0	61.0	37.0
63	29	Romania	64.2	1.0	72.5	87.5	85.8	59.8	73.3	75.0	50.0	40.0	38.0	60.4
64	30	France	64.2	0.9	86.3	82.5	51.9	17.9	79.7	50.0	70.0	80.0	69.0	54.7
67	31	Turkey	63.8	2.2	68.9	86.4	78.1	82.9	70.0	65.0	50.0	50.0	46.0	41.1
68	32	Montenegro	63.6	5.4	70.1	83.2	90.0	54.4	73.2	55.0	50.0	40.0	34.0	86.4
71	33	Poland	63.2	2.9	62.2	87.5	74.9	46.8	78.1	60.0	60.0	55.0	46.0	61.5
73	34	Greece	62.7	1.9	77.4	82.5	65.9	41.9	77.6	60.0	60.0	60.0	47.0	55.1
74	35	Italy	62.7	1.3	77.9	87.5	55.2	31.2	79.0	75.0	60.0	55.0	48.0	58.2
75	36	Bulgaria	62.3	−2.3	77.8	87.4	86.3	48.3	69.5	50.0	60.0	30.0	36.0	78.1
92	37	Croatia	59.2	4.1	61.5	87.8	70.3	47.1	75.8	65.0	60.0	40.0	44.0	40.8
104	38	Serbia	56.9	0.3	58.9	75.2	83.2	41.4	64.5	50.0	50.0	40.0	34.0	72.2
110	39	Bosnia and Herzegovina	56.2	3.1	61.3	80.8	83.2	28.8	74.7	70.0	60.0	10.0	32.0	61.2
125	40	Moldova	53.7	−1.2	70.2	79.9	85.1	43.0	67.5	30.0	50.0	40.0	29.0	42.7
143	41	Russia	50.3	−0.5	52.2	68.4	82.3	66.5	62.6	25.0	40.0	25.0	21.0	59.6
150	42	Belarus	48.7	3.7	72.1	80.3	85.2	32.0	62.6	20.0	10.0	20.0	20.0	84.8
162	43	Ukraine	46.4	−2.4	38.7	82.6	77.9	41.1	61.2	20.0	30.0	30.0	25.0	57.7
n/a	n/a	Liechtenstein	n/a	n/a	n/a	n/a	n/a	n/a	n/a	n/a	n/a	n/a	n/a	n/a

■ 70%–79.9% Mostly Free   □ 50%–59.9% Mostly Unfree

▨ 60%–69.9% Moderately Free   □ 0%–49.9% Repressed

Table 4 ☎ heritage.org

2010 Index of Economic Freedom

between 60 and 80, achieving the status of either "moderately free" or "mostly free." Only Ukraine and Belarus remain "repressed" with scores below 50.

SOUTH AND CENTRAL AMERICA/CARIBBEAN

The countries of the South and Central America/Caribbean region range from prosperous Chile and the developing economic colossus of Brazil to the small island economies of the Caribbean Sea. The region, which consists of 29 economies, is one of the world's most diverse, economically as well as politically.

Despite strong economic progress in many countries as the result of policy liberalization, governments and even electorates in some countries have been turning away from free-market policies and embracing a new populism that looks very much like the old corrupt cronyism that characterized the region before the outbreak of democracy in the 1980s and 1990s. This newly packaged but really old-fashioned authoritarianism, backed by the oil revenue of an increasingly anti-democratic Venezuela, increases the risk, especially in the poorer countries of Central America or the smaller islands of the Caribbean, that economic freedom and long-term prosperity could be sacrificed for short-term payoffs and political expediency.

The countries in the South and Central America/Caribbean region perform better than the world average in four of the 10 components of economic freedom measured in the *Index*. (See Chart 4.) Corruption and a lack of protection for property rights are the major problem areas, reflecting long-standing issues of poor governance and weak rule of law.

The typical country in the region stands out positively in terms of limited taxation and government expenditures. The freedom to trade and invest is slightly better protected than in other parts of the developing world.

The region has maintained an overall level of economic freedom that is slightly higher than the global average of 59.4. Colombia is the most improved country in the region, gaining 3.2 points in the 2010 *Index*. (See Table 5.) It has become one of South America's most stable economies. Improvements in its entrepreneurial environment, facilitated by openness to trade and investment, have led to steady economic growth. Recent reforms have focused on improving regulation and fostering a strong private sector. Bolivia has recorded the hemisphere's worst performance this year, losing about four points in overall economic freedom. Half-measures of privatization and liberalization have resulted in marginal investments and slow economic growth. Bolivia's overall economic development has been uneven, and poverty remains a daunting challenge.

One of the 29 countries in the South and Central America/Caribbean region ranks among the top 20 in the world: Chile (10th). Chile's continuing commitment to economic freedom and its dynamic private sector have facilitated steady economic growth.

Noticeably, the region's countries are distributed throughout the rankings in a more balanced fashion than are the countries of any other region, almost like a bell curve. All but seven countries receive an economic freedom score between 50 and 70, and 16 countries fall in the middle category of "moderately free."

Economic Freedom in South and Central America/Caribbean

Overall Eco. Fdm.	59.7	▽
Business Freedom	63.1	▽
Trade Freedom	74.3	▲
Fiscal Freedom	76.4	▽
Government Spending	71.9	▽
Monetary Freedom	70.4	▽
Investment Freedom	49.7	▽
Financial Freedom	47.9	▽
Property Rights	42.2	▽
Fdm. from Corruption	39.3	▲
Labor Freedom	61.3	▲

0 least free — 50 — 100 most free

| = world average

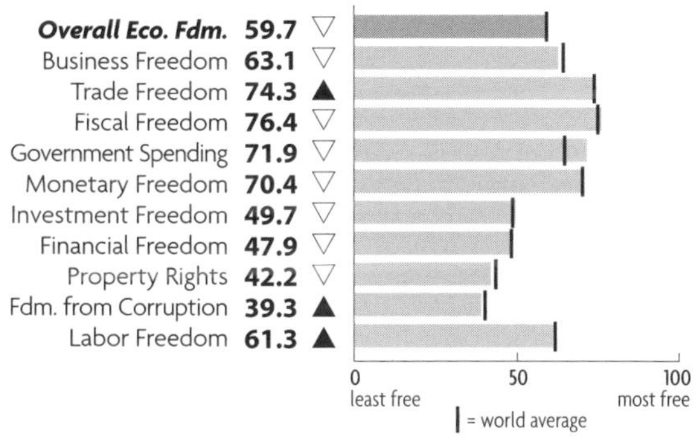

Source: Terry Miller and Kim R. Holmes, *2010 Index of Economic Freedom* (Washington, D.C.: The Heritage Foundation and Dow Jones & Company, Inc., 2010), at *www.heritage.org/index*.

Chart 4 ☎ heritage.org

Economic Freedom in South and Central America/ Caribbean Countries

World Rank	Region Rank	Country	Overall Score	Change from 2009	Business Freedom	Trade Freedom	Fiscal Freedom	Government Spending	Monetary Freedom	Investment Freedom	Financial Freedom	Property Rights	Freedom from Corruption	Labor Freedom
10	1	Chile	**77.2**	−1.1	64.8	88.0	77.5	89.6	73.0	80.0	70.0	85.0	69.0	75.4
25	2	Saint Lucia	**70.5**	1.7	88.4	71.9	73.2	71.4	80.1	55.0	40.0	70.0	71.0	84.2
32	3	El Salvador	**69.9**	0.1	67.4	83.8	85.7	89.2	74.1	75.0	70.0	50.0	39.0	64.5
33	4	Uruguay	**69.8**	0.7	63.1	82.8	81.7	72.6	72.3	75.0	30.0	75.0	69.0	76.2
40	5	Barbados	**68.3**	−3.2	90.0	60.5	70.1	54.6	73.1	45.0	60.0	80.0	70.0	80.0
45	6	Peru	**67.6**	3.0	65.8	85.0	79.5	92.3	81.6	70.0	60.0	40.0	36.0	66.1
47	7	The Bahamas	**67.3**	−3.0	73.4	42.2	95.2	83.6	72.7	30.0	70.0	70.0	55.0	81.0
49	8	Saint Vincent and The Grenadines	**66.9**	2.6	79.9	73.3	72.5	64.1	71.3	55.0	40.0	70.0	65.0	77.6
54	9	Costa Rica	**65.9**	−0.5	59.3	82.5	82.4	87.0	67.8	70.0	50.0	50.0	51.0	59.0
55	10	Trinidad and Tobago	**65.7**	−2.3	59.0	81.7	80.8	72.3	69.3	60.0	70.0	50.0	36.0	78.0
57	11	Jamaica	**65.5**	0.3	87.0	72.2	74.8	61.8	68.4	85.0	60.0	45.0	31.0	70.0
58	12	Colombia	**65.5**	3.2	83.6	72.5	74.3	74.8	74.0	55.0	60.0	50.0	38.0	72.7
60	13	Panama	**64.8**	0.1	75.9	75.8	82.6	90.0	73.2	65.0	70.0	40.0	34.0	41.3
70	14	Dominica	**63.2**	0.6	75.4	74.3	67.7	49.8	80.0	65.0	30.0	65.0	60.0	65.2
79	15	Belize	**61.5**	−1.5	74.1	71.5	68.3	74.9	75.6	50.0	50.0	40.0	29.0	81.7
81	16	Paraguay	**61.3**	0.3	60.9	83.5	96.6	91.7	75.4	65.0	60.0	30.0	24.0	26.1
83	17	Guatemala	**61.0**	1.6	52.5	84.0	79.3	93.9	70.2	60.0	50.0	35.0	31.0	54.3
86	18	Dominican Republic	**60.3**	1.1	62.4	80.0	85.3	90.2	70.8	55.0	40.0	30.0	30.0	59.6
98	19	Nicaragua	**58.3**	−1.5	55.7	82.8	78.4	78.5	64.1	55.0	50.0	25.0	25.0	68.3
99	20	Honduras	**58.3**	−0.4	63.0	83.7	84.7	73.5	70.2	60.0	60.0	30.0	26.0	31.6
113	21	Brazil	**55.6**	−1.1	54.5	69.2	68.4	50.3	75.8	45.0	50.0	50.0	35.0	57.5
131	22	Suriname	**52.5**	−1.6	41.0	66.4	66.9	77.8	67.8	15.0	30.0	40.0	36.0	84.5
135	23	Argentina	**51.2**	−1.1	62.1	69.5	69.5	75.6	61.2	45.0	30.0	20.0	29.0	50.1
141	24	Haiti	**50.8**	0.3	36.0	79.1	81.5	91.3	67.1	30.0	30.0	10.0	14.0	69.2
146	25	Bolivia	**49.4**	−4.2	57.3	76.9	84.3	67.5	63.2	15.0	50.0	10.0	30.0	39.4
147	26	Ecuador	**49.3**	−3.2	52.9	71.8	79.3	77.5	63.9	25.0	40.0	20.0	20.0	42.2
153	27	Guyana	**48.4**	0.0	63.4	71.3	55.9	26.2	71.0	30.0	40.0	35.0	26.0	65.2
174	28	Venezuela	**37.1**	−2.8	50.3	57.2	74.0	61.8	47.7	5.0	20.0	0.0	19.0	36.2
177	29	Cuba	**26.7**	−1.2	10.0	61.7	45.9	0.0	66.7	0.0	10.0	10.0	43.0	20.0

■ 70%–79.9% Mostly Free   ▢ 50%–59.9% Mostly Unfree

■ 60%–69.9% Moderately Free   ▢ 0%–49.9% Repressed

Table 5 ☎ heritage.org

MIDDLE EAST/NORTH AFRICA

The Middle East/North Africa region remains central to world affairs. Encompassing some of the world's most ancient civilizations, it consists of 17 countries. Although the region's overall economic freedom has increased by 0.4 point since the 2009 *Index*, many of its economies remain only "moderately free" or "mostly unfree." Cursed in some ways by enormous natural oil resources, most of the local populations still suffer from extreme concentrations of wealth and poverty.

Despite some progress in recent years, structural problems clearly abound. The regional unemployment rate, which averages more than 10 percent, is among the highest in the world and is most pronounced among younger members of the labor force. Despite the outflow of crude oil, the actual trade flows of the region's countries remain relatively low, indicating a lack of economic dynamism. The oil industry requires very little investment in labor or human capital and only a marginal amount of investment in the land. People need freedom to be productive, but oil does not generate the incentives needed for societies to embrace openness. To the contrary, an abundance of oil seems most often to inspire repression.

As shown in Chart 5, the region's overall economic freedom score is slightly above the world average of 59.4, mainly due to a high degree of fiscal freedom that reflects low income and corporate tax rates. However, other institutional problems pose serious impediments to creating more dynamic private sectors and diverse economies. Investment freedom, financial freedom, property rights, and freedom from corruption all score below world averages, holding down the region's overall economic freedom and its economic potential.

The ongoing transformation of innovative and reform-oriented states like Bahrain, Qatar, Kuwait, Oman, and Israel may pave the way for more robust and dynamic regional economic growth.

As Table 6 shows, scores for most of the 17 countries in the region are concentrated between 50 and 70. Qatar and the United Arab Emirates made the biggest leaps forward with gains of over four points in economic freedom. Improving the entrepreneurial environment and broadening the economic base beyond the energy sector, a series of economic reforms has made Qatar and the United Arab Emirates, respectively, the 10th and 14th most improved economies in the 2010 *Index*.

Bahrain, ranked 13th globally with an economic freedom score of 74.8, is the only Middle Eastern country among the world's 20 freest economies. Structural reforms and openness to global commerce have made Bahrain a financial hub and the regional leader in economic freedom. One of the region's least oil-dependent economies, it has a competitive tax regime and sophisticated financial sector that facilitates the flow of capital and foreign investment.

Seven "moderately free" economies ranging from Israel to Saudi Arabia—while politically very different—share a common commitment to economic freedom that is significantly greater than that of other countries in the region.

The lowest-ranking countries in the region continue to be Iran and Libya, bonded together by economic freedom scores that are among the worst in the world.

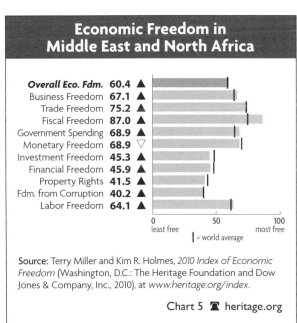

Economic Freedom in Middle East and North Africa

Overall Eco. Fdm.	60.4	▲
Business Freedom	67.1	▲
Trade Freedom	75.2	▲
Fiscal Freedom	87.0	▲
Government Spending	68.9	▲
Monetary Freedom	68.9	▽
Investment Freedom	45.3	▲
Financial Freedom	45.9	▲
Property Rights	41.5	▲
Fdm. from Corruption	40.2	▲
Labor Freedom	64.1	▲

0 least free   50   100 most free

| = world average

Source: Terry Miller and Kim R. Holmes, *2010 Index of Economic Freedom* (Washington, D.C.: The Heritage Foundation and Dow Jones & Company, Inc., 2010), at *www.heritage.org/index*.

Chart 5 ☎ heritage.org

Economic Freedom in Middle East/North African Countries

World Rank	Region Rank	Country	Overall Score	Change from 2009	Business Freedom	Trade Freedom	Fiscal Freedom	Government Spending	Monetary Freedom	Investment Freedom	Financial Freedom	Property Rights	Freedom from Corruption	Labor Freedom
13	1	Bahrain	**76.3**	1.5	77.8	82.9	99.9	80.8	73.4	65.0	80.0	60.0	54.0	89.4
39	2	Qatar	**69.0**	3.2	73.7	82.2	99.9	73.7	65.9	45.0	50.0	65.0	65.0	69.1
42	3	Kuwait	**67.7**	2.1	65.8	82.5	99.9	76.6	66.4	55.0	50.0	50.0	43.0	88.0
43	4	Oman	**67.7**	0.7	66.9	83.4	98.5	57.4	64.8	55.0	60.0	50.0	55.0	86.4
44	5	Israel	**67.7**	0.1	66.4	87.8	58.4	35.4	78.2	85.0	70.0	70.0	60.0	65.4
46	6	United Arab Emirates	**67.3**	2.6	67.4	82.8	99.9	80.9	68.8	35.0	50.0	50.0	59.0	79.3
52	7	Jordan	**66.1**	0.7	65.6	78.8	83.0	55.1	73.2	65.0	60.0	55.0	51.0	74.2
65	8	Saudi Arabia	**64.1**	−0.2	84.6	82.5	99.6	68.1	62.3	45.0	50.0	40.0	35.0	74.4
89	9	Lebanon	**59.5**	1.4	56.6	80.5	91.6	62.8	71.4	55.0	60.0	30.0	30.0	57.0
91	10	Morocco	**59.2**	1.5	76.1	71.2	68.5	81.5	78.4	60.0	60.0	40.0	35.0	21.7
94	11	Egypt	**59.0**	1.0	65.0	74.0	89.7	73.4	64.2	50.0	50.0	40.0	28.0	55.6
95	12	Tunisia	**58.9**	1.0	80.2	53.5	74.4	78.5	76.5	35.0	30.0	50.0	44.0	67.4
105	13	Algeria	**56.9**	0.3	71.2	70.7	83.5	73.4	77.2	45.0	30.0	30.0	32.0	56.4
121	14	Yemen	**54.4**	−2.5	74.4	76.1	83.2	51.3	65.1	45.0	30.0	30.0	23.0	65.4
145	15	Syria	**49.4**	−1.9	59.2	54.0	87.0	80.2	63.3	20.0	20.0	25.0	21.0	64.7
168	16	Iran	**43.4**	−1.2	69.9	50.2	81.1	79.6	54.7	0.0	10.0	10.0	23.0	55.1
173	17	Libya	**40.2**	−3.3	20.0	85.0	81.7	62.8	66.4	10.0	20.0	10.0	26.0	20.0
n/a	n/a	Iraq	**n/a**	n/a	n/a	n/a	n/a	n/a	n/a	n/a	n/a	n/a	n/a	n/a

■ 70%–79.9% Mostly Free   □ 50%–59.9% Mostly Unfree

▨ 60%–69.9% Moderately Free   □ 0%–49.9% Repressed

Table 6 ☎ heritage.org

ASIA–PACIFIC

With 3.7 billion inhabitants, the Asia–Pacific region contains over half of the world's population: one-third in China and nearly another third in India. The region has achieved an average annual economic growth rate of around 8 percent over the past five years, largely driven by China, India, and other export-oriented economies.

What sets the Asia–Pacific region apart from other regions is the extraordinary disparity in levels of economic freedom. Four of the world's 10 freest economies—Hong Kong, Singapore, Australia, and New Zealand—are in this region, yet most of its other countries remain "mostly unfree." Countries such as Turkmenistan, Bangladesh, and Burma have economies that are "repressed." North Korea remains the least free economy, both in the region and in the world. The region's overall economic freedom score is below the world average of 59.4.

The Asia–Pacific region, which consists of 41 economies, scores higher than the world average in three of the 10 economic freedoms: fiscal freedom, government spending, and labor freedom. (See Chart 6.) Lower government expenditures result in a regional government spending score that is about five points better than the world average. The region's labor freedom score is also better than the world average by four points, although many small Pacific island economies still lack fully developed formal labor markets.

The typical Asian country has notably lower scores in four components: investment freedom, financial freedom, property rights, and freedom from corruption. Asian countries could make the most progress by strengthening their banking and investment institutions and by enhancing transparency and corporate governance.

With the top scores in four of the 10 economic freedoms, Hong Kong once again is the freest economy in the 2010 *Index*. (See Table 7.) Singapore is the top country in labor freedom and second overall, both in the region and in the world. Singapore grants private firms the most flexibility in hiring and firing workers. New Zealand sets the standard for clean, corruption-free government and benefits significantly from its transparent and straightforward business environment.

About two-thirds of the 41 countries in the Asia–Pacific region score between 40 and 60 on the economic freedom scale, remaining either "mostly unfree" or "repressed." In the 2010 *Index*, the scores of 13 countries in the region have improved, while those of 27 are worse. Bangladesh and Indonesia are the region's most improved countries. Timor-Leste and the

Economic Freedom in Asia–Pacific

	Score	
Overall Eco. Fdm.	**57.0**	▽
Business Freedom	64.5	▲
Trade Freedom	71.0	▲
Fiscal Freedom	77.2	▲
Government Spending	70.2	▽
Monetary Freedom	69.0	▽
Investment Freedom	36.1	▽
Financial Freedom	41.2	▲
Property Rights	38.9	▲
Fdm. from Corruption	36.1	▽
Labor Freedom	66.0	▽

0 least free — 50 — 100 most free

| = world average

Source: Terry Miller and Kim R. Holmes, *2010 Index of Economic Freedom* (Washington, D.C.: The Heritage Foundation and Dow Jones & Company, Inc., 2010), at *www.heritage.org/index.*

Chart 6 ☎ heritage.org

Economic Freedom in Asia–Pacific Countries

World Rank	Region Rank	Country	Overall Score	Change from 2009	Business Freedom	Trade Freedom	Fiscal Freedom	Government Spending	Monetary Freedom	Investment Freedom	Financial Freedom	Property Rights	Freedom from Corruption	Labor Freedom
1	1	Hong Kong	**89.7**	−0.3	98.7	90.0	93.0	93.7	83.1	90.0	90.0	90.0	81.0	87.4
2	2	Singapore	**86.1**	−1.0	98.2	90.0	90.7	95.3	80.9	75.0	50.0	90.0	92.0	98.9
3	3	Australia	**82.6**	0.0	90.3	85.1	61.4	64.9	82.7	80.0	90.0	90.0	87.0	94.9
4	4	New Zealand	**82.1**	0.1	99.9	86.0	63.6	51.3	83.1	80.0	80.0	95.0	93.0	88.8
19	5	Japan	**72.9**	0.1	84.5	82.4	67.2	61.1	88.8	60.0	50.0	80.0	73.0	82.4
20	6	Macau	**72.5**	0.5	60.0	90.0	77.8	95.2	77.5	80.0	70.0	60.0	54.0	60.0
27	7	Taiwan	**70.4**	0.9	83.0	85.8	75.9	90.5	79.3	65.0	50.0	70.0	57.0	47.7
31	8	South Korea	**69.9**	1.8	91.9	70.8	71.1	74.9	77.4	70.0	70.0	70.0	56.0	47.1
59	9	Malaysia	**64.8**	0.2	69.9	78.7	84.3	81.3	76.7	30.0	50.0	55.0	51.0	71.4
66	10	Thailand	**64.1**	1.1	70.7	75.9	74.7	89.8	66.4	40.0	70.0	45.0	35.0	73.6

(continued on next page)

■ 80%–100% Free
▨ 70%–79.9% Mostly Free
▢ 60%–69.9% Moderately Free

Table 7 ☎ heritage.org

Economic Freedom in Asia–Pacific Countries (continued)

World Rank	Region Rank	Country	Overall Score	Change from 2009	Business Freedom	Trade Freedom	Fiscal Freedom	Government Spending	Monetary Freedom	Investment Freedom	Financial Freedom	Property Rights	Freedom from Corruption	Labor Freedom
80	11	Kyrgyz Republic	*61.3*	−0.5	76.6	75.9	92.9	80.2	62.2	50.0	50.0	25.0	18.0	82.6
82	12	Kazakhstan	*61.0*	0.9	73.5	85.9	87.9	82.1	65.6	30.0	50.0	30.0	22.0	83.1
84	13	Samoa	*60.4*	0.9	73.2	70.0	79.6	67.5	73.8	30.0	30.0	55.0	44.0	80.8
85	14	Fiji	*60.3*	−0.7	63.5	71.0	75.7	80.6	73.6	25.0	60.0	30.0	40.0	84.0
88	15	Mongolia	*60.0*	−2.8	69.0	79.8	81.9	56.7	66.5	50.0	60.0	30.0	30.0	75.9
96	16	Azerbaijan	*58.8*	0.8	74.6	77.1	79.5	77.5	62.7	55.0	40.0	20.0	19.0	82.5
103	17	Bhutan	*57.0*	−0.7	60.5	52.0	84.1	58.3	73.4	15.0	30.0	60.0	52.0	85.1
107	18	Cambodia	*56.6*	0.0	39.9	70.0	91.0	92.9	70.5	60.0	50.0	30.0	18.0	43.6
108	19	Vanuatu	*56.4*	−2.0	68.7	55.1	94.9	84.3	76.8	20.0	40.0	40.0	29.0	55.0
109	20	The Philippines	*56.3*	−0.4	48.1	77.8	78.8	91.2	72.7	40.0	50.0	30.0	23.0	51.9
114	21	Indonesia	*55.5*	2.1	53.1	77.9	81.9	89.1	70.8	35.0	40.0	30.0	26.0	50.8
117	22	Pakistan	*55.2*	−1.8	71.7	67.0	80.5	88.8	69.4	30.0	40.0	30.0	25.0	49.8
120	23	Sri Lanka	*54.6*	−1.4	71.8	62.2	73.5	83.9	56.8	15.0	40.0	40.0	32.0	70.7
124	24	India	*53.8*	−0.6	36.3	67.9	73.4	76.1	67.5	35.0	40.0	50.0	34.0	57.7
126	25	Papua New Guinea	*53.5*	−1.3	59.1	86.2	65.0	63.3	72.6	35.0	30.0	20.0	20.0	83.3
127	26	Tonga	*53.4*	−0.7	78.2	56.2	82.8	70.8	63.5	25.0	20.0	20.0	24.0	93.7
128	27	Tajikistan	*53.0*	−1.6	57.4	82.5	88.9	78.0	58.4	25.0	40.0	25.0	20.0	54.4
130	28	Nepal	*52.7*	−0.5	59.4	58.8	86.6	92.3	77.8	15.0	30.0	35.0	27.0	44.7
137	29	Bangladesh	*51.1*	3.6	59.4	58.0	72.8	93.9	66.6	45.0	20.0	20.0	21.0	53.8
138	30	Laos	*51.1*	0.7	59.4	68.4	80.1	90.3	73.5	25.0	20.0	15.0	20.0	58.9
140	31	China	*51.0*	−2.2	49.7	72.2	70.2	88.1	70.6	20.0	30.0	20.0	36.0	53.2
142	32	Micronesia	*50.6*	−1.1	59.1	81.0	97.5	0.0	76.7	20.0	30.0	30.0	30.0	81.8
144	33	Vietnam	*49.8*	−1.2	60.7	68.9	76.1	73.4	58.1	20.0	30.0	15.0	27.0	68.4
148	34	Maldives	*49.0*	−2.3	82.3	44.5	95.5	0.0	69.7	35.0	30.0	30.0	28.0	75.3
158	35	Uzbekistan	*47.5*	−3.0	67.8	65.1	88.4	72.6	62.4	10.0	10.0	20.0	18.0	61.1
164	36	Timor-Leste	*45.8*	−4.7	46.2	73.0	64.7	54.1	72.5	20.0	20.0	20.0	22.0	65.6
166	37	Kiribati	*43.7*	−2.0	65.6	55.4	42.2	0.0	71.9	25.0	30.0	30.0	31.0	86.1
170	38	Solomon Islands	*42.9*	−3.1	63.2	65.2	67.9	0.0	65.5	10.0	30.0	30.0	29.0	68.4
171	39	Turkmenistan	*42.5*	−1.7	30.0	79.2	90.2	94.7	62.8	0.0	10.0	10.0	18.0	30.0
175	40	Burma	*36.7*	−1.0	20.0	72.3	81.9	98.4	46.5	0.0	10.0	5.0	13.0	20.0
179	41	North Korea	*1.0*	−1.0	0.0	0.0	0.0	0.0	0.0	0.0	0.0	5.0	5.0	0.0
n/a	n/a	Afghanistan	*n/a*	n/a	n/a	n/a	n/a	n/a	n/a	n/a	n/a	n/a	n/a	n/a

60%–69.9% Moderately Free
50%–59.9% Mostly Unfree
0%–49.9% Repressed

Table 7 ☎ heritage.org

Solomon Islands, by contrast, lost the most economic freedom.

India and China are ranked 24th and 31st, respectively, in the region, and both remain "mostly unfree." Despite these seemingly low scores, however, there can be no denying that the winds of change are still blowing in Asia, particularly in these two economic leviathans. Notwithstanding very slow progress, it should be noted that economic freedom has been improving gradually in India and China over the years.

SUB-SAHARAN AFRICA

The Sub-Saharan Africa region continues to be characterized primarily by poverty and instability. Civil wars flare sporadically from the Horn of Africa to the Atlantic Coast. HIV/AIDS is a continuing burden. Mass unemployment is common. Unsurprisingly, with just a fraction of the population of Asia, Sub-Saharan Africa receives more absolute foreign aid, both multilateral and bilateral, than any other region.

Africa's overall level of economic freedom is weaker than that of any other region. Sub-Saharan Africa is ranked last in seven of the 10 components of economic freedom and performs especially poorly in terms of property rights and freedom from corruption. (See Chart 7.)

Economic Freedom in Sub-Saharan Africa

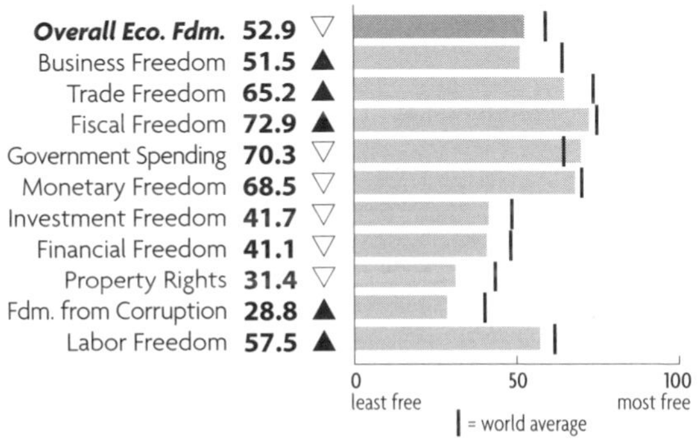

Overall Eco. Fdm.	**52.9**	▽
Business Freedom	**51.5**	▲
Trade Freedom	**65.2**	▲
Fiscal Freedom	**72.9**	▲
Government Spending	**70.3**	▽
Monetary Freedom	**68.5**	▽
Investment Freedom	**41.7**	▽
Financial Freedom	**41.1**	▽
Property Rights	**31.4**	▽
Fdm. from Corruption	**28.8**	▲
Labor Freedom	**57.5**	▲

0 least free   50   100 most free

| = world average

Source: Terry Miller and Kim R. Holmes, *2010 Index of Economic Freedom* (Washington, D.C.: The Heritage Foundation and Dow Jones & Company, Inc., 2010), at *www.heritage.org/index*.

Chart 7 ☎ heritage.org

Some of the gaps between Sub-Saharan Africa's scores and world averages are especially striking. It lags by over 10 points in business freedom and by about 12 points in both property rights and freedom from corruption. Labor freedom is restricted, reflecting in part the region's lack of progress in developing modern and efficient labor markets.

Thankfully, there are some success stories. Mauritius remains among the world's 20 freest economies. (See Table 8.) With an economic freedom score of 76.3, it is both the 12th freest economy in the world and the leader in economic freedom in the region. It scores above the global average in eight economic freedoms, including trade freedom, investment freedom, property rights, freedom from corruption, and fiscal freedom. Mauritius has also demonstrated its strong commitment to enhancing economic freedom by accelerating major tax reforms. Botswana remains the region's second freest economy, followed by Madagascar and South Africa.

Unlike other regions that have a more diverse range of "free" economies, in Sub-Saharan Africa, there are only distinctions among less free economies. A majority of nations in the region are ranked either "mostly unfree" with scores between 50 and 60 or "repressed" with scores below 50.

With its economic freedom continuing to deteriorate, Eritrea recorded the region's biggest overall score reduction. Eritrea's institutional capacity and support for economic freedom have deteriorated significantly. Poor management of macroeconomic policies, coupled with political instability over the past decade, severely impedes overall economic development. A harsh regulatory environment and pervasive corruption undermine the business and investment climates.

Zimbabwe's economy has also continued to crumble under the tyrannical and oppressive rule of Robert Mugabe. All components of economic freedom score below or far below world averages. Having caused one of the worst periods of hyperinflation in world history, the gov-

Economic Freedom in Sub-Saharan Africa Countries

World Rank	Region Rank	Country	Overall Score	Change from 2009	Business Freedom	Trade Freedom	Fiscal Freedom	Government Spending	Monetary Freedom	Investment Freedom	Financial Freedom	Property Rights	Freedom from Corruption	Labor Freedom
12	1	Mauritius	76.3	2.0	82.2	85.6	92.5	83.4	71.2	85.0	70.0	60.0	55.0	78.5
28	2	Botswana	70.3	0.6	70.5	73.9	74.1	67.1	68.8	80.0	70.0	70.0	58.0	70.8
69	3	Madagascar	63.2	1.1	71.9	73.2	87.3	88.8	75.4	60.0	50.0	45.0	34.0	46.9
72	4	South Africa	62.8	−1.0	73.0	76.0	69.1	76.8	70.2	45.0	60.0	50.0	49.0	59.0
76	5	Uganda	62.2	−1.3	57.0	72.1	80.5	85.5	78.1	45.0	60.0	30.0	26.0	88.1
77	6	Namibia	62.2	−0.2	73.3	87.8	68.3	69.5	71.0	50.0	40.0	30.0	45.0	87.2
78	7	Cape Verde	61.8	0.5	63.3	65.5	65.6	65.3	74.5	60.0	60.0	65.0	51.0	48.1
87	8	Ghana	60.2	2.1	56.8	65.3	83.5	58.9	65.9	65.0	60.0	50.0	39.0	57.4
90	9	Burkina Faso	59.4	−0.1	60.0	71.3	80.4	80.0	73.0	50.0	50.0	30.0	35.0	64.4
93	10	Rwanda	59.1	4.9	74.5	67.4	77.1	75.6	66.9	40.0	40.0	30.0	30.0	89.2
97	11	Tanzania	58.3	0.0	45.5	70.5	80.3	82.6	70.8	65.0	50.0	30.0	30.0	58.4
100	12	Zambia	58.0	1.4	66.4	79.9	72.4	82.6	63.3	50.0	50.0	30.0	28.0	57.0
101	13	Kenya	57.5	−1.2	63.4	67.9	78.1	83.1	72.7	45.0	50.0	30.0	21.0	63.7
102	14	Swaziland	57.4	−1.7	67.2	74.9	63.1	55.5	68.8	55.0	40.0	45.0	36.0	68.4
106	15	Nigeria	56.8	1.7	53.2	67.2	84.4	64.7	75.4	40.0	40.0	30.0	27.0	85.7
111	16	Mozambique	56.0	0.3	58.7	74.5	77.6	76.1	74.9	50.0	50.0	30.0	26.0	42.0
112	17	Mali	55.6	0.0	47.5	69.6	60.2	81.1	73.8	50.0	40.0	35.0	31.0	67.9
115	18	Benin	55.4	0.0	42.3	57.0	75.9	85.2	74.6	60.0	50.0	30.0	31.0	47.8
116	19	Gabon	55.4	0.4	58.8	62.1	61.5	86.4	71.4	45.0	40.0	40.0	31.0	57.4
118	20	The Gambia	55.1	−0.7	58.5	60.6	71.9	75.3	71.6	55.0	50.0	25.0	19.0	63.8
119	21	Senegal	54.6	−1.7	63.1	69.7	64.7	77.8	75.2	35.0	40.0	45.0	34.0	41.9
122	22	Malawi	54.1	0.4	44.8	68.6	78.9	45.8	71.0	50.0	50.0	45.0	28.0	59.3
123	23	Côte d'Ivoire	54.1	−0.9	43.7	64.3	78.3	87.1	76.0	35.0	50.0	30.0	20.0	56.1
129	24	Niger	52.9	−0.9	37.2	75.7	65.1	85.1	77.6	50.0	40.0	30.0	28.0	40.7
132	25	Cameroon	52.3	−0.6	37.2	59.7	71.8	92.7	71.9	35.0	50.0	30.0	23.0	52.2
133	26	Mauritania	52.0	−1.9	48.3	69.9	75.1	73.4	78.0	30.0	40.0	25.0	28.0	52.5
134	27	Guinea	51.8	0.8	43.7	60.0	69.9	93.1	57.4	40.0	40.0	20.0	16.0	78.0
136	28	Ethiopia	51.2	−1.8	66.3	61.9	77.7	82.9	60.4	25.0	20.0	30.0	26.0	61.5
139	29	Djibouti	51.0	−0.2	35.7	31.9	78.2	58.9	70.5	60.0	60.0	30.0	30.0	55.3
149	30	São Tomé and Príncipe	48.8	5.0	43.5	66.6	87.1	52.5	59.0	45.0	30.0	30.0	27.0	47.6
151	31	Equatorial Guinea	48.6	−2.7	44.8	58.9	75.5	83.9	80.9	20.0	40.0	20.0	17.0	44.8
152	32	Central African Republic	48.4	0.1	37.5	58.1	65.5	94.1	68.3	40.0	30.0	20.0	20.0	50.7
154	33	Angola	48.4	1.4	43.4	70.4	85.1	62.8	62.6	35.0	40.0	20.0	19.0	45.2

■ 70%–79.9% Mostly Free   □ 50%–59.9% Mostly Unfree

■ 60%–69.9% Moderately Free   □ 0%–49.9% Repressed

(continued on next page)

Table 8 ☎ heritage.org

Economic Freedom in Sub-Saharan Africa Countries (continued)

World Rank	Region Rank	Country	Overall Score	Change from 2009	Business Freedom	Trade Freedom	Fiscal Freedom	Government Spending	Monetary Freedom	Investment Freedom	Financial Freedom	Property Rights	Freedom from Corruption	Labor Freedom
155	34	Lesotho	***48.1***	–1.6	62.0	63.5	52.0	30.0	70.3	25.0	40.0	40.0	32.0	66.1
156	35	Seychelles	***47.9***	0.1	64.2	33.4	76.4	9.3	57.9	50.0	30.0	50.0	48.0	59.8
157	36	Sierra Leone	***47.9***	0.1	54.6	62.8	80.9	80.5	71.7	40.0	20.0	10.0	19.0	39.0
159	37	Chad	***47.5***	0.0	32.7	58.4	50.5	89.2	76.7	45.0	40.0	20.0	16.0	46.9
160	38	Burundi	***47.5***	–1.3	37.8	68.6	72.2	42.7	62.7	50.0	30.0	25.0	19.0	66.9
161	39	Togo	***47.1***	–1.5	36.8	62.8	56.2	86.0	74.5	25.0	30.0	30.0	27.0	43.3
163	40	Liberia	***46.2***	–1.9	52.8	53.8	67.8	82.3	65.4	20.0	20.0	25.0	24.0	51.3
165	41	Comoros	***44.9***	1.6	43.7	62.4	65.0	85.1	76.4	10.0	20.0	30.0	25.0	31.4
167	42	Guinea–Bissau	***43.6***	–1.8	23.4	58.2	88.6	47.3	67.0	30.0	30.0	20.0	19.0	52.5
169	43	Rep. of Congo	***43.2***	–2.2	48.7	61.0	60.3	69.3	70.8	15.0	30.0	10.0	19.0	48.1
172	44	Demo. Rep. of Congo	***41.4***	–1.4	33.5	61.7	74.0	90.5	58.7	15.0	20.0	10.0	17.0	33.4
176	45	Eritrea	***35.3***	–3.2	18.0	69.1	73.0	6.9	59.0	0.0	20.0	10.0	26.0	70.8
178	46	Zimbabwe	***21.4***	–1.3	30.0	44.8	58.4	0.0	0.0	0.0	10.0	5.0	18.0	48.2
n/a	n/a	Sudan	***n/a***	n/a	n/a	n/a	n/a	n/a	n/a	n/a	n/a	n/a	n/a	n/a

0%–49.9% Repressed

Table 8 heritage.org

ernment's continuing control of the economy has put the population at great risk.

PRESERVING ECONOMIC FREEDOM

In recent months, economies in every region have shown some vital signs of economic recovery after the turbulence of the previous two years. Today's world economy can emerge stronger if the right policy choices are made at this critical juncture. Abruptly halting the long-standing commitment to economic freedom will only prolong the current economic downturn and weaken the foundation for solid economic growth.

The recent financial and economic turmoil vividly illustrates the interdependence of economies in different regions. Bad policy choices that hurt economic freedom and retard economic performance in one country may have profoundly negative effects in others. Wise policymakers, therefore, will defend progress in economic freedom not only in their own countries, but in others as well. That challenge will require strong commitment and political leadership.

Economic freedom is the indispensable link between economic opportunity and prosperity. With a renewed commitment to the principles of economic freedom, the global economy can emerge quickly with institutions better-equipped to foster growth and provide the resources to deal more effectively both with today's challenges and with those of the future.

Chapter 7

The Countries

This chapter reports data on economic freedom in each of the 183 countries covered in the *Index of Economic Freedom*. Of these 183 countries, 179 are fully scored and ranked. Because of data constraints, the remaining four—Afghanistan, Iraq, Sudan, and Liechtenstein—are covered without numerical grading. Each graded country is given a score ranging from 0 to 100 for all 10 components of overall economic freedom, and these scores are then averaged (using equal weights) to get the country's final *Index of Economic Freedom* score.

In addition to these scores, the country pages include a brief introduction describing economic strengths and weaknesses and the political and economic background influencing a country's performance, as well as a statistical profile giving the country's main economic indicators. These statistics and their sources are outlined in detail below.

Three charts are included for each country. (The charts for Albania presented here are

examples of what the reader will see on each country page.)

The first indicates the total economic freedom score earned in the 2010 *Index*. The range of scores, from 0 to 100, is displayed on a 180 degree arc, and a pointer indicates the country's exact score.

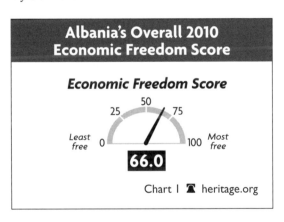

The second shows a time series of the country's overall economic freedom score for each year from 1995 (or the earliest year for which

Albania's Economic Freedom Score Over Time

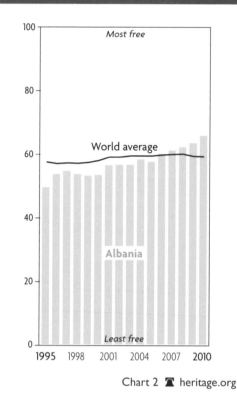

Chart 2 ☎ heritage.org

the countries are graded, every effort has been made to use the same source consistently for all countries; when data are unavailable from the primary source, secondary sources are used. (See appendix, "Methodology for the 10 Economic Freedoms.")

DEFINING THE "QUICK FACTS"

Each country page includes "Quick Facts" with eight different categories of information. Unless otherwise indicated, the data in each country's profile are for 2008 (the year for which the most recent data are widely available) and in current 2008 U.S. dollars (also the most recent available). The few cases in which no reliable statistical data were available are indicated by "n/a." Definitions and sources for each category of information are as follows.

Population: 2008 data from World Bank, *World Development Indicators Online*. For some countries, another source is the country's statistical agency and/or central bank.

GDP: Gross domestic product—total production of goods and services—adjusted to reflect purchasing power parity (PPP). The primary source for GDP data is World Bank, *World Development Indicators Online 2009*. The major secondary source is International Monetary Fund, *World Economic Outlook Database April 2009*. Other sources include a country's statistical agency and/or central bank.

data are available) through 2010, compared to the world average. In some cases, a country is not graded continuously for all 16 years, often because grading did not begin in the 1995 edition and frequently because violence, political instability, or natural disaster has resulted in a lack of reliable information, making continuous scoring impossible.

The third chart graphs the country's 10 freedom component scores for 2010 using horizontal bars. A hash mark is included to show the world average so that one can quickly identify the comparative strengths and weaknesses of economic freedom in each country. Additionally, up or down arrows are placed to illustrate the direction of score changes from the 2009 *Index* to the 2010 *Index*.

To assure consistency and reliability for each of the 10 components on which

Ten Components of Albania's 2010 Economic Freedom Score

Chart 3 ☎ heritage.org

GDP growth rate: Annual percentage growth rate of real GDP derived from constant national currency units, based on country-specific years. Annual percent changes are year-on-year. The primary source is International Monetary Fund, *World Economic Outlook Database April 2009*. Secondary sources include World Bank, *World Development Indicators Online 2009*; Economist Intelligence Unit, *Country Reports*, 2008–2009; Asian Development Bank, *Asian Development Outlook 2009*; and a country's statistical agency and/or central bank.

GDP five-year compound annual growth: The geometric average growth rate measured over a specified period of time. The compound annual growth rate is measured using data from 2003 to 2008, based on real GDP expressed in constant national currency units, based on country-specific years. It is calculated by taking the *n*th root of the total percentage growth rate, where *n* is the number of years in the period being considered. The primary source is International Monetary Fund, *World Economic Outlook Database*, *April 2009*. Secondary sources are World Bank, *World Development Indicators Online 2009*, and Asian Development Bank, *Asian Development Outlook 2009*.

GDP per capita: Gross domestic product (adjusted for PPP) divided by total population. The sources for these data are World Bank, *World Development Indicators Online 2009*; International Monetary Fund, *World Economic Outlook Database April 2009*; U.S. Central Intelligence Agency, *The World Factbook 2009*; and a country's statistical agency and/or central bank.

Unemployment rate: A measure of the portion of the workforce that is not employed but is actively seeking work. The primary sources are U.S. Central Intelligence Agency, *The World Factbook 2009*; Economist Intelligence Unit, *Country Reports*, 2008–2009, and *Country Profiles*, 2007–2009; International Monetary Fund, *Article IV Staff Reports*, 2008–2009; and a country's statistical agency.

Inflation: The annual percent change in consumer prices as measured for 2008 (or the most recent available year). The primary source for 2008 data is International Monetary Fund, *World Economic Outlook Database, April 2009*. Secondary sources are Economist Intelligence Unit, *Country Reports*, 2008–2009, and *Country Profiles*, 2007–2009; Asian Development Bank, *Asian Development Outlook 2009*; and a country's statistical agency and/or central bank.

Foreign direct investment (FDI) inward flow: This series indicates the total annual inward flow of FDI. Data are in current 2008 U.S. dollars, reported in millions. FDI flows are defined as investments that acquire a lasting management interest (10 percent or more of voting stock) in a local enterprise by an investor operating in another country. Such investment is the sum of equity capital, reinvestment of earnings, other long-term capital, and short-term capital as shown in the balance of payments and both short-term and long-term international loans. Data are from United Nations Conference on Trade and Development, *World Investment Report 2009*, and Economist Intelligence Unit, *Country Reports*, 2008–2009, and *Country Profiles*, 2008–2009.

COMMONLY USED ACRONYMS

CARICOM: Caribbean Community and Common Market, comprised of Antigua and Barbuda, the Bahamas, Barbados, Belize, Dominica, Grenada, Guyana, Haiti, Jamaica, Montserrat, Saint Lucia, St. Kitts and Nevis, St. Vincent and the Grenadines, Suriname, and Trinidad and Tobago.

CEMAC: Central African Economic and Monetary Community, which includes Cameroon, the Central African Republic, Chad, the Republic of Congo, Equatorial Guinea, and Gabon.

CIS: Commonwealth of Independent States, consisting of Azerbaijan, Armenia, Belarus, Georgia, Kazakhstan, the Kyrgyz Republic, Moldova, Russia, Tajikistan, Turkmenistan, Ukraine, and Uzbekistan.

EU: European Union, consisting of Austria, Belgium, Bulgaria, Cyprus, the Czech Republic, Denmark, Estonia, Finland, France, Germany, Greece, Hungary, Ireland, Italy, Latvia, Lithuania, Luxembourg, Malta, the Netherlands, Poland, Portugal, Romania, Slovakia, Slovenia, Spain, Sweden, and the United Kingdom.

IMF: International Monetary Fund, established in 1945 to help stabilize countries during crises, that now includes 186 member countries.

MERCOSUR: Customs union that includes Argentina, Brazil, Paraguay, Uruguay, and Venezuela.

OECD: Organisation for Economic Co-operation and Development, an international organization of developed countries, founded in 1948, that now includes 30 member countries.

SACU: Southern African Customs Union, consisting of Botswana, Lesotho, Namibia, South Africa, and Swaziland.

WTO: World Trade Organization, founded in 1995 as the central organization dealing with the rules of trade between nations and based on signed agreements among 153 member countries.

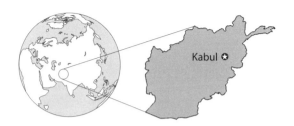

Kabul ◉

AFGHANISTAN

Economic Freedom Score

The economy is not graded

Afghanistan's economic freedom cannot be fully assessed because of a lack of reliable data. Political uncertainty and security challenges remain considerable, and the government's periodic compilations of official economic data have been inadequate. The country will receive an economic freedom score and ranking in future editions when more reliable information becomes available.

Undergoing substantial political, economic, and social transformation since the fall of the Taliban regime in late 2001, Afghanistan has achieved rapid economic growth averaging close to 10 percent over the past five years. The construction sector has been the key contributor to growth because of its close link to the economic reconstruction process. Facilitated by economic development, there also have been noticeable improvements in such areas as health, education, microfinance, and public finance management.

However, the economy lacks the overall capacity to enhance productivity as well as to improve the standard of living. Although progress has been made in developing the private sector, it remains too small and informal to provide real impetus for more vibrant entrepreneurial activity.

BACKGROUND: Afghanistan, which has been roiled by conflict since the 1978 Communist coup, is one of the world's poorest countries. After an American-led coalition ousted the Taliban government in 2001, a U.N.-sponsored conference established a framework that led to a new constitution and successful elections for a president in 2004 and parliament in 2005. GDP grew by more than 7 percent in 2008, largely as a result of foreign aid, but the economy remains hobbled by poor infrastructure, a Taliban insurgency, and the government's inability to extend the rule of law to many rural areas. The economic dominance of illegal opium production is a major impediment to political stability and sustainable development.

Country's Score Over Time

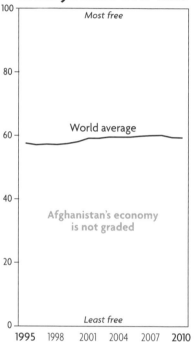

Quick Facts

Population: 27.4 million

GDP (PPP): $30.6 billion
    12.1% growth in 2007
    9.8% 5-year compound
    annual growth

Unemployment: 40.0% (2007)

Inflation (CPI): 27.2%

FDI Inflow: $300 million

2008 data unless otherwise noted
Data compiled as of September 2009

How Do We Measure Economic Freedom?
See page 457 for an explanation of the methodology or visit the *Index* Web site at *heritage.org/index.*

83

BUSINESS FREEDOM — NOT GRADED

The overall freedom to start, operate, and close a business remains constrained by an underdeveloped regulatory environment. Starting a business and obtaining a business license have been relatively streamlined, but other structural barriers and political instability persist. Business reform has been too weak to spark sustainable business activity.

TRADE FREEDOM — NOT GRADED

Afghanistan's weighted average tariff rate in 2008 was 7.7 percent. Inefficient customs administration, inadequate economic and physical infrastructure, undeveloped regulatory administration, and corruption delay trade and increase costs. If Afghanistan were being graded, 15 points would be deducted from its trade freedom score to account for non-tariff barriers.

FISCAL FREEDOM — NOT GRADED

Afghanistan has relatively low tax rates. The top income and corporate tax rates are 20 percent. There is also a 2 percent to 5 percent sales tax. In the most recent year, overall tax revenue as a percentage of GDP was 5.2 percent. Authorities are working to improve and automate the tax system, but governance and security issues impede tax collection, especially at the regional level. A business receipts tax on imports was implemented as of March 2009.

GOVERNMENT SPENDING — NOT GRADED

Total government expenditures, including consumption and transfer payments, are low. In the most recent year, government spending equaled 19.9 percent of GDP. Restructuring of state-owned enterprises has been slow and uneven. Commercial laws to lay the foundation for further privatization have yet to be implemented.

MONETARY FREEDOM — NOT GRADED

Inflation spiked in 2008 as a result of dramatically increased costs for food and fuel, bringing the average between 2006 and 2008 to a very high 21.7 percent. Price controls exist in major cities, and controls on egg, milk, cheese, bread, meat, fruit, and vegetable prices vary by municipality. If Afghanistan were being graded, 15 points would be deducted from its monetary freedom score to adjust for price controls.

INVESTMENT FREEDOM — NOT GRADED

Foreign and domestic firms are treated equally under the law, but foreign investment in certain sectors, such as non-banking financial activities, insurance, natural resources, power, water, sewage, waste treatment, airports, telecommunications, and health and education facilities, receives special scrutiny. Foreign investors may not own land but may lease parcels for up to 50 years. Foreigners may own 100 percent of a company, and there are no capital or currency controls. The state can expropriate an investment or asset for the purpose of public interest and on a non-discriminatory basis. No seizures of foreign-owned assets have been reported. Investment is discouraged by security concerns, inadequate regulations, lack of financial capacity, corruption, inefficient bureaucracy, and slow privatization of the many state-owned enterprises.

FINANCIAL FREEDOM — NOT GRADED

Afghanistan's financial sector has undergone two phases of major development since 2001, the first laying the foundation for a basic legal framework for modern banking and the second encouraging the establishment of formal financial services. The banking sector now consists of two state-owned commercial banks, 10 private commercial banks, and five branches of foreign commercial banks. Restructuring of state-owned banks has progressed, and domestic private banks account for around half of total assets. Nevertheless, the financial sector, with its lack of adequate management and irregularities concerning insider lending, remains weak and a key impediment to private-sector development. Most bank credit is short-term, and regulatory inefficiency has undermined development.

PROPERTY RIGHTS — NOT GRADED

Afghanistan's judicial system is severely underdeveloped. Property rights protection is weak due to a lack of property registries or a land titling database, disputed land titles, lack of capacity by commercial courts, and widespread corruption. The bankruptcy law is ineffective. Afghanistan has no legislation on intellectual property rights and does not belong to any international IPR-protection organizations.

FREEDOM FROM CORRUPTION — NOT GRADED

Corruption is perceived as rampant. Afghanistan ranks 176th out of 179 countries in Transparency International's Corruption Perceptions Index for 2008. Corruption permeates all sectors and levels of government and poses a serious risk to the rebuilding of state institutions. The very large opium economy is the most significant source of corruption.

LABOR FREEDOM — NOT GRADED

Political and security instability prevent the development of a modern labor market. Laws and regulations concerning wage rates and work hours are inconsequential. The prevalence of opium-related activities and a large informal economy further dampen development of a functioning labor market.

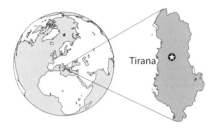

Tirana ✪

ALBANIA

Economic Freedom Score

25 50 75

Least free 0   100 Most free

66.0

World Rank: 53   **Regional Rank: 25**

Albania's economic freedom score is 66.0, making its economy the 53rd freest in the 2010 *Index*. Its level of economic freedom increased by 2.3 points during the past year, due primarily to increases in trade freedom, property rights, freedom from corruption, and labor freedom. Albania is ranked 25th freest among the 43 countries in the Europe region, and its overall score is above the world average.

Despite the global economic slowdown, Albania has been able to maintain relatively sound macroeconomic stability. It has acted to enhance its business and investment environment. Albania now has a flat rate of 10 percent for individual and corporate taxes, and structural reforms to foster private-sector growth have led to increased production and consumption, as well as a substantially reduced poverty rate.

Albania's economic freedom is comparable to that of other developing Balkan states like Croatia and Macedonia. Fiscal freedom, investment freedom, and financial freedom rate significantly higher than typical levels. However, Albania's overall score is reduced by weak property rights and pervasive corruption. Money laundering remains a significant problem in the cash-based economy. The low property rights score is largely a result of political interference in the judiciary.

BACKGROUND: Albania is one of Europe's poorest countries despite some economic and political reform since 1992, when nearly 50 years of Communist rule ended. The government has been pursuing greater integration into the Euro–Atlantic community for several years. In June 2006, Albania signed a Stabilization and Association Agreement with the European Union as the first step toward EU membership, as well as a free trade agreement giving Albanians duty-free access to key EU markets and opening the country to imports. In April 2009, it also achieved full membership in NATO. Albania's transportation and energy infrastructure are poor by European standards, and its agricultural sector remains the largest source of employment.

Country's Score Over Time

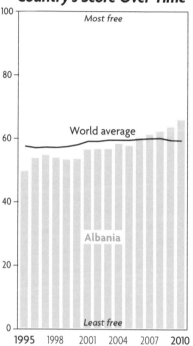

Quick Facts

Population: 3.1 million

GDP (PPP): $24.3 billion
6.0% growth in 2008
6.1% 5-year compound annual growth
$7,715 per capita

Unemployment: 12.5% (2007)

Inflation (CPI): 3.4%

FDI Inflow: $656.0 million

2008 data unless otherwise noted
Data compiled as of September 2009

How Do We Measure Economic Freedom?
See page 457 for an explanation of the methodology or visit the *Index* Web site at *heritage.org/index.*

ALBANIA'S TEN ECONOMIC FREEDOMS

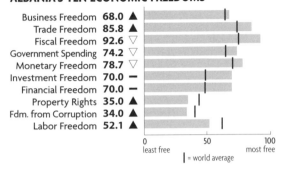

Business Freedom	68.0 ▲	
Trade Freedom	85.8 ▲	
Fiscal Freedom	92.6 ▽	
Government Spending	74.2 ▽	
Monetary Freedom	78.7 ▽	
Investment Freedom	70.0 —	
Financial Freedom	70.0 —	
Property Rights	35.0 ▲	
Fdm. from Corruption	34.0 ▲	
Labor Freedom	52.1 ▲	

0 least free   50   100 most free

| = world average

BUSINESS FREEDOM — 68

Despite some improvement, Albania's business freedom remains constrained by a burdensome regulatory environment. Starting a business takes five days, compared to the world average of 35. Obtaining a business license requires 24 procedures, compared to the world average of 18, and almost 100 more days than the world average of 218.

TRADE FREEDOM — 85.8

Albania's weighted average tariff rate in 2008 was 2.1 percent. Import taxes may be based on a government-determined fair market price, regardless of the actual price paid. Weak enforcement of intellectual property rights, inadequate trade capacity, and administrative bureaucracy delay trade and increase costs. Ten points were deducted from Albania's trade freedom score to account for non-tariff barriers.

FISCAL FREEDOM — 92.6

Albania's tax rates are low. Personal income and corporate tax rates are a flat 10 percent. Other taxes include a value-added tax (VAT), a property tax, and an excise tax. In the most recent year, overall tax revenue as a percentage of GDP was 23.3 percent.

GOVERNMENT SPENDING — 74.2

Total government expenditures, including consumption and transfer payments, are moderate. In the most recent year, government spending equaled 29.3 percent of GDP. Privatization in the strategic sectors of energy and insurance has been completed, but planned divestment of water utilities and telecommunications has stalled. Although the fiscal deficit has been under control, public debt has increased and amounts to around 56 percent of GDP.

MONETARY FREEDOM — 78.7

Inflation has been relatively low, averaging 3.2 percent between 2006 and 2008. Regulatory agencies continue to oversee prices, and the government raised pensions and public-sector wages in May 2009 against the advice of the IMF. Ten points were deducted from Albania's monetary freedom score to account for wage and price interventions.

INVESTMENT FREEDOM — 70

Foreign and domestic firms are treated equally under the law, and nearly all sectors are open to foreign investment. Foreigners may not purchase agricultural land but may rent it for up to 99 years. They also may purchase commercial property if the proposed investment is worth three times the price of the land. There are no restrictions on foreign ownership of other property. Foreigners may own 100 percent of Albanian companies, and monetary expatriation is legal. Residents and non-residents may hold foreign exchange accounts. The state can expropriate an investment or asset for the purpose of public interest, but there are legal provisions for compensation. Inadequate infrastructure, lack of reliable power, weak rule of law, poorly defined property rights, inefficient bureaucracy, and corruption discourage foreign investment.

FINANCIAL FREEDOM — 70

Albania's financial sector has grown rapidly, and credit is generally allocated on market terms. Banking is increasingly dominated by foreign banks, which account for about 90 percent of total assets. This has led to more competition and better availability of services. Supervisory regulations have been strengthened to preserve financial stability. In response to the global financial crisis, the Bank of Albania has acted to increase liquidity and maintain public confidence. With little or no direct exposure to recently troubled international financial assets, Albania's banking system has been able to withstand the global financial shock with little disruption.

PROPERTY RIGHTS — 35

Albania's constitution provides for an independent judiciary, but political pressure, intimidation, widespread corruption, limited resources, and organized crime are obstacles to the effective administration of justice. Overall protection of intellectual property rights is weak, although there has been some progress with respect to industrial property and trademarks. Property registration has improved, but the security of land rights remains a problem in coastal areas where there is potential for tourism development.

FREEDOM FROM CORRUPTION — 34

Corruption is perceived as widespread. Albania ranks 85th out of 179 countries in Transparency International's Corruption Perceptions Index for 2008, a significant improvement over 2007, due to the work of the Government Corruption and Organized Crime Task Force and reforms in tax administration, procurement, and business registration. Albania is a major transit country for human trafficking and illegal arms and narcotics.

LABOR FREEDOM — 52.1

Rigid employment regulations hinder productivity growth. The non-salary cost of employing a worker is high, and dismissing a redundant employee is relatively costly. The high cost of laying off workers is a disincentive for companies that would otherwise increase employment.

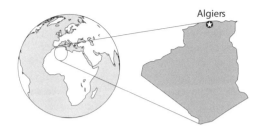

ALGERIA

Economic Freedom Score

Least free 0 — 25 — 50 — 75 — 100 Most free

56.9

A lgeria's economic freedom score is 56.9, making its economy the 105th freest in the 2010 *Index*. Its overall score is 0.3 point higher than last year due to improved fiscal freedom and small gains in trade freedom, freedom from corruption, and labor freedom. Algeria is ranked 13th among the 17 countries in the Middle East and North Africa region, and its score remains below both the regional and world averages.

Algeria has recorded several years of strong economic growth, largely because of its hydrocarbon sector. Government revenue from hydrocarbons has allowed reductions in external debt, but Algeria still faces critical challenges in fostering a more dynamic economic environment. Structural reforms to diversify the economic base have achieved only marginal success, and the inefficient business environment impedes the development of the non-hydrocarbon sector and more job creation.

In six of the 10 economic freedoms, Algeria performs below world averages. Persistent problems include an underdeveloped financial sector, corruption, and political interference in the judiciary. The government also needs to strengthen fiscal governance and modernize budget management. A broader economic base would be facilitated by more flexibility in a labor market that is burdened with high youth unemployment.

BACKGROUND: After Algeria gained its independence from France in 1962 following eight years of civil war, the new revolutionary government adopted a socialist economic model that held back economic development. Violent conflict in the 1990s between Islamist militants and the government claimed more than 100,000 lives. President Abdelaziz Bouteflika negotiated a peace accord in 1999 that delivered greater political stability, but some Islamist militants merged with al-Qaeda in 2006 and remain a threat. Algeria is the world's fourth-largest exporter of natural gas and has the world's eighth-largest natural gas reserves and 15th-largest oil reserves. The government hopes to diversify the economy by attracting foreign and domestic private investment in non-energy sectors.

Country's Score Over Time

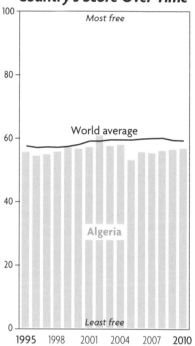

Quick Facts

Population: 34.4 million

GDP (PPP): $276.0 billion
3.0% growth in 2008
3.3% 5-year compound annual growth
$8,033 per capita

Unemployment: 12.5% (2007)

Inflation (CPI): 4.5%

FDI Inflow: $1.7 billion

2008 data unless otherwise noted
Data compiled as of September 2009

How Do We Measure Economic Freedom?
See page 457 for an explanation of the methodology or visit the *Index* Web site at *heritage.org/index*.

ALGERIA'S TEN ECONOMIC FREEDOMS

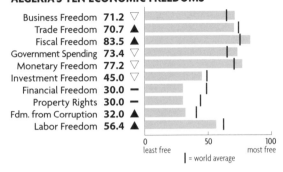

Business Freedom	71.2 ▽	
Trade Freedom	70.7 ▲	
Fiscal Freedom	83.5 ▲	
Government Spending	73.4 ▽	
Monetary Freedom	77.2 ▽	
Investment Freedom	45.0 ▽	
Financial Freedom	30.0 —	
Property Rights	30.0 —	
Fdm. from Corruption	32.0 ▲	
Labor Freedom	56.4 ▲	

0 least free — 50 — 100 most free

| = world average

BUSINESS FREEDOM — 71.2

The overall freedom to start, operate, and close a business is relatively well protected by Algeria's regulatory environment. Starting a business takes an average of 24 days, compared to the world average of 35 days. Obtaining a business license requires slightly more than the global average of 18 procedures and 218 days.

TRADE FREEDOM — 70.7

Algeria's weighted average tariff rate in 2008 was 9.7 percent. Customs clearance procedures, value-added taxes, inconsistent enforcement of property rights, import and export controls, and restrictive labeling, sanitary, and phytosanitary regulations continue to delay trade and increase costs. Ten points were deducted from Algeria's trade freedom score to adjust for non-tariff barriers.

FISCAL FREEDOM — 83.5

The top income tax rate has been reduced from 40 percent to 35 percent. The top corporate tax rate has been lowered to 19 percent from 25 percent. Other major taxes include a value-added tax (VAT) and a withholding tax on dividends. In the most recent year, overall tax revenue as a percentage of GDP was 7.9 percent. Other reform efforts have centered on improving collection of non-hydrocarbon taxes.

GOVERNMENT SPENDING — 73.4

Algeria's economy is dominated by the public sector, which is still the largest employer. Better prioritization of large public spending projects is necessary to keep a growing wage bill and non-hydrocarbon debt from undermining long-term fiscal stability. In the most recent year, government spending equaled 29.8 percent of GDP.

MONETARY FREEDOM — 77.2

Inflation averaged 4.1 percent between 2006 and 2008. The government incurred large fiscal deficits in the wake of the global financial crisis as it expanded civil service wages and government subsidies, although it was able to use significant savings accumulated during years of high energy prices to fund these increases. Distortionary subsidies and direct price controls on some essential commodities including water, energy, and agricultural products remain in place. Ten points were deducted from Algeria's monetary freedom score to account for price-control measures.

INVESTMENT FREEDOM — 45

Foreign and domestic firms are treated equally under the law, and most of the economy is open to foreign investment. Foreign ownership is limited to joint-venture relationships in hydrocarbons and some other sectors. Privatization has stalled due to limited interest among foreign investors and the government's lack of confidence in privatization. The global financial crisis has put bank privatization on hold. The investment code is transparent, but administration and bureaucracy can be burdensome. Residents and non-residents may hold foreign exchange, subject to some restrictions. Foreign investors may repatriate profits, subject to restrictions. The tax law was modified in August 2008 to require companies to reinvest within four years the value of any tax incentives received or face a 30-percent penalty, and a 15 percent tax was imposed on foreign companies transferring profits out of Algeria.

FINANCIAL FREEDOM — 30

The financial sector remains subject to considerable government interference. Delays in modernizing the banking sector and reducing state involvement have led to inefficient credit allocation and have kept the non-hydrocarbon sector from developing. The banking sector is dominated by state-owned banks, which account for around 90 percent of assets. Banking and financial reform, ostensibly a goal since 1999, has been uneven and slow. In late 2007, citing the slowdown of global financial markets, the government delayed the privatization of one of the state-owned banks, Credit Populaire d'Algerie. Privatization of the CPA has since been suspended indefinitely. Six state-owned firms dominate the small insurance sector. The stock exchange, established in 1999, remains undeveloped with only three companies listed.

PROPERTY RIGHTS — 30

The constitution provides for an independent judiciary, but the legal system functions inefficiently, and the executive branch influences judicial actions. Most real property is government-owned, and conflicting title claims make buying and financing real estate difficult.

FREEDOM FROM CORRUPTION — 32

Corruption is perceived as widespread. Public procurement is often tainted with irregularities, including the excessive use of private agreements. Algeria ranks 92nd out of 179 countries in Transparency International's Corruption Perceptions Index for 2008, a slight improvement from 2007. The government has acted on several high-profile cases of official corruption.

LABOR FREEDOM — 56.4

Restrictive labor regulations hinder employment and productivity growth. The non-salary cost of employing a worker is high, although dismissing a redundant employee is relatively easy and inexpensive.

ANGOLA

Economic Freedom Score

Least free 0   100 Most free

48.4

A ngola's economic freedom score is 48.4, making its economy the 154th freest in the 2010 *Index*. Its overall score has improved 1.4 points, primarily because of increased investment freedom. Angola is ranked 33rd out of 46 countries in the Sub-Saharan Africa region.

In recent years, robust economic growth facilitated by the booming oil industry has allowed Angola to sustain macroeconomic stability in rebuilding its post–civil war economy. Structural reforms have progressed in public financial management and trade liberalization.

Pervasive corruption and a lack of institutional capacity continue to undermine the implementation of other important reform policies. Angola scores poorly in most of the 10 economic freedoms. Monetary stability remains fragile, regulation chokes private business investment, and the judiciary is politically influenced. Inconsistent and confusing regulations make entrepreneurial activity costly and difficult. Despite the government's plan to diversify its economic base away from oil and diamonds, progress in stimulating the development of the non-oil private sector has been sluggish. Monopolies and quasi-monopolies still dominate the leading sectors of the economy.

BACKGROUND: Since the end of a 27-year civil war in 2002, Angola has been repairing and improving ravaged infrastructure and weakened political and social institutions. President José Eduardo dos Santos has ruled since 1979, and his Popular Movement for the Liberation of Angola (MPLA) won a strong victory in the 2008 parliamentary elections. A long-delayed presidential election is supposed to be held in late 2009 or 2010. Despite extensive oil and gas resources, diamonds, hydroelectric potential, and rich agricultural land, many Angolans remain poor and dependent on subsistence agriculture. The recent decline in international oil prices has depressed economic growth and strained the budget. Corruption and public-sector mismanagement are pervasive, particularly in the oil sector, which accounts for approximately 60 percent of GDP, 95 percent of exports, and 80 percent of government revenue.

Country's Score Over Time

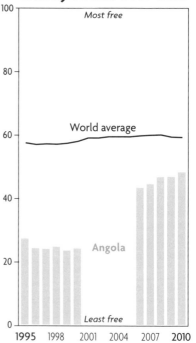

Quick Facts

Population: 18.0 million

GDP (PPP): $106.3 billion
14.8% growth in 2008
18.5% 5-year compound annual growth
$5,899 per capita

Unemployment: n/a

Inflation (CPI): 12.5%

FDI Inflow: –$1.5 billion

2008 data unless otherwise noted
Data compiled as of September 2009

How Do We Measure Economic Freedom?
See page 457 for an explanation of the methodology or visit the *Index* Web site at *heritage.org/index*.

ANGOLA'S TEN ECONOMIC FREEDOMS

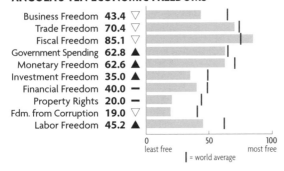

Business Freedom	43.4 ▽	
Trade Freedom	70.4 ▽	
Fiscal Freedom	85.1 ▽	
Government Spending	62.8 ▲	
Monetary Freedom	62.6 ▲	
Investment Freedom	35.0 ▲	
Financial Freedom	40.0 —	
Property Rights	20.0 ▽	
Fdm. from Corruption	19.0 ▽	
Labor Freedom	45.2 ▲	

0 least free   50   100 most free

| = world average

BUSINESS FREEDOM — 43.4

The overall freedom to start, operate, and close a business is constrained by Angola's regulatory environment. Starting a business takes an average of 68 days, compared to the world average of 35 days. Obtaining a business license requires more than the global average of 218 days.

TRADE FREEDOM — 70.4

Angola's weighted average tariff rate was 7.3 percent in 2008. Despite progress in trade reform, restrictions on some imports, variable and high customs fees and taxes, import licensing, government import authorizations, the regulatory environment, non-transparent government procurement, subsidies, inadequate customs capacity, and issues involving enforcement of intellectual property rights add to the cost of trade. Fifteen points were deducted from Angola's trade freedom score to account for non-tariff barriers.

FISCAL FREEDOM — 85.1

Angola has a relatively low income tax rate but a burdensome corporate tax rate. The top income tax rate is 15 percent, and the top corporate tax rate is 35 percent. Other taxes include a fuel tax and a consumption tax. In the most recent year, overall tax revenue as a percentage of GDP was 6.2 percent.

GOVERNMENT SPENDING — 62.8

Total government expenditures, including consumption and transfer payments, are moderate. In the most recent year, government spending equaled 35.2 percent of GDP. The transparency of government fiscal accounts and government budgetary management is somewhat improved, but an expanded wage bill and higher fuel subsidies have increased the fiscal deficit.

MONETARY FREEDOM — 62.6

Inflation, though high at an average rate of 12.5 percent between 2006 and 2008, has moderated somewhat, largely due to central bank intervention in foreign-exchange markets, but the government still needs to improve fiscal management and deal with excess liquidity. Key sectors remain government-owned, and price controls are pervasive in many sectors, including fuel and electricity. Fifteen points were deducted from Angola's monetary freedom score to adjust for price-control measures.

INVESTMENT FREEDOM — 35

Foreign investors receive equal treatment, but investment in certain sectors is restricted, and ministry regulations can take precedence over the law. Foreign investments exceeding $100,000 and investments that require a concession (such as oil and mining) or involve participation by a parastatal require approval. The regulatory system is non-transparent and time-consuming, lacks capacity, and is subject to corruption. Companies familiar with the business environment's bureaucratic and legal complexities often hold an advantage. There are few specific performance requirements on foreign investments, but "Angolanization" of companies and greater use of Angolan suppliers are encouraged. Reforms have improved local access to foreign exchange, and repatriation of profits for officially approved foreign investment is guaranteed, subject to some restrictions. All land is ultimately state-owned but can be leased to private entities. Direct expropriation of foreign investors' assets is relatively unlikely.

FINANCIAL FREEDOM — 40

Liberalization and privatization of the previously state-controlled banking system has progressed. Banking is relatively well capitalized, in part due to foreign banks, which have driven growth. In 2008, there were 18 commercial banks, but three major banks (two of them government-owned) still dominate the system. The granting of credit to the private sector has increased sharply. In 2008, deposits rose by around 45 percent, and loans expanded by over 80 percent. Banking, however, remains rudimentary. Fewer than 10 percent of Angolans have bank accounts. After years of delays, the opening of the Luanda Stock Exchange has been further postponed.

PROPERTY RIGHTS — 20

Angola's legal and judicial system is inefficient and subject to executive influence. Legal fees are high, and most businesses avoid taking commercial disputes to court. The state owns all land, but long-term renewable leases are available for most urban and some non-urban land. Property registration is lengthy and expensive. Angola is ranked 114th out of 115 countries in the 2009 International Property Rights Index.

FREEDOM FROM CORRUPTION — 19

Corruption is perceived as rampant, especially among government officials at all levels, and investigations and prosecutions of government officials are practically non-existent. Angola ranks 158th out of 179 countries in Transparency International's Corruption Perceptions Index for 2008, a decline from 2007.

LABOR FREEDOM — 45.2

Restrictive labor regulations hinder employment and productivity growth. The non-salary cost of employing a worker is low, but dismissing a redundant employee is relatively costly. The high cost of laying off workers creates a disincentive for employment expansion.

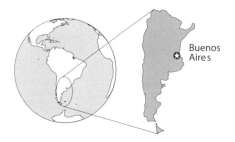

Buenos Aires

ARGENTINA

Economic Freedom Score

25   50   75

Least free 0   100 Most free

51.2

A rgentina's economic freedom score is 51.2, making its economy the 135th freest in the 2010 *Index*. Its overall score has declined 1.1 points from the 2009 *Index*. Argentina is ranked 23rd out of 29 countries in the South and Central America/Caribbean region, and its overall score is below the regional and world averages.

Ten years of structural change have encouraged investment and diversified Argentina's productive structure. Public external debt has fallen to around 40 percent of GDP from 140 percent in 2003. Despite a contraction in 2009, the economy has grown by around 8 percent annually for five years.

However, institutional weaknesses, including onerous regulations, corruption, and a weak judiciary, could make the high growth rate unsustainable. The state's role in the economy has grown. Financial freedom remains constrained by government influence, political interference with an inefficient judiciary hinders foreign investment, and there are reports of official and informal obstructions to due process. The tax burden is relatively low, primarily because of avoidance and evasion. Despite efforts to reform labor regulations, non-wage costs limit flexibility.

BACKGROUND: Argentina has been politically unstable since World War II, and three democratically elected presidents in the past quarter-century have left office early. Cristina Fernandez de Kirchner succeeded her husband as president in late 2007 and retained most of his cabinet. Her popularity began a steady decline in early 2008 after attempts to impose steep export taxes on soybeans and other commodities. The global economic downturn later in the year added to resentment of heavy-handed government interventionism, illustrated by the seizure of more than $25 billion in private pension funds to replenish the public treasury. Argentina is South America's second-largest country and has vast agricultural and mineral resources. Agriculture accounts for more than half of exports; food and beverage processing, chemicals, petrochemicals, and automotive manufacturing are the most important industrial sectors.

Country's Score Over Time

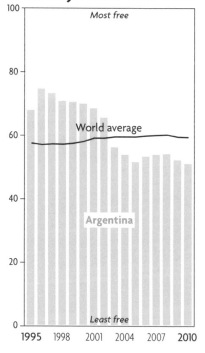

Most free

World average

Argentina

Least free

1995   1998   2001   2004   2007   2010

Quick Facts

Population: 39.9 million

GDP (PPP): $571.5 billion
7.0% growth in 2008
8.3% 5-year compound
annual growth
$14,333 per capita

Unemployment: 7.9%

Inflation (CPI): 8.6%

FDI Inflow: $8.9 billion

2008 data unless otherwise noted
Data compiled as of September 2009

How Do We Measure Economic Freedom?
See page 457 for an explanation of the methodology or visit the *Index* Web site at *heritage.org/index.*

ARGENTINA'S TEN ECONOMIC FREEDOMS

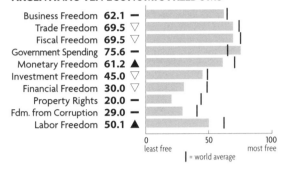

Business Freedom	62.1	—
Trade Freedom	69.5	▽
Fiscal Freedom	69.5	▽
Government Spending	75.6	—
Monetary Freedom	61.2	▲
Investment Freedom	45.0	▽
Financial Freedom	30.0	▽
Property Rights	20.0	—
Fdm. from Corruption	29.0	—
Labor Freedom	50.1	▲

0 least free   50   100 most free

| = world average

BUSINESS FREEDOM — *62.1*

Argentina's regulatory environment remains burdensome, inconsistent, and not fully transparent. Starting a business takes an average of 27 days, compared to the world average of 35 days. Obtaining a business license requires more that the global average of 18 procedures and 218 days.

TRADE FREEDOM — *69.5*

Argentina's weighted average tariff rate was 5.3 percent in 2008. Import and export bans and controls, restrictions on trade in services, tariff escalation, import and export taxes and fees, minimum and reference pricing, regulations and licensing provisions, sanitary and phytosanitary rules, subsidies, restrictions on ports of entry, domestic preference in government procurement, and issues involving enforcement of intellectual property rights add to the cost of trade. Twenty points were deducted from Argentina's trade freedom score to account for non-tariff barriers.

FISCAL FREEDOM — *69.5*

Argentina has relatively high tax rates. The top income and flat corporate tax rates are 35 percent. Other taxes include a value-added tax (VAT) and a wealth tax. In the most recent year, overall tax revenue as a percentage of GDP was 24.5 percent.

GOVERNMENT SPENDING — *75.6*

Total government expenditures, including consumption and transfer payments, are moderate. In the most recent year, government spending equaled 28.5 percent of GDP. In November 2008, the private pension system was nationalized. Price setting still prevails in energy and transportation, but some subsidies have been eased because of growing public debt and shrinking revenues.

MONETARY FREEDOM — *61.2*

Government statistics show inflation to be relatively high, averaging 8.9 percent between 2006 and 2008; private measures put the annual rate as of mid-2009 even higher, at 10 percent–15 percent. The government subsidizes or regulates prices of electricity, water, retail-level gas distribution, urban transport, and local telephone services. It also pressures companies to fix prices and wages to contain rising inflationary pressures. Twenty points were deducted from Argentina's monetary freedom score to adjust for measures that distort prices.

INVESTMENT FREEDOM — *45*

Foreign and domestic investors have equal rights to establish and own businesses, but foreign investment is prohibited in a few sectors. Foreign exchange and capital flows are subject to restrictions. Foreign companies may send profits abroad; export proceeds must be repatriated to Argentina. Inflows of foreign funds from certain private-sector debt, inflows for most fiduciary funds, and investments in public-sector securities purchased in the secondary market are restricted. Foreign and domestic institutional investors are restricted to total currency transactions of $2 million per month; transactions by institutions acting as intermediaries do not count against this limit. Investments may be expropriated or nationalized only for public purpose and upon prompt payment of compensation at fair market value. Corruption, weak institutions, and uncertain creditor, contract, and property rights are serious deterrents to investment.

FINANCIAL FREEDOM — *30*

Argentina's largest bank is state-owned and the sole financial institution in some areas. Since the 2001–2002 debt default and banking crisis, regulation and supervision have become more prudential. The banking sector has expanded faster than the overall economy since 2005 but is struggling to regain confidence and stability. Mortgages and personal loans are increasing, and non-performing bank loans are declining. International banks that have returned have not recovered their former prominence. Capital controls remain in place. The stock exchange is active, but the investor base is small. Nationalization of private pension funds in late 2008 triggered widespread outrage.

PROPERTY RIGHTS — *20*

The executive branch influences Argentina's judiciary. The courts are notoriously slow, inefficient, secretive, and corrupt, and many foreign investors resort to international arbitration. In November 2008, the government seized more than $25 billion in private pension funds to replenish the public treasury. Patent protection is problematic, and pirated copies of copyrighted products are widely available. Government manipulation of inflation statistics has caused foreign and domestic bondholders to lose billions in interest payments.

FREEDOM FROM CORRUPTION — *29*

Corruption is perceived as widespread. Argentina ranks 109th out of 179 countries in Transparency International's Corruption Perceptions Index for 2008. Foreign investors complain about government and private-sector corruption. Money laundering, trafficking in narcotics and contraband, and tax evasion plague the financial system.

LABOR FREEDOM — *50.1*

Inflexible labor regulations continue to hinder employment creation and productivity growth. The non-salary cost of employing a worker is high, and dismissing a redundant employee can be costly.

ARMENIA

Economic Freedom Score

Least free 0   25   50   75   100 Most free

69.2

World Rank: 38   **Regional Rank: 21**

A rmenia's economic freedom score is 69.2, making its economy the 38th freest in the 2010 *Index*. Its overall score decreased by 0.7 point from last year. Armenia is ranked 21st freest among the 43 countries in the Europe region, and its score puts it above the world and regional averages.

Armenia has implemented substantial economic reforms in many parts of its economy over the past decade, making considerable gains in income growth and poverty reduction while maintaining macroeconomic stability. Low tax rates and moderate government spending contribute to an impressive degree of fiscal freedom.

However, widespread corruption and weak protection of property rights continue to reduce Armenia's overall level of economic freedom. Burdensome bureaucratic procedures and discretionary decisions by individual officials encourage petty corruption. Sluggish structural reforms also keep the Armenian economy from diversifying its productive base.

BACKGROUND: Armenia gained its independence from the Soviet Union in 1991. President Serge Sargsyan's government still faces domestic unrest stemming from the disputed February 2008 election, a weakening economy, and opposition to proposed normalization of relations with Turkey. The 21-year dispute with Azerbaijan over the Nagorno–Karabakh region remains unresolved. Although a cease-fire has been in effect since 1994 and most ethnic Armenians displaced by the conflict have returned home, more than 500,000 Azeris still live as refugees in Azerbaijan, and borders with Azerbaijan and Turkey remain closed. In April 2009, Armenia and Turkey signed a "road map" for gradual normalization of relations. Armenia's economy relies on manufacturing, services, remittances, and agriculture. Most sectors are in recession. The government relies on financial assistance and loans from the World Bank, the International Monetary Fund, and Russia and is running a large budget deficit.

Country's Score Over Time

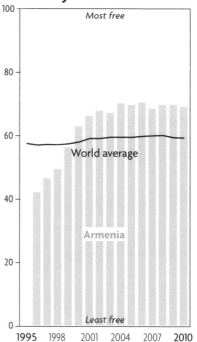

Quick Facts

Population: 3.1 million

GDP (PPP): $18.7 billion
6.8% growth in 2008
11.9% 5-year compound annual growth
$6,070 per capita

Unemployment: 7.1% (2007)

Inflation (CPI): 9.0%

FDI Inflow: $661.0 million

2008 data unless otherwise noted
Data compiled as of September 2009

How Do We Measure Economic Freedom?
See page 457 for an explanation of the methodology or visit the *Index* Web site at *heritage.org/index*.

93

ARMENIA'S TEN ECONOMIC FREEDOMS

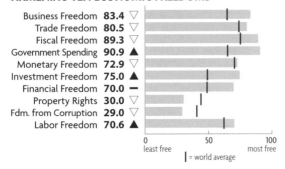

Business Freedom	83.4 ▽	
Trade Freedom	80.5 ▽	
Fiscal Freedom	89.3 ▽	
Government Spending	90.9 ▲	
Monetary Freedom	72.9 ▽	
Investment Freedom	75.0 ▲	
Financial Freedom	70.0 —	
Property Rights	30.0 ▽	
Fdm. from Corruption	29.0 ▽	
Labor Freedom	70.6 ▲	

0 least free — 50 — 100 most free
| = world average

BUSINESS FREEDOM — 83.4

The freedom to start, operate, and close a business is well protected under Armenia's regulatory environment. Starting a business takes an average of 15 days, compared to the world average of 35 days. Obtaining a business license requires about the world average of 18 procedures and less than the world average of 218 days.

TRADE FREEDOM — 80.5

Armenia's weighted average tariff rate was 2.3 percent in 2008. Excise taxes and fees, inadequate infrastructure, unpredictable customs valuation, inefficient customs administration, weak enforcement of property rights, import monopolies, and corruption add to the cost of trade. Fifteen points were deducted from Armenia's trade freedom score to account for non-tariff barriers.

FISCAL FREEDOM — 89.3

Armenia has relatively low tax rates. The top income and corporate tax rates are 20 percent. Other taxes include a value-added tax (VAT) and excise taxes. In the most recent year, overall tax revenue as a percentage of GDP was 16.5 percent. In response to a dramatic shortfall in tax revenue in early 2009 (due in large part to low collection of VAT and profit taxes), authorities announced intentions to improve tax administration through major policy changes in 2010. No legislation had been put forth as of July 2009.

GOVERNMENT SPENDING — 90.9

Total government expenditures, including consumption and transfer payments, are low. In the most recent year, government spending equaled 17.4 percent of GDP. Authorities have been forced to limit nonessential spending but are still not meeting expenditure targets.

MONETARY FREEDOM — 72.9

Inflation has increased, averaging 7.3 percent between 2006 and 2008. Government subsidies and regulations distort prices in some sectors, such as public transportation, electricity, and gas. Ten points were deducted from Armenia's monetary freedom score to adjust for measures that distort domestic prices.

INVESTMENT FREEDOM — 75

Officially, foreign and domestic investors are treated equally and have the same right to establish businesses in nearly all sectors. Privatization, though generally successful and legally open to all bidders, has not been transparent, and some sectors are uncompetitive, dominated by a few domestic firms. There are no restrictions or controls on foreign exchange accounts, invisible transactions, or current transfers, and there are no repatriation requirements. Investment regulations can be burdensome and lack transparency, and their administration is inefficient and prone to corruption. Non-residents may lease but not own land. By law, foreign investments cannot be expropriated except in extreme cases of a natural or state emergency, upon a decision by the courts, and with compensation.

FINANCIAL FREEDOM — 70

Armenia has accelerated the pace of legal and regulatory reform in order to restructure its financial sector. The government has embarked on privatization and regulatory reform that includes adopting international accounting standards, and many banks have closed or merged. The state no longer has a stake in any bank, and all 22 are privately owned. Financial-sector infrastructure has been enhanced through improved market transparency. However, the banking sector, which accounts for over 90 percent of total financial-sector assets, still suffers from insufficient long-term funding and market segmentation. Capital markets and insurance are not fully developed. There are no limitations on conversion and transfer of money or repatriation of capital and earnings. The securities market has a legal framework in place but remains small. Due to the limited external exposure of local banks, the global financial turmoil has not had a direct adverse impact on the financial system's stability.

PROPERTY RIGHTS — 30

Armenia ranks 98th out of 115 countries in the 2009 International Property Rights Index (IPRI). Its score on the component of the IPRI concerned with intellectual property rights was the lowest in the world. The judicial system is still recovering from underdevelopment and corruption—legacies of the Soviet era that substantially impede the enforcement of contracts.

FREEDOM FROM CORRUPTION — 29

Corruption is perceived as widespread on all levels and in all sectors. Demands for bribes by government officials are routine. Government-connected businesses hold monopolies on the importation of numerous vital products. Armenia ranks 109th out of 179 countries in Transparency International's Corruption Perceptions Index for 2008, a decline from 2007.

LABOR FREEDOM — 70.6

Armenia's somewhat rigid labor regulations remain barriers to employment and productivity growth. The non-salary cost of employing a worker is moderate, and dismissing a redundant employee is relatively inexpensive.

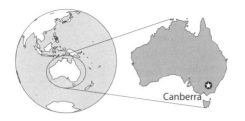

AUSTRALIA

Economic Freedom Score

25   50   75

Least free 0   100 Most free

82.6

World Rank: **3**   Regional Rank: **3**

Australia's economic freedom score is 82.6, making its economy the 3rd freest in the 2010 *Index*. Its overall score is unchanged from last year. Australia is ranked 3rd out of 41 countries in the Asia–Pacific region, and its score is well above the regional and world averages.

Sound macroeconomic policies and well-implemented structural reforms have allowed the Australian economy to weather the recent global financial and economic crisis better than many other advanced economies. Facilitated by robust supervision and sound regulation, Australia's banks have coped well with the financial turmoil. Unemployment has been rising since the start of 2009 but remains well below the OECD average. With growth recovering, the government's temporary stimulus measures are scheduled to phase out in 2010.

Overall, the Australian economy is well equipped in terms of its structural strength. Monetary stability and openness to global commerce continue to facilitate a competitive financial and investment environment based on market principles. A strong rule of law protects property rights, and corruption is perceived as minimal. Both foreign and domestically owned businesses enjoy considerable flexibility under licensing and regulatory schemes and in their employment practices. Measures to enhance public finance and maintain long-term fiscal sustainability are focused on achieving better efficiency and effectiveness.

BACKGROUND: Australia is one of the Asia–Pacific's richest countries. Over a period of more than three decades, successive Labor and Liberal governments have deregulated financial and labor markets and reduced trade barriers. Now in its 18th year of uninterrupted economic expansion, Australia is an internationally competitive producer of services, technologies, and high-value-added manufactured goods. Its export sector remains heavily focused on mining and agriculture.

Country's Score Over Time

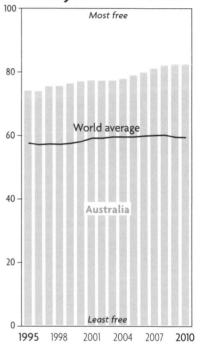

Quick Facts

Population: 21 million

GDP (PPP): $762.6 billion
3.7% growth in 2008
2.9% 5-year compound annual growth
$35,677 per capita

Unemployment: 4.2%

Inflation (CPI): 4.4%

FDI Inflow: $46.8 billion

2008 data unless otherwise noted
Data compiled as of September 2009

How Do We Measure Economic Freedom?
See page 457 for an explanation of the methodology or visit the *Index* Web site at *heritage.org/index*.

AUSTRALIA'S TEN ECONOMIC FREEDOMS

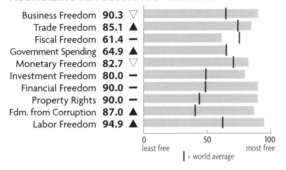

Business Freedom	90.3 ▽
Trade Freedom	85.1 ▲
Fiscal Freedom	61.4 —
Government Spending	64.9 ▲
Monetary Freedom	82.7 ▽
Investment Freedom	80.0 —
Financial Freedom	90.0 —
Property Rights	90.0 —
Fdm. from Corruption	87.0 ▲
Labor Freedom	94.9 ▲

0 least free   50   100 most free

❘ = world average

BUSINESS FREEDOM — 90.3

The overall freedom to start, operate, and close a business is strongly protected under Australia's regulatory environment. Starting a business takes two days, compared to the world average of 35 days. Obtaining a business license requires less than the global average of 18 procedures. Bankruptcy procedures are straightforward and not burdensome. The government generally follows a hands-off approach to sectors dominated by small businesses.

TRADE FREEDOM — 85.1

Australia's weighted average tariff rate was 2.5 percent in 2008. Import restrictions and bans, stringent sanitary and biotechnology measures, a quarantine regime, subsidies and other support programs for agriculture and manufacturing products, and barriers to trade in services raise the cost of trade. Exports of bulk wheat and containerized wheat have been liberalized, but bulk exports still require a license before shipment. Ten points were deducted from Australia's trade freedom score to account for non-tariff barriers.

FISCAL FREEDOM — 61.4

Australia has a high income tax rate and a moderately high corporate tax rate. The top income tax rate is 45 percent (plus a Medicare levy of 1.5 percent). The corporate tax rate is a flat 30 percent. Other taxes include a goods and services tax (GST) and a tax on the transfer of real property (applied at the state level). In the most recent year, overall tax revenue as a percentage of GDP was 30.6 percent.

GOVERNMENT SPENDING — 64.9

Total government expenditures, including consumption and transfer payments, are moderate. In the most recent year, government spending equaled 34.2 percent of GDP. A large stimulus package of transfers to households and increased infrastructure spending shifted the fiscal balance into deficit. State corporations increased public investment spending.

MONETARY FREEDOM — 82.7

Inflation has been moderate, averaging 3.8 percent between 2006 and 2008. The government can impose price controls, but competition reforms are reducing the range of goods subject to control. Retail gas and electricity prices are regulated, causing five points to be deducted from Australia's monetary freedom score.

INVESTMENT FREEDOM — 80

Foreign and domestic investors receive equal treatment, but foreign investments may be screened. The government generally must be notified about proposals to start new businesses in sensitive sectors, acquisitions of substantial interests in existing businesses, plans to establish new businesses involving a total investment of A$10 million or more, significant portfolio investments and all non-portfolio investments in the media, takeovers of offshore companies with Australian subsidiaries valued at A$200 million or more, direct investments by foreign governments or their agencies, and certain acquisitions of interests in urban land. The government may reject proposals deemed inconsistent with the "national interest." Foreign investors may own land, subject to approval and a number of restrictions. Residents and non-residents have access to foreign exchange and may conduct international payments and capital transactions. There are no controls on capital repatriation. Private property can be expropriated for public purposes in accordance with international law, and compensation is paid.

FINANCIAL FREEDOM — 90

Australia's well-developed and highly competitive financial sector includes banking, insurance, and equity industries. All banks are privately owned. Government regulation is minimal, and foreign banks, licensed as branches or subsidiaries, offer a full range of services. As of June 2009, there were 58 licensed banks: 14 Australian-owned and 44 foreign-owned. The sector is dominated by four major Australian banks that are not allowed to merge. Relatively low leverage and a high ratio of capital adequacy, coupled with banks' limited exposure to securitized assets, helped to avert a sharp credit contraction during the global financial crisis. Foreign insurance companies are permitted, and regulation is focused on capital adequacy, solvency, and prudential behavior.

PROPERTY RIGHTS — 90

Property rights are well protected. The rule of law is seen as fundamental, and enforcement is even-handed. The government respects the independence of the judiciary. Protection of intellectual property rights meets or exceeds world standards. Contracts are secure, and expropriation is highly unusual.

FREEDOM FROM CORRUPTION — 87

Corruption is perceived as minimal. Australia ranks 9th out of 179 countries in Transparency International's Corruption Perceptions Index for 2008, and the government actively promotes international efforts to curb the bribing of foreign officials.

LABOR FREEDOM — 94.9

Highly flexible employment regulations enhance employment and productivity growth. The non-salary cost of employing a worker is moderate, and dismissing a redundant employee is costless.

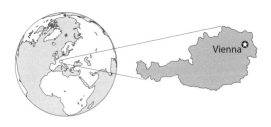

AUSTRIA

Economic Freedom Score

World Rank: **22**   Regional Rank: **11**

71.6

Least free 0   25   50   75   100   Most free

A ustria's economic freedom score is 71.6, making its economy the 22nd freest in the 2010 *Index*. Its score is slightly improved from last year. Austria is ranked 11th out of 43 countries in the Europe region, and its overall score is well above the regional and world averages.

2009 marked Austria's first major recession since the early 1980s, although the contraction has not been as severe as in other advanced economies. Austrian banks, with their large exposure to Central and Eastern European countries that have been hit hard by the global financial crisis, have been under considerable strain.

Austria's international orientation and traditions of property rights and clean government are the backbone of its economic growth. Monetary stability is well established. The government has streamlined time-consuming regulations, and a comprehensive legal framework promotes competition. Foreign investment requirements are not particularly stringent, and the financial market facilitates entrepreneurial activity. The corporate tax regime is competitive, although individuals still face high rates and an onerous overall tax burden. Government spending has been close to 50 percent of GDP in recent years.

BACKGROUND: During the Cold War, Austria's affinity for the West was apparent in its adherence to democratic government and increasingly market-oriented economic policies. Austria joined the European Union in 1995, and other EU member states now account for more than 80 percent of trade. The government has gradually relinquished control of formerly nationalized oil, gas, steel, and engineering companies and has deregulated telecommunications and electricity. From 2000–2007, People's Party Chancellor Wolfgang Schüssel accelerated market reform and significantly limited government intervention in the economy. The subsequent coalition government of Social Democrat Alfred Gusenbauer dissolved after 18 months. In the September 2008 parliamentary elections, far-right anti-immigrant parties made significant gains, but Social Democrat Werner Faymann was able to form a center-right coalition government with the People's Party.

Country's Score Over Time

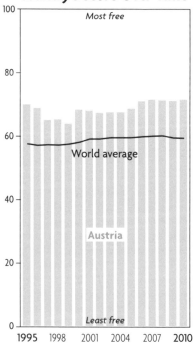

Quick Facts

Population: 8.3 million

GDP (PPP): $318.4 billion
1.8% growth in 2008
2.8% 5-year compound annual growth
$38,152 per capita

Unemployment: 3.8%

Inflation (CPI): 3.2%

FDI Inflow: $13.6 billion

2008 data unless otherwise noted
Data compiled as of September 2009

How Do We Measure Economic Freedom?
See page 457 for an explanation of the methodology or visit the *Index* Web site at *heritage.org/index*.

AUSTRIA'S TEN ECONOMIC FREEDOMS

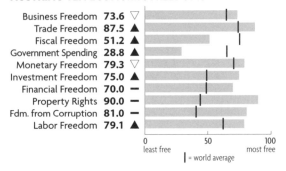

Business Freedom	73.6	▽
Trade Freedom	87.5	▲
Fiscal Freedom	51.2	▲
Government Spending	28.8	▲
Monetary Freedom	79.3	▽
Investment Freedom	75.0	▲
Financial Freedom	70.0	—
Property Rights	90.0	—
Fdm. from Corruption	81.0	—
Labor Freedom	79.1	▲

0   least free   50   100   most free

| = world average

BUSINESS FREEDOM — 73.6

The overall freedom to start, operate, and close a business is relatively well protected under Austria's regulatory environment. Starting a business takes an average of 28 days, compared to the world average of 35 days. Obtaining a business license involves less than the global average of 18 procedures, and bankruptcy procedures are straightforward.

TRADE FREEDOM — 87.5

Austria's trade policy is the same as that of other members of the European Union. The common EU weighted average tariff rate was 1.3 percent in 2008. However, the EU has high or escalating tariffs for agricultural and manufacturing products, and its MFN tariff code is complex. EU-wide non-tariff barriers include agricultural and manufacturing subsidies, quotas, import restrictions and bans on some goods and services, market access restrictions in some services sectors, non-transparent and restrictive regulations and standards, and inconsistent regulatory and customs administration. Austria maintains additional restrictions on biotechnology and certain service sectors. Ten points were deducted from Austria's trade freedom score to account for non-tariff barriers.

FISCAL FREEDOM — 51.2

Austria has a high income tax rate and a moderate corporate tax rate. The top income tax rate is 50 percent, and the top corporate tax rate is 25 percent. Other taxes include a value-added tax (VAT), a tax on insurance contracts, and a tax on real estate transfers. In the most recent year, overall tax revenue as a percentage of GDP was 41.9 percent.

GOVERNMENT SPENDING — 28.8

Total government expenditures, including consumption and transfer payments, are very high. In the most recent year, government spending equaled 48.7 percent of GDP. Sustained wage increases have been implemented, and a stimulus package passed in 2009 will further drive up public-sector debt.

MONETARY FREEDOM — 79.3

Austria is a member of the euro zone. From 2006 to 2008, its weighted average annual rate of inflation was 2.8 percent. As a participant in the EU's Common Agricultural Policy, the government subsidizes agricultural production,

distorting the prices of agricultural products. It also subsidizes rail transportation and operates some state-owned firms, utilities, and services. Ten points were deducted from Austria's monetary freedom score to account for policies that distort domestic prices.

INVESTMENT FREEDOM — 75

For foreign investors, at least one manager must meet residency and other legal qualifications, and non-residents must appoint a representative in Austria. Foreign and domestic private enterprises may establish, acquire, and dispose of business interests, except in some infrastructure areas and utilities and a few state monopolies. Environmental restrictions are strict, and many industries fall under a greenhouse-gas emissions trading system. There are no controls or requirements on current transfers, access to foreign exchange, or repatriation of profits. Real estate transactions are subject to approval by local authorities. Legal, regulatory, and accounting systems are transparent, but bureaucracy can be cumbersome and unpredictable. Expropriation is rare and requires special legal authorization.

FINANCIAL FREEDOM — 70

Banks provide a wide range of credit and financial services, credit is allocated at market terms, and domestic and foreign investors enjoy unrestricted access to capital markets. Austria's five largest banking groups account for around 60 percent of total assets. Financial regulations are consistent with international norms. Foreign exchange is fully liberalized, and there are no limitations on cross-border transactions. Austrian banks have been stressed by their considerable exposure to troubled assets in Central and Eastern Europe. The government has responded with a deposit guarantee and capital injections.

PROPERTY RIGHTS — 90

Private property is very secure. Contractual agreements are enforced, and the protection of intellectual property is well established. The rule of law is respected, and the judiciary is independent.

FREEDOM FROM CORRUPTION — 81

Corruption is perceived as minimal. Austria ranks 12th out of 179 countries in Transparency International's Corruption Perceptions Index for 2008. Bribery of an Austrian or foreign government official is subject to criminal penalties. The government has tightened corruption regulations and is establishing a central public prosecution department for corruption cases.

LABOR FREEDOM — 79.1

Austria's relatively flexible labor regulations enhance employment and productivity growth. However, the non-salary cost of employing a worker is high, and the cost of fringe benefits per employee is among the EU's highest. There is no nationally mandated minimum wage. Companies may employ workers on short working hours for up to 24 months.

AZERBAIJAN

Economic Freedom Score

25   50   75

Least free   0   100   Most free

58.8

World Rank: 96   **Regional Rank: 16**

Azerbaijan's economic freedom score is 58.8, making its economy the 96th freest in the 2010 *Index*. Its overall score is 0.8 point higher than last year, reflecting a significant improvement in investment freedom offset by modest declines in several other factors. Azerbaijan is ranked 16th out of 41 countries in the Asia–Pacific region, and its overall score is above the regional average but just below the world average.

Azerbaijan's impressive economic growth has been driven mainly by oil and gas. Continued transformation and restructuring are needed, both to capitalize on Azerbaijan's well-educated labor force and tradition of entrepreneurship and to diversify production. The government has implemented wide-ranging reforms to improve economic freedom. Openness to global trade, relatively moderate taxation, streamlined business processes, and improved public-sector management have aided the transition to a market-based system.

Despite considerable gains in regulatory reform and economic diversification led by the services sectors, substantial challenges remain, particularly in implementing more institutional and systemic reforms. Property rights and freedom from corruption remain weak, and government interference and control hurt overall monetary stability and foreign investment.

BACKGROUND: Oil-rich Azerbaijan's dispute with Armenia over Nagorno–Karabakh has cost thousands of lives and much territory. Despite a cease-fire since 1994, over 500,000 Azeris from the disputed territory still live as refugees in Azerbaijan, and tensions with Turkey have increased because of Ankara's rapprochement with Armenia. Azerbaijan is exploring Russian mediation of the conflict with Armenia and Moscow's offers to buy and ship more of its natural gas to Europe. It also has suspended in-country foreign radio broadcasts. A constitutional amendment to abolish presidential term limits, passed by national referendum in 2009, will allow President Ilham Aliyev to seek a third term. Falling oil and gas revenues and shrinking foreign direct investment because of the 2009 global crisis have led to a budget deficit.

Country's Score Over Time

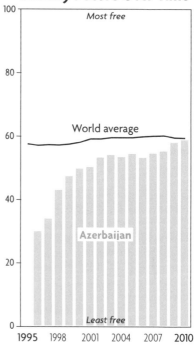

Quick Facts

Population: 8.7 million

GDP (PPP): $76.1 billion
10.8% growth in 2008
22.3% 5-year compound annual growth
$8,765 per capita

Unemployment: 6.1% (2008)

Inflation (CPI): 20.8%

FDI Inflow: $11 million

2008 data unless otherwise noted
Data compiled as of September 2009

How Do We Measure Economic Freedom?
See page 457 for an explanation of the methodology or visit the *Index* Web site at *heritage.org/index.*

AZERBAIJAN'S TEN ECONOMIC FREEDOMS

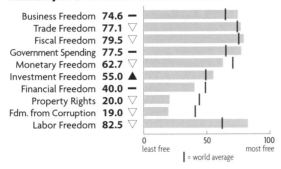

Business Freedom	74.6 —
Trade Freedom	77.1 ▽
Fiscal Freedom	79.5 ▽
Government Spending	77.5 ▽
Monetary Freedom	62.7 ▽
Investment Freedom	55.0 ▲
Financial Freedom	40.0 —
Property Rights	20.0 ▽
Fdm. from Corruption	19.0 ▽
Labor Freedom	82.5 ▽

0 least free   50   100 most free
| = world average

BUSINESS FREEDOM — 74.6

Azerbaijan's overall regulatory environment has improved. Starting a business takes less than half the world average of 35 days. Obtaining a business license involves more than the global average of 18 procedures, but closing a business is relatively easy.

TRADE FREEDOM — 77.1

Azerbaijan's weighted average tariff rate was 3.9 percent in 2008. A weak legal regime, arbitrary customs administration, regulatory conflicts of interest, subsidies, import and export controls and restrictions, weak enforcement of property rights, and customs corruption add to the cost of trade. Fifteen points were deducted from Azerbaijan's trade freedom score to account for non-tariff barriers.

FISCAL FREEDOM — 79.5

Azerbaijan has a relatively high income tax rate and a moderate corporate tax rate. On January 1, 2010, the top income tax rate of 35 percent will be lowered to 30 percent, and the top corporate tax rate of 22 percent will be lowered to 20 percent. Other taxes include a value-added tax (VAT) and a property tax. In the most recent year, overall tax revenue as a percentage of GDP was 18.4 percent.

GOVERNMENT SPENDING — 77.5

Total government spending, including consumption and transfer payments, is relatively low. In the most recent year, government spending was 27.4 percent of GDP. Power supply and water companies remain in state hands.

MONETARY FREEDOM — 62.7

Inflation has accelerated rapidly, averaging 18.6 percent between 2006 and 2008. The government controls prices on most energy products and operates several state-owned enterprises. Monopolist importers in many sectors prevent declines in commodity prices from being fully passed on to consumers. Ten points were deducted from Azerbaijan's monetary freedom score to adjust for price-control policies.

INVESTMENT FREEDOM — 55

Foreign direct investment is allowed in most sectors. Investment in areas related to national security and defense is prohibited, and the government controls other key sectors, such as energy and communications. The regulatory sys-

tem has been improved, but non-transparency, corruption, weak legal institutions, politically connected monopoly interests, and informal bureaucratic control impede application of laws and regulations and hinder competition. The law provides that foreign investors be "not less favored" than local investors and allows repatriation of profits, revenues, and other investment-related funds as long as applicable taxes are paid. The exchange system is generally liberal; there are few restrictions on converting or transferring investment-associated funds into freely tradable currency. Foreign citizens and enterprises may lease but not own land. Expropriation may occur in the event of natural disaster, epidemic, or other extraordinary situation, and foreign investors are entitled to adequate compensation.

FINANCIAL FREEDOM — 40

Azerbaijan's banking sector has been growing rapidly. Bank credit has expanded by more than 50 percent per year since 2004. Prudential regulation and supervision have been the central bank's priority to contain potential risks from the rapid expansion. Private banks have grown faster than state-owned banks and account for around 60 percent of total assets. However, availability of long-term financial instruments remains limited. The market for government and corporate bonds remains small and illiquid. There are no limits on foreign ownership of domestic banks, and some international banks have opened representative offices. The state-owned International Bank of Azerbaijan still dominates the banking sector. The government sold a 50 percent stake in the state-owned Kapital Bank in 2007 and further privatized the bank in 2008.

PROPERTY RIGHTS — 20

Azerbaijan's judicial system, filled with bureaucratic requirements and generally seen as corrupt and inefficient, does not function independently of the executive. The poor quality, reliability, and transparency of governance, as well as regulatory abuse and poor contract enforcement, significantly impede the ability of many companies to do business.

FREEDOM FROM CORRUPTION — 19

Corruption is perceived as rampant. Azerbaijan ranks 158th out of 179 countries in Transparency International's Corruption Perceptions Index for 2008. Judicial and police corruption are widespread. Arbitrary tax and customs administration create opportunities for graft, regulatory practices favor monopolies, and corruption appears at all levels. Politically connected businesses seem to have benefited from government regulatory and other decisions and have achieved control of several lucrative sectors of the economy.

LABOR FREEDOM — 82.5

Azerbaijan's labor market is relatively free, and flexible employment regulations have been implemented as a result of recent reforms. The non-salary cost of employing a worker is moderate, and dismissing a redundant employee is not burdensome.

THE BAHAMAS

Economic Freedom Score

Least free 0 — 25 — 50 — 75 — 100 Most free

67.3

The Bahamas' economic freedom score is 67.3, making its economy the 47th freest in the 2010 *Index*. Its overall score is 3 points lower than last year, primarily due to lower scores in trade freedom, investment freedom, and property rights. The Bahamas is ranked 7th out of 29 countries in the South and Central America/Caribbean region, and its overall score is higher than the regional and world averages.

A relatively high degree of economic freedom has made the Bahamas one of the most prosperous countries in the Caribbean region. The financial services sector's domestic and offshore activities contribute around 15 percent of GDP. The economy has a very competitive tax regime. There is no personal income tax, corporate tax, or value-added tax (VAT). The labor market is very flexible, and the overall regulatory environment is relatively efficient.

Burdensome tariff and non-tariff barriers remain an area that needs proactive reform. A poor investment climate characterized by government interference and lingering corruption also undermines the Bahamas' overall economic freedom score.

BACKGROUND: The Bahamas is a parliamentary democracy with two main parties, the Free National Movement and the Progressive Liberal Party. It is also one of the Caribbean's most prosperous nations and a prime tourist destination. Tourism generates about half of all jobs, but the number of visitors has dropped significantly since the beginning of the global economic downturn during the last quarter of 2008. Banking and international financial services also have contracted, and the Bahamas is one of 34 secrecy jurisdictions that would be subject to the Stop Tax Haven Abuse Act, introduced in the U.S. Congress. The Bahamas archipelago is a way station for drug smugglers and illegal aliens seeking to enter the United States. Aggressive anti–money laundering efforts have caused some offshore banks to incur losses and leave the country.

Country's Score Over Time

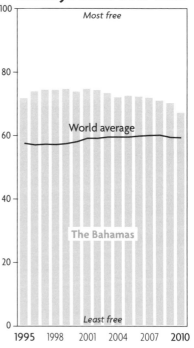

Quick Facts

Population: 337,000

GDP (PPP): $9.2 billion
–1.2% growth in 2008
2.3% 5-year compound annual growth
$27,470 per capita

Unemployment: 7.6% (2006)

Inflation (CPI): 4.5%

FDI Inflow: $700 million

2008 data unless otherwise noted
Data compiled as of September 2009

How Do We Measure Economic Freedom?
See page 457 for an explanation of the methodology or visit the *Index* Web site at *heritage.org/index*.

THE BAHAMAS' TEN ECONOMIC FREEDOMS

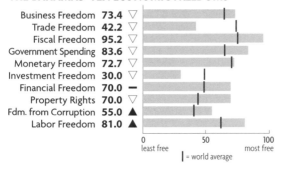

Business Freedom	73.4	▽
Trade Freedom	42.2	▽
Fiscal Freedom	95.2	▽
Government Spending	83.6	▽
Monetary Freedom	72.7	▽
Investment Freedom	30.0	▽
Financial Freedom	70.0	—
Property Rights	70.0	▽
Fdm. from Corruption	55.0	▲
Labor Freedom	81.0	▲

0   50   100
least free   most free
| = world average

BUSINESS FREEDOM — 73.4

Overall, the regulatory environment is conducive to development of the private sector, but the process for obtaining a business license is not fully transparent, and officials have considerable discretionary power.

TRADE FREEDOM — 42.2

According to the World Bank, the Bahamas' weighted average tariff rate was a high 23.9 percent in 2006. High tariffs and a "stamp" tax on certain imports, high duties that protect a few agricultural items and consumer goods, occasional import bans, and some import licensing and permits add to the cost of trade. Ten points were deducted from the Bahamas' trade freedom score to account for non-tariff barriers.

FISCAL FREEDOM — 95.2

The Bahamas' tax burden is one of the world's lowest. The government imposes national insurance, property, and stamp taxes but no income tax, corporate income tax, capital gains tax, value-added tax (VAT), or wealth tax. In the most recent year, overall tax revenue as a percentage of GDP was 21.8 percent. Authorities are trying to increase tax compliance and collection in the wake of the global crisis.

GOVERNMENT SPENDING — 83.6

Total government spending, including consumption and transfer payments, is relatively low. In the most recent year, government spending equaled 23.4 percent of GDP. Authorities are committed to improving the transparency of budget planning. Central government debt rose in the first half of 2009 as government turned to international loans to compensate for revenue shortfalls.

MONETARY FREEDOM — 72.7

Inflation has been moderate, averaging 3.7 percent between 2006 and 2008. Fifteen points were deducted from the Bahamas' monetary freedom score to adjust for measures that distort domestic prices for such "breadbasket" items as medicines, gasoline, diesel oil, and petroleum gas.

INVESTMENT FREEDOM — 30

Activities reserved exclusively for Bahamians include wholesale and retail operations, commission import–export agencies, real estate and property management,

newspaper and magazine publication, advertising and public relations firms, nightclubs and certain restaurants, security services, distribution and building supplies, certain construction, personal cosmetics and beauty services, certain fishing operations, auto and appliance service operations, and public transportation. All other foreign direct investment must be approved by the government. New foreign ventures perceived as competing with existing Bahamian businesses may face loss or refusal of business licenses. All outward capital transfers and inward transfers by non-residents require approval, but exchange controls are not known to hamper repatriation of approved investment capital. To buy real estate for commercial purposes or to buy more than five acres, foreigners must obtain a permit from the Investments Board.

FINANCIAL FREEDOM — 70

The financial sector is the economy's second most important sector, accounting for around 20 percent of GDP. The government has adopted incentives to encourage foreign financial business, and further banking and finance reforms are in progress. The government plans to merge the regulatory functions of key financial institutions, including the Central Bank of the Bahamas (CBB) and the Securities and Exchange Commission. Restrictions and controls on capital and money market instruments exist, and the CBB administers exchange controls. The development of local capital markets has accelerated. The Bahamas International Securities Exchange currently consists of 19 listed public companies. Reflecting the relative soundness of the banking system, the impact of the global financial crisis on the financial sector has been limited.

PROPERTY RIGHTS — 70

The Bahamas has an efficient legal system based on British common law. The judiciary is independent. The judicial process tends to be very slow, and some investors have complained of malfeasance by court officials. Copyright laws are widely ignored, and there is widespread piracy of video and music recordings and broadcasts.

FREEDOM FROM CORRUPTION — 55

The law provides criminal penalties for official corruption, and the government generally implements these laws effectively. Piracy of software, music, and videos is a problem. Illegal drug trafficking and money laundering reportedly involve police, coast guard, and other government employees. Violent crimes have escalated sharply. Even though Internet gambling is illegal, more than 10 online gambling sites are reportedly based in the Bahamas. The Bahamas has neither signed nor ratified the U.N. Convention Against Corruption.

LABOR FREEDOM — 81

Flexible employment regulations generally enhance overall productivity growth and job creation. Employment contracts, though not mandatory, are often used. There is no legal entitlement to notice of termination.

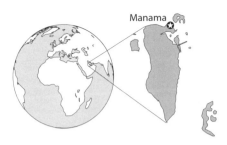

Manama

BAHRAIN

Economic Freedom Score

Least free 0   100 Most free

76.3

Bahrain's economic freedom score is 76.3, making its economy the 13th freest in the 2010 *Index*. Its overall score is 1.5 points higher than last year, with improvements in trade freedom, investment freedom, labor freedom, and freedom from corruption. Bahrain is ranked 1st out of 17 countries in the Middle East/North Africa region, and its economic freedom score is well above the world average.

Overall economic growth has slowed, but the impact of the global financial crisis on banking has been relatively muted. There has been no severe liquidity contraction, and the financial sector's resilience has helped to minimize any adverse effects on the economy. Bahrain has maintained monetary stability despite inflationary pressure.

Structural reforms and openness to global commerce have made Bahrain a financial hub and the regional leader in economic freedom. One of the region's least oil-dependent economies, it has a competitive tax regime and a sophisticated financial sector that facilitates the flow of capital and foreign investment. The government has modernized the regulatory framework and continues to focus on diversifying the productive base. Despite more flexible employment regulations, unemployment remains a serious problem.

BACKGROUND: Bahrain has developed one of the Persian Gulf's most advanced economies and most progressive political systems since gaining its independence from Great Britain in 1971. Under a constitution promulgated by Sheikh Hamad bin Isa al-Khalifa, the country became a constitutional monarchy in 2002, and the government has sought to reduce dependence on declining oil reserves and encourage foreign investment by diversifying the economy. Bahrain is home to many multinational firms that do business in the region. It has a modern communications and transportation infrastructure, a reliable regulatory structure, and a cosmopolitan outlook. In 2006, the U.S. and Bahrain implemented the first free trade agreement between the U.S. and a Persian Gulf state.

Country's Score Over Time

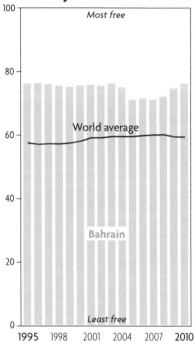

Quick Facts

Population: 0.8 million

GDP (PPP): $26.9 billion
6.1% growth in 2008
7.2% 5-year compound annual growth
$34,605 per capita

Unemployment: 15.0% (2007)

Inflation (CPI): 3.5%

FDI Inflow: $1.8 billion

2008 data unless otherwise noted
Data compiled as of September 2009

How Do We Measure Economic Freedom?
See page 457 for an explanation of the methodology or visit the *Index* Web site at *heritage.org/index*.

BAHRAIN'S TEN ECONOMIC FREEDOMS

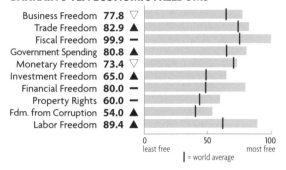

Business Freedom	77.8	▽
Trade Freedom	82.9	▲
Fiscal Freedom	99.9	—
Government Spending	80.8	▲
Monetary Freedom	73.4	▽
Investment Freedom	65.0	▲
Financial Freedom	80.0	—
Property Rights	60.0	—
Fdm. from Corruption	54.0	▲
Labor Freedom	89.4	▲

0 least free 50 100 most free

| = world average

BUSINESS FREEDOM — 77.8

Bahrain's commercial law system is relatively straightforward, but establishing and running a business can be slowed by the uncoordinated regulatory environment. The government is working to streamline regulations and create the necessary infrastructure in partnership with the private sector.

TRADE FREEDOM — 82.9

Bahrain's weighted average tariff rate was 3.5 percent in 2008. There are few non-tariff barriers, but a limited number of products are subject to import and export prohibitions or restrictions, and standards can be inconsistent. While improving, the enforcement of intellectual property rights can be a problem. Ten points were deducted from Bahrain's trade freedom score to account for non-tariff barriers.

FISCAL FREEDOM — 99.9

Historically, Bahrain has imposed no taxes on personal income. However, the government levies a 1 percent tax on the salaries of Bahraini nationals and 3 percent on the salaries of expatriate employees working for companies with more than 50 employees as a way to fund job training. Most companies are not subject to corporate tax, but a 46 percent corporate tax is levied on oil companies. A small stamp duty is collected on property transfers. In the most recent year, overall tax revenue as a percentage of GDP was 2.7 percent.

GOVERNMENT SPENDING — 80.8

Total government expenditures, including consumption and transfer payments, are relatively low. In the most recent year, government spending equaled 25.3 percent of GDP. Privatization has slowed in recent years and is expected to stall further in 2010.

MONETARY FREEDOM — 73.4

Inflation has been relatively low, averaging 3.3 percent between 2006 and 2008. Fifteen points were deducted from Bahrain's monetary freedom score to account for extensive price controls and subsidies that distort domestic prices for many food products, electricity, water, and petroleum.

INVESTMENT FREEDOM — 65

The government generally welcomes foreign investment, but certain sectors are restricted. Bahrain permits 100 percent foreign ownership of new industrial entities and the establishment of representative offices or branches of foreign companies without local sponsors. Wholly foreign-owned companies may be established for regional distribution services and may operate within the domestic market if they do not pursue domestic commercial sales exclusively. Gulf Cooperation Council nationals may own 100 percent of the shares of firms listed on the stock exchange; non-GCC nationals are limited to 49 percent. There are no restrictions on the repatriation of profits or capital, no exchange controls, and no restrictions on converting or transferring funds, whether associated with an investment or not. In 2006, the Cabinet passed an edict opening ownership of "free hold" properties being constructed throughout the kingdom and allowing all nationalities to own commercial or investment (but not residential) properties.

FINANCIAL FREEDOM — 80

As a regional financial hub, Bahrain has a modern and competitive financial sector. Foreign and local individuals and companies enjoy access to credit on market terms. With more than 400 banks and financial institutions in 2008, the financial sector accounts for over 25 percent of GDP. The banking system provides a wide range of financial services for foreign and domestic investors. Financial regulation has become more flexible and comprehensive. With passage of the Central Bank of Bahrain and Financial Institutions Law in 2006, the CBB became a single regulator of the financial services industry, with more enforcement powers and operational independence. The impact of the global financial turmoil on the banking sector has been relatively muted.

PROPERTY RIGHTS — 60

Property ownership is secure, and expropriation is unlikely. The king has the right to appoint judges and amend the constitution, but the legal system is well regarded, and foreign firms can resolve disputes satisfactorily through the local courts. There are no prohibitions on the use of international arbitration to safeguard contracts. Bahrain was ranked 44th out of 115 countries in the 2009 International Property Rights Index.

FREEDOM FROM CORRUPTION — 54

Corruption is perceived as present. Bahrain ranks 43rd out of 179 countries in Transparency International's Corruption Perceptions Index for 2008. Corruption affects the management of scarce water resources, and significant areas of government activity lack transparency.

LABOR FREEDOM — 89.4

Bahrain needs more flexible labor regulations to establish a more dynamic labor market. There is no nationally mandated minimum wage, and the government has launched a four-pillar labor reform process to enhance productivity and create more private-sector job opportunities.

BANGLADESH

Economic Freedom Score

Least free 0   50   100 Most free
25   75

51.1

Bangladesh's economic freedom score is 51.1, making its economy the 137th freest in the 2010 *Index*. Its overall score is 3.6 points higher than last year, mainly reflecting improvements in trade freedom and investment freedom. Bangladesh is ranked 29th out of 41 countries in the Asia–Pacific region.

Bangladesh has enjoyed impressive economic growth of around 6 percent per year over the past five years, driven mainly by its limited but growing services and industrial sectors.

Structural and institutional weaknesses remain serious impediments to sustaining such high economic growth rates. Bangladesh's economy remains overly dependent on agriculture, which accounts for almost 20 percent of GDP and employs more than half of the labor force. State-owned enterprises (SOEs) are a significant presence in most productive sectors, including those that are usually dominated by the private sector in other economies. Further, the weak regulatory regime is often heavily politicized, and SOEs tend to crowd out private investment. Corruption, coupled with onerous bureaucracy, is still perceived as pervasive, and the underdeveloped financial sector impedes the growth of a more dynamic private sector, as does a haphazard and politicized approach to the rule of law.

BACKGROUND: After nearly two years of military-backed rule, the People's Republic of Bangladesh returned to democracy after successful elections in December 2008. The secular Awami League party won over two-thirds of the 300 parliamentary seats, returning Sheikh Hasina Wajed as prime minister, a post she had held from 1996–2001. Bangladesh is one of the world's poorest and most densely populated nations, and the majority of its people work in agriculture, though service industries now account for around half of GDP. The formal financial system remains weak, and inadequate infrastructure discourages investment. Weak institutions continue to undermine economic development and fuel corruption.

Country's Score Over Time

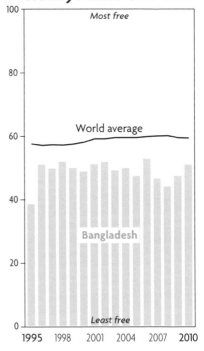

Quick Facts

Population: 160 million

GDP (PPP): $213.5 billion
6.2% growth in 2008
6.2% 5-year compound
annual growth
$1,334 per capita

Unemployment: 4.2% (2006)

Inflation (CPI): 8.4%

FDI Inflow: $1.1 billion

2008 data unless otherwise noted
Data compiled as of September 2009

How Do We Measure Economic Freedom?
See page 457 for an explanation of the methodology or visit the *Index* Web site at *heritage.org/index*.

BANGLADESH'S TEN ECONOMIC FREEDOMS

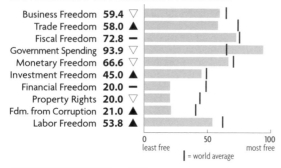

Business Freedom	59.4 ▽	
Trade Freedom	58.0 ▲	
Fiscal Freedom	72.8 —	
Government Spending	93.9 ▽	
Monetary Freedom	66.6 ▽	
Investment Freedom	45.0 ▲	
Financial Freedom	20.0 —	
Property Rights	20.0 ▽	
Fdm. from Corruption	21.0 ▲	
Labor Freedom	53.8 ▲	

0   50   100
least free   most free
| = world average

BUSINESS FREEDOM — 59.4

The overall freedom to start, operate, and close a business is limited by Bangladesh's regulatory environment. Starting a business takes an average of 44 days, compared to the world average of 35 days. Obtaining a business license requires less than the world average of 18 procedures.

TRADE FREEDOM — 58

Bangladesh's weighted average tariff rate was 11 percent in 2007. Import and export restrictions, numerous border taxes and fees, restrictive labeling requirements, burdensome import licensing rules, export subsidies and other support programs, government monopolies and state trading boards, complex and non-transparent government procurement, inefficient and corrupt customs administration, and weak enforcement of intellectual property rights also add to the cost of trade. Twenty points were deducted from Bangladesh's trade freedom score to account for non-tariff barriers.

FISCAL FREEDOM — 72.8

Bangladesh has a moderate income tax rate and a high corporate tax rate. The top income tax rate is 25 percent, and the top corporate tax rate is 45 percent. Other taxes include a value-added tax (VAT) and a tax on interest. The Administration Capacity and Taxpayer Services (TACTS) program, created to enhance transparency and to help authorities encourage tax compliance, has been implemented successfully. In the most recent year, overall tax revenue as a percentage of GDP was 8.4 percent.

GOVERNMENT SPENDING — 93.9

Total government expenditures, including consumption and transfer payments, are low. In the most recent year, government spending equaled 14.3 percent of GDP. Expenditures on social safety nets are increasing as a response to the global crisis.

MONETARY FREEDOM — 66.6

Inflation is accelerating, averaging 8.4 percent between 2006 and 2008. Subsidies and other government assistance to the agriculture sector have doubled since 2005. Fifteen points were deducted from Bangladesh's monetary freedom score to adjust for price-control measures that distort domestic prices for petroleum products, some pharmaceuticals, and goods produced in state-owned enterprises.

INVESTMENT FREEDOM — 45

Officially, foreign investment is welcomed, but certain sectors are restricted, and potential investors face a host of challenges: delays in project approvals, burdensome bureaucratic procedures, high levels of corruption, and uncertainty about contract and regulatory enforcement. The Foreign Investment Act of 1980 guarantees the right of repatriation of invested capital, profits, capital gains, post-tax dividends, and approved royalties and fees. Foreign firms are able to repatriate funds without much difficulty, provided the appropriate documentation is in order. In general, government laws and regulations and their implementation create rather than reduce distortions or impediments to investment.

FINANCIAL FREEDOM — 20

The financial sector is underdeveloped and provides a limited range of banking services. Bangladesh's state-owned commercial banks account for more than 30 percent of total banking system assets, undermining the sector's efficiency. Behind the high level of non-performing loans often stand weak financial supervision, fraudulent transactions, mismanagement, and political influence in lending practices. The financial system consists of the central Bangladesh Bank, four nationalized commercial banks, five government-owned specialized banks, 30 domestic private banks, 10 foreign banks, and 28 non-bank financial institutions. An extensive microfinance presence remains largely unsupervised. There are two stock exchanges, but market capitalization is low. There are controls and limits on transactions regarding money market instruments. Bangladesh has made modest progress in recent years in its banking sector. There has been noticeable credit and deposit growth as well as a reduction in non-performing loans, particularly those of state-owned commercial banks.

PROPERTY RIGHTS — 20

Bangladesh has a civil court system based on the British model. Although the constitution provides for an independent judiciary, the lower courts are considered to be part of the executive branch and suffer from serious corruption. Contract enforcement is weak, and dispute settlement is further hampered by shortcomings in accounting practices and real property registration.

FREEDOM FROM CORRUPTION — 21

Corruption is perceived as pervasive. Bangladesh ranks 147th out of 179 countries in Transparency International's Corruption Perceptions Index for 2008, a slight improvement from 2007. Widespread and severe corruption among government officials and police, who engage in corrupt practices with impunity, facilitates trafficking in persons. Given that corruption blights all other economic freedoms, this is a key area for improvement.

LABOR FREEDOM — 53.8

Inflexible employment regulations hinder job creation and productivity growth. The non-salary cost of employing a worker is low, but dismissing a redundant employee can be difficult.

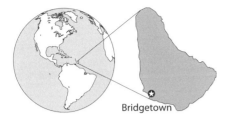

BARBADOS

Economic Freedom Score

Least free 0

Most free 100

68.3

World Rank: 40   **Regional Rank: 5**

Barbados's economic freedom score is 68.3, making its economy the 40th freest in the 2010 *Index*. Its score is 3.2 points lower than last year because of significant declines in its property rights and government spending scores. Barbados has slipped from 2nd to 5th out of 29 countries in the South and Central America/Caribbean region, but its overall score remains well above global and regional averages.

Despite its size, Barbados is one of the Caribbean region's most prosperous economies. Offshore finance and tourism are important sources of economic growth. The sugar industry, though declining, remains an important employer and exporter. Overall, government economic policies are focused on attracting international companies.

Business regulations, laid out in commercial laws and evenly applied, facilitate private-sector growth. Labor policies are relatively flexible, and transparency levels the playing field for domestic and foreign businesses, despite certain restrictions on foreign investment. The legal system adjudicates business disputes effectively and encourages a relatively low level of corruption. The financial sector has been little affected by the global financial turmoil, and the overall macroeconomic situation remains stable.

BACKGROUND: The Democratic Labor Party won the 2008 elections, ousting the business-friendly Barbados Labor Party after 14 years in power. Prime Minister David Thompson is struggling to fulfill promises to increase spending on social services, fight crime, and stimulate job creation as the government copes with declining tax revenues. The Central Bank of Barbados has loosened monetary policy in response to decelerating economic growth, and there are concerns about the country's credit rating. Many construction jobs depend on tourism, which accounts for more than 15 percent of GDP and has been hurt by the global downturn. Informatics and light manufacturing are also important, and the offshore financial sector, though smaller than others in the Caribbean, earns significant foreign exchange and is generally well regulated.

Country's Score Over Time

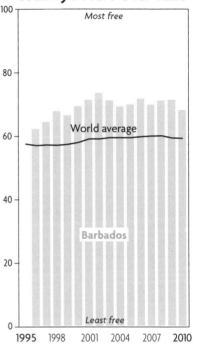

Quick Facts

Population: 0.27 million

GDP (PPP): $5.2 billion
0.6% growth in 2006
2.8% 5-year compound
annual growth
$19,025 per capita

Unemployment: n/a

Inflation (CPI): 8.3%

FDI Inflow: $133 million

2008 data unless otherwise noted
Data compiled as of September 2009

How Do We Measure Economic Freedom?
See page 457 for an explanation of the methodology or visit the *Index* Web site at *heritage.org/index*.

BARBADOS'S TEN ECONOMIC FREEDOMS

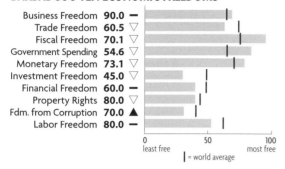

Business Freedom	90.0	—
Trade Freedom	60.5	▽
Fiscal Freedom	70.1	▽
Government Spending	54.6	▽
Monetary Freedom	73.1	▽
Investment Freedom	45.0	▽
Financial Freedom	60.0	—
Property Rights	80.0	▽
Fdm. from Corruption	70.0	▲
Labor Freedom	80.0	—

0 least free — 50 — 100 most free

| = world average

BUSINESS FREEDOM — 90

The overall process for obtaining licenses and starting a business is straightforward. The Company Act ensures flexibility and simplicity in establishing and operating companies. Transparent policies and effective laws enhance competition.

TRADE FREEDOM — 60.5

Barbados's weighted average tariff rate was 14.8 percent in 2007. Import levies and fees; requirements for permits, licenses, or permission before importation; labeling, sanitary, and phytosanitary policies; and direct and indirect export subsidies add to the cost of trade. State trading is limited to imports of chicken and turkey wings. Certain state companies are de facto sole traders. Ten points were deducted from Barbados's trade freedom score to account for non-tariff barriers.

FISCAL FREEDOM — 70.1

Barbados has a relatively high income tax rate and a moderate corporate tax rate. The top income tax rate is 35 percent, and the top corporate tax rate is 25 percent. Other taxes include a value-added tax (VAT) and a property tax. In the most recent year, overall tax revenue as a percentage of GDP was 33.8 percent.

GOVERNMENT SPENDING — 54.6

Total government expenditures, including consumption and transfer payments, are relatively high. Efforts to reform budget management and overhaul the pension system were halted in 2009. Public-sector debt is rising. In the most recent year, government spending equaled 38.9 percent of GDP.

MONETARY FREEDOM — 73.1

Inflation has been up, averaging 7.1 percent between 2006 and 2008. Although prices are generally set by the market, 10 points were deducted from Barbados's monetary freedom score to adjust for measures that distort domestic prices for basic food items, transportation, and fuel.

INVESTMENT FREEDOM — 45

Barbados is generally open to foreign investors. Tour operators, travel agents, certain ground transport, and food retail services are reserved for locally domiciled firms. There are few monopolies other than utilities and some state trading enterprises. Purchases of securities abroad by residents require exchange control approval, and earnings must be repatriated and surrendered to an authorized dealer. Credit operations and direct investments also require exchange control approval. The central bank regulates investment transfers and capital remittances. In general, foreign currency funds may be freely repatriated for current transactions; if substantial capital gains have been realized, repatriation must generally be phased over a period determined by the central bank. Companies can freely repatriate profits and capital from foreign direct investment if they registered with the central bank at the time of investment. Central bank approval is required for residents and non-residents to hold and transact in foreign exchange accounts. Despite transparent policies and effective laws, bureaucracy can be cumbersome. The government can acquire property for public use upon prompt payment of compensation at fair market value. Acquisition of real estate by foreigners requires permission from the central bank.

FINANCIAL FREEDOM — 60

Barbados's six commercial banks are dominated by Caribbean Community and Common Market and Canadian institutions. The banking sector has grown rapidly and provides a wide range of services for domestic and foreign investors. While maintaining strong regulatory standards, the government also seeks to expand product offerings in other financial services. Compliance with international supervisory standards is high for offshore and onshore banking institutions. Revised guidelines have further refined controls on money laundering. Exchange controls are being eased. CARICOM-related exchange controls have been abolished, and restrictions on non-CARICOM transactions are to be removed eventually. The securities markets are illiquid and lack depth, partly because of restrictions on capital movements.

PROPERTY RIGHTS — 80

Barbados has an efficient legal system based on British common law. Private property is well protected. The Caribbean Court of Justice is the court of final appeal for Barbados and other CARICOM member states. By regional standards, the police and courts are efficient and unbiased.

FREEDOM FROM CORRUPTION — 70

Corruption is perceived as present. Barbados ranks 22nd out of 179 countries in Transparency International's Corruption Perceptions Index for 2008. There are criminal penalties for official corruption, and the government generally implements these laws effectively. Barbados is a narcotics trafficking transit country and attracts drug money–laundering operations.

LABOR FREEDOM — 80

Flexible employment regulations enhance overall productivity growth and job creation. Employees are guaranteed a minimum of two weeks of annual leave and are covered by unemployment benefits and national insurance legislation. Employers are not legally obligated to recognize unions.

BELARUS

Economic Freedom Score

25 50 75

Least free 0 | Most free 100

48.7

World Rank: 150   **Regional Rank: 42**

Belarus's economic freedom score is 48.7, making its economy the 150th freest in the 2010 *Index*. The persistence of Soviet-era policies and practices continues to deny Belarus the benefits of economic freedom enjoyed in most other former Soviet republics, although its low score has improved by 3.7 points after four years of decline. Belarus is ranked 42nd among the 43 countries in the Europe region.

Reforms undertaken to reduce regulatory costs and enhance the business and investment climate have led to improved business freedom and labor freedom scores. Most of Belarus's 10 economic freedom scores, however, are considerably lower than world averages.

Belarus's economy is still characterized by pervasive state involvement and control. Restructuring is very slow, and the small private sector remains marginalized. Though tax rates are moderate, there is no comprehensive tax code. Regulations are confusing and applied unevenly. Financial freedom, investment freedom, property rights, and freedom from corruption are 20–40 points below world averages. The government controls many financial institutions, directly or partially. Besides insecure property rights and corruption, foreign investment faces restrictions and bureaucratic inefficiency.

BACKGROUND: In October 2004, President Alexander Lukashenko, in power since 1994, changed the constitution, effectively becoming president for life. In 2005, he vowed to guide Belarus toward "market socialism," and the economy has been deteriorating ever since. Industry and state-controlled agriculture are uncompetitive, and GDP is expected to contract by 4 percent in 2009. In 2008, Russia extended a $2 billion loan to Belarus that was linked to the creation of a single currency between the two countries. The International Monetary Fund approved a $2.46 billion loan in January 2009. Growing ties with Iran, Venezuela, and China have not improved economic prospects; nor has Belarus's effort to move toward a customs union with Russia and Kazakhstan as a part of the Eurasian Economic Community.

Country's Score Over Time

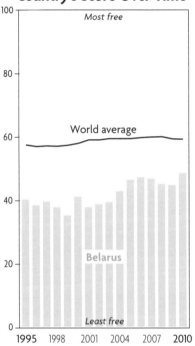

Quick Facts

Population: 9.7 million

GDP (PPP): $118.7 billion
10.0% growth in 2008
9.5% 5-year compound annual growth
$12,261 per capita

Unemployment: n/a

Inflation (CPI): 14.8%

FDI Inflow: $2.2 billion

2008 data unless otherwise noted
Data compiled as of September 2009

How Do We Measure Economic Freedom?
See page 457 for an explanation of the methodology or visit the *Index* Web site at *heritage.org/index.*

109

BELARUS'S TEN ECONOMIC FREEDOMS

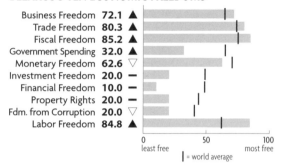

Business Freedom	72.1 ▲	
Trade Freedom	80.3 ▲	
Fiscal Freedom	85.2 ▲	
Government Spending	32.0 ▲	
Monetary Freedom	62.6 ▽	
Investment Freedom	20.0 —	
Financial Freedom	10.0 —	
Property Rights	20.0 —	
Fdm. from Corruption	20.0 ▽	
Labor Freedom	84.8 ▲	

0 least free   50   100 most free
| = world average

BUSINESS FREEDOM — *72.1*

Recent reforms have somewhat enhanced the overall freedom to establish and run a business. Starting a business now requires about six days, compared to the world average of 35 days, and obtaining a business license takes less than the global average of 218 days.

TRADE FREEDOM — *80.3*

Belarus's weighted average tariff rate was 2.3 percent in 2008. Extensive import restrictions and quotas, licensing requirements, non-transparent and arbitrary regulations, weak enforcement of property rights, domestic preference in government procurement, and government subsidies add to the cost of trade. Fifteen points were deducted from Belarus's trade freedom score to account for non-tariff barriers.

FISCAL FREEDOM — *85.2*

Belarus has a relatively low income tax rate and a moderate corporate tax rate. In 2008, the top income tax rate dropped to a flat 12 percent from 30 percent. The top corporate tax rate is 24 percent. Other taxes include a value-added tax (VAT), a turnover tax on production of goods and provision of services, and an environmental tax for legal entities. Excise taxes on alcohol and tobacco were raised as of July 1, 2009. In the most recent year, overall tax revenue as a percentage of GDP was 27.5 percent.

GOVERNMENT SPENDING — *32*

Belarus's economy is highly centralized. Total government expenditures, including consumption and transfer payments, are high. In the most recent year, government spending equaled 47.6 percent of GDP. The government is seeking buyers for state-owned enterprises in energy and telecommunications, but privatization has stagnated.

MONETARY FREEDOM — *62.6*

Inflation has been very high, averaging 12.6 percent between 2006 and 2008. The government subsidizes many basic goods and services, sets prices of products made by state-owned enterprises, controls wages, and regulates retail-sector prices. Fifteen points were deducted from Belarus's monetary freedom score to adjust for measures that distort domestic prices.

INVESTMENT FREEDOM — *20*

The government discriminates against domestic and for-eign private parties in favor of state-owned businesses. Foreign investments undergo additional screening and are allowed only case-by-case. The government openly states that it wants to control all economic activity. Numerous industries remain the exclusive domain of the state, and profitable and strategic sectors are often under de facto government control. Inefficient bureaucracy, corruption, contradictory enforcement of regulations, lack of respect for law, and official resistance to the private sector hinder foreign investment. Foreigners and businesses may not own land. Capital transactions, resident and non-resident accounts, and current transfers are subject to restrictions. When expropriating property, the government generally alleges breaches of business law and offers no compensation.

FINANCIAL FREEDOM — *10*

Belarus's banking system remains heavily government-influenced, with commercial banks' lending practices subject to state pressure. Although 14 banks have been sold to foreign investors since 2006, the four largest state-owned banks account for more than 70 percent of total assets. Foreign banks face major impediments, and barriers to credit remain high. Businesses have access to various credit mechanisms, but long bureaucratic delays discourage smaller companies. The small non-bank financial sector is inhibited by state intervention and irregular regulatory enforcement. The stock market is small and largely dormant.

PROPERTY RIGHTS — *20*

The structure of property rights is unchanged since the Soviet period, with state ownership of land and government-controlled collective and state farms. The legal system does not fully protect private property, and inefficient courts do not enforce contracts consistently. The judiciary is neither independent nor objective by international standards. The government has wide scope to interfere in commercial transactions. In 2008, the government made registration, assessment, sales, and purchases of property somewhat less cumbersome, but the procedures are still highly bureaucratic and time-consuming. Independent lawyers cannot practice without a special license from the Ministry of Justice. Protection of intellectual property is weak.

FREEDOM FROM CORRUPTION — *20*

Corruption is perceived as pervasive. Belarus ranks 151st out of 179 countries in Transparency International's Corruption Perceptions Index for 2007. Owners of import–export businesses in particular complain of corruption at every point in a transaction. According to independent polls, corruption is most pervasive among local government officials, directors of large state enterprises, police, doctors, and teachers.

LABOR FREEDOM — *84.8*

Relatively flexible labor market regulations promote more job creation and productivity growth. The non-salary cost of employing a worker remains high, but dismissing a redundant employee is relatively easy.

BELGIUM

Economic Freedom Score

Least free 0   25   50   75   100 Most free

70.1

World Rank: **30**	Regional Rank: **16**

Belgium's economic freedom score is 70.1, making its economy the 30th freest in the 2010 *Index*. Its overall score has decreased 2.0 points from last year, primarily due to reductions in investment freedom and financial freedom. Belgium is ranked 16th freest among the 43 countries in the Europe region, and its overall score is above the regional and global averages.

The global financial crisis has sparked a sharp economic slowdown in Belgium. In response to the turmoil in the banking sector and the subsequent contraction in overall economic activity, the government has intervened to support the financial system and implement a moderate-sized fiscal stimulus package.

Although Belgium's economy has benefited from a long-standing commitment to economic freedom, there are lingering structural weaknesses that hinder reforms to enhance economic freedom and competitiveness. The tax system still relies too much on relatively growth-distorting taxes, and individual and corporate income tax rates are burdensome. Belgium's extensive welfare state is supported by exceptionally high government spending, and labor market rigidities remain a considerable barrier to facilitating productivity and job growth.

BACKGROUND: Belgium is a federal state consisting of three culturally different regions: Flanders, Wallonia, and the capital city of Brussels, which houses the headquarters of NATO and the European Union. Services account for 75 percent of economic activity. Leading exports are electrical equipment, vehicles, diamonds, and chemicals. After eight years in office, Guy Verhofstadt and his Liberal Party lost the 2007 general election, although they remained in office until March 2008 because of political deadlock. Christian Democrat Yves Leterme took over as premier, but his government resigned *en masse* in the wake of a bank scandal in December 2008. Christian Democrat Herman van Rompuy, formerly president of the Chamber of Representatives, became prime minister on January 5, 2009.

Country's Score Over Time

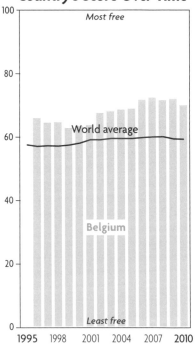

Quick Facts

Population: 10.7 million

GDP (PPP): $369.2 billion
     1.1% growth in 2008
     2.2% 5-year compound
       annual growth
     $34,493 per capita

Unemployment: 7.0%

Inflation (CPI): 4.5%

FDI Inflow: $59.7 billion

2008 data unless otherwise noted
Data compiled as of September 2009

How Do We Measure Economic Freedom?
See page 457 for an explanation of the methodology or visit the *Index* Web site at *heritage.org/index*.

BELGIUM'S TEN ECONOMIC FREEDOMS

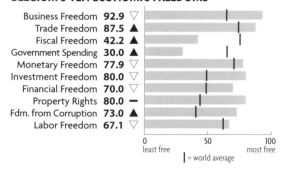

Business Freedom	92.9	▽
Trade Freedom	87.5	▲
Fiscal Freedom	42.2	▲
Government Spending	30.0	▲
Monetary Freedom	77.9	▽
Investment Freedom	80.0	▽
Financial Freedom	70.0	▽
Property Rights	80.0	—
Fdm. from Corruption	73.0	▲
Labor Freedom	67.1	▽

0 least free   50   100 most free

| = world average

BUSINESS FREEDOM — 92.9

The overall freedom to establish and run a business is strongly protected under Belgium's regulatory environment. Starting a business takes an average of four days, compared to the world average of 35 days. Obtaining a business license requires less than the world average of 18 procedures and 218 days.

TRADE FREEDOM — 87.5

Belgium's trade policy is the same as that of other members of the European Union. The common EU weighted average tariff rate was 1.3 percent in 2008. However, the EU has high or escalating tariffs for agricultural and manufacturing products, and its MFN tariff code is complex. Non-tariff barriers reflected in EU and Belgian policy include agricultural and manufacturing subsidies, quotas, import restrictions and bans for some goods and services, market access restrictions in some services sectors, non-transparent and restrictive regulations and standards, and inconsistent regulatory and customs administration among EU members. Ten points were deducted from Belgium's trade freedom score to account for non-tariff barriers.

FISCAL FREEDOM — 42.2

Belgium's income tax rate is one of the world's highest, and its corporate tax rate is moderately high. The top income tax rate is 50 percent, and the top corporate tax rate is effectively 34 percent (33 percent plus a 3 percent austerity tax charged on the income tax due). Other taxes include a value-added tax (VAT), a real property tax, and an estate tax. Rates of the latter two vary by region. In the most recent year, overall tax revenue as a percentage of GDP was 46.1 percent.

GOVERNMENT SPENDING — 30

Total government expenditures, including consumption and transfer payments, are very high. In the most recent year, government spending equaled 48.3 percent of GDP. A stimulus package includes utility subsidies, reduced social security contributions, and higher unemployment benefits.

MONETARY FREEDOM — 77.9

Belgium is a member of the euro zone. Between 2006 and 2008, the weighted average annual rate of inflation rose to 3.6 percent. As a participant in the EU's Common Agricultural Policy, the government subsidizes agricultural production, distorting the prices of agricultural products. Price-control policies affect water supply, waste handling, homes for the elderly, medicines and implantable medical devices, certain cars, compulsory insurance, fire insurance, petroleum products, cable television, and certain types of bread. Ten points were deducted from Belgium's monetary freedom score to account for these policies.

INVESTMENT FREEDOM — 80

Foreign investors may enter into joint ventures and partnerships on the same basis as domestic parties, except for such professions as doctors, lawyers, accountants, and architects. Permission is required to open department stores, provide transportation and security services, produce and sell certain food items, cut and polish diamonds, or sell firearms and ammunition. Bureaucracy can be cumbersome. There are no restrictions on the purchase of real estate, resident and non-resident foreign exchange accounts, repatriation of profit, or transfer of capital. If the government acquires property for a public purpose, adequate compensation is paid.

FINANCIAL FREEDOM — 70

Belgium's five largest banks account for around 85 percent of deposits, but domestic and foreign banks operate in a very competitive environment. Credit is allocated at market terms, but regional authorities may subsidize medium- and long-term borrowing. The insurance sector is smaller than the banking sector. Capital markets are integrated into Euronext, a broader European exchange. Responding to the global financial crisis, the government has bailed out several major banks. Other financial groups have received additional recapitalization, and the government has offered inter-bank loan guarantees.

PROPERTY RIGHTS — 80

Property ownership is protected, and contracts are secure. Laws are codified, and the judiciary and civil service, while often slow, are of high quality. Intellectual property rights are protected, but implementation of relevant EU directives is slow.

FREEDOM FROM CORRUPTION — 73

Corruption is perceived as minimal. Belgium ranks 18th out of 179 countries in Transparency International's Corruption Perceptions Index for 2008. Belgium outlaws both active bribery and "passive bribery," whereby officials request or accept bribes to benefit themselves or others in exchange for certain behavior.

LABOR FREEDOM — 67.1

Employment regulations are relatively flexible, but further reform would foster job creation and productivity growth. The non-salary cost of employing a worker remains high, and dismissing a redundant employee is relatively costly.

BELIZE

Economic Freedom Score

Least free 0   25   50   75   100   Most free

61.5

Belize's economic freedom score is 61.5, making its economy the 79th freest in the 2010 *Index*. Its overall score has declined 1.5 points from last year, primarily as a result of problems with respect for property rights and the rule of law. Belize is ranked 15th out of 29 countries in the South and Central America/Caribbean region.

Belize's macroeconomic performance has been uneven, and growth is affected by structural weaknesses in the economy. Burdensome tariff and non-tariff barriers, together with the high cost of domestic financing, hinder private-sector development. Infrastructure is inadequate and raises the cost of conducting entrepreneurial activity.

Belize's overall economic freedom remains constrained by other institutional weaknesses. Special licensing requirements discourage foreign investment in many sectors, and foreign exchange regulations are inconsistent and non-transparent. The judicial system remains vulnerable to political interference, and corruption is common. Despite a high top income tax rate, corporate taxes are relatively low, and the tax burden is not particularly large as a percentage of GDP. The government has explored the idea of tax reform to enhance competitiveness.

BACKGROUND: Belize is a parliamentary democracy and member of the British Commonwealth. In February 2008, the United Democratic Party defeated the incumbent People's United Party amid allegations of corruption, mismanagement of state-owned enterprises, botched telecommunications privatization, and extensive social problems. Prime Minister Dean Barrow has worked to restore confidence in government, but high public-sector debt leaves him little fiscal room to maneuver. Tourism and agriculture contribute significantly to the economy, but the growth of tourism and remittances has slowed. Output of sugar, the principal export, is falling, and reduced export demand has hurt citrus and shrimp production and depressed prices. Belize is plagued by crime, money-laundering, and one of the region's highest murder rates. International relations are dominated by a long-running territorial dispute with Guatemala and membership in CARICOM.

Country's Score Over Time

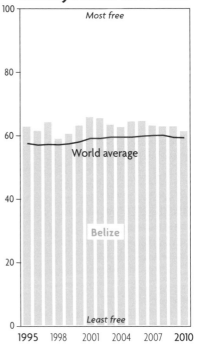

Quick Facts

Population: 0.3 million

GDP (PPP): $2.2 billion
3.0% growth in 2008
3.0% 5-year compound annual growth
$6,941 per capita

Unemployment: 8.1% (2007)

Inflation (CPI): 6.4%

FDI Inflow: $179 million

2008 data unless otherwise noted
Data compiled as of September 2009

How Do We Measure Economic Freedom?
See page 457 for an explanation of the methodology or visit the *Index* Web site at *heritage.org/index*.

BELIZE'S TEN ECONOMIC FREEDOMS

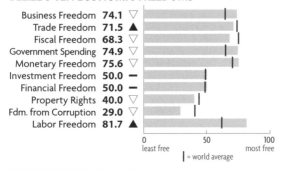

Business Freedom	74.1	▽
Trade Freedom	71.5	▲
Fiscal Freedom	68.3	▽
Government Spending	74.9	▽
Monetary Freedom	75.6	▽
Investment Freedom	50.0	—
Financial Freedom	50.0	—
Property Rights	40.0	▽
Fdm. from Corruption	29.0	▽
Labor Freedom	81.7	▲

0 least free — 50 — 100 most free

| = world average

BUSINESS FREEDOM — *74.1*

The overall freedom to start, operate, and close a business is relatively well protected under Belize's regulatory environment. Obtaining a business license takes less than the world average of 18 procedures and 218 days. The process for closing a business is relatively easy.

TRADE FREEDOM — *71.5*

Belize's weighted average tariff rate was 9.3 percent in 2008. Import restrictions, import licensing rules for some products, customs corruption, and weak enforcement of intellectual property rights add to the cost of trade. Ten points were deducted from Belize's trade freedom score to account for non-tariff barriers.

FISCAL FREEDOM — *68.3*

Belize has high income tax rates and a moderate corporate tax rate. The top income tax rate is 45 percent, and the top corporate tax rate is 25 percent. Other taxes include a goods and services tax (GST) and a stamp duty. In the most recent year, overall tax revenue as a percentage of GDP was 22.7 percent.

GOVERNMENT SPENDING — *74.9*

Total government expenditures, including consumption and transfer payments, are moderate. In the most recent year, government spending equaled 28.9 percent of GDP. Public debt is high, but continued and transparent fiscal consolidation should help to achieve the long-term debt strategy.

MONETARY FREEDOM — *75.6*

Inflation is increasing, averaging 5.2 percent between 2006 and 2008. The government maintains the prices of some basic commodities, such as rice, flour, beans, sugar, bread, butane gas, and fuel, and controls the retail price of electricity. Price controls are enforced only with respect to a handful of goods, although regulations define administrative prices or mark-ups for several other products. Ten points were deducted from Belize's monetary freedom score to adjust for measures that distort domestic prices.

INVESTMENT FREEDOM — *50*

Belize generally is non-discriminatory toward foreign investment, but there are restrictions in certain sectors. Full foreign ownership of businesses is legal, although the government encourages local partnerships. Laws and regulations do not significantly distort or impede investment, but bureaucracy can be non-transparent, and dispute resolution can be time-consuming. Residents and non-residents may hold foreign exchange accounts subject to government approval. Officially, no person other than authorized dealers and depositories may retain any foreign currency without the consent of the central bank. All capital transactions must be notified to or approved by the central bank. Applications to buy more than 10 acres of land require approval by the Ministerial Cabinet, and non-residents must obtain approval for the transfer of any land or buildings. The government must assess and pay appropriate compensation if it expropriates an asset.

FINANCIAL FREEDOM — *50*

Belize's financial system is small but growing, and obtaining credit is relatively straightforward. Bank credit to the private sector reached approximately 70 percent of GDP in 2008. There are five commercial banks, eight international banks, and several quasi-government banks. Over the past decade, government policy has fostered development of offshore financial activities. Subsidiaries of foreign banks are competitive, but approval is required to secure a foreign currency loan from outside Belize, and only authorized dealers may retain foreign currency. The government influences the allocation of credit through the quasi-government banks. Although the financial system has remained largely insulated from the global financial crisis, non-performing loans increased considerably in 2008.

PROPERTY RIGHTS — *40*

The judiciary, though constitutionally independent, is subject to political influence. There is a severe lack of trained prosecutors, and police officers often assume that role in the magistrates' courts. There are lengthy trial backlogs. Expropriation of personal property is relatively rare. Many property disputes involve foreign investors and landowners, and it is often difficult to trace the ownership history or specific borders of land holdings. Protection of intellectual property rights is lax.

FREEDOM FROM CORRUPTION — *29*

Corruption is perceived as widespread. Belize ranks 109th out of 179 countries in Transparency International's Corruption Perceptions Index for 2008, a decline from 2007. Money laundering, primarily related to narcotics trafficking and contraband smuggling, occurs through banks operating in Belize. The former prime minister and former minister of home affairs were arrested in 2008 and charged with theft of $10 million, the proceeds of a grant from Venezuela.

LABOR FREEDOM — *81.7*

Flexible employment regulations enhance employment and productivity growth. The non-salary cost of employing a worker is low, and dismissing a redundant employee can be costless.

● Porto-Novo

BENIN

Economic Freedom Score

25   50   75

Least free 0 .... 100 Most free

55.4

Benin's economic freedom score is 55.4, making its economy the 115th freest in the 2010 *Index*. Its overall score is unchanged from last year because improved scores in fiscal freedom and investment freedom were largely countered by reductions in trade freedom and financial freedom. Benin is ranked 18th out of 46 countries in the Sub-Saharan Africa region, and its overall score is slightly higher than the regional average.

Although the economy is not very diversified, Benin's entrepreneurial environment benefits from a relatively stable political and macroeconomic situation. The government has introduced structural reforms to revitalize the economy, and privatization of state-owned enterprises has continued. Inefficient regulation and the lack of institutional capacity to fully implement necessary reforms are the main obstacles to greater economic freedom.

The most visible constraints on private-sector development are related to fiscal pressure, administrative complexities, and lack of respect for contracts. Bureaucratic inefficiency and corruption affect much of the economy. Court enforcement of property rights remains vulnerable to political interference. High individual and corporate income tax rates impede entrepreneurial activity and fuel the growth of the informal sector.

BACKGROUND: President Mathieu Kérékou, who ruled in Marxist–Leninist fashion for almost 20 years following a military coup, stepped down following a democratic transition in the early 1990s and later served two five-year elected terms. Current President Boni Yayi, former head of the West African Development Bank, came to power in 2006 in elections that were generally regarded as free and fair. Benin remains underdeveloped and dependent on subsistence agriculture and cotton, which is the main commercial crop and accounts for over 40 percent of foreign exchange earnings, 17 percent of exports, and about 7 percent of GDP. Trade with neighboring countries, particularly re-export of goods to Nigeria, is extensive, though much economic activity, including trade, is in the informal sector.

Country's Score Over Time

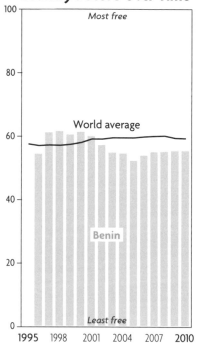

Quick Facts

Population: 8.7 million

GDP (PPP): $12.7 billion
     5.1% growth in 2008
     4.1% 5-year compound
       annual growth
     $1,468 per capita

Unemployment: n/a

Inflation (CPI): 8.0%

FDI Inflow: $120 million

2008 data unless otherwise noted
Data compiled as of September 2009

How Do We Measure Economic Freedom?
See page 457 for an explanation of the methodology or visit the *Index* Web site at *heritage.org/index*.

BENIN'S TEN ECONOMIC FREEDOMS

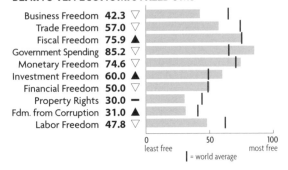

Business Freedom	42.3 ▽	
Trade Freedom	57.0 ▽	
Fiscal Freedom	75.9 ▲	
Government Spending	85.2 ▽	
Monetary Freedom	74.6 ▽	
Investment Freedom	60.0 ▲	
Financial Freedom	50.0 ▽	
Property Rights	30.0 —	
Fdm. from Corruption	31.0 ▲	
Labor Freedom	47.8 ▽	

0 least free   50   100 most free

| = world average

BUSINESS FREEDOM — 42.3

The overall freedom to start, operate, and close a business is significantly limited by Benin's regulatory environment. Starting a business takes an average of 31 days, compared to the world average of 35 days. Obtaining a business license takes more than the world average of 218 days. Closing a business can be burdensome.

TRADE FREEDOM — 57

Benin's weighted average tariff rate was 16.5 percent in 2008. Customs inefficiency and corruption, restrictions on some imports, and import taxes add to the cost of trade, and the enforcement of intellectual property rights is inadequate. Ten points were deducted from Benin's trade freedom score to account for non-tariff barriers.

FISCAL FREEDOM — 75.9

Benin has relatively high tax rates. The top income tax rate is 35 percent, and the top corporate tax rate is 30 percent. Oil companies are subject to a special rate of 45 percent. Other taxes include a value-added tax (VAT), a property tax, and a tax on insurance contracts. In the most recent year, overall tax revenue as a percentage of GDP was 16.9 percent.

GOVERNMENT SPENDING — 85.2

Total government expenditures, including consumption and transfer payments, are relatively low. In the most recent year, government spending equaled 22.2 percent of GDP. In 2008, partial privatization of the state-owned Sonapra cotton company and Continental Bank–Benin was completed. Energy shortages and high electricity costs cripple the private sector.

MONETARY FREEDOM — 74.6

As a member of the West African Economic and Monetary Union, Benin uses the CFA franc, which is pegged to the euro. Inflation is moderate but rising, averaging 5.9 percent between 2006 and 2008. The government regulates prices in the state-owned water, telecommunications, and electricity sectors, and the parastatal cotton sector benefits from government subsidies and price supports. State subsidies to the troubled electricity sector have jumped, as have public-sector wages. Ten points were deducted from Benin's monetary freedom score to adjust for measures that distort domestic prices.

INVESTMENT FREEDOM — 60

Benin officially encourages foreign investment, and foreign investors have taken advantage of opportunities linked to the privatization of state-owned enterprises, which have been reduced from 130 in 1980 to four today. Bureaucracy is inefficient and subject to corruption. Judicial resolution of civil disputes is time-consuming. International intellectual property agreements are not adequately enforced. Transfers exceeding 300,000 FCFA (approximately $600) to a Western country other than France require central bank and government approval. There are no restrictions on remittance of profits by companies, but remittances by individual resident investors can be restricted. There are no controls on the purchase of land by non-residents, except for investments in enterprises, branches, or corporations. The government can seize property by eminent domain but is required to pay compensation to the owners.

FINANCIAL FREEDOM — 50

Benin's financial sector has been expanding. Enforcement of contracts, transparency, and fraud prevention are weak. The Central Bank of West African States governs Benin's financial institutions, and regulatory oversight can be unwieldy. Banking is predominantly private, and foreign ownership in banking and insurance is allowed. Credit is allocated on market terms and available without discrimination. Banks experience difficulty with non-performing loans and recovering collateral on those loans. There has been noticeable development of microfinance institutions, but bank penetration remains low. The government has pursued the National Microfinance Development Strategy and taken steps to support activities in the financial sector.

PROPERTY RIGHTS — 30

Benin's legal system is weak and subject to corruption. Businesses and other litigants routinely complain that corruption is particularly widespread at the trial court level and in administrative hearings. There are no separate commercial courts, and backlogs of civil cases cause long delays. International donor assistance projects aim to improve the judiciary by training staff and expanding physical capacity.

FREEDOM FROM CORRUPTION — 31

Corruption is perceived as widespread. Benin ranks 96th out of 179 countries in Transparency International's Corruption Perceptions Index for 2008, an improvement over 2007. Despite prosecution of several high-profile cases against corrupt officials, government corruption continues to blight economic growth and deter investment.

LABOR FREEDOM — 47.8

Restrictive employment regulations hinder job creation and productivity growth. Restrictions on increasing or contracting the number of working hours are rigid. The non-salary cost of employing a worker is high, but dismissing a redundant employee can be relatively inexpensive.

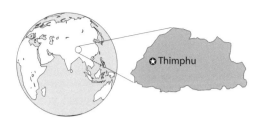

BHUTAN

World Rank: 103   **Regional Rank: 17**

Bhutan's economic freedom score is 57.0, making its economy the 103rd freest in the 2010 *Index*. Its score has declined 0.7 point from last year, primarily because of a reduction in investment freedom that was only partially offset by a gain in trade freedom. Bhutan is ranked 17th freest among the 41 countries in the Asia–Pacific region, and its overall score is slightly below the global average.

Despite strong economic growth over the past five years, driven largely by hydropower, Bhutan remains an underdeveloped economy with a poverty rate of around 30 percent. The public sector has long been the main source of economic growth, but the government now recognizes that developing the private sector is critical. The government has placed a higher priority on efforts to diversify the economy, particularly in light of demographic shifts that will bring more young people into the labor market.

Key constraints on private-sector development include inefficient and arbitrary regulation, limited access to financing, and an underdeveloped investment code. The financial sector remains small and without adequate regulation or supervision. Bhutan scores above the world average in fiscal freedom, monetary freedom, freedom from corruption, and labor freedom. Taxation of personal and corporate income is moderate, and flexible employment regulations and stable labor relations are potential advantages for private-sector development.

BACKGROUND: Bhutan, a small Himalayan constitutional monarchy that made the transition from absolute monarchy to parliamentary democracy in March 2008, has one of the world's smallest and least-developed economies. Until a few decades ago, this still largely agrarian country had no roads, electricity, or hospitals. Rugged terrain makes the development of infrastructure difficult, but recent interregional economic cooperation, particularly the development of trade with Bangladesh and India, is helping to spur economic growth. Bhutan's international trade has long been dominated by India, and connections to global markets are limited.

Country's Score Over Time

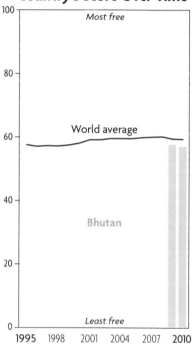

Quick Facts

Population: 0.7 million

GDP (PPP): $3.3 billion
13.8% growth in 2008
10.0% 5-year compound annual growth
$4,755 per capita

Unemployment: 3.7% (2007)

Inflation (CPI): 7.7%

FDI Inflow: $30 million

2008 data unless otherwise noted
Data compiled as of September 2009

How Do We Measure Economic Freedom?
See page 457 for an explanation of the methodology or visit the *Index* Web site at *heritage.org/index.*

BHUTAN'S TEN ECONOMIC FREEDOMS

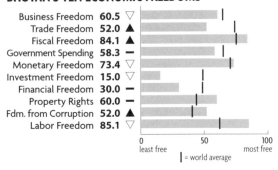

Business Freedom	60.5	▽
Trade Freedom	52.0	▲
Fiscal Freedom	84.1	▲
Government Spending	58.3	—
Monetary Freedom	73.4	▽
Investment Freedom	15.0	▽
Financial Freedom	30.0	—
Property Rights	60.0	—
Fdm. from Corruption	52.0	▲
Labor Freedom	85.1	▽

0 least free   50   100 most free

| = world average

BUSINESS FREEDOM — 60.5

The overall freedom to establish and run a business is constrained by Bhutan's regulatory environment. Starting a business takes an average of 46 days, compared to the world average of 35 days. Obtaining a business license requires 25 procedures, compared to the world average of 18.

TRADE FREEDOM — 52

Bhutan's weighted average tariff rate in 2007 was 16.5 percent. Import and export restrictions, services market access restrictions, inadequate infrastructure and trade capacity, underdeveloped markets, and non-transparent and arbitrary regulation add to the cost of trade. Fifteen points were deducted from Bhutan's trade freedom score to account for non-tariff barriers.

FISCAL FREEDOM — 84.1

Bhutan has moderate income and corporate tax rates. The top income tax rate is 25 percent, and the corporate tax rate is 30 percent. Other taxes include a motor vehicle tax, a property tax, and an excise tax. In the most recent year, overall tax revenue as a percentage of GDP was 7.9 percent. A long-term economic development policy under consideration is expected to include criteria for broad tax exemptions.

GOVERNMENT SPENDING — 58.3

Total government expenditures, including consumption and transfer payments, are relatively high. In the most recent year, government spending equaled 37.3 percent of GDP. The tenth five-year development plan (2008–2013) advocates tightened fiscal management. Public spending is targeted toward transportation infrastructure and hydropower.

MONETARY FREEDOM — 73.4

Inflation has been high, averaging 6.8 percent between 2006 and 2008. The government maintains an effective monopoly on imports of rationed goods such as fertilizer, kerosene, and liquefied petroleum gas, providing these goods to domestic users at subsidized prices. Ten points were deducted from Bhutan's monetary freedom score to adjust for the lack of competition and broad-based ownership in the economy.

INVESTMENT FREEDOM — 15

All foreign investments are approved on a case-by-case

basis, and no firm has had majority foreign ownership until recently. Foreign direct investment has been a sensitive issue, largely because of concerns about its effect on culture and traditions and possibly because of the domestic private sector's unwillingness to lose the benefits that restrictions provide. Foreign exchange and capital transactions are subject to government controls. Foreign investors may not purchase land.

FINANCIAL FREEDOM — 30

Bhutan's financial sector is small, and an underdeveloped regulatory framework limits access to capital for local entrepreneurs. Two state-owned commercial banks have branches around the country. The Bank of Bhutan enjoyed a monopoly for many years, but competition has improved with the establishment of the Bhutan National Bank and the opening of the sector to more foreign partnerships. There has been rapid expansion of bank credit to the private sector, with private credit reaching about 20 percent of GDP. The government owns the Bhutan Development Finance Corporation and the Royal Insurance Corporation of Bhutan; both have high levels of non-performing loans. Credit is not always allocated on market terms. Foreign exchange is tightly regulated, and the currency is not convertible. The four state-owned financial institutions dominate the Royal Securities Exchange. Bhutan needs a more efficient and competitive financial sector to mobilize savings and channel long-term capital to facilitate development of the private sector.

PROPERTY RIGHTS — 60

In trying to integrate its small economy into the world, Bhutan has taken steps to facilitate development of the private sector. Protections of intellectual property rights are stipulated in the Industrial Property Act of the Kingdom of Bhutan and the Copyright Act of the Kingdom of Bhutan. The Ministry of Trade and Industry's Intellectual Property Division is responsible for implementing intellectual property policies. Property rights are more equally protected than in most of South Asia, with women rather than men inheriting and owning property in some areas.

FREEDOM FROM CORRUPTION — 52

Corruption is perceived as present. Bhutan ranks 45th out of 179 countries in Transparency International's Corruption Perceptions Index for 2008. The government's Anti-Corruption Commission has identified misuse of resources, bribery and collusion, and nepotism as major forms of corruption.

LABOR FREEDOM — 85.1

Flexible employment regulations facilitate overall productivity growth. The non-salary cost of employing a worker is moderate, and dismissing a redundant employee is relatively easy. However, the formal labor market is not fully developed, and a more dynamic private sector is critical to correcting the imbalance between labor supply and demand.

BOLIVIA

World Rank: 146   **Regional Rank: 25**

Economic Freedom Score

25   50   75

Least free 0   100 Most free

49.4

Bolivia's economic freedom score is 49.4, making its economy the 146th freest in the 2010 *Index*. Its overall score is 4.2 points worse than last year, with declines in nine of the 10 economic freedoms. Bolivia is ranked 25th out of 29 countries in the South and Central America/Caribbean region, and its overall score is below the world and regional averages.

Privatization and liberalization half-measures have led to marginal investment and economic growth. The hydrocarbon sector has been the major source of relatively high income growth in the past five years. Overall economic development has been uneven, and poverty remains daunting. Improving the investment and business climate remains an urgent priority.

Persistent institutional weaknesses impede creation of a more vibrant private sector. Pervasive corruption and onerous regulation are major hurdles for foreign and domestic investment. Rule of law is weak, and private property is vulnerable to bureaucratic interference or even expropriation. Restrictive labor laws hamper employment and productivity growth. More than half of the workforce is estimated to work in the shadow economy.

BACKGROUND: Almost two-thirds of Bolivia's people live in poverty, engaged primarily in subsistence agriculture. From the mid-1980s until 2005, successive elected governments pursued economic and social reform. The government of President Sanchez de Lozada (1993–1997) reduced government intervention through partial privatization and lower taxes and tariffs. A 1999 economic downturn created fiscal pressures, and proposed tax hikes sparked social unrest. Mobs removed two presidents from office in 2003 and 2005, and anti-market populist Evo Morales took office in 2006. Morales engineered a new constitution that expanded executive power, land redistribution, and state control of key natural resources and industries. His concentration of power has been somewhat contained by the opposition-controlled Senate and state governors seeking greater autonomy. Internal divisions led to a serious outbreak of violence in September 2008.

Country's Score Over Time

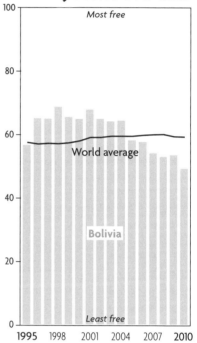

Quick Facts

Population: 9.7 million

GDP (PPP): $41.4 billion
6.1% growth in 2008
4.9% 5-year compound annual growth
$4,278 per capita

Unemployment: 7.5% (2007)

Inflation (CPI): 14.0%

FDI Inflow: $513 million

2008 data unless otherwise noted
Data compiled as of September 2009

How Do We Measure Economic Freedom?
See page 457 for an explanation of the methodology or visit the *Index* Web site at *heritage.org/index.*

BOLIVIA'S TEN ECONOMIC FREEDOMS

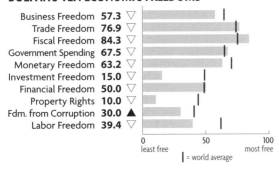

Business Freedom	57.3 ▽	
Trade Freedom	76.9 ▽	
Fiscal Freedom	84.3 ▽	
Government Spending	67.5 ▽	
Monetary Freedom	63.2 ▽	
Investment Freedom	15.0 ▽	
Financial Freedom	50.0 ▽	
Property Rights	10.0 ▽	
Fdm. from Corruption	30.0 ▲	
Labor Freedom	39.4 ▽	

0 least free   50   100 most free

| = world average

BUSINESS FREEDOM — 57.3

The overall freedom to establish and run a business is restricted by Bolivia's regulatory environment. Starting a business takes an average of 50 days, compared to the world average of 35 days. Obtaining a business license requires about the world average of 18 procedures and more than the world average of 218 days.

TRADE FREEDOM — 76.9

Bolivia's weighted average tariff rate was 4.1 percent in 2008. Inconsistent customs valuation, import bans and restrictions, domestic preference in government procurement, inconsistent sanitary and phytosanitary rules, export subsidies, customs corruption, weak infrastructure, and issues related to the enforcement and protection of intellectual property rights add to the costs of trade. Fifteen points were deducted from Bolivia's trade freedom score to account for non-tariff barriers.

FISCAL FREEDOM — 84.3

Bolivia has a relatively low income tax and a moderate corporate tax. The top income tax rate is 13 percent, and the corporate tax rate is 25 percent. Other taxes include a value-added tax (VAT) and a transaction tax. In the most recent year, overall tax revenue as a percentage of GDP was 27.8 percent.

GOVERNMENT SPENDING — 67.5

Total government expenditures, including consumption and transfer payments, are moderate. In the most recent year, government spending equaled 32.9 percent of GDP. Strategic sectors (hydrocarbons and telecommunications) are nationalized, public spending is on the rise, and budgetary management is weak.

MONETARY FREEDOM — 63.2

Inflation has accelerated rapidly, averaging 11.8 percent between 2006 and 2008. Regulations control prices for most public utilities, petroleum products, and potable water. Fifteen points were deducted from Bolivia's monetary freedom score to adjust for measures that distort domestic prices.

INVESTMENT FREEDOM — 15

The law provides for equal treatment of foreign and domestic firms. Residents and non-residents may hold foreign exchange accounts. President Morales has "nationalized"

the hydrocarbons industry (forcing companies to negotiate new contracts and offering the state-owned oil company majority control of five firms) and telecommunications, with mining, forestry, electricity, and transportation as other possible targets. Under the 2009 constitution, all hydrocarbon deposits belong to the government. Despite a relatively transparent investment code, private investment is hindered by arbitrary implementation, cumbersome bureaucracy, pervasive corruption, uncertainty about future nationalizations, and social unrest. There are minimal restrictions on currency transfers or remittances. The government can expropriate property, and competing claims to land titles and the absence of reliable dispute resolution create risk and uncertainty in real property acquisition.

FINANCIAL FREEDOM — 50

Bolivia's financial system remains generally weak and poorly supervised, but it has grown and become more open. There are 12 commercial banks, of which three are foreign-owned, and 45 non-bank financial institutions. Credit is generally allocated on market terms, but domestic collateral is required. Credit to the private sector has expanded very slowly. The development of a modern securities exchange is undermined by political and social unrest. Capital markets are focused on trading in government bonds, although corporate debt and mutual funds have grown. There are no restrictions on remittances or currency transfers.

PROPERTY RIGHTS — 10

Article 308 of a new constitution promulgated in 2009 states that "the private accumulation of economic power" will not be permitted to "endanger the economic sovereignty of the State" and that the "the right to own private property either individually or collectively [must] fulfill a social function" and "not harm the collective interest." Although other statutes guarantee property rights, the judicial process is subject to political influence and corruption. Enforcement of intellectual property rights is erratic and largely ineffective. Competing claims to land titles and the absence of reliable dispute resolution make acquisition of real property risky. Expropriation is a real possibility, as is illegal squatting on rural private property.

FREEDOM FROM CORRUPTION — 30

Corruption is perceived as pervasive. Bolivia ranks 102nd out of 179 countries in Transparency International's Corruption Perceptions Index for 2008. Officials accused of corruption are rarely prosecuted or convicted. A government report has rated the national police, customs, and justice system as the most corrupt institutions.

LABOR FREEDOM — 39.4

Restrictive employment regulations hinder job creation and productivity growth. The government has established minimum wages for the public and private sectors. The non-salary cost of employing a worker is moderate, but overall rigidity in hiring and firing is quite high.

BOSNIA AND HERZEGOVINA

Sarajevo◉

World Rank: 110   **Regional Rank: 39**

Economic Freedom Score

25   50   75

Least free 0   100 Most free

56.2

Bosnia and Herzegovina's economic freedom score is 56.2, making its economy the 110th freest in the 2010 *Index*. Its overall score is 3.1 points higher than last year, with significant improvements in fiscal freedom, investment freedom, and labor freedom. Bosnia and Herzegovina is ranked 39th freest among the 43 countries in the Europe region, and its overall score remains well below the regional average.

After several years of robust growth and monetary stability, the economy of Bosnia and Herzegovina deteriorated markedly in 2009, partly because of the global economic crisis and the generally slow pace of transition to greater economic freedom. The entrepreneurial environment has been improving but remains one of the region's most difficult and inefficient.

Further reforms are needed to tackle bureaucracy and reduce petty corruption. Without significant progress in revitalizing the privatization of large-scale enterprises, reforming the judicial system, and improving the enforcement of laws on competition and bankruptcy procedures, the encouraging growth of previous years is unlikely to resume, leaving much of the country mired in poverty and high unemployment.

BACKGROUND: The 1995 Dayton Agreement ended three years of fighting and finalized Bosnia and Herzegovina's secession from the former Yugoslavia. Under a loose central government, two separate entities exist along ethnic lines: the Republika Srpska (Serbian) and the Federation of Bosnia and Herzegovina (Muslim/Croat). The rule of law is weak, and local courts are subject to substantial political interference and lack the resources to prosecute complex crimes. Intrusive bureaucracy and costly registration procedures reflect a history of central planning. The economy relies heavily on agriculture. The European Union signed a Stabilization and Association Agreement with Bosnia and Herzegovina in June 2008, moving closer to EU membership. Progress toward membership in NATO slowed somewhat in 2009 because of member countries' concerns about the lack of progress on needed reform.

Country's Score Over Time

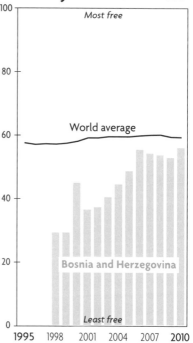

100 — Most free

80 —

60 — World average

40 —

20 — Bosnia and Herzegovina

0 — Least free

1995   1998   2001   2004   2007   2010

Quick Facts

Population: 3.8 million

GDP (PPP): $31.7 billion
6.0% growth in 2008
5.8% 5-year compound annual growth
$8,390 per capita

Unemployment: 29.0% (2007)

Inflation (CPI): 7.4%

FDI Inflow: $1.0 billion

2008 data unless otherwise noted
Data compiled as of September 2009

How Do We Measure Economic Freedom?
See page 457 for an explanation of the methodology or visit the *Index* Web site at *heritage.org/index.*

BOSNIA & HERZEGOVINA'S TEN ECONOMIC FREEDOMS

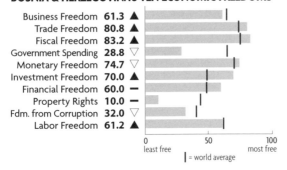

Business Freedom	61.3	▲
Trade Freedom	80.8	▲
Fiscal Freedom	83.2	▲
Government Spending	28.8	▽
Monetary Freedom	74.7	▽
Investment Freedom	70.0	▲
Financial Freedom	60.0	—
Property Rights	10.0	—
Fdm. from Corruption	32.0	▽
Labor Freedom	61.2	▲

0 least free — 50 — 100 most free
| = world average

BUSINESS FREEDOM — 61.3

The overall freedom to establish and run a business is limited by Bosnia and Herzegovina's national regulatory environment. Starting a business takes an average of 60 days, compared to the world average of 35 days. Obtaining a business license takes more than the world average of 218 days.

TRADE FREEDOM — 80.8

Bosnia and Herzegovina's weighted average tariff rate was 4.6 percent in 2008. Import and export restrictions, non-transparent regulations and government procurement, additional import duties on agriculture products, and numerous border fees add to the cost of trade. Enforcement of intellectual property rights remains problematic. Ten points were deducted from Bosnia and Herzegovina's trade freedom score to account for non-tariff barriers.

FISCAL FREEDOM — 83.2

Bosnia and Herzegovina's various governing entities have different tax policies. The top income tax rate is 10 percent, down from 15 percent. The top corporate tax rate is also 10 percent, down from 30 percent. Other taxes include a value-added tax (VAT), a sales tax, and a property tax. In the most recent year, overall tax revenue as a percentage of GDP was 38.5 percent.

GOVERNMENT SPENDING — 28.8

Total government expenditures, including consumption and transfer payments, are high. Privatization efforts have had mixed success. A Fiscal Council was established in 2008 to address problems with national fiscal coordination. In the most recent year, government spending equaled 48.7 percent of GDP.

MONETARY FREEDOM — 74.7

Inflation is rising, averaging 5.8 percent between 2006 and 2008. Price controls apply to electricity, gas, and telecommunications services. Ten points were deducted from Bosnia and Herzegovina's monetary freedom score to adjust for measures that distort domestic prices.

INVESTMENT FREEDOM — 70

The law accords foreign investors the same rights as domestic investors. With the exception of armaments and media, where foreign control is limited to 49 percent, there are no restrictions on investment. The right to transfer and repatriate profits and remittances immediately is guaranteed, and local and foreign companies may hold accounts in one or more banks that are authorized to initiate or receive payments in foreign currency. A multi-tiered and divided two-entity government creates a confusing array of regulations, fees, taxation, and standards requirements. Foreign investors continue to face serious obstacles, including a complex legal and regulatory framework, non-transparent business procedures, and a weak judiciary. Myriad state and municipal administrations result in a non-transparent bureaucratic system that creates opportunities for corruption. Privatization of state-owned enterprises has lagged behind the other countries in the region. There are few restrictions on capital transactions and foreign exchange accounts. The law prohibits expropriation and nationalization of assets, except under special circumstances and with due compensation.

FINANCIAL FREEDOM — 60

More reform has taken place in the financial sector than in any other area of economic activity. The banking system has expanded quickly in recent years, and consolidation and privatization have followed. Most banks are in private hands, accounting for more than 80 percent of banking capital. There is easy access to capital and a wide range of services. The presence of foreign-owned banks is strong, accounting for over 90 percent of total banking assets. Long-term lending is still hindered by insufficient enforcement of contracts and the poor regulatory environment. The central bank has attempted to consolidate financial oversight, but the process has stalled. Capital markets remain underdeveloped. Each region has a slowly growing non-bank financial sector and a small stock exchange. There are no restrictions on payments and transfers related to international current and capital transactions.

PROPERTY RIGHTS — 10

Property registers are largely unreliable, leaving property transfers open to dispute. The judicial system does not cover commercial activities adequately. Court decisions are difficult to enforce. Contracts are almost unenforceable, and the implementation of laws protecting intellectual property rights is inadequate.

FREEDOM FROM CORRUPTION — 32

Corruption is perceived as widespread. Bosnia and Herzegovina ranks 92nd out of 179 countries in Transparency International's Corruption Perceptions Index for 2008. Corruption remains prevalent in many political and economic institutions. Judges typically request bribes and respond to pressure from public officials. Business registration and licensing are particularly vulnerable to corruption.

LABOR FREEDOM — 61.2

Relatively inflexible employment regulations hinder employment creation and productivity growth. The non-salary cost of employing a worker is moderate, but an inflexible wage-determination system hinders job creation and mobility.

BOTSWANA

Economic Freedom Score

Least free 0   25   50   75   100 Most free

70.3

B otswana's economic freedom score is 70.3, making its economy the 28th freest in the 2010 *Index*. Its overall score is 0.6 point better than last year. Botswana is ranked 2nd out of 46 countries in the Sub-Saharan Africa region, and its overall score is well above the regional and world averages.

Botswana is a regional leader in economic freedom. Competitiveness and flexibility are promoted by a sensible business regulatory environment, openness to foreign investment and trade, and relatively flexible employment regulations. The financial sector remains relatively well developed, with an independent central bank and little government intervention. The independent judiciary provides strong protection of property rights.

The economy depends heavily on exports, particularly of minerals, and has contracted because of the global recession. Monetary stability has deteriorated as well. In an effort to move away from dependence on diamond production, the government has instituted competitive corporate tax rates, streamlined the application process for business ventures, and committed to increased transparency. Another priority has been to enhance business profitability and regional competitiveness with a more efficient investment code.

BACKGROUND: The Botswana Democratic Party has governed this multi-party democracy since the achievement of independence in 1966. Ian Khama assumed the presidency in 2008 as hand-picked successor to former President Festus Mogae. With significant natural resources and a market-oriented economy that encourages private enterprise, Botswana has Africa's highest sovereign credit rating. Despite efforts to diversify the economy, minerals (principally diamonds) accounted for 75 percent of exports in 2006 and 42 percent of GDP and 50 percent of government revenue in 2006–2007. Botswana has worked with other countries in the Southern African Development Community to address the political turmoil in neighboring Zimbabwe and the influx of Zimbabwean refugees. The country has one of the world's highest HIV/AIDS infection rates.

Country's Score Over Time

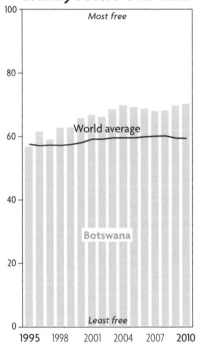

Quick Facts

Population: 1.9 million

GDP (PPP): $25.5 billion
   −1.0% growth in 2008
   3.5% 5-year compound
      annual growth
   $13,392 per capita

Unemployment: 7.5% (2007)

Inflation (CPI): 12.6%

FDI Inflow: −$4 million

2008 data unless otherwise noted
Data compiled as of September 2009

How Do We Measure Economic Freedom?
See page 457 for an explanation of the methodology or visit the *Index* Web site at *heritage.org/index*.

BOTSWANA'S TEN ECONOMIC FREEDOMS

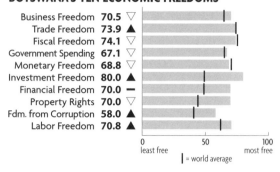

Business Freedom	70.5	▽
Trade Freedom	73.9	▲
Fiscal Freedom	74.1	▽
Government Spending	67.1	▽
Monetary Freedom	68.8	▽
Investment Freedom	80.0	▲
Financial Freedom	70.0	—
Property Rights	70.0	▽
Fdm. from Corruption	58.0	▲
Labor Freedom	70.8	▲

0 least free — 50 — 100 most free

| = world average

BUSINESS FREEDOM — 70.5

The overall freedom to establish and run a business is relatively well protected under Botswana's regulatory environment. Obtaining a business license takes less than the world average of 218 days. The government has established a one-stop shop for investors, and the process for closing a business is easy and straightforward.

TRADE FREEDOM — 73.9

Botswana's weighted average tariff rate was 8 percent in 2008. There are very few non-tariff barriers, but import bans and restrictions on some products, import taxes, import licensing, domestic bias in government procurement, and weak enforcement of intellectual property rights add to the cost of trade. Ten points were deducted from Botswana's trade freedom score to account for non-tariff barriers.

FISCAL FREEDOM — 74.1

Botswana's tax rates remain among the lowest in Southern Africa. Both the top income tax rate and the top corporate tax rate are 25 percent. Other taxes include a value-added tax (VAT), a property tax, and an inheritance tax. In the most recent year, overall tax revenue as a percentage of GDP was 36.6 percent.

GOVERNMENT SPENDING — 67.1

Total government expenditures, including consumption and transfer payments, are moderate. In the most recent year, government spending equaled 33.1 percent of GDP. Parliament began a review of the draft National Development Plan in 2009, but implementation is expected to be put off until mid-2010 at the earliest.

MONETARY FREEDOM — 68.8

Inflation has been high, averaging 11.2 percent between 2006 and 2008. Most prices are set by the market, but the government maintains price policies for some agricultural and livestock goods and is able to influence prices through numerous state-owned enterprises and service providers. Ten points were deducted from Botswana's monetary freedom score to adjust for measures that distort domestic prices.

INVESTMENT FREEDOM — 80

While generally open to foreign participation in its econ-omy, Botswana reserves a number of sectors for citizen participation. Increased foreign investment plays a significant role in the privatization of state-owned enterprises. Investment regulations are transparent, and bureaucratic procedures are streamlined and open, although somewhat slow. Investment returns such as profits and dividends, debt service, capital gains, returns on intellectual property, royalties, franchise fees, and service fees can be repatriated without limits. Foreign exchange is not difficult to obtain, and there are no restrictions on foreign exchange accounts or international transfers. The constitution prohibits the nationalization of private property.

FINANCIAL FREEDOM — 70

Botswana's competitive banking system is one of Africa's most advanced. Generally adhering to global standards in the transparency of financial policies and banking supervision, the financial sector provides ample access to credit for entrepreneurs. The opening of Capital Bank in 2008 brought the total number of licensed banks to eight. The government is involved in banking through state-owned financial institutions and a special financial incentives program that is aimed at increasing Botswana's status as a financial center. Credit is allocated on market terms, although the government provides subsidized loans. Reform of non-bank financial institutions has continued in recent years, notably through the establishment of a single financial regulatory agency that provides more effective supervision. The government has abolished exchange controls, and with the resulting creation of new portfolio investment options, the Botswana Stock Exchange is growing.

PROPERTY RIGHTS — 70

The constitution prohibits the nationalization of private property and provides for an independent judiciary, and the government respects this in practice. The legal system is sufficient to conduct secure commercial dealings, although a serious and growing backlog of cases prevents timely trials. The protection of intellectual property rights has improved significantly. Botswana is ranked second only to South Africa among sub-Saharan Africa countries in the 2009 International Property Rights Index.

FREEDOM FROM CORRUPTION — 58

Corruption is perceived as present. Botswana ranks 36th out of 179 countries in Transparency International's Corruption Perceptions Index for 2008 and remains Africa's least corrupt country. It is ahead of many European and Asian countries and has a proven record of honest economic governance.

LABOR FREEDOM — 70.8

Botswana's employment regulations are relatively flexible. The non-salary cost of employing a worker is very low, and dismissing a redundant employee can be almost costless. Employers are not required to make pension, health insurance, and unemployment insurance contributions.

BRAZIL

Economic Freedom Score

Least free 0 — 25 — 50 — 75 — 100 Most free

55.6

| World Rank: **113** | Regional Rank: **21** |

Brazil's economic freedom score is 55.6, making its economy the 113th freest in the 2010 *Index*. Its score is 1.1 points lower than last year as a result of declines in investment freedom and labor freedom. Brazil is ranked 21st out of 29 countries in the South and Central America/Caribbean region, and its overall score is below the regional and world averages.

In addition to its large agricultural and industrial base, Brazil's economy is driven by a growing services sector that has accounted for over 60 percent of GDP in recent years. The global financial and economic turmoil's impact on the financial sector has been moderate, and monetary stability has been maintained.

The state presence in many areas of the economy is heavy, and the efficiency and overall quality of government services remain poor despite high government spending as a percentage of GDP. Other barriers to entrepreneurial activity and job creation include a heavy overall tax burden, inefficient regulation, the relatively high cost of credit, and a rigid labor market. The judicial system remains vulnerable to political influence and corruption.

BACKGROUND: Brazil's democratic constitution dates from 1988. Workers' Party President Luiz Inacio "Lula" da Silva was elected in 2002 and re-elected in 2006, and despite his socialist rhetoric, he has operated as a pragmatist. He and his economic team have implemented prudent fiscal and monetary policies and pursued microeconomic reforms, and Brazil has benefited from surging prices for its booming exports of commodities. A strong currency regime has contributed to rising living standards, and the middle class is growing. Brazil is the world's fifth-largest country and is dominated geographically by the Amazon River basin and the world's largest rain forest. Its almost 200 million people are heavily concentrated on the coast, where a dozen major metropolitan areas offer direct access to the Atlantic Ocean.

Country's Score Over Time

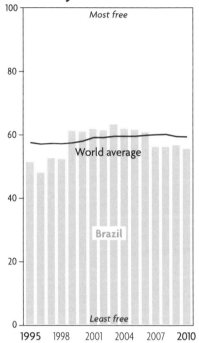

Quick Facts

Population: 192.0 million

GDP (PPP): $2.0 trillion
5.1% growth in 2008
4.5% 5-year compound
annual growth
$10,296 per capita

Unemployment: 7.9%

Inflation (CPI): 5.7%

FDI Inflow: $45.1 billion

2008 data unless otherwise noted
Data compiled as of September 2009

How Do We Measure Economic Freedom?
See page 457 for an explanation of the methodology or visit the *Index* Web site at *heritage.org/index.*

BRAZIL'S TEN ECONOMIC FREEDOMS

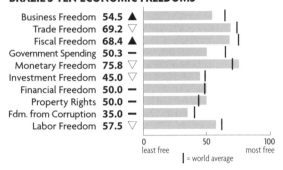

Business Freedom	54.5 ▲	
Trade Freedom	69.2 ▽	
Fiscal Freedom	68.4 ▲	
Government Spending	50.3 —	
Monetary Freedom	75.8 ▽	
Investment Freedom	45.0 ▽	
Financial Freedom	50.0 —	
Property Rights	50.0 —	
Fdm. from Corruption	35.0 —	
Labor Freedom	57.5 ▽	

0 least free — 50 — 100 most free

| = world average

BUSINESS FREEDOM — 54.5

The overall freedom to start, operate, and close a business is limited by Brazil's regulatory environment. Starting a business takes more than three times the world average of 35 days, and obtaining a business license takes much longer than the global average of 218 days.

TRADE FREEDOM — 69.2

Brazil's weighted average tariff rate was 7.9 percent in 2008. Import bans and restrictions, market access barriers in services, high tariffs, border taxes and fees, restrictive regulatory and licensing rules, subsidies, complex customs procedures, and problematic protection of intellectual property rights add to the cost of trade. Fifteen points were deducted from Brazil's trade freedom score to account for non-tariff barriers.

FISCAL FREEDOM — 68.4

Brazil's top income tax rate is 27.5 percent. The standard corporate tax rate is 15 percent, but a surtax of 10 percent and a 9 percent social contribution on net profit paid by most industries bring the effective rate to 34 percent. There is also a real estate transfer tax. In the most recent year, overall tax revenue as a percentage of GDP was 35.3 percent.

GOVERNMENT SPENDING — 50.3

Total government expenditures, including consumption and transfer payments, are relatively high. In the most recent year, government spending equaled 40.7 percent of GDP. Public debt is just below 50 percent of GDP. Privatization efforts have been unremarkable in the past year. Besides debt service, government spending is focused mainly on pensions, transfers to local governments, and bureaucracy.

MONETARY FREEDOM — 75.8

Inflation has been better controlled in recent years, averaging 5.0 percent between 2006 and 2008. Prudent fiscal and monetary policies are credited with helping Brazil to avoid the worst of the global financial crisis of 2008 and 2009. Although such public services as railways, telecommunications, and electricity have been privatized, regulatory agencies oversee prices. The National Petroleum Agency fixes the wholesale price of fuel, and the government controls airfares. Ten points were deducted from Brazil's mon-

etary freedom score to account for the presence of price controls.

INVESTMENT FREEDOM — 45

Foreign investors are granted national treatment, but foreign investment is restricted in nuclear energy, health services, media, rural and border property, fishing, mail and telegraph services, aviation, and aerospace. In general, Brazilian nationals must constitute at least two-thirds of all employees and receive at least two-thirds of total payroll in firms employing three or more persons. Bureaucracy and administration are non-transparent, burdensome, complex, and subject to corruption. Legal disputes can be time-consuming. There are few restrictions on foreign exchange transactions. Foreign investors, upon registering their investments with the central bank, may remit dividends, capital (including capital gains), and royalties. The central bank regulates outward direct investment in some cases, including transfers and remittances. Foreign investors must obtain specific authorization to purchase land along borders.

FINANCIAL FREEDOM — 50

Banking and capital markets are increasingly diversified, dynamic, and competitive. The 10 largest domestic banks account for more than 60 percent of total assets. Three of the top 10 banks are foreign-owned. The two largest state-owned banks control about 25 percent of total assets. The state requires banks to channel loans to preferred sectors. Brazil's insurance sector is now the region's largest, and the reinsurance market was opened to private-sector competition in 2008. The government currently is allowed to take shares in struggling banks through the two largest state-owned banks, and a Credit Guarantee Fund introduced in March 2009 provides state guarantees on bank certificates of deposit.

PROPERTY RIGHTS — 50

Contracts are generally considered secure, but Brazil's judiciary is inefficient, is subject to political and economic influence, and lacks resources and staff training. Decisions can take years, and judgments by the Supreme Federal Tribunal are not automatically binding on lower courts. Protection of intellectual property rights has improved, but piracy of copyrighted material persists.

FREEDOM FROM CORRUPTION — 35

Corruption is perceived as significant. Brazil ranks 80th out of 179 countries in Transparency International's Corruption Perceptions Index for 2008. Businesses bidding on government procurement contracts can encounter corruption, which is also a problem in the lower courts.

LABOR FREEDOM — 57.5

Inflexible labor regulations hinder employment and productivity growth. The non-salary cost of employing a worker is high, and dismissing a redundant employee can be costly. Mandated benefits amplify overall labor costs.

BULGARIA

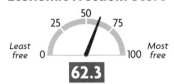
World Rank: **75**   Regional Rank: **36**

Bulgaria's economic freedom score is 62.3, making its economy the 75th freest in the 2010 *Index*. Its overall score is 2.3 points lower than last year, reflecting losses in investment freedom and freedom from corruption and growth in government spending. Bulgaria is ranked 36th freest among the 43 countries in the Europe region, and its overall score is above the world average but below the regional average.

Bulgaria has made substantial progress toward long-term stability and sustained growth. Comprehensive economic reform and trade liberalization have led to annual growth of over 6 percent over the past five years, supporting considerable increases in investment and job creation. Competitive flat tax rates facilitate dynamic entrepreneurial activity.

Bulgaria's substantially reduced public debt (less than 20 percent of GDP in recent years) is a result of prudent public financial management. However, there are some institutional weaknesses that could hamper macroeconomic stability and retard growth. Weak property rights, lingering corruption, and burdensome bureaucracy continue to reduce economic freedom, and developing a more independent judicial system would appear to be a key area for reform.

BACKGROUND: Bulgaria held its first multi-party election since World War II in 1990 and joined the European Union in January 2007. Tourism, agriculture, and natural resource exports, including exports of coal, copper, and zinc, are important to the economy. Since the signing of an EU accession agreement in 2004, Bulgaria has experienced a vast inflow of capital and high rates of growth, though the economy was contracting in 2009. Sergei Stanishev of the Bulgarian Socialist Party (BSP) has been prime minister since 2005. Relations between the BSP and its main coalition partner, the National Movement for Stability and Progress (NMSP), remain troubled. Scandals involving the handling of EU funds have hurt the ruling parties, but the governing coalition survived three no-confidence votes in 2008.

Country's Score Over Time

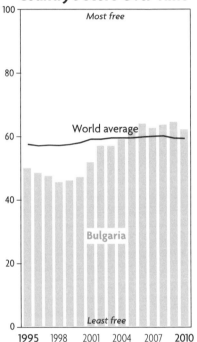

Quick Facts

Population: 7.6 million

GDP (PPP): $94.5 billion
6.0% growth in 2008
6.2% 5-year compound
annual growth
$12,393 per capita

Unemployment: 5.6%

Inflation (CPI): 12.0%

FDI Inflow: $9.2 billion

2008 data unless otherwise noted
Data compiled as of September 2009

How Do We Measure Economic Freedom?
See page 457 for an explanation of the methodology or visit the *Index* Web site at *heritage.org/index*.

BULGARIA'S TEN ECONOMIC FREEDOMS

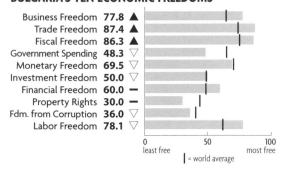

Business Freedom	77.8	▲
Trade Freedom	87.4	▲
Fiscal Freedom	86.3	▲
Government Spending	48.3	▽
Monetary Freedom	69.5	▽
Investment Freedom	50.0	▽
Financial Freedom	60.0	—
Property Rights	30.0	—
Fdm. from Corruption	36.0	▽
Labor Freedom	78.1	▽

0 least free   50   100 most free

| = world average

BUSINESS FREEDOM — 77.8

The overall freedom to establish and run a business is relatively well protected under Bulgaria's regulatory environment. Starting a business takes about half the world average of 35 days. Obtaining a business license takes less than the world average of 218 days.

TRADE FREEDOM — 87.4

Bulgaria's trade policy is the same as that of other members of the European Union. The common EU weighted average tariff rate was 1.3 percent in 2008. However, the EU has high or escalating tariffs for agricultural and manufacturing products, and its MFN tariff code is complex. Non-tariff barriers reflected in EU and Bulgarian policy include agricultural and manufacturing subsidies, quotas, import restrictions and bans for some goods and services, market access restrictions in some services sectors, non-transparent and restrictive regulations and standards, and inconsistent regulatory and customs administration among EU members. Enforcement of intellectual property rights and non-transparent government procurement remain problematic. Ten points were deducted from Bulgaria's trade freedom score to account for non-tariff barriers.

FISCAL FREEDOM — 86.3

Bulgaria has low tax rates. The corporate and income tax rates are a flat 10 percent. Other taxes include a value-added tax (VAT), an estate tax, and a vehicle tax. In the most recent year, overall tax revenue as a percentage of GDP was 34.2 percent.

GOVERNMENT SPENDING — 48.3

Total government expenditures, including consumption and transfer payments, are relatively high. In the most recent year, government spending equaled 41.5 percent of GDP. Authorities are trying to keep spending 10 percent below levels set in the 2009 budget.

MONETARY FREEDOM — 69.5

Inflation has been high, averaging 10.5 percent between 2006 and 2008. Privatization of state-owned firms has progressed, and the market determines most prices, but regulation affects the prices of electricity, water, natural gas, and pharmaceuticals. As a participant in the EU's Common Agricultural Policy, the government subsidizes agricultural production, distorting the prices of agricultural products. Ten points were deducted from Bulgaria's monetary freedom score to adjust for measures that distort domestic prices.

INVESTMENT FREEDOM — 50

Foreign and domestic investors are treated equally. Government approval is required for majority foreign ownership in some sectors. Licensing, regulation, and arbitrary bureaucracy deter investment, as do pervasive corruption, a slow-moving judiciary, and the influence of organized crime in some sectors of the economy. Foreign exchange and capital transactions may be subject to restrictions and require prior registration with the central bank. Foreign ownership of land is permitted if the owners are from EU countries or countries with an international agreement permitting such purchases. There are no legal restrictions on acquisition of land by locally registered companies with majority foreign participation. If public needs cannot be met by other means, expropriation may be undertaken, provided that the owner is adequately compensated.

FINANCIAL FREEDOM — 60

Introduction of a currency board, stronger supervision, and tighter prudential rules have helped to transform Bulgaria's banking sector. Consolidation began in 2004, and privatization of state-owned banks is complete. Combined assets of the 30 commercial banks exceed 100 percent of GDP. The three largest banks account for more than 30 percent of assets. In the domestic credit market, foreign banks account for more than 80 percent of total assets. Credit is generally allocated on market terms. Insurance, with strong foreign participation, is private and expanding. Strong banking supervision and prudential regulations are likely to lessen the impact of global financial turmoil.

PROPERTY RIGHTS — 30

Although the law protects the acquisition and disposition of property, the judicial system does not solve commercial disputes, register businesses, or enforce judgments effectively. The constitution provides for an independent judiciary, but ineffective rule of law limits investor confidence in the enforcement of contracts, ownership and shareholders rights, and intellectual property rights.

FREEDOM FROM CORRUPTION — 36

Corruption is perceived as widespread. Bulgaria ranks 72nd out of 179 countries in Transparency International's Corruption Perceptions Index for 2008. Despite advances in laws and legal instruments, organized crime and government and judicial corruption persist. Corruption's threat to the security of the common border is a matter of great concern to the EU.

LABOR FREEDOM — 78.1

Relatively flexible labor regulations enhance employment and productivity growth, although there is room for further reforms. The non-salary cost of employing a worker is high, but the dismissal cost is moderate.

BURKINA FASO

Ouagadougou

Economic Freedom Score

Least free 0   25   50   75   Most free 100

59.4

urkina Faso's economic freedom score is 59.4, making its economy the 90th freest in the 2010 *Index*. Its overall score is almost identical to last year, with a loss of monetary freedom offset by a gain in investment freedom. Burkina Faso is ranked 9th out of 46 countries in the Sub-Saharan Africa region, and its overall score is equal to the world average.

Progress in opening the economy and developing the private sector has promoted relatively sound macroeconomic performance with an annual growth rate of over 5 percent over the past five years. Burkina Faso scores relatively well in fiscal freedom, government spending, and monetary freedom. The overall tax burden is low, and privatization has been resumed.

Deeper structural and institutional reforms remain critical to maintaining stable growth, diversifying the production base, and continuing the transition to greater economic freedom. There are systemic weaknesses in business freedom, property rights, investment freedom, and freedom from corruption. Extensive regulations hinder the development of a more entrepreneurial environment, and the weak judicial system fuels corruption.

BACKGROUND: Burkina Faso has been ruled for over two decades by former army officer Blaise Compaoré, who seized power in a 1987 coup and executed his predecessor. Compaoré won a third term as president in November 2005, though a constitutional amendment that entered into force that same year should limit the presidency to two terms in the future. Burkina Faso is a very poor agrarian country that is beset by frequent drought. Over 80 percent of the population is engaged in subsistence agriculture. Many Burkinabé live and work abroad, with as many as 4 million living in or migrating annually to neighboring Côte d'Ivoire for seasonal agricultural work. Remittances are a substantial source of income. Inadequate communications, poor infrastructure, and a high rate of illiteracy have slowed development.

Country's Score Over Time

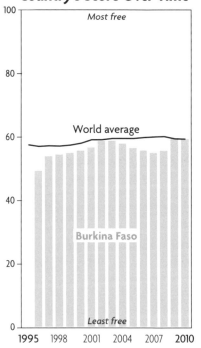

Quick Facts

Population: 15.2 million

GDP (PPP): $17.7 billion
4.5% growth in 2008
5.3% 5-year compound annual growth
$1,161 per capita

Unemployment: estimated to be over 20%

Inflation (CPI): 10.7%

FDI Inflow: $137 million

2008 data unless otherwise noted
Data compiled as of September 2009

How Do We Measure Economic Freedom?
See page 457 for an explanation of the methodology or visit the *Index* Web site at *heritage.org/index*.

BURKINA FASO'S TEN ECONOMIC FREEDOMS

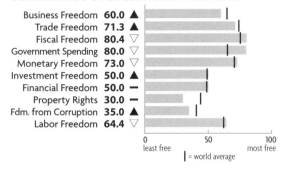

Business Freedom	60.0 ▲	
Trade Freedom	71.3 ▲	
Fiscal Freedom	80.4 ▽	
Government Spending	80.0 ▽	
Monetary Freedom	73.0 ▽	
Investment Freedom	50.0 ▲	
Financial Freedom	50.0 —	
Property Rights	30.0 —	
Fdm. from Corruption	35.0 ▲	
Labor Freedom	64.4 ▽	

0   50   100
least free   most free

❘ = world average

BUSINESS FREEDOM — 60

The overall freedom to start, operate, and close a business remains constrained by Burkina Faso's regulatory environment. Business registration is more streamlined, and obtaining a business license requires less than the world average of 18 procedures. The process for closing a business can be lengthy.

TRADE FREEDOM — 71.3

Burkina Faso's weighted average tariff rate was 9.3 percent in 2008. Despite steps to reform the trade regime, supplementary taxes on imports, import fees and bans, import authorization for certain products, customs corruption, and weak enforcement of intellectual property rights add to the cost of trade. Ten points were deducted from Burkina Faso's trade freedom score to account for non-tariff barriers.

FISCAL FREEDOM — 80.4

Burkina Faso has moderate tax rates. The top income and corporate tax rates are 30 percent. Other taxes include a value-added tax (VAT) and a tax on insurance contracts. In the most recent year, overall tax revenue as a percentage of GDP was 12.5 percent. Full introduction of the new tax management system should simplify tax collection. The government remains committed to reforming the corporate tax and the VAT.

GOVERNMENT SPENDING — 80

Burkina Faso's total government expenditures, including consumption and transfer payments, are moderate. In the most recent year, government spending equaled 25.8 percent of GDP. The national telephone company was privatized in March 2009.

MONETARY FREEDOM — 73

Inflation rose dramatically in 2008 and averaged 7.3 percent between 2006 and 2008, driven by sharp increases in the prices of food and imported oil. A record cereal harvest and lower international oil prices are expected to reduce inflation in 2009. The regional Banque Centrale des Etats de l'Afrique de l'Ouest maintains the CFA franc's peg to the euro. The market determines most prices, but the government maintains price supports for cotton and influences prices through the public sector. Ten points were deducted from Burkina Faso's monetary freedom score to adjust for measures that distort domestic prices.

INVESTMENT FREEDOM — 50

The law guarantees equal treatment of foreign and domestic investors. Investments are screened to determine eligibility for incentives. The government is liberalizing most monopolies and adopting transparent laws to foster competition, but inadequate infrastructure, a weak legal system, and corruption remain deterrents to investment. Foreign investors are guaranteed the right to transfer abroad any investment-associated funds, including dividends, receipts from liquidation, assets, and salaries. Payments and transfers over a specified amount require supporting documents, and proceeds from non–West African Economic and Monetary Union countries must be surrendered to an authorized dealer. If property is expropriated, the government must compensate the property holder in advance, except in the event of an emergency.

FINANCIAL FREEDOM — 50

Burkina Faso's financial system is small and underdeveloped. Microfinance has expanded rapidly. Reforms aimed at tightening supervision and improving credit access are ongoing. The government has pursued banking liberalization and restructuring since the 1990s and limits its direct participation. The banking sector consists of 11 commercial subsidiaries of major multinational banks. In 2008, the government held around 20 percent of total banking capital. Credit is generally allocated on market terms, but the government still influences lending. The financial sector remains hampered by difficulties in mobilizing long-term resources. Due to limited exposure to international financial markets, the impact of the global financial crisis on banking has not been significant.

PROPERTY RIGHTS — 30

Burkina Faso's judicial system is weak. Villagers have their own customary or traditional courts. The executive has extensive appointment and other judicial powers. Systemic weaknesses include arbitrary removal of judges, outdated legal codes, too few courts, a lack of financial and human resources, and excessive legal costs.

FREEDOM FROM CORRUPTION — 35

Corruption is perceived as pervasive. Burkina Faso ranks 80th out of 179 countries in Transparency International's Corruption Perceptions Index for 2008, a substantial improvement over 2007. Persistent deficiencies include a weak judiciary, limited enforcement powers of anti-corruption institutions, misappropriation of public funds, and a lack of separation of powers. According to a June 2009 poll, two-thirds of the population believes that corruption is becoming more prevalent. Almost half reported that they had been directly affected by corrupt practices.

LABOR FREEDOM — 64.4

Relatively flexible employment regulations enhance employment and productivity growth. The non-salary cost of employing a worker is high, but dismissing a redundant employee is generally costless.

Rangoon

BURMA

Economic Freedom Score

Least free 0   100 Most free

36.7

Burma's economic freedom score is 36.7, making its economy the 5th worst in the 2010 *Index*. Its score is one point lower than last year as a result of worsened investment freedom. Burma is ranked 40th out of 41 countries in the Asia–Pacific region, and its overall score is much lower than the regional average.

Long-standing structural problems include a wide fiscal deficit due to poor public finance management, continuing losses by state-owned enterprises, and underdeveloped legal and regulatory frameworks. Repressive governance interferes heavily with economic activity. The efficiency and overall quality of government services remain very poor. The junta's woeful response in the aftermath of the May 2008 cyclone—the country's worst-ever humanitarian crisis—showed callous disregard for the welfare of the country's people.

Historically scoring far below the world average, Burma's economic freedom has deteriorated even more in recent years. Investment freedom, financial freedom, property rights, and freedom from corruption are extraordinarily weak. Monetary stability remains fragile, and inflation is very high, largely reflecting excessive money creation to fund fiscal deficits.

BACKGROUND: Burma has been ruled by a military junta since 1962. After the opposition National League for Democracy won a large majority in the 1990 legislative elections, the junta redoubled its efforts to crack down on dissent. Political instability continues, and the United Nations estimates that the violent government response to pro-democracy demonstrations in September 2007 resulted in over 30 fatalities. A new constitution approved by referendum in 2008 is regarded by international observers as deeply flawed. Burma is richly endowed with natural resources, but government intervention in the economy has made it one of the world's poorest countries. An estimated one million Burmese have sought refuge in neighboring countries, and Cyclone Nargis, which struck in May 2008, is estimated to have killed well over 100,000 people.

Country's Score Over Time

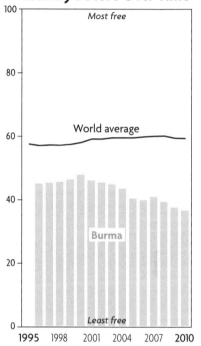

Quick Facts

Population: 58.8 million

GDP (PPP): $67.9 billion
4.0% growth in 2008
10.8% 5-year compound annual growth
$1,156 per capita

Unemployment: 9.5%

Inflation (CPI): 26.4%

FDI Inflow: $283 million

2008 data unless otherwise noted
Data compiled as of September 2009

How Do We Measure Economic Freedom?
See page 457 for an explanation of the methodology or visit the *Index* Web site at *heritage.org/index*.

BURMA'S TEN ECONOMIC FREEDOMS

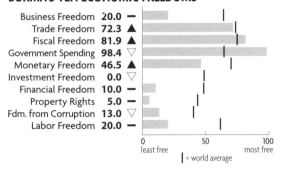

Business Freedom	20.0 ▬
Trade Freedom	72.3 ▲
Fiscal Freedom	81.9 ▲
Government Spending	98.4 ▽
Monetary Freedom	46.5 ▲
Investment Freedom	0.0 ▽
Financial Freedom	10.0 ▬
Property Rights	5.0 ▬
Fdm. from Corruption	13.0 ▽
Labor Freedom	20.0 ▬

0   50   100
least free   most free
❙ = world average

BUSINESS FREEDOM — 20

Entrepreneurial activity is restricted by a lack of legal and regulatory transparency. Inconsistent enforcement of laws and bureaucratic red tape severely hinder the development of a critically needed private sector.

TRADE FREEDOM — 72.3

Burma's weighted average tariff rate was 3.9 percent in 2007. Import and export bans and restrictions, high import and export taxes and fees, non-transparent import and export permit and licensing rules, arbitrary policy changes, non-transparent and outdated regulations and standards, customs corruption, state trading, poor intellectual property rights protection, and inefficient regulatory and customs bureaucracy add to the cost of trade. Twenty points were deducted from Burma's trade freedom score to account for non-tariff barriers.

FISCAL FREEDOM — 81.9

Burma has moderately high tax rates. The top income and corporate tax rates are 30 percent. In the most recent year, overall tax revenue as a percentage of GDP was 3.0 percent.

GOVERNMENT SPENDING — 98.4

Total government expenditures, including consumption and transfer payments, are low. In the most recent year, government spending equaled only 7.2 percent of GDP, but the resulting high score reflects a lack of government capacity rather than policy restraint. The government is relying primarily on international donors to rebuild the transportation, energy, and health infrastructures damaged by the May 2008 cyclone. Soaring deficits are driven by military spending.

MONETARY FREEDOM — 46.5

Inflation continues to be extremely high, averaging 26 percent between 2006 and 2008, although it slowed somewhat in 2009 due to falling fuel and food prices and continuing recovery from the May 2008 cyclone. The state is heavily engaged in mining and power, and state-owned firms are prominent in transport, trade, and manufacturing. The government uses price controls and subsidies to maintain below-market prices for such staples as gasoline, cooking oil, propane, and soap. Such products are strictly rationed, so retailers often sell on the black market. Twenty points

were deducted from Burma's monetary freedom score to adjust for measures that distort domestic prices.

INVESTMENT FREEDOM — 0

Foreign and domestic private investment is approved case by case. Many sectors are reserved for domestic and government-controlled activity. Once permission is granted, foreign investors need business licenses, which are rarely granted. Investment is severely limited by government design, corruption, cronyism, political intervention, complex and capricious regulation, no rule of law, and poor infrastructure. All official trade in goods, extractive industries, sources of capital, movement of labor, and access to information are government-controlled. Manufacturing and services remain undeveloped. Access to capital is very limited, and the government favors state-owned banks over the few private banks. The government restricts foreign exchange accounts and current transfers and controls all capital transactions. Multiple exchange rates make conversion and repatriation of foreign exchange complex and prone to corruption. Foreign firms may not own land but may lease it from the government.

FINANCIAL FREEDOM — 10

The government directs loans to government projects, and entrepreneurs' access to credit is highly constrained. Banking is dominated by five state-owned banks, but there are several private banks and 13 foreign banks. Opaque regulatory and legal institutions add to a fairly hostile financial climate. The government tightly controls banking. Money laundering continues to grow. Conversion and repatriation of foreign exchange are ripe for corruption due to the multiple exchange rate system. Only three state banks are permitted to deal with foreign exchange transactions.

PROPERTY RIGHTS — 5

Private real property and intellectual property are not protected. Private and foreign companies are at a disadvantage in disputes with governmental and quasi-governmental organizations. Foreign investors who have conflicts with the local government or whose businesses are illegally expropriated have little success in obtaining compensation.

FREEDOM FROM CORRUPTION — 13

Corruption is perceived as pervasive. Burma ranks 178th out of 179 countries in Transparency International's Corruption Perceptions Index for 2008. Burma is a major source of opium, and most Burmese view corruption as necessary for survival. Investors complain of official corruption in taxation, investment permission, import and export licenses, and land and real estate lease approvals.

LABOR FREEDOM — 20

Burma's formal labor market remains distorted by state intervention. Regulations regarding wage rates and maximum work hours are not uniformly observed. The government sets public-sector wages and influences wage-setting in the private sector. The state uses forced labor to construct military buildings and commercial enterprises.

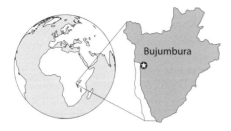

Bujumbura

BURUNDI

Economic Freedom Score

25   50   75

Least free 0   100 Most free

47.5

Burundi's economic freedom score is 47.5, making its economy the 160th freest in the 2010 *Index*. Its overall score is 1.3 points lower than last year, reflecting lower scores for government spending and monetary freedom that are only partly offset by an increase in investment freedom. Burundi is ranked 38th out of 46 countries in the Sub-Saharan Africa region and scores much worse than the world average.

Following years of political instability, Burundi faces major challenges. Law enforcement is weak and vulnerable to political influence. Economic expansion averaging 3 percent per year for the past five years is at risk due to over-reliance on the widely fluctuating agricultural sector, the principal source of jobs for 80 percent of the population.

Burundi scores significantly below world averages in many of the 10 economic freedoms. The lack of institutional capacity still delays reforms needed to restructure and modernize the economy. Many aspects of doing business, from obtaining licenses to attracting foreign investment, are subject to intrusive and inefficient regulations. The weak judiciary fuels corruption.

BACKGROUND: Since becoming fully independent in 1962, Burundi has suffered from tension between the dominant Tutsi minority and the Hutu majority. The 1993 assassination of the first Hutu president, Melchior Ndadaye, sparked a civil war, and the violence following the death of his successor, Cyprien Ntayamira, and Rwandan President Juvenal Habyarimana in a 1994 plane crash led to an estimated 300,000 deaths and the beginnings of the Rwandan genocide. Negotiations mediated by South Africa resulted in a power-sharing government in 2001, and the last active rebel group signed a cease-fire in 2008. In 2005, a new constitution was adopted by referendum and the National Assembly elected Pierre Nkurunziza president. Burundi remains very poor. A majority of the population depends on subsistence agriculture, and agriculture accounted for 34 percent of GDP in 2007.

Country's Score Over Time

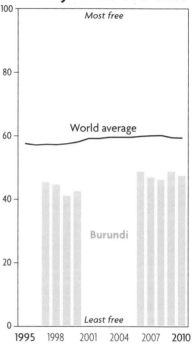

Quick Facts

Population: 8.1 million

GDP (PPP): $3.1 billion
4.5% growth in 2008
3.5% 5-year compound annual growth
$383 per capita

Unemployment: n/a

Inflation (CPI): 24.4%

FDI Inflow: $1 million

2008 data unless otherwise noted
Data compiled as of September 2009

How Do We Measure Economic Freedom?
See page 457 for an explanation of the methodology or visit the *Index* Web site at *heritage.org/index*.

BURUNDI'S TEN ECONOMIC FREEDOMS

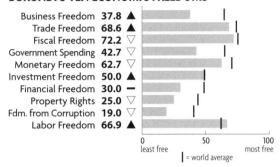

Business Freedom	37.8 ▲	
Trade Freedom	68.6 ▲	
Fiscal Freedom	72.2 ▽	
Government Spending	42.7 ▽	
Monetary Freedom	62.7 ▽	
Investment Freedom	50.0 ▲	
Financial Freedom	30.0 —	
Property Rights	25.0 ▽	
Fdm. from Corruption	19.0 ▽	
Labor Freedom	66.9 ▲	

0   50   100
least free   most free
❙ = world average

BUSINESS FREEDOM — 37.8

The overall freedom to establish and run a business is constrained by Burundi's regulatory environment. Despite new regulations, continuing instability and a massive, corrupt bureaucracy make it difficult to conduct entrepreneurial activity. Obtaining a business license requires more than the world average of 18 procedures.

TRADE FREEDOM — 68.6

Burundi's weighted average tariff rate was 10.7 percent in 2008. The government has adopted a relatively open trade regime, but import restrictions, inadequate administrative capacity, poor infrastructure, and customs corruption add to the cost of trade. Ten points were deducted from Burundi's trade freedom score to account for non-tariff barriers.

FISCAL FREEDOM — 72.2

Burundi has relatively high tax rates. The top income and corporate tax rates are 35 percent. A value-added tax (VAT) replaced the general sales tax on July 1, 2009. In the most recent year, overall tax revenue as a percentage of GDP was 18.3 percent.

GOVERNMENT SPENDING — 42.7

Total government expenditures in Burundi, including consumption and transfer payments, are high. In the most recent year, government spending equaled 43.7 percent of GDP. Much-needed privatization of the coffee industry remains stalled.

MONETARY FREEDOM — 62.7

Inflation has been high, averaging 18.6 percent between 2006 and 2008, but falling international food and fuel prices helped to ease pressure in 2009. The government influences prices through state-owned enterprises, subsidies, and agriculture-support programs. Ten points were deducted from Burundi's monetary freedom score to adjust for measures that distort domestic prices.

INVESTMENT FREEDOM — 50

Foreign investment receives equal treatment. The 2008 investment code, established to attract and reassure investors, is vague and dependent on further tax and customs reform. Corruption, underdeveloped markets, the state of post-conflict infrastructure, geographic isolation, and proximity to regional conflicts discourage large foreign invest-

ment. In theory, there are no limitations on the flow of funds for remittance of profits, debt service, capital, capital gains, returns on intellectual property, or imported inputs; however, there are no significant foreign enterprises to test the effectiveness of this policy. In principle, there are no restrictions on converting or transferring funds associated with foreign investment; in practice, limitations depend on the availability of hard currency. The government may expropriate property for "exceptional and state-approved reasons," but "a just and prior compensatory allowance is required."

FINANCIAL FREEDOM — 30

Burundi's small financial sector provides a very limited range of services. Retail and corporate banking are at a relatively early stage of development. Many people still rely on microcredit or informal lending. The state dominates the two largest commercial banks. It is not easy for small enterprises to get credit, and the lack of domestic investment opportunity also hinders bank development. The many loans made to the government and to state-owned enterprises have resulted in non-performing loans that have reached around 19 percent of gross total lending. Banking regulation is bureaucratic and arduous. Other difficulties include the largely inadequate availability of long-term capital and an undeveloped payments system.

PROPERTY RIGHTS — 25

Private property is subject to government expropriation and armed banditry. The constitution guarantees the independence of the judiciary, but judges are appointed by the executive branch and subject to political pressure. Judicial personnel, predominantly Tutsi, have shown increasing signs of independence under Hutu presidents. A large number of refugees and internally displaced persons are blocked from resettlement by weak land tenure and property rights systems and by the lack of ownership records.

FREEDOM FROM CORRUPTION — 19

Corruption is perceived as pervasive. Burundi ranks 158th out of 179 countries in Transparency International's Corruption Perceptions Index for 2008, a significant deterioration from 2007. From senior government officials demanding large kickbacks on procurement tenders to low-level civil servants demanding petty bribes for services, licenses, or permits, corruption is present in every area of life. Corruption is most pervasive in government procurement, where the purchase and sale of government property frequently leads to allegations of bribery and cronyism. The ruling party has been accused of using arbitrary arrests, detentions without trial, and even torture against political adversaries.

LABOR FREEDOM — 66.9

Rigid employment regulations and an underdeveloped labor market hinder productivity growth and job creation. The non-salary cost of employing a worker is low, but the difficulty of dismissing a worker creates a disincentive for companies that would otherwise hire more people.

CAMBODIA

Economic Freedom Score

Least free 0   100 Most free

56.6

Cambodia's economic freedom score is 56.6, making its economy the 107th freest in the 2010 *Index*. Its overall score is almost the same as last year, with improvements in trade freedom and investment freedom balanced by declines in monetary freedom and several other factors. Cambodia is ranked 18th out of 41 countries in the Asia–Pacific region, and its overall score is slightly lower than the regional average.

Cambodia's economic growth has averaged about 10 percent over the past five years, considerably reducing poverty. There has been notable progress in the management of public finance, and the trade regime is more open and transparent.

There is, however, a lack of reform in other areas that are indispensable to sustaining high economic growth. Monetary stability has been in decline, and the business environment is not conducive to private-sector development. Pervasive corruption and weak rule of law further constrain entrepreneurial activity and increase its cost. The rigidity of the formal labor market is partly responsible for the existence of an underground dual labor market.

BACKGROUND: Cambodia's multigenerational effort to recover from war and the brutal Khmer Rouge regime of Pol Pot continues. An estimated 3 million people were killed by the government or died as a result of the forced evacuation of cities, torture, or starvation between 1975 and 1979. A tribunal established under an agreement with the United Nations to try senior officials involved in the atrocities held its first trial in 2009. Though nominally a democracy, Cambodia has been ruled either formally or de facto by Prime Minister Hun Sen since 1993. The former Khmer Rouge leader's Cambodian People's Party won a renewed mandate in mid-2008, taking a large majority of the seats in the National Assembly, and Hun Sen was re-elected prime minister. Cambodia's economy is heavily dependent on tourism and garment exports.

Country's Score Over Time

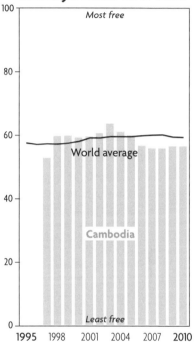

Quick Facts

Population: 14.7 million

GDP (PPP): $28.0 billion
    5.2% growth in 2008
    10.0% 5-year compound
        annual growth
    $1,905 per capita

Unemployment: 3.5% (2007)

Inflation (CPI): 19.7%

FDI Inflow: $815 million

2008 data unless otherwise noted
Data compiled as of September 2009

How Do We Measure Economic Freedom?
See page 457 for an explanation of the methodology or visit the *Index* Web site at *heritage.org/index*.

CAMBODIA'S TEN ECONOMIC FREEDOMS

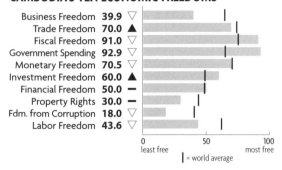

Business Freedom	39.9	▽
Trade Freedom	70.0	▲
Fiscal Freedom	91.0	▽
Government Spending	92.9	▽
Monetary Freedom	70.5	▽
Investment Freedom	60.0	▲
Financial Freedom	50.0	—
Property Rights	30.0	—
Fdm. from Corruption	18.0	▽
Labor Freedom	43.6	▽

0 least free   50   100 most free

❙ = world average

BUSINESS FREEDOM — 39.9

The overall freedom to establish and run a business is constrained significantly by Cambodia's regulatory environment. Starting a business takes more than twice the world average of 35 days. Obtaining a business license requires more than the world average of 18 procedures and 218 days.

TRADE FREEDOM — 70

Cambodia's weighted average tariff rate was 10 percent in 2007. Cambodia continues to improve its trade regime, but import bans and restrictions, discretionary tax levies, non-automatic import licensing, non-transparent government procurement, weak enforcement of intellectual property rights, and inconsistent and cumbersome customs administration add to the cost of trade. Ten points were deducted from Cambodia's trade freedom score to account for non-tariff barriers.

FISCAL FREEDOM — 91

Cambodia's tax rates are relatively low. The top income and corporate tax rates are 20 percent. Other taxes include an excise tax and a value-added tax (VAT), which may be broadened in 2009. In the most recent year, overall tax revenue was 10.2 percent of GDP.

GOVERNMENT SPENDING — 92.9

Total government expenditures, including consumption and transfer payments, are low. In the most recent year, government spending equaled 15.4 percent of GDP. Efforts to improve tax administration and budget management are ongoing.

MONETARY FREEDOM — 70.5

Inflation has been very high, averaging 15 percent between 2006 and 2008 and reaching 25 percent in 2008 as a result of rapid growth in the money supply and high global prices for food and fuel. The market determines most prices, but the government attempts to maintain stable retail prices for fuel through subsidies. The effectiveness of monetary policy is limited, owing to the high degree of dollarization of the economy. Five points were deducted from Cambodia's monetary freedom score to adjust for measures that distort domestic prices.

INVESTMENT FREEDOM — 60

Foreign capital and domestic capital are treated equally in most sectors. In a few sectors, foreign investment is subject to conditions, local equity participation, or prior authorization from authorities. Investment can be limited by regulatory inconsistencies, corruption, and a non-transparent court system. The privatization of state enterprises and transactions involving state property have not always been carried out in a transparent manner. There are no restrictions or controls on the holding of foreign exchange accounts by residents or non-residents. Non-residents may lease but not own land. The government may expropriate property only in the public interest and with advance compensation.

FINANCIAL FREEDOM — 50

Cambodia's financial system is segmented, underdeveloped, and subject to government influence. Efficiency has gradually improved as a result of some privatization and consolidation since 2000. In addition to the National Bank of Cambodia, which is solely a regulatory and supervisory agency, the financial system consists of 16 commercial banks, seven specialized financial institutions, two representative offices of foreign banks, 17 licensed and 26 registered microfinance institutions, and six insurance companies. The banking sector is market-oriented, and credit to the private sector has increased to over 10 percent of GDP from 6 percent in 2001. The foreign presence has been growing, with eight commercial banks majority owned by foreign investors. Credit is allocated on market terms, but the government influences lending decisions. There are no bond or securities markets.

PROPERTY RIGHTS — 30

Cambodia's legal system does not protect private property effectively, and there are many gaps in company law, bankruptcy procedures, and arbitration. The executive branch usually dominates the legislature and the judiciary. Inconsistent judicial rulings and outright corruption are common. The land titling system is not fully functional, and most property owners do not have documentation to prove their ownership.

FREEDOM FROM CORRUPTION — 18

Corruption is perceived as rampant. Cambodia ranks 166th out of 179 countries in Transparency International's Corruption Perceptions Index for 2008. Business people, both local and foreign, have identified corruption, particularly within the judiciary, as the single biggest deterrent to investment in Cambodia. Corruption hampers economic opportunity and competitiveness, and demands for petty bribes are common. Pervasive corruption makes Cambodia highly vulnerable to penetration by drug traffickers and foreign crime syndicates.

LABOR FREEDOM — 43.6

Inflexible employment regulations impede job creation and productivity growth. The non-salary cost of employing a worker is low, but work hours are regulated rigidly.

CAMEROON

Economic Freedom Score

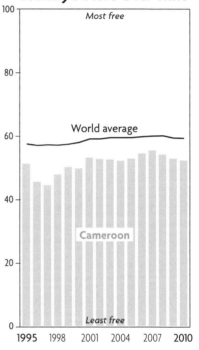

25 50 75

Least free 0   100 Most free

52.3

World Rank: **132**   Regional Rank: **25**

Cameroon's economic freedom score is 52.3, making its economy the 132nd freest in the 2010 *Index*. Its overall score is 0.6 point lower than last year, primarily as a result of worsened investment freedom and monetary freedom. Cameroon is ranked 25th out of 46 countries in the Sub-Saharan Africa region, and its overall score is slightly lower than the regional average.

Cameroon faces challenges common to developing African nations: inefficient bureaucracy, an unreliable legal system, and poor infrastructure. Restrictive regulations hurt employment and productivity growth. Restrictions on trade are common, and the weak judicial system allows pervasive corruption and erodes the potential for long-term economic growth.

Despite progress in privatizing management of the national water company, other important enterprises remain state-controlled. Because of the recent global financial turmoil, Cameroon has struggled with reduced exports, and investment projects have been delayed by difficulties in obtaining financing. In response to a potential fiscal deficit, the government has tried to improve transparency while further developing non-oil sources of revenue. Progress on access to financial services has been sluggish.

BACKGROUND: President Paul Biya has held office since 1982, and political reforms have been largely ignored or overturned. In 2008, Biya's supporters in parliament, having won a strong majority in 2007, passed constitutional amendments granting the president immunity for acts committed while in office and enabling Biya to run for a third term in 2011. Despite abundant natural resources, over half of the population depends on agriculture, and the National Statistics Office estimates that the informal sector accounts for over 90 percent of employment and over 60 percent of economic output. Rising oil prices have added to GDP growth and government revenues; with international oil prices declining, economic growth is expected to decline. The transparency of oil-related public finances is improved, but economic mismanagement continues to inhibit development.

Country's Score Over Time

100 — Most free

80

60 — World average

Cameroon

40

20

0 — Least free

1995 1998 2001 2004 2007 **2010**

Quick Facts

Population: 18.9 million

GDP (PPP): $41.9 billion
3.9% growth in 2008
3.1% 5-year compound annual growth
$2,215 per capita

Unemployment: estimated to be over 10%

Inflation (CPI): 5.3%

FDI Inflow: $260 million

2008 data unless otherwise noted
Data compiled as of September 2009

How Do We Measure Economic Freedom?
See page 457 for an explanation of the methodology or visit the *Index* Web site at *heritage.org/index.*

CAMEROON'S TEN ECONOMIC FREEDOMS

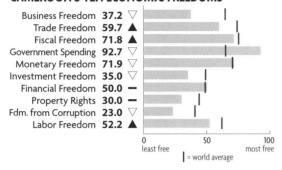

Business Freedom	37.2 ▽	
Trade Freedom	59.7 ▲	
Fiscal Freedom	71.8 ▲	
Government Spending	92.7 ▽	
Monetary Freedom	71.9 ▽	
Investment Freedom	35.0 ▽	
Financial Freedom	50.0 —	
Property Rights	30.0 —	
Fdm. from Corruption	23.0 ▽	
Labor Freedom	52.2 ▲	

0 least free   50   100 most free

| = world average

BUSINESS FREEDOM — 37.2

The overall freedom to establish and run a business is seriously limited by Cameroon's regulatory environment. Obtaining a business license requires 15 procedures, compared to the global average of 18, but takes much longer than the world average of 218 days. Bankruptcy procedures remain onerous and costly.

TRADE FREEDOM — 59.7

Cameroon's weighted average tariff rate was 12.7 percent in 2007. Surcharges and inconsistent customs valuation, import and export restrictions, import and export taxes and fees, import registration and licensing, domestic preference in government procurement, corruption, and inadequate enforcement of intellectual property rights add to the cost of trade. Fifteen points were deducted from Cameroon's trade freedom score to account for non-tariff barriers.

FISCAL FREEDOM — 71.8

Cameroon has relatively high tax rates. The top income tax rate is 35 percent, and the top corporate tax rate is 38.5 percent (35 percent plus a 10 percent council tax). Other taxes include a value-added tax (VAT), a transfer tax on businesses sold, a property tax, and an inheritance tax. In the most recent year, overall tax revenue as a percentage of GDP was 10.8 percent.

GOVERNMENT SPENDING — 92.7

Total government expenditures, including consumption and transfer payments, are low. In the most recent year, government spending equaled 15.6 percent of GDP. Budget management, especially in the non-oil sector, is weak.

MONETARY FREEDOM — 71.9

Inflation has been moderate, averaging 4.3 percent between 2006 and 2008. The regional Banque des Etats de l'Afrique Centrale (BEAC) prioritizes the control of inflation and maintenance of the CFA franc's peg to the euro. The market determines most prices, but the government provides subsidies and controls prices for such "strategic" goods and services as rice, flour, consumer goods, agriculture inputs, electricity, water, petroleum products, telecommunications, cooking gas, pharmaceuticals, and cotton. Fifteen points were deducted from Cameroon's monetary freedom score to adjust for measures that distort domestic prices.

INVESTMENT FREEDOM — 35

The government permits 100 percent foreign equity ownership. All investments face government screening. Corruption, cumbersome bureaucracy, and decision-making delays burden investment. The government generally holds at least 30 percent–45 percent shares of "privatized" companies. Dividends, capital returns, interest and principal on foreign debt, lease payments, royalties and management fees, and returns on liquidation can be freely remitted abroad. Liquidation of foreign direct investment must be declared at the Ministry of Finance and the central bank. Residents may open foreign exchange accounts with central bank and Ministry of Finance approval. Many capital transactions, including foreign borrowing, foreign direct investment, liquidation, and foreign securities, are subject to controls and generally require the approval of or declaration to the government. Delay and corruption are encountered in resolving commercial disputes. Local ownership of land is not required.

FINANCIAL FREEDOM — 50

Cameroon's financial system is not fully developed. Three banks control two-thirds of all assets. The cost of financing is high, and access to credit is very limited in rural areas. There is a wide network of microfinance institutions. Four companies account for about 60 percent of the insurance market. The largest insurer is foreign-owned, but Cameroonian ownership is increasing. The stock exchange remains small. The government has continued its efforts to shore up financial intermediation by setting up a regional market in government bonds, enhancing supervision of microfinance, and expanding access to banking services.

PROPERTY RIGHTS — 30

Corruption and legal uncertainty can lead to confiscation of private property. Courts and administrative agencies often favor domestic firms and have been accused of corruption. Some foreign companies allege that unfavorable judgments are obtained through fraud or frivolous lawsuits. Trademarks and copyrights are routinely violated, and software piracy is widespread. Cameroon is ranked 96th out of 115 countries in the 2009 International Property Rights Index.

FREEDOM FROM CORRUPTION — 23

Corruption is perceived as pervasive. Cameroon ranks 141st out of 179 countries in Transparency International's Corruption Perceptions Index for 2008. Courts and government agencies have been accused of corrupt practices, and there continue to be reports of beatings of detainees, arbitrary arrests, and illegal searches.

LABOR FREEDOM — 52.2

Relatively inflexible employment regulations hinder job creation and productivity growth. The non-salary cost of employing a worker is moderate, and dismissing a redundant employee is relatively easy, though labor legislation mandates retraining or replacement before firing a worker.

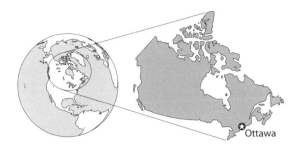

CANADA

Economic Freedom Score

Least free 0   100 Most free

80.4

Canada's economic freedom score is 80.4, making its economy the 7th freest in the 2010 *Index*. Its overall score is almost unchanged from last year. Canada is ranked 1st out of three countries in the North America region.

Scoring high in many of the 10 economic freedoms, Canada performs particularly well in business freedom, financial freedom, property rights, and freedom from corruption. Straightforward regulations facilitate entrepreneurial activity. Overall, regulation is thorough but essentially transparent. A strong rule of law ensures property rights and equitable application of the commercial code. A high level of economic freedom, coupled with a sound and prudent banking sector, has enabled Canada to emerge from the global downturn relatively unscathed.

Canada's economic freedom trails the world average only in government spending. Elaborate social and welfare state programs swell overall government expenditures. Government spending has also increased slightly due to implementation of a significant stimulus package. However, good fiscal management and federal budget surpluses have enabled the economy to undertake stimulus measures without undermining fiscal soundness and long-term economic competitiveness.

BACKGROUND: Canada has a strong and stable democratic political system that has proven itself capable of handling occasional ethnic tensions. It is also one of the world's leading free-market economies and a major exporter of oil, minerals, automobiles, manufactured goods, and forest products. Over 75 percent of its exports are to the United States. Despite one of the most restrictive foreign ownership policies in telecommunications, publishing, broadcasting, aviation, mining, and fishing among all Organisation for Economic Co-operation and Development countries, macroeconomic fundamentals remain strong. In May and June 2008, Canada strengthened its commitment to become a more active economic partner in the Americas by concluding free trade negotiations with Colombia and signing a similar agreement with Peru.

Country's Score Over Time

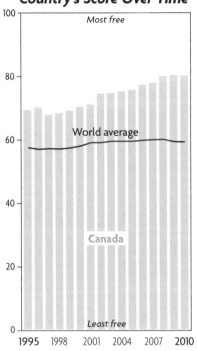

Quick Facts

Population: 33.3 million

GDP (PPP): $1.2 trillion
0.4% growth in 2008
2.3% 5-year compound annual growth
$36,444 per capita

Unemployment: 6.1%

Inflation (CPI): 2.4%

FDI Inflow: $44.7 billion

2008 data unless otherwise noted
Data compiled as of September 2009

How Do We Measure Economic Freedom?
See page 457 for an explanation of the methodology or visit the *Index* Web site at *heritage.org/index*.

CANADA'S TEN ECONOMIC FREEDOMS

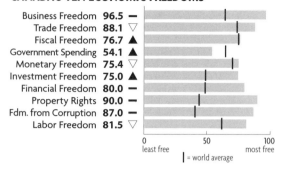

Business Freedom	96.5	▬
Trade Freedom	88.1	▽
Fiscal Freedom	76.7	▲
Government Spending	54.1	▲
Monetary Freedom	75.4	▽
Investment Freedom	75.0	▲
Financial Freedom	80.0	▬
Property Rights	90.0	▬
Fdm. from Corruption	87.0	▬
Labor Freedom	81.5	▽

0 least free — 50 — 100 most free

| = world average

BUSINESS FREEDOM — 96.5

The overall freedom to establish and run a business is strongly protected under Canada's regulatory environment. Starting a business takes an average of five days, compared to the world average of 35 days. Obtaining a business license requires less than the world average of 18 procedures and 218 days.

TRADE FREEDOM — 88.1

Canada's weighted average tariff rate was 1 percent in 2008. Federal and provincial non-tariff barriers, restrictions on imports of domestic "supply managed" agricultural products, restricted access to certain service industries, import taxes, export-support programs for industry and agriculture producers, cumbersome standards and import licensing, and state trading boards for some agriculture products add to the cost of trade. Ten points were deducted from Canada's trade freedom score to account for non-tariff barriers.

FISCAL FREEDOM — 76.7

Canada has moderate tax rates. The top federal income tax rate is 29 percent, and provincial rates range from 10 percent to 24 percent. The general corporate tax rate is 19.5 percent. Other taxes include a value-added tax (VAT) and a property tax. In the most recent year, overall tax revenue as a percentage of GDP was 33.3 percent.

GOVERNMENT SPENDING — 54.1

Total government expenditures, including consumption and transfer payments, are relatively high. In the most recent year, government spending equaled 39.1 percent of GDP. Privatization is widespread, and the government encourages competition even in sectors formerly operated by government or privately owned monopolies. With the lowest debt-to-GDP ratio in the G-7, Canada was well positioned to finance a significant stimulus plan in the wake of the global downturn.

MONETARY FREEDOM — 75.4

Inflation has been low, averaging 2.3 percent between 2006 and 2008. The market determines most prices, but the government regulates the prices of some utilities, subsidizes industry and agriculture producers, controls prices for some agricultural products, and influences prices through state-owned enterprises. The government controls virtually all prices for health care services through its manda-

tory "single-payer" nationalized program. Fifteen points were deducted from Canada's monetary freedom score to account for measures that distort domestic prices.

INVESTMENT FREEDOM — 75

Canada treats foreign and domestic capital equally in almost all situations. A federal agency must approve all direct foreign investment. Canada remains one of the few OECD countries to require such approval (which is usually granted). Restricted sectors include media, telecommunications, fishing, mining, and aviation. There are no restrictions on current transfers, repatriation of profits, or access to foreign exchange. Prince Edward Island, Saskatchewan, and Nova Scotia all limit real estate sales to out-of-province parties.

FINANCIAL FREEDOM — 80

Canada's financial system provides many options for businesses and competitive services for investors. Credit is allocated on market terms. The "big six" domestic banks account for around 90 percent of total assets; foreign banks, around 8 percent. It has become easier for foreign banks to enter the market, and their regulatory burden has been reduced. Revisions of the Bank Act in 2007 focused on streamlining regulation and enhancing consumer protection. Mergers between large banks are restricted, and large banks may not buy large insurance companies. The largest insurance companies conduct more than half of their business overseas. Securities markets are well developed, but the regulatory system is fragmented. The Montreal and Toronto exchanges merged in May 2008 while maintaining areas of specialization. Banking has weathered the recent financial crisis with no need for an injection of state funds.

PROPERTY RIGHTS — 90

Private property is well protected. The judiciary is independent, and judges and civil servants are generally honest. Foreign investors have full access to the legal system, and private property rights are limited only by the rights of governments to establish monopolies and expropriate for public purposes. Canada has yet to ratify the World Intellectual Property Organization's Internet Treaties, which it signed in 1997. Enforcement against counterfeiting and piracy is reportedly cumbersome and ineffective.

FREEDOM FROM CORRUPTION — 87

Corruption is perceived as minimal. Canada ranks 9th out of 179 countries in Transparency International's Corruption Perceptions Index for 2008. Bribery and other forms of corruption are rare. Canada has signed the U.N. Convention Against Corruption.

LABOR FREEDOM — 81.5

Flexible labor regulations enhance employment and productivity growth. The non-salary cost of employing a worker is moderate, and dismissing a redundant employee is relatively inexpensive. Rules on work hours are flexible.

CAPE VERDE

Praia

Economic Freedom Score

Least free 0   25   50   75   100 Most free

61.8

Cape Verde's economic freedom score is 61.8, making its economy the 78th freest in the 2010 *Index*. Its overall score is 0.5 point higher than last year, mainly as a result of enhanced business freedom. Cape Verde is ranked 7th out of 46 countries in the Sub-Saharan Africa region, and its overall score is much higher than the regional average.

Cape Verde has achieved an annual growth rate of close to 8 percent over the past five years. As a result of strong investments in infrastructure and ongoing trade liberalization, the entrepreneurial environment has gradually improved and become more streamlined. Cape Verde scores relatively well in monetary freedom, investment freedom, and especially property rights. Monetary stability is well maintained. Property rights are strongly protected by the rule of law in comparison to other countries in the region.

A number of challenges remain in the ongoing transition to greater economic freedom. High tax rates, inefficient state-owned enterprises, and a rigid labor market impede private investment and entrepreneurship and risk undermining long-term competitiveness.

BACKGROUND: Cape Verde, a West African archipelago, is a multi-party parliamentary democracy. Political power has changed hands peacefully since 1991. The country has few natural resources and is subject to frequent droughts and serious water shortages. The economy is dominated by services, but light industry, agriculture, and fishing employ a majority of the workforce. Cape Verde has close economic and political ties to the European Union, and its currency is pegged to the euro. The EU has granted Cape Verde special partnership status, under which Cape Verde and the EU cooperate to improve governance, security and stability, regional integration, and antipoverty efforts. The World Bank notes that remittances from the many Cape Verdeans who live abroad declined in 2007 and 2008. Cape Verde joined the World Trade Organization in 2007.

Country's Score Over Time

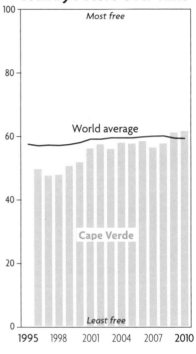

Quick Facts

Population: 0.5 million

GDP (PPP): $1.7 billion
6.0% growth in 2008
7.7% 5-year compound annual growth
$3,504 per capita

Unemployment: estimated to be over 15%

Inflation (CPI): 6.8%

FDI Inflow: $209 million

2008 data unless otherwise noted
Data compiled as of September 2009

How Do We Measure Economic Freedom?
See page 457 for an explanation of the methodology or visit the *Index* Web site at *heritage.org/index.*

CAPE VERDE'S TEN ECONOMIC FREEDOMS

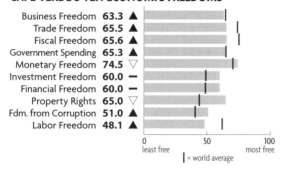

Business Freedom	63.3	▲
Trade Freedom	65.5	▲
Fiscal Freedom	65.6	▲
Government Spending	65.3	▲
Monetary Freedom	74.5	▽
Investment Freedom	60.0	—
Financial Freedom	60.0	—
Property Rights	65.0	▽
Fdm. from Corruption	51.0	▲
Labor Freedom	48.1	▲

0 least free   50   100 most free
| = world average

BUSINESS FREEDOM — *63.3*

The efficiency of Cape Verde's business environment has been improved. Starting a business takes less than the world average of 35 days. Obtaining a business license requires less than the world average of 218 days, but bankruptcy procedures are not fully developed.

TRADE FREEDOM — *65.5*

Cape Verde's weighted average tariff rate was 12.2 percent in 2008. Reform has progressed slowly, and import restrictions, services market access restrictions, import fees, inefficient regulatory and customs processes, non-transparent sanitary and phytosanitary regulations, state trade in certain products, weak enforcement of intellectual property rights, and export incentives still add to the cost of trade. Ten points were deducted from Cape Verde's trade freedom score to account for non-tariff barriers.

FISCAL FREEDOM — *65.6*

Cape Verde has a high income tax rate and a moderate corporate tax rate. The top income tax rate is 45 percent, and the top corporate tax rate is 30 percent. Other taxes include a value-added tax (VAT) and a special consumption tax. The stamp duty on sales and checks was abolished in 2009. In the most recent year, tax revenue as a percentage of GDP was 22.8 percent.

GOVERNMENT SPENDING — *65.3*

Total government expenditures, including consumption and transfer payments, are moderate. In the most recent year, government spending equaled 34 percent of GDP. State ownership is high, and nationalized companies are poorly run. The government now plans to re-structure rather than completely divest the national airline and electric companies.

MONETARY FREEDOM — *74.5*

Inflation has been moderately high, averaging 6.0 percent between 2006 and 2008. The market determines most prices, but the government controls the prices of water and electricity and regulates some others, including those for petroleum products and basic food items. Ten points were deducted from Cape Verde's monetary freedom score to adjust for measures that distort domestic prices.

INVESTMENT FREEDOM — *60*

Foreign investment is officially encouraged and receives equal treatment. Most sectors are open, but all foreign investment requires prior authorization. The government has simplified and expedited registration, opening most privatization to foreign investors. Cumbersome and time-consuming bureaucracy and inadequate institutional capacity and infrastructure undermine investment. Residents and non-residents may hold foreign exchange accounts, subject to some restrictions. Most capital transactions are permitted but are also subject to advance approval by the central bank or other controls.

FINANCIAL FREEDOM — *60*

Cape Verde's financial sector has been growing, albeit from a low base. The sector is highly concentrated, and two dominant commercial banks account for around 90 percent of assets and deposits. Credit is allocated on market terms and is available to foreign and domestic investors without discrimination. Credit to the private sector has climbed to around 50 percent of GDP. The non-performing loan ratio has improved significantly. Legislation implemented in 2002 gave more independence to the central bank, promoting its financial intermediary role, and the financial sector has been strengthened by improved regulations and monetary policy autonomy. New financial instruments including tax-free government bonds have been introduced. The government remains active in financial institutions that handle public investment and international aid. The legal and institutional framework for the Cape Verde Stock Exchange has been strengthened, and the stock market has been reinvigorated with increasing market capitalization equivalent to around 25 percent of GDP.

PROPERTY RIGHTS — *65*

Private property is fairly well protected. The constitutional provision for an independent judiciary is generally respected by the government, but the judicial system is overburdened, understaffed, and inefficient. The case backlog leads to delays of six months or more. Several recently signed treaties provide protection for intellectual property.

FREEDOM FROM CORRUPTION — *51*

Corruption is perceived as significant. Cape Verde ranks 47th out of 179 countries in Transparency International's Corruption Perceptions Index for 2008. Its political and economic governance is generally regarded as Africa's third best, behind Botswana and South Africa. The economy is about 40 percent informal. The government has adopted laws and regulations to make customs corruption criminally punishable.

LABOR FREEDOM — *48.1*

Employment regulations are relatively rigid. The non-salary cost of employing a worker is moderate, but the cost of dismissing a worker is relatively high. The effect of a 2008 labor reform aimed at increasing flexibility and competitiveness has been mixed.

CENTRAL AFRICAN REPUBLIC

★ Bangui

| World Rank: **152** | Regional Rank: **32** |

Economic Freedom Score

25   50   75

Least free 0   100 Most free

48.4

The Central African Republic's economic freedom score is 48.4, making its economy the 152nd freest in the 2010 *Index*. Its overall score is 0.1 point higher than last year, primarily because of improving trade freedom. The CAR is ranked 32nd out of 46 countries in the Sub-Saharan Africa region, and its overall score is lower than the regional average.

The recent financial and economic crisis has led to reduced growth prospects, largely because of a decrease in the country's principal exports. Medium-term structural reforms include a government financial management information system, an enhanced debt management plan, and systematic tax audits.

The overall efficiency and quality of government remain poor. Monetary stability has been affected by inflationary pressures, and government interference with market prices is extensive. Regulation is burdensome, and business operations remain constrained by government interference and bureaucratic delays. Rigid labor regulations and an underdeveloped labor market impose additional costs on establishing and expanding businesses. Access to financing is limited. The protection of property rights remains weak, and corruption is rampant.

BACKGROUND: The Central African Republic (CAR) has a history of political instability. General François Bozizé overthrew the civilian government in 2003 and won the 2005 election. Fighting between rebels and government troops in the North has displaced tens of thousands of people. A December 2008 agreement between Bozizé, opposition leaders, and some rebel groups established a consensus government, and presidential elections are scheduled for 2010. Other rebel groups remain active. In March 2009, an EU peacekeeping force was replaced by the U.N. mission in the CAR and Chad. Despite abundant timber, diamonds, gold, and uranium, the CAR is one of the world's least-developed countries. Most of its people are subsistence farmers, and agriculture and forestry account for over half of GDP. Infrastructure is poor, institutions are weak, and corruption is prevalent.

Country's Score Over Time

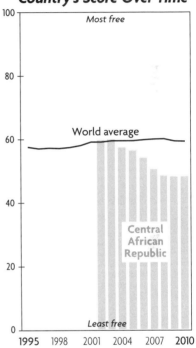

Quick Facts

Population: 4.4 million

GDP (PPP): $3.3 billion
2.8% growth in 2008
3.0% 5-year compound annual growth
$736 per capita

Unemployment: n/a

Inflation (CPI): 9.3%

FDI Inflow: $121 million

2008 data unless otherwise noted
Data compiled as of September 2009

How Do We Measure Economic Freedom?
See page 457 for an explanation of the methodology or visit the *Index* Web site at *heritage.org/index.*

143

CENTRAL AFRICAN REP.'S TEN ECONOMIC FREEDOMS

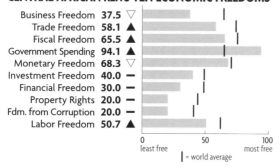

Business Freedom	37.5 ▽	
Trade Freedom	58.1 ▲	
Fiscal Freedom	65.5 ▲	
Government Spending	94.1 ▲	
Monetary Freedom	68.3 ▽	
Investment Freedom	40.0 —	
Financial Freedom	30.0 —	
Property Rights	20.0 —	
Fdm. from Corruption	20.0 —	
Labor Freedom	50.7 ▲	

0   50   100
least free   most free
| = world average

BUSINESS FREEDOM — 37.5

The overall freedom to start, operate, and close a business is impeded by the Central African Republic's regulatory environment. Starting a business takes less than the world average of 35 days, but obtaining a business license requires slightly more than the world average of 18 procedures and 218 days.

TRADE FREEDOM — 58.1

The Central African Republic's weighted average tariff rate was 13.5 percent in 2007. Limits on imports of sugar and coffee, import and export taxes, inappropriate customs valuation for certain imports, inadequate infrastructure, weak regulatory and customs administration, and customs fraud and inefficiency add to the cost of trade. Fifteen points were deducted from the CAR's trade freedom score to account for non-tariff barriers.

FISCAL FREEDOM — 65.5

The Central African Republic has a high income tax rate and a moderate corporate tax rate. The top income tax rate is 50 percent, and the top corporate tax rate is 30 percent. Other taxes include a value-added tax (VAT). The excise tax on fuel was increased in 2008. In the most recent year, overall tax revenue as a percentage of GDP was 7.3 percent.

GOVERNMENT SPENDING — 94.1

Total government expenditures, including consumption and transfer payments, are low. In the most recent year, government spending equaled 14.0 percent of GDP. Fiscal management needs improvement, and energy remains under state control.

MONETARY FREEDOM — 68.3

Inflation has jumped, averaging 7.0 percent between 2006 and 2008, although inflationary pressures are expected to decrease in 2009–2010 because of falling international energy and food prices and rising production of food crops. The government influences most prices through the public sector, subsidies, and price controls on 17 food staples, coffee, cotton, electricity, water, and petroleum. Fifteen points were deducted from the CAR's monetary freedom score to account for measures that distort domestic prices.

INVESTMENT FREEDOM — 40

Foreign and domestic investors are treated equally, but several sectors are closed to private investment. A weak security environment, non-transparent and corrupt bureaucracy, and inadequate infrastructure are significant deterrents. Residents may hold foreign exchange accounts. All capital transactions, transfers, and payments to countries other than certain regional nations, France, and Monaco are subject to government approval and reporting requirements. Sale or issue of capital market securities and commercial credits likewise require government approval.

FINANCIAL FREEDOM — 30

The CAR's financial sector is underdeveloped, and access to financing for businesses remains limited. Less than 1 percent of the population has access to banking services. Regulation and supervision are inadequate. The regional Central African Economic and Monetary Community countries share a common central bank and a common currency pegged to the euro. In addition to a branch of the regional central bank, there are three commercial banks, two microfinance institutions, and two postal financial institutions. The two largest commercial banks, Banque Internationale pour le Centrafrique and Commercial Bank Centrafrique, have been privatized, but the Banque Populaire Maroco-Centrafricaine is still partly government-owned. The banking sector is used to finance government expenditures, and the accumulation of state debt and lack of promised credits have undermined the system. Since the state borrows at the maximum possible interest rate, commercial banks have little incentive to lend to the private sector.

PROPERTY RIGHTS — 20

Protection of property rights is weak. The constitution has been suspended, allowing the president to rule by decree. Judges are appointed by the president, and the judiciary is subject to executive interference. Because of inefficient administration, a shortage of trained personnel, growing salary arrears, and a lack of material resources, the courts are barely functioning.

FREEDOM FROM CORRUPTION — 20

Corruption is perceived as pervasive. The Central African Republic ranks 151st out of 179 countries in Transparency International's Corruption Perceptions Index for 2008. Informal market activity and smuggling, especially in diamonds, are extensive. Misappropriation of public funds and corruption are widespread, and government officials engage in corrupt practices with impunity. The formal sector has contracted significantly because of regulation and corruption, and a large part of the population works informally. The police and the judiciary are among the country's most corrupt institutions.

LABOR FREEDOM — 50.7

Rigid labor regulations hinder employment and productivity growth. The non-salary cost of employing a worker is moderate, and dismissing a redundant employee is relatively difficult. Regulations on the number of work hours are rigid.

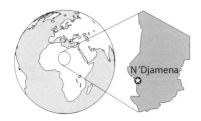

CHAD

Economic Freedom Score

47.5

25 · 50 · 75

Least free 0 · 100 Most free

Chad's economic freedom score is 47.5, making its economy the 159th freest in the 2010 *Index*. Its overall score is virtually unchanged from last year. Chad is ranked 37th out of 46 countries in the Sub-Saharan Africa region, and its overall score is lower than the regional average.

Development of a more dynamic climate for investment and entrepreneurship has stalled. Inflation has been contained, but the government still intervenes in the prices of certain goods. Improving fiscal governance and the efficiency of government services is critical to stabilizing an economy that is strained by security expenditures and overly reliant on oil revenues. Only the informal economy offers a large number of jobs to relatively unskilled labor.

Chad scores very poorly on such institutional factors as the business and investment climate, labor market flexibility, and taxation. Taxes are burdensome, starting a business takes over two months, and both licensing and closing a business remain time-consuming and costly. The weak rule of law and rampant corruption seriously impede economic development.

BACKGROUND: President Idriss Deby seized power in 1990 and in 2006 won a third term in an election that was boycotted by the main opposition parties. Conflict with rebels in eastern Chad and unrest in Sudan's Darfur region have resulted in hundreds of thousands of Chadian and Sudanese refugees, and each country has accused the other of supporting rebels in its territory. In March 2009, an EU peacekeeping force was replaced by the U.N. mission in the Central African Republic and Chad. Chad is thinly populated, landlocked, unstable, and impoverished, and over 70 percent of its people depend on subsistence agriculture, herding, and fishing. Investments in the oil sector since 2001 and receipts of oil revenues since 2003 have encouraged economic growth, and oil now accounts for about half of GDP.

Country's Score Over Time

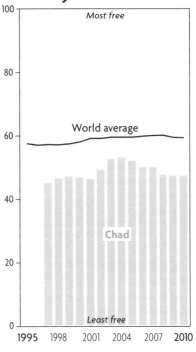

100 — Most free

80

60 — World average

40

Chad

20

0 — Least free

1995   1998   2001   2004   2007   **2010**

Quick Facts

Population: 11.1 million

GDP (PPP): $16.1 billion
−0.4% growth in 2008
1.9% 5-year compound annual growth
$1,455 per capita

Unemployment: 8.3%

Inflation (CPI): 8.3%

FDI Inflow: $834 million

2008 data unless otherwise noted
Data compiled as of September 2009

How Do We Measure Economic Freedom?
See page 457 for an explanation of the methodology or visit the *Index* Web site at *heritage.org/index.*

CHAD'S TEN ECONOMIC FREEDOMS

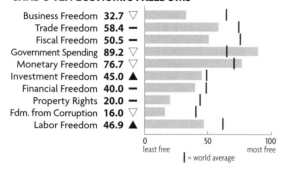

Business Freedom	32.7 ▽
Trade Freedom	58.4 —
Fiscal Freedom	50.5 —
Government Spending	89.2 ▽
Monetary Freedom	76.7 ▽
Investment Freedom	45.0 ▲
Financial Freedom	40.0 —
Property Rights	20.0 —
Fdm. from Corruption	16.0 ▽
Labor Freedom	46.9 ▲

0 least free   50   100 most free

| = world average

BUSINESS FREEDOM — *32.7*

The overall freedom to start, operate, and close a business is seriously limited under Chad's regulatory environment. Starting a business takes almost twice the world average of 35 days, and the cost of establishing a business remains quite high.

TRADE FREEDOM — *58.4*

Chad's weighted average tariff rate was 13.3 percent in 2007. Import and export restrictions, import fees, inappropriate customs valuation for some products, a non-transparent customs code, weak enforcement of intellectual property rights, non-transparent government procurement, subsidies, corruption, and inefficient customs administration add to the cost of trade. Fifteen points were deducted from Chad's trade freedom score to account for non-tariff barriers.

FISCAL FREEDOM — *50.5*

Chad has very high tax rates. The top income tax rate is 60 percent, and the top corporate tax rate is 40 percent. Other taxes include a value-added tax (VAT), a property tax, and an apprenticeship tax. In the most recent year, overall tax revenue as a percentage of GDP was 4.2 percent.

GOVERNMENT SPENDING — *89.2*

Total government expenditures, including consumption and transfer payments, are low. In the most recent year, government spending equaled 19.0 percent of GDP. Privatization has slowed, and the state retains control of cotton, water, and electricity. Chad's economy is highly vulnerable to changes in the price of oil. The non-oil deficit has climbed to nearly 25 percent of GDP.

MONETARY FREEDOM — *76.7*

Inflation has been moderate, averaging 4 percent between 2006 and 2008. The Banque des Etats de l'Afrique Centrale maintains the CFA franc's peg to the euro. Most prices are determined in the market, but the government influences prices through state-owned enterprises and regulation of such key goods and services as cotton, telecommunications, water, road transportation, and energy. Ten points were deducted from Chad's monetary freedom score to adjust for measures that distort domestic prices.

INVESTMENT FREEDOM — *45*

Chad allows foreign ownership and provides equal treatment to foreign investors, subject to certain bureaucratic requirements and restrictions in some sectors. Investment is inhibited by inadequate infrastructure and technical expertise, burdensome taxes, underdeveloped markets, weak dispute mechanisms, and corruption. Bureaucracy is burdensome and non-transparent and can be arbitrary. Residents and non-residents may hold foreign exchange accounts with government approval. Capital transactions, payments, and transfers to certain countries are subject to some controls and restrictions.

FINANCIAL FREEDOM — *40*

The financial system is small and suffers from weak market infrastructure and legal and judicial frameworks. Chad and the five other countries in the Central African Economic and Monetary Community share a common central bank and a common currency pegged to the euro. Significant banking privatization has been completed, and there are now five commercial banks. However, informal financial services are common, and supervision and regulation are insufficient. Difficult access to credit and its high cost hinder private-sector development. Small and medium enterprises rely mainly on self-financing or mutual aid systems. The small insurance sector is dominated by the formerly state-owned Star Nationale. There are no capital or money markets.

PROPERTY RIGHTS — *20*

Protection of private property is weak. It is widely felt that the courts should be avoided at all costs, and most disputes are settled privately. The constitution guarantees judicial independence, but most key judicial officials are named by the president and assumed to be subject to political influence. Legal clerks often obstruct procedures in order to elicit bribes. Chad is ranked 109th out of 115 countries in the 2009 International Property Rights Index.

FREEDOM FROM CORRUPTION — *16*

Corruption is perceived as rampant. Chad ranks 173rd out of 179 countries in Transparency International's Corruption Perceptions Index for 2008. Although Chad has a "Ministry of Morality" that is responsible for fighting corruption and conducts anti-corruption seminars for government employees, corruption exists at all levels of government. It may be most pervasive in the customs and tax enforcement services, but it is notable in the judiciary and the government procurement office as well. The government actively obstructs the work of domestic human rights organizations through arrest, detention, and intimidation of their members.

LABOR FREEDOM — *46.9*

Burdensome employment regulations hinder job creation and productivity growth. The non-salary cost of employing a worker is high, and dismissing a redundant employee is relatively costly.

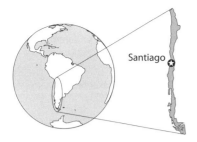

Santiago

CHILE

Economic Freedom Score

25 50 75
Least free 0   100 Most free

77.2

Chile's economic freedom score is 77.2, making its economy the 10th freest in the 2010 *Index*. Its overall score is 1.1 points lower than last year, reflecting small declines in six of the 10 economic freedoms. Chile enjoys the highest degree of economic freedom in the South and Central America/Caribbean region.

Openness to global trade and investment and a dynamic private sector have facilitated steady economic growth. Chile has pursued free trade agreements with countries around the world. The financial sector is diversified and stable compared to other regional economies, and prudent lending and regulations have allowed the banking sector to withstand the global financial crisis with little disruption. Other institutional strengths include transparent and stable public finance management and strong protection of property rights, although protection of intellectual property rights still needs to be strengthened.

Chile trails behind other comparable economies in business freedom, fiscal freedom, and labor freedom. Income taxes on individuals remain burdensome. Although overall regulatory licensing is easy, bankruptcy procedures remain cumbersome and costly.

BACKGROUND: Since 1990, successive governments, though left-of-center, have largely maintained the market-based institutions and policies established under the 17-year rule of General Augusto Pinochet. Socialist President Michele Bachelet's coalition government has done so as well, although her rhetoric emphasizes income equality over freedom. Chile is the world's leading producer of copper, and exports of minerals, wood, fruit, seafood, and wine drive GDP growth. An Economic and Social Stabilization Fund manages taxes on copper revenues to maintain social spending during downturns. Chile belongs to the Asia–Pacific Economic Cooperation forum and has signed or is negotiating trade agreements with China and other Pacific Rim countries to supplement its agreement with the U.S. It also is on track to become the first South American country to join the Organisation for Economic Co-operation and Development.

Country's Score Over Time

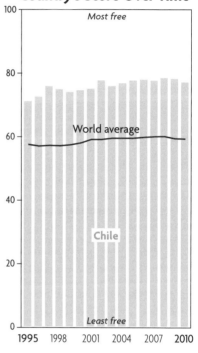

Quick Facts

Population: 16.8 million

GDP (PPP): $242.4 billion
3.2% growth in 2008
4.5% 5-year compound annual growth
$14,465 per capita

Unemployment: 7.8%

Inflation (CPI): 8.7%

FDI Inflow: $16.8 billion

2008 data unless otherwise noted
Data compiled as of September 2009

How Do We Measure Economic Freedom?
See page 457 for an explanation of the methodology or visit the *Index* Web site at *heritage.org/index*.

CHILE'S TEN ECONOMIC FREEDOMS

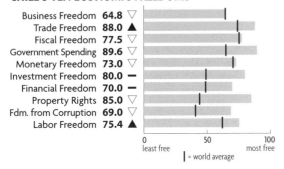

Business Freedom	64.8 ▽
Trade Freedom	88.0 ▲
Fiscal Freedom	77.5 ▽
Government Spending	89.6 ▽
Monetary Freedom	73.0 ▽
Investment Freedom	80.0 —
Financial Freedom	70.0 —
Property Rights	85.0 ▽
Fdm. from Corruption	69.0 ▽
Labor Freedom	75.4 ▲

0 least free   50   100 most free

| = world average

BUSINESS FREEDOM — 64.8

The overall freedom to establish and run a business is relatively well protected under Chile's regulatory environment. Starting a business takes an average of 27 days, compared to the world average of 35 days. Obtaining a business license takes the world average of 18 procedures and less than the world average of 218 days. Bankruptcy procedures can be burdensome and lengthy.

TRADE FREEDOM — 88

Chile's weighted average tariff rate was 1 percent in 2008. Chile is phasing out price bands for wheat, flour, and sugar, but approval requirements and stringent sanitary and phytosanitary regulations on imports of agricultural products and processed food, import bans, import taxes, export subsidies for some sectors, and issues related to the protection of intellectual property rights add to the cost of trade. Ten points were deducted from Chile's trade freedom score to account for non-tariff barriers.

FISCAL FREEDOM — 77.5

Chile's income tax rate is well above average, but its corporate tax rate is well below average. The top income tax rate is 40 percent, and the top standard corporate tax rate is 17 percent. Other taxes include a value-added tax (VAT) and a property tax. In the most recent year, overall tax revenue as a percentage of GDP was 18.9 percent.

GOVERNMENT SPENDING — 89.6

Total government expenditures, including consumption and transfer payments, are low. In the most recent year, government spending equaled 18.6 percent of GDP.

MONETARY FREEDOM — 73

Inflation has been high, averaging 7.2 percent between 2006 and 2008. Many prices are determined in the market, but the government controls prices for utilities, and price bands for certain agricultural products remain in effect. Ten points were deducted from Chile's monetary freedom score to adjust for measures that distort domestic prices.

INVESTMENT FREEDOM — 80

Foreign and domestic investments generally receive equal treatment. The Ministry of Economy reviews foreign investment and sets the terms and conditions for contracts involving foreign direct investment. Foreigners may invest in fishing companies and media only if their countries have reciprocity arrangements with Chile. Regulation tends to be transparent and efficient. Residents and non-residents may hold foreign exchange accounts, and there are no restrictions on repatriation. There are few controls on current transfers and capital transactions. The government can expropriate property for public or national interests, on a non-discriminatory basis and in accordance with the due process of law.

FINANCIAL FREEDOM — 70

Chile's financial system is among the region's and the world's most stable and developed. Reforms that include capitalization requirements and shareholder obligations have increased competition and widened the range of operations. Twelve foreign banks and 13 domestic banks compete on an equal footing. The four largest banks control about 65 percent of total assets. The state-owned Banco Estado is Chile's third largest bank and accounts for about 15 percent of assets. Credit is issued on market terms. Domestic and foreign banking and insurance companies receive equal treatment. Chile's liberal capital market is the region's largest. Legislation to enhance access to financing for individuals and firms was passed in April 2009. The banking system has withstood the global financial turmoil well because of prudential lending and sound regulations.

PROPERTY RIGHTS — 85

Private property is well protected. Contracts are secure, and courts are transparent and efficient. Expropriation is rare, and owners receive compensation. Intellectual property rights laws and regulations are substantively deficient, and IPR enforcement is inadequate. Principal concerns involve protection of pharmaceutical patents and test data and copyright piracy of movies, music, and software. In 2008, the government created the National Industrial Property Institute to streamline IPR procedures.

FREEDOM FROM CORRUPTION — 69

Corruption is perceived as minimal. Chile ranks 23rd out of 179 countries in Transparency International's Corruption Perceptions Index for 2008. Contractual agreements are the most secure in Latin America, and local public administration is generally considered honest. Nevertheless, the ruling coalition is increasingly accused of corruption. Chile has ratified the Organization of American States Convention Against Corruption and the OECD Convention on Combating Bribery. Judicial corruption is rare.

LABOR FREEDOM — 75.4

The non-salary cost of employing a worker is low, but dismissing a redundant employee is relatively costly. The labor market has become more rigid as regulations and minimum wage increases have exceeded overall productivity growth.

PEOPLE'S REPUBLIC OF **CHINA**

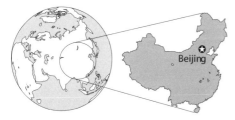
Beijing

World Rank: 140   **Regional Rank: 31**

Economic Freedom Score

25   50   75

Least free 0   100 Most free

51.0

China's economic freedom score is 51, making its economy the 140th freest in the 2010 *Index*. Its overall score is 2.2 points lower than last year, with significant declines recorded in investment freedom and labor freedom. China is ranked 31st out of 41 countries in the Asia–Pacific region, and its overall score is lower than the global and regional averages.

The world's most populous economy has benefited from global trade and investment and periodic bursts of reform for three decades. The state still directs most economic activity, and the Communist Party, while allowing some response to market forces, still maintains ultimate authority over economic decisions.

China's transition to greater economic freedom has been sluggish over the life of the *Index*. Efforts to embrace market principles have been made from time to time, but overall progress has been modest. Rapid development of coastal cities has resulted in increasing disparities in economic freedom and standards of living across the country. Foreign investment is controlled and regulated, and the judicial system is highly vulnerable to political influence. The state maintains tight control of the financial sector and directly or indirectly owns all banks.

BACKGROUND: China has liberalized parts of its economy to a notable degree since the early 1980s. It joined the World Trade Organization in 2001, and its industrial and manufacturing sector is now second in size only to that of the United States. At the same time, however, China remains a one-party state in which the Communist Party maintains tight control of political expression, speech, religion, and assembly. Any social group that can organize on a large scale is deemed a threat, as are many individual dissidents. The government is struggling to manage environmental degradation, demographic pressure, and the world's largest-ever migration from rural to urban areas, all of which contribute to social unrest.

Country's Score Over Time

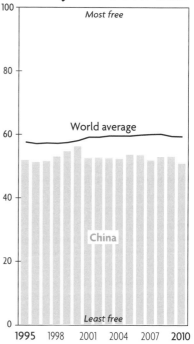

Quick Facts

Population: 1.3 billion

GDP (PPP): $7.9 trillion
9.0% growth in 2008
11.0% 5-year compound annual growth
$5,962 per capita

Unemployment: 4.2% (urban area)
Substantial unemployment and underemployment in rural areas

Inflation (CPI): 5.9%

FDI Inflow: $108.3 billion

2008 data unless otherwise noted
Data compiled as of September 2009

How Do We Measure Economic Freedom?
See page 457 for an explanation of the methodology or visit the *Index* Web site at *heritage.org/index.*

CHINA'S TEN ECONOMIC FREEDOMS

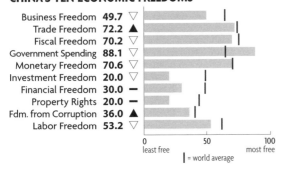

Business Freedom	49.7	▽
Trade Freedom	72.2	▲
Fiscal Freedom	70.2	▽
Government Spending	88.1	▽
Monetary Freedom	70.6	▽
Investment Freedom	20.0	▽
Financial Freedom	30.0	—
Property Rights	20.0	▽
Fdm. from Corruption	36.0	▲
Labor Freedom	53.2	▽

0 least free   50   100 most free

| = world average

BUSINESS FREEDOM — 49.7

The overall freedom to establish and run a business is constrained by China's regulatory environment. Starting a business takes about the world average of 35 days, but obtaining a business license requires more than the world average of 18 procedures and 218 days. China lacks legal and regulatory transparency.

TRADE FREEDOM — 72.2

China's weighted average tariff rate was 3.9 percent in 2008. Despite lower non-tariff barriers pursuant to World Trade Organization requirements, import and export bans and restrictions, import and export licensing, non-transparent tariff classifications, complex regulations and standards, subsidies, state trading in certain goods, services market restrictions, issues involving the protection of intellectual property rights, and inconsistent and corruption-prone customs administration add to the cost of trade. Twenty points were deducted from China's trade freedom score to account for non-tariff barriers.

FISCAL FREEDOM — 70.2

China has a high income tax rate and a moderate corporate tax rate. The top income tax rate is 45 percent, and the top corporate tax rate is 25 percent. The government encourages new-technology businesses with a reduced corporate rate of 15 percent. Other taxes include a value-added tax (VAT) and a real estate tax. As of October 2008, individual income tax is no longer paid on interest on bank deposits. In the most recent year, overall tax revenue as a percentage of GDP was 18.3 percent.

GOVERNMENT SPENDING — 88.1

Government expenditures, including consumption and transfer payments, are low. In the most recent year, central government spending equaled 19.9 percent of GDP. State ownership of enterprises persists in most sectors. Mergers have been more frequent than divestments. The first anti-monopoly law was enacted in August 2008.

MONETARY FREEDOM — 70.6

Inflation has been moderate, averaging 5.2 percent between 2006 and 2008. The market determines the prices of most traded products, but the government maintains prices for petroleum, electricity, pharmaceuticals, coal, agricultural products, and other "essential" goods. Subsidies allow state-owned enterprises to produce and sell goods to wholesalers and retailers at artificially low prices. Fifteen points were deducted from China's monetary freedom score to adjust for measures that distort domestic prices.

INVESTMENT FREEDOM — 20

China's Foreign Investment Catalogue delineates sectors in which foreign investment is encouraged, permitted, restricted, and prohibited, as well as such specific restrictions as caps on foreign ownership and permissible types of investment. Investors face regulatory non-transparency, complex and inconsistently enforced laws and regulations, weak protection of intellectual property rights, corruption, industrial policies protecting local firms, and a legal system that cannot guarantee the sanctity of contracts. Foreign investors may access foreign exchange for current account transactions like repatriating profits, but capital account transactions are tightly regulated. Chinese law prohibits nationalization of foreign investment except under "special" circumstances.

FINANCIAL FREEDOM — 30

China's complex financial system is tightly controlled by the government. The China Banking Regulatory Commission supervised roughly 5,600 financial institutions in 2008. China has only two private banks; four state-owned banks account for over 50 percent of total assets. The state directs the allocation of credit, and the big four state banks lend primarily to state-owned enterprises. Since joining the WTO, China has gradually removed barriers to foreign banks, but cumbersome regulations remain. Foreign banks account for only about 2 percent of total assets. Foreign participation in capital markets remains limited. Expanding access to financial services still remains a challenge.

PROPERTY RIGHTS — 20

China's judicial system is weak, and many companies resort to arbitration. Local officials can ignore court decision with impunity. All land is state-owned, but individuals and firms may own and transfer long-term leases (subject to many restrictions) as well as structures and personal property. Intellectual property rights are not enforced effectively. Copyrights, patents, brand names, trademarks, and trade secrets are routinely stolen.

FREEDOM FROM CORRUPTION — 36

Corruption is perceived as widespread. China ranks 72nd out of 179 countries in Transparency International's Corruption Perceptions Index for 2008. Corruption affects banking, finance, government procurement, and construction most severely, and there is a lack of independent investigative bodies and courts.

LABOR FREEDOM — 53.2

China's labor regulations hinder overall employment and productivity growth. The non-salary cost of employing a worker is high. Dismissing an employee may require prior consultation with the local labor bureau and labor union.

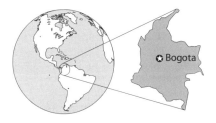

COLOMBIA

Economic Freedom Score

Colombia's economic freedom score is 65.5, making its economy the 58th freest in the 2010 *Index*. Its overall score is 3.2 points higher than last year, reflecting improved business and labor freedom, better protection of property rights, and reduced corruption. Colombia is ranked 12th out of 29 countries in the South and Central America/Caribbean region, and its overall score is higher than the regional average.

As one of South America's most stable economies, Colombia continues its transition to greater economic freedom. Improvements in its entrepreneurial environment, facilitated by openness to trade and investment, have led to steady economic growth. Recent reforms have focused on improving regulation and fostering a strong private sector.

Colombia's overall economic freedom remains obstructed by persistent institutional weaknesses. The rule of law remains problematic. Despite nominal openness to foreign investment, regulations are complex and uncertain. Business contracts are generally respected, but judicial corruption undermines legal transparency and efficiency. State ownership is limited to a few utilities, but public expenditure is high because of large transfers to regional state-owned enterprises.

BACKGROUND: Colombia is one of South America's oldest continuous democracies. President Alvaro Uribe, re-elected by a landslide in 2006, has restored security by enforcing the law against both the Revolutionary Armed Forces of Colombia and its anti-Communist paramilitary nemesis. He has also waged a vigorous war on narcotics trafficking. The quality of life has improved substantially, and unemployment has dropped significantly. Like all of Latin America, Colombia was buffeted by global economic turbulence in 2008–2009. The economy depends heavily on exports of petroleum, coffee, and cut flowers. A trade agreement with the U.S. that would encourage economic diversification and stimulate further growth was submitted to the U.S. Congress in 2008 but is still awaiting action. Uribe has been seeking constitutional changes to allow him to run for a third consecutive term.

Country's Score Over Time

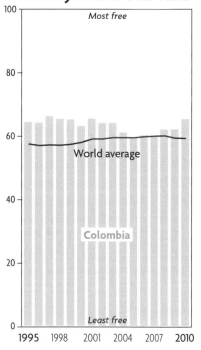

Quick Facts

Population: 44.5 million

GDP (PPP): $395.7 billion
2.5% growth in 2008
5.7% 5-year compound
annual growth
$8,885 per capita

Unemployment: 11.3%

Inflation (CPI): 7.0%

FDI Inflow: $10.6 billion

2008 data unless otherwise noted
Data compiled as of September 2009

How Do We Measure Economic Freedom?
See page 457 for an explanation of the methodology or visit the *Index* Web site at *heritage.org/index.*

COLOMBIA'S TEN ECONOMIC FREEDOMS

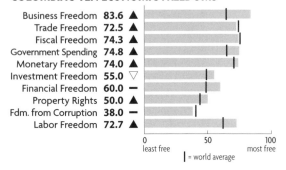

Business Freedom	83.6 ▲	
Trade Freedom	72.5 ▲	
Fiscal Freedom	74.3 ▲	
Government Spending	74.8 ▲	
Monetary Freedom	74.0 ▲	
Investment Freedom	55.0 ▽	
Financial Freedom	60.0 —	
Property Rights	50.0 ▲	
Fdm. from Corruption	38.0 —	
Labor Freedom	72.7 ▲	

0 least free — 50 — 100 most free

| = world average

BUSINESS FREEDOM — 83.6

The overall freedom to start, operate, and close a business is relatively well protected under Colombia's regulatory environment. Starting a business takes 20 days, compared to the world average of 35 days. Obtaining a business license takes much less than the world average of 18 procedures and 218 days.

TRADE FREEDOM — 72.5

Colombia's weighted average tariff rate was 8.7 percent in 2008. Import bans and restrictions, import price bands for certain goods, services market access limits, restrictive standards and regulations, restrictive import licensing, issues involving the enforcement of intellectual property rights, non-transparent customs administration and valuation, export-promotion programs, and corruption add to the cost of trade. Ten points were deducted from Colombia's trade freedom score to account for non-tariff barriers.

FISCAL FREEDOM — 74.3

The top income and corporate tax rates are 33 percent. Other taxes include a value-added tax (VAT) and a financial transactions tax. In the most recent year, overall tax revenue as a percentage of GDP was 19.8 percent. Tax evasion, though on the decline, is still relatively high.

GOVERNMENT SPENDING — 74.8

Total government expenditures, including consumption and transfer payments, are moderate. In the most recent year, government spending equaled 29.0 percent of GDP.

MONETARY FREEDOM — 74

Inflation has been relatively moderate, averaging 6.4 percent between 2006 and 2008. The government controls prices for ground and air transport, some pharmaceutical products, petroleum derivatives, natural gas, some petrochemicals, public utility services, residential rents, schoolbooks, and school tuition, and the Agriculture Ministry may intervene temporarily to freeze prices of basic foodstuffs through agreements with regional wholesalers. Ten points were deducted from Colombia's monetary freedom score to adjust for measures that distort domestic prices.

INVESTMENT FREEDOM — 55

Foreign investment receives national treatment, and 100 percent foreign ownership is permitted in most sectors. Foreign investment in television concessions and nation-wide private television operators, radio broadcasting, movie production, maritime agencies, national airlines, and shipping companies is limited to minority stakes. The legal and regulatory systems are generally transparent and consistent with international norms. Frequent changes in business rules and a burdensome judiciary impede investment. For firms with more than 10 employees, no more than 10 percent of the general workforce and 20 percent of specialists can be foreign nationals. Foreign investments must be registered with the central bank to allow repatriation of profits and remittances and to access foreign exchange. Residents who work in certain internationally related companies may hold foreign exchange accounts. Assets expropriated by eminent domain will be compensated.

FINANCIAL FREEDOM — 60

Colombia's relatively large financial sector has become more stable and modern. Banking has undergone significant consolidation and privatization since early 2000. The government has strengthened regulations and seized some banks for falling below solvency requirements. Seven of the 17 commercial banks are foreign-owned. Two private financial groups account for about 45 percent of bank assets. Foreign banks accounted for less than 20 percent of total assets in 2008. Credit is allocated on market terms. As of early 2008, the government retained 15 percent of total banking assets. Foreign companies are prominent in the insurance sector, and competition has intensified since 2003. Colombia's small capital market provides limited access to long-term credit. The market is heavily concentrated in government bonds. Accounting for only 5 percent of total trading, equity trading is dominated by a few listed companies.

PROPERTY RIGHTS — 50

Colombia's constitution explicitly protects the right to private property. Contracts are generally respected. Arbitration is complex and dilatory, especially with regard to the enforcement of awards. The law guarantees indemnification in expropriation cases. Enforcement of intellectual property rights remains erratic. Infringements, especially unauthorized use of trademarks, are common. In areas still controlled by terrorist groups, property rights cannot be guaranteed.

FREEDOM FROM CORRUPTION — 38

Corruption is perceived as significant. Colombia ranks 70th out of 179 countries in Transparency International's Corruption Perceptions Index for 2008. Despite notable improvements in fighting corruption and narcotics trafficking, concerns remain over the influence of criminal organizations on the police, the military, and lower levels of the judiciary and civil service.

LABOR FREEDOM — 72.7

Labor regulations have become more flexible. The non-salary cost of employing a worker remains somewhat burdensome, but dismissing a redundant employee can be relatively inexpensive. Regulations controlling work hours are relatively flexible.

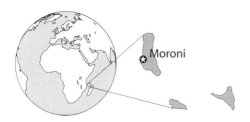
Moroni

COMOROS

Economic Freedom Score

25   50   75

Least free 0   100 Most free

44.9

World Rank: **165**	Regional Rank: **41**

Comoros's economic freedom score is 44.9, making its economy the 165th freest in the 2010 *Index*. Its overall score improved 1.6 points as a result of a large improvement in trade freedom. Comoros is ranked 41st out of 46 countries in the Sub-Saharan Africa region, and its overall score is lower than the regional average.

Economic freedom remains severely constrained in Comoros. Poor management of macroeconomic policies, coupled with political crises over the past decade, has hindered overall economic development. The economy remains highly dependent on foreign aid and remittances.

The public sector is inefficient and lacks capacity to support or provide such basic public goods as secure property rights, a sound legal system, efficient infrastructure, and transparent regulations. Poor access to credit and the high costs of financing for entrepreneurial activity severely limit the development of a vibrant private sector, driving a large portion of the workforce into the small retail services sector.

BACKGROUND: After declaring its independence from France in 1975, Comoros experienced political instability and numerous coups. A 2001 constitution granting the islands of Grande Comore, Anjouan, and Moheli increased autonomy provided some stability. The presidency rotates among the three islands. President Ahmed Abdallah Sambi's 2006 election was the country's first democratic transition of leadership. Remittances by Comorans living abroad are an important source of income and were estimated to have equaled 18 percent of GDP in 2006. Fishing, agriculture, and forestry employ approximately 80 percent of the population and provide over 50 percent of GDP. Though much of the terrain is not suitable for agriculture, Comoros is among the world's leading producers of ylang-ylang (a perfume ingredient), cloves, and vanilla. Basic infrastructure, such as ports and roads, is severely underdeveloped.

Country's Score Over Time

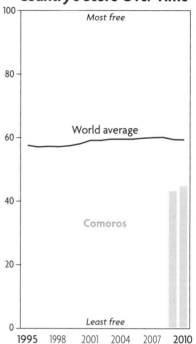

Quick Facts

Population: 0.6 million

GDP (PPP): $0.8 billion
1.0% growth in 2008
1.7% 5-year compound annual growth
$1,169 per capita

Unemployment: n/a

Inflation (CPI): 4.8%

FDI Inflow: $8 million

2008 data unless otherwise noted
Data compiled as of September 2009

How Do We Measure Economic Freedom?
See page 457 for an explanation of the methodology or visit the *Index* Web site at *heritage.org/index*.

COMOROS'S TEN ECONOMIC FREEDOMS

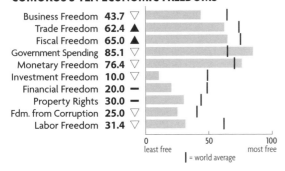

Business Freedom	43.7 ▽	
Trade Freedom	62.4 ▲	
Fiscal Freedom	65.0 ▲	
Government Spending	85.1 ▽	
Monetary Freedom	76.4 ▽	
Investment Freedom	10.0 ▽	
Financial Freedom	20.0 —	
Property Rights	30.0 —	
Fdm. from Corruption	25.0 ▽	
Labor Freedom	31.4 ▽	

0 least free — 50 — 100 most free

| = world average

BUSINESS FREEDOM — 43.7

The overall freedom to start, operate, and close a business is constrained by Comoros's regulatory environment. Starting a business takes only 24 days, compared to the world average of 35 days, but regulations can be inconsistent. Obtaining a business license requires about the world average of 18 procedures.

TRADE FREEDOM — 62.4

Comoros's simple average tariff rate was 11.3 percent in 2008, less than half the rate in 2006. Import bans and restrictions, import fees, inadequate infrastructure and trade capacity, fragmented and non-transparent customs administration, inefficient regulation, state trading, and underdeveloped markets add to the cost of trade. Fifteen points were deducted from Comoros's trade freedom score to account for non-tariff barriers.

FISCAL FREEDOM — 65

Comoros has a moderate income tax rate and a high corporate tax rate. The top income tax rate is 30 percent, and the top corporate tax rate is 50 percent. Other taxes include a value-added tax (VAT), an insurance tax, a vehicle tax, and a tax on real estate transactions. In the most recent year, overall tax revenue as a percentage of GDP was 10.0 percent.

GOVERNMENT SPENDING — 85.1

Total government expenditures, including consumption and transfer payments, are relatively low. The wage bill accounts for the majority of government spending. In the most recent year, government spending equaled 22.3 percent of GDP. Per a September 2008 policy aimed at increasing transparency, authorities from each island have been conducting monthly budget execution reports and meeting quarterly.

MONETARY FREEDOM — 76.4

Inflation has been moderate, averaging 4.6 percent between 2006 and 2008. Comoros's membership in the Franc Zone has a restraining effect on inflation, limiting the government's ability to print money to finance deficits and curtailing growth of the money supply. However, an underperforming agricultural sector, which is vulnerable to adverse weather conditions, and increases in global prices for oil and food added to inflationary pressures in 2008. Ten points were deducted from Comoros's monetary freedom score to adjust for measures that distort domestic prices.

INVESTMENT FREEDOM — 10

The Investment Division of the Ministry of Finance, Budget, Economy, Commerce, and Investments monitors and facilitates investment in Comoros. Investments are reviewed by the government. Non-transparent investment regulations, corruption, weak enforcement of contracts, inadequate infrastructure, political instability, and underdeveloped markets inhibit investment. Capital transfers are subject to prior approval, and foreign exchange is controlled by the central bank.

FINANCIAL FREEDOM — 20

Comoros's financial sector remains small, without adequate regulation or supervision. Bank penetration is low, and many people still rely on informal lending and have no bank account. Microfinance institutions account for around 20 percent of lending. Access to credit for entrepreneurial activities is limited. The banking system consists mainly of the central bank; the Banque de Développement des Comores, which focuses on development lending, and the Banque pour l'Industrie et le Commerce des Comores, which provides full banking services as well as international trade finance. Overall, the financial system lacks an effective regulatory structure that can facilitate dynamic business investment. The central bank controls foreign exchange, and capital transfers need prior authorization from various government agencies. Comoros has no capital market.

PROPERTY RIGHTS — 30

Protection of property rights is weak, and registration of real property is time-consuming and expensive. Although women do not have the same legal protections as men, traditional custom grants women favorable inheritance and property rights. The judicial system is ineffective, contracts are weakly enforced, and courts are relatively inexperienced in commercial litigation. Despite an adequate legal regime for the protection of intellectual property rights, the government lacks the capacity to enforce copyright violations.

FREEDOM FROM CORRUPTION — 25

Corruption is perceived as pervasive. Comoros ranks 134th out of 179 countries in Transparency International's Corruption Perceptions Index for 2008, a decline from 2007. The law provides criminal penalties for official corruption, but the government does not implement the law effectively, and officials engage in corrupt practices with impunity.

LABOR FREEDOM — 31.4

Inflexible employment regulations hinder overall productivity growth. The non-salary cost of employing a worker is very high, and dismissing a redundant employee is relatively costly. The high cost of laying off workers creates a serious disincentive for companies that might hire additional staff.

DEMOCRATIC REPUBLIC OF **CONGO**

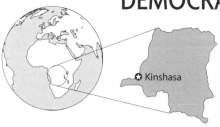

⊙ Kinshasa

Economic Freedom Score

25　**50**　75

Least free　0　　　　　100　Most free

41.4

The Democratic Republic of Congo (DRC) has an economic freedom score of 41.4, making it the 172nd freest economy in the 2010 *Index*. Its overall score is 1.4 points lower than last year, reflecting a decline particularly in investment freedom. The DRC is ranked 44th out of 46 countries in the Sub-Saharan Africa region, and its score is far below the regional average.

The DRC has been emerging from a long period of instability and violence. Poor economic management, worsened by repeated political crises, has severely hindered economic development and constrained economic freedom. The government's failure to provide basic public goods further reduces citizens' economic opportunities.

Economic activity is curtailed by an underdeveloped regulatory environment and the absence of institutional capacity or apparent desire to facilitate private-sector development. Arbitrary taxation, poor infrastructure, marginal enforcement of property rights, and weak rule of law have driven many people and enterprises into the informal sector, which accounts for more than 80 percent of economic activity.

BACKGROUND: After Laurent Kabila overthrew Mobutu Sese Seko in 1997, a five-year conflict between government forces supported by Angola, Namibia, and Zimbabwe and rebels backed by Rwanda and Uganda claimed an estimated 3 million lives. Kabila was assassinated in 2001. His son Joseph assumed power and in 2006 won the first multiparty election in 40 years. Rebel groups remain active in the eastern region bordering Burundi, Rwanda, Sudan, and Uganda, and a U.N. mission has struggled to address the resulting instability. The DRC's immense natural resources, including copper, cobalt, and diamonds, seem to have fueled conflict as much as development. Agriculture and forestry account for just under half of GDP. Corruption and mismanagement have driven much economic activity into the informal sector, and infrastructure is virtually nonexistent in many areas.

Country's Score Over Time

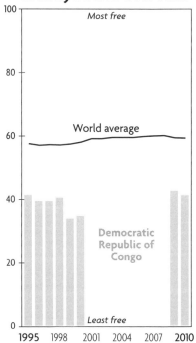

Quick Facts

Population: 64.2 million

GDP (PPP): $20.6 billion
　　　　　6.2% growth in 2008
　　　　　6.5% 5-year compound
　　　　　　annual growth
　　　　　$321 per capita

Unemployment: n/a

Inflation (CPI): 18.0%

FDI Inflow: $1 billion

2008 data unless otherwise noted
Data compiled as of September 2009

How Do We Measure Economic Freedom?
See page 457 for an explanation of the methodology or visit the *Index* Web site at *heritage.org/index*.

DEMO. REP. OF CONGO'S TEN ECONOMIC FREEDOMS

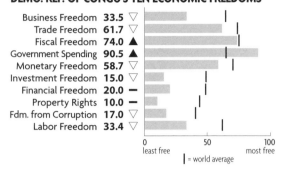

Business Freedom	33.5 ▽	
Trade Freedom	61.7 ▽	
Fiscal Freedom	74.0 ▲	
Government Spending	90.5 ▲	
Monetary Freedom	58.7 ▽	
Investment Freedom	15.0 ▽	
Financial Freedom	20.0 —	
Property Rights	10.0 —	
Fdm. from Corruption	17.0 ▽	
Labor Freedom	33.4 ▽	

0 least free   50   100 most free

▌ = world average

BUSINESS FREEDOM — 33.5

The overall freedom to start, operate, and close a business is heavily restricted by the Democratic Republic of Congo's regulatory environment. Starting a business takes an average of 149 days, compared to the world average of 35 days. Obtaining a business license takes about 322 days and involves 14 procedures, compared to the world average of 218 days and 18 procedures.

TRADE FREEDOM — 61.7

The DRC's weighted average tariff rate was 11.6 percent in 2008. Import restrictions, import taxes, services market restrictions, inadequate infrastructure, complex regulations, bureaucracy, inefficient customs administration, and corruption add to the cost of trade, and there is substantial unrecorded trade. Fifteen points were deducted from the DRC's trade freedom score to account for non-tariff barriers.

FISCAL FREEDOM — 74

The Democratic Republic of Congo has a moderate income tax rate and a relatively high corporate tax rate. The top income tax rate is 30 percent, and the top corporate tax rate is 40 percent. Other taxes include a sales tax and a tax on vehicles. In the most recent year, overall tax revenue as a percentage of GDP was 10.0 percent.

GOVERNMENT SPENDING — 90.5

Total government expenditures, including consumption and transfer payments, are low. In the most recent year, government spending equaled 17.8 percent of GDP.

MONETARY FREEDOM — 58.7

Inflation has been very high, averaging 17.2 percent between 2006 and 2008. The DRC has turned to the IMF for help in restoring value to the Congolese franc, which dropped 45 percent between the third quarter of 2008 and the first quarter of 2009. The central bank is also maintaining a tight monetary stance. Despite partial liberalization, some prices are still controlled through the public sector. Import price controls can be significant because nearly all manufactured goods and many food items are imported. Fifteen points were deducted from the Democratic Republic of Congo's monetary freedom score to adjust for price-control measures.

INVESTMENT FREEDOM — 15

Regulations do not generally discriminate against foreign investors, but there are restrictions in retail commerce, artisanal production, small public transport firms, small restaurants, and hotels with fewer than 10 beds. There are no formal limits on foreign ownership of businesses. Underdeveloped infrastructure, inadequate contract enforcement, limited access to credit, physical insecurity, lack of property rights, non-transparent bureaucracy, and corruption constrain private-sector development. The granting of permits and licenses is often subject to corruption. All investors are subject to audits by government agencies seeking evidence of violations of tax laws or price controls. Restructuring of approximately 60 state-owned enterprises is slow. International transfers of funds take place freely when transacted through a local commercial bank. Official channels often do not provide recourse in the event of property seizure.

FINANCIAL FREEDOM — 20

The financial system is small and provides a minimal range of banking services. Access to financing for entrepreneurial activity remains poor. The government retains shares in two of the 11 commercial banks. Financial intermediation is minimal. Credit to the private sector accounts for less than 3 percent of GDP. Most banks act as financial agents for the government or extend credit to international institutions operating in the country. More than 80 percent of the money supply is held outside the banking system. Larger banks are mostly subsidiaries of foreign banks. Informal lending is an important source of finance, and microfinance is beginning to emerge. There is no stock exchange.

PROPERTY RIGHTS — 10

Despite a new constitution and enhanced attempts at enforcement, protection of property rights remains weak and dependent on a dysfunctional public administration and judicial system. Fighting, banditry, and abuses of human rights threaten property rights and deter economic activity. Courts suffer from widespread corruption, public administration is unreliable, and individuals are subject to selective application of a complex legal code.

FREEDOM FROM CORRUPTION — 17

Corruption is perceived as rampant. The Democratic Republic of Congo ranks 171st out of 179 countries in Transparency International's Corruption Perceptions Index for 2008. Foreign businessmen often cite corruption as a principal obstacle to doing business. Corruption and government policies have given rise to a parallel economy.

LABOR FREEDOM — 33.4

Formal-sector employment is negligible. Highly restrictive employment regulations hinder job growth and reduce productivity. The non-salary cost of employing a worker is low, but dismissing an employee is costly.

REPUBLIC OF **CONGO**

Brazzaville

Economic Freedom Score

Least free 0   Most free 100

25   50   75

43.2

The Republic of Congo's economic freedom score is 43.2, making its economy the 169th freest in the 2010 *Index*. Its overall score has dropped 2.2 points from last year, due largely to declining scores for government spending and investment freedom. Congo is ranked 43rd out of 46 countries in the Sub-Saharan Africa region, and its overall score is much lower than the global and regional averages.

The Congolese economy, long afflicted with structural problems that severely undermine the development of a more dynamic private sector, lags in productivity growth. Entrepreneurs face extensive state controls that persist from the country's period of state socialism. At the same time, the government has failed to provide basic public goods and infrastructure.

The economy achieved marginal improvement in trade freedom, but it scores poorly in investment freedom, financial freedom, property rights, and labor freedom. Foreign investment restrictions, domestic regulations, and an inflexible labor market create a hostile business climate. The worst barrier to economic development is a profound lack of property rights, exacerbated by pervasive corruption.

BACKGROUND: Congo has endured internal conflict and coups since becoming independent in 1960. After seizing power in 1979, President Denis Sassou-Nguesso governed the country as a Marxist–Leninist state before moderating economic policy and making the transition to multi-party democracy in 1992. Sassou-Nguesso lost the 1992 election to Pascal Lissouba. Then, backed by Angolan troops, he again seized power following a 1997 civil war, won a flawed 2002 election, and was re-elected in July 2009. The 2003 and 2007 peace agreements with rebel groups have curtailed unrest in the Pool region, but many of the rebels have turned to banditry and criminality. Although most Congolese are engaged in agriculture, oil accounted for about 65 percent of GDP, over 90 percent of exports, and 85 percent of government revenue in 2008.

Country's Score Over Time

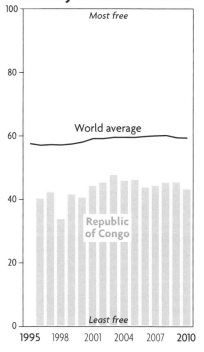

Most free

World average

Republic of Congo

Least free

1995   1998   2001   2004   2007   2010

Quick Facts

Population: 3.6 million

GDP (PPP): $14.3 billion
5.6% growth in 2008
4.4% 5-year compound annual growth
$3,946 per capita

Unemployment: n/a

Inflation (CPI): 6.0%

FDI Inflow: $2.6 billion

2008 data unless otherwise noted
Data compiled as of September 2009

How Do We Measure Economic Freedom?
See page 457 for an explanation of the methodology or visit the *Index* Web site at *heritage.org/index.*

REPUBLIC OF CONGO'S TEN ECONOMIC FREEDOMS

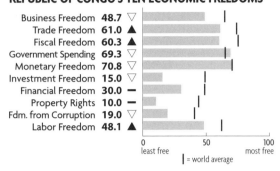

Business Freedom	48.7	▽
Trade Freedom	61.0	▲
Fiscal Freedom	60.3	▲
Government Spending	69.3	▽
Monetary Freedom	70.8	▽
Investment Freedom	15.0	▽
Financial Freedom	30.0	—
Property Rights	10.0	—
Fdm. from Corruption	19.0	▽
Labor Freedom	48.1	▲

0 least free   50   100 most free

▮ = world average

BUSINESS FREEDOM — 48.7

The overall freedom to start, operate, and close a business is seriously limited by Congo's regulatory environment. Starting a business takes about the world average of 35 days. The cost of launching a business is high, and closing a business is relatively easy but costly.

TRADE FREEDOM — 61

Congo's weighted average tariff rate was 14.5 percent in 2007. Import and export quotas, restrictive import licensing rules, burdensome and non-transparent bureaucracy, government export-promotion programs, an inefficient customs service, and corruption add to the cost of trade. Ten points were deducted from Congo's trade freedom score to adjust for non-tariff barriers.

FISCAL FREEDOM — 60.3

Congo has high tax rates. The top income tax rate is 50 percent, and the top corporate tax rate is 38 percent. Other taxes include a value-added tax (VAT), a tax on rental values, and an apprenticeship tax. In the most recent year, overall tax revenue as a percentage of GDP was 5.4 percent.

GOVERNMENT SPENDING — 69.3

Total government expenditures, including consumption and transfer payments, are moderate. In the most recent year, government spending equaled 32.0 percent of GDP. The government has agreed to implement public-sector reforms aimed at stronger, more transparent fiscal management, but political pressure has held up such reforms in the past, and the administrative capacity needed to implement reforms is lacking.

MONETARY FREEDOM — 70.8

Inflation has been moderate, averaging 5.1 percent between 2006 and 2008. The regional Banque des Etats de l'Afrique Centrale (BEAC) prioritizes the control of inflation and the maintenance of the CFA franc's peg to the euro. The prices of rail transport, telecommunications, electricity, water, and other goods and services are affected by government ownership and subsidization of the large public sector. Fifteen points were deducted from Congo's monetary freedom score to adjust for measures that distort domestic prices.

INVESTMENT FREEDOM — 15

Congo does not generally discriminate against foreign investors, but retail and bakery trades and urban and long-haul transport are limited to Congolese nationals. Investments of over CFAF100 million require Ministry of Economy, Finance, and Budget approval within 30 days unless they involve creation of an enterprise with public–private ownership. The few state-owned enterprises have a disproportionate influence on economic performance and business conditions. Privatization has been slow. Bureaucracy and corruption are significant impediments to investment. Residents may not hold foreign exchange accounts; companies may hold such accounts with special approval. Non-residents may hold foreign exchange accounts subject to government approval. Payments and transfers to most countries are subject to documentation requirements. Capital transactions require approval.

FINANCIAL FREEDOM — 30

Congo's underdeveloped financial sector remains significantly hindered by instability and poor regulation. Bank development has been stunted by poor management, bad loans, and government interference. Congo shares a common central bank with the other five members of the Central African Economic and Monetary Community. The banking system dominates Congo's financial sector, and there are six banks that are privately owned. Banking-sector weakness limits access to credit for business and investment. Bank accounts are held by less than 3 percent of the population, many of whom still face high financing costs due to limited competition and poor financial infrastructure. Bank credit to the private sector represents around 3 percent of GDP, but microfinance has been expanding rapidly.

PROPERTY RIGHTS — 10

The 1997–2003 civil war left the judiciary corrupt, overburdened, underfinanced, subject to political influence and bribery, and almost without records. Security of contracts and the enforcement of justice cannot be guaranteed, and protection of intellectual property is virtually nonexistent. In rural areas, traditional courts handle many local disputes, especially those involving inheritance and property.

FREEDOM FROM CORRUPTION — 19

Corruption is perceived as pervasive. The Republic of Congo ranks 158th out of 179 countries in Transparency International's Corruption Perceptions Index for 2008. Corruption is seen as permeating the government, and financial non-transparency, inadequate internal controls and accounting systems, and conflicts of interest in the state-owned oil company's marketing of oil are concerns. Low-level corruption among security personnel and customs and immigrations officials is widespread.

LABOR FREEDOM — 48.1

Burdensome employment regulations restrict job opportunities and productivity growth. The non-salary cost of employing a worker is high; dismissing an employee can be difficult and inexpensive. Rigid restrictions control hours worked.

COSTA RICA

Economic Freedom Score

25   50   75
Least free 0   100 Most free

65.9

Costa Rica's economic freedom score is 65.9, making its economy the 54th freest in the 2010 *Index*. Its overall score is 0.5 point lower than last year, reflecting small decreases in five of the 10 economic freedoms. Costa Rica is ranked 9th out of 29 countries in the South and Central America/ Caribbean region, and its overall score is higher than the global and regional averages.

Costa Rica's average annual growth rate has been over 6 percent for the past five years. Personal and corporate tax rates are moderate, and the overall burden is not high. The trade regime is more open, and management of public finance is sound. Costa Rica has been working to improve financial-sector freedom by consolidating private banks, easing procedures for foreign banks' operations, and introducing a new development bank structure.

Bureaucratic procedures continue to discourage dynamic entrepreneurial activity, and privatization and fiscal reform have slowed. Inflation has been hovering at around 12 percent due to rising commodity prices. The court system, while transparent and not corrupt, is inefficient, and enforcement is weak.

BACKGROUND: With a strong tradition of democracy and respect for human rights, and with no standing army, Costa Rica has avoided the political violence that has afflicted other Central American countries over the past half-century. Former President Oscar Arias (1986–1990) was elected for a second time in 2006 on a pledge to break up state monopolies, especially in telecommunications and insurance, but unions have resisted his gradual approach to privatization. An important producer of bananas, pineapples, and coffee, Costa Rica has benefited from industrialization in electronics and health care, and per capita income is high by regional standards. In October 2007, a slender majority of Costa Ricans voted for the Central America–Dominican Republic–United States Free Trade Agreement, which entered into force on January 1, 2009.

Country's Score Over Time

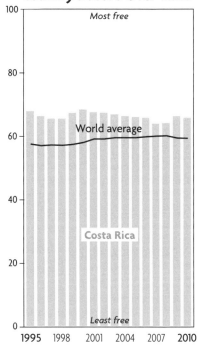

Quick Facts

Population: 4.5 million

GDP (PPP): $50.9 billion
2.9% growth in 2008
6.3% 5-year compound annual growth
$11,241 per capita

Unemployment: 4.9%

Inflation (CPI): 13.4%

FDI Inflow: $2 billion

2008 data unless otherwise noted
Data compiled as of September 2009

How Do We Measure Economic Freedom?
See page 457 for an explanation of the methodology or visit the *Index* Web site at *heritage.org/index.*

COSTA RICA'S TEN ECONOMIC FREEDOMS

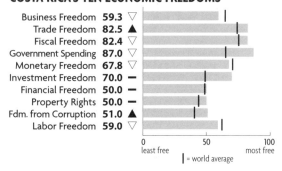

Business Freedom	59.3 ▽	
Trade Freedom	82.5 ▲	
Fiscal Freedom	82.4 ▽	
Government Spending	87.0 ▽	
Monetary Freedom	67.8 ▽	
Investment Freedom	70.0 —	
Financial Freedom	50.0 —	
Property Rights	50.0 —	
Fdm. from Corruption	51.0 ▲	
Labor Freedom	59.0 ▽	

0 least free — 50 — 100 most free

| = world average

BUSINESS FREEDOM — 59.3

The overall freedom to start, operate, and close a business is limited by Costa Rica's regulatory environment. Starting a business takes an average of 60 days, compared to the world average of 35 days, although obtaining a business license requires less than the world average of 218 days.

TRADE FREEDOM — 82.5

Costa Rica's weighted average tariff rate was 3.8 percent in 2007. Peak tariffs, import and export controls, import taxes, services market access restrictions, sanitary and phytosanitary requirements, bureaucratic customs administration, and issues involving the enforcement of intellectual property rights add to the cost of trade. Ten points were deducted from Costa Rica's trade freedom score to account for non-tariff barriers.

FISCAL FREEDOM — 82.4

Costa Rica has moderate tax rates. The top income tax rate is 25 percent, and the top corporate tax rate is 30 percent. Other taxes include a general sales tax and a real property tax. In the most recent year, overall tax revenue as a percentage of GDP was 15.2 percent.

GOVERNMENT SPENDING — 87

Total government expenditures, including consumption and transfer payments, are low. In the most recent year, government spending equaled 20.8 percent of GDP. Prudent fiscal management allowed some leeway with stimulus spending. Though privatization has been successful in some sugar production and transportation, state ownership persists, particularly in banking and insurance. Government intervention is highest in utilities, education, and hydrocarbons.

MONETARY FREEDOM — 67.8

Inflation has been high, averaging 12.3 percent between 2006 and 2008. The government controls the prices of goods on a basic consumption list, including energy, petroleum, telecommunications, and water. Ten points were deducted from Costa Rica's monetary freedom score to adjust for measures that distort domestic prices.

INVESTMENT FREEDOM — 70

Costa Rica treats foreign and domestic investors equally, but electrical power generation, broadcasting, professional services, wholesale distribution, fixed-line telecommunications, energy generation and distribution, transportation, and petroleum are reserved for state companies or require participation of a certain percentage of Costa Rican citizens or residents. Laws, regulations, and practices are generally transparent, although bureaucratic procedures are often burdensome. There are no controls on capital flows, but reporting requirements are mandatory for some transactions. There are no restrictions or controls on the holding of foreign exchange accounts, which are readily transferable and available at market rates. There are no restrictions on land purchases, but some land owned by foreign investors has been expropriated.

FINANCIAL FREEDOM — 50

Costa Rica's small but growing financial sector functions relatively well. Three state-owned banks account for about 50 percent of the financial system's assets. Some consolidation of private banks has occurred, and the combined assets of the 11 private commercial banks represent about 25 percent of the country's total. A new development bank structure draws in private and public banks. Procedures for operation of foreign banks have been simplified and streamlined. Credit is generally available on market terms, although the government retains some influence over lending. Accounting has become more transparent and consistent with international norms. Earlier financial reforms have liberalized Costa Rica's capital account and guarantee the free exchange of foreign currency. The banking sector has little exposure to structured financial products, and the impact of the global financial turmoil has been relatively muted. In late 2008, the government injected capital into the six largest institutions, including the three state-owned banks.

PROPERTY RIGHTS — 50

The judicial system can be slow and complicated. Contracts are generally upheld, and investments are secure, but it takes an average of more than 1.5 years to resolve a contract-related legal complaint. The system quickly recognizes rights acquired by squatters, especially when land is rural and not actively worked. Despite a legal framework, enforcement of intellectual property rights is often ineffective.

FREEDOM FROM CORRUPTION — 51

Corruption is perceived as present. Costa Rica ranks 47th out of 179 countries in Transparency International's Corruption Perceptions Index for 2008. The government does not emphasize enforcement of anti-corruption laws, regulations, and penalties. Allegations of lower-level corruption are common, and some prosecutions have resulted. Some foreign firms complain of corruption in the administration of public tenders.

LABOR FREEDOM — 59

Employment regulations are relatively flexible. The nonsalary cost of employing a worker is high, but dismissing an employee is relatively inexpensive. Rules on work hours are flexible.

CÔTE D'IVOIRE

Yamoussoukro

Economic Freedom Score

25   50   75

Least free 0   100 Most free

54.1

Côte d'Ivoire's economic freedom score is 54.1, making its economy the 123rd freest in the 2010 *Index*. Its score is 0.9 point lower than last year, reflecting moderate decreases in eight of the 10 economic freedoms that are partially offset by a significant gain in fiscal freedom. Côte d'Ivoire is ranked 23rd out of 46 countries in the Sub-Saharan Africa region, and its overall score is above the regional average.

One of the region's largest economies, Côte d'Ivoire is trying to promote much-delayed economic reform and development. Significant tax relief is intended to foster a more dynamic private sector. Despite slow progress in public-sector reform, the government has maintained its policy of divesting state-owned enterprises.

The overall business climate, hurt especially by political instability, remains unfavorable to private investment and productivity growth. Commercial regulations and bureaucratic red tape are burdensome. Property rights are undermined by an inefficient judiciary, and corruption is debilitating. Despite improvements in tax administration, budget management has been strained by higher electricity subsidies and delayed tax collection from the national oil company.

BACKGROUND: In 2002, civil war split Côte d'Ivoire between a rebel-controlled North and a government-controlled South. Despite the 2007 Ouagadougou Accord, the country remains divided, and U.N. peacekeepers are still present. U.N. Security Council resolutions have extended the mandate of President Laurent Gbagbo, whose five-year term expired in 2005. A transition government, with rebel leader Guillaume Soro as prime minister and Gbagbo as president, was formed in 2007, and presidential and legislative elections were scheduled for 2009 and 2010, respectively. Côte d'Ivoire is the world's leading cocoa producer, and the agricultural sector employs roughly half of the labor force and accounted for 26 percent of GDP in 2005. Much economic activity, including regional trade, has moved to the informal sector, and most businesses are operating at far below capacity.

Country's Score Over Time

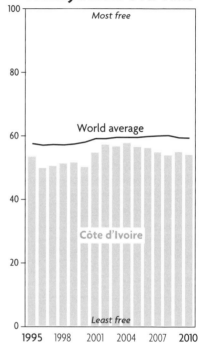

Most free

World average

Côte d'Ivoire

Least free

1995   1998   2001   2004   2007   **2010**

Quick Facts

Population: 20.6 million

GDP (PPP): $34.0 billion
    2.2% growth in 2008
    1.6% 5-year compound
        annual growth
    $1,651 per capita

Unemployment: n/a

Inflation (CPI): 6.3%

FDI Inflow: $353 million

2008 data unless otherwise noted
Data compiled as of September 2009

How Do We Measure Economic Freedom?
See page 457 for an explanation of the methodology or visit the *Index* Web site at *heritage.org/index.*

161

CÔTE D'IVOIRE'S TEN ECONOMIC FREEDOMS

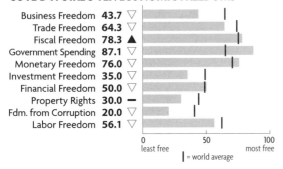

Business Freedom	43.7 ▽	
Trade Freedom	64.3 ▽	
Fiscal Freedom	78.3 ▲	
Government Spending	87.1 ▽	
Monetary Freedom	76.0 ▽	
Investment Freedom	35.0 ▽	
Financial Freedom	50.0 ▽	
Property Rights	30.0 —	
Fdm. from Corruption	20.0 ▽	
Labor Freedom	56.1 ▽	

0 least free   50   100 most free

▮ = world average

BUSINESS FREEDOM — 43.7

The overall freedom to start, run, and close a business is seriously restricted by Côte d'Ivoire's regulatory environment. Starting a business takes an average of 40 days, compared to the world average of 35 days. Obtaining a business license requires more than the world average of 18 procedures and 218 days.

TRADE FREEDOM — 64.3

Côte d'Ivoire's weighted average tariff rate was 10.3 percent in 2008. Import prohibitions and restrictions, import authorization requirements for certain goods, import fees and taxes, services market access restrictions, minimum price floors for some imports, corruption in customs and government procurement, and weak enforcement of intellectual property rights add to the cost of trade. Fifteen points were deducted from Côte d'Ivoire's trade freedom score to account for non-tariff barriers.

FISCAL FREEDOM — 78.3

Côte d'Ivoire has a relatively high income tax rate and a moderate corporate tax rate. The top income tax rate is 36 percent, and the top corporate tax rate has been reduced to 25 percent. Other taxes include a value-added tax (VAT) and a tax on interest. In the most recent year, overall tax revenue as a percentage of GDP was 15.7 percent.

GOVERNMENT SPENDING — 87.1

Total government expenditures, including consumption and transfer payments, are low. In the most recent year, government spending equaled 20.7 percent of GDP. Social and political instability have prevented meaningful progress in privatization.

MONETARY FREEDOM — 76

Inflation has been moderate, averaging 4.9 percent between 2006 and 2008. The regional Banque Centrale des Etats de l'Afrique de l'Ouest (BCEAO) prioritizes control of inflation and maintenance of the CFA franc's peg to the euro. If international food and oil prices remain depressed, average annual inflation is expected to drop to around 2 percent by the end of 2009. The government regulates prices of pharmaceuticals, petroleum products, and public-sector goods and services, and cocoa and coffee prices and quotas are part of a price stabilization program. Ten points were deducted from Côte d'Ivoire's monetary freedom score to account for policies that distort domestic prices.

INVESTMENT FREEDOM — 35

In general, foreign and domestic investors are treated equally. Proposed investment is not screened. Approval is required for investment in the health sector, travel agencies, and law and accounting firms, and majority foreign ownership is not permitted in these sectors. Bureaucracy, ad hoc tax policy, corruption, and burdensome contract enforcement inhibit investment. Residents may hold foreign exchange accounts with government and BCEAO approval; non-residents may hold them with BCEAO approval. Transfers to countries other than France, Monaco, and certain regional countries require government approval. Some other transfers are subject to requirements, controls, and authorization. Many capital transactions require government authorization. Despite land reform, freehold tenure outside of urban areas is difficult, and most businesses opt for long-term leases.

FINANCIAL FREEDOM — 50

The financial sector, dominated by banking, is small and underdeveloped. Despite some bank modernization and restructuring since 2004, it lacks the capacity to support development of the private sector and economic diversification. The banking system consists of 19 banks and two other financial institutions. There are also over 100 active microfinance institutions. The largest banks include foreign ownership and are regarded as more reliable in the unstable climate. The government has sold its shares in smaller banks, but has minority holdings in several larger institutions. Trading on the Côte d'Ivoire–based regional stock market is minimal despite 45 company listings.

PROPERTY RIGHTS — 30

The judiciary is constitutionally independent but slow, inefficient, and subject to executive branch, military, and other influences. Judges serve at the discretion of the executive, and some are open to bribery. Outside of urban areas, traditional property rights of villages and ethnic groups prevent the sale of land.

FREEDOM FROM CORRUPTION — 20

Corruption is perceived as pervasive. Côte d'Ivoire ranks 151st out of 179 countries in Transparency International's Corruption Perceptions Index for 2008. Domestic laws and regulations to combat corruption are neither generally nor effectively enforced. Government corruption and lack of transparency affect judicial proceedings, contract awards, customs and tax issues, and the accountability of security forces.

LABOR FREEDOM — 56.1

Burdensome labor regulations hinder employment opportunities and productivity growth. The non-salary cost of employing a worker is relatively low, but dismissing an employee is costly. Regulations on work hours are rigid.

CROATIA

Economic Freedom Score

25   50   75

Least
free   0   100   Most
free

59.2

World Rank: 92   **Regional Rank: 37**

Croatia's economic freedom score is 59.2, making its economy the 92nd freest in the 2010 *Index*. Its overall score is 4.1 points higher than last year, reflecting significantly improved scores for government spending, investment freedom, and protection of property rights. Croatia has moved up 24 places in the world rankings and from 38th to 37th out of 43 countries in the Europe region; its overall score is still below the regional and world averages.

Croatia has made notable improvements that have affected its overall economic freedom score and scores above the world average in trade freedom, investment freedom, and monetary freedom. Management of public finance has been enhanced, and regulation is more streamlined. Croatia has also created a more competitive financial system by implementing efficient regulatory frameworks and privatization.

Croatia's overall weakness stems from excessive government interference that erodes the economy's efficiency and flexibility. In addition to high levels of government spending, government intervention in other key areas of the economy is considerable. Burdensome and non-transparent administrative regulations, particularly at the local level, continue to challenge entrepreneurs, resulting in lower levels of productivity and job growth. Corruption and political interference, especially with regard to the judiciary, also restrict economic freedom.

BACKGROUND: Rapid industrialization in the years following World War II made Croatia the most prosperous area of the former Yugoslavia. As Communism collapsed throughout Eastern Europe and Yugoslavia began to unravel along ethnic and religious lines, Croatia declared its independence in 1991. Years of ensuing conflict between Croats and Serbs ended formally in 1995 with the Dayton Peace Accords. Croatia has actively pursued greater integration into the Euro–Atlantic community. It became a full member of NATO in April 2009 and hopes to join the European Union in 2011, although political violence and allegations of government corruption may slow the process.

Country's Score Over Time

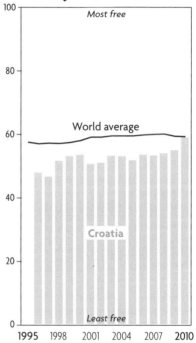

Quick Facts

Population: 4.4 million

GDP (PPP): $84.6 billion
2.4% growth in 2008
4.2% 5-year compound
annual growth
$19,084 per capita

Unemployment: 13.7%

Inflation (CPI): 6.1%

FDI Inflow: $4.4 billion

2008 data unless otherwise noted
Data compiled as of September 2009

How Do We Measure Economic Freedom?
See page 457 for an explanation of the methodology or visit the *Index* Web site at *heritage.org/index*.

163

CROATIA'S TEN ECONOMIC FREEDOMS

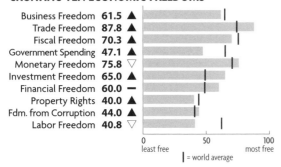

Business Freedom	61.5	▲
Trade Freedom	87.8	▲
Fiscal Freedom	70.3	▲
Government Spending	47.1	▲
Monetary Freedom	75.8	▽
Investment Freedom	65.0	▲
Financial Freedom	60.0	—
Property Rights	40.0	▲
Fdm. from Corruption	44.0	▲
Labor Freedom	40.8	▽

0 least free   50   100 most free

| = world average

BUSINESS FREEDOM — *61.5*

Despite some progress, Croatia's overall regulatory environment remains burdensome and inefficient. Starting a business takes 22 days, less than the world average of 35 days. Obtaining a business license takes much longer than the world average of 218 days. Closing a business is relatively simple.

TRADE FREEDOM — *87.8*

Croatia's weighted average tariff rate was 1.1 percent in 2008. Some additional customs duties, import licensing for certain goods, burdensome regulations and standards, inefficient customs administration, and weak enforcement of intellectual property rights add to the cost of trade. Ten points were deducted from Croatia's trade freedom score to account for non-tariff barriers.

FISCAL FREEDOM — *70.3*

Croatia has a high income tax rate but a low corporate tax rate. The top income tax rate is 45 percent, and the top corporate tax rate is 20 percent. There is also a value-added tax (VAT). In the most recent year, overall tax revenue as a percentage of GDP was 23.4 percent.

GOVERNMENT SPENDING — *47.1*

Total government expenditures, including consumption and transfer payments, are relatively high. In the most recent year, government spending equaled 42 percent of GDP. The government's total debt is around 35 percent of GDP.

MONETARY FREEDOM — *75.8*

Inflation has been moderate, averaging 5.0 percent between 2006 and 2008. Many price supports and subsidies have been eliminated, but proposed price changes on some 30 products require Ministry of Economy approval. The government also influences prices through state-owned enterprises. The state still controls a significant part of the economy. Ten points were deducted from Croatia's monetary freedom score to adjust for measures that distort domestic prices.

INVESTMENT FREEDOM — *65*

Foreign investors receive national treatment. Despite economic and administrative reforms, an inefficient bureaucracy can inhibit economic activity. Corruption remains a problem. There is steady pressure to increase transparency and fulfill commitments to adopt EU laws, norms, and practices. The constitution guarantees the free transfer and repatriation of profits and invested capital for foreign investments. Some capital transactions, such as inward portfolio investment, are subject to government conditions. To acquire property by means other than inheritance, reciprocity, or as an incorporated Croatian legal entity, foreign investors need Ministry of Justice approval.

FINANCIAL FREEDOM — *60*

Undergoing restructuring and modernization, Croatia's financial system has become more efficient and competitive, and access to financing for entrepreneurial activity is not difficult. After significant market consolidation, there are fewer than 35 banks. Two national commercial banks are majority foreign-owned and control almost half of all assets, and foreign banks own the majority of total assets. Supervisory and regulatory frameworks for the financial sector are more efficient, and credit is allocated on market terms. Privatization and regulatory improvements have done much to re-establish confidence in banking. The stock exchange has been growing rapidly, with more than 200 companies now listed, and securities markets are open to foreign investors. The Capital Market Act, which aims to strengthen securities regulation and transparency, came into force in January 2009.

PROPERTY RIGHTS — *40*

The right to ownership of private property is established in the constitution and protected by numerous acts and regulations. Observers view the judicial system as most affected by corruption. The court system is cumbersome and inefficient, and backlogs cause business disputes to drag on for years. Some investors insist that contract arbitration take place outside of Croatia. The government is committed to judicial reform, but much remains to be done. Despite intellectual property rights legislation, piracy of digital media and counterfeiting continue. Croatia is ranked 60th out of 115 countries in the 2009 International Property Rights Index.

FREEDOM FROM CORRUPTION — *44*

Corruption is perceived as significant. Croatia ranks 62nd out of 179 countries in Transparency International's Corruption Perceptions Index for 2008. The government has initiated a process to overhaul areas particularly afflicted by corruption: the judicial and health systems, local governments, political party financing, public administration, and economic agencies. Citizens continue to cite corruption as one of Croatia's most important problems.

LABOR FREEDOM — *40.8*

Burdensome labor regulations limit employment and productivity growth. The non-salary cost of employing a worker is high, and dismissing an employee can be difficult and costly. The labor code mandates retraining or replacement before firing a worker.

CUBA

Economic Freedom Score

Least free 0   100 Most free

26.7

Cuba's economic freedom score is 26.7, making its economy one of the world's least free, ahead of only Zimbabwe and North Korea. Its overall score is 1.2 points lower than last year, reflecting primarily a worsened score in investment freedom. Cuba is ranked at the bottom of 29 countries in the South and Central America/Caribbean region, and its overall score is less than half of the regional average.

Cuba's overall economic freedom remains severely hampered by institutional constraints, and the private sector is very limited. Because the government dictates most economic policies, many aspects of economic activity are tightly controlled by the state. No courts are free of political interference, entrepreneurship is impeded, and private property is strictly regulated. Lack of transparency and excessive regulations limit trade and investment.

The economy performs relatively well in terms of trade and monetary freedom. Cuba has a moderate average tariff rate but maintains very restrictive non-tariff barriers. Inflation is also moderate. In an effort to court foreign investment, Cuba has been building closer ties with China and Venezuela.

BACKGROUND: A one-party Communist state with a command economy, Cuba continues to depend heavily on external assistance (chiefly oil provided by Venezuela's Hugo Chávez and remittances from Cubans overseas) and a captive labor force. The regime refuses to allow free elections; restricts freedom of expression, property ownership, and other basic rights; and holds hundreds of political prisoners. In February 2008, Fidel Castro's 75-year-old brother Raul became head of state, but an ailing Fidel reportedly still influences the Communist Party and decision-making from behind the scenes. Little reliable economic information is available, and official figures on per capita GDP may not reflect actual incomes. Damage from hurricanes in 2008, falling revenue from tourism and commodity sales, and an unwillingness to introduce meaningful economic reform have further weakened economic performance.

Country's Score Over Time

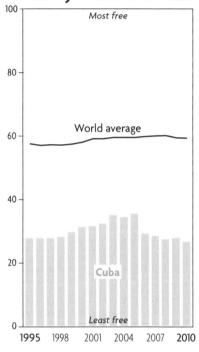

Quick Facts

Population: 11.2 million

GDP (PPP): $108.2 billion
4.3% growth in 2008
5-year compound annual growth n/a
$9,500 per capita

Unemployment: 1.6% (estimate)

Inflation (CPI): 3.4%

FDI Inflow: $36 million

2008 data unless otherwise noted
Data compiled as of September 2009

How Do We Measure Economic Freedom?
See page 457 for an explanation of the methodology or visit the *Index* Web site at *heritage.org/index.*

CUBA'S TEN ECONOMIC FREEDOMS

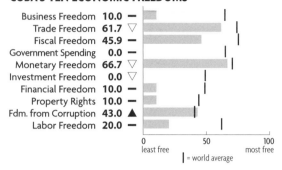

Business Freedom	10.0	▬
Trade Freedom	61.7	▽
Fiscal Freedom	45.9	▬
Government Spending	0.0	▬
Monetary Freedom	66.7	▽
Investment Freedom	0.0	▽
Financial Freedom	10.0	▬
Property Rights	10.0	▬
Fdm. from Corruption	43.0	▲
Labor Freedom	20.0	▬

0 least free — 50 — 100 most free
| = world average

BUSINESS FREEDOM — *10*

The overall freedom to start, operate, and close a business remains constrained by the state. Only limited private entrepreneurship exists. Inconsistent and non-transparent application of regulations impedes entrepreneurial activity.

TRADE FREEDOM — *61.7*

Cuba's weighted average tariff rate was 9.1 percent in 2008. The trade regime remains largely non-transparent, customs corruption is common, rules and regulations are burdensome, and imports and exports are dominated by the government. Twenty points were deducted from Cuba's trade freedom score to account for non-tariff barriers.

FISCAL FREEDOM — *45.9*

Cuba has a high income tax rate of 50 percent. The top corporate tax rate is 30 percent (35 percent for companies with entirely foreign capital). In the most recent year, tax revenue as a percentage of GDP was 44.8 percent. Other taxes include a tax on property transfers and a sales tax.

GOVERNMENT SPENDING — *0*

Total government expenditures, including consumption and transfer payments, are very high. In the most recent year, government spending equaled 68.2 percent of GDP. Expansive government employment commitments are an obstacle to sound fiscal management.

MONETARY FREEDOM — *66.7*

Inflation has been moderate, averaging 4.4 percent between 2006 and 2008. Official year-end inflation of only 0.8 percent in 2008 was achieved by imposing price caps in agricultural markets to suppress real food costs; average inflation, which reflects the underlying trend in market prices over the year, was 3.4 percent. The government determines prices for most goods and services and subsidizes much of the economy, although some private and informal market retail activity is not government-controlled. Twenty points were deducted from Cuba's monetary freedom score to adjust for measures that distort domestic prices.

INVESTMENT FREEDOM — *0*

The Foreign Investment Act theoretically guarantees transferability of profits to foreign countries, bans expropriation without compensation, allows transfer of ownership to other foreign investors, and permits three types of foreign investment: international association contracts, joint ventures, and totally foreign-owned companies. In practice, investment is inhibited by a lack of business policy, arbitrary and non-transparent regulation, discrimination against foreign and private domestic investment, and state control of the economy. Private-sector opportunities are limited. The government is aggressively pursuing recentralization of economic activity and maintains strict capital and exchange controls. Some restrictions have been loosened to permit investment commitments and credit lines from China and Venezuela. There is no foreign ownership of land.

FINANCIAL FREEDOM — *10*

Cuba's financial sector remains underdeveloped, and credit for entrepreneurial activity is seriously impeded by inefficient regulation and bureaucracy. Despite a decade of incremental changes, the government remains firmly in control. The Cuban peso is the domestic currency; a separate convertible peso is required for foreign exchange and nonessential retail purchases. Over a dozen foreign banks have opened offices but are not allowed to operate freely. New products, such as travel and medical insurance and personal pensions, are being introduced. The government established a central bank in 1997 and converted the Banco Nacional de Cuba into one of a new set of state banks. Central bank authority was enhanced in 2005 to allow closer control of the use of hard currency and convertible pesos. Credit and insurance markets remain government-controlled.

PROPERTY RIGHTS — *10*

Cuban citizens may own land and productive capital for farming and self-employment. The constitution subordinates the courts to the National Assembly of People's Power and the Council of State. The NAPP and its lower-level counterparts choose all judges. The law and trial practices do not meet international standards for fair public trials.

FREEDOM FROM CORRUPTION — *43*

Corruption is perceived as significant. Cuba ranks 65th out of 179 countries in Transparency International's Corruption Perceptions Index for 2008. Customs officials reportedly have requested unauthorized fees or have confiscated the belongings of citizens legally residing overseas who were returning to Cuba after visiting relatives, and senior officials in large state-run tourism organizations have been jailed for corruption.

LABOR FREEDOM — *20*

Rigid labor regulations hinder employment and productivity growth. The formal labor market is not fully developed, and the government-controlled labor market has helped to create a large informal economy. A labor code aimed at improving the efficiency of entrepreneurial activities and providing strict penalties for the use of work time for personal benefit took effect in 2007.

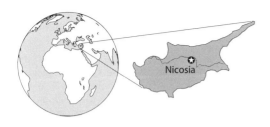

CYPRUS

Economic Freedom Score

70.9

World Rank: **24**	Regional Rank: **13**

Cyprus's economic freedom score is 70.9, making its economy the 24th freest in the 2010 *Index*. Its overall score is almost unchanged from last year, with significant declines in property rights and labor freedom balanced by improvements in business freedom and freedom from corruption. Cyprus is ranked 13th out of 43 countries in the Europe region, and its overall score is higher than the regional and global averages.

Cyprus performs well in many of the 10 economic freedoms. Business growth is facilitated by a relatively transparent and efficient regulatory framework. The financial sector has also become more open and efficient with strict but sensible supervision, and the government has taken measures to improve its public finance.

A high level of government spending is the primary weakness that holds down Cyprus's overall economic freedom. There is also room for improvement in trade freedom. While tariff barriers are low, there are significant non-tariff barriers. Monetary stability has deteriorated somewhat due to rising inflation and government price-fixing practices.

BACKGROUND: A U.N. buffer zone divides the Greek Cypriot Republic of Cyprus (a member of the European Union) and the Turkish Republic of Northern Cyprus (not a member). The Republic of Cyprus acts as the island's internationally recognized administration, and there is deep hostility between the two sides. Tourism and financial services drive the Greek Cypriot economy, and restrictions on foreign investment have been lifted. Economic liberalization was enhanced for Greek Cypriots in 2004 with EU membership, but telecommunications and utilities are still not privatized or deregulated. Cyprus joined the euro zone on January 1, 2008. Formerly robust growth in the Turkish Cypriot economy has been undermined by political and legal uncertainty, and Turkish Cypriots remain heavily dependent on trade and aid from Turkey. Greek and Turkish leaders continue to negotiate on possible reunification.

Country's Score Over Time

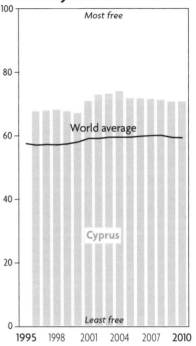

Quick Facts

Population: 0.8 million

GDP (PPP): $22.7 billion
3.6% growth in 2008
4.0% 5-year compound annual growth
$29,853 per capita

Unemployment: 3.6%

Inflation (CPI): 4.4%

FDI Inflow: $2.2 billion

2008 data unless otherwise noted
Data compiled as of September 2009

How Do We Measure Economic Freedom?
See page 457 for an explanation of the methodology or visit the *Index* Web site at *heritage.org/index*.

CYPRUS'S TEN ECONOMIC FREEDOMS

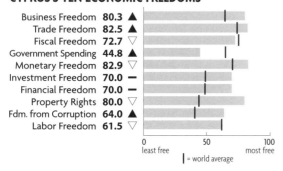

Business Freedom	80.3 ▲	
Trade Freedom	82.5 ▲	
Fiscal Freedom	72.7 ▽	
Government Spending	44.8 ▲	
Monetary Freedom	82.9 ▽	
Investment Freedom	70.0 —	
Financial Freedom	70.0 —	
Property Rights	80.0 ▽	
Fdm. from Corruption	64.0 ▲	
Labor Freedom	61.5 ▽	

0 least free   50   100 most free

| = world average

BUSINESS FREEDOM — *80.3*

The overall freedom to start, operate, and close a business is relatively well protected under Cyprus's regulatory environment. Regulations have been streamlined, administrative procedures have been simplified, and business regulations are transparent and consistently applied.

TRADE FREEDOM — *82.5*

Cyprus's trade policy is the same as that of other members of the European Union. The common EU weighted average tariff rate was 1.3 percent in 2008. However, the EU has high or escalating tariffs for agricultural and manufacturing products, and its MFN tariff code is complex. Non-tariff barriers reflected in EU and Cypriot policy include agricultural and manufacturing subsidies, quotas, import restrictions and bans for some goods and services, market access restrictions in some services sectors, non-transparent and restrictive regulations and standards, and inconsistent regulatory and customs administration among EU members. Pharmaceutical and biotechnology regulations are more burdensome than EU policy, services markets are further restricted, enforcement of intellectual property rights remains problematic, and there is a dichotomy between the trade regimes of Greek and Turkish areas. Fifteen points were deducted from Cyprus's trade freedom score to account for non-tariff barriers.

FISCAL FREEDOM — *72.7*

Cyprus has a moderate income tax rate and a low corporate tax rate. The top income tax rate is 30 percent, and the flat corporate tax rate is 10 percent (25 percent for vaguely defined public corporate bodies). Other taxes include a value-added tax (VAT) and a real estate tax. In the most recent year, tax revenue as a percentage of GDP was 41.6 percent.

GOVERNMENT SPENDING — *44.8*

Total government expenditures, including consumption and transfer payments, are high. In the most recent year, government spending equaled 42.9 percent of GDP.

MONETARY FREEDOM — *82.9*

Inflation has been relatively low, averaging 3.6 percent between 2006 and 2008. Weaker consumer demand and softer international commodity prices caused inflation to ease toward the end of 2008. The government controls prices of some agricultural products. Five points were deducted from Cyprus's monetary freedom score to reflect this practice.

INVESTMENT FREEDOM — *70*

The government grants national treatment to foreign investors. In the government-controlled area, business-related procedures and regulations are generally transparent and evenly applied. The area administered by Turkish Cypriots has adopted more transparent regulation but still lags behind European or U.S. standards. Non-EU investors may not invest in tertiary education, mass media, banking, and construction. Accession to the EU has reduced barriers to investment, but some have been replaced by EU-wide barriers. EU residents may own 100 percent of local companies and any company listed on the stock exchange. Some payments, current transfers, and capital transactions are subject to central bank approval or restriction. Cypriot law restricts foreign, non-EU ownership of real property.

FINANCIAL FREEDOM — *70*

Cyprus's financial sector is diverse and relatively sound. Regulation and supervision of banking and finance are efficient, and access to credit is not constrained. Financing for domestic and foreign investors is available at market rates. The three dominant banks' lending practices are prudent and conservative. Total credit to the private sector has increased. There are no exchange controls and no interest rate ceiling. Cyprus has developed into a center for non-banking offshore activity, facilitated by a competitive tax regime and double-taxation treaties with many countries. The stock exchange is one of the smallest in Europe, with a capitalization of around $5 billion in early 2009.

PROPERTY RIGHTS — *80*

Contracts and property rights are generally enforced. The civil judiciary is independent constitutionally but not always in practice. Intellectual property rights are not adequately protected in the area administered by Turkish Cypriots. Real property remains contested. The absence of a political settlement poses an inherent risk for the foreign investor interested in buying or leasing property in the North.

FREEDOM FROM CORRUPTION — *64*

Corruption is perceived as present. Cyprus ranks 31st out of 179 countries in Transparency International's Corruption Perceptions Index for 2008. Some foreign companies complain of bias and a lack of transparency in government consideration of competing bids. Corruption and patronage appear to continue in the Turkish Cypriot area.

LABOR FREEDOM — *61.5*

Relatively flexible labor regulations facilitate employment and productivity growth. The government mandates a minimum wage and minimum standards for terms and conditions of employment. Cyprus's unemployment rate is one of the EU's lowest.

CZECH REPUBLIC

Economic Freedom Score

Least free 0   100 Most free

69.8

The Czech Republic's economic freedom score is 69.8, making its economy the 34th freest in the 2010 *Index*. Its overall score is 0.4 point higher than last year, primarily reflecting improved labor freedom. The Czech Republic is ranked 17th out of 43 countries in the Europe region, and its overall score is higher than the regional and global averages.

The Czech Republic's transition to greater economic freedom has been facilitated by structural reforms and an increasingly vibrant private sector that accounts for more than 80 percent of GDP. As reflected in relatively high scores for fiscal and investment freedom, competitive taxation and openness to foreign direct investment have contributed to a strong economy. An extensive banking sector includes significant foreign ownership and a well-established supervisory framework. The government has pursued reform measures to curb relatively high levels of government spending.

Although the regulatory environment is generally consistent with a market economy, bureaucracy and red tape slow entrepreneurial dynamism. Corruption is still perceived as significant, as evidenced by the slow pace of legislative and judicial reform. Structural reforms in the labor market are also needed.

BACKGROUND: The Velvet Revolution of 1989 peacefully overthrew a Communist dictatorship and led to the election of dissident playwright Vaclav Havel as president of a democratic Czechoslovakia. The Czech Republic separated from Slovakia, became an independent nation in 1993, and joined the European Union in 2004. In March 2009, Prime Minister Mirek Topolanek's center-right coalition cabinet left office after a parliamentary vote of no confidence; in April, Jan Fischer, nonpartisan head of the Czech Statistical Office, became interim prime minister. Elections scheduled for October were halted by the Constitutional Court. Historically, Czech lands have been among the world's most industrialized, but industrial production and exports to the EU declined in 2009, and GDP was projected to contract sharply.

Country's Score Over Time

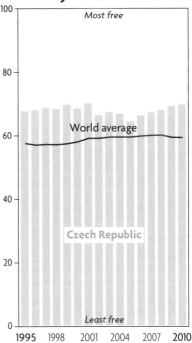

Quick Facts

Population: 10.4 million

GDP (PPP): $257.7 billion
  3.2% growth in 2008
  5.6% 5-year compound
    annual growth
  $24,712 per capita

Unemployment: 4.4%

Inflation (CPI): 6.3%

FDI Inflow: $10.7 billion

2008 data unless otherwise noted
Data compiled as of September 2009

How Do We Measure Economic Freedom?
See page 457 for an explanation of the methodology or visit the *Index* Web site at *heritage.org/index.*

CZECH REPUBLIC'S TEN ECONOMIC FREEDOMS

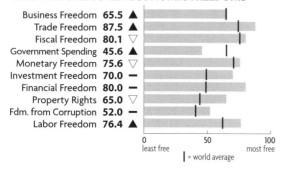

Business Freedom	65.5	▲
Trade Freedom	87.5	▲
Fiscal Freedom	80.1	▽
Government Spending	45.6	▲
Monetary Freedom	75.6	▽
Investment Freedom	70.0	—
Financial Freedom	80.0	—
Property Rights	65.0	▽
Fdm. from Corruption	52.0	▽
Labor Freedom	76.4	▲

0 least free — 50 — 100 most free
| = world average

BUSINESS FREEDOM — 65.5

The Czech Republic's overall regulatory environment remains somewhat inefficient. Starting a business takes an average of 15 days, compared to the world average of 35 days. Obtaining a business license requires twice the world average of 18 procedures. Closing a business is burdensome.

TRADE FREEDOM — 87.5

The Czech Republic's trade policy is the same as that of other members of the European Union. The common EU weighted average tariff rate was 1.3 percent in 2008. However, the EU has high or escalating tariffs for agricultural and manufacturing products, and its MFN tariff code is complex. Non-tariff barriers reflected in EU and Czech policy include agricultural and manufacturing subsidies, quotas, import restrictions and bans for some goods and services, market access restrictions in some services sectors, non-transparent and restrictive regulations and standards, and inconsistent regulatory and customs administration among EU members. Services market restrictions exceed EU policy, and non-transparent government procurement and the enforcement of intellectual property rights remain problematic. Ten points were deducted from the Czech Republic's trade freedom score to account for non-tariff barriers.

FISCAL FREEDOM — 80.1

The Czech Republic has relatively low tax rates. The flat income tax rate is 15 percent, and the top corporate tax rate has been reduced to 20 percent. Other taxes include a value-added tax (VAT), a real estate transfer tax, and an inheritance tax on non-family recipients. In the most recent year, overall tax revenue as a percentage of GDP was 36.9 percent.

GOVERNMENT SPENDING — 45.6

Total government expenditures, including consumption and transfer payments, are high. In the most recent year, government spending equaled 42.6 percent of GDP. The government has sold its remaining stakes in a telecommunications company and a petrochemicals refiner.

MONETARY FREEDOM — 75.6

Inflation has been moderate, averaging 5.1 percent between 2006 and 2008. As a participant in the EU's Common Agricultural Policy, the government subsidizes agricultural production, distorting the prices of agricultural products. The Ministry of Finance can fix prices, set minimum or maximum commercial transaction prices, and establish periods when prices may not change. Energy, some raw materials, domestic rents, and rail and bus transport are subject to controls. Maximum prices apply to mail and tele-communications tariffs. Ten points were deducted from the Czech Republic's monetary freedom score to account for these policies.

INVESTMENT FREEDOM — 70

Legally, foreign and domestic investors are treated identically. The government screens foreign investment projects in banking, insurance, and defense, where the state is a partner. Slow legislative and judicial reform, uneven contract enforcement, bureaucracy, and corruption are continuing obstacles. Most major state-owned companies have been privatized with foreign participation. There are no restrictions on payments or current transfers, and residents and non-residents may hold foreign exchange accounts. Branches or offices of foreign companies may buy local real estate, except for farmland or woodland.

FINANCIAL FREEDOM — 80

The Czech Republic's financial sector is one of Central and Eastern Europe's most advanced. The state is controlling shareholder in two banks. Foreign-controlled banks account for over 80 percent of assets. Insurance companies and pension funds include significant foreign participation. The supervisory framework is well established. Capital markets are small and lack transparency, but regulatory bodies have been merged to streamline oversight. The impact of the global financial turmoil on the banking sector has been relatively modest.

PROPERTY RIGHTS — 65

Property rights are protected by law, and contracts are generally secure. The judiciary is independent, but decisions vary from court to court. Commercial disputes can take years to resolve. Company registration is controlled by the courts and can be slow and complicated. Enforcing judgments and foreclosing security interests in land and personal property can still be difficult.

FREEDOM FROM CORRUPTION — 52

Corruption is perceived as significant. The Czech Republic ranks 45th out of 179 countries in Transparency International's Corruption Perceptions Index for 2008. Convictions for bribery result in long prison terms, but prosecution of high-level corruption is infrequent. Allegations of corruption most often involve the court-controlled company registration system and the police. The Czech Republic has ratified the OECD's anti-bribery convention and has signed but not ratified the U.N. Convention Against Corruption.

LABOR FREEDOM — 76.4

Labor regulations are relatively flexible. The non-salary cost of employing a worker can be high, but dismissing an employee is relatively easy and inexpensive.

Copenhagen

DENMARK

Economic Freedom Score

25   50   75

Least free 0   100 Most free

77.9

Denmark's economic freedom score is 77.9, making its economy the 9th freest in the 2010 *Index*. Its overall score is 1.7 points lower than last year, due mainly to reduced scores in monetary freedom, property rights, and labor freedom. Denmark is now ranked 3rd freest among the 43 countries in the European region, and its overall score is well above the regional average.

Denmark's modern and competitive economy performs well on many of the 10 economic freedoms, enhancing entrepreneurship and macroeconomic stability. The country has a strong tradition of openness to global trade and investment, and transparent and efficient regulations are applied evenly in most cases. Denmark also boasts an efficient, independent judiciary that protects property rights, and the level of corruption is extraordinarily low. The financial sector is competitive, and its efficiency is supported by prudent lending practices and sound oversight. The impact of the global financial crisis on the banking sector has been relatively small.

Two significant weaknesses continue to hold down Denmark's overall economic freedom. Despite a gradual decline over the past years, government spending remains over 50 percent of GDP. While the corporate tax rate is moderate, personal income taxes are very high, and the overall tax burden is significant.

BACKGROUND: Denmark's strong economy depends heavily on foreign trade, and the private sector is characterized by many small and medium-size companies. A large welfare state provides public education, lifelong health care coverage, and subsidized care for children and the elderly. Relations between Denmark and the Muslim world have been precarious ever since September 2005 when several cartoon caricatures of the Prophet Muhammad were printed in Danish newspapers. Prime Minister Anders Fogh Rasmussen resigned in April 2009 to become Secretary General of NATO and was succeeded as prime minister by former Minister of Finance Lars Løkke Rasmussen.

Country's Score Over Time

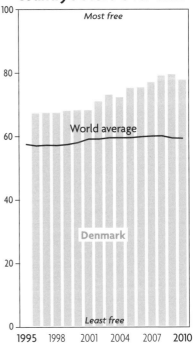

Quick Facts

Population: 5.5 million

GDP (PPP): $201.2 billion
–1.1% growth in 2008
1.6% 5-year compound annual growth
$36,607 per capita

Unemployment: 3.3%

Inflation (CPI): 3.4%

FDI Inflow: $10.9 billion

2008 data unless otherwise noted
Data compiled as of September 2009

How Do We Measure Economic Freedom?
See page 457 for an explanation of the methodology or visit the *Index* Web site at *heritage.org/index*.

DENMARK'S TEN ECONOMIC FREEDOMS

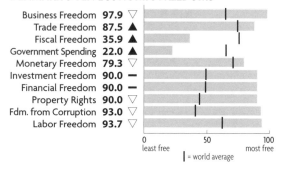

Business Freedom	97.9 ▽	
Trade Freedom	87.5 ▲	
Fiscal Freedom	35.9 ▲	
Government Spending	22.0 ▲	
Monetary Freedom	79.3 ▽	
Investment Freedom	90.0 —	
Financial Freedom	90.0 —	
Property Rights	90.0 ▽	
Fdm. from Corruption	93.0 ▽	
Labor Freedom	93.7 ▽	

0 least free   50   100 most free

| = world average

BUSINESS FREEDOM — 97.9

The overall freedom to start, operate, and close a business is well protected under Denmark's regulatory environment. Starting a business takes an average of six days, compared to the world average of 35 days. Obtaining a business license requires much less than the world average of 18 procedures and 218 days.

TRADE FREEDOM — 87.5

Denmark's trade policy is the same as that of other members of the European Union. The common EU weighted average tariff rate was 1.3 percent in 2008. However, the EU has high or escalating tariffs for agricultural and manufacturing products, and its MFN tariff code is complex. Non-tariff barriers reflected in EU and Danish policy include agricultural and manufacturing subsidies, quotas, import restrictions and bans for some goods and services, market access restrictions in some services sectors, non-transparent and restrictive regulations and standards, and inconsistent regulatory and customs administration among EU members. The lack of transparency in pharmaceuticals regulation exceeds EU policy. Ten points were deducted from Denmark's trade freedom score to account for non-tariff barriers.

FISCAL FREEDOM — 35.9

Denmark has a very high income tax rate and a moderate corporate tax rate. The top income tax rate of 59 percent is scheduled to be lowered to 51.5 percent in January 2010. The top corporate tax rate is 25 percent. County municipal taxes range from 22.7 percent to 27.8 percent. State taxes vary from 5 percent to 15 percent. Other taxes include a value-added tax (VAT), a vehicle tax, and an 8 percent health tax. In the most recent year, overall tax revenue as a percentage of GDP was 49.5 percent.

GOVERNMENT SPENDING — 22

Total government expenditures, including consumption and transfer payments, are very high. In the most recent year, government spending equaled 51 percent of GDP. Most industries and businesses are now in private hands.

MONETARY FREEDOM — 79.3

Inflation has been relatively low, averaging 2.9 percent between 2006 and 2008. As a participant in the EU's Common Agricultural Policy, the government subsidizes agricultural production, distorting the prices of agricultural products. Medications are heavily subsidized, and rents are generally fixed by law. Ten points were deducted from Denmark's monetary freedom score to account for policies that distort domestic prices.

INVESTMENT FREEDOM — 90

As a rule, foreign direct investment is not restricted or prescreened, but Denmark restricts the establishment of companies that provide legal, accounting, auditing, and medical services. The investment code is relatively transparent, and bureaucracy is streamlined and transparent. Incentive financing is available to foreign and domestic businesses. There are no restrictions on converting or transferring investment-associated funds into or out of Denmark. EU citizens and companies from EU member states may purchase any type of real estate (except vacation properties) without prior authorization; non-EU citizens and companies not previously based in Denmark for at least five years need government permission.

FINANCIAL FREEDOM — 90

Denmark's financial system is competitive, though the two largest banks account for about 75 percent of assets. No banks are state-owned, and the central bank is independent. Supervision and regulation are based on EU legislation. The securities market is highly developed, and the bond market is one of the world's largest. The global financial turmoil caused the collapse of several small and medium-sized banks. In October 2008, the parliament passed legislation calling for a joint financing program by private banks and the government. As a result of relatively prudent lending in a sound regulatory framework, Denmark has weathered the financial crisis with resilience.

PROPERTY RIGHTS — 90

The judiciary is independent and generally fair and efficient. Commercial and bankruptcy laws are consistently applied, and secured interests in property are recognized and enforced. Denmark adheres to key international conventions and treaties on the protection of intellectual property rights.

FREEDOM FROM CORRUPTION — 93

Denmark (along with two other countries) is ranked 1st out of 179 countries in Transparency International's Corruption Perceptions Index for 2008 for the second year in a row. Denmark has signed the OECD Anti-Bribery Convention. The Public Prosecutor for Serious Economic Crime has investigated the involvement of Danish firms in the U.N. Oil-for-Food scandal.

LABOR FREEDOM — 93.7

Flexible labor regulations enhance employment opportunities and productivity growth. The non-salary cost of employing a worker is low, and dismissing an employee is relatively easy and inexpensive.

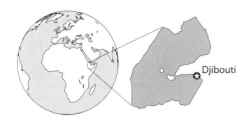

DJIBOUTI

Economic Freedom Score

51.0

25 — 50 — 75
Least free 0 — 100 Most free

World Rank: 139   **Regional Rank: 29**

Djibouti's economic freedom score is 51.0, making its economy the 139th freest in the 2010 *Index*. Its overall score is almost the same as last year, with small declines in five economic freedoms offset by a gain in investment freedom. Djibouti is ranked 29th out of 46 countries in the Sub-Saharan Africa region, and its overall score is slightly lower than the regional average.

Djibouti's economy is driven mainly by services, with industry accounting for less than 20 percent of GDP. Increased investment, particularly in construction and port operations, has led to relatively high economic growth. The financial sector is growing and, with new banking laws, becoming more efficient. Capitalizing on its geographical advantage, Djibouti is trying to transform itself into a regional trade, finance, and telecommunications hub.

Overall economic development is undermined by very weak business freedom and trade freedom. Limited privatization and weak infrastructure result in persistently high unemployment. Tariff and non-tariff barriers are high, and bureaucratic inefficiency, burdensome regulations, widespread corruption, and weak rule of law hamper many areas of the economy.

BACKGROUND: Djibouti has struggled toward multi-party democracy since gaining its independence in 1977. President Ismael Omar Guelleh was elected in 1999 and re-elected in 2005, and his multi-party, multi-ethnic coalition controls all levels of government. Opposition groups boycotted the 2005 presidential election and the February 2008 legislative election. An effort is underway to amend the constitution to permit Guelleh to run for a third term in 2011. Djibouti is strategically located at the mouth of the Red Sea along the shipping route between the Mediterranean Sea and the Indian Ocean. Its economy is centered on port facilities, the railway, and foreign military bases, and services accounted for nearly 80 percent of GDP in 2007. The population is concentrated in the capital city, though a minority continues its nomadic desert existence.

Country's Score Over Time

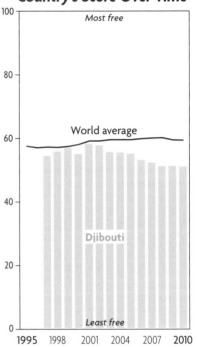

Quick Facts

Population: 0.8 million

GDP (PPP): $1.8 billion
3.9% growth in 2008
4.7% 5-year compound annual growth
$2,140 per capita

Unemployment: estimated to be more than 30%

Inflation (CPI): 12.0%

FDI Inflow: $234 million

2008 data unless otherwise noted
Data compiled as of September 2009

How Do We Measure Economic Freedom?
See page 457 for an explanation of the methodology or visit the *Index* Web site at *heritage.org/index*.

DJIBOUTI'S TEN ECONOMIC FREEDOMS

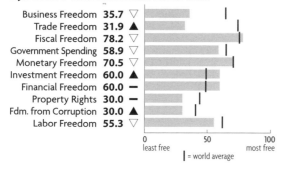

Business Freedom	35.7 ▽	
Trade Freedom	31.9 ▲	
Fiscal Freedom	78.2 ▽	
Government Spending	58.9 ▽	
Monetary Freedom	70.5 ▽	
Investment Freedom	60.0 ▲	
Financial Freedom	60.0 —	
Property Rights	30.0 —	
Fdm. from Corruption	30.0 ▲	
Labor Freedom	55.3 ▽	

0 least free   50   100 most free

| = world average

BUSINESS FREEDOM — 35.7

Overall business freedom remains constrained by the burdensome regulatory environment. Obtaining a business license requires slightly less than the world average of 18 procedures and 218 days, but licensing costs and the entry cost of launching a business are high.

TRADE FREEDOM — 31.9

Djibouti's weighted average tariff rate was 29.1 percent in 2006. Despite some reforms, the prohibition of certain imports, variable and sometimes high import taxes and fees, import licensing requirements, market access restrictions in the services sector, weak enforcement of intellectual property rights, and insufficient capacity in older port facilities add to the cost of trade. Ten points were deducted from Djibouti's trade freedom score to account for non-tariff barriers.

FISCAL FREEDOM — 78.2

Djibouti has average tax rates. The top income tax rate is 32 percent, and the top corporate tax rate is 25 percent. Other taxes include a property tax, an excise tax, and a value-added tax (VAT). The sales tax and services tax are being replaced by the VAT and restructured tariffs. In the most recent year, overall tax revenue as a percentage of GDP was 23.1 percent.

GOVERNMENT SPENDING — 58.9

Total government expenditures, including consumption and transfer payments, are relatively high. In the most recent year, government spending equaled 37 percent of GDP. Privatization has been slow, and private enterprises are hampered by weak infrastructure and the high costs of labor, power, and telecommunications. Over the past year, authorities have exhibited spending restraint, resisting calls to expand the already large wage bill with salary increases.

MONETARY FREEDOM — 70.5

Inflation has been rising, averaging 9.5 percent between 2006 and 2008. Goods and services such as medicines, bread, water, electricity, telecommunications, postal services, and urban transport are subject to price controls. The government also influences prices through its regulation of state-owned enterprises. Ten points were deducted from Djibouti's monetary freedom score to account for measures that distort domestic prices.

INVESTMENT FREEDOM — 60

No major laws discriminate against foreign investment. Certain sectors, such as public utilities, are state-owned and not open. Privatization has progressed, but the private sector remains underdeveloped outside of Djibouti's free trade zone. Reforms are being introduced, but bureaucratic procedures are complicated, and the legal system, derived from French civil law, is complex, opaque, and slow. Corruption deters investment. Residents and non-residents may hold foreign exchange accounts, and there are no restrictions on payments or transfers.

FINANCIAL FREEDOM — 60

Djibouti's underdeveloped financial sector has been growing as more banks, particularly foreign banks, enter the market. One majority French-owned bank and one fully French-owned bank together still dominate banking. Since 2006, the central bank has permitted more foreign banks to operate. The government retains a minority stake in Banque pour le Commerce et l'Industrie-Mer Rouge, the largest commercial bank. The government has acted to promote the integrity and efficiency of the banking sector and has adopted new banking laws. Credit is allocated on market terms, but access to credit for entrepreneurial activity is still limited by high costs and the lack of other available financing instruments. Commercial banks generally provide only short-term financing and lending. The government imposes no limitations on international fund conversions or transfers, and there are no foreign exchange controls. Capital markets are undeveloped.

PROPERTY RIGHTS — 30

Protection of private property is weak. Courts are frequently overburdened, and enforcement of contracts can be time-consuming. Trials and judicial proceedings are subject to corruption. Political manipulation undermines the judicial system's credibility. Commercial and bankruptcy laws are not applied consistently. The government does not enforce laws protecting intellectual property rights. Pirated goods are sold openly in the informal markets.

FREEDOM FROM CORRUPTION — 30

Corruption is perceived as widespread. Djibouti ranks 102nd out of 179 countries in Transparency International's Corruption Perceptions Index for 2008. It is estimated that more than 80 percent of enterprises are within the informal sector, including microenterprises that play a key role in the economy. Anti-corruption laws are rarely enforced. Administrative delays, demands for petty bribes, and a non-transparent judicial system are barriers to foreign direct investment.

LABOR FREEDOM — 55.3

Relatively inflexible labor regulations hinder employment and productivity growth. The non-salary cost of employing a worker is moderate, but dismissing an employee can be relatively difficult and costly. Work hours are not fully flexible.

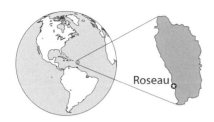

DOMINICA

Economic Freedom Score

25 — 50 — 75

Least free 0   100 Most free

63.2

World Rank: 70   **Regional Rank: 14**

Dominica's economic freedom score is 63.2, making its economy the 70th freest in the 2010 *Index*. Its overall score is 0.6 point higher than last year, with only small changes in any of the 10 economic freedoms. Dominica is ranked 14th out of 29 countries in the South and Central America/Caribbean region, and its overall score is above the world and regional averages.

Dominica scores above the world average in six of the 10 economic freedoms. The entrepreneurial environment is relatively efficient, and foreign investors receive treatment generally equal to nationals. Property rights are respected, although pirated materials are bought and sold without consequence.

Two major weaknesses limit Dominica's overall economic freedom. Sounder and more prudent public finance management is needed to promote long-term economic growth. Government expenditure equals nearly 40 percent of GDP, and the efficiency of government services has been poor, undermining the economy's overall productivity. Dominica's low score in financial freedom reflects problems with bank supervision and the regulatory framework.

BACKGROUND: Dominica has a unicameral parliamentary government with a president and prime minister. Tourism is less significant than on other Eastern Caribbean islands, although ecotourists are drawn to the rugged mountains and rain forests. Bananas, citrus, coconuts, coconut soap, and cocoa dominate the economy, and nearly one-third of the labor force works in agriculture. Banana producers continue to struggle to recover from the effects of 2007's Hurricane Dean. The government has tried to diversify agriculture by encouraging the growing of coffee, patchouli, aloe vera, cut flowers, and exotic fruits. In 2008, after Venezuela promised millions in funding for agricultural and industrial development, Dominica's government decided to join Venezuela's Bolivarian Alternative for the Americas (ALBA) socialist trade scheme. This could undermine regional economic integration under the CARICOM Single Market and Economy.

Country's Score Over Time

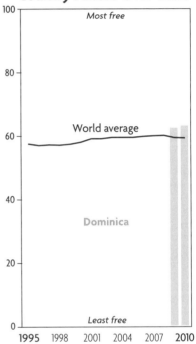

Quick Facts

Population: 73.2 thousand

GDP (PPP): $0.6 billion
3.4% growth in 2008
2.9% 5-year compound annual growth
$8,696 per capita

Unemployment: estimated to be more than 10%

Inflation (CPI): 6.9%

FDI Inflow: $60 million

2008 data unless otherwise noted
Data compiled as of September 2009

How Do We Measure Economic Freedom?
See page 457 for an explanation of the methodology or visit the *Index* Web site at *heritage.org/index*.

DOMINICA'S TEN ECONOMIC FREEDOMS

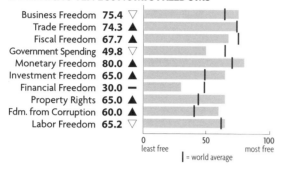

Business Freedom	75.4 ▽	
Trade Freedom	74.3 ▲	
Fiscal Freedom	67.7 ▲	
Government Spending	49.8 ▽	
Monetary Freedom	80.0 ▲	
Investment Freedom	65.0 ▲	
Financial Freedom	30.0 —	
Property Rights	65.0 ▲	
Fdm. from Corruption	60.0 ▲	
Labor Freedom	65.2 ▽	

0 least free   50   100 most free

| = world average

BUSINESS FREEDOM — 75.4

The overall freedom to conduct a business is relatively well protected under Dominica's regulatory environment. Starting a business takes less than half of the world average of 35 days. Obtaining a business license requires 13 procedures, compared to the world average of 18, and almost 40 days less than the world average of 218 days.

TRADE FREEDOM — 74.3

Dominica's weighted average tariff rate was 7.9 percent in 2007. Dominica is trying to improve customs efficiency, modernize customs operations, and address inefficiencies in the clearance of goods, but some import and export bans and restrictions, import taxes and fees, export fees, restrictions on services markets, import licensing, export subsidies, and limited state trading add to the cost of trade. Ten points were deducted from Dominica's trade freedom score to account for non-tariff barriers.

FISCAL FREEDOM — 67.7

The top income tax rate is 38 percent; a reduction planned for January 2009 did not take place. The corporate tax rate is 30 percent. Tax reforms begun in 2008 continued in 2009 with income tax cuts for lower brackets. Other taxes include a value-added tax (VAT), an environmental tax, and excise taxes on food and fuel that were reduced in late 2008. In the most recent year, overall tax revenue as a percentage of GDP was 29.8 percent.

GOVERNMENT SPENDING — 49.8

Total government expenditures, including consumption and transfer payments, are relatively high. In the most recent year, government spending equaled 40.9 percent of GDP. Prudent management of aid inflows remains central to sound fiscal management.

MONETARY FREEDOM — 80

Inflation has been moderate, averaging 5.6 percent between 2006 and 2008. Dominica's currency is the Eastern Caribbean Dollar, a regional currency. The Eastern Caribbean Central Bank issues the EC$, manages monetary policy, and regulates and supervises commercial banking in member countries. In 2003, the government began a comprehensive restructuring of the economy, including elimination of price controls and privatization of the state banana com-

pany. Five points were deducted from Dominica's monetary freedom score to adjust for remaining price controls on fuel.

INVESTMENT FREEDOM — 65

Foreign investment is subject to little restriction, and foreign investors generally receive national treatment. Foreign investors may hold up to 100 percent of an investment. Dominica reserves many small-business opportunities for nationals. Investment is hindered by non-transparent bureaucracy and regulation, infrastructure constraints, underdeveloped markets, and inefficient contract enforcement and land registration. There are no restrictions on the repatriation of dividends for totally foreign-owned firms; a mixed foreign–domestic company may repatriate profits to the extent of its foreign participation. In general, non-national investors must obtain an Alien Landholding License to purchase up to one acre of land for residential use and up to three acres for trade or business purposes.

FINANCIAL FREEDOM — 30

Dominica's underdeveloped financial sector is dominated by banking, and regulation and supervision are poor. Shallow markets and a lack of available financial instruments restrict access to credit. One of the four banks is government-owned. In the past few years, offshore financial services have expanded rapidly. Dominica is one of nine members of the Eastern Caribbean Central Bank. Nonperforming loans have declined from over 20 percent of total assets in 2003 to around 10 percent. The government hopes that implementing its Financial Services Act will strengthen the regulatory and prudential framework for non-bank financial institutions, which are dominated by insurance companies and credit unions. Regulation of the non-bank financial sector remains uneven.

PROPERTY RIGHTS — 65

Dominica has an efficient legal system based on British common law. The judiciary is independent, and public trials are generally fair. When the male head of household dies without a will, the wife may not inherit or sell the property, but she may live in it and pass it to her children. Pirated copyrighted material is sold openly.

FREEDOM FROM CORRUPTION — 60

Corruption is perceived as significant. Dominica ranks 33rd out of 179 countries in Transparency International's Corruption Perceptions Index for 2008. There are criminal penalties for official corruption, but the law is not implemented effectively. Monitoring of non-bank financial institutions needs to be strengthened to deter money laundering.

LABOR FREEDOM — 65.2

Dominica's employment regulations are relatively inflexible. The non-salary cost of employing a worker is moderate, and dismissing an employee is difficult or costly.

DOMINICAN REPUBLIC

Santo Domingo

World Rank: 86 **Regional Rank: 18**

Economic Freedom Score

Least free 0 — 25 — 50 — 75 — 100 Most free

60.3

T he Dominican Republic's economic freedom score is 60.3, making its economy the 86th freest in the 2010 *Index*. Its overall score increased 1.1 points, led by improvements in trade freedom, investment freedom and labor freedom. The Dominican Republic is ranked 18th out of 29 countries in the South and Central America/Caribbean region.

Trade freedom has increased significantly in the Dominican Republic as a result of a drop in the average tariff rate. Government spending is low, and investment freedom has been improved by provisions that strengthen investor protections and improve transparency and efficiency.

The Dominican Republic scores poorly in financial freedom and property rights. The financial sector suffers from poor supervision and regulation as well as from limited access to credit. Additionally, corruption (in the form of drug trafficking, violence, and organized crime) and poor enforcement of the rule of law are widespread, hurting the investment and entrepreneurial climate.

BACKGROUND: Leonel Fernandez of the Dominican Liberation Party, president from 1996 to 2000 and elected again in 2004, was re-elected to a third term in 2008. A 1990s economic boom, led by tourism, telecommunications, and *maquiladora* manufacturing, slowed to negative growth by 2003. The economy rebounded somewhat, helped by implementation of the Central America–Dominican Republic–United States Free Trade Agreement in 2007, but a severe economic downturn in 2009 has fueled public anger about government corruption and wasteful spending. The government also needs to manage a fiscal adjustment, deal with an energy crisis, rebuild infrastructure, and finance trade and budget deficits. The highly politicized electricity sector is plagued by "distribution losses" (theft) of more than one-third of its output, seasonal drought that reduces hydroelectric production, and rising world oil prices.

Country's Score Over Time

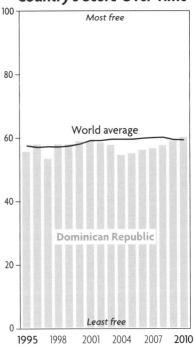

Quick Facts

Population: 9.8 million

GDP (PPP): $80.8 billion
5.3% growth in 2008
8.3% 5-year compound
annual growth
$8,217 per capita

Unemployment: 15.5%

Inflation (CPI): 10.6%

FDI Inflow: $2.9 billion

2008 data unless otherwise noted
Data compiled as of September 2009

How Do We Measure Economic Freedom?
See page 457 for an explanation of the methodology or visit the *Index* Web site at *heritage.org/index.*

DOMINICAN REPUBLIC'S TEN ECONOMIC FREEDOMS

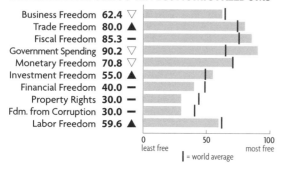

Business Freedom	62.4 ▽
Trade Freedom	80.0 ▲
Fiscal Freedom	85.3 —
Government Spending	90.2 ▽
Monetary Freedom	70.8 ▽
Investment Freedom	55.0 ▲
Financial Freedom	40.0 —
Property Rights	30.0 —
Fdm. from Corruption	30.0 —
Labor Freedom	59.6 ▲

0 least free — 50 — 100 most free
| = world average

BUSINESS FREEDOM — 62.4

The overall freedom to start, operate, and close a business is limited by the Dominican Republic's regulatory environment. Starting a business takes less than the world average of 35 days, but closing a business is a lengthy and costly process.

TRADE FREEDOM — 80

The Dominican Republic's weighted average tariff rate was 5 percent in 2008. High agriculture tariffs, import permit requirements, non-transparent and restrictive regulations and standards, non-transparent government procurement, inefficient customs administration, and corruption add to the cost of trade. Ten points were deducted from the Dominican Republic's trade freedom score to account for non-tariff barriers.

FISCAL FREEDOM — 85.3

The Dominican Republic has moderate tax rates. The top income tax rate is 25 percent. Corporations are subject to a flat rate of 25 percent. Other taxes include a value-added tax (VAT), an estate tax, and a net wealth tax. In the most recent year, overall tax revenue as a percentage of GDP was 15.0 percent.

GOVERNMENT SPENDING — 90.2

Total government expenditures, including consumption and transfer payments, are low. In the most recent year, government spending equaled 18.1 percent of GDP.

MONETARY FREEDOM — 70.8

Inflation has been high, averaging 9.2 percent between 2006 and 2008. The government applies price controls to electricity and fuel and subsidizes some agricultural products and electricity generation. Ten points were deducted from the Dominican Republic's monetary freedom score to account for policies that distort domestic prices.

INVESTMENT FREEDOM — 55

Unlimited foreign investment is permitted in all sectors with the exception of disposal and storage of toxic or radioactive waste not produced in the country, activities negatively affecting public health and the environment, and the production of goods directly linked to national security, unless authorized by the president. Despite reforms aimed at improving the transparency and effectiveness of laws affecting competition, efforts to establish the rule of law in many sectors have been impeded or soundly defeated by special interests. Foreign investors cite a lack of clear, standardized rules by which to compete and a lack of enforcement. Complaints have included corruption, requests for bribes, delays in government payments, and failure to honor contracts. Eighty percent of the labor force of a foreign or national company, including free trade zone companies, must be composed of Dominican nationals (the management or administrative staff of a foreign company is exempt). Residents and non-residents may hold foreign exchange accounts. Payments and transfers are subject to documentation requirements. Some capital transactions are subject to approval, documentation, or reporting requirements. Foreign investors and citizens have the same rights to own property.

FINANCIAL FREEDOM — 40

The Dominican Republic's small financial sector is poorly supervised and regulated, limiting access to credit. The sector has achieved modest liberalization and consolidation. Assets are largely controlled by 14 multiple-service banks. An attempt to create a new financial regulatory network was circumvented by a government bailout of several banks during a 2003 banking crisis, and confidence in banking has been shaky since then. However, credit to the private sector has bounced back in recent years. Pension funds and insurance companies account for less than 10 percent of financial-sector assets. Distortions in the foreign exchange market have been gradually eliminated. In an effort to strengthen the regulatory framework for the banking sector, amendments to the Monetary and Finance Law were proposed in 2008.

PROPERTY RIGHTS — 30

The court system is inefficient, and red tape is common. The government can expropriate property arbitrarily. Most confiscated property has been used for infrastructure or commercial development. Although the government has slowly improved its patent and trademark laws, enforcement of intellectual property rights remains poor. The Dominican Republic has a history of problems resulting from conflicting property titles.

FREEDOM FROM CORRUPTION — 30

Corruption is perceived as widespread. The Dominican Republic ranks 102nd out of 179 countries in Transparency International's Corruption Perceptions Index for 2008. Corruption remains endemic in government, the private sector, and the security forces. Despite recent reforms, Dominican and foreign business leaders complain that judicial and administrative corruption affects the settlement of business disputes.

LABOR FREEDOM — 59.6

Employment regulations are relatively burdensome. The non-salary cost of employing a worker is moderate, but dismissing an employee can be difficult and costly. Restrictions on work hours are rigid.

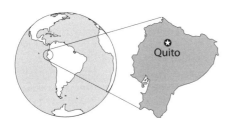

ECUADOR

Economic Freedom Score

World Rank: **147**	Regional Rank: **26**

49.3

E cuador's economic freedom score is 49.3, making its economy the 147th freest in the 2010 *Index*. Its overall score is 3.2 points lower than last year, continuing a sharp downward trend with declines in eight of the 10 economic freedoms. Ecuador is ranked 26th out of 29 countries in the South and Central America/Caribbean region, and its overall score is significantly below the world and regional averages.

Ecuador's new constitution, approved by referendum in September 2008, increases the state's role in management of the economy and expands government spending. As a result, government interference has increased in key industries such as energy, banking, and telecommunications, and it is estimated that the government now spends over 40 percent of GDP.

Ecuador performs particularly poorly in business freedom, property rights, investment freedom, and freedom from corruption. Burdensome regulations restrict business and labor flexibility, the rule of law is politically influenced and inefficient, and expropriation of private property is a concern. The judiciary rules erratically and remains vulnerable to corruption.

BACKGROUND: In January 2007, economist Rafael Correa was elected president on a populist platform of tighter government control of banking and oil production. He also promised to default on debt owed to international lenders and to oppose any free trade agreement with the United States. Capital flight has soared, and foreign direct investment has fallen. Aligned with Venezuela's leftist President Hugo Chávez, Correa has consolidated his political power under a new constitution and won re-election to a second term in April 2009. Ecuador is the world's largest banana exporter. It also has ample petroleum reserves, but the government-run oil industry is mismanaged and corrupt, and production is declining. Factions in the legislature fuel political and institutional instability, and there is a lack of respect for the rule of law.

Country's Score Over Time

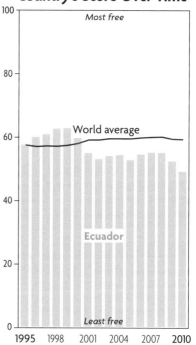

Quick Facts

Population: 13.5 million

GDP (PPP): $107.9 billion
6.5% growth in 2008
4.4% 5-year compound
annual growth
$8,009 per capita

Unemployment: 8.7%

Inflation (CPI): 8.4%

FDI Inflow: $974 million

2008 data unless otherwise noted
Data compiled as of September 2009

How Do We Measure Economic Freedom?
See page 457 for an explanation of the methodology or visit the *Index* Web site at *heritage.org/index*.

ECUADOR'S TEN ECONOMIC FREEDOMS

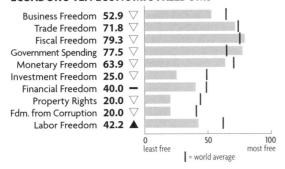

Business Freedom	52.9 ▽	
Trade Freedom	71.8 ▽	
Fiscal Freedom	79.3 ▽	
Government Spending	77.5 ▽	
Monetary Freedom	63.9 ▽	
Investment Freedom	25.0 ▽	
Financial Freedom	40.0 —	
Property Rights	20.0 ▽	
Fdm. from Corruption	20.0 ▽	
Labor Freedom	42.2 ▲	

0   50   100
least free   most free
| = world average

BUSINESS FREEDOM — 52.9

The overall freedom to conduct business is limited by Ecuador's regulatory environment. Starting a business takes an average of 64 days, compared to the world average of 35 days. Obtaining a business license takes about the world average of 18 procedures. Closing a business is a lengthy process.

TRADE FREEDOM — 71.8

Ecuador's weighted average tariff rate was 6.6 percent in 2008. Import restrictions, price bands and variable levies against certain agriculture goods, import taxes against certain products, import licenses, mandatory pre-approval for imports of certain agriculture products, inefficient administration of tariff rate quotas, discriminatory standards and regulations, non-transparent government procurement, and issues involving the enforcement of intellectual property rights add to the cost of trade. Fifteen points were deducted from Ecuador's trade freedom score to account for non-tariff barriers.

FISCAL FREEDOM — 79.3

Ecuador has an above-average income tax rate and an average corporate tax rate. The top income tax rate is 35 percent, and the corporate tax rate is 25 percent. Other taxes include a value-added tax (VAT) and an inheritance tax. In the most recent year, overall tax revenue as a percentage of GDP was 14.9 percent.

GOVERNMENT SPENDING — 77.5

Total government expenditures, including consumption and transfer payments, have been relatively low. Government spending equaled 27.4 percent of GDP in the reference year of 2007 but has been rising rapidly since then. State-owned electricity and telecommunications enterprises remain inefficient.

MONETARY FREEDOM — 63.9

Inflation, restrained somewhat by Ecuador's use of the U.S. dollar as its currency, averaged 6.4 percent between 2006 and 2008 and is climbing. Only public or mixed enterprises (with a public majority stake) may provide public services or control strategic sectors. The government sets domestic prices for bread, noodles, sugar, tuna, vegetable oil, rice, oats, milk, chicken, bananas, coffee, cocoa, fuels, and pharmaceuticals. Twenty points were deducted from Ecuador's monetary freedom score to account for measures that distort domestic prices.

INVESTMENT FREEDOM — 25

Foreign investment receives national treatment, but investment in petroleum, mining, domestic fishing, electricity, telecommunications, broadcast media, coastal and border real estate, and national security is subject to government approval and additional regulations. Rules are complex and non-transparent. There are no antitrust laws, and industry is relatively concentrated. Systemic weaknesses and political pressure are significant problems. Profit repatriation and foreign access to the credit market are allowed. There are no restrictions on foreign exchange, direct investment, or transfers. In some cases, the judicial system has failed to provide adequate protection from unlawful expropriations or effective compensation for expropriated property.

FINANCIAL FREEDOM — 40

Ecuador's financial sector is not fully developed, and access to credit can be costly. Banking has undergone consolidation and restructuring since the late 1990s. There are now 25 banks; the four largest account for more than 60 percent of deposits. The state controls about 10 percent of bank assets. The U.S. dollar is the official currency. Credit is available on market terms, but lack of options hampers entrepreneurial activity. The financial system lacks efficiency and depth, and capital markets remain underdeveloped. There are two stock markets, but little equity has been traded. Foreign takeovers of banks and insurance companies are restricted.

PROPERTY RIGHTS — 20

The rule of law is weak, and intellectual property rights are not enforced. Court delays are significant, judgments are unpredictable and inconsistent, and the judicial system is subject to corruption. Expropriation is possible, and agricultural land may be seized by squatters. The new constitution increases the state's role in the economy and enshrines the government's right to control strategic sectors such as natural resources and telecommunications. Ecuador is ranked 90th out of 115 countries in the 2009 International Property Rights Index.

FREEDOM FROM CORRUPTION — 20

Corruption is perceived as pervasive. Ecuador ranks 151st out of 179 countries in Transparency International's Corruption Perceptions Index for 2008. Laws and regulations to combat official corruption are inadequately enforced. Illicit payments for official favors and theft of public funds take place frequently. Dispute settlement procedures are complicated by the lack of transparency and inefficiency in the judicial system. Local authorities often demand gratuities to issue necessary permits.

LABOR FREEDOM — 42.2

Burdensome labor regulations hinder employment opportunities and productivity growth. Job-tenure regulations create a disincentive for new hiring. Many employers resort to short-term outsourcing contracts.

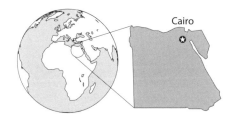

EGYPT

Economic Freedom Score

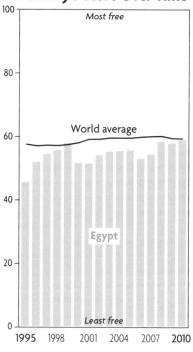

59.0

25 — 50 — 75
Least free 0 — 100 Most free

World Rank: 94　　　　　　**Regional Rank: 11**

Egypt's economic freedom score is 59.0, making its economy the 94th freest in the 2010 *Index*. Its overall score increased by one point over the past year, with noticeable improvements in trade freedom and government spending. Egypt is ranked 11th out of 17 countries in the Middle East/ North Africa region, and its overall score is just below the world and regional averages.

Steady reform measures that Egypt has taken since 2004 have resulted in progress toward greater economic freedom. Trade freedom has improved significantly due to large reductions in the average tariff rate. Competitive tax rates are in place, and public finance management has become more efficient. In the financial sector, the state's presence has been gradually phased out, and restructuring is underway. Egypt's entrepreneurial environment has been enhanced by regulatory reforms.

Continuing the solid track record of economic transformation now requires deeper reforms in order to sustain the country's long-term economic growth. Those reforms include strengthening the judicial system, better protecting property rights, and effective eradication of corruption that is perceived to be widespread.

BACKGROUND: Egypt is the most populous Arab country and a major force in Middle Eastern affairs. President Hosni Mubarak has held power since 1981, but supporters of the radical (and illegal) Muslim Brotherhood hold 20 percent of the seats in Parliament, having campaigned as "independents" in 2005. Despite incremental reforms to liberalize the socialist economic system, the government still heavily subsidizes food, energy, and other key commodities. Economic reform became a higher priority under Prime Minister Ahmed Nazif, who took office in 2004 and placed liberal reformers in key positions. In 2005, the government reduced personal and corporate tax rates, cut energy subsidies, and privatized several enterprises. Since then, the economy has been bolstered by growing foreign investment and revenues from the production and export of oil and gas.

Country's Score Over Time

Most free
100

80

World average
60

40

Egypt

20

Least free
0

1995　1998　2001　2004　2007　**2010**

Quick Facts

Population: 81.5 million

GDP (PPP): $441.6 billion
　7.1% growth in 2008
　6.4% 5-year compound
　　annual growth
　$5,416 per capita

Unemployment: 8.4%

Inflation (CPI): 11.7%

FDI Inflow: $9.5 billion

2008 data unless otherwise noted
Data compiled as of September 2009

How Do We Measure Economic Freedom?
See page 457 for an explanation of the methodology or visit the *Index* Web site at *heritage.org/index.*

EGYPT'S TEN ECONOMIC FREEDOMS

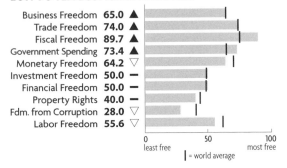

Business Freedom	65.0 ▲	
Trade Freedom	74.0 ▲	
Fiscal Freedom	89.7 ▲	
Government Spending	73.4 ▲	
Monetary Freedom	64.2 ▽	
Investment Freedom	50.0 —	
Financial Freedom	50.0 —	
Property Rights	40.0 —	
Fdm. from Corruption	28.0 ▽	
Labor Freedom	55.6 ▽	

0   50   100
least free   most free

| = world average

BUSINESS FREEDOM — 65

The government has established a "one-stop shop" for business investment and revamped regulation. Starting a business takes an average of seven days, compared to the world average of 35 days. Obtaining a business license still takes more than the world average of 18 procedures.

TRADE FREEDOM — 74

Egypt's weighted average tariff rate was 8 percent in 2008. Customs administration is improving, but import bans and restrictions, services market access restrictions, non-transparent sanitary and phytosanitary measures, import licensing, domestic preference in government procurement, inconsistent customs valuation, and weak enforcement of intellectual property rights add to the cost of trade. Ten points were deducted from Egypt's trade freedom score to account for non-tariff barriers.

FISCAL FREEDOM — 89.7

Egypt has below-average personal income and corporate tax rates. The top individual and corporate income tax rates are 20 percent. A special tax of 40.55 percent remains in effect for oil, gas, and exploration companies. Other taxes include a property tax and general sales tax (GST) that functions as a value-added tax (VAT). The Industrial Development Authority exempted 67 items from sales tax in June 2009. In the most recent year, overall tax revenue as a percentage of GDP was 15.3 percent.

GOVERNMENT SPENDING — 73.4

Total government expenditures, including consumption and transfer payments, are moderate. In the most recent year, government spending equaled 29.8 percent of GDP. Despite announced plans to privatize 152 state-owned enterprises, no progress had been made as of mid-2009. The government is using revenue from reductions in gas and fuel subsidies to increase other social spending.

MONETARY FREEDOM — 64.2

Inflation has been high, averaging 10.8 percent between 2006 and 2008. The government controls prices for some basic foods, energy (including fuel), transport, and medicine and subsidizes basic food items, sugar, pharmaceuticals, and public transportation. Fifteen points were deducted from Egypt's monetary freedom score to adjust for measures that distort domestic prices.

INVESTMENT FREEDOM — 50

All investment projects must be reviewed to gain legal status and qualify for incentives. Foreigners may own up to 100 percent of a project, but approval is easier for joint ventures with domestic partners, and certain sectors remain restricted. Reforms are increasing regulatory transparency and reducing bureaucracy; however, regulations may be inconsistently enforced, and the judicial system is slow and subject to political influence. Residents and non-residents may hold foreign exchange accounts. There are no restrictions on repatriating capital. Real estate laws are complex, but there are few restrictions on foreign ownership of non-agricultural real estate.

FINANCIAL FREEDOM — 50

The government has moved gradually from direct intervention to indirect control of monetary aggregates through such measures as bond issues. Full private-sector ownership, including foreign ownership, is allowed in banking and insurance, but five public banks dominate the sector. Many large international financial institutions in commercial and investment banking, mutual funds, insurance, and securities trading now operate in Egypt. The government sold a majority stake in the Bank of Alexandria in 2006. Sale of Banque du Caire has been indefinitely delayed following the failure of the government's attempt to sell its stake in June 2008. Capital markets are developing, and the stock exchange has been expanding as a key source of financing.

PROPERTY RIGHTS — 40

The government sometimes uses fast-track military courts to circumvent the judiciary. On average, it takes six years to decide commercial cases, and appeal procedures can extend cases beyond 15 years. Local contractual arrangements are generally secure. Laws on real estate ownership are complex, and titles to real property may be difficult to establish and trace. Judicial procedures tend to be protracted, costly, and subject to political pressure. Enforcement of intellectual property rights is seriously deficient.

FREEDOM FROM CORRUPTION — 28

Corruption is perceived as widespread. Egypt ranks 115th out of 179 countries in Transparency International's Corruption Perceptions Index for 2008. Bribery of low-level civil servants seems to be a part of daily life, and there are allegations of significant corruption among high-level officials.

LABOR FREEDOM — 55.6

The government has adopted a new labor code, but employment regulations are not flexible enough to enhance employment opportunities and productivity growth. Restrictions on work hours are relatively flexible, but the non-salary cost of employing a worker remains high.

EL SALVADOR

Economic Freedom Score

Least free 0   100 Most free

69.9

El Salvador's economic freedom score is 69.9, making its economy the 32nd freest in the 2010 *Index*. Its overall score is 0.1 point higher than last year, with only small movements in any of the 10 economic freedoms. El Salvador is ranked 3rd out of 29 countries in the South and Central America/Caribbean region, and its overall score is well above the world average.

El Salvador has a solid record of economic and structural reform, and its economy has become more modern and service-based. General openness to international commerce, privatizations of state-owned enterprises, and a moderate tax regime have contributed to progress toward greater economic freedom. The economy performs well in many of the 10 economic freedoms, particularly trade freedom, fiscal freedom, and investment freedom.

El Salvador's overall economic freedom remains diluted by two institutional weaknesses. Property rights are moderately well protected, but the relatively weak and inefficient judicial system remains a critical area in need of reform. Freedom from corruption is the only economic freedom indicator where El Salvador scores below the world average.

BACKGROUND: An estimated 75,000 Salvadorans died in the 1980–1992 civil war. Since the 1992 peace accord, political parties have cooperated on political and economic reforms, the restoration of civil liberties, and respect for human rights. Steady economic growth and poverty reduction are due in part to the National Republican Alliance (ARENA) party's free-market policies in the mid and late 1990s. Coffee exports remain significant, but much growth has come from *maquila* industries and the services sector. Annual emigrants' remittances of roughly $3 billion are also vital. El Salvador participates in the Central America–Dominican Republic–United States Free Trade Agreement. In March 2009, Farabundo Marti Liberation Front (FMLN) leader Mauricio Funes became El Salvador's first leftist president. A poor government education system and increasing gang violence are major problems.

Country's Score Over Time

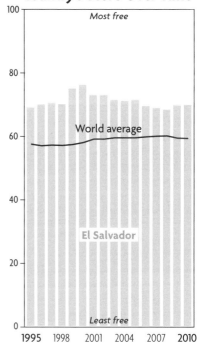

Quick Facts

Population: 6.1 million

GDP (PPP): $41.7 billion
2.5% growth in 2008
3.6% 5-year compound annual growth
$6,794 per capita

Unemployment: 6.3%

Inflation (CPI): 7.3%

FDI Inflow: $784 million

2008 data unless otherwise noted
Data compiled as of September 2009

How Do We Measure Economic Freedom?
See page 457 for an explanation of the methodology or visit the *Index* Web site at *heritage.org/index*.

183

EL SALVADOR'S TEN ECONOMIC FREEDOMS

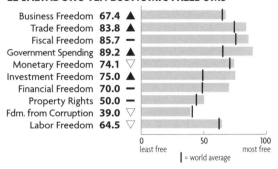

Business Freedom	67.4	▲
Trade Freedom	83.8	▲
Fiscal Freedom	85.7	—
Government Spending	89.2	▲
Monetary Freedom	74.1	▽
Investment Freedom	75.0	▲
Financial Freedom	70.0	—
Property Rights	50.0	—
Fdm. from Corruption	39.0	▽
Labor Freedom	64.5	▽

0 least free 50 100 most free

| = world average

BUSINESS FREEDOM — 67.4

The overall freedom to conduct a business is relatively well protected under El Salvador's regulatory environment. Starting a business takes about half the world average of 35 days. Obtaining a business license takes less than the world average of 218 days. Bankruptcy is somewhat lengthy but not costly.

TRADE FREEDOM — 83.8

El Salvador's weighted average tariff rate was 3.1 percent in 2008. Import restrictions and bans, services market access barriers, restrictive sanitary and phytosanitary regulations, export subsidies, and a few other discriminatory applications of standards add to the cost of trade. Ten points were deducted from El Salvador's trade freedom score to account for non-tariff barriers.

FISCAL FREEDOM — 85.7

El Salvador has average tax rates. The top personal and corporate income tax rates are 25 percent. Other taxes include a value-added tax (VAT), a tax on insurance contracts, and excise taxes. In the most recent year, overall tax revenue as a percentage of GDP was 13.4 percent.

GOVERNMENT SPENDING — 89.2

Total government expenditures, including consumption and transfer payments, are low. In the most recent year, government spending equaled 19 percent of GDP. The economy is largely privatized, but monopolies persist in transportation, banking, and electricity distribution.

MONETARY FREEDOM — 74.1

Although the economy is fully dollarized, inflation has risen, averaging 6.3 percent between 2006 and 2008. The government controls the price of some goods and services, including liquid propane gas, public transport, and electricity. Government ministries directly subsidize water services and set the distribution-service price. The government subsidizes diesel, petroleum, and liquid propane gas. Ten points were deducted from El Salvador's monetary freedom score to adjust for measures that distort domestic prices.

INVESTMENT FREEDOM — 75

The law grants equal treatment to foreign and domestic investors. Investors who begin operations with 10 or fewer employees must present plans to increase employment to the Ministry of Economy. Small-business concerns and investment in certain sectors face additional regulation or restriction. Laws and regulations are relatively transparent and generally foster competition. Bureaucratic procedures are relatively streamlined, although commercial law enforcement remains inefficient and inconsistent. Regulatory agencies are often understaffed and inexperienced. There are no controls or requirements on current transfers, access to foreign exchange, or most capital transactions. El Salvador's 1983 constitution allows the government to expropriate private property for reasons of public utility or social interest, and indemnification can take place either before or after the fact. No single domestic or foreign entity can own more than 245 hectares of land. Rural lands may not be acquired by foreigners from countries where Salvadorans do not enjoy the same right.

FINANCIAL FREEDOM — 70

El Salvador's financial sector is one of Central America's most advanced. Banking is sound and relatively well managed, and credit is easily accessible. Following a decade of liberalization and consolidation, there has been robust growth in deposits and domestic assets. Banks are now largely foreign-owned, but two of the 12 operating in the country are state-owned. The four largest banks account for over 80 percent of total assets. A wide range of financial services are available, and non-performing loans, which have climbed since 2006, account for about 3 percent of the total. Banking regulations are open and transparent. Non-bank financial institutions are limited by the lack of personal savings and low disposable income. El Salvador's well-capitalized banking sector has not been adversely affected by the global financial turmoil.

PROPERTY RIGHTS — 50

Private property rights are moderately well protected. Lawsuits move very slowly and can be costly and unproductive. The legal system is subject to manipulation by private interests, and final rulings may not be enforced. Judicial inefficiency and crime are among the main constraints on business. There have been credible complaints about judicial corruption.

FREEDOM FROM CORRUPTION — 39

Corruption is perceived as significant. El Salvador ranks 67th out of 179 countries in Transparency International's Corruption Perceptions Index for 2008. It is against the law to solicit, offer, or accept a bribe. Most government corruption occurs at lower levels of the bureaucracy.

LABOR FREEDOM — 64.5

Relatively flexible labor regulations enhance employment opportunities and productivity growth. Restrictions on work hours are not rigid. The non-salary cost of employing a worker is low, but dismissing an employee is difficult.

EQUATORIAL GUINEA

Malabo

World Rank: 151   **Regional Rank: 31**

Economic Freedom Score

25   50   75

Least   0   100   Most
free   free

48.6

Equatorial Guinea's economic freedom score is 48.6, making its economy the 151st freest in the 2010 *Index*. Its overall score fell 2.7 points, with the biggest declines in investment freedom and protection of property rights. Equatorial Guinea is ranked 31st out of 46 countries in the Sub-Saharan Africa region.

Equatorial Guinea's rapid economic growth has been driven mainly by oil. However, overall economic development remains severely hampered by structural and institutional problems, and growth has not translated into improvements in ordinary citizens' quality of life. Heavily dependent on petroleum, which accounts for almost 90 percent of GDP, the economy suffers from a lack of dynamism. Poor economic infrastructure and weak regulatory and judicial frameworks impede expansion and diversification of the productive base.

Equatorial Guinea's overall economic freedom is beset by serious institutional distortions. The judicial system is vulnerable to political interference, and corruption under the weak rule of law is prevalent in nearly all facets of the economy. The lack of access to financing precludes entrepreneurial growth, and the investment regime lacks transparency.

BACKGROUND: One-party rule ended in 1991, but opposition parties have won few victories. President Teodoro Obiang Nguema Mbasogo seized power in a 1979 coup and won a fourth seven-year term in 2002 in severely flawed elections. Obiang still tightly controls the military and the government. Equatorial Guinea, though small, is now sub-Saharan Africa's third-largest oil producer and one of Africa's fastest growing economies. Oil and gas accounted for 91 percent of GDP, 91 percent of government revenue, and 99 percent of exports in 2007. Government management of oil wealth is not transparent. The combination of massive oil wealth and a small population makes Equatorial Guinea one of Africa's richest countries per capita, yet most of its people rely on subsistence farming, hunting, and fishing.

Country's Score Over Time

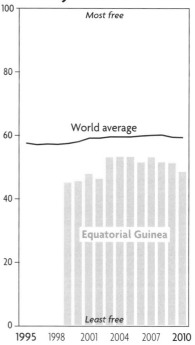

Quick Facts

Population: 0.7 million

GDP (PPP): $22.3 billion
11.3% growth in 2008
10.7% 5-year compound
annual growth
$33,873 per capita

Unemployment: n/a

Inflation (CPI): 5.9%

FDI Inflow: $1.3 billion

2008 data unless otherwise noted
Data compiled as of September 2009

How Do We Measure Economic Freedom?
See page 457 for an explanation of the methodology or visit the *Index* Web site at *heritage.org/index*.

185

EQUATORIAL GUINEA'S TEN ECONOMIC FREEDOMS

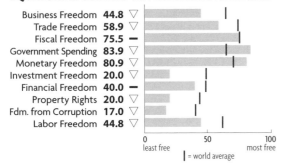

Business Freedom	**44.8** ▽	
Trade Freedom	**58.9** ▽	
Fiscal Freedom	**75.5** —	
Government Spending	**83.9** ▽	
Monetary Freedom	**80.9** ▽	
Investment Freedom	**20.0** ▽	
Financial Freedom	**40.0** —	
Property Rights	**20.0** ▽	
Fdm. from Corruption	**17.0** ▽	
Labor Freedom	**44.8** ▽	

0 least free   50   100 most free

❙ = world average

BUSINESS FREEDOM — 44.8

Equatorial Guinea's burdensome regulatory environment impedes the overall freedom to conduct business. Starting a business takes more than three times the world average of 35 days. Obtaining a business license takes about the world average of 18 procedures and 218 days. Modern bankruptcy procedures have not been developed.

TRADE FREEDOM — 58.9

Equatorial Guinea's weighted average tariff rate was 15.5 percent in 2007. Burdensome and corrupt customs, extensive and non-transparent regulations, inadequate infrastructure, export licenses for timber and cocoa, and government subsidies of cocoa and other exports add to the cost of trade. Ten points were deducted from Equatorial Guinea's trade freedom score to account for non-tariff barriers.

FISCAL FREEDOM — 75.5

Equatorial Guinea has relatively high tax rates. The top income and corporate tax rates are 35 percent. Other taxes include a value-added tax (VAT) and a tax on inheritance. In the most recent year, overall tax revenue as a percentage of GDP was 1.7 percent. Oil and gas account for more than 85 percent of total government revenue.

GOVERNMENT SPENDING — 83.9

Total government expenditures, including consumption and transfer payments, are relatively low. In the most recent year, government spending equaled 23.2 percent of GDP. Falling oil prices have forced the government to clamp down on public spending. Transparency and responsible management of oil revenues are crucial to long-term fiscal stability.

MONETARY FREEDOM — 80.9

Inflation has been moderate, averaging 5.0 percent between 2006 and 2008. The regional Banque des Etats de l'Afrique Centrale (BEAC) prioritizes control of inflation and maintenance of the CFA franc's peg to the euro. Nevertheless, Equatorial Guinea's inflation has been consistently higher than in other Franc Zone countries over the past 10 years. Inflation is forecast to fall to 4 percent in 2009 because of a decline in global food and oil prices and lower government spending. The government sets the price of electricity and subsidizes electricity and cocoa production. Five points were deducted from Equatorial

Guinea's monetary freedom score to adjust for measures that distort domestic prices.

INVESTMENT FREEDOM — 20

The government welcomes foreign investment, but complex bureaucracy and non-transparent regulation, underdeveloped markets, insufficiently qualified staff, poor data, corruption, and lax or arbitrary enforcement of investment law are serious impediments. Foreign investment is not screened, and foreign equity ownership is not subject to limitation, although additional advantages can be gained by having a national majority partner. Residents and non-residents may hold foreign exchange accounts, subject to approval. Capital transactions, payments, and transfers to countries other than France, Monaco, and regional partners are subject to restrictions.

FINANCIAL FREEDOM — 40

Equatorial Guinea's small financial system remains underdeveloped. The banking sector, which has expanded as a result of high economic growth in recent years, dominates the financial system. However, the high costs of finance and limited access to credit instruments hinder dynamic entrepreneurial activities. The banking sector consists of four main banks, all mostly foreign-owned. Compliance with banking regulations is mixed, but non-performing loans have declined to around 10 percent of total loans. The insurance sector is very small, consisting of three insurance companies and one reinsurance company. Equatorial Guinea, a member of the Central African Economic and Monetary Community (CEMAC), has no stock exchange or securities market. Capital transfers within the CEMAC region are unrestricted, but there are restrictions on capital accounts transactions with other countries.

PROPERTY RIGHTS — 20

Application of the laws is selective. Some government officials have attempted to extort money from foreign companies by threatening to take away concessions, and the judicial system is open to political influence. Equatorial Guinea is a member of OHADA (Organisation pour l'Harmonisation en Afrique du Droit des Affaires), a regional organization that trains judges and lawyers to help reform the enforcement of contracts. Enforcement of intellectual property rights is weak.

FREEDOM FROM CORRUPTION — 17

Corruption is perceived as rampant. Equatorial Guinea ranks 171st out of 179 countries in Transparency International's Corruption Perceptions Index for 2008. Corruption among officials is pervasive, particularly in connection with the oil sector, and many business deals are concluded under non-transparent circumstances.

LABOR FREEDOM — 44.8

Restrictive labor regulations hinder employment and productivity growth. Restrictions on work hours are rigid. The non-salary cost of employing a worker is high, and dismissing an employee is costly.

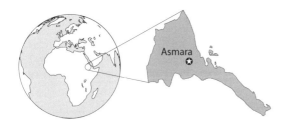

ERITREA

Economic Freedom Score

Least free 0 — 25 — **50** — 75 — 100 Most free

35.3

ritrea's economic freedom score is 35.3, making its economy the world's 4th least free in the 2010 *Index*. It scores far below the world average in eight of 10 economic freedoms and in its overall score. Eritrea is ranked 45th out of the 46 countries in the Sub-Saharan Africa region.

Eritrea's institutional capacity or support for economic freedom remains very weak. Poor management of macroeconomic policies, coupled with political instability over the past decade, has hindered overall economic development. Consequently, the fragile economy remains highly dependent on foreign aid.

A harsh regulatory environment and pervasive corruption undermine the business and investment climates. Investment freedom has fallen to zero because the investment sector lacks structure, procedural consistency, and transparency in light of the pervasive state presence in economic activity. The government uses the judicial system as a coercive tool to promote its own interests, making the courts a biased arbiter in legal disputes. Fiscal, trade, and monetary freedom are also undermined by distortions in prices, exchange rates, and interest rates.

BACKGROUND: Eritrea won independence from Ethiopia in 1993, but conflict soon resumed. A U.N. peacekeeping mission ended in 2008 because of Eritrean-imposed restrictions, and relations with Ethiopia remain tense. Eritrea has also ignored a U.N. resolution instructing it to remove troops from a disputed region on the border with Djibouti. President Isaias Afwerki has ruled since independence; political pluralism, enshrined in the 1997 constitution, has yet to materialize; and elections have not been held. Judicial independence is limited, and journalists and others have been held without trial for speaking against the government. There are no private radio or television stations. Roughly three-quarters of Eritreans depend on small-scale agriculture and fishing. Productivity is very low, and the International Monetary Fund estimates that remittances from overseas Eritreans were equivalent to 23 percent of GDP in 2007.

Country's Score Over Time

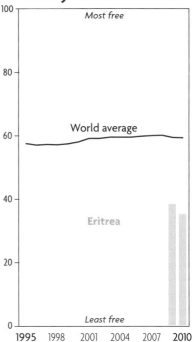

Quick Facts

Population: 5.0 million

GDP (PPP): $3.2 billion
2.0% growth in 2008
1.0% 5-year compound annual growth
$632 per capita

Unemployment: n/a

Inflation (CPI): 11.0%

FDI Inflow: n/a

2008 data unless otherwise noted
Data compiled as of September 2009

How Do We Measure Economic Freedom?
See page 457 for an explanation of the methodology or visit the *Index* Web site at *heritage.org/index.*

ERITREA'S TEN ECONOMIC FREEDOMS

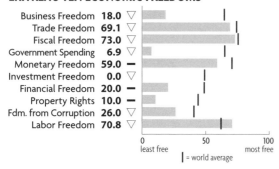

Business Freedom	18.0 ▽	
Trade Freedom	69.1 ▽	
Fiscal Freedom	73.0 ▽	
Government Spending	6.9 ▽	
Monetary Freedom	59.0 —	
Investment Freedom	0.0 ▽	
Financial Freedom	20.0 —	
Property Rights	10.0 —	
Fdm. from Corruption	26.0 ▽	
Labor Freedom	70.8 ▽	

0 least free   50   100 most free

| = world average

BUSINESS FREEDOM — *18*

The overall freedom to start, operate, and close a business is seriously limited by Eritrea's burdensome regulatory environment. Starting a business takes an average of 84 days, compared to the world average of 35 days. Procedures for obtaining a business license are not formally established.

TRADE FREEDOM — *69.1*

Eritrea's weighted average tariff rate was 5.4 percent in 2006. Import licensing for all private imports, inadequate infrastructure, inefficient and cumbersome customs administration, weak protection and enforcement of intellectual property rights, corruption, and limited export activity delay trade and increase its costs. Twenty points were deducted from Eritrea's trade freedom score to account for non-tariff barriers.

FISCAL FREEDOM — *73*

Eritrea's fiscal regime and tax administration lack transparency, and there are no available data on tax revenue collection as a percentage of GDP. Remittances from the diaspora are the main source of income. The top income and corporate tax rates are 30 percent.

GOVERNMENT SPENDING — *6.9*

Total government expenditures, including consumption and transfer payments, are well above average. In the most recent year, government spending equaled 55.7 percent of GDP. There is hardly a functioning economy independent of resource exports and foreign aid.

MONETARY FREEDOM — *59*

Inflation has been high, averaging 11.0 percent between 2006 and 2008. The government maintains a firm grip on Eritrea's command economy, using the military and party-owned businesses to implement its development agenda. The government strictly controls the use of foreign currency, limiting access and availability. Few private enterprises remain. Twenty points were deducted from Eritrea's monetary freedom score to adjust for extreme monetary-control measures.

INVESTMENT FREEDOM — *0*

Eritrea remains a strict command economy, eliminating most private investment. Large-scale projects must be approved by the appropriate minister or the Office of the President. The government has selectively and narrowly courted foreign investors to explore underexploited resources, primarily in mineral extraction, but also in energy, fisheries, and tourism. There is no clearly organized regulatory system; procedures are haphazard and irregularly enforced. Additional impediments to both domestic and foreign private investment include severe limits on the possession and exchange of foreign currency, lack of objective dispute settlement mechanisms, difficulty in obtaining licenses, large-scale use of conscripted labor, and expropriation of private assets. The government uses the judicial system to promote its own interests, making the courts a biased arbiter in legal disputes.

FINANCIAL FREEDOM — *20*

Eritrea's small financial system remains poorly developed, and government interference is significant. High credit costs and scarce access to financing severely impede private investment and dynamic economic growth. All banks are majority-owned by the government, and private-sector involvement in the financial system remains limited. The Commercial Bank of Eritrea, the country's largest commercial bank, has been chartered by the government to provide a range of financial services to the public, but very high collateral requirements for loans prohibit many small entrepreneurs from establishing and expanding their businesses.

PROPERTY RIGHTS — *10*

The government exercises strict control of political, social, and economic systems, with almost no civil liberties allowed. The independence of the judiciary is limited. The government has a history of expropriating houses, businesses, and other private property without notice, explanation, or compensation. The government has imposed an arbitrary and complex set of regulatory requirements that discourage investment from both foreign and domestic sources, and it often reclaims successful private enterprises and property. In theory, women have the legal right to equal educational opportunities, equal pay for equal work, and equal property rights; in practice, men retain privileged access to education, employment, and control of economic resources, particularly in rural areas.

FREEDOM FROM CORRUPTION — *26*

Corruption is perceived as pervasive. Eritrea ranks 126th out of 179 countries in Transparency International's Corruption Perceptions Index for 2008. The government controls all foreign exchange, making it virtually the only legal source of imports and creating illicit profit opportunities for smugglers (who are often high-ranking Eritrean military officers). Eritrea is not known to be a party to any international anti-corruption agreements. Individuals requesting exit visas or passports reportedly have had to pay bribes.

LABOR FREEDOM — *70.8*

Employment regulations are flexible. The non-salary cost of employing a worker is moderate, but dismissing an employee can be difficult and costly. The formal labor market remains severely underdeveloped.

ESTONIA

Economic Freedom Score

Least free 0   100 Most free

74.7

Estonia's economic freedom score is 74.7, making its economy the 16th freest in the 2010 *Index*. Its overall score decreased 1.7 points, as improved business freedom was offset by lower scores in monetary freedom and protection of property rights. Estonia is ranked 7th out of 43 countries in the Europe region, and its overall score is well above the regional and world averages.

Estonia performs well in most of the 10 economic freedoms. A reform bill that facilitates insolvent firms' restructuring and makes overall bankruptcy procedures easier and less costly has enhanced the entrepreneurial environment. The financial sector's efficiency and competitiveness are facilitated by a sound regulatory environment and relatively prudent lending. The overall investment code is simple and transparent, and an independent judiciary protects property rights.

In January 2009, the parliament implemented amendments to the Income and Value Added Tax Act and delayed the planned reduction of the corporate income tax rate to 20 percent by one year. Overall economic freedom has been curbed by relatively high government spending and lingering labor-market rigidity.

BACKGROUND: Since the fall of the Soviet Union, Estonia has been one of the most determined reformers among the former Soviet nations and has transformed itself into one of the world's most dynamic and modern economies. A credit bubble in 2005–2007 ended two decades of strong growth, and the economy contracted significantly in 2009. Estonia has strong trade ties to Finland, Sweden, and Germany and is sensitive to any weakness in those economies. The country became a member of NATO and the European Union in 2004 and aims to join the euro zone in 2010 if it can stick to the Maastricht deficit rules despite its current economic difficulties. A model of stable multi-party democracy, Estonia has experienced seven peaceful changes in leadership since regaining its independence in 1991.

Country's Score Over Time

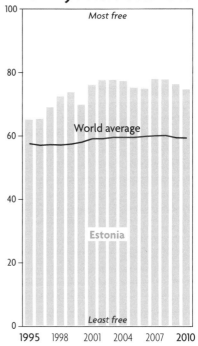

Quick Facts

Population: 1.3 million

GDP (PPP): $27.7 billion
 −3.6% growth in 2008
 5.4% 5-year compound
 annual growth
 $20,662 per capita

Unemployment: 5.5%

Inflation (CPI): 10.4%

FDI Inflow: $2.5 billion

2008 data unless otherwise noted
Data compiled as of September 2009

How Do We Measure Economic Freedom?
See page 457 for an explanation of the methodology or visit the *Index* Web site at *heritage.org/index*.

ESTONIA'S TEN ECONOMIC FREEDOMS

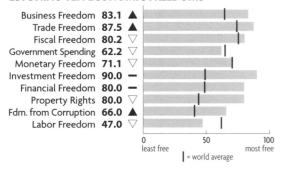

Business Freedom	83.1	▲
Trade Freedom	87.5	▲
Fiscal Freedom	80.2	▽
Government Spending	62.2	▽
Monetary Freedom	71.1	▽
Investment Freedom	90.0	—
Financial Freedom	80.0	—
Property Rights	80.0	▽
Fdm. from Corruption	66.0	▲
Labor Freedom	47.0	▽

0 least free   50   100 most free

| = world average

BUSINESS FREEDOM — 83.1

The overall freedom to conduct a business is relatively well protected under Estonia's transparent regulatory environment. Starting a business takes an average of seven days, compared to the world average of 35 days. Obtaining a business license requires less than the world average of 18 procedures and 218 days.

TRADE FREEDOM — 87.5

Estonia's trade policy is the same as that of other members of the European Union. The common EU weighted average tariff rate was 1.3 percent in 2008. However, the EU has high or escalating tariffs for agricultural and manufacturing products, and its MFN tariff code is complex. Non-tariff barriers reflected in EU and Estonian policy include agricultural and manufacturing subsidies, quotas, import restrictions and bans for some goods and services, market access restrictions in some services sectors, non-transparent and restrictive regulations and standards, and inconsistent regulatory and customs administration among EU members. Ten points were deducted from Estonia's trade freedom score to reflect these factors.

FISCAL FREEDOM — 80.2

Estonia has relatively low tax rates. The personal income tax rate is a flat 21 percent. The corporate tax is also 21 percent. Undistributed profits are not subject to taxation. Other taxes include excise taxes and a value-added tax (VAT). In the most recent year, overall tax revenue as a percentage of GDP was 33.2 percent.

GOVERNMENT SPENDING — 62.2

Total government expenditures, including consumption and transfer payments, are moderate. In the most recent year, government spending equaled 35.5 percent of GDP. The private sector generates more than 80 percent of GDP. Privatization of remaining state-owned enterprises in transportation and electricity is under consideration.

MONETARY FREEDOM — 71.1

Inflation has been relatively high, averaging 8.9 percent between 2006 and 2008. As a participant in the EU's Common Agricultural Policy, the government subsidizes agricultural production, distorting the prices of agricultural products. It also subsidizes fuel and rent. Ten points

were deducted from Estonia's monetary freedom score to account for policies that distort domestic prices.

INVESTMENT FREEDOM — 90

Foreign and domestic investments are treated equally under the law. Foreigners may invest in all sectors and own real estate, but there are restrictions on land purchases exceeding 10 hectares. Licenses required for investment in banking, mining, gas and water supply, railroads and transport, energy, and communications are allocated in a non-discriminatory manner. The foreign investment code is transparent. The commercial community's small size can encourage favoritism. Residents and non-residents may hold foreign exchange accounts, and payments, transfers, and most capital transactions are not subject to controls.

FINANCIAL FREEDOM — 80

Financial regulatory and supervisory frameworks are efficient and transparent. As of mid-2008, there were more than 50 financial institutions, including six commercial banks and 10 foreign bank branches. The banking sector is highly profitable and provides a wide range of financial services. Four banks still control over 90 percent of assets. The government has no financial stake in any local credit institution. Foreign financial institutions are welcome, and foreign firms dominate the insurance sector. Credit is allocated on market terms, and foreign investors may obtain credit freely. The small but active stock exchange is part of a network of Scandinavian and Baltic exchanges. The financial sector weathered the global financial turmoil relatively well owing to sound regulations and supportive measures. The commercial banks have remained well capitalized, and no extensive state intervention in sustaining financial stability has been carried out. Nonperforming loans have climbed to around 4 percent of total loans.

PROPERTY RIGHTS — 80

Estonia's judiciary is insulated from government influence. Property rights and contracts are enforced, and the commercial code is applied consistently. Estonian law is in compliance with EU directives protecting intellectual property rights. Estonia is ranked 27th out of 115 countries in the 2009 International Property Rights Index.

FREEDOM FROM CORRUPTION — 66

Corruption is perceived as present. Estonia ranks 27th out of 179 countries in Transparency International's Corruption Perceptions Index for 2008. Estonia has laws, regulations, and penalties to combat corruption, and the corruption that does exist is generally not targeted at foreign investors.

LABOR FREEDOM — 47

Rigid labor regulations impede job creation and productivity growth. The non-salary cost of employing a worker can be high, and dismissing an employee is relatively difficult and costly. Restrictions on the number of work hours remain rigid.

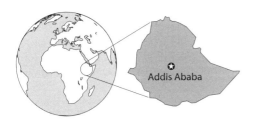

ETHIOPIA

World Rank: **136**　　　　　Regional Rank: **28**

E thiopia's economic freedom score is 51.2, making its economy the 136th freest in the 2010 *Index*. Its overall score fell 1.8 points as a result of deteriorating trade freedom, monetary freedom, and investment freedom. Ethiopia is ranked 28th out of 46 countries in the Sub-Saharan Africa region, and its overall score is just below the regional average.

Ethiopia has achieved considerable economic growth over the past five years, driven mainly by exports of agricultural products. The double-digit growth rate of over 10 percent, however, is fragile due to the lack of economic dynamism, and the economy remains highly vulnerable to external shocks. Progress toward greater economic freedom has been uneven and sluggish.

Ethiopia underperforms in many of the 10 economic freedoms. The business and investment regime is burdensome and opaque. The overall quality and efficiency of government services have been poor and are further undermined by weak rule of law and pervasive corruption. Monetary stability is hampered by state distortions in prices and interest rates, and trade freedom is hurt by high tariff and non-tariff barriers.

BACKGROUND: Ethiopia is Africa's oldest independent country and is moving toward multi-party democracy, but obstacles are abundant, as demonstrated by the 2005 post-election crackdown on protestors. Following war with Eritrea in the late 1990s, a U.N. peacekeeping mission was established on the border. The mission was terminated in 2008, but relations between the two countries remain tense. Ethiopia invaded Somalia in support of Somalia's transitional federal government in 2006 and withdrew in 2009 following a peace deal concluded between the Somali government and moderate Islamic factions. Despite frequent drought and famine, agriculture contributes over 40 percent of GDP, accounts for over 70 percent of exports, and employs about 80 percent of the population. Privatization of state-owned enterprises has proceeded slowly, and the government remains involved in key sectors.

Country's Score Over Time

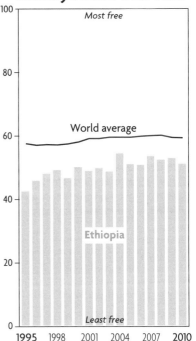

Quick Facts

Population: 80.7 million

GDP (PPP): $70.1 billion
　　11.3% growth in 2008
　　11.8% 5-year compound
　　annual growth
　　$868 per capita

Unemployment: n/a

Inflation (CPI): 25.3%

FDI Inflow: $93 million

2008 data unless otherwise noted
Data compiled as of September 2009

How Do We Measure Economic Freedom?
See page 457 for an explanation of the methodology or visit the *Index* Web site at *heritage.org/index*.

ETHIOPIA'S TEN ECONOMIC FREEDOMS

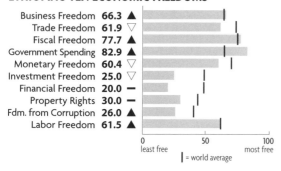

Business Freedom	66.3	▲
Trade Freedom	61.9	▽
Fiscal Freedom	77.7	▲
Government Spending	82.9	▲
Monetary Freedom	60.4	▽
Investment Freedom	25.0	▽
Financial Freedom	20.0	—
Property Rights	30.0	—
Fdm. from Corruption	26.0	▲
Labor Freedom	61.5	▲

0   least free   50   100   most free

| = world average

BUSINESS FREEDOM — 66.3

The overall freedom to conduct a business remains constrained by Ethiopia's regulatory environment. Starting a business takes an average of nine days, compared to the world average of 35 days. Obtaining a business license requires less than the world average of 218 days, but the minimum capital investment to start a business is high.

TRADE FREEDOM — 61.9

Ethiopia's weighted average tariff rate was 11.5 percent in 2008. Import taxes, import restrictions, restrictive foreign exchange controls, services market barriers, non-transparent government procurement, import licensing, cumbersome customs clearance, and inadequate infrastructure add to the cost of trade. All imports must be channeled through Ethiopian nationals registered as official import or distribution agents with the Ministry of Trade and Industry. Fifteen points were deducted from Ethiopia's trade freedom score to account for non-tariff barriers.

FISCAL FREEDOM — 77.7

Ethiopia has above-average tax rates. The top income tax rate is 35 percent, and the top corporate tax rate is 30 percent. Other taxes include a value-added tax (VAT) and a capital gains tax. In the most recent year, overall tax revenue as a percentage of GDP was 10.3 percent.

GOVERNMENT SPENDING — 82.9

Total government expenditures, including consumption and transfer payments, are relatively low. In the most recent year, government spending equaled 23.9 percent of GDP.

MONETARY FREEDOM — 60.4

Inflation has skyrocketed, averaging 21.8 percent between 2006 and 2008. Inflation averaged 44.4 percent in 2008 owing to strong increases in food and oil prices. The government influences prices through its regulation of state-owned enterprises and utilities, subsidizes and controls the prices of petroleum products, and controls the prices of pharmaceuticals and fertilizers. Ten points were deducted from Ethiopia's monetary freedom score to adjust for measures that distort domestic prices.

INVESTMENT FREEDOM — 25

Foreign participation is prohibited in domestic banking, insurance and microcredit services, and several other activities. All investments must be approved and certified and may be subject to additional restrictions. The judicial system remains poorly staffed and inexperienced. Foreign exchange accounts, payments, and current transfers are subject to tight controls and restrictions. Investors may remit profits and dividends, principal and interest on foreign loans, and other capital transactions with few restrictions. While government law states that no assets of a domestic investor or a foreign investor, enterprise, or expansion may be nationalized, except when required by public interest and in compliance with the laws and payment of adequate compensation, there were new reports of threatened or actual property expropriation cases and business disputes involving foreign investors and the government during 2008. All land is owned by the state and can be leased for up to 99 years.

FINANCIAL FREEDOM — 20

Ethiopia's small financial sector remains underdeveloped. The government strongly influences lending and owns the largest bank, which dominates the banking sector. The state has allowed the local private sector to participate in banking, but foreign ownership and branch operations remain strictly barred. As of 2008, there were three government-owned banks, nine private banks, and nine insurance firms. The ratio of domestic credit to GDP has fallen to under 40 percent. The share of non-performing loans has decreased from over 50 percent to just under 10 percent. About 30 microfinance institutions have become major sources of financial services. Reflecting the financial system's lack of efficiency and depth, capital markets are poorly developed, and there is no stock market.

PROPERTY RIGHTS — 30

Enforcement of property rights is weak. The judicial system is underdeveloped, poorly staffed, and inexperienced. Property and contractual rights are recognized, but judges lack an understanding of commercial issues. An international arbitration body's decision may not be fully accepted and implemented. A highly restrictive land-tenure policy makes it very difficult to register property. Land must be leased from the state.

FREEDOM FROM CORRUPTION — 26

Corruption is perceived as pervasive. Ethiopia ranks 126th out of 179 countries in Transparency International's Corruption Perceptions Index for 2008. Despite legal restrictions, officials have been accused of manipulating the privatization process, and state-owned and party-owned businesses receive preferential access to land leases and credit.

LABOR FREEDOM — 61.5

Relatively rigid labor regulations hinder employment and productivity growth. The non-salary cost of employing a worker is very low, but firing unneeded or poorly performing employees is difficult. Restrictions on work hours are inflexible.

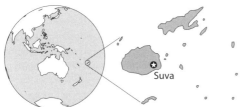

FIJI

Economic Freedom Score

25   50   75

Least free   0   100   Most free

60.3

World Rank: **85**	Regional Rank: **14**

Fiji's economic freedom score is 60.3, making its economy the 85th freest in the 2010 *Index*. Its overall score decreased by 0.7 point from last year, reflecting deterioration in five of the 10 economic freedoms. Fiji is ranked 14th out of 41 countries in the Asia–Pacific region, and its overall score is slightly above the world average.

Fiji has recorded dismal economic performance over the past five years, in large part due to the country's repressed entrepreneurial environment and considerable political instability. The lack of business and investment opportunities, coupled with regulatory uncertainties, has led to economic stagnation. Fiji performs relatively well in only a few of the 10 economic freedoms. Trade and financial freedoms have been facilitated by sluggish but ongoing modernization and liberalization.

The overall efficiency of government is poor and distorted by the lack of transparency. Considerable corruption under the weak rule of law further undermines the effectiveness and productivity of the public sector, prolonging the country's lack of economic dynamism. Fiji's investment freedom has deteriorated in light of the state's continuing tight control. Monetary freedom also remains constrained by the government's interference in the market.

BACKGROUND: The Pacific island nation of Fiji is ruled by an interim government that is backed by military forces led by Commodore Frank Bainimarama, who seized power in 2006 and dismissed the elected government. Fiji has long suffered from ethnic tension between the indigenous, mostly Christian population and a large minority of Hindu or Muslim Indo–Fijians. The resultant political convulsions have stunted the crucial tourism industry. Sanctions imposed by Fiji's main trading partners, including the European Union and Australia, have hurt the vital agriculture, clothing, and fishing industries.

Country's Score Over Time

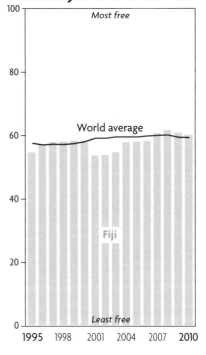

Quick Facts

Population: 0.8 million

GDP (PPP): $3.7 billion
     0.2% growth in 2008
     −0.7% 5-year compound
       annual growth
     $4,382 per capita

Unemployment: n/a

Inflation (CPI): 8.0%

FDI Inflow: $274 million

2008 data unless otherwise noted
Data compiled as of September 2009

How Do We Measure Economic Freedom?
See page 457 for an explanation of the methodology or visit the *Index* Web site at *heritage.org/index*.

FIJI'S TEN ECONOMIC FREEDOMS

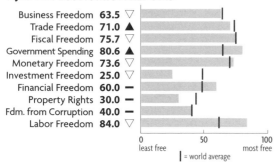

Business Freedom	63.5 ▽	
Trade Freedom	71.0 ▲	
Fiscal Freedom	75.7 ▽	
Government Spending	80.6 ▲	
Monetary Freedom	73.6 ▽	
Investment Freedom	25.0 ▽	
Financial Freedom	60.0 —	
Property Rights	30.0 —	
Fdm. from Corruption	40.0 —	
Labor Freedom	84.0 ▽	

0 least free   50   100 most free

| = world average

BUSINESS FREEDOM — 63.5

The overall freedom to conduct a business is relatively well protected under Fiji's regulatory environment. Starting a business takes an average of 46 days, compared to the world average of 35 days. Obtaining a business license takes about the world average of 18 procedures. Bankruptcy is generally straightforward.

TRADE FREEDOM — 71

Fiji's weighted average tariff rate was 9.5 percent in 2008. Import restrictions, import taxes, import and export licensing, weak enforcement of intellectual property rights, corrupt and inefficient customs, state trading, and subsidies for exporters add to the cost of trade. Ten points were deducted from Fiji's trade freedom score to account for non-tariff barriers.

FISCAL FREEDOM — 75.7

Fiji has moderately high tax rates. The top income and corporate tax rates are 31 percent. Other taxes include a value-added tax (VAT) and a land sales tax. In the most recent year, overall tax revenue as a percentage of GDP was 22.6 percent.

GOVERNMENT SPENDING — 80.6

Total government expenditures, including consumption and transfer payments, are relatively low. In the most recent year, government spending equaled 25.4 percent of GDP. Public debt hovers around an unsustainable 50 percent of GDP.

MONETARY FREEDOM — 73.6

Inflation has been relatively high, averaging 6.7 percent between 2006 and 2008. In April 2009, the central bank devalued the Fiji dollar by 20 percent and imposed capital controls. The devaluation will increase inflation. The government influences prices through state-owned utilities and controls the prices of various products, including food. Ten points were deducted from Fiji's monetary freedom score to adjust for measures that distort domestic prices.

INVESTMENT FREEDOM — 25

Fiji restricts and requires government approval for all foreign investment. A number of areas are reserved for Fijian nationals or the state, and investors must meet certain conditions before investing in other restricted industries.

Foreign acquisition of controlling interest in or takeovers of established, locally owned enterprises are discouraged. Despite some reforms, a lack of transparency in government procurement, inadequate technical expertise, and regulatory uncertainty persist. Bureaucracy and regulation can be burdensome, and the independence of the judiciary has come into question. Residents may hold foreign exchange accounts subject to government approval and restrictions; non-residents also face certain restrictions. Most payments and transfers (including capital) are subject to government approval and limitations on amounts. Foreign real estate ownership is technically permitted but heavily restricted. Leasing is the typical approach to land use.

FINANCIAL FREEDOM — 60

Fiji's financial system is relatively well developed. Banking accounts for about 35 percent of financial system assets and is largely private, though the state-owned Fiji Development Bank offers business development loans and some commercial banking services. The government withdrew from commercial banking in 2006, selling its minority stake in the National Bank. Foreign participation in banking is significant. The two largest banks are Australian and account for 80 percent of the market; three other foreign banks operate freely. The insurance sector consists of 10 companies and is dominated by foreign firms. Fiji's stock exchange has listed fewer than 20 companies but is developing.

PROPERTY RIGHTS — 30

Protection of property is highly uncertain. The backlog of cases is significant, and there is a shortage of prosecutors. Government actions undermine the judiciary's independence, and several judges have resigned. Obtaining land titles is difficult, and the enforcement of intellectual property rights is inadequate.

FREEDOM FROM CORRUPTION — 40

Corruption is perceived as significant. Fiji was ranked 55th out of 158 countries in Transparency International's Corruption Perceptions Index for 2005. (It was not ranked in 2006, 2007, or 2008.) Credible allegations regarding misuse of government funds or abuse of public office have been raised repeatedly. Limited accountability for corruption, inefficient government systems, and lack of effective disciplinary processes pose major challenges to entrepreneurs. Because of Fiji's relatively small population and limited circles of power, personal relationships often play a major role in business and government decisions. The military cited corruption in government and the civil service as a major justification for its overthrow of Fiji's democratically elected government in 2006.

LABOR FREEDOM — 84

Labor regulations are flexible, but the labor market is not fully developed. The non-salary cost of employing a worker is low, and dismissing an employee is straightforward. Restrictions on work hours have become more flexible.

Helsinki

FINLAND

Economic Freedom Score

Least free 0   Most free 100

73.8

Finland's economic freedom score is 73.8, making its economy the 17th freest in the 2010 *Index*. Its score declined by 0.7 point as a result of modest reductions in monetary freedom, property rights, and freedom from corruption. Finland is ranked 8th out of 43 countries in the Europe region, and its overall score is well above the world average.

The modern and competitive Finnish economy has long benefited from high levels of economic freedom. The economy remains a world leader in business freedom, trade freedom, property rights, and freedom from corruption. Private enterprises continue to blossom and promote innovation in an efficient regulatory and legal environment. With prudent and sound banking practices, the financial sector has weathered the global financial turbulence relatively well.

Finland's overall high level of economic freedom is curbed by high government spending and the rigidity of the labor market. As in many other European social democracies, high government spending (close to half of Finland's GDP) supports an extensive welfare state. Restrictive labor regulations undermine employment and productivity growth.

BACKGROUND: Finland joined the European Union in 1995 and adopted the euro as its currency in 1999. The country is sparsely populated, with about one-fourth of its land mass above the Arctic Circle, but boasts a modern, competitive, and transparent economy with vibrant information and communications technology sectors. Previously robust economic growth slowed in 2009 due to the global recession, and Finland, like many other European nations, faces demographic challenges in the form of an aging population and shrinking workforce that could threaten future growth and the government's ability to maintain generous social spending programs. Finland became a member of NATO's Partnership for Peace program in 1994 but has not pursued full NATO membership because of its neutral military status.

Country's Score Over Time

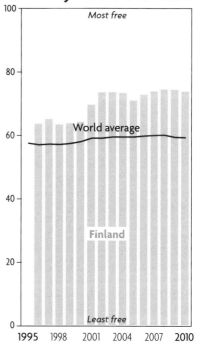

Quick Facts

Population: 5.3 million

GDP (PPP): $188.2 billion
0.9% growth in 2007
3.2% 5-year compound annual growth
$35,427 per capita

Unemployment: 6.4%

Inflation (CPI): 3.9%

FDI Inflow: −$4.2 billion

2008 data unless otherwise noted
Data compiled as of September 2009

How Do We Measure Economic Freedom?
See page 457 for an explanation of the methodology or visit the *Index* Web site at *heritage.org/index*.

195

FINLAND'S TEN ECONOMIC FREEDOMS

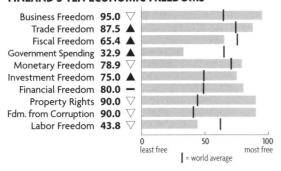

Business Freedom	95.0 ▽	
Trade Freedom	87.5 ▲	
Fiscal Freedom	65.4 ▲	
Government Spending	32.9 ▲	
Monetary Freedom	78.9 ▽	
Investment Freedom	75.0 ▲	
Financial Freedom	80.0 —	
Property Rights	90.0 ▽	
Fdm. from Corruption	90.0 ▽	
Labor Freedom	43.8 ▽	

0 least free — 50 — 100 most free
❙ = world average

BUSINESS FREEDOM — 95

The overall freedom to start, operate, and close a business is strongly protected under Finland's regulatory environment. Starting a business takes an average of 14 days, compared to the world average of 35 days. Obtaining a business license requires much less than the world average of 18 procedures and 218 days. Bankruptcy is straightforward and not costly.

TRADE FREEDOM — 87.5

Finland's trade policy is the same as that of other members of the European Union. The common EU weighted average tariff rate was 1.3 percent in 2008. However, the EU has high or escalating tariffs for agricultural and manufacturing products and its MFN tariff code is complex. Non-tariff barriers reflected in EU and Finnish policy include agricultural and manufacturing subsidies, quotas, import restrictions and bans for some goods and services, market access restrictions in some services sectors, non-transparent and restrictive regulations and standards, and inconsistent regulatory and customs administration among EU members. Ten points were deducted from Finland's trade freedom score to account for non-tariff barriers.

FISCAL FREEDOM — 65.4

Finland has moderate tax rates but a relatively high level of overall taxation. The top income tax rate is 30.5 percent, with municipal rates between 16.5 percent and 20 percent. The top corporate tax rate is 26 percent. Other taxes include a value-added tax (VAT), an inheritance tax, and a flat 28 percent tax on capital income. In the most recent year, overall tax revenue as a percentage of GDP was 43.1 percent.

GOVERNMENT SPENDING — 32.9

Total government expenditures, including consumption and transfer payments, are high. In the most recent year, government spending equaled 47.3 percent of GDP. State ownership of productive assets is considerable.

MONETARY FREEDOM — 78.9

Finland uses the euro as its currency. Between 2006 and 2008, Finland's weighted average annual rate of inflation was 3.1 percent. As a participant in the EU's Common Agricultural Policy, the government subsidizes agricultural production, distorting the prices of agricultural products.

It also imposes artificially low prices on pharmaceutical products. Ten points were deducted from Finland's monetary freedom score to account for measures that distort domestic prices.

INVESTMENT FREEDOM — 75

Finland is open to foreign direct investment. Certain acquisitions of large companies may require follow-up clearance from the Ministry of Trade and Industry. Non–European Economic Area investors must apply for a license to invest in security, electrical contracting, alcohol, telecommunications, aviation, and restaurants. Regulation is relatively transparent and efficient. There are no exchange controls and no restrictions on current transfers or repatriation of profits, and residents and non-residents may hold foreign exchange accounts. Restrictions on the purchase of land apply only to non-residents purchasing land in the Aaland Islands.

FINANCIAL FREEDOM — 80

Finland's sophisticated financial system provides a wide range of services, guided by sound regulations and prudent lending. There are more than 300 domestic banks, but three bank groups (Nordea, OP Bank Group, and the Sampo Group) dominate the system. The government owns about 14 percent of the Sampo Group. Banking is open to foreign competition, and about 60 percent of assets are foreign-owned. Capital markets determine interest rates, and credit is available to nationals and foreigners. The stock exchange is part of a Baltic–Nordic exchange network. Merger of the Financial Supervision Authority and Insurance Supervisory Authority came into force in January 2009. The impact of the global financial turmoil on the banking sector has been relatively muted.

PROPERTY RIGHTS — 90

Property rights are well protected, and contractual agreements are strictly honored. The quality of the judiciary and civil service is generally high. Expropriation is unlikely. Finland adheres to numerous international agreements concerning the protection of intellectual property.

FREEDOM FROM CORRUPTION — 90

Corruption is perceived as almost nonexistent. Finland is tied for 5th place out of 179 countries in Transparency International's Corruption Perceptions Index for 2008. Finland is a signatory to the OECD Anti-Bribery Convention. The Council of Europe's Group of States against Corruption has recommended that Finland sharpen its controls over political financing and increase the transparency of donations to political parties and election candidates.

LABOR FREEDOM — 43.8

Burdensome labor market regulations hamper employment opportunities and productivity growth. The nonsalary cost of employing a worker is high, and dismissing an employee can be costly. Restrictions on work hours are rigid.

FRANCE

Economic Freedom Score

Least free 0 — Most free 100

25 50 75

64.2

World Rank: **64**   Regional Rank: **30**

France's economic freedom score is 64.2, making its economy the 64th freest in the 2010 *Index*. Its overall score has increased slightly due to improvements in six of the 10 economic freedoms. France is ranked 30th out of 43 countries in the Europe region, and its overall score is higher than the world average.

The French economy is well diversified and modern, with institutional strengths such as strong protection of property rights and a relatively efficient legal framework. The entrepreneurial environment is generally facilitated by a sophisticated financial sector that has demonstrated relative resilience during the recent global financial turmoil. The government has pursued various reform measures to increase the competitiveness and flexibility of the economy, but overall progress has been slow.

France's economic freedom remains curtailed by the pervasive presence of the state in economic activity. Spending more than half of GDP, the government's dominance continues in major sectors of the economy. The government also interferes in the market as a large shareholder in many semi-public enterprises. Despite recent reforms, the labor market remains rigid, with multiple restrictions that undermine productivity and employment growth.

BACKGROUND: France was a founding member of the European Union, and French leaders across the political spectrum have championed European integration. Europe was shocked when French voters rejected the European Constitution in a popular referendum in 2003. The government passed the constitution's successor, the Lisbon Treaty, without a public vote. France has a diversified, modern industrial economy but remains the top recipient of market-distorting agricultural subsidies under the EU's Common Agricultural Policy. President Nicolas Sarkozy has pledged to introduce revolutionary market reforms that were neglected in the 1990s, but progress has been slow. In April 2009, France cohosted NATO's 60th anniversary summit in Strasbourg and was formally reintegrated into NATO's military command structures.

Country's Score Over Time

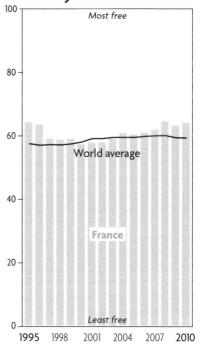

Quick Facts

Population: 62.0 million

GDP (PPP): $2.1 trillion
0.4% growth in 2007
1.8% 5-year compound
annual growth
$34,045 per capita

Unemployment: 7.8%

Inflation (CPI): 3.2%

FDI Inflow: $117.5 billion

2008 data unless otherwise noted
Data compiled as of September 2009

How Do We Measure Economic Freedom?
See page 457 for an explanation of the methodology or visit the *Index* Web site at *heritage.org/index*.

FRANCE'S TEN ECONOMIC FREEDOMS

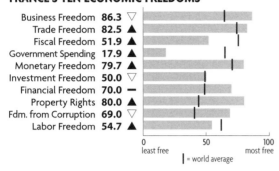

Business Freedom	86.3	▽
Trade Freedom	82.5	▲
Fiscal Freedom	51.9	▲
Government Spending	17.9	▲
Monetary Freedom	79.7	▲
Investment Freedom	50.0	▽
Financial Freedom	70.0	—
Property Rights	80.0	▲
Fdm. from Corruption	69.0	▽
Labor Freedom	54.7	▲

0 least free — 50 — 100 most free
| = world average

BUSINESS FREEDOM — 86.3

France's regulatory environment makes it relatively easy to establish and run a business. Starting a business takes an average of seven days, compared to the world average of 35 days. Obtaining a business license requires less than the world average of 18 procedures and 218 days. Closing a business is relatively easy.

TRADE FREEDOM — 82.5

France's trade policy is the same as that of other members of the European Union. The common EU weighted average tariff rate was 1.3 percent in 2008. However, the EU has high or escalating tariffs for agricultural and manufacturing products, and its MFN tariff code is complex. Non-tariff barriers reflected in EU and French policy include agricultural and manufacturing subsidies, quotas, import restrictions and bans for some goods and services, market access restrictions in some services sectors, non-transparent and restrictive regulations and standards, and inconsistent regulatory and customs administration among EU members. Lack of transparency in standards and regulations, barriers to services market access, and pharmaceutical restrictions exceed EU policy. Fifteen points were deducted from France's trade freedom score to account for these factors.

FISCAL FREEDOM — 51.9

France has relatively high tax rates. The top personal income tax rate is 40 percent. The top corporate tax rate is 34.4 percent (33.3 percent plus a 3.3 percent surcharge that is applicable only to companies with turnover exceeding a certain threshold). Other taxes include a value-added tax (VAT) and a household wealth tax. In the most recent year, overall tax revenue as a percentage of GDP was 45 percent.

GOVERNMENT SPENDING — 17.9

Total government expenditures, including consumption and transfer payments, are very high. In the most recent year, government spending equaled 52.3 percent of GDP. State-owned or state-controlled enterprises dominate such industries as postal services, electricity, and rail. Semi-public companies in which the state holds shares employ almost 4 percent of the labor force.

MONETARY FREEDOM — 79.7

France is a member of the euro zone. Between 2006 and 2008, France's weighted average annual rate of inflation was 2.7 percent. Inflation peaked at 3.6 percent in July 2008. As a participant in the EU's Common Agricultural Policy, the government subsidizes agricultural production, distorting the prices of agricultural products. Prices of health care, pharmaceuticals, books, electricity, gas, and rail transportation are regu-ated. Ten points were deducted from France's monetary policy score to adjust for measures that distort domestic prices.

INVESTMENT FREEDOM — 50

There is no generalized screening of foreign investment, but acquisitions in some sensitive sectors, including public health, defense, agriculture, aircraft production, air transport, audiovisuals, insurance, and maritime transport, require approval. Investments involving large stakes in firms are subject to government review. Regulations are transparent, but officials have wide discretion to impose "unwritten" performance requirements. Attitudes toward foreign investors can be negative. Residents and non-residents may hold foreign exchange accounts. There are no restrictions or controls on payments, transfers, or repatriation of profits, and non-residents may purchase real estate.

FINANCIAL FREEDOM — 70

France's financial, regulatory, and accounting systems are bureaucratic but consistent with international norms. The nine largest banks control more than 70 percent of assets. Most loans are provided on market terms. The government still owns the Caisse des Depots et Consignations and holds minority stakes elsewhere. The Credit Establishments Committee must grant permission for foreign branches from countries outside the European Economic Area. Foreign companies hold around 20 percent of the insurance market. The government owns stakes in several insurance companies. Capital markets are well developed, and foreign investors participate freely. There are no foreign exchange controls. The banking sector has been relatively resilient during the global financial turmoil, but the government has established agencies to recapitalize banks and provide government guarantees for bank refinancing.

PROPERTY RIGHTS — 80

Contractual agreements are secure, and the judiciary is professional. Any company defined as a national public service or natural monopoly must pass into state ownership. Protection of intellectual property rights is very strong.

FREEDOM FROM CORRUPTION — 69

Corruption is perceived as present. France ranks 23rd out of 179 countries in Transparency International's Corruption Perceptions Index for 2008. France enforces the OECD Anti-Bribery Convention.

LABOR FREEDOM — 54.7

Burdensome regulations hamper productivity and job growth. The non-salary cost of employing a worker is very high, and dismissing an employee can be difficult.

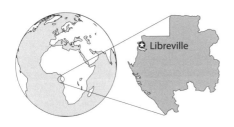

GABON

Economic Freedom Score

55.4

Gabon's economic freedom score is 55.4, making its economy the 116th freest in the 2010 *Index*. Its overall score is 0.4 point higher than last year, reflecting higher trade and investment freedom scores. Gabon is ranked 19th out of 46 countries in the Sub-Saharan Africa region, and its overall score is lower than the world average.

Government efforts to promote economic diversification have met with little success. Heavy reliance on the oil sector makes the economy highly vulnerable to fluctuations in global oil prices and undermines long-term economic competiveness. Despite its relatively minor contribution to overall economic growth, the oil sector accounts for over 50 percent of GDP.

Fostering a more vibrant private sector remains challenging, in large part due to Gabon's lack of institutional capacity to facilitate development. The legal and regulatory environment is not conducive to entrepreneurial activity, and the efficiency of government spending is severely undermined by bureaucracy and poor public finance management. Widespread corruption and the weak rule of law further dampen the fragile entrepreneurial environment.

BACKGROUND: In 1968, President Omar Bongo declared Gabon to be a one-party state. Domestic unrest led to reforms under the 1991 constitution, including multi-party democracy with freedom of assembly and the press, but the democratic process remains deeply flawed. Bongo died in June 2009, and his son, Ali Ben Bongo, won election to replace him and took office in October. Gabon's economy is driven by oil, forestry, and minerals. In 2006, oil accounted for over 50 percent of GDP, over 60 percent of government revenues, and over 80 percent of exports. Despite relatively high average per capita income from oil revenue, most people live in poverty. Oil production is declining as fields are exhausted, and Gabon needs to diversify its economy.

Country's Score Over Time

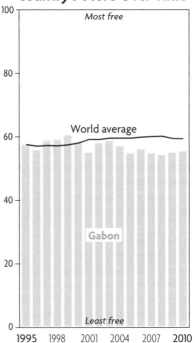

Quick Facts

Population: 1.4 million

GDP (PPP): $21.0 billion
2.1% growth in 2008
2.9% 5-year compound annual growth
$14,527 per capita

Unemployment: 21.0% (2006)

Inflation (CPI): 5.3%

FDI Inflow: $20 million

2008 data unless otherwise noted
Data compiled as of September 2009

How Do We Measure Economic Freedom?
See page 457 for an explanation of the methodology or visit the *Index* Web site at *heritage.org/index.*

GABON'S TEN ECONOMIC FREEDOMS

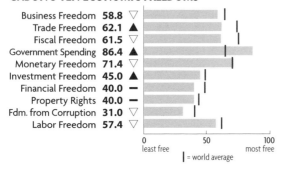

Business Freedom	58.8	▽
Trade Freedom	62.1	▲
Fiscal Freedom	61.5	▽
Government Spending	86.4	▲
Monetary Freedom	71.4	▽
Investment Freedom	45.0	▲
Financial Freedom	40.0	—
Property Rights	40.0	—
Fdm. from Corruption	31.0	▽
Labor Freedom	57.4	▽

0 least free   50   100 most free
| = world average

BUSINESS FREEDOM — 58.8

The overall freedom to conduct a business is restricted by Gabon's regulatory environment. Starting a business takes an average of 58 days, compared to the world average of 35 days. Obtaining a business license requires less than the world average of 18 procedures and 218 days. Closing a business can be lengthy and costly.

TRADE FREEDOM — 62.1

Gabon's weighted average tariff rate was 14 percent in 2008. Tariff escalation, import bans, import and export taxes, inadequate administrative and trade capacity, and lack of customs transparency add to the cost of trade. Ten points were deducted from Gabon's trade freedom score to account for non-tariff barriers.

FISCAL FREEDOM — 61.5

Gabon has high tax rates. The top income tax rate is 50 percent, and the top corporate tax rate is 35 percent. The value-added tax (VAT) was temporarily waived on basic goods to alleviate pressure during the 2008 food crisis. In the most recent year, overall tax revenue as a percentage of GDP was 11.1 percent.

GOVERNMENT SPENDING — 86.4

Total government expenditures, including consumption and transfer payments, are low. In the most recent year, government spending equaled 21.3 percent of GDP.

MONETARY FREEDOM — 71.4

Inflation is relatively moderate, averaging 4.6 percent between 2006 and 2008. The regional Banque des Etats de l'Afrique Centrale (BEAC) maintains the CFA franc's peg to the euro. The government influences prices through subsidies to state-owned enterprises and controls the prices of various products, including fuel, pharmaceuticals, and medical equipment. Fifteen points were deducted from Gabon's monetary freedom score to adjust for measures that distort domestic prices.

INVESTMENT FREEDOM — 45

Foreign investment and domestic capital are legally equal. Certain economic sectors have their own business code. There is no requirement that nationals own shares in foreign investments, though many investors find it useful to have a local partner. An unpredictable legal system, politi-

cal influence, corruption, underdeveloped markets, and inadequate infrastructure impede investment. Residents may hold foreign exchange accounts subject to some restrictions. Non-residents may hold foreign exchange accounts but must report them to the government. Transfers and payments to most countries must be officially approved. Capital transactions are subject to reporting requirements, controls, and official authorization. All real estate transactions must be reported.

FINANCIAL FREEDOM — 40

Gabon's small financial system remains government-influenced. Credit costs are high, and access to financing is scarce. The government still plays a considerable role in long-term lending through the state-owned development bank. Most banks are at least partly state-owned, and competition is limited. Gabon shares certain financial institutions, such as a common central bank and common currency, with other West African countries. The banking sector includes five commercial banks and is open to foreign competition. Three banks are affiliated with French banks, and another is entirely foreign-owned. Domestic credit is limited and expensive, though available without discrimination to foreign investors with prior authorization. Poorly developed capital markets cannot provide alternative financing instruments. A small regional stock exchange headquartered in Gabon began operation in 2008.

PROPERTY RIGHTS — 40

Private property is moderately well protected. Expropriation is unlikely. The president influences the judiciary and parliament. Foreign investors are largely treated in the same manner as their Gabonese counterparts with regard to the purchase of real estate. As a member of the Central African Economic and Monetary Community and the Economic Community of Central African States, Gabon adheres to the standards of the African Intellectual Property Office.

FREEDOM FROM CORRUPTION — 31

Corruption is perceived as widespread. Gabon ranks 96th out of 179 countries in Transparency International's Corruption Perceptions Index for 2008, a decline from 2007. The lack of accountability and oversight that afflicts the budget process can be seen in other areas of the economy as well. Companies have complained of a lack of transparency in customs and other government activities. In the past, fiscal shortfalls, weak financial management, and suspected corruption have contributed to significant arrears in domestic and external debt payments. Gabon participates in the Extractive Industries Transparency Initiative, which aims to provide better accounting for revenues from petroleum and mining industries.

LABOR FREEDOM — 57.4

Labor regulations hinder employment opportunities and productivity growth. The non-salary cost of employing a worker is high, and dismissing an employee is relatively costly. Regulations on work hours remain rigid.

THE GAMBIA

Economic Freedom Score

25   50   75

Least free   0 100   Most free

55.1

World Rank: 118   **Regional Rank: 20**

T he Gambia's economic freedom score is 55.1, making its economy the 118th freest in the 2010 *Index*. Its overall score is 0.7 point lower than last year, reflecting in particular lower scores in property rights and freedom from corruption. The Gambia is ranked 20th out of 46 countries in the Sub-Saharan Africa region, and its overall score is lower than the world average.

The Gambian economy is highly concentrated in the agricultural sector, reflecting a lack of entrepreneurial dynamism. Economic growth, though around 6 percent over the past five years, remains fragile in the absence of a vibrant private sector. The government presence is pervasive, and state-controlled enterprises dominate key sectors. Despite some progress in easing barriers to establishing and running businesses, the overall regulatory environment remains burdened by red tape and a lack of transparency.

Other institutional impediments to economic freedom include the inefficient protection of property rights, corruption, and the weak rule of law. Pervasive corruption is a serious deterrent to translating economic growth into the effective reduction of poverty throughout the population.

BACKGROUND: President Sir Dawda Kairaba Jawara ruled for almost 30 years until 1994, when he was ousted by a military coup led by Lieutenant Yahya Jammeh. Jammeh won flawed multi-party presidential elections in 1996, 2001, and 2006. International rights groups have criticized the government's restraints on civil liberties and political opponents, and journalists have frequently been imprisoned without charge. Geographically, the country tracks the banks of the Gambia River. It has few natural resources. Agriculture employs over 70 percent of the labor force and accounted for 33 percent of GDP in 2007. Tourism is an important source of foreign exchange. Groundnuts are the most important agricultural crop, accounting for over half of domestic exports. The infrastructure is improving but remains inadequate, with frequent power shortages and poor roads.

Country's Score Over Time

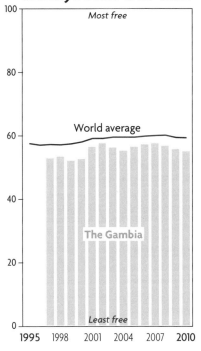

Quick Facts

Population: 1.7 million

GDP (PPP): $2.3 billion
  5.9% growth in 2008
  6.0% 5-year compound
    annual growth
  $1,363 per capita

Unemployment: n/a

Inflation (CPI): 4.5%

FDI Inflow: $63.0 million

2008 data unless otherwise noted
Data compiled as of September 2009

How Do We Measure Economic Freedom?
See page 457 for an explanation of the methodology or visit the *Index* Web site at *heritage.org/index*.

THE GAMBIA'S TEN ECONOMIC FREEDOMS

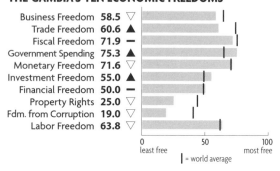

Business Freedom	58.5 ▽	
Trade Freedom	60.6 ▲	
Fiscal Freedom	71.9 —	
Government Spending	75.3 ▲	
Monetary Freedom	71.6 ▽	
Investment Freedom	55.0 ▲	
Financial Freedom	50.0 —	
Property Rights	25.0 ▽	
Fdm. from Corruption	19.0 ▽	
Labor Freedom	63.8 ▽	

0 least free — 50 — 100 most free
| = world average

BUSINESS FREEDOM — 58.5

The overall freedom to conduct business remains limited by The Gambia's regulatory environment. Starting a business takes an average of 27 days, compared to the world average of 35 days. Obtaining a business license requires less than the world average of 18 procedures and 218 days. Closing a business can be burdensome and costly.

TRADE FREEDOM — 60.6

The Gambia's weighted average tariff rate was 14.7 percent in 2008. Inefficient and sometimes corrupt regulatory administration, restrictive licensing, sanitary and phytosanitary prohibitions, and a large informal trade sector add to the cost of trade. Ten points were deducted from The Gambia's trade freedom score to account for non-tariff barriers.

FISCAL FREEDOM — 71.9

The Gambia has relatively high tax rates. The top income and corporate tax rates are 35 percent. Other taxes include a capital gains tax and a sales tax on goods and services. In the most recent year, overall tax revenue as a percentage of GDP was 19.0 percent.

GOVERNMENT SPENDING — 75.3

Total government expenditures, including consumption and transfer payments, are moderate. In the most recent year, government spending equaled 28.7 percent of GDP.

MONETARY FREEDOM — 71.6

Inflation has been moderate but rising, averaging 4.5 percent between 2006 and 2008. The government influences prices through a large public sector, and most leading companies, including those in agriculture, water, electricity, maritime services, public transportation, and telecommunications, remain in government hands. Fifteen points were deducted from The Gambia's monetary freedom score to adjust for measures that distort domestic prices.

INVESTMENT FREEDOM — 55

Foreign and domestic investments generally receive equal treatment. There are no limits on foreign ownership or control of businesses except in the operations of foreign exchange bureaus and in television broadcasting and defense industries, which are closed to private-sector participation.

There is an embargo on establishing new private security companies. Joint ventures are encouraged, but foreign investors may invest without a local partner. Investment is hindered by political influence in the bureaucracy, government corruption, and limited access to financing. Residents and non-residents may hold foreign exchange accounts, and there are few restrictions on foreign exchange and capital transactions. Repatriation of profits is permitted.

FINANCIAL FREEDOM — 50

The Gambia's small financial system is dominated by banking. The banking sector is not fully developed but is relatively sound, despite non-performing loans that are estimated at slightly over 10 percent of total loans. Credit to the private sector has increased. Supervision and regulation remain deficient due to weak institutional capacity. There are 11 banks, including an Islamic development bank. Almost all commercial banks are majority-owned by foreign banks. The insurance sector is small but growing. Two commercial banks have entered the microfinance industry. The government has created a Credit Reference Bureau, but its operation has been delayed. The central bank has established prudential guidelines aimed at reducing barriers to new non-bank financial institutions. Capital markets consist only of government securities; there is no stock exchange.

PROPERTY RIGHTS — 25

The judicial system is inefficient and, especially at the lower levels, subject to pressure from the executive branch. Intimidation of lawyers, a lack of independence, and a lack of technical support severely undermine the administration of justice. Lack of judicial security is one of the main deterrents to doing business. Although the constitution and law provide for protection of most human rights, there are problems in many areas. For example, prisoners are held incommunicado without charge, face prolonged pretrial detention, are denied access to families and lawyers, and are tortured and denied due process. The government restricts freedom of speech and press through intimidation, detention, and restrictive legislation, and several journalists have been murdered. Nevertheless, the law provides adequate protection for intellectual property, patents, copyrights, and trademarks.

FREEDOM FROM CORRUPTION — 19

Corruption is perceived as pervasive. The Gambia ranks 158th out of 179 countries in Transparency International's Corruption Perceptions Index for 2008, a decline from 2007. Corruption among senior government officials is serious, and the few prosecutions of high-profile politicians have not been conducted in a way that bespeaks serious intent.

LABOR FREEDOM — 63.8

Labor regulations are relatively flexible. The non-salary cost of employing a worker is moderate, and dismissing an employee is relatively easy. Restrictions on work hours are fairly flexible.

GEORGIA

Economic Freedom Score

Least free 0   100 Most free

70.4

Georgia's economic freedom score is 70.4, making its economy the 26th freest in the 2010 *Index*. Its overall score is 0.6 point higher than last year due to improvements in trade freedom, property rights, and freedom from corruption. Georgia is ranked 14th out of 43 countries in the Europe region, and its overall score is higher than the world average.

With impressive progress toward greater economic freedom, Georgia for the first time has achieved "mostly free" status. This is particularly justified by high ratings in business freedom, trade freedom, fiscal freedom, and labor freedom. With its strong commitment to economic reform, Georgia has revitalized its historic tradition of entrepreneurship.

The economy has recorded high growth rates averaging over 8 percent over the past five years but experienced a sharp contraction in 2008 due to the Russian invasion. Georgia is well positioned, however, to restart its economic expansion; growth should be facilitated by a competitive tax regime and efficient regulatory framework. Although corruption is still a significant hindrance to overall economic freedom, anti-corruption measures since 2003 have made notable progress.

BACKGROUND: Since the collapse of the Soviet Union in 1991, independent Georgia has survived civil wars and the instability generated by secessionist movements. President Mikheil Saakashvili and his center-right United National Movement took power in the Rose Revolution of 2003 and won presidential and parliamentary elections in 2008. Completion of the Baku–Tbilisi–Ceyhan oil pipeline from Azerbaijan to Turkey has helped the economy, but Russian economic sanctions levied since 2006, the 2008 war with Russia, and Russia's continued military presence in Abkhazia and South Ossetia contribute to political and economic instability. Despite significant international assistance, GDP growth decelerated to 2 percent in 2008 and only 1 percent in early 2009, down from an annualized growth rate of 7 percent from 2000–2007.

Country's Score Over Time

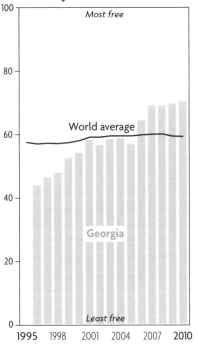

Quick Facts

Population: 4.4 million

GDP (PPP): $21.4 billion
2.0% growth in 2008
8.3% 5-year compound annual growth
$4,896 per capita

Unemployment: 16.5 %

Inflation (CPI): 10.0%

FDI Inflow: $1.6 billion

2008 data unless otherwise noted
Data compiled as of September 2009

How Do We Measure Economic Freedom?
See page 457 for an explanation of the methodology or visit the *Index* Web site at *heritage.org/index*.

GEORGIA'S TEN ECONOMIC FREEDOMS

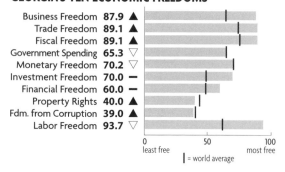

Business Freedom	87.9	▲
Trade Freedom	89.1	▲
Fiscal Freedom	89.1	▲
Government Spending	65.3	▽
Monetary Freedom	70.2	▽
Investment Freedom	70.0	—
Financial Freedom	60.0	—
Property Rights	40.0	▲
Fdm. from Corruption	39.0	▲
Labor Freedom	93.7	▽

0 = least free   50   100 = most free

| = world average

BUSINESS FREEDOM — 87.9

The overall freedom to conduct a business is relatively well protected under Georgia's regulatory environment. Starting a business takes an average of three days, compared to the world average of 35 days. Obtaining a business license requires much less than the world average of 18 procedures and 218 days. Closing a business is relatively simple.

TRADE FREEDOM — 89.1

Georgia's weighted average tariff rate was 0.5 percent in 2008. Georgia has made progress in liberalizing trade, but import restrictions, import taxes, agriculture subsidies, import and export licensing, weak enforcement of intellectual property rights, and inadequate infrastructure and trade capacity still add to the cost of trade. Some border trade goes unreported. Ten points were deducted from Georgia's trade freedom score to account for non-tariff barriers.

FISCAL FREEDOM — 89.1

Georgia has relatively low taxes. The income tax rate is a flat 20 percent, down from 25 percent as of January 1, 2009. The corporate tax rate is 15 percent. Other taxes include a value-added tax (VAT), a tax on interest, and a tax on dividends (reduced as of January 1, 2009). In the most recent year, overall tax revenue as a percentage of GDP was 21.6 percent.

GOVERNMENT SPENDING — 65.3

Total government expenditures, including consumption and transfer payments, are moderate but increasing. In the most recent year, government spending rose to 34 percent of GDP. Privatization of state-owned enterprises is winding down, and proceeds are being used to offset social welfare and defense spending increases.

MONETARY FREEDOM — 70.2

Inflation has been relatively high, averaging 9.7 percent between 2006 and 2008. Prices are generally set in the market, but the government may impose controls through state-owned enterprises. It also provides subsidies for agricultural products and energy. Ten points were deducted from Georgia's monetary freedom score to adjust for measures that distort domestic prices.

INVESTMENT FREEDOM — 70

Foreign and domestic investments receive equal treatment. Exceptions may be made for certain sectors, including maritime fisheries, air and maritime transport, and broadcasting. The government continues to implement reforms, but legal disputes can be lengthy and susceptible to pressure from the government or other outside influences. Foreign firms may participate freely in privatizations, though transparency has been an issue. Residents and non-residents may hold foreign exchange accounts. There are few limits for international payments and current transfers; capital transactions are not restricted but must be registered. Foreign individuals and companies may buy non-agricultural land. Agricultural land can be purchased by forming a Georgian corporation that may be up to 100 percent foreign-owned.

FINANCIAL FREEDOM — 60

Georgia's financial sector has undergone substantial liberalization. There are 20 banks, and the foreign presence is strong. In March 2008, the Georgian Parliament approved the Global Competitiveness of the Financial Services Sector Act to enhance the sector's efficiency. Eight banks account for about 90 percent of total assets. Loans to the private sector have increased rapidly. There are no formal barriers to foreign bank branches and subsidiaries. The government does not have a financial stake in any bank. Significant informal transactions undermine the banking sector to some degree, and the stock exchange is small and underdeveloped. With bank deposits and foreign reserves falling, Georgia's financial system underwent considerable stress during the August 2008 Russian invasion. Restoring stability and confidence has been slowed by the global financial turmoil. Although the financial system has shown a considerable degree of resilience to the external shocks, non-performing loans had increased to around 13 percent at the end of 2008.

PROPERTY RIGHTS — 40

Judges now have to pass tests before appointment, but foreigners and Georgians continue to doubt the judicial system's ability to protect private property and contracts. Enforcement of laws protecting intellectual property rights is weak.

FREEDOM FROM CORRUPTION — 39

Corruption is perceived as significant. Georgia ranks 67th out of 179 countries in Transparency International's Corruption Perceptions Index for 2008, an improvement over 2007. The government has improved its performance in fighting corruption; it has fired thousands of civil servants and police, and several high-level officials have been prosecuted for corruption-related offenses.

LABOR FREEDOM — 93.7

Labor regulations are very flexible. The non-salary cost of employing a worker can be moderate, and dismissing an employee is costless. Rules on work hours are very flexible.

GERMANY

Economic Freedom Score

25   50   75

Least free   0   100   Most free

71.1

Germany's economic freedom score is 71.1, making its economy the 23rd freest in the 2010 *Index*. Its overall score has improved slightly due to modest improvements in freedom from corruption and government spending. Germany is ranked 12th out of 43 countries in the Europe region, and its overall score is significantly higher than the world average.

Germany's economy has long benefited from openness to trade and investment. Reform has facilitated greater economic freedom and dynamic entrepreneurial activity. The judicial system is efficient and independent, and tolerance for corruption is low. Business freedom and investment freedom are strong. Foreign and national investors are treated equally under the law. Although investors continue to face bureaucratic red tape, regulations are clear and evenly enforced.

As in many other European social democracies, government expenditures and the tax burden remain high in support of an extensive welfare state. Government spending and fiscal freedom scores are well below the world average. The downward trend in government spending since 2003 is likely to be reversed in light of the global recession.

BACKGROUND: Germany is Europe's largest economy. Reintegration of the East and West German economies has been difficult, and unemployment, particularly in the East, remains high. Germany is home to many world-class companies and has an enormous export industry and one of the world's highest incomes per capita. The election of conservative Angela Merkel to the chancellorship in 2006 led to some economic reforms, but inclusion of the Social Democrats in a grand coalition seriously limited the government's ability to carry out structural reforms. With the advent of the global economic crisis in 2009, Germany decided not to increase stimulus spending despite pressure from other countries, including the United States. Chancellor Merkel, who is committed to non-inflationary policies, won reelection in September 2009.

Country's Score Over Time

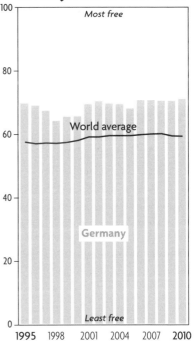

Quick Facts

Population: 82.1 million

GDP (PPP): $2.9 trillion
1.3% growth in 2008
1.9% 5-year compound annual growth
$35,613 per capita

Unemployment: 7.3%

Inflation (CPI): 2.8%

FDI Inflow: $24.9 billion

2008 data unless otherwise noted
Data compiled as of September 2009

How Do We Measure Economic Freedom?
See page 457 for an explanation of the methodology or visit the *Index* Web site at *heritage.org/index.*

GERMANY'S TEN ECONOMIC FREEDOMS

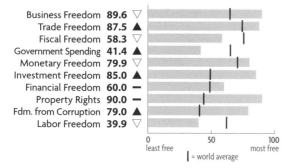

Business Freedom	89.6	▽
Trade Freedom	87.5	▲
Fiscal Freedom	58.3	▽
Government Spending	41.4	▲
Monetary Freedom	79.9	▽
Investment Freedom	85.0	▲
Financial Freedom	60.0	—
Property Rights	90.0	—
Fdm. from Corruption	79.0	▲
Labor Freedom	39.9	▽

0 least free   50   100 most free

| = world average

BUSINESS FREEDOM — 89.6

The overall freedom to establish and run a business is well protected under Germany's regulatory environment. Starting a business takes an average of 18 days, compared to the world average of 35 days. Obtaining a business license requires less than the world average of 18 procedures and 218 days.

TRADE FREEDOM — 87.5

Germany's trade policy is the same as that of other members of the European Union. The common EU weighted average tariff rate was 1.3 percent in 2008. However, the EU has high or escalating tariffs for agricultural and manufacturing products, and its MFN tariff code is complex. Non-tariff barriers reflected in EU and German policy include agricultural and manufacturing subsidies, quotas, import restrictions and bans for some goods and services, market access restrictions in some services sectors, non-transparent and restrictive regulations and standards, and inconsistent regulatory and customs administration among EU members. Restrictions in services markets and the burden of regulations and standards exceed EU policy. Ten points were deducted from Germany's trade freedom score to account for non-tariff barriers.

FISCAL FREEDOM — 58.3

Germany has a high income tax rate and a relatively low corporate tax rate. The top income tax rate is 47.5 percent (45 percent plus a 5.5 percent solidarity surcharge). The federal corporate tax rate is 15.8 percent (15 percent plus a 5.5 percent solidarity tax), but a 7 percent to 17 percent trade tax raises the effective top rate to roughly 33 percent. Other taxes include a value-added tax (VAT) and a flat tax of 25 percent on capital gains income (streamlined as of January 2009). In the most recent year, overall tax revenue as a percentage of GDP was 40.8 percent.

GOVERNMENT SPENDING — 41.4

Total government expenditures, including consumption and transfer payments, are high. In the most recent year, government spending equaled 44.2 percent of GDP. Privatization of the railway company has stalled. The state remains the largest employer.

MONETARY FREEDOM — 79.9

Germany is a member of the euro zone. Between 2006 and 2008, its weighted average annual rate of inflation was 2.5 percent. As a participant in the EU's Common Agricultural Policy, the government subsidizes agricultural production, distorting the prices of agricultural products. It also regulates prices for pharmaceuticals, electricity, telecommunications, and other public services. Ten points were deducted from Germany's monetary freedom score to adjust for measures that distort domestic prices.

INVESTMENT FREEDOM — 85

Foreign and domestic investors are treated equally. Some businesses, including certain financial institutions, passenger transport businesses, and real estate agencies, require licenses. There are no permanent currency controls on foreign investments and no serious limitations on new projects, except for the sale of defense companies. New rules have helped to cut red tape, but bureaucracy remains burdensome. There are no restrictions on capital transactions or current transfers, real estate purchases, repatriation of profits, or access to foreign exchange.

FINANCIAL FREEDOM — 60

Banking consolidation has accelerated dramatically, but Germany's traditional three-tiered system of private, public, and co-operative banks remains intact. Most of the roughly 2,000 banks are local savings banks and cooperative institutions. Private banks account for less than 30 percent of the market, and government-linked publicly owned banks account for nearly 50 percent. The foreign presence is not strong. Regulations are generally transparent and consistent with international norms. All types of capital are available to foreign and domestic businesses, and banks offer a full range of services. Interest rates are market-determined, and foreign investors can access credit freely. The insurance sector and capital markets are open to foreign participation. The government established a financial stabilization fund for troubled banks in October 2008.

PROPERTY RIGHTS — 90

Contractual arrangements are secure, and commercial law and private contracts are respected. All property is protected, and the judiciary and civil service are highly professional. Separate supreme courts deal with commercial, tax, labor, and constitutional cases.

FREEDOM FROM CORRUPTION — 79

Corruption is perceived as minimal. Germany ranks 14th out of 179 countries in Transparency International's Corruption Perceptions Index for 2008. Strict anti-corruption laws are enforced, and Germany has ratified the OECD Anti-Bribery Convention.

LABOR FREEDOM — 39.9

Labor regulations are restrictive. The non-salary cost of employing a worker is high, and dismissing an employee is costly. Wages and fringe benefits remain among the world's highest.

GHANA

Economic Freedom Score

G hana's economic freedom score is 60.2, making its economy the 87th freest in the 2010 *Index*. Its overall score is 2.1 points higher than last year due to improvements in five of the 10 economic freedoms, including freedom from corruption and trade freedom. Ghana is ranked 8th out of 46 countries in the Sub-Saharan Africa region, and its overall score is above the world average.

Prudent macroeconomic policies and structural reforms have enabled Ghana to achieve average growth of over 6 percent during the past five years. Many state-owned or state-controlled enterprises that the government identified for privatization in 2007 have been divested. An expanding private sector, macroeconomic stability, and financial-sector reform have contributed to relatively steady expansion and poverty reduction. As a result, Ghana for the first time has achieved the status of "moderately free."

Ghana's overall economic freedom is mainly curtailed by an ineffective judicial system that remains vulnerable to political influence. Corruption and the weak rule of law undermine Ghana's capacity to attract more foreign investment.

BACKGROUND: In 1957, Ghana was the first Sub-Saharan African nation to achieve independence from a colonial power. It has been a stable democracy since 1992. Long-time opposition party candidate John Atta Mills was elected president in December 2008 by the narrowest margin in African history. Ghana is rich in natural resources, including gold, diamonds, manganese ore, and bauxite. The industrial sector, at about 30 percent of GDP in 2007, is somewhat more developed than those of many other African countries, but agriculture is the key economic pillar and in 2007 accounted for 50 percent of employment, 43 percent of GDP, and 39 percent of exports (predominantly cocoa, cocoa products, and timber). Ghana is the world's second-largest producer of cocoa. Significant oil reserves, discovered in 2007, have yet to be fully exploited.

Country's Score Over Time

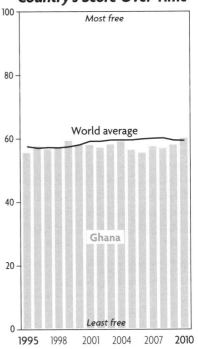

Quick Facts

Population: 23.4 million

GDP (PPP): $33.9 billion
6.2% growth in 2008
6.4% 5-year compound
annual growth
$1,452 per capita

Unemployment: estimated to be
over 10%

Inflation (CPI): 16.5%

FDI Inflow: $855.0 million

2008 data unless otherwise noted
Data compiled as of September 2009

How Do We Measure Economic Freedom?
See page 457 for an explanation of the methodology or visit the *Index* Web site at *heritage.org/index*.

GHANA'S TEN ECONOMIC FREEDOMS

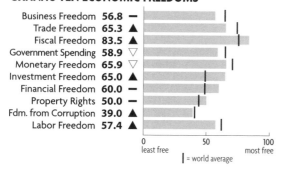

Business Freedom	56.8 —	
Trade Freedom	65.3 ▲	
Fiscal Freedom	83.5 ▲	
Government Spending	58.9 ▽	
Monetary Freedom	65.9 ▽	
Investment Freedom	65.0 ▲	
Financial Freedom	60.0 —	
Property Rights	50.0 —	
Fdm. from Corruption	39.0 ▲	
Labor Freedom	57.4 ▲	

0 least free — 50 — 100 most free
| = world average

BUSINESS FREEDOM — 56.8

The overall freedom to conduct a business remains relatively constrained. Starting a business takes about the world average of 35 days. Obtaining a business license takes about the same as the world average of 18 procedures and 218 days.

TRADE FREEDOM — 65.3

Ghana's weighted average tariff rate was 9.8 percent in 2008. Import bans and restrictions, services market barriers, import fees and taxes, cumbersome and non-transparent standards and regulations, weak enforcement of intellectual property rights, non-transparent government procurement, export promotion schemes, and complex and corruption-prone customs procedures add to the cost of trade. Fifteen points were deducted from Ghana's trade freedom score to account for non-tariff barriers.

FISCAL FREEDOM — 83.5

Ghana has moderate tax rates. The top personal and corporate tax rates are 25 percent. Other taxes include a value-added tax (VAT) and a capital gains tax. Taxes on food products have been reinstated. In the most recent year, overall tax revenue as a percentage of GDP was 20 percent.

GOVERNMENT SPENDING — 58.9

Total government expenditures, including consumption and transfer payments, are relatively high. In the most recent year, government spending equaled 37 percent of GDP. A bloated wage bill is largely responsible for high levels of spending, but expenditure management is generally sound.

MONETARY FREEDOM — 65.9

Inflation has been high, averaging 14.5 percent between 2006 and 2008. The government influences prices through its regulation of state-owned utilities and controls the prices of petroleum products. Ten points were deducted from Ghana's trade freedom score to adjust for measures that distort domestic prices.

INVESTMENT FREEDOM — 65

The foreign investment code eliminates screening of foreign investment, guarantees capital repatriation, and does not discriminate against foreign investors. Sector-specific laws further regulate banking, non-banking financial insti-

tutions, insurance, fishing, securities, telecommunications, energy, and real estate and may limit or deny foreign participation. Non-transparent and burdensome bureaucracy, political influence, and corruption are deterrents. Foreign investors must register with the government and satisfy minimum capital requirements. Residents and non-residents may hold foreign exchange accounts, and payments and current transfers are subject to few restrictions. Foreign investors may lease but not own land.

FINANCIAL FREEDOM — 60

Ghana's financial system has undergone restructuring and transformation. There are 24 banks, and the government has a majority share in the largest bank and full ownership in two others. Bank credit to the private sector has increased. Since the introduction in 2003 of a Universal Banking Business License intended to create more competition in the banking industry, the financial sector has continued to deepen its operations. The relatively developed insurance sector is dominated by two state-owned companies. In 2008, the Non-Bank Financial Institutions Bill was enacted to strengthen regulation and supervision of non-bank financial institutions, including microcredit institutions. Capital markets are developing, and the stock exchange, with over 30 listed companies, has achieved a 45 percent increase in market capitalization. Foreigners may invest in securities listed on the stock exchange without exchange-control restrictions. In 2008, the financial system's efficiency was enhanced by institutional changes that include the establishment of a common National Payment System Platform and full automation of the stock exchange.

PROPERTY RIGHTS — 50

Ghana's judicial system suffers from corruption, albeit less than the systems in some other African countries, and political influence. The courts are slow to dispose of cases and face challenges in enforcing decisions, largely because of resource constraints and institutional inefficiencies. The legal system recognizes and enforces secured interest in property, but getting clear title to land is often difficult, complicated, and lengthy. Despite laws to protect intellectual property rights, very few cases have been filed.

FREEDOM FROM CORRUPTION — 39

Corruption is perceived as significant. Ghana ranks 67th out of 179 countries in Transparency International's Corruption Perceptions Index for 2008, a slight improvement for the second consecutive year. Corruption is comparatively less prevalent than in other countries in the region. A poll measuring public trust in the government found that the courts were one of the least trusted institutions, second only to the police.

LABOR FREEDOM — 57.4

Despite some improvements, labor regulations remain restrictive. The non-salary cost of employing a worker is moderate, but dismissing an employee is costly and difficult.

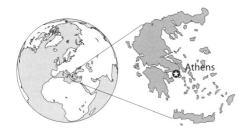

GREECE

Economic Freedom Score

62.7

Greece's economic freedom score is 62.7, making its economy the 73rd freest in the 2010 *Index*. Its overall score has improved by 1.9 points from last year, reflecting better scores in five of the 10 economic freedoms. Greece is ranked 34th out of 43 countries in the Europe region, and its overall score is above the world average.

The Greek economy has been gradually transforming in ways that improve flexibility and openness, but progress has been sluggish. Privatization has reduced the state's dominant role in the economy, and the overall entrepreneurial environment has been enhanced by implementation of a more competitive corporate tax rate and more efficient regulation. Following mergers and privatizations, the financial sector has become more open and more efficient.

Challenges to economic freedom remain in such areas as government spending and labor freedom. High government spending chronically causes budget deficits and places upward pressure on an already high public debt. The rigidity of the labor market impedes productivity and job growth, undermining long-term competitiveness. Corruption is another lingering problem.

BACKGROUND: Greece became the 10th member of the European Union in 1981 and adopted the euro in 2002. The economy depends heavily on tourism and other services. More than half of Greek industry is located in the Greater Athens area and is focused on agriculture, tourism, construction, and shipping. Greece has been a member of NATO since 1952 but has enjoyed uninterrupted democratic rule only since 1974. Political life is dominated by the rivalry between the socialist PASOK party and the more centrist New Democracy party of Prime Minister Konstantinos Karamanlis. Political disputes with neighboring countries, especially Macedonia, simmer in political channels; a more deep-rooted rivalry with Turkey, focused on Cyprus but dating back to the Ottoman Empire or earlier, has come close to armed conflict, though not in the past decade.

Country's Score Over Time

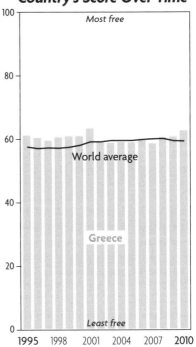

Quick Facts

Population: 11.2 million

GDP (PPP): $330.0 billion
2.9% growth in 2007
3.6% 5-year compound
annual growth
$29,361 per capita

Unemployment: 7.7%

Inflation (CPI): 4.2%

FDI Inflow: $5.1 billion

2008 data unless otherwise noted
Data compiled as of September 2009

How Do We Measure Economic Freedom?
See page 457 for an explanation of the methodology or visit the *Index* Web site at *heritage.org/index*.

209

GREECE'S TEN ECONOMIC FREEDOMS

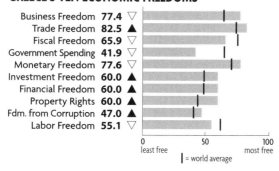

Business Freedom	77.4	▽
Trade Freedom	82.5	▲
Fiscal Freedom	65.9	▽
Government Spending	41.9	▽
Monetary Freedom	77.6	▽
Investment Freedom	60.0	▲
Financial Freedom	60.0	▲
Property Rights	60.0	▲
Fdm. from Corruption	47.0	▲
Labor Freedom	55.1	▽

0 least free   50   100 most free

| = world average

BUSINESS FREEDOM — 77.4

The overall freedom to start, operate, and close a business is relatively well protected by Greece's regulatory environment. Starting a business takes about half of the world average of 35 days. Obtaining a business license requires less than the world average of 18 procedures and 218 days. Closing a business is relatively easy.

TRADE FREEDOM — 82.5

Greece's trade policy is the same as that of other members of the European Union. The common EU weighted average tariff rate was 1.3 percent in 2008. However, the EU has high or escalating tariffs for agricultural and manufacturing products, and its MFN tariff code is complex. Non-tariff barriers reflected in EU and Greek policy include agricultural and manufacturing subsidies, quotas, import restrictions and bans for some goods and services, market access restrictions in some services sectors, non-transparent and restrictive regulations and standards, and inconsistent regulatory and customs administration among EU members. Subsidies, regulations, and services market access restrictions exceed EU policy, and the enforcement of intellectual property rights is problematic. Fifteen points were deducted from Greece's trade freedom score to account for non-tariff barriers.

FISCAL FREEDOM — 65.9

Greece has a relatively high income tax rate and a moderate corporate tax rate. The top income tax rate is 40 percent, and the top corporate tax rate is 25 percent. Other taxes include a value-added tax (VAT), an inheritance tax, and a tax on interest. In the most recent year, overall tax revenue as a percentage of GDP was 34.4 percent.

GOVERNMENT SPENDING — 41.9

Total government expenditures, including consumption and transfer payments, are high. In the most recent year, government spending equaled 44.0 percent of GDP. Progress has been made in reforming and privatizing state-owned enterprises.

MONETARY FREEDOM — 77.6

Greece is a member of the euro zone. Between 2006 and 2008, Greece's weighted average annual rate of inflation was 3.8 percent. As a participant in the EU's Common Agricultural Policy, the government subsidizes agricultural production, distorting the prices of agricultural products. It also can set a ceiling on retail prices and regulates prices for pharmaceuticals, transportation, and energy while setting margins for wholesalers and retailers. Ten points were deducted from Greece's monetary freedom score to account for policies that distort domestic prices.

INVESTMENT FREEDOM — 60

Greece officially welcomes foreign investment but restricts investment in some utilities, and non-EU investors in banking, mining, broadcasting, maritime, and air transport must obtain licenses and other approvals that are not required of Greek and EU investors. Bureaucracy is non-transparent and inefficient. The government caps private investment in companies of "strategic importance" at 20 percent without special approval. Residents and non-residents may hold foreign exchange accounts. There are no restrictions or controls on payments, real estate transactions, transfers, or repatriation of profits. Restrictions exist on land purchases in border regions and on certain islands due to national security considerations.

FINANCIAL FREEDOM — 60

Privatization and mergers have considerably reduced the government's influence in banking. Private banks account for 70 percent of assets. There are more than 60 domestic and foreign banks along with other special credit institutions. Foreign-owned banks are around 11 percent of the market. Five large commercial groups operate as private universal banks. The state directly controls one bank, indirectly controls another, and holds an approximately 30 percent stake in the Postal Savings Bank. Capital markets provide a wide range of financial instruments. A combination of state guarantees and participation in share capital has increased flows in financial markets.

PROPERTY RIGHTS — 60

The judiciary is nominally nonpartisan but tends to reflect government sensibilities. Expropriation is unlikely. The lack of a land registry and the multiple layers of authority concerning land use and zoning permits are among the most significant disincentives to Greenfield investments. Enforcement of intellectual property rights is not rigorous.

FREEDOM FROM CORRUPTION — 47

Corruption is perceived as significant. Greece ranks 57th out of 179 countries in Transparency International's Corruption Perceptions Index for 2008. Bribery is considered a criminal act, and the law provides severe penalties for infractions, but implementation and enforcement remain problematic.

LABOR FREEDOM — 55.1

Labor regulations are restrictive. The non-salary cost of employing a worker is high, and regulations on work hours remain rigid, although employers have greater flexibility under a labor law passed in 2005.

GUATEMALA

Economic Freedom Score

25   50   75

Least free   0   100   Most free

61.0

World Rank: 83   **Regional Rank: 17**

Guatemala's economic freedom score is 61, making its economy the 83rd freest in the 2010 *Index*. Its score has increased by 1.6 points, reflecting improvements in trade freedom, property rights, and freedom from corruption. Guatemala is ranked 17th out of 29 countries in the South and Central America/Caribbean region, and its overall score is above the world average.

Gradually advancing its economic freedom, Guatemala has regained its status as a "moderately free" economy. It scores particularly well in government spending while also scoring well in trade freedom and fiscal freedom. Government expenditures are effectively controlled, with stable fiscal and public finance management, including throughout the global financial crisis. Public debt is among the region's lowest. Personal and corporate tax rates are moderate, and the overall tax burden is relatively low.

Guatemala's overall economic freedom is curbed by a relative lack of business freedom and respect for property rights and widespread corruption. Business licensing procedures are burdensome, and bureaucratic impediments persist. Judicial inefficiency undermines the rule of law.

BACKGROUND: President Alvaro Colom of the leftist National Unity for Hope Party was elected in 2007, promising social democracy, accelerated rural development, improved education, and access to health care. Ongoing issues include crime; rising youth gang membership; judicial weakness and corruption; and participation in Petrocaribe, Venezuela's long-term oil loans and subsidies program, designed to create loyalty to and dependence on Hugo Chávez. About 80 percent of Guatemalans live below the poverty line, less than half of all age-appropriate youth are enrolled in secondary schools, and nearly half of the labor force works in agriculture. The most advanced sector, telecommunications, is fully deregulated. The Central America–Dominican Republic–United States Free Trade Agreement has led to greater trade and employment. Leading exports include coffee, sugar, bananas, winter vegetables, cut flowers, and textiles.

Country's Score Over Time

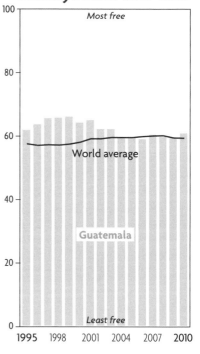

Most free

100

80

60   World average

40

Guatemala

20

0   Least free

1995   1998   2001   2004   2007   **2010**

Quick Facts

Population: 13.7 million

GDP (PPP): $65.1 billion
4.0% growth in 2008
4.7% 5-year compound annual growth
$4,760 per capita

Unemployment: estimated at over 40% (including underemployment)

Inflation (CPI): 11.4%

FDI Inflow: $838.0 million

2008 data unless otherwise noted
Data compiled as of September 2009

How Do We Measure Economic Freedom?
See page 457 for an explanation of the methodology or visit the *Index* Web site at *heritage.org/index.*

GUATEMALA'S TEN ECONOMIC FREEDOMS

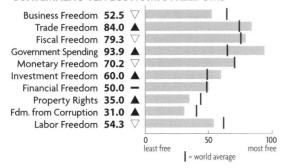

Business Freedom	52.5 ▽	
Trade Freedom	84.0 ▲	
Fiscal Freedom	79.3 ▽	
Government Spending	93.9 ▲	
Monetary Freedom	70.2 ▽	
Investment Freedom	60.0 ▲	
Financial Freedom	50.0 ▬	
Property Rights	35.0 ▲	
Fdm. from Corruption	31.0 ▲	
Labor Freedom	54.3 ▽	

0 least free   50   100 most free

| = world average

BUSINESS FREEDOM — 52.5

The overall freedom to conduct a business is restricted by Guatemala's regulatory environment. Starting a business takes an average of 29 days, compared to the world average of 35 days. Obtaining a business license requires less than the world average of 218 days.

TRADE FREEDOM — 84

Guatemala's weighted average tariff rate was 3 percent in 2008. Import taxes, import licensing, non-transparent sanitary and phytosanitary regulations, services market access restrictions, inconsistent customs valuation and administration, problems enforcing intellectual property rights, and inadequate infrastructure add to the cost of trade. Ten points were deducted from Guatemala's trade freedom score to account for non-tariff barriers.

FISCAL FREEDOM — 79.3

Guatemala's tax rates are moderately high. The top income and corporate tax rates are 31 percent. Other taxes include a value-added tax (VAT) and a tax on real estate. In the most recent year, overall tax revenue as a percentage of GDP increased slightly to 12.1 percent, reflecting efforts to improve tax administration.

GOVERNMENT SPENDING— 93.9

Total government expenditures, including consumption and transfer payments, are low. In the most recent year, government spending equaled 14.3 percent of GDP. State ownership of enterprises, though not extensive, persists in telecommunications and port control. Overall, stable budgetary management has maintained Guatemala's solid fiscal situation through the global downturn.

MONETARY FREEDOM — 70.2

Inflation has been high, averaging 9.8 percent between 2006 and 2008. Inflation peaked at more than 14 percent on an annualized basis in July 2008 but fell below 4 percent by early 2009 as the price of commodities on global markets declined. The government maintains few price controls but subsidizes numerous economic activities and products, such as fuel and housing construction. Ten points were deducted from Guatemala's monetary freedom score to adjust for measures that distort domestic prices.

INVESTMENT FREEDOM — 60

Foreign investors receive national treatment. Some profes-sional services may be supplied only by professionals with locally recognized academic credentials, and mining activities face additional restrictions as minerals and petroleum are the property of the state. While the government has instituted many reforms, complex and non-transparent laws and regulations, inconsistent judicial decisions, burdensome bureaucracy, and corruption continue to deter investment. Residents and non-residents may hold foreign exchange accounts. There are no restrictions or controls on payments, transactions, and transfers. Foreign investors may not own land immediately adjacent to rivers, oceans, or international borders.

FINANCIAL FREEDOM — 50

Guatemala's small financial system is dominated by bank-centered financial conglomerates, and banking has undergone drastic reorganization. Since the banking crises of 2006 and 2007, the government has modernized regulation and strengthened supervision. There are 20 banks, one of which is foreign-owned. The five largest banks account for almost 80 percent of total assets. Sixteen non-bank financial institutions carry out investment banking and medium-term and long-term lending. Foreign banks' presence is small, and their market share accounts for about 8 percent of deposits. Bank supervision and transparency have been strengthened under a legal and regulatory framework adopted in 2002 and legislation passed in 2005 and 2006, which also makes government intervention easier. Capital markets are small and not fully developed. Two commercial exchanges deal almost exclusively in commercial paper and government bonds. The Stock Market Law, intended to improve mechanisms to make information concerning issuing institutions more readily available, was signed into law in 2008.

PROPERTY RIGHTS — 35

Judicial resolution of disputes is time-consuming and often unreliable. Civil cases can take as long as a decade. Judicial corruption is not uncommon. Inadequately documented titles and gaps in the public record can lead to conflicting claims of land ownership. Land invasions by squatters are increasingly common in rural areas, and evicting squatters can be difficult. Successful prosecution of intellectual property rights cases is rare. Guatemala is ranked 80th out of 115 countries in the 2009 International Property Rights Index.

FREEDOM FROM CORRUPTION — 31

Corruption is perceived as widespread. Guatemala ranks 96th out of 179 countries in Transparency International's Corruption Perceptions Index for 2008. Guatemala has ratified the U.N. Convention Against Corruption, but corruption remains a serious problem in customs transactions and at many levels of government.

LABOR FREEDOM — 54.3

Labor regulations are rigid. The non-salary cost of employing a worker is moderate, but dismissing an employee is relatively costly.

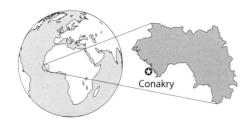

Conakry

GUINEA

Economic Freedom Score

25   50   75

Least free   0   100   Most free

51.8

World Rank: 134   **Regional Rank: 27**

Guinea's economic freedom score is 51.8, making its economy the 134th freest in the 2010 *Index*. Its overall score is 0.8 point better than last year, reflecting improvements in labor freedom and trade freedom. Guinea is ranked 27th out of 46 countries in the Sub-Saharan Africa region, and its overall score is below the world and regional averages.

Guinea has undertaken much-delayed economic reforms to improve macroeconomic stability and enhance economic growth. These measures include reforming fiscal policies, strengthening management of public finance, and implementing other institutional reforms. However, the reforms have not been implemented effectively, and there has been little progress in terms of privatization.

Overall, the entrepreneurial environment is hardly encouraging. Although progress has been made in streamlining bankruptcy procedures, establishing and running a business still requires overcoming numerous bureaucratic hurdles. The application of commercial law is non-transparent and inconsistent. The judiciary is subject to pervasive political interference, and there is corruption in many parts of the economy.

BACKGROUND: After despotic President Lansana Conté died in December 2008, a military junta led by Captain Moussa Dadis Camara seized power, suspended the constitution, and dissolved the parliament, supreme court, and other government institutions. A National Council for Democracy and Development was set up, and Camara was declared president. Under international and domestic pressure, the junta agreed to hold legislative elections in October 2009 and presidential elections in December 2009. Fighting and instability in Côte d'Ivoire, Sierra Leone, and Liberia have often spilled over into Guinea, which has hosted hundreds of thousands of refugees. Guinea possesses rich mineral resources, including iron, gold, diamonds, and perhaps half of the world's bauxite reserves, but infrastructure is poor, electricity and water shortages are common, and much of the population depends on subsistence agriculture.

Country's Score Over Time

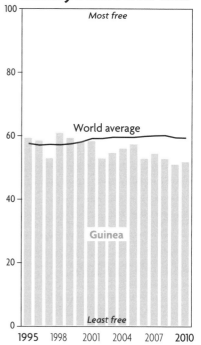

Most free

World average

Guinea

Least free

1995   1998   2001   2004   2007   **2010**

Quick Facts

Population: 9.8 million

GDP (PPP): $11.8 billion
8.4% growth in 2008
2.8% 5-year compound annual growth
$1,204 per capita

Unemployment: n/a

Inflation (CPI): 22.9%

FDI Inflow: $1.4 billion

2008 data unless otherwise noted
Data compiled as of September 2009

How Do We Measure Economic Freedom?
See page 457 for an explanation of the methodology or visit the *Index* Web site at *heritage.org/index*.

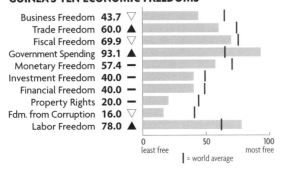

GUINEA'S TEN ECONOMIC FREEDOMS

Business Freedom	43.7	▽
Trade Freedom	60.0	▲
Fiscal Freedom	69.9	▽
Government Spending	93.1	▲
Monetary Freedom	57.4	—
Investment Freedom	40.0	—
Financial Freedom	40.0	—
Property Rights	20.0	—
Fdm. from Corruption	16.0	▽
Labor Freedom	78.0	▲

0 least free   50   100 most free

| = world average

BUSINESS FREEDOM — 43.7

The overall freedom to conduct a business is very restricted by Guinea's burdensome regulatory environment. Starting a business takes an average of 41 days, compared to the world average of 35 days. Obtaining a business license requires more than the world average of 18 procedures and 218 days.

TRADE FREEDOM — 60

Guinea's weighted average tariff rate was 12.5 percent in 2008. Import taxes, pre-import and export authorization requirements, non-transparent and corrupt customs administration, a lack of foreign currency for transacting formal trade, state-owned import and export monopolies, subsidies, and inadequate infrastructure add to the cost of trade. Fifteen points were deducted from Guinea's trade freedom score to account for non-tariff barriers.

FISCAL FREEDOM — 69.9

Guinea has high tax rates. The top income tax rate is 40 percent, and the top corporate tax rate is 35 percent. Other taxes include a value-added tax (VAT) and an inheritance tax. In the most recent year, overall tax revenue as a percentage of GDP was 13.5 percent.

GOVERNMENT SPENDING — 93.1

Total government expenditures, including consumption and transfer payments, are low. In the most recent year, government spending equaled 15.2 percent of GDP. Poor spending management and excessive reliance on the declining mining sector have contributed to fiscal deficits. Political instability and government interference in the provision of water and electricity have hurt fiscal management.

MONETARY FREEDOM — 57.4

Inflation has been extremely high, averaging 26.5 percent between 2006 and 2008. The government influences prices through the regulation of state-owned enterprises and administrative price controls for cement, petroleum products, water, and electricity. It also subsidizes rice importers. Ten points were deducted from Guinea's monetary freedom score to adjust for measures that distort domestic prices.

INVESTMENT FREEDOM — 40

Foreign investment and domestic investment generally receive equal treatment; however, foreign majority ownership in media and mining are subject to ad hoc government review and approval. Investment is deterred by bureaucratic inefficiency, inadequate infrastructure and regulatory capacity, a weak and corrupt judiciary, political uncertainty, opaque procedures, and corruption. Residents and non-residents may hold foreign exchange accounts, and payments and transfers are allowed with some restrictions. Barring a foreign exchange crisis, such transactions can take place upon request, although business owners complain of periodic delays, shortages, and unofficial caps on amounts exchanged. Foreigners and nationals may own property, though individuals have found it difficult on occasion to exercise this right.

FINANCIAL FREEDOM — 40

Guinea's small financial system is dominated by banking. Regulation is inefficient and poorly enforced. With fewer than 10 commercial banks, services are largely concentrated in the capital. Branches and subsidiaries of foreign or regional banks play a relatively important role in financial intermediation. Considerable economic activity remains outside the formal banking sector, and bank lending to the private sector remains, on average, under 10 percent of GDP. About 30 percent of total loans are non-performing. The banking sector, supervised by the Central Bank of Guinea, has some foreign ownership, particularly by French financial institutions. Microfinance has expanded rapidly, and five institutions operate in Guinea. Commercial banks are the main source of financing for private businesses, and capital markets are underdeveloped, reflecting the lack of efficiency and depth in the financial system. There have been no corporate issuances in the debt market.

PROPERTY RIGHTS — 20

Enforcement of property rights depends on a corrupt and inefficient legal and administrative system. Poorly trained magistrates, corruption, and nepotism reportedly plague the administration of justice. The government has expressed its intention to reform the judiciary with the help of international donor agencies, but there are few cases to demonstrate that the system can provide effective protection of real or intellectual property rights.

FREEDOM FROM CORRUPTION — 16

Corruption is perceived as pervasive. Guinea ranks 173rd out of 179 countries in Transparency International's Corruption Perceptions Index for 2008. The business and political cultures, poor formal salaries, and a very large informal economy encourage corruption. Business is routinely conducted through the payment of bribes; government officials commonly demand everything from money to gasoline to perform their routine duties.

LABOR FREEDOM — 78

Labor regulations are relatively flexible. The non-salary cost of employing a worker is modest, and regulations on work hours are not burdensome. The formal labor market is not fully developed.

2010 Index of Economic Freedom

GUINEA–BISSAU

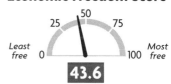

Bissau

World Rank: 167   **Regional Rank: 42**

Economic Freedom Score

Least free 0   25   50   75   100 Most free

43.6

Guinea–Bissau's economic freedom score is 43.6, making its economy the 167th freest in the 2010 *Index*. Its score has declined by 1.8 points, largely due to significant deterioration in trade freedom and monetary freedom. Guinea–Bissau is ranked 42nd out of 46 countries in the Sub-Saharan Africa region, and its overall score is well below the world and regional averages.

Guinea-Bissau's progress in structural reform has been undercut by political and institutional instability. An unsustainable level of public debt has long been a major impediment to development. Economic freedom is severely constrained, and state involvement in the economy is widespread and inefficient.

The economy scores well below the world average in many of the 10 economic freedoms, including business freedom, investment freedom, property rights, and freedom from corruption. Normal business operations are extremely difficult. Restrictions on foreign investment, combined with domestic regulations, create a business environment that is not conducive to private enterprise. Weak rule of law jeopardizes property rights, and corruption is so rampant that the informal market dwarfs the legitimate market.

BACKGROUND: Guinea–Bissau is one of the world's poorest countries. Joao Vieira overthrew post-independence leader Luis Cabral in 1980, won the country's first multi-party elections in 1994, and was ousted in 1998. Kumba Yala, elected in 2000, was ousted by the military in 2003. Vieira won the presidency again in 2005 and was assassinated in March 2009. A presidential candidate and a prominent member of parliament were killed in June 2009, shortly before elections won in a runoff by former interim President Malam Bacai Sanha. Agriculture accounts for over 60 percent of GDP, employs over 80 percent of the labor force, and comprises about 90 percent of exports. Cashew nuts are the primary export. Guinea–Bissau has become a major transshipment point for drugs and light arms by international criminal gangs.

Country's Score Over Time

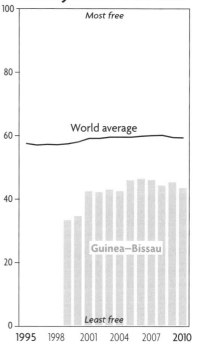

Most free

World average

Guinea–Bissau

Least free

1995   1998   2001   2004   2007   2010

Quick Facts

Population: 1.6 million

GDP (PPP): $0.8 billion
2.7% growth in 2008
2.5% 5-year compound annual growth
$538 per capita

Unemployment: n/a

Inflation (CPI): 10.4%

FDI Inflow: $15 million

2008 data unless otherwise noted
Data compiled as of September 2009

How Do We Measure Economic Freedom?
See page 457 for an explanation of the methodology or visit the *Index* Web site at *heritage.org/index.*

GUINEA–BISSAU'S TEN ECONOMIC FREEDOMS

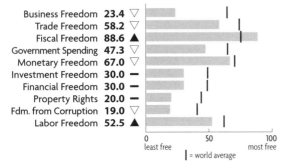

Business Freedom	23.4	▽
Trade Freedom	58.2	▽
Fiscal Freedom	88.6	▲
Government Spending	47.3	▽
Monetary Freedom	67.0	▽
Investment Freedom	30.0	—
Financial Freedom	30.0	—
Property Rights	20.0	—
Fdm. from Corruption	19.0	▽
Labor Freedom	52.5	▲

0   50   100
least free   most free
| = world average

BUSINESS FREEDOM — 23.4

The overall freedom to conduct a business remains severely limited by Guinea–Bissau's regulatory environment. Starting a business takes more than five times the world average of 35 days. The entry costs of launching a business are very high.

TRADE FREEDOM — 58.2

Guinea–Bissau's weighted average tariff rate was 13.4 percent in 2008. Irregularities in import valuation, difficulty tracking and monitoring goods, inadequate infrastructure and trade capacity, and customs corruption add to the cost of trade. The government intervenes in the export of cashews, the principal export. Fifteen points were deducted from Guinea–Bissau's trade freedom score to account for non-tariff barriers.

FISCAL FREEDOM — 88.6

Guinea–Bissau has a relatively low income tax rate but a moderate corporate tax rate. The top income tax rate is 20 percent, and the top corporate tax rate is 25 percent. In the most recent year, overall tax revenue as a percentage of GDP was 10.9 percent.

GOVERNMENT SPENDING — 47.3

Total government expenditures, including consumption and transfer payments, are relatively high. In the most recent year, government spending equaled 41.9 percent of GDP. State-owned water and electricity enterprises struggle to maintain stability. Fiscal management is shaky and focused on meeting current-year expenditure demands without increasing domestic arrears. With the economy heavily dependent on foreign aid, political uncertainty has only exacerbated the situation.

MONETARY FREEDOM — 67

Inflation has been high, averaging 8.1 percent between 2006 and 2008. The regional Banque centrale des Etats de l'Afrique de l'ouest (BCEAO) maintains the CFA franc's peg to the euro. Its monetary policies and the agriculture sector's improving performance will help to control inflation. However, food prices, which depend on the annual harvest, are the main component of the consumer price index and will continue to have the largest impact. The government influences prices through state-owned utilities and controls prices for cashew nuts, the primary export

and source of roughly 30 percent of GDP. Fifteen points were deducted from Guinea–Bissau's monetary freedom score to adjust for measures that distort domestic prices.

INVESTMENT FREEDOM — 30

The investment code provides for national treatment of foreign investors, as well as incentives and guarantees against nationalization and expropriation. Political and economic instability, inadequate regulatory capacity and infrastructure, corruption, and an unskilled workforce discourage foreign investment. Non-residents may hold foreign exchange accounts with permission of the BCEAO, and residents may hold them with the permission of the Ministry of Finance and the BCEAO. Capital transfers to most foreign countries are restricted. The government must approve most personal capital movements between residents and non-residents.

FINANCIAL FREEDOM — 30

Guinea–Bissau's small financial sector remains hampered by economic and institutional instability. The banking system has not been revitalized since the end of the civil war in the late 1990s. Guinea–Bissau is one of eight members of the West African Economic and Monetary Union, which governs banking and other financial institutions. Four banks were in operation as of 2007. The government, regional government institutions, and foreign investors participate in banking. A large part of the population is still outside of the formal banking sector. High credit costs and scarce access to financing severely impede entrepreneurial activity. The first microfinance institution opened at the end of 2005 as a subsidiary of a regional development bank. There is no stock exchange.

PROPERTY RIGHTS — 20

Protection of property rights is extremely weak. The judiciary is influenced by the executive. Judges are poorly trained, poorly paid, and subject to corruption. Traditional practices prevail in most rural areas, and persons who live in urban areas often bring judicial disputes to traditional counselors to avoid the official system's costs and bureaucratic impediments. The police often resolve disputes without recourse to the courts.

FREEDOM FROM CORRUPTION — 19

Corruption is perceived as pervasive. Guinea–Bissau ranks 158th out of 179 countries in Transparency International's Corruption Perceptions Index for 2008. The informal sector eclipses the formal economy. Trade in smuggled diamonds, food, and fishing products is significant. Corruption and lack of transparency pervade all levels of government. Customs officers frequently accept bribes.

LABOR FREEDOM — 52.5

Labor regulations are burdensome. The non-salary cost of employing a worker is high, and dismissing an employee is relatively costly. Restrictions on work hours are not flexible.

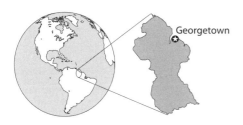
Georgetown

GUYANA

Economic Freedom Score

Least free 0

Most free 100

48.4

G uyana's economic freedom score is 48.4, making its economy the 153rd freest in the 2010 *Index*. Its overall score remains the same as last year because improvements in three of the 10 economic freedoms were offset by declines in investment freedom and property rights. Guyana is ranked 27th out of 29 countries in the South and Central America/Caribbean region, and its overall score is well below the world and regional averages.

Guyana does not perform well in any of the 10 economic freedoms and is slightly above the world average only in labor freedom and monetary freedom. Average economic growth over the past five years has been only about 3 percent, lagging behind other developing countries.

Long-standing constraints on overall economic freedom include property rights protected only erratically under the weak rule of law and widespread corruption in all areas of government. The biggest barrier to development is Guyana's oversized government, with expenditures that often exceed half of GDP. Significant restrictions on foreign investment, combined with an inefficient bureaucracy, substantially depress the entrepreneurial environment.

BACKGROUND: Guyana gained its independence in 1966. Support for the two major parties is ethnically and racially polarized, and attempts at reform have been made only under framework agreements with international organizations. In August 2006, President Bharrat Jagdeo of the People's Progressive Party–Civic was returned to office in the first nonviolent elections in more than 20 years. Although the main opposition parties accepted the election result and the risk of political violence is at its lowest since the early 1990s, relations between the PPP–Civic and the People's National Congress–Reform remain hostile. Guyana is one of the poorest countries in the Western Hemisphere, and its state-dominated economy, dependent mainly on agriculture and mining, has been stagnant for many years. Violent crime and drug trafficking are serious concerns.

Country's Score Over Time

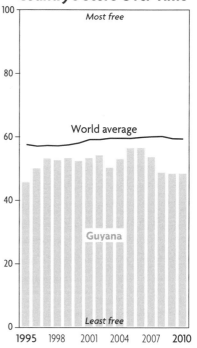

Quick Facts

Population: 0.8 million

GDP (PPP): $1.9 billion
3.0% growth in 2008
2.9% 5-year compound annual growth
$2,542 per capita

Unemployment: 11.0% (2007)

Inflation (CPI): 8.1%

FDI Inflow: $178 million

2008 data unless otherwise noted
Data compiled as of September 2009

How Do We Measure Economic Freedom?
See page 457 for an explanation of the methodology or visit the *Index* Web site at *heritage.org/index.*

GUYANA'S TEN ECONOMIC FREEDOMS

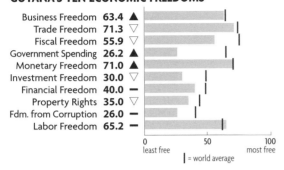

Business Freedom	63.4	▲
Trade Freedom	71.3	▽
Fiscal Freedom	55.9	▽
Government Spending	26.2	▲
Monetary Freedom	71.0	▲
Investment Freedom	30.0	▽
Financial Freedom	40.0	—
Property Rights	35.0	▽
Fdm. from Corruption	26.0	—
Labor Freedom	65.2	—

0   50   100
least free   most free
| = world average

BUSINESS FREEDOM — 63.4

Despite some progress, the overall freedom to conduct a business remains restricted by Guyana's regulatory environment. Starting a business takes about the world average of 35 days. Obtaining a business license requires less than the world average of 18 procedures, but closing a business can be costly.

TRADE FREEDOM — 71.3

Guyana's weighted average tariff rate was 6.9 percent in 2008. Import restrictions, import taxes, import-licensing requirements for a relatively large number of products, burdensome standards and regulations, inefficient customs administration, weak intellectual property rights enforcement, inadequate infrastructure, and corruption add to the cost of trade. Fifteen points were deducted from Guyana's trade freedom score to account for non-tariff barriers.

FISCAL FREEDOM — 55.9

Guyana has relatively high tax rates. The top income tax rate is 33.3 percent, and the top corporate tax rate is 45 percent. Other taxes include a property tax and a value-added tax (VAT). Excise taxes on fuel were temporarily suspended in 2008. In the most recent year, overall tax revenue as a percentage of GDP was 35.7 percent.

GOVERNMENT SPENDING — 26.2

Total government expenditures, including consumption and transfer payments, are high. Privatization of state-owned enterprises has achieved mixed results. Poor management of public expenditures has led to persistent fiscal deficits. In the most recent year, government spending equaled 49.6 percent of GDP.

MONETARY FREEDOM — 71

Inflation has been high, averaging 9.0 percent between 2006 and 2008, but has been falling steadily from a peak of nearly 12 percent in March 2008. It was 6.4 percent at the end of 2008 and is expected to continue to fall in 2009, barring a renewed shock to global energy prices. Guyana has made progress in removing price controls and privatizing the large public sector, but the government still influences prices through the regulation of state-owned utilities and enterprises. Ten points were deducted from Guyana's monetary freedom score to adjust for measures that distort domestic prices.

INVESTMENT FREEDOM — 30

Guyana has been moving toward a more welcoming environment for foreign investors, but major foreign investments receive intense political scrutiny in an economy still dominated by the state. The approval process for investments can be burdensome and non-transparent. While there is no mandatory screening of foreign investment, the government conducts a de facto screening of most investments to determine eligibility for special tax treatment, access to licenses, availability of land, and approval for investment incentives. Investment is hindered by crime, corruption, inefficient and burdensome government bureaucracy, non-transparent regulations, a weak and burdensome judiciary, and an inadequately educated workforce. Foreign exchange, credit, and capital transactions face some restrictions and controls. The constitution guarantees the right of foreigners to own property or land.

FINANCIAL FREEDOM — 40

Guyana's underdeveloped financial system remains plagued by inefficiency and a poor institutional framework. High credit costs and scarce access to financing remain barriers to more dynamic entrepreneurial activity. The percentage of loans that are considered non-performing is a relatively high 14 percent. Six commercial banks operate in Guyana, and the two largest are foreign-owned. There are restrictions on financial transactions with non-residents. Guyana has six insurance companies and a small stock exchange, which lists 15 companies.

PROPERTY RIGHTS — 35

Guyana's judicial system is often slow and inefficient. It is also subject to corruption. Law enforcement officials and prominent lawyers question the independence of the judiciary and accuse the government of intervening in some cases. A shortage of trained court personnel and magistrates, poor resources, and persistent bribery prolong the resolution of court cases unreasonably. There is no enforcement mechanism to protect intellectual property rights. Guyana is ranked 109th out of 115 countries in the 2009 International Property Rights Index.

FREEDOM FROM CORRUPTION — 26

Corruption is perceived as widespread. Guyana ranks 126th out of 179 countries in Transparency International's Corruption Perceptions Index for 2008. There is extensive corruption at every level of law enforcement and government. Public officials are required to disclose their assets to an Integrity Commission before assuming office, but the commission had not been constituted as of mid-2009. Widespread corruption undermines poverty-reduction efforts by international aid donors and discourages foreign investors.

LABOR FREEDOM — 65.2

Labor regulations are relatively flexible. The non-salary cost of employing a worker is low, but dismissing an employee is fairly costly.

Port-au-Prince

HAITI

Economic Freedom Score

25   50   75

Least free 0   100 Most free

50.8

Haiti's economic freedom score is 50.8, making its economy the 141st freest in the 2010 *Index*. With improvements in fiscal and labor freedoms, its overall score is 0.3 point higher than last year. Haiti is ranked 24th out of 29 countries in the South and Central America/Caribbean region, and its overall score is lower than the world and regional averages.

Haiti's overall economic freedom remains curtailed by a number of institutional factors, and the progress in the country's reform efforts has been marginal. Government spending has been largely directed toward mitigating the effects of several natural disasters, but the effectiveness of public finance is severely undermined by political volatility and corruption that exacerbate the weak rule of law.

Low tariff barriers give Haiti a relatively good score in trade freedom, and overall government expenditures are low, but economic freedom in other areas is weak. Reforms to improve the business and investment climates have had little effect. Rampant corruption and an inefficient judicial system are serious obstacles to entrepreneurial activity.

BACKGROUND: Haiti, the Western Hemisphere's poorest country and one of the world's least-developed nations, is plagued by corruption, gang violence, drug trafficking, and organized crime. The justice system is non-functional. A democratic constitution was adopted in 1986, but the 1990 election of President Jean-Bertrand Aristide began 13 years of intense polarization that culminated in his second exile in February 2004. Rene Préval, who won a U.N.-supervised election in 2006, maintains close ties to Cuba and Venezuela. Despite the U.N. Stability Mission and a better trained and equipped national police force, disorder is easily sparked by paid gangs. Haiti is 95 percent deforested, and its infrastructure is decimated. Unemployment is very high, most economic activity is informal, and emigrants' remittances have declined to about 17 percent of GDP. Secondary education is available to few children.

Country's Score Over Time

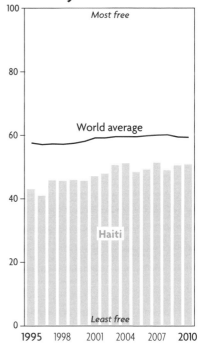

Quick Facts

Population: 9.8 million

GDP (PPP): $11.5 billion
1.3% growth in 2008
2.2% 5-year compound annual growth
$1,177 per capita

Unemployment: n/a

Inflation (CPI): 14.4%

FDI Inflow: $30.0 million

2008 data unless otherwise noted
Data compiled as of September 2009

How Do We Measure Economic Freedom?
See page 457 for an explanation of the methodology or visit the *Index* Web site at *heritage.org/index.*

HAITI'S TEN ECONOMIC FREEDOMS

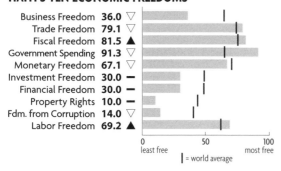

Business Freedom	36.0 ▽	
Trade Freedom	79.1 ▽	
Fiscal Freedom	81.5 ▲	
Government Spending	91.3 ▽	
Monetary Freedom	67.1 ▽	
Investment Freedom	30.0 —	
Financial Freedom	30.0 —	
Property Rights	10.0 —	
Fdm. from Corruption	14.0 ▽	
Labor Freedom	69.2 ▲	

0 least free — 50 — 100 most free
| = world average

BUSINESS FREEDOM — 36

The overall freedom to conduct a business is severely impeded by Haiti's burdensome regulatory environment. Starting a business takes an average of 195 days, compared to the world average of 35 days. Obtaining a business license takes about five times longer than the world average of 218 days.

TRADE FREEDOM — 79.1

Haiti's weighted average tariff rate was 3 percent in 2008. Import controls, import quotas on some food products, import licensing requirements, inadequate trade capacity and infrastructure, inefficient port administration, and customs corruption add to the cost of trade. Fifteen points were deducted from Haiti's trade freedom score to account for non-tariff barriers.

FISCAL FREEDOM — 81.5

Haiti has moderate tax rates. The top income and corporate tax rates are 30 percent. Other taxes include a value-added tax (VAT) and a capital gains tax. In the most recent year, overall tax revenue as a percentage of GDP was 6.9 percent.

GOVERNMENT SPENDING — 91.3

Total government expenditures, including consumption and transfer payments, are low. In the most recent year, government spending equaled 17.0 percent of GDP. Political instability has made government economic and financial management weak and inconsistent.

MONETARY FREEDOM — 67.1

Inflation has been high, averaging 13.1 percent between 2006 and 2008. Annual inflation increased rapidly in most of 2008, owing to sharp rises in international fuel and food prices, but declined to around zero by June 2009. Prices are generally determined by the market, but the government restricts markups of some products (retailers, for example, may not mark up pharmaceutical products by more than 40 percent) and strictly controls the prices of petroleum products. Ten points were deducted from Haiti's monetary freedom score to adjust for measures that distort domestic prices.

INVESTMENT FREEDOM — 30

Foreign investors are granted national treatment, but investment in sensitive sectors such as public health, agri-culture, electricity, water, and telecommunications requires special authorization. In general, natural resources are considered to be the property of the state, and mining activities require concessions and permits. Laws are transparent but not consistently enforced. Bureaucracy and red tape are burdensome. Privatization advances slowly, and inadequate institutional capacity, corruption, and political instability deter investment. Residents may hold foreign exchange accounts for specified purposes; non-residents may hold them without restriction. There are no restrictions on payments, transfers, or capital transactions. Foreign ownership of land is restricted.

FINANCIAL FREEDOM — 30

Haiti's small financial sector remains underdeveloped and fragile. Many economic transactions are conducted outside the formal banking sector, and scarce access to financing severely hinders entrepreneurial activity. Supervision and regulation of the financial system are poor and not consistent with international norms. The legal and institutional framework is not conducive to deepening financial intermediation. The banking sector is highly concentrated, with around 80 percent of assets held by the three largest banks. The two state-owned banks, privatization of which has been delayed repeatedly by political and economic crises, account for slightly less than 10 percent of assets. Capital markets are poorly developed.

PROPERTY RIGHTS — 10

Protection of investors and property is severely compromised by weak enforcement, a paucity of updated laws to handle modern commercial practices, and a dysfunctional and resource-poor legal system. Most commercial disputes are settled out of court if at all. Widespread corruption allows disputing parties to purchase favorable outcomes. Real property interests are handicapped by the absence of a comprehensive civil registry. Bona fide property titles, when they exist, often conflict with other titles for the same property. Despite statutes protecting intellectual property, the weak judiciary and a lack of political will hinder enforcement.

FREEDOM FROM CORRUPTION — 14

Corruption is perceived as rampant. Haiti ranks 177th out of 179 countries in Transparency International's Corruption Perceptions Index for 2008. Customs officers often demand bribes to clear shipments. Smuggling is a major problem, and contraband accounts for a large percentage of the manufactured consumables market. International donors have pushed the government to take a few steps to enforce public accountability and transparency, but substantive institutional reforms are still needed.

LABOR FREEDOM — 69.2

Labor regulations are relatively flexible, but the formal labor market is not fully developed. The non-salary cost of employing a worker is moderate, but dismissing an employee is relatively costly. Restrictions on work hours are not flexible.

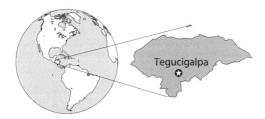

Tegucigalpa

HONDURAS

Economic Freedom Score

25　　50　　75

Least free　0　　　　　100　Most free

58.3

Honduras's economic freedom score is 58.3, making its economy the 99th freest in the 2010 *Index*. Its overall score is 0.4 point lower than last year, partially reflecting lower scores in labor freedom and government spending. Honduras is ranked 20th out of 29 countries in the South and Central America/Caribbean region, and its overall score is lower than the world and regional averages.

Honduras's overall economic freedom suffers greatly from pervasive corruption and the lack of institutional capacity to protect property rights. Coupled with ongoing political instability, corruption and the inefficiency of the judicial system have had far-reaching effects on the overall entre-preneurial environment.

Honduras receives relatively high scores for trade freedom and fiscal freedom. It has benefited from freer trade, especially following the implementation of the Central America–Dominican Republic–United States Free Trade Agreement (CAFTA) and other free trade agreements that have resulted in overall tariff reductions. These agreements have also helped to enhance the investment environment. Fiscal freedom is facilitated by moderate personal and corporate income tax rates and a moderate overall tax burden.

BACKGROUND: President Jose Manuel Zelaya Rosales, who supports closer ties with Venezuela and Cuba, was removed from office in 2009 following a constitutional dispute related to lifting the prohibition on presidential re-election. Honduras is one of Central America's poorest countries; two-thirds of its people live below the poverty line, and unemployment is about 28 percent. Ongoing concerns include political instability, drug trafficking, violent crime, and youth gangs. The economy has diversified beyond traditional exports of coffee and bananas to include shrimp, melons, tourism, and textiles, but more than one-third of the labor force works in agriculture. The government has met targeted macroeconomic objectives, is shedding debt under World Bank and International Monetary Fund initiatives, and hopes that CAFTA will expand trade and investment.

Country's Score Over Time

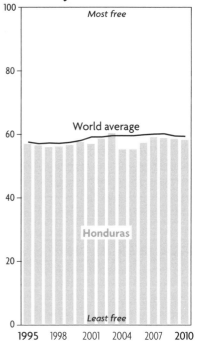

Quick Facts

Population: 7.2 million

GDP (PPP): $28.7 billion
4.2% growth in 2008
5.8% 5-year compound
annual growth
$3,965 per capita

Unemployment: 3.5%
A substantial level of
underemployment exists

Inflation (CPI): 11.4%

FDI Inflow: $877.0 million

2008 data unless otherwise noted
Data compiled as of September 2009

How Do We Measure Economic Freedom?
See page 457 for an explanation of the methodology or visit the *Index* Web site at *heritage.org/index.*

HONDURAS'S TEN ECONOMIC FREEDOMS

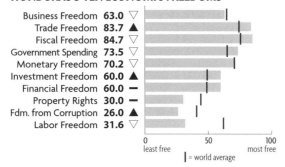

Business Freedom	63.0	▽
Trade Freedom	83.7	▲
Fiscal Freedom	84.7	▽
Government Spending	73.5	▽
Monetary Freedom	70.2	▽
Investment Freedom	60.0	▲
Financial Freedom	60.0	▬
Property Rights	30.0	▬
Fdm. from Corruption	26.0	▲
Labor Freedom	31.6	▽

0 least free   50   100 most free

| = world average

BUSINESS FREEDOM — 63

The overall freedom to conduct a business remains limited by Honduras's regulatory environment. Starting a business takes slightly more than half the world average of 35 days. The entry cost of launching a business is high, and closing a business is relatively costly.

TRADE FREEDOM — 83.7

Honduras's weighted average tariff rate was 3.2 percent in 2008. Some import taxes, price bands for products, import restrictions, limitations on market access in the services sector, non-transparent government procurement, restrictive sanitary and phytosanitary regulations, weak enforcement of intellectual property rights, and subsidies add to the cost of trade. Ten points were deducted from Honduras's trade freedom score to account for non-tariff barriers.

FISCAL FREEDOM — 84.7

Honduras has moderate tax rates. The top income and corporate tax rates are 25 percent. Other taxes include a 5 percent social contribution tax, a capital gains tax, and a general sales tax (not applicable to food staples). In the most recent year, overall tax revenue as a percentage of GDP was 16.7 percent.

GOVERNMENT SPENDING — 73.5

Total government expenditures, including consumption and transfer payments, are moderate. In the most recent year, government spending equaled 29.7 percent of GDP. Privatization of state-owned enterprises has been stagnant since 2000. The government holds monopolies in many sectors including electricity, railways, and telecommunications.

MONETARY FREEDOM — 70.2

Inflation has been high, averaging 9.8 percent between 2006 and 2008. The government regulates the prices of petroleum products, steel, pharmaceuticals, and services from state-owned utilities and can impose price controls on other goods and services as desired. Ten points were deducted from Honduras's monetary freedom score to adjust for measures that distort domestic prices.

INVESTMENT FREEDOM — 60

Foreign investment is generally accorded the same rights as domestic investment. Government authorization must be obtained to invest in basic health services, telecommunications, electricity, air transport, fishing, hunting and aquaculture, forestry, mining, large-scale agricultural, insurance and financial services, and private education services. For all investments, at least 90 percent of a company's labor force must be Honduran, and at least 85 percent of the payroll must be paid to Hondurans. Corruption, crime, red tape, inadequate infrastructure, and the lack of judicial security are deterrents to investment. Residents and non-residents may hold foreign exchange accounts. Payments and transfers are not restricted, and few capital transactions require approval. There is no foreign ownership of land within 40 kilometers of international borders and shorelines, although Honduran law now permits foreign individuals to purchase properties in designated "tourism zones."

FINANCIAL FREEDOM — 60

Honduras's financial system has undergone consolidation through mergers and closures. The banking sector has two state-owned banks and 17 commercial banks, 10 of which are majority foreign-owned. Honduras has few legal and regulatory barriers to entry in the banking sector, but most foreign banks' participation has been at a regional level rather than at a national level. Three foreign-bank representative offices operate in Honduras, and they have a small client base. In recent years, the government has passed five banking reform laws aimed at strengthening the nation's financial system. Capital markets are not fully developed, and the stock exchange (the Central American Stock Exchange) remains small.

PROPERTY RIGHTS — 30

Protection of property is weak. The lack of judicial security, a deteriorating security environment, and endemic corruption make it difficult to resolve business disputes. Expropriation of property is possible, and compensation, when awarded, is in 20-year government bonds. Honduran laws and practices regarding real estate differ substantially from those in more developed countries, and fraudulent deeds and titles are common. There is no title insurance in Honduras. In addition, the judicial system is weak and inefficient, often prolonging disputed cases for many years before resolution. Approximately 80 percent of the privately held land in the country is untitled.

FREEDOM FROM CORRUPTION — 26

Corruption is perceived as pervasive. Honduras ranks 126th out of 179 countries in Transparency International's Corruption Perceptions Index for 2008. Corruption appears to be most pervasive in government procurement, government permits, and land titling. Decades of cronyism, nepotism, secrecy, and prevarication have removed the stigma that once attached to corruption.

LABOR FREEDOM — 31.6

Labor regulations are burdensome. The non-salary cost of employing a worker can be low, but dismissing an employee is costly. Regulations on work hours are not flexible.

HONG KONG

Economic Freedom Score

Least free 0 — 25 — 50 — 75 — 100 Most free

89.7

Hong Kong's economic freedom score is 89.7, making its economy the freest in the 2010 *Index*. Its score is 0.3 point lower than last year, reflecting increases in business and labor freedom that were offset by modest declines in several factors, particularly trade freedom, monetary freedom, and freedom from corruption. Hong Kong is ranked 1st out of 41 countries in the Asia–Pacific region.

Hong Kong's competitive tax regime, respect for property rights, and flexible labor market, coupled with an educated and highly motivated workforce, have stimulated an innovative, prosperous economy. Hong Kong is one of the world's leading financial and business centers, and its legal and regulatory framework for the financial sector is transparent and efficient. Business regulation is straightforward. Despite the global economic slowdown, Hong Kong has maintained its status as Asia's second-largest destination for foreign direct investment, attracting over $60 billion in 2008.

Even in an economy as free as Hong Kong's, threats to freedom can arise. Though the introduction of competition legislation was postponed in April 2009, a minimum wage bill was introduced in June, with implementation forecast for late 2010 or early 2011. The government has also set out strategies to promote development in six specific industrial and services sectors, a priority-setting exercise for which the free market would seem better suited.

BACKGROUND: The Special Administrative Region of Hong Kong is part of the People's Republic of China, but it governs its own affairs on a day-to-day basis and enjoys a wide range of freedoms under the territory's mini-constitution, the Basic Law. The government has promised to advance universal suffrage but so far has not delivered. Hong Kong boasts one of the world's most prosperous economies, thanks to small government, low taxes, and light regulation. Major industries include financial services and shipping, while manufacturing has migrated largely to the mainland. Ongoing concerns include cronyism in government policymaking and self-censorship in media and restrictions on the free flow of information.

Country's Score Over Time

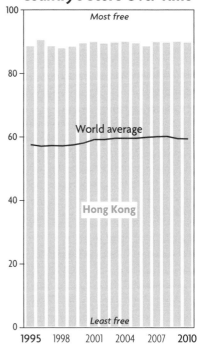

Quick Facts

Population: 7.0 million

GDP (PPP): $306.5 billion
2.4% growth in 2007
5.7% 5-year compound annual growth
$43,924 per capita

Unemployment: 3.5%

Inflation (CPI): 4.3%

FDI Inflow: $63 billion

2008 data unless otherwise noted
Data compiled as of September 2009

How Do We Measure Economic Freedom?
See page 457 for an explanation of the methodology or visit the *Index* Web site at *heritage.org/index.*

HONG KONG'S TEN ECONOMIC FREEDOMS

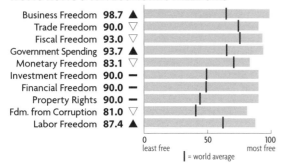

Business Freedom	98.7	▲
Trade Freedom	90.0	▽
Fiscal Freedom	93.0	▽
Government Spending	93.7	▲
Monetary Freedom	83.1	▽
Investment Freedom	90.0	—
Financial Freedom	90.0	—
Property Rights	90.0	—
Fdm. from Corruption	81.0	▽
Labor Freedom	87.4	▲

0 least free   50   100 most free

| = world average

BUSINESS FREEDOM — 98.7

The overall freedom to start, operate, and close a business is well protected under Hong Kong's regulatory environment. Starting a business takes six days, compared to the world average of 35 days, and obtaining necessary licenses takes less than the world average of 218 days.

TRADE FREEDOM — 90

Hong Kong's weighted average tariff rate was 0 percent in 2008. Some import taxes, restrictive pharmaceuticals regulation, market access restrictions for some services, food and energy labeling regulations, and issues involving the enforcement of intellectual property rights add to the cost of trade. Ten points were deducted from Hong Kong's trade freedom score to account for non-tariff barriers.

FISCAL FREEDOM — 93

Hong Kong's effective tax rates are among the lowest in the world. Individuals are taxed either progressively, between 2 percent and 17 percent on income adjusted for deductions and allowances, or at a flat 15 percent of gross income, depending on which liability is lower. The top corporate income tax rate is 16.5 percent. Excise duties on beer and wine were removed in 2008. In the most recent year, overall tax revenue as a percentage of GDP was 14.2 percent.

GOVERNMENT SPENDING— 93.7

Total government expenditures, including consumption and transfer payments, are low. In the most recent year, government spending equaled 14.5 percent of GDP. Disciplined fiscal management has helped Hong Kong to weather the global downturn. The government has made efforts to maintain a balanced budget. State ownership is mostly limited to transportation.

MONETARY FREEDOM — 83.1

Inflation has been relatively low, averaging 3.5 percent between 2006 and 2008. Since the Hong Kong dollar maintains a fixed exchange rate with the U.S. dollar, interest rates and currency movements follow trends in the United States. Hong Kong has efficient clearing and settlement systems. China's rapid food inflation in 2008 affected Hong Kong, as the mainland is the leading source of food imports. The rise in private rental prices is moderating

because of the weakening economy. The government regulates the prices of public transport and electricity and some residential rents. Five points were deducted from Hong Kong's monetary freedom score to adjust for measures that distort domestic prices.

INVESTMENT FREEDOM — 90

Foreign capital receives domestic treatment, and foreign investment is strongly encouraged. There are no limits on foreign ownership and no screening or special approval procedures to set up a foreign firm except in broadcasting, where foreign entities may own no more than 49 percent of the local stations, and certain legal services. There are no controls or requirements on current transfers, access to foreign exchange, or repatriation of profits. Bureaucracy is efficient and transparent.

FINANCIAL FREEDOM — 90

Hong Kong is a global financial center with a regulatory and legal environment focused on enforcing prudent minimum standards and transparency. At the end of 2008, there were 201 authorized banking institutions, including 122 incorporated outside of Hong Kong. Banks are overseen by the independent Hong Kong Monetary Authority. Credit is allocated on market terms. There are no restrictions on foreign banks, which are treated the same as domestic institutions. The Hong Kong Stock Exchange is one of the world's 10 most capitalized, but it felt the effects of the global financial crisis. The Hang Seng Index fell almost 50 percent in 2008, and the number of successful initial public offerings decreased significantly. Overall, however, the financial system has weathered the global financial turmoil relatively well, and banks remain well capitalized.

PROPERTY RIGHTS — 90

Contracts are strongly protected. Hong Kong's legal system is based on common law, and its constitution strongly supports private property and freedom of exchange. Despite government public awareness campaigns, pirated and counterfeit products such as CDs, DVDs, software, and designer apparel are sold openly. The government controls all land and, through public auctions, grants renewable leases that are valid up to 2047.

FREEDOM FROM CORRUPTION — 81

Corruption is perceived as minimal. Hong Kong ranks 12th out of 179 countries in Transparency International's Corruption Perceptions Index for 2008. Giving or accepting a bribe is a criminal act.

LABOR FREEDOM — 87.4

Labor regulations are flexible. The labor code is strictly enforced but not burdensome. The non-salary cost of employing a worker is low, but dismissing an employee can be relatively costly. Regulations on work hours are flexible.

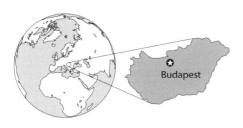

HUNGARY

Economic Freedom Score

Least free 0   25   50   75   100   Most free

66.1

Hungary's economic freedom score is 66.1, making its economy the 51st freest in the 2010 *Index*. Its score has decreased by 0.6 point, reflecting declines in six of the 10 economic freedoms that offset improvements in three others. Hungary is ranked 24th out of 43 countries in the Europe region, and its overall score is well above the world average.

Greater openness and flexibility have led to robust entrepreneurial activity and substantial inflows of foreign direct investment. The overall business environment is aided by strong trade freedom, business freedom, property rights, and investment freedom. Investing is easy, and foreign capital and domestic capital enjoy virtually the same protections. The rule of law is respected, and corruption is perceived as moderate.

Hungary needs fiscal consolidation and better management of public finance. The size of government is Hungary's biggest weakness, with its score far below the world average. The fiscal deficit is high, and economic competitiveness has declined somewhat with worsening economic fundamentals and a growing tax burden. The global financial turmoil led to immediate financing difficulties for the government, with its already high levels of official debt.

BACKGROUND: Hungary emerged from 40 years of Communist rule more politically and economically open than its formerly Communist neighbors. It rapidly transformed itself into a market economy and in 2004 joined the European Union. The ruling coalition of the Hungarian Socialist Party and the liberal Alliance of Free Democrats collapsed in April 2008, but the Socialists have continued in power as a minority government with slightly less than half of the seats in Parliament. With Hungary hit hard by the global financial crisis and the economy contracting, Socialist Prime Minister Ferenc Gyurcsany resigned in May 2009. Former economy minister Gordon Bajnai took over as prime minister and has enacted spending cuts and other reforms intended to enhance competitiveness.

Country's Score Over Time

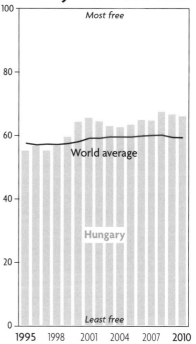

Quick Facts

Population: 10.0 million

GDP (PPP): $194.0 billion
0.6% growth in 2008
2.4% 5-year compound annual growth
$19,330 per capita

Unemployment: 7.8%

Inflation (CPI): 6.1%

FDI Inflow: $6.5 billion

2008 data unless otherwise noted
Data compiled as of September 2009

How Do We Measure Economic Freedom?
See page 457 for an explanation of the methodology or visit the *Index* Web site at *heritage.org/index.*

HUNGARY'S TEN ECONOMIC FREEDOMS

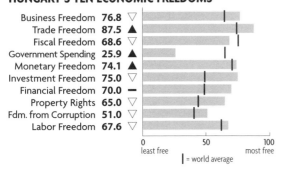

Business Freedom	76.8 ▽
Trade Freedom	87.5 ▲
Fiscal Freedom	68.6 ▽
Government Spending	25.9 ▲
Monetary Freedom	74.1 ▲
Investment Freedom	75.0 ▽
Financial Freedom	70.0 —
Property Rights	65.0 ▽
Fdm. from Corruption	51.0 ▽
Labor Freedom	67.6 ▽

0
least free

50

100
most free

I = world average

BUSINESS FREEDOM — 76.8

The overall freedom to start, operate, and close a business is relatively well protected under Hungary's regulatory environment. Starting a business takes four days, compared to the world average of 35 days, but obtaining a business license requires more than the world average of 18 procedures.

TRADE FREEDOM — 87.5

Hungary's trade policy is the same as that of other members of the European Union. The common EU weighted average tariff rate was 1.3 percent in 2008. However, the EU has high or escalating tariffs for agricultural and manufacturing products, and its MFN tariff code is complex. Non-tariff barriers reflected in EU and Hungarian policy include agricultural and manufacturing subsidies, quotas, import restrictions and bans for some goods and services, market access restrictions in some services sectors, non-transparent and restrictive regulations and standards, and inconsistent regulatory and customs administration among EU members. Restrictive biotechnology regulations, non-transparent government procurement, and weak enforcement of intellectual property rights add to the cost of trade. Ten points were deducted from Hungary's trade freedom score to account for non-tariff barriers.

FISCAL FREEDOM — 68.6

Hungary has a relatively high income tax rate but a relatively low corporate tax rate. The top income tax rate is 36 percent, and the top corporate tax rate is 16 percent. Other taxes include a value-added tax (VAT), a property tax, and a gift tax. In the most recent year, overall tax revenue as a percentage of GDP was 39.9 percent.

GOVERNMENT SPENDING — 25.9

Total government expenditures, including consumption and transfer payments, are high. In the most recent year, government spending equaled 49.7 percent of GDP. The government remains directly involved in agriculture, electric power, and railways.

MONETARY FREEDOM — 74.1

Inflation has been relatively high, averaging 6.3 percent between 2006 and 2008. As a participant in the EU's Common Agricultural Policy, the government subsidizes agricultural production, distorting the prices of agricultural products. It also regulates prices for energy, telecommunications services, and subsidized pharmaceutical products, among others. Ten points were deducted from Hungary's monetary freedom score to account for policies that distort domestic prices.

INVESTMENT FREEDOM — 75

Foreign capital receives domestic legal treatment, and foreign companies account for a large share of manufacturing, telecommunications, and energy. The government allows 100 percent foreign ownership with the exception of some defense-related industries. Deterrents include bureaucracy, inadequate judicial capacity, and a non-transparent investment code. Residents and non-residents may hold foreign exchange accounts. There are no restrictions or controls on current transfers or repatriation of profits and no restrictions on issues or sales of capital market instruments; there are some reporting requirements. Only private Hungarian citizens and EU citizens resident in Hungary and engaged in agricultural activity may purchase farmland; others may lease it.

FINANCIAL FREEDOM — 70

Hungary's financial sector is dominated by banking. There are 29 commercial banks and eight special credit institutions. The government has largely withdrawn from banking, and over two-thirds of the sector is foreign-owned. Capital markets are relatively developed, and foreign investors participate freely. The Budapest Stock Exchange has low volumes of trading and lists about 60 companies. After years of robust growth, banking expansion has slowed considerably, and profitability is down. With mutual funds heavily exposed to the real estate market, the financial sector has been severely strained by the global financial crisis.

PROPERTY RIGHTS — 65

Secured interests in property are recognized and enforced, but there is no title insurance. The judiciary is constitutionally independent, and this is respected in practice. The threat of expropriation is low. The courts are slow and severely overburdened, and a final ruling on a contract dispute can take more than a year. Protection of intellectual property rights has improved somewhat.

FREEDOM FROM CORRUPTION — 51

Corruption is perceived as present. Hungary ranks 47th out of 179 countries in Transparency International's Corruption Perceptions Index for 2008. There are persistent reports of corruption in government procurement. Hungary is a party to the OECD Anti-Bribery Convention and has incorporated its provisions into the penal code, as it has with subsequent OECD and EU requirements on the prevention of bribery.

LABOR FREEDOM — 67.6

Labor regulations are relatively inflexible. The non-salary cost of employing a worker is burdensome, and dismissing an employee is relatively costly. Regulations on work hours are not flexible.

ICELAND

Economic Freedom Score

Least free 0   100 Most free

73.7

Iceland's economic freedom score is 73.7, making its economy the 18th freest in the 2010 *Index*. Its overall score has declined by 2.2 points from last year, reflecting drops in seven of the 10 economic freedoms. Iceland is ranked 9th out of 43 countries in the Europe region, and its overall score is higher than the world and regional averages.

Iceland's economy has contracted significantly, with its financial sector severely affected by the global financial turmoil. Aggressive overseas expansion of bank lending, unchecked by the domestic regulatory environment, caused the buildup of considerable systemic risk for such a small economy. The resulting collapse of the banking sector has increased government debt, triggering a sharp surge in the fiscal deficit.

Nevertheless, Iceland's overall levels of economic freedom are still relatively high. Such institutional strengths as the strong rule of law, low levels of corruption, efficient business regulations, and competitive tax rates are good foundations on which to build recovery, curb long-term high unemployment, and restore economic stability, but they need to be supported by further reforms in financial management and the labor market.

BACKGROUND: Iceland is a centuries-old democracy that traditionally has enjoyed low unemployment and a growing economy. However, in October 2008, the banking sector collapsed, sparking a currency crisis. Prime Minister Geir Haarde of the Independence Party and his cabinet were forced to resign, and the Social Democrats took over on February 2, 2009, with Johanna Sigurðardóttir as prime minister. A deep recession has taken hold, and unemployment is high. Reversing its long-held opposition to joining the European Union, Iceland's parliament voted in July 2009 to apply for EU membership. Iceland is already a member of the European Free Trade Association and the European Economic Area, which allows for free cross-border movement of capital, labor, goods, and services with the EU.

Country's Score Over Time

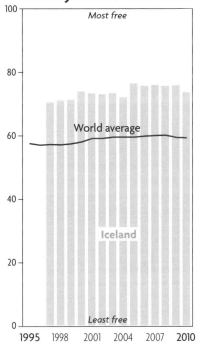

Quick Facts

Population: 0.3 million

GDP (PPP): $11.7 billion
0.3% growth in 2007
4.4% 5-year compound annual growth
$36,775 per capita

Unemployment: 7.1% (1st quarter of 2009)

Inflation (CPI): 12.4%

FDI Inflow: –$2.6 billion

2008 data unless otherwise noted
Data compiled as of September 2009

How Do We Measure Economic Freedom?
See page 457 for an explanation of the methodology or visit the *Index* Web site at *heritage.org/index.*

ICELAND'S TEN ECONOMIC FREEDOMS

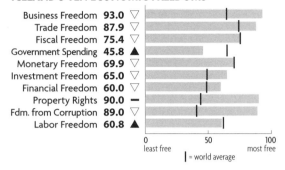

Business Freedom	93.0	▽
Trade Freedom	87.9	▽
Fiscal Freedom	75.4	▽
Government Spending	45.8	▲
Monetary Freedom	69.9	▽
Investment Freedom	65.0	▽
Financial Freedom	60.0	▽
Property Rights	90.0	—
Fdm. from Corruption	89.0	▽
Labor Freedom	60.8	▲

0 least free   50   100 most free

| = world average

BUSINESS FREEDOM — 93

The overall freedom to start, operate, and close a business is strongly protected under Iceland's regulatory environment. Starting a business takes an average of five days, compared to the world average of 35 days. Obtaining a business license requires much less than the world average of 18 procedures and 218 days. Bankruptcy proceedings are straightforward.

TRADE FREEDOM — 87.9

Iceland's weighted average tariff rate was 1.1 percent in 2008. High agriculture tariffs, import bans and restrictions, import taxes, strict sanitary and phytosanitary regulations, and government support programs for the agricultural sector add to the cost of trade. Ten points were deducted from Iceland's trade freedom score to account for non-tariff barriers.

FISCAL FREEDOM — 75.4

Iceland has a competitive flat-tax system. The main income tax rate is 22.75 percent (which, combined with the local government rate, can rise to 35.72 percent). Investment income is subject to a flat 10 percent rate. The corporate tax rate is a flat 15 percent. Other taxes include a value-added tax (VAT) and an estate tax. Excise taxes on tobacco, alcohol and fuel were raised in 2009. In the most recent year, overall tax revenue as a percentage of GDP was 41.4 percent.

GOVERNMENT SPENDING — 45.8

Total government expenditures, including consumption and transfer payments, are high. In the most recent year, government spending equaled 42.5 percent of GDP. Privatization of state-owned enterprises has progressed over the past 10 years. A mounting fiscal deficit was projected to reach 13 percent of GDP in 2009.

MONETARY FREEDOM — 69.9

Inflation has been high, averaging 10.1 percent between 2006 and 2008. Inflation fell from nearly 19 percent in January 2009 to 11.3 percent in July and would have fallen further were it not for the depreciation of the krona since March, which has boosted import prices. The government subsidizes agricultural production; milk is subject to production-linked direct payments, production quotas, and administered prices; and sheep farmers receive direct payments based on support targets and quality-dependent payments. Ten points were deducted from Iceland's monetary freedom score to account for policies that distort domestic prices.

INVESTMENT FREEDOM — 65

The 1996 Act on Investment by Non-Residents in Business Enterprises grants national treatment to non-residents of the European Economic Area (EEA). Under the law, foreign ownership of businesses is generally unrestricted, but there are limitations in fishing, energy, and aviation. Investment regulations are transparent, although bureaucratic delays can occur. Until recently, Icelandic law provided for full convertibility and transferability of dividends, profits, interest on loans, debentures, mortgages, lease payments, and invested capital. However, following the financial turmoil in 2008, movements of capital to and from Iceland have faced new restrictions. Foreign investors from outside the EEA may purchase land or real estate in Iceland upon government approval.

FINANCIAL FREEDOM — 60

Iceland's financial sector, which remains dominated by banking, has been under considerable strain. While undergoing rapid transformation and restructuring over the past decade, the banking sector grew to about eight times GDP by 2007, mostly through aggressive expansion of overseas lending. Regulatory oversight proved insufficient to deal with such an anomalous situation. Macroeconomic imbalances and private-sector borrowers' high indebtedness added to the instability, rendering banks highly vulnerable to any external shock. The three main banks, which accounted for over 80 percent of the banking system, collapsed in late 2008 and have been brought under the government's control since then. Efforts to shore up stability and confidence have been made, but vulnerabilities linger.

PROPERTY RIGHTS — 90

Private property is well protected. The constitution provides for an independent judiciary, and the government respects this in practice. Trials are generally public and conducted fairly. Iceland is one of the few countries with efficient, property rights–based fisheries management.

FREEDOM FROM CORRUPTION — 89

Corruption is perceived as minimal. Iceland ranks 7th out of 179 countries in Transparency International's Corruption Perceptions Index for 2008. Isolated cases of corruption are not an obstacle to foreign investment. Iceland's 1,000-year history of parliamentary government has encouraged the institutionalization of accountability and transparency.

LABOR FREEDOM — 60.8

Labor regulations are relatively rigid. The non-salary cost of employing a worker is moderate, but dismissing an employee can be costly. The labor market remains highly centralized, with broad wage settlements and over 80 percent unionization.

INDIA

Economic Freedom Score

Least free 0
25
50
75
100 Most free

53.8

| World Rank: **124** | Regional Rank: **24** |

India's economic freedom score is 53.8, making its economy the 124th freest in the 2010 *Index*. Its score is 0.6 point lower than last year as a result of declines in freedom from corruption, business freedom, and monetary freedom. India is ranked 24th out of 41 countries in the Asia–Pacific region, and its overall score is below the world average.

India continues to move forward with market-oriented economic reforms and has achieved average growth of about 9 percent over the past five years. The economy has been driven by information technology and other business process sectors. Despite sluggish progress in reducing onerous non-tariff barriers, the trade regime has gradually become more open, with its average tariff rate decreasing.

The state still plays a major role in over 200 public-sector enterprises. Public debt is 80 percent of GDP, leaving little fiscal room to react to the global downturn. India's overly restrictive regulatory environment does not facilitate entrepreneurship or realization of the economy's full potential. Corruption is pervasive, and the judicial system remains inefficient and clogged by a large backlog of cases. Labor freedom is especially weak, with rigid regulations a costly impediment to further economic growth and job creation.

BACKGROUND: India is the world's most populous democracy and one of Asia's fastest-growing economies. Its 1991 "big bang" liberalization ended decades of cumbersome regulations and protectionism, and the economy has since grown rapidly, first in services and more recently in manufacturing. The Congress Party government was re-elected to another five-year term in May 2009 on a populist platform that included a social welfare scheme that guarantees employment for rural households. Though over 80 percent of the population is Hindu, the country has one of the world's largest Muslim populations. Conflict with Pakistan over Kashmir, which has simmered since independence and twice boiled over into war, continues unresolved.

Country's Score Over Time

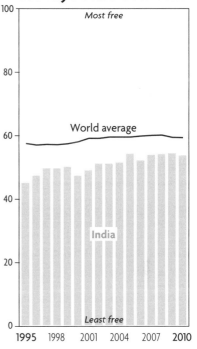

Quick Facts

Population: 1.1 billion

GDP (PPP): $3.4 trillion
7.1% growth in 2008
8.9% 5-year compound annual growth
$2,972 per capita

Unemployment: 6.8%

Inflation (CPI): 8.3%

FDI Inflow: $41.6 billion

2008 data unless otherwise noted
Data compiled as of September 2009

How Do We Measure Economic Freedom?
See page 457 for an explanation of the methodology or visit the *Index* Web site at *heritage.org/index.*

INDIA'S TEN ECONOMIC FREEDOMS

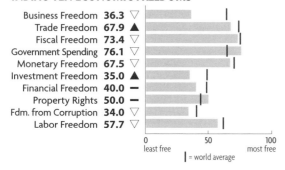

Business Freedom	36.3	▽
Trade Freedom	67.9	▲
Fiscal Freedom	73.4	▽
Government Spending	76.1	▽
Monetary Freedom	67.5	▽
Investment Freedom	35.0	▲
Financial Freedom	40.0	—
Property Rights	50.0	—
Fdm. from Corruption	34.0	▽
Labor Freedom	57.7	▽

0 least free   50   100 most free
| = world average

BUSINESS FREEDOM — 36.3

The overall freedom to start, operate, and close a business remains restricted by India's regulatory environment. Starting a business takes an average of 30 days, compared to the world average of 35 days. Obtaining a business license requires more than the world average of 18 procedures and 218 days.

TRADE FREEDOM — 67.9

India's weighted average tariff rate was 6 percent in 2008. Large differences between bound and applied tariff rates, import and export restrictions, services market access restrictions, import taxes and fees, complex and non-transparent regulation, onerous standards and certifications, discriminatory sanitary and phytosanitary measures, restrictive import licensing, domestic bias in government procurement, problematic enforcement of intellectual property rights, export subsidies, inadequate infrastructure, and complex and non-transparent customs add to the cost of trade. Twenty points were deducted from India's trade freedom score to account for non-tariff barriers.

FISCAL FREEDOM — 73.4

India's tax rates are relatively high. The top income and corporate tax rates are 33.99 percent (30 percent plus a 10 percent surcharge and a 3 percent education tax on that total). Other taxes include a dividend distribution tax, a tax on interest, and a value-added tax (VAT). In the most recent year, overall tax revenue as a percentage of GDP was 18.8 percent.

GOVERNMENT SPENDING — 76.1

Total government expenditures, including consumption and transfer payments, are relatively low. In the most recent year, government spending equaled 28.2 percent of GDP.

MONETARY FREEDOM — 67.5

Inflation has been relatively high, averaging 7.7 percent between 2006 and 2008. The government subsidizes agricultural, gas, and kerosene production; applies factory, wholesale, and retail price controls on "essential" commodities, 25 crops, services, electricity, water, some petroleum products, and certain types of coal; and controls the prices of 74 bulk drugs that cover 40 percent of the market. Another 354 drugs are to be brought under controls by a new pharmaceutical policy. Domestic price and marketing arrangements

apply to commodities like sugar and certain cereals. Fifteen points were deducted from India's monetary freedom score to account for policies that distort domestic prices.

INVESTMENT FREEDOM — 35

Foreign investors generally receive national treatment. If licensing is required, procedures do not discriminate against foreign companies; however, in certain consumer-goods industries, export obligations and local content requirements are imposed. Foreign investment is prohibited in multi-brand retailing, legal services, security services, nuclear energy, and railways. Foreign investment in real estate is limited to company property used to do business and the development of some types of new commercial and residential properties. Bureaucracy is non-transparent and burdensome, and contract enforcement can be difficult. Foreign exchange, capital transactions, and some credit operations are subject to approvals, restrictions, and additional requirements.

FINANCIAL FREEDOM — 40

Liberalization and modernization have allowed more private banks to compete, but state-owned institutions continue to dominate the banking sector and capital markets. Currently, 28 state-owned banks control about 70 percent of commercial banking assets. Access to financial services varies sharply around the country. High credit costs and scarce access to financing still impede private-sector development. Foreign banks account for less than 10 percent of total assets. Foreign banks operating in India may not directly or indirectly retain more than a 5 percent equity stake in a domestic private bank. Insurance is partially liberalized. Capital markets have been developing but remain illiquid, with foreign participation limited.

PROPERTY RIGHTS — 50

The legal system imposes a number of restrictions on the transfer of land, and titling problems can make buying and selling difficult. There is no reliable system for recording secured interests in property. Because of large backlogs, courts take years to reach decisions, and foreign corporations often resort to international arbitration. Protection of intellectual property rights is problematic. Proprietary test results and other data about patented products submitted to the government by foreign pharmaceutical companies have been used by domestic companies without any legal penalties.

FREEDOM FROM CORRUPTION — 34

Corruption is perceived as significant. India ranks 85th out of 179 countries in Transparency International's Corruption Perceptions Index for 2008. Corruption remains a major concern, especially in government procurement of telecommunications, power, and defense contracts.

LABOR FREEDOM — 57.7

India's informal economy remains an important source of employment. The non-salary cost of employing a worker is moderate, but dismissing an employee is costly.

INDONESIA

Economic Freedom Score

25   50   75

Least free   0   100   Most free

55.5

Indonesia's economic freedom score is 55.5, making its economy the 114th freest in the 2010 *Index*. Its score has improved by 2.1 points since last year, reflecting improvements in business freedom, fiscal freedom, and freedom from corruption. Indonesia is ranked 21st out of 41 countries in the Asia–Pacific region, and its overall score is below the world average.

The Indonesian economy has demonstrated a moderate degree of resilience in recent years, weathering the global financial turmoil relatively well. Recent reform measures have put greater emphasis on improving the entrepreneurial environment, enhancing regional competitiveness, and creating a more vibrant private sector through decentralization. Management of public finance has improved, and tariff barriers have been lowered.

Lingering institutional impediments to greater economic freedom, however, continue to undermine Indonesia's growth potential. Starting a business takes more than twice as long as the world average, and regulations are onerous. Despite some progress, investment freedom remains curtailed by government interference that discourages domestic as well as foreign investment. Because of pervasive corruption, impartial adjudication of cases is not guaranteed, and judicial enforcement is both erratic and non-transparent.

BACKGROUND: Indonesia is the world's most populous Muslim-majority democracy. In the years since 1998, when long-standing authoritarian ruler General Suharto stepped down, Indonesia's nearly 250 million people have enjoyed the blossoming of a wide range of political freedoms, and political participation is high. President Susilo Bambang Yudhoyono has cracked down on corruption and tried to draw in much-needed foreign investment, but the weak rule of law remains a major impediment to attracting capital. As a member of the G-20, Indonesia is playing an increasingly important role in international economic policy discussions.

Country's Score Over Time

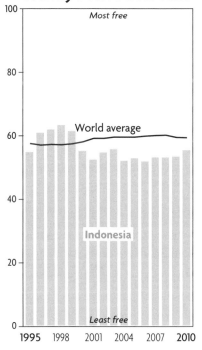

Quick Facts

Population: 228.2 million

GDP (PPP): $907.3 billion
6.1% growth in 2008
5.9% 5-year compound annual growth
$3,975 per capita

Unemployment: 8.4%

Inflation (CPI): 9.8%

FDI Inflow: $7.9 billion

2008 data unless otherwise noted
Data compiled as of September 2009

How Do We Measure Economic Freedom?
See page 457 for an explanation of the methodology or visit the *Index* Web site at *heritage.org/index.*

INDONESIA'S TEN ECONOMIC FREEDOMS

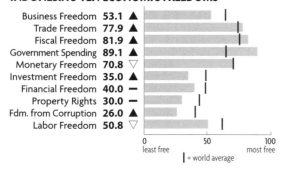

Business Freedom	53.1 ▲	
Trade Freedom	77.9 ▲	
Fiscal Freedom	81.9 ▲	
Government Spending	89.1 ▲	
Monetary Freedom	70.8 ▽	
Investment Freedom	35.0 ▲	
Financial Freedom	40.0 —	
Property Rights	30.0 —	
Fdm. from Corruption	26.0 ▲	
Labor Freedom	50.8 ▽	

0 least free   50   100 most free

| = world average

BUSINESS FREEDOM — 53.1

Despite some progress, the overall freedom to start, operate, and close a business remains hampered by Indonesia's regulatory environment. Starting a business takes more than the world average of 35 days. Obtaining a business license requires about the world average of 18 procedures. Closing a business is difficult and costly.

TRADE FREEDOM — 77.9

Indonesia's weighted average tariff rate was 3.6 percent in 2007. Import and export bans and restrictions, services market access barriers, non-transparent and arbitrary regulations, import and export licensing requirements, restrictive sanitary and phytosanitary regulations, state trading, weak enforcement of intellectual property rights, and inconsistent and corruption-prone customs valuation add to the cost of trade. Fifteen points were deducted from Indonesia's trade freedom score to account for non-tariff barriers.

FISCAL FREEDOM — 81.9

Indonesia has reduced taxes to moderate levels as part of broader fiscal reform. The top individual income tax rate is 30 percent, down from 35 percent. The top corporate tax rate is 28 percent, down from 30 percent. Other taxes include a value-added tax (VAT) and a property tax. In the most recent year, overall tax revenue as a percentage of GDP was 11.3 percent.

GOVERNMENT SPENDING — 89.1

Total government expenditures, including consumption and transfer payments, are low. In the most recent year, government spending equaled 19.1 percent of GDP. State control of the economy is widespread, but relative stability in fiscal management has enabled Indonesia to weather the economic downturn.

MONETARY FREEDOM — 70.8

Inflation has been high, averaging 9.2 percent between 2006 and 2008. Fuel, housing, and health care are subsidized, and prices of gasoline, electricity, liquefied petroleum gas, rice, cigarettes, cement, hospital services, potable/piped water, city transport, air transport, telephone charges, trains, salt, toll-road tariffs, and postage are set by the government. Ten points were deducted from Indonesia's monetary freedom score to account for policies that distort domestic prices.

INVESTMENT FREEDOM — 35

Foreign investors face significant restrictions. After approval of an Investment Law in March 2007, the government issued a revised "Investment Negative List" that identified sectors closed to foreign investment or subject to conditions. Corruption; unpredictable, inconsistent, and non-transparent regulations; weak contract enforcement; labor market rigidities; and inadequate infrastructure add to the cost of investment. Subject to approvals and restrictions, residents and non-residents may engage in foreign exchange and capital transactions. Non-residents may not purchase real estate.

FINANCIAL FREEDOM — 40

Indonesia's financial system has undergone restructuring and consolidation since the late 1990s, and the number of banks has been reduced to less than 130. Overall, banking supervision has been strengthened, and the efficiency of the banking system has increased. The state still owns five banks, three of which are among the largest in terms of assets. Non-performing loans in the banking sector have declined and account for less than 5 percent of total loans. The government has taken steps to establish a new Financial Services Authority, which should become operational by late 2010, to monitor and regulate the financial system. Capital markets are developing, and the previous two stock exchanges were merged into the Indonesia Stock Exchange in 2007. The impact of the global financial turmoil on the banking sector has been relatively minor, but due to a considerable degree of market segmentation, smaller banks have been more adversely affected.

PROPERTY RIGHTS — 30

Court rulings can be arbitrary and inconsistent, and corruption is substantial. Judges have been known to rule against foreigners in commercial disputes, ignoring contracts between the parties. It is difficult to get the courts to enforce international arbitration awards. Lack of clear land titles and the inability to own land in "fee simple" are also problems. Enforcement of intellectual property rights is weak.

FREEDOM FROM CORRUPTION — 26

Corruption is perceived as pervasive. Indonesia ranks 126th out of 179 countries in Transparency International's Corruption Perceptions Index for 2008, an improvement over 2007. There remains, however, a widespread domestic and international perception that corruption is a necessary part of daily life. Companies cite demands for irregular fees to obtain required permits or licenses, as well as the awarding of government contracts and concessions based on personal relationships.

LABOR FREEDOM — 50.8

Labor regulations are restrictive. The non-salary cost of employing a worker is moderate, but dismissing an employee can be costly.

IRAN

Economic Freedom Score

Least free 0 — 25 — 50 — 75 — 100 Most free

43.4

Iran's economic freedom score is 43.4, making its economy the 168th freest in the 2010 *Index*. Its score has decreased by 1.2 points from last year, driven by lower scores in freedom from corruption and monetary freedom. Iran is ranked 16th out of 17 countries in the Middle East/North Africa region, and its overall score is below the world and regional averages.

Protectionism and heavy state involvement in many aspects of economic activity have led to economic stagnation in Iran's non-oil sector and a lack of overall economic dynamism. A restrictive business and investment environment depresses development of a viable private sector. More than 500 companies are state-owned, and privatization has been negligible in the past year.

Business licensing and closure are regulated heavily by an intrusive and inefficient bureaucracy. High tariff rates and non-tariff barriers impede trade and foreign investment. Corruption is rampant, and fair adjudication of property rights cannot be guaranteed. The judicial system is vulnerable to political influence and lacks transparency. The oil sector accounts for nearly 50 percent of the government budget.

BACKGROUND: Iran's economy, once one of the most advanced in the Middle East, has been crippled by the 1979 Islamic revolution, the Iran–Iraq war, chronic economic mismanagement, and corruption. International concern about Iran's nuclear development activities and support for terrorism remains high. The United Nations Security Council has imposed three rounds of economic sanctions against the country. Mahmoud Ahmadinejad, who was re-elected president in June 2009 in an election of questionable legitimacy, has halted tentative efforts to reform the state-dominated economy and has greatly expanded government spending. In 2008, high world oil prices significantly boosted oil export revenues, which provide about 85 percent of government revenues, but Iran's economy remains burdened by high unemployment, rising inflation, corruption, costly subsidies, and an increasingly bloated and inefficient public sector.

Country's Score Over Time

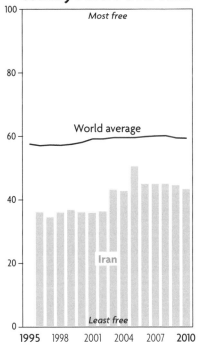

Quick Facts

Population: 72.0 million

GDP (PPP): $839.4 billion
5.6% growth in 2008
5.7% 5-year compound annual growth
$11,666 per capita

Unemployment: 12.5%

Inflation (CPI): 26.0%

FDI Inflow: $1.5 million

2008 data unless otherwise noted
Data compiled as of September 2009

How Do We Measure Economic Freedom?
See page 457 for an explanation of the methodology or visit the *Index* Web site at *heritage.org/index*.

IRAN'S TEN ECONOMIC FREEDOMS

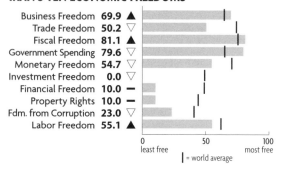

Business Freedom	69.9 ▲	
Trade Freedom	50.2 ▽	
Fiscal Freedom	81.1 ▲	
Government Spending	79.6 ▽	
Monetary Freedom	54.7 ▽	
Investment Freedom	0.0 ▽	
Financial Freedom	10.0 —	
Property Rights	10.0 —	
Fdm. from Corruption	23.0 ▽	
Labor Freedom	55.1 ▲	

0   50   100
least free   most free
| = world average

BUSINESS FREEDOM — 69.9

The overall freedom to start, operate, and close a business remains limited by Iran's regulatory environment. Starting a business takes an average of 9 days, much less than the world average of 35 days, but obtaining a business license takes 322 days, compared to the world average of 218 days.

TRADE FREEDOM — 50.2

Iran's weighted average tariff rate was 17.4 percent in 2008. Import bans and restrictions, high tariffs and import taxes, export licensing requirements, restrictive sanitary and phytosanitary regulations, burdensome customs procedures, state trading, arbitrary changes in tariff and tax schedules, and weak enforcement of intellectual property rights add to the cost of trade. Fifteen points were deducted from Iran's trade freedom score to account for non-tariff barriers.

FISCAL FREEDOM — 81.1

Iran has a relatively high income tax rate and a moderate corporate tax rate. The top income tax rate is 35 percent, and the flat corporate tax rate is 25 percent. All property transfers are subject to a standard tax. A value-added tax (VAT) has been collected and then not collected intermittently since 2005. In the most recent year, overall tax revenue as a percentage of GDP was 6.1 percent.

GOVERNMENT SPENDING — 79.6

Total government expenditures, including consumption and transfer payments, are relatively low. In the most recent year, government spending equaled 26.1 percent of GDP.

MONETARY FREEDOM — 54.7

Inflation is very high, averaging 22.9 percent between 2006 and 2008. The government controls the prices of petroleum products, electricity, water, and wheat; provides economic subsidies; and influences prices through regulation of Iran's many state-owned enterprises. Fifteen points were deducted from Iran's monetary freedom score to adjust for measures that distort domestic prices.

INVESTMENT FREEDOM — 0

Foreign investment faces considerable government hostility and is restricted or banned in many activities, including banking, telecommunications, transport, oil, and gas.

All investments must be approved, and the process is not straightforward. The method of calculating the maximum share that foreign-owned entities are allowed can be non-transparent. The parliament can veto projects in which foreign investors have a majority stake. Political unrest and uncertainty over international sanctions further deter investment. Most payments, transfers, credit operations, and capital transactions are subject to restrictions or approval requirements. Only legal permanent residents of Iran may purchase land. Foreign companies may own property in Iran only if they are registered both in Iran and in their respective countries and make the purchase using their Iranian business identity.

FINANCIAL FREEDOM — 10

Iran's financial sector remains heavily influenced by the government. All banks were nationalized following the 1979 revolution, but six private banks have come into operation since then. These small private banks operate under strict restrictions regarding de facto interest rates and capital requirements. Stringent government controls have kept the banks' lending scope from expanding, limiting access to financing for businesses. State-owned commercial banks and specialized financial institutions account for a majority of the banking sector's total assets. The government directs credit allocation, though credit is often supplied by traditional money lenders in the bazaar in support of small cash-based businesses. The non-banking financial sector remains dominated by state-owned companies. Capital markets are not fully developed.

PROPERTY RIGHTS — 10

The constitution allows the government to confiscate property acquired either illicitly or in a manner not in conformance with Islamic law. Resorting to the courts is often counterproductive; finding an influential local business partner with substantial political patronage is a more effective way to protect contracts. Few laws protect intellectual property; computer software piracy is extensive; and infringement of industrial designs, trademarks, and copyrights is widespread.

FREEDOM FROM CORRUPTION — 23

Corruption is perceived as pervasive. Iran ranks 141st out of 179 countries in Transparency International's Corruption Perceptions Index for 2008, a decline from 2007. The law provides criminal penalties for official corruption, but it is not implemented effectively, and official corruption is found in all three branches of government. Graft is extensive, and the anti-corruption agency has fewer than 1,000 inspectors to monitor the 2.3 million full-time civil servants and numerous government contractors who control most of Iran's economy.

LABOR FREEDOM — 55.1

Labor regulations are restrictive. The non-salary cost of employing a worker is high, and firing a worker requires approval of the Islamic Labor Council or the Labor Discretionary Board.

IRAQ

Economic Freedom Score

The economy is not graded

The level of economic freedom in Iraq remains unrated in the 2010 *Index* because of the lack of sufficiently reliable data for the economy. The Iraqi economy has slowly recovered from the hostilities that began in 2003. However, progress has been uneven, and the country faces continuing tension among different ethnic and religious factions. Iraq was last graded in the 2002 *Index*, when it received an overall score of 15.6.

The Iraqi economy has adopted institutional reforms that have been put in place since 2003, including tax reforms, simple and low tariffs, new investment laws, microfinance initiatives, and a significantly liberalized and modernized banking system.

However, the absence of the rule of law is impeding the development of a vibrant private sector and hurts overall economic growth, especially by hindering the creation of a stable investment and entrepreneurial climate. Economic progress rests on a fragile foundation, undermined continuously by weak physical security and persistent corruption.

BACKGROUND: A U.S.-led coalition removed Saddam Hussein's dictatorship in 2003, and an elected government led by Prime Minister Nuri al-Maliki took office in May 2006. Iraq's oil industry provides more than 90 percent of hard-currency earnings but has been hurt by pipeline sabotage, electricity outages, and years of neglect and postponed maintenance. Economic recovery, though helped by relatively high oil prices and aid from the United States and other donors, is hampered by ongoing insurgency and instability. Improved security and the gradual restoration of oil exports have increased the prospects for steady economic growth. The oil industry, still in government hands, is both the glue that holds Iraq's disparate factions together and a source of ongoing tension among them. Successful provincial elections in January 2009 weakened extremist political parties and encouraged an atmosphere of political compromise.

Country's Score Over Time

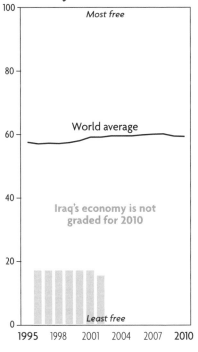

Quick Facts

Population: 29.6 million

GDP (PPP): $105.7 billion
9.5% growth in 2008
4.1% 5-year compound annual growth
$3,570 per capita

Unemployment: 18.2% (unofficial estimates as high as 30%)

Inflation (CPI): 3.5%

FDI Inflow: $20.2 billion

2008 data unless otherwise noted
Data compiled as of September 2009

How Do We Measure Economic Freedom?
See page 457 for an explanation of the methodology or visit the *Index* Web site at *heritage.org/index*.

235

BUSINESS FREEDOM — NOT GRADED

Despite some progress in establishing an investment-friendly business environment, significant problems remain to be addressed as Iraq tries to deal with challenges to its security and stability.

TRADE FREEDOM — NOT GRADED

Iraq is trying to re-establish more broad-based trade. According to the U.S. Department of Commerce, Iraq applied a flat tariff rate of 5 percent in 2004. Non-tariff barriers include inadequate infrastructure and trade capacity, significant customs delays, security concerns, and some import and export bans.

FISCAL FREEDOM — NOT GRADED

Individual and corporate income tax rates are capped at 15 percent. Tax revenue as a percentage of GDP is negligible. Further modernization of the tax system and introduction of a sales tax as a precursor to a value-added tax (VAT) are under consideration, but the weakness of the central government limits effective reform.

GOVERNMENT SPENDING — NOT GRADED

Total government expenditures in Iraq, including consumption and transfer payments, are very high. It is estimated that government spending equals about 70 percent of GDP. The oil sector accounts for over 95 percent of exports and government revenue, and attempts to sell state-owned oil fields in the past year were not successful.

MONETARY FREEDOM — NOT GRADED

Inflation in Iraq has been high, averaging 14.6 percent between 2006 and 2008. Consumer price growth has slowed from its peaks (inflation reached 65 percent at the end of 2006), in large part because of improvement in the supply of basic items, especially fuel, as the security situation has stabilized. The government maintains a large public sector, provides a number of subsidies, and imposes a number of price controls.

INVESTMENT FREEDOM — NOT GRADED

Iraq is open to foreign capital in principle, but inadequate regulatory capacity, policy uncertainty, security concerns, and corruption deter investment. There are no restrictions on current and capital transactions involving currency exchange as long as underlying transactions are supported by valid documentation. The National Investment Law, which is not yet implemented, would allow investors to bank and transfer capital inside or outside of Iraq. Foreigners may not own land, but foreign investors are permitted renewable leases for up to 50 years.

FINANCIAL FREEDOM — NOT GRADED

Iraq's financial system remains poorly developed, and the legal and institutional framework is not conducive to deepening financial intermediation. A March 2004 law liberalized and modernized the banking system, allowing allocation of credit on market terms and making the central bank independent. There are seven state-owned banks, 32 private banks, and six Islamic banks. The two largest state-owned banks (Al-Rafidain and Al-Rasheed) account for over 90 percent of assets. Four specialized state-owned banks serve the agricultural, industrial, real estate, and social sectors. The major activity of private banks is financial transfers from the government to local authorities or individuals. The insurance sector and the new stock exchange are very small.

PROPERTY RIGHTS — NOT GRADED

There is very little protection of property in Iraq. Foreigners may only rent or lease land for up to 50 years, but leases are renewable. Foreign investors may own investment portfolios in shares and securities. The Commission for the Resolution of Real Property Disputes is an independent governmental commission established to resolve claims for real property confiscated, forcibly acquired, or otherwise taken for less than fair value by the former regime between 1968 and 2003 for reasons other than land reform or lawfully applied eminent domain. The legal system remains very weak. U.S. forces, working with Iraqi military and police units, have improved the rule of law but still face daunting challenges. Iraq does not have adequate statutory protection for intellectual property rights.

FREEDOM FROM CORRUPTION — NOT GRADED

Corruption is perceived as rampant. Iraq ranks 178th out of 179 countries in Transparency International's Corruption Perceptions Index for 2008, unchanged from 2007. Under Hussein, corruption was a fact of life and touched every economic transaction. Undoing this legacy will be a long process, and investors still may have to contend with requests for bribes or kickbacks from government officials at all levels.

LABOR FREEDOM — NOT GRADED

Iraq's formal labor market is not yet fully developed. Most private-sector jobs are informal. It is estimated that unemployment and underemployment combined affect about half of the labor force.

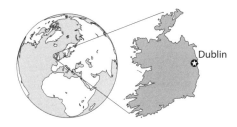

IRELAND

Economic Freedom Score

Least free 0 — 100 Most free

81.3

I reland's economic freedom score is 81.3, making its economy the 5th freest in the 2010 *Index*. Its score has decreased by 0.9 point from last year, reflecting lower scores in monetary freedom, government spending, and financial freedom. The Irish economy was able to maintain its status as freest economy in the Europe region in the 2010 *Index*.

Though Ireland's dynamic economy has benefited substantially from its openness and flexibility in recent years, the financial sector was affected by the global financial turmoil, and the economy has suffered sharp economic adjustments since late 2008. The budget deficit has been on the rise, putting greater pressure on balancing the government budget. Despite the government's efforts at stabilization, the banking system's health remains precarious. The government plans to buy up non-performing loans, estimated to be equivalent to about 45 percent of GDP.

Despite the crisis, Ireland's overall levels of economic freedom remain high, sustained by such institutional strengths as strong protection of property rights, a low level of corruption, efficient business regulations, and competitive tax rates. These strengths provide solid foundations on which to build recovery and curb long-term unemployment.

BACKGROUND: The Anglo–Irish Treaty of 1921 formally partitioned the Irish Free State, roughly along Catholic–Protestant lines, into Ireland, which in 1948 became the Republic of Ireland, and Northern Ireland, which remained under British rule. Sectarian violence declined in the 1990s, and the Irish Republican Army formally renounced armed struggle in 2005. Ireland's modern, highly industrialized economy performed extraordinarily well throughout the 1990s, but the burst of a speculative housing bubble in 2008 sent the economy into a tailspin. Reversing the outcome of an earlier referendum, Irish voters approved the Lisbon treaty in 2009.

Country's Score Over Time

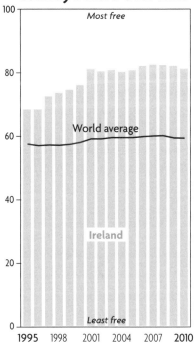

Quick Facts

Population: 4.5 million

GDP (PPP): $197.1 billion
    −2.3% growth in 2007
    3.9% 5-year compound
      annual growth
    $44,200 per capita

Unemployment: 6%

Inflation (CPI): 3.1%

FDI Inflow: −$20 billion

2008 data unless otherwise noted
Data compiled as of September 2009

How Do We Measure Economic Freedom?
See page 457 for an explanation of the methodology or visit the *Index* Web site at *heritage.org/index*.

IRELAND'S TEN ECONOMIC FREEDOMS

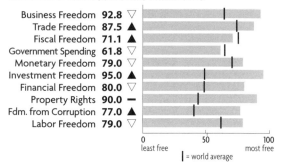

Business Freedom	92.8	▽
Trade Freedom	87.5	▲
Fiscal Freedom	71.1	▲
Government Spending	61.8	▽
Monetary Freedom	79.0	▽
Investment Freedom	95.0	▲
Financial Freedom	80.0	▽
Property Rights	90.0	—
Fdm. from Corruption	77.0	▲
Labor Freedom	79.0	▽

0 least free   50   100 most free

| = world average

BUSINESS FREEDOM — 92.8

The overall freedom to conduct a business is well protected under Ireland's regulatory environment. Starting a business takes an average of 13 days, compared to the world average of 35 days. Obtaining a business license requires less than the world average of 18 procedures and 218 days. Bankruptcy procedures are straightforward.

TRADE FREEDOM — 87.5

Ireland's trade policy is the same as that of other members of the European Union. The common EU weighted average tariff rate was 1.3 percent in 2008. However, the EU has high or escalating tariffs for agricultural and manufacturing products, and its MFN tariff code is complex. Non-tariff barriers reflected in EU and Irish policy include agricultural and manufacturing subsidies, quotas, import restrictions and bans for some goods and services, market access restrictions in some services sectors, non-transparent and restrictive regulations and standards, and inconsistent regulatory and customs administration among EU members. Government procurement rules are restrictive. Ten points were deducted from Ireland's trade freedom score to account for non-tariff barriers.

FISCAL FREEDOM — 71.1

Ireland has a relatively high income tax rate but a relatively low corporate tax rate. The top income tax rate is 41 percent, and the top corporate tax rate is 12.5 percent. Other taxes include a value-added tax (VAT) and a tax on interest. In the most recent year, overall tax revenue as a percentage of GDP was 32.5 percent.

GOVERNMENT SPENDING — 61.8

Total government expenditures, including consumption and transfer payments, are moderate. In the most recent year, government spending equaled 35.7 percent of GDP. Public expenditures on an aging population and the slowdown in overall economic activity have contributed to a growing fiscal deficit.

MONETARY FREEDOM — 79

Ireland is a member of the euro zone. Inflation has been relatively low, averaging 3.0 percent between 2006 and 2008. As a participant in the EU's Common Agricultural Policy, the government subsidizes agricultural production, distorting the prices of agricultural products. It also influences prices through state-owned enterprises. Ten points were deducted from Ireland's monetary freedom score to account for policies that distort domestic prices.

INVESTMENT FREEDOM — 95

Ireland welcomes foreign investment, and domestic and foreign firms incorporated in Ireland receive equal treatment. There is no approval process for foreign investment or capital inflows unless the company is applying for incentives. The regulatory regime is generally transparent and efficient. There are no restrictions or barriers with respect to current transfers, repatriation of profits, or access to foreign exchange. Residents and non-residents may own land.

FINANCIAL FREEDOM — 80

Ireland has suffered severe economic and financial challenges as a result of the recent financial and banking crisis. Its competitive financial system was compromised by the collapse of a property bubble in which banks were highly exposed. Government action in response to the financial crisis included the establishment of a single fully integrated regulatory institution. The government also restructured the financial sector, creating the National Asset Management Agency to stabilize the banking sector and restore liquidity. The government nationalized the Anglo Irish bank in early 2009. The country's two largest banks, Bank of Ireland and Allied Irish Bank, have received capital injections, and the government has taken a 25 percent stake in the Bank of Ireland.

PROPERTY RIGHTS — 90

Secured interests in property, both chattel and real estate, are recognized and enforced. An efficient, non-discriminatory legal system is accessible to foreign investors to protect and facilitate acquisition and disposition of all property rights. Expropriation is highly unlikely. The courts protect property, and contracts are secure. Ireland has one of Europe's most comprehensive legal frameworks for the protection of intellectual property rights.

FREEDOM FROM CORRUPTION — 77

Corruption is perceived as minimal. Ireland ranks 16th out of 179 countries in Transparency International's Corruption Perceptions Index for 2008. Corruption is not a serious problem for foreign investors in Ireland. It is illegal for public servants to accept bribes, and the police investigate allegations of corruption. Ireland has ratified the OECD Anti-Bribery Convention and is a member of the OECD Working Group on Bribery and the Group of States Against Corruption.

LABOR FREEDOM — 79

Labor regulations are flexible. The non-salary cost of employing a worker is low, and dismissing an employee is relatively easy. Restrictions on work hours are flexible.

ISRAEL

Economic Freedom Score

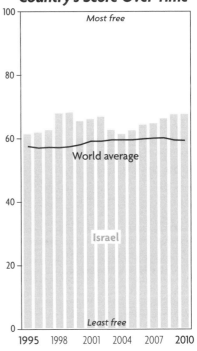

67.7

Israel's economic freedom score is 67.7, making its economy the 44th freest in the 2010 *Index*. Its overall score has increased slightly, reflecting improvements in fiscal freedom and investment freedom. Israel is ranked 5th out of 17 countries in the Middle East/North Africa region.

The Israeli economy has increasingly diversified its productive base and has enjoyed steady growth of close to 5 percent over the past five years. Along with its openness to global trade and investment, Israel's overall economic competitiveness is supported by strong protection of property rights and relatively low levels of corruption.

Israel's commitment to economic restructuring and development continues, and there is room for improvement in implementing more effective public finance management. Government spending equals almost half of GDP. Income and corporate tax rates remain relatively burdensome, but implementation of further cuts in both individual and corporate income tax rates is scheduled.

BACKGROUND: After more than 60 years, Israel continues to live under the threat of war and terrorist violence, and its vibrant democracy is unique in the region. Having moved away from the socialist economic model in the mid-1980s, Israel made dramatic free-market gains in the 1990s. The collapse of the 1993 Oslo peace agreement and onset of the "Second Intifada" in 2000 depressed tourism, discouraged foreign investment, and contributed to economic recession; the economy rebounded by 2004 as a result of increased foreign investment, restored tourism, and a greater demand for Israeli exports, especially high-technology goods and services. Despite the 2006 war against Hezbollah in Lebanon, the December 2008 war against Hamas in Gaza, and continued Palestinian terrorism, the economy has grown significantly. Prime Minister Benjamin Netanyahu leads a coalition government formed after the February 2009 elections.

Country's Score Over Time

Quick Facts

Population: 7.3 million

GDP (PPP): $201.3 billion
  4.2% growth in 2008
  4.9% 5-year compound
    annual growth
  $27,548 per capita

Unemployment: 6.2%

Inflation (CPI): 4.7%

FDI Inflow: $9.6 billion

2008 data unless otherwise noted
Data compiled as of September 2009

How Do We Measure Economic Freedom?
See page 457 for an explanation of the methodology or visit the *Index* Web site at *heritage.org/index.*

ISRAEL'S TEN ECONOMIC FREEDOMS

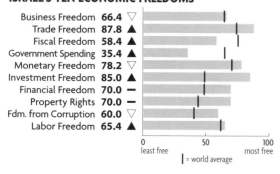

Business Freedom	66.4 ▽	
Trade Freedom	87.8 ▲	
Fiscal Freedom	58.4 ▲	
Government Spending	35.4 ▲	
Monetary Freedom	78.2 ▽	
Investment Freedom	85.0 ▲	
Financial Freedom	70.0 —	
Property Rights	70.0 —	
Fdm. from Corruption	60.0 ▽	
Labor Freedom	65.4 ▲	

0 least free   50   100 most free

| = world average

BUSINESS FREEDOM — 66.4

The overall freedom to conduct a business is relatively well protected under Israel's regulatory environment. Starting a business takes an average of 34 days, compared to the world average of 35 days. Obtaining a business license requires slightly more than the world average of 18 procedures and 218 days. Bankruptcy can be lengthy and costly.

TRADE FREEDOM — 87.8

Israel's weighted average tariff rate was 1.1 percent in 2008. Import bans and restrictions, high agriculture tariffs, import fees and taxes, a complex and non-transparent tariff rate quota system, restrictive labeling requirements, import licensing, and non-transparent government procurement add to the cost of trade. Ten points were deducted from Israel's trade freedom score to account for non-tariff barriers.

FISCAL FREEDOM — 58.4

The top income tax rate has been lowered from 47 percent to 46 percent. The top corporate tax rate has been reduced to 26 percent from 27 percent. Both rates are scheduled for further reduction in 2010. Other taxes include a value-added tax (VAT) and a capital gains tax. In the most recent year, overall tax revenue as a percentage of GDP was 37 percent.

GOVERNMENT SPENDING — 35.4

Total government expenditures, including consumption and transfer payments, are high. In the most recent year, government spending equaled 46.4 percent of GDP. Privatization has accelerated in recent years. Years of prudent fiscal policy have reduced public debt from 100 percent of GDP in 2003 to below 80 percent.

MONETARY FREEDOM — 78.2

Inflation has been moderate, averaging 3.5 percent between 2006 and 2008. The government influences prices through the public sector and provides some subsidies, especially for agriculture production. The energy sector remains largely state-owned and heavily regulated, and the government can impose price controls on vital goods and services. Ten points were deducted from Israel's monetary freedom score to account for policies that distort domestic prices.

INVESTMENT FREEDOM — 85

Foreign investment is restricted in a few sectors, such as defense, but is not screened. Regulations on acquisitions, mergers, and takeovers apply equally to foreign and domestic investors. Investments in regulated industries, such as banking, require prior government approval, as does the receipt of investment incentive benefits. Commercial law is consistent and standardized, and international arbitration is binding in dispute settlements with the state. Bureaucracy can be complex and burdensome. Residents and non-residents may hold foreign exchange accounts, and there are no controls or restrictions on current transfers, repatriation of profits, or other transactions.

FINANCIAL FREEDOM — 70

Israel's financial sector has undergone restructuring and consolidation. The banking sector is highly concentrated, and the five principal banking groups together hold more than 95 percent of total assets. Commercial banks provide a full range of financial services that facilitate entrepreneurial activity and private-sector development. Credit is available on market terms, and financial institutions offer a wide array of financial instruments. Supervision is prudent, and regulations conform to international norms. The 2005 Bachar Reform bars commercial banks from owning holdings in mutual funds and provident funds that resemble pension accounts. Capital markets have been largely liberalized as part of Israel's effort to reinvent itself as a finance hub. The financial market achieved a sharp recovery during the first half of 2009, offsetting most of the losses triggered by the global financial crisis in 2008.

PROPERTY RIGHTS — 70

Israel has a modern legal system based on British common law. Property rights and contracts are enforced effectively. Courts are independent, and commercial law is clear and consistently applied. Expropriation occurs only if property is linked to a terrorist threat and expropriation is deemed to be in the interest of national security. Jurisdiction for the enforcement of intellectual property rights is problematic, especially since responsibility in the West Bank and Gaza rests with the Palestinian Authority.

FREEDOM FROM CORRUPTION — 60

Corruption is perceived as present. Israel ranks 33rd out of 179 countries in Transparency International's Corruption Perceptions Index for 2008. Bribery and other forms of corruption are illegal. Israel became a signatory to the OECD Bribery convention in November 2008. Several non-governmental organizations focus on public-sector ethics.

LABOR FREEDOM — 65.4

Labor regulations are relatively flexible. The non-salary cost of employing a worker is low, but dismissing an employee is relatively costly. Restrictions on work hours are not flexible.

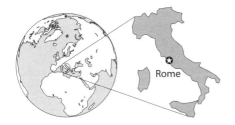

ITALY

Economic Freedom Score

62.7

Least free 0   25   50   75   Most free 100

I taly's economic freedom score is 62.7, making its economy the 74th freest in the 2010 *Index*. Its overall score is 1.3 points higher than last year, reflecting modest improvements in trade freedom and investment freedom. Italy is ranked 35th out of 43 countries in the Europe region, and its score is slightly above the world average.

The regional disparities in Italy's economic development remain distinctive. The northern part of the country has well-established traditions of private-sector entrepreneurship, while the southern part of the country has long been dependent on the agricultural sector and government welfare. The Italian economy on the whole has become increasingly dominated by the services sector, which accounts for around 70 percent of GDP.

Italy's overall economic freedom is curbed by ineffective public finance management, considerable corruption, and a high tax burden. Government spending remains over 45 percent of GDP. Reduction of the chronic budget deficit has proved difficult, and public debt still hovers around 105 percent of GDP. A considerable level of economic activity takes place outside of the formal economy.

BACKGROUND: The volatile and vibrantly democratic Italian political landscape is dominated currently by a center-right coalition led by Silvio Berlusconi, who was elected prime minister for a third time in 2008. Italy is a member of the European Union, NATO, and the G-8, which it hosted in July 2009. Small and medium-size enterprises dominate key industries such as manufacturing and high-end design. The export market for luxury goods was hard-hit by the global economic downturn, and the economy experienced a deep recession. The informal sector still accounts for a sizeable portion of economic activity. Persistent problems in other areas include organized crime, increasing unemployment, and the long-standing imbalance between the prosperous and industrialized North and the less developed South.

Country's Score Over Time

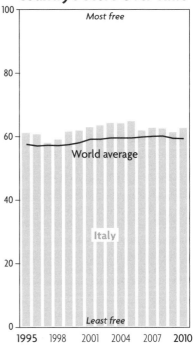

Quick Facts

Population: 59.9 million

GDP (PPP): $1.8 trillion
 –1.0% growth in 2008
 0.8% 5-year compound annual growth
 $30,756 per capita

Unemployment: 6.8%

Inflation (CPI): 3.5%

FDI Inflow: $17 billion

2008 data unless otherwise noted
Data compiled as of September 2009

How Do We Measure Economic Freedom?
See page 457 for an explanation of the methodology or visit the *Index* Web site at *heritage.org/index*.

ITALY'S TEN ECONOMIC FREEDOMS

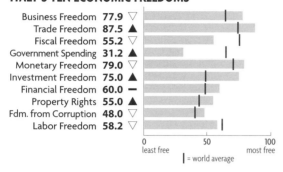

Business Freedom	77.9 ▽	
Trade Freedom	87.5 ▲	
Fiscal Freedom	55.2 ▽	
Government Spending	31.2 ▲	
Monetary Freedom	79.0 ▽	
Investment Freedom	75.0 ▲	
Financial Freedom	60.0 —	
Property Rights	55.0 ▲	
Fdm. from Corruption	48.0 ▽	
Labor Freedom	58.2 ▽	

0 least free   50   100 most free

∎ = world average

BUSINESS FREEDOM — 77.9

The overall freedom to start, operate, and close a business is relatively well protected under Italy's regulatory environment. Starting a business takes an average of 10 days, compared to the world average of 35 days. Obtaining a business license requires less than the world average of 18 procedures and slightly more than the world average of 218 days.

TRADE FREEDOM — 87.5

Italy's trade policy is the same as that of other members of the European Union. The common EU weighted average tariff rate was 1.3 percent in 2008. However, the EU has high or escalating tariffs for agricultural and manufacturing products, and its MFN tariff code is complex. Non-tariff barriers reflected in EU and Italian policy include agricultural and manufacturing subsidies, quotas, import restrictions and bans for some goods and services, market access restrictions in some services sectors, non-transparent and restrictive regulations and standards, and inconsistent regulatory and customs administration among EU members. Ten points were deducted from Italy's trade freedom score to account for non-tariff barriers.

FISCAL FREEDOM — 55.2

Italy has a high income tax and a moderate corporate tax. The top income tax rate is 43 percent, and the top corporate tax rate is 27.5 percent. Individuals are also subject to small regional and municipal income taxes, and corporations are subject to a regional tax of 3.9 percent. Other taxes include a value-added tax (VAT), a tax on interest, a property transfer tax, and an inheritance tax. In the most recent year, overall tax revenue as a percentage of GDP was 43.3 percent.

GOVERNMENT SPENDING — 31.2

Total government expenditures, including consumption and transfer payments, are high. In the most recent year, government spending equaled 47.9 percent of GDP. The state still controls some strategic enterprises, mainly in transportation and energy.

MONETARY FREEDOM — 79

Italy is a member of the euro zone. Inflation is relatively low, averaging 3.0 percent between 2006 and 2008. As a participant in the EU's Common Agricultural Policy, the government subsidizes agricultural production, distorting agricultural prices. Items subject to price controls at the national level include drinking water, electricity, gas, highway tolls, prescription drugs reimbursed by the national health service, telecommunications, and domestic travel. Ten points were deducted from Italy's monetary freedom score to account for policies that distort domestic prices.

INVESTMENT FREEDOM — 75

Italy welcomes foreign investment, but the government can veto acquisitions involving foreign investors. National treatment is provided to foreign investors established in Italy or another EU member state, except in defense, aircraft manufacturing, petroleum exploration and development, domestic airlines, and shipping. The government often retains a "golden share" in privatized companies. An inefficient judicial system, bureaucracy, rigid labor laws, inefficient infrastructure, regulatory non-transparency, the possibility of government intervention, and hostile labor unions are deterrents. There are no barriers to repatriation of profits. Foreigners may not buy land along the border.

FINANCIAL FREEDOM — 60

The financial sector is relatively well developed and provides a wide range of services. Banking has undergone consolidation. Credit is allocated on market terms, and foreign participation is welcome. Only three major financial institutions remain state-controlled. However, banks are not free from political interference. The five largest banks account for over 50 percent of assets. Regulations and prohibitions can be burdensome, and approval is needed to gain control of a financial institution. The government has acted to reform underdeveloped capital markets. The global financial turmoil's impact on the banking sector has been relatively modest, with Italian banks less exposed to troubled financial instruments than banks in some other countries.

PROPERTY RIGHTS — 55

Property rights and contracts are secure, but judicial procedures are extremely slow, and many companies choose to settle out of court. Many judges are politically oriented. Enforcement of intellectual property rights falls below the standards of other developed Western European countries.

FREEDOM FROM CORRUPTION — 48

Corruption is perceived as present. Italy ranks 48th out of 179 countries in Transparency International's Corruption Perceptions Index for 2008. Corruption and organized crime are significant impediments to investment and economic growth in southern Italy, and Italians regard investment-related sectors as corrupt.

LABOR FREEDOM — 58.2

Labor regulations are relatively rigid. The non-salary cost of employing a worker is very high, but dismissing an employee can be costless. Rules on work hours are relatively inflexible.

JAMAICA

Economic Freedom Score

25   50   75

Least   0   100   Most
free   free

65.5

World Rank: 57   **Regional Rank: 11**

Jamaica's economic freedom score is 65.5, making its economy the 57th freest in the 2010 *Index*. Its score is 0.3 point better than last year, reflecting improvements in four of the 10 economic freedoms. Jamaica ranks 11th out of 29 countries in the South and Central America/Caribbean region.

Jamaica has implemented reforms to develop its private sector. The economy scores very high in investment freedom and business freedom and above the world average in three other areas. Procedures for conducting a business are straightforward and simple. Foreign investment is welcome in many sectors, and steps have been taken to enhance the regulatory environment for the financial sector.

Jamaica's overall economic freedom is hurt by significant corruption and relatively high government spending. Excessive public debt renders Jamaica's fiscal situation unstable. Efforts to restrict spending have generally fallen short. Undermining anti-corruption efforts, the judicial system remains inefficient and clogged by a significant backlog of cases.

BACKGROUND: Once a major sugar producer, Jamaica is now a net sugar importer. The economy is diverse, but industries need modernization and lack investment capital. Most foreign exchange comes from remittances, tourism, and bauxite. The downturn in U.S. demand for Jamaica's major exports (particularly agricultural, mining, and services), a decline in remittances, and a contraction of consumer demand led to a deep recession in 2009 with stubbornly high unemployment and underemployment. Jamaica's public debt equals more than 120 percent of GDP, and more than half of government revenue goes to debt service and recurrent expenditures. These factors, in addition to money laundering and drug-related violence, are among the challenges facing Prime Minister Bruce Golding, who took office in late 2007 with his Jamaica Labour Party holding a slim parliamentary majority.

Country's Score Over Time

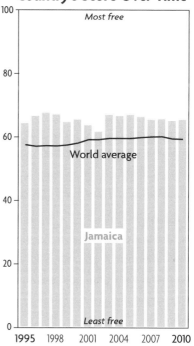

Quick Facts

Population: 2.7 million

GDP (PPP): $20.7 billion
  −1.3% growth in 2008
  1.0% 5-year compound
    annual growth
  $7,705 per capita

Unemployment: 11.0%

Inflation (CPI): 22.0%

FDI Inflow: $789.0 million

2008 data unless otherwise noted
Data compiled as of September 2009

How Do We Measure Economic Freedom?
See page 457 for an explanation of the methodology or visit the *Index* Web site at *heritage.org/index.*

JAMAICA'S TEN ECONOMIC FREEDOMS

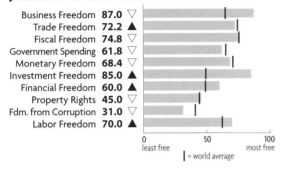

Business Freedom	87.0 ▽
Trade Freedom	72.2 ▲
Fiscal Freedom	74.8 ▽
Government Spending	61.8 ▽
Monetary Freedom	68.4 ▽
Investment Freedom	85.0 ▲
Financial Freedom	60.0 ▲
Property Rights	45.0 ▽
Fdm. from Corruption	31.0 ▽
Labor Freedom	70.0 ▲

0 least free   50   100 most free

▎= world average

BUSINESS FREEDOM — 87

The overall freedom to start, operate, and close a business is relatively well protected by Jamaica's regulatory environment. Starting a business takes eight days, compared to the world average of 35 days. Obtaining a business license requires 10 procedures and takes less than the world average of 218 days.

TRADE FREEDOM — 72.2

Jamaica's weighted average tariff rate was 8.9 percent in 2006. The government has been implementing reforms of the trade regime, but some high tariffs, import fees and taxes, import and export bans and restrictions, restrictive pharmaceuticals regulations, inefficient regulatory administration, and weak enforcement of intellectual property rights add to the cost of trade. Ten points were deducted from Jamaica's trade freedom score to account for non-tariff barriers.

FISCAL FREEDOM — 74.8

Jamaica has a moderate income tax rate and a relatively high corporate tax rate. The flat income tax rate is 25 percent, and the top corporate tax rate is 33.3 percent. Other taxes include a value-added tax (called a general consumption tax), a property transfer tax, and a tax on interest. In the most recent year, overall tax revenue as a percentage of GDP was 28.1 percent.

GOVERNMENT SPENDING — 61.8

Total government expenditures, including consumption and transfer payments, are moderately high. In the most recent year, government spending equaled 35.7 percent of GDP. Despite identifying two potential buyers for the national airline (Air Jamaica), the government has missed two of its self-imposed divestment deadlines.

MONETARY FREEDOM — 68.4

Inflation has been very high, averaging 17.7 percent between 2006 and 2008. Most prices are set by the market, but the government regulates utility services, including electricity, water, and bus fares. There are no official policies on price regulation or control, but the government monitors the pricing of consumer items. Five points were deducted from Jamaica's monetary freedom score to account for policies that distort domestic prices.

INVESTMENT FREEDOM — 85

Jamaica encourages foreign investment in all sectors. Foreign and domestic investors receive equal treatment, and foreign investors can acquire privatized state-owned enterprises. There is no screening, but projects that affect national security, have a negative impact on the environment, or involve such sectors as life insurance, media, or mining are subject to some restrictions. There are no limits on foreign control of companies. The legal system upholds the sanctity of contracts. The government is steadily improving bureaucratic efficiency and transparency. Residents and non-residents may hold foreign exchange accounts. There are no restrictions on international transactions, transfers, or the repatriation of funds, and non-residents may purchase real estate.

FINANCIAL FREEDOM — 60

Jamaica's financial sector has undergone major consolidation and restructuring. Government efforts to strengthen supervision and regulation of banking and insurance continue. Although some financial products are still not available, the private sector has access to a wide range of credit instruments. Despite the global financial turmoil, the banking sector remains relatively sound and well capitalized. The three largest commercial banks account for about 85 percent of commercial bank assets, and five of the seven commercial banks are foreign-owned. Credit is generally allocated on market terms. Capital markets are underdeveloped and centered on the stock exchange. In 2008, the government continued to enhance the regulatory framework for the financial sector, moving forward the Credit Reporting Bill and reform of the National Payments System.

PROPERTY RIGHTS — 45

Jamaica's legal system is based on English common law, but the judiciary lacks adequate resources, and trials can be delayed for years. Bureaucracy can cause significant delays in securing land titles. An inadequate police force weakens the security of property rights, and crime threatens foreign investment. Jamaica's patent law is not WTO/TRIPS-compliant.

FREEDOM FROM CORRUPTION — 31

Corruption is perceived as significant. Jamaica ranks 96th out of 179 countries in Transparency International's Corruption Perceptions Index for 2008, a decline from 2007. Corruption may well be the single greatest concern among Jamaicans, most of whom believe it to be one of the root causes of the high crime rate. The executive and legislative branches of government, as well as the Jamaica Constabulary Force, are widely regarded as subject to corruption.

LABOR FREEDOM — 70

Labor regulations are relatively flexible. The non-salary cost of employing a worker is moderate, but dismissing an employee is costly. Regulations on work hours are flexible.

JAPAN

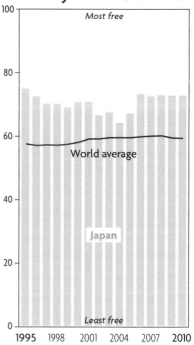

Economic Freedom Score

Least free 0 — 25 — 50 — 75 — 100 Most free

72.9

Japan's economic freedom score is 72.9, making its economy the 19th freest in the 2010 *Index*. Its score is almost the same as last year. Japan is ranked 5th out of 41 countries in the Asia–Pacific region.

The export-oriented Japanese economy has long benefited from global trade, although non-tariff barriers linger, hurting overall trade freedom. The economy scores above the world average in many of the 10 economic freedoms, including business freedom, property rights, freedom from corruption, and labor freedom. The regulatory environment is efficient and facilitates overall entrepreneurial activity. Property rights are generally well respected, and corruption is perceived as minimal.

Japan still faces a number of challenges in trying to revitalize its stagnant economy. Together with deflationary pressure, which increased during the course of 2009, a large and growing public debt (around 180 percent of GDP) has crowded out private-sector economic activity. Disparities in productivity between different segments of the economy have continued to widen. The financial sector is modern and well developed, but it remains subject to government influence and a host of restrictions. Taxation is fairly burdensome, and Japan's corporate tax rate is becoming increasingly uncompetitive.

BACKGROUND: Japan is the world's second-largest economy, but its "lost decade" of the 1990s has extended well into a second decade. The economy is smaller than it was in the first quarter of 1992. Japan's brief period of economic expansion earlier this decade under Prime Minister Junichiro Koizumi was driven primarily by reliance on exports. Market reform is now urgently needed to create domestic sources of growth. The Democratic Party of Japan won a historic victory in August 2009, capturing both houses of parliament and elevating Yukio Hatoyama to the prime ministership.

Country's Score Over Time

Most free

World average

Japan

Least free

1995   1998   2001   2004   2007   **2010**

Quick Facts

Population: 127.7 million

GDP (PPP): $4.4 trillion
−0.7% growth in 2008
1.4% 5-year compound
annual growth
$34,099 per capita

Unemployment: 4.0%

Inflation (CPI): 1.4%

FDI Inflow: $24.4 billion

*2008 data unless otherwise noted
Data compiled as of September 2009*

How Do We Measure Economic Freedom?
See page 457 for an explanation of the methodology or visit the *Index* Web site at *heritage.org/index.*

JAPAN'S TEN ECONOMIC FREEDOMS

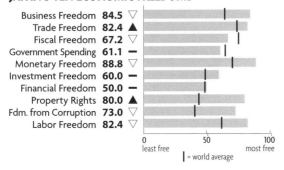

Business Freedom	84.5	▽
Trade Freedom	82.4	▲
Fiscal Freedom	67.2	▽
Government Spending	61.1	—
Monetary Freedom	88.8	▽
Investment Freedom	60.0	—
Financial Freedom	50.0	—
Property Rights	80.0	▲
Fdm. from Corruption	73.0	▽
Labor Freedom	82.4	▽

0 least free   50   100 most free

| = world average

BUSINESS FREEDOM — 84.5

The overall freedom to start, operate, and close a business is strongly protected under Japan's regulatory environment. Starting a business takes 23 days, compared to the world average of 35 days. Obtaining a business license takes less than the world average of 18 procedures and 218 days. Bankruptcy proceedings are easy and straightforward.

TRADE FREEDOM — 82.4

Japan's weighted average tariff rate was 1.3 percent in 2008. Import and export bans and restrictions, import quotas and licensing, services market access barriers, non-transparent and burdensome regulations and standards, restrictive sanitary and phytosanitary rules, restrictions in government procurement, state trade in some goods, subsidies, and inefficient customs administration add to the cost of trade. Fifteen points were deducted from Japan's trade freedom score to account for non-tariff barriers.

FISCAL FREEDOM — 67.2

Japan has a high income tax rate and a moderate corporate tax rate. The top income tax rate is 40 percent, which rises to almost 50 percent when local taxes are included. The standard corporate tax rate is 30 percent, which local taxes can raise to around 41 percent. Other taxes include a value-added tax (VAT), a tax on interest, and an estate tax. In the most recent year, overall tax revenue as a percentage of GDP was 27.9 percent.

GOVERNMENT SPENDING — 61.1

Total government expenditures, including consumption and transfer payments, are relatively high. In the most recent year, government spending equaled 36 percent of GDP. Efforts to reinvigorate the economy and the rising cost of social welfare for an aging population have put government spending on an upward trend.

MONETARY FREEDOM — 88.8

Inflation is minimal and falling, averaging 1.0 percent between 2006 and 2008. Japan is struggling with its second round of deflation this decade, with the corporate goods price index falling at a record pace while the jobless rate rose to near an all-time high. Other product prices are also expected to drop as retailers slash prices to encourage recession-wary consumers to spend. Formal price controls apply to rice, but major producers, backed by regulators, are able to dictate retail and wholesale prices. Five points were deducted from Japan's monetary freedom score to account for policies that distort domestic prices.

INVESTMENT FREEDOM — 60

Foreign investment is officially welcomed, and inward direct investment is subject to few restrictions. However, foreign acquisition of Japanese firms is inhibited by insufficient financial disclosure and cross-holding of shares among companies in the same business grouping (*keiretsu*). Further deterrents include public resistance to foreign acquisitions, overregulation, and a slow court system. Government approval is needed for investments in agriculture, forestry, petroleum, electricity, gas, water, aerospace, telecommunications, and leather manufacturing. There are few controls on the holding of foreign exchange accounts or on current transfers, repatriation of profits, or real estate transactions by residents or non-residents.

FINANCIAL FREEDOM — 50

Japan's modern financial system remains subject to government influence. Overall transparency is still weak despite gradual improvement. Deregulation and competition have led to consolidation in an effort to create banks large enough to be major players abroad. The government supports bank mergers and continues to update laws and regulations to facilitate them. The government-owned postal savings system is Japan's biggest financial institution by assets. In late 2007, under a 10-year privatization plan, the Japanese post office was divided into four commercial entities: a bank, an insurance company, a mail-delivery service, and a branch-management entity. Capital markets are relatively well developed. The impact of the global financial turmoil on the Japanese banking sector has been relatively modest because of its limited exposure to troubled assets.

PROPERTY RIGHTS — 80

Real and intellectual property rights are generally secure, but obtaining and protecting patents and trademarks can be time-consuming and costly. The courts do not discriminate against foreign investors, but they are not well suited to litigation of business disputes. Contracts are highly respected.

FREEDOM FROM CORRUPTION — 73

Corruption is perceived as minimal. Japan ranks 18th out of 179 countries in Transparency International's Corruption Perceptions Index for 2008.

LABOR FREEDOM — 82.4

Japan's labor regulations are relatively flexible. The non-salary cost of employing a worker is moderate, and dismissing an employee is not difficult. Regulations on work hours are rigid.

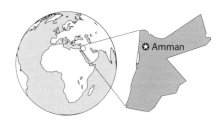

JORDAN

Economic Freedom Score

Least free 0 — 100 Most free
25 · 50 · 75

66.1

Jordan's economic freedom score is 66.1, making its economy the 52nd freest in the 2010 *Index*. Its score has increased by 0.7 point since last year, reflecting improvements in three of the 10 economic freedoms. Jordan is ranked 7th out of 17 countries in the Middle East/North Africa region, and its score is above the world and regional averages.

The Jordanian economy benefits from relatively high levels of trade freedom, fiscal freedom, and investment freedom. Economic reforms have promoted the transition to a more open and flexible economy. Well-developed and increasingly modern, the financial sector has taken steps to meet international standards. In the past five years, the economy has recorded an average annual economic growth rate of over 7 percent.

Sound public finance management and privatization have been key parts of the reform agenda. Total public debt has been reduced to about 60 percent of GDP in 2008 from over 80 percent in 2005. Overall economic freedom is curtailed by such lingering challenges as corruption and the judicial system's vulnerability to political influence.

BACKGROUND: Jordan, which gained its independence from Britain in 1946, is a constitutional monarchy with a relatively well-educated population. The economy is supported to a significant degree by foreign loans, international aid, and remittances from expatriate workers, many of whom work in the Persian Gulf oil kingdoms. King Abdullah II has undertaken political, economic, and regulatory reforms since coming to power in 1999. In 2000, Jordan joined the World Trade Organization and signed a free trade agreement with the United States; in 2001, it signed an association agreement with the European Union. In addition, Qualifying Industrial Zones allow duty-free exports to the United States of goods made with some content from Israel. Ongoing problems include high unemployment, heavy debt, an influx of Iraqi refugees, and the high cost of oil imports.

Country's Score Over Time

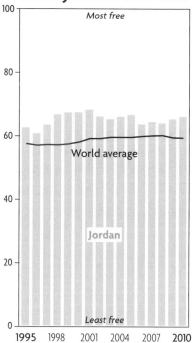

Most free
World average
Jordan
Least free

1995 1998 2001 2004 2007 2010

Quick Facts

Population: 5.9 million

GDP (PPP): $31.2 billion
5.6% growth in 2008
7.2% 5-year compound annual growth
$5,283 per capita

Unemployment: 12.6%

Inflation (CPI): 14.9%

FDI Inflow: $1.9 billion

2008 data unless otherwise noted
Data compiled as of September 2009

How Do We Measure Economic Freedom?
See page 457 for an explanation of the methodology or visit the *Index* Web site at *heritage.org/index.*

JORDAN'S TEN ECONOMIC FREEDOMS

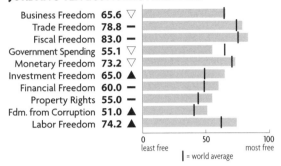

Business Freedom	65.6	▽
Trade Freedom	78.8	—
Fiscal Freedom	83.0	—
Government Spending	55.1	▽
Monetary Freedom	73.2	▽
Investment Freedom	65.0	▲
Financial Freedom	60.0	—
Property Rights	55.0	—
Fdm. from Corruption	51.0	▲
Labor Freedom	74.2	▲

0 least free — 50 — 100 most free
| = world average

BUSINESS FREEDOM — 65.6

The overall freedom to establish and run a business is somewhat restricted by Jordan's regulatory environment. Starting a business takes an average of 13 days, compared to the world average of 35 days, and obtaining a business license requires less than the world average of 218 days. Closing a business, however, is difficult. Despite efforts at reform, bureaucratic obstacles and delays persist.

TRADE FREEDOM — 78.8

Jordan's weighted average tariff rate was 5.6 percent in 2007. Import bans and restrictions, import taxes and fees, licensing requirements, export subsidies, weak enforcement of intellectual property rights, and inefficient customs administration add to the cost of trade. Ten points were deducted from Jordan's trade freedom score to account for non-tariff barriers.

FISCAL FREEDOM — 83

Jordan has moderate tax rates. The top income and corporate tax rates are 25 percent (35 percent for banks and financial institutions). Other taxes include a value-added tax (VAT) and a property tax. In the most recent year, overall tax revenue as a percentage of GDP was 21.1 percent.

GOVERNMENT SPENDING — 55.1

Total government expenditures, including consumption and transfer payments, are relatively high. In the most recent year, government spending equaled 38.7 percent of GDP. Some 19 companies were slated for privatization in 2008. Fiscal policy has been stable and effective. Expenditure reductions, the result of removing barley and fuel subsidies, will be offset by higher capital spending and lower tax revenues.

MONETARY FREEDOM — 73.2

Inflation has been high, averaging 11.8 percent between 2006 and 2008. Most controls have been eliminated, but the government sets prices for electricity, telecommunications, and water. Five points were deducted from Jordan's monetary freedom score to account for policies that distort domestic prices.

INVESTMENT FREEDOM — 65

Foreign and domestic investments receive equal treatment. There is no formal screening, but there are minimum capital requirements. Additionally, foreign investments may not exceed 50 percent in sectors like construction, wholesale and retail trade, transport, import and export services, and advertising. Foreigners may not invest in investigative and security services, sports clubs, stone quarrying, customs clearance services, and land transportation. Excessive bureaucracy, red tape, a judicial system susceptible to political pressure, and inconsistent enforcement of regulations inhibit investment. Residents and non-residents may hold foreign exchange accounts. There are no restrictions or controls on payments, transactions, transfers, or repatriation of profits. Certain real estate purchases require approval.

FINANCIAL FREEDOM — 60

Jordan's fairly well developed financial sector is dominated by banking. Along with financial-sector policies that are intended to enhance competition and efficiency, the government has brought supervision and regulation into line with international standards. More than 20 banks, including nine domestic commercial banks and eight foreign banks, operate in Jordan. The Arab Bank dominates the sector, accounting for about 60 percent of total assets. Government-encouraged consolidation among smaller banks has progressed. The government owns no commercial banks but does own five specialized credit institutions focused on agricultural credit, housing, rural and urban development, and industry. The insurance sector is small but open to foreign competition. Capital markets are not fully developed but are fairly robust by regional standards. An anti–money laundering bill went into effect in July 2007.

PROPERTY RIGHTS — 55

Interest in property (moveable and real) is recognized, enforced, and recorded through reliable legal processes and registries. The legal system protects the acquisition and disposition of all property rights. The judiciary is generally independent, but the king is the ultimate authority. Despite a law passed in 2001 to limit its influence, the Ministry of Justice significantly influences judges' careers. Expropriation is unlikely. Jordan's record in protecting intellectual property rights has improved.

FREEDOM FROM CORRUPTION — 51

Corruption is perceived as present. Jordan ranks 51st out of 179 countries in Transparency International's Corruption Perceptions Index for 2008. Influence peddling and a lack of transparency have been alleged in government procurement and dispute settlement. The use of family, business, and other personal connections to advance personal business interests at the expense of others is endemic and seen by many Jordanians as a normal part of doing business.

LABOR FREEDOM — 74.2

Labor regulations are relatively flexible. The non-salary cost of employing a worker is moderate, but dismissing an employee is not easy. Regulations on work hours are not rigid.

KAZAKHSTAN

World Rank: 82　　　　　　　　　**Regional Rank: 12**

Economic Freedom Score

25　50　75

Least free　0　　　　　　100　Most free

61.0

Kazakhstan's economic freedom score is 61, making its economy the 82nd freest in the 2010 *Index*. Its score is 0.9 point higher than last year, primarily reflecting improvements in business freedom, property rights, and labor freedom. Kazakhstan ranks 12th out of 41 countries in the Asia–Pacific region, and its overall score is above the world and regional averages.

A series of economic reforms, along with high oil prices, allowed Kazakhstan to achieve economic growth of over 8 percent annually over the past five years. However, the global financial turmoil and economic slowdown have taken a considerable toll on the economy. Kazakhstan's financial freedom has eroded, but its fiscal freedom has improved as a result of reduction of the corporate tax rate to 20 percent at the beginning of 2009. Business competitiveness is up as a result.

Challenges to economic freedom remain considerable. The economy exhibits significant shortcomings in three areas: investment freedom, property rights, and freedom from corruption. Foreign investment is hindered by ad hoc barriers and favoritism toward domestic firms. Red tape and overly burdensome restrictions still hamper business freedom. The weak rule of law allows for significant corruption and insecure property rights.

BACKGROUND: Kazakhstan is an important energy and commodity producer in Central Asia and an economic development leader in the region. Oil output is projected to reach 3.5 million barrels a day in 2020. Excessive dependence on commodity exports makes the economy particularly vulnerable to global price changes, and the 2009 global recession has led to weakness and contraction in construction, banking, and commodities. Kazakhstan possesses an estimated 20 percent of the world's uranium reserves, but resource nationalism and corruption encourage investor uncertainty. President Nursultan Nazarbayev's Nur Otan party won all of the seats in the lower house of parliament in 2007, and presidential term limits have been abolished.

Country's Score Over Time

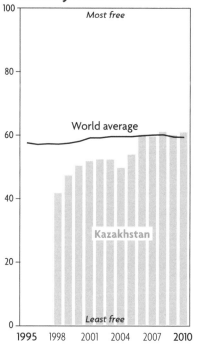

Quick Facts

Population: 15.7 million

GDP (PPP): $177.4 billion
　3.2% growth in 2008
　8.1% 5-year compound
　　annual growth
　$11,315 per capita

Unemployment: 6.6%

Inflation (CPI): 17.2%

FDI Inflow: $14.5 billion

2008 data unless otherwise noted
Data compiled as of September 2009

How Do We Measure Economic Freedom?
See page 457 for an explanation of the methodology or visit the *Index* Web site at *heritage.org/index.*

KAZAKHSTAN'S TEN ECONOMIC FREEDOMS

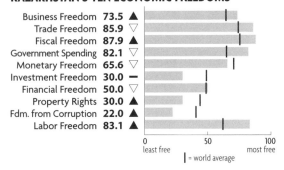

Business Freedom	73.5	▲
Trade Freedom	85.9	▽
Fiscal Freedom	87.9	▲
Government Spending	82.1	▽
Monetary Freedom	65.6	▽
Investment Freedom	30.0	—
Financial Freedom	50.0	▽
Property Rights	30.0	▲
Fdm. from Corruption	22.0	▲
Labor Freedom	83.1	▲

0 least free   50   100 most free

| = world average

BUSINESS FREEDOM — 73.5

The overall freedom to start, operate, and close a business is limited by Kazakhstan's regulatory environment. Starting a business takes an average of 20 days, compared to the world average of 35 days. Obtaining a business license requires more than the world average of 18 procedures, and fees are high.

TRADE FREEDOM — 85.9

Kazakhstan's weighted average tariff rate was 2.1 percent in 2008. Liberalization has progressed, but services market access barriers, import licensing requirements, non-transparent regulations and standards, opaque government procurement, weak enforcement of intellectual property rights, and customs inefficiency and complexity add to the cost of trade. Ten points were deducted from Kazakhstan's trade freedom score to account for non-tariff barriers.

FISCAL FREEDOM — 87.9

Kazakhstan has a low income tax rate and a relatively low corporate tax rate. The flat income tax rate is 10 percent, and the standard corporate tax rate has been reduced to 20 percent from 30 percent. Other taxes include a value-added tax (VAT), property tax, excise taxes, and a minerals extraction tax implemented in 2009. In the most recent year, overall tax revenue as a percentage of GDP was 26.7 percent.

GOVERNMENT SPENDING — 82.1

Total government expenditures, including consumption and transfer payments, are relatively low. In the most recent year, government spending equaled 24.4 percent of GDP. Much of the economy is now in private hands, but government economic intervention will continue to rise under the Action Plan 2009.

MONETARY FREEDOM — 65.6

Inflation has been high, averaging 14.8 percent between 2006 and 2008. The market sets most prices, but the government retains the right to control prices, influences them through state-owned enterprises and manufacturing subsidies, and has made little progress in promoting competition in agriculture. Ten points were deducted from Kazakhstan's monetary freedom score to account for policies that distort domestic prices.

INVESTMENT FREEDOM — 30

The government plays a large role in overseeing foreign investment. Screening of foreign investment proposals is often non-transparent, arbitrary, and slow, and foreign ownership in some sectors is limited. An investor may be obligated to use local content in production or to train local specialists and contribute to the social development of the region. An unclear legal code, legislative favoritism toward Kazakh companies, inconsistent application of investment regulations, and government interference in commercial operations further deter investment. Subject to restrictions, foreign exchange accounts may be held by residents and non-residents. Most capital transactions, payments, and transfers are permitted with few restrictions. The Investment Law of 2003 weakened protections related to expropriation and compensation and provides no clear guidance for either process. Land ownership is restricted.

FINANCIAL FREEDOM — 50

Although Kazakhstan's financial sector had experienced deeper reforms than other areas of the economy, the global financial crisis has revealed continuing weaknesses in regulation and supervision. Domestic banks expanded rapidly on the back of foreign borrowing, and much of their lending was directed to construction and real estate development. Weak risk management and overexposure to the property market have taken a severe toll on the country's banking stability. Non-performing loans reached about 10 percent in early 2009, and in the face of systemic risk, the government stepped in, taking up to a 25 percent stake in each of the four largest troubled banks. Capital markets remain underdeveloped, though the bond market has been growing. The insurance sector is small, and foreign companies are limited to joint ventures with local companies.

PROPERTY RIGHTS — 30

Most legal disputes arise from breaches of contract or non-payment by the government. Corruption is widespread, and the judiciary views itself more as an arm of the executive than as an enforcer of contracts or property rights. Some foreign investors encounter serious problems short of expropriation. Piracy of copyrighted products is widespread, and enforcement of intellectual property rights is weak.

FREEDOM FROM CORRUPTION — 22

Corruption is perceived as pervasive. Kazakhstan ranks 145th out of 179 countries in Transparency International's Corruption Perceptions Index for 2008. Corruption is a significant obstacle to investment, and law enforcement agencies occasionally pressure foreign investors to cooperate with government demands.

LABOR FREEDOM — 83.1

Kazakhstan's labor regulations are flexible. The non-salary cost of employing a worker is moderate, and dismissing an employee is not costly. Regulations on work hours can be rigid.

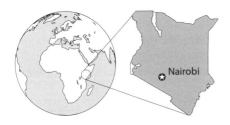

KENYA

Economic Freedom Score

25 — 50 — 75
Least free 0 — 100 Most free

57.5

World Rank: 101   **Regional Rank: 13**

Kenya's economic freedom score is 57.5, making its economy the 101st freest in the 2010 *Index*. Its score has decreased by 1.2 points since last year, reflecting slight deterioration in trade freedom, monetary freedom, and business freedom. Kenya is ranked 13th out of 46 countries in the Sub-Saharan Africa region, and its overall score is below the world average.

Kenya is one of Africa's most developed economies and has a tradition of private-sector entrepreneurial activity. Domestic debt as a percentage of GDP has been declining incrementally in recent years, and there have been a number of initial public offerings and some divestment of state-owned enterprises. Reforms in public financial management have continued, though progress has been sluggish.

Lax property rights and extensive corruption limit Kenya's overall economic freedom. Corruption is perceived as pervasive, giving Kenya one of the world's lower scores in this vital area. Non-transparent trade regulations and customs inefficiency hurt overall trade freedom. As in many other Sub-Saharan African nations, Kenya's judiciary is underdeveloped and subject to political influence.

BACKGROUND: Kenya was a one-party state until 1992. Widespread violence followed the 2007 election when both Mwai Kibaki, who had won the presidency in 2002, and rival Raila Odinga claimed victory. After months of negotiations, they agreed to a power-sharing arrangement. Corruption remains commonplace despite government pledges to combat it. Kenya is the transportation, communication, and financial hub of East Africa. Economic growth, hindered for decades by government mismanagement, counterproductive economic policies, and corruption, was improving before the instability that followed the 2007 election. Civil service reform has been slow, and the government employs about one-third of the formal labor force. According to the Kenya Bureau of Statistics, nearly 80 percent of employment is informal. Agriculture accounts for about a quarter of GDP and employs a majority of the population.

Country's Score Over Time

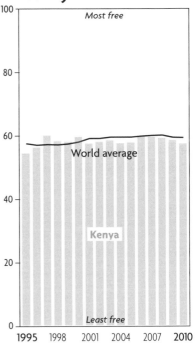

Quick Facts

Population: 38.5 million

GDP (PPP): $61.3 billion
3.6% growth in 2008
5.3% 5-year compound annual growth
$1,590 per capita

Unemployment: 40%

Inflation (CPI): 13.1%

FDI Inflow: $96.0 million

2008 data unless otherwise noted
Data compiled as of September 2009

How Do We Measure Economic Freedom?
See page 457 for an explanation of the methodology or visit the *Index* Web site at *heritage.org/index.*

KENYA'S TEN ECONOMIC FREEDOMS

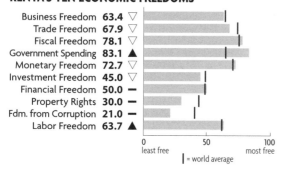

Business Freedom	63.4 ▽	
Trade Freedom	67.9 ▽	
Fiscal Freedom	78.1 ▽	
Government Spending	83.1 ▲	
Monetary Freedom	72.7 ▽	
Investment Freedom	45.0 ▽	
Financial Freedom	50.0 —	
Property Rights	30.0 —	
Fdm. from Corruption	21.0 —	
Labor Freedom	63.7 ▲	

0 least free   50   100 most free
| = world average

BUSINESS FREEDOM — 63.4

The overall freedom to start, operate, and close a business is relatively respected under Kenya's regulatory environment. Starting a business takes an average of 34 days, compared to the world average of 35 days. Obtaining a business license requires less than the world average of 18 procedures. Closing a business is lengthy and costly.

TRADE FREEDOM — 67.9

Kenya's weighted average tariff rate was 8.6 percent in 2008. Import and export bans and restrictions, import and export taxes, import and export licensing requirements, non-transparent and restrictive regulations, opaque government procurement, subsidies, weak enforcement of intellectual property rights, and customs corruption add to the cost of trade. Fifteen points were deducted from Kenya's trade freedom score to account for non-tariff barriers.

FISCAL FREEDOM — 78.1

Kenya has moderate income and corporate tax rates. The top income and corporate tax rates are 30 percent. Other taxes include a value-added tax (VAT) and a tax on interest. In the most recent year, overall tax revenue as a percentage of GDP was 19.7 percent.

GOVERNMENT SPENDING — 83.1

Total government expenditures, including consumption and transfer payments, are relatively low. In the most recent year, government spending equaled 23.7 percent of GDP. A special panel has been formed to oversee the divestment of 16 state-owned enterprises.

MONETARY FREEDOM — 72.7

Inflation has been high, averaging 12.4 percent between 2006 and 2008. Price controls were officially dismantled in 1994, but the government reserves the right to set maximum prices in certain cases and influences prices through agricultural marketing boards and state-owned utilities and enterprises. Five points were deducted from Kenya's monetary freedom score to account for policies that distort domestic prices.

INVESTMENT FREEDOM — 45

Foreign and local investors generally receive equal treatment, but there are exceptions. The government screens private-sector projects to determine their viability and implications for national development. Private foreign and domestic investments are constrained in certain sectors to include those where state corporations have a statutory monopoly. There is a minimum foreign investment threshold, and foreign investors must sign an agreement defining training arrangements intended to phase out expatriates. Poor infrastructure, restrictive labor laws, burdensome regulation, inefficient bureaucracy, and crime are disincentives. Residents and non-residents may hold foreign exchange accounts. There are no controls or requirements on payments and transfers. Most capital transactions are permitted, but the sale or issue of capital and money market instruments may require government approval. Real estate purchases by non-residents are subject to government approval.

FINANCIAL FREEDOM — 50

Kenya's financial system remains vulnerable to government influence and inadequate supervision. The five largest banks account for just over 50 percent of assets. The government owns or holds shares in several other domestic financial institutions and influences the allocation of credit. Non-performing loans, particularly from state-owned banks to state-owned enterprises, remain a problem but have been declining. The 45 financial institutions include two Islamic banking institutions that came into operation in 2008. About 20 percent of the adult population has bank accounts and access to formal financial services. The Microfinance Act took effect in 2008. Capital markets are relatively small, and just over 50 companies are listed on the Nairobi Stock Exchange. Foreign investors may acquire shares in the stock market, subject to specified limits.

PROPERTY RIGHTS — 30

Kenya's judicial system is modeled on the British system. Commercial courts deal with commercial cases. Enforcement of property and contractual rights is subject to long delays. The process for acquiring land titles is often non-transparent and cumbersome. Courts generally do not permit sales of land by mortgage lenders to collect debts. Protection of intellectual property rights is weak.

FREEDOM FROM CORRUPTION — 21

Corruption is perceived as pervasive. Kenya ranks 147th out of 179 countries in Transparency International's Corruption Perceptions Index for 2008. Corruption has led to foreign disinvestment and has drained resources needed for education, health, and infrastructure. Kenyans view the police as the most corrupt public institution. Corruption involving food and fuel oil may have far-reaching consequences as the administration of President Kibaki tries to tackle a looming food crisis. The government has taken some halting steps to address judicial corruption.

LABOR FREEDOM — 63.7

Labor regulations are relatively rigid. The non-salary cost of employing a worker is relatively low, but dismissing an employee can be costly.

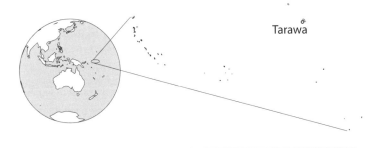

Tarawa

KIRIBATI

Economic Freedom Score

25   50   75

Least free 0   100 Most free

43.7

World Rank: 166   **Regional Rank: 37**

K iribati's economic freedom score is 43.7, making its economy the 166th freest in the 2010 *Index*. Its score has decreased by 2 points since last year, reflecting deterioration in freedom from corruption and monetary freedom. Kiribati is ranked 37th out of 41 countries in the Asia–Pacific region, and its overall score is below the world and regional averages.

The Kiribati economy is dominated by a large public sector that accounts for two-thirds of employment and about half of GDP. Only about 10 percent of the population is employed on wages or salaries; the rest work in subsistence farming or fishing. The economy relies heavily on foreign assistance and remittances. The country has undergone a period of fiscal pressure in light of monetary instability combined with falling external income.

Challenges to overall economic freedom remain daunting, and geographical remoteness increases the costs of interaction with the world economy. Economic growth potentials are also undermined by a glut of state-owned enterprises and regulations that hinder private-sector development. The government has made efforts to decentralize economic activity from the main islands, but progress has been very limited. The financial sector remains underdeveloped, leaving a large portion of the population without formal access to banking services. Corruption also poses considerable impediments to entrepreneurial activity.

BACKGROUND: An archipelago spread across the equator in the Pacific, Kiribati gained its independence from Britain in 1979 and enjoys democratic government under a national constitution. President Anote Tong was elected to a second term in 2007. Kiribati was once rich in phosphates and highly dependent on mining, but deposits were exhausted in 1979. Today, it depends on a $500 million Revenue Equalization Reserve Fund created with the profits from phosphates earnings, foreign assistance, remittances from overseas, sale of fishing licenses, and exports of fish and coconuts.

Country's Score Over Time

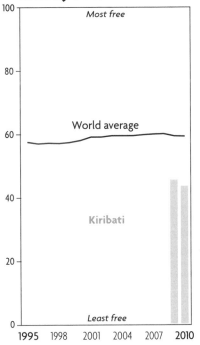

Quick Facts

Population: 0.1 million

GDP (PPP): $0.2 billion
3.4% growth in 2008
1.7% 5-year compound annual growth
$2,484 per capita

Unemployment: n/a

Inflation (CPI): 11.0%

FDI Inflow: $2.0 million

2008 data unless otherwise noted
Data compiled as of September 2009

How Do We Measure Economic Freedom?
See page 457 for an explanation of the methodology or visit the *Index* Web site at *heritage.org/index.*

KIRIBATI'S TEN ECONOMIC FREEDOMS

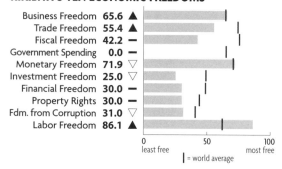

Business Freedom	65.6 ▲	
Trade Freedom	55.4 ▲	
Fiscal Freedom	42.2 —	
Government Spending	0.0 —	
Monetary Freedom	71.9 ▽	
Investment Freedom	25.0 ▽	
Financial Freedom	30.0 —	
Property Rights	30.0 —	
Fdm. from Corruption	31.0 ▽	
Labor Freedom	86.1 ▲	

0 least free   50   100 most free

❙ = world average

BUSINESS FREEDOM — 65.6

The overall freedom to establish and run a business remains constrained by Kiribati's regulatory environment. Starting a business takes an average of 21 days, compared to the world average of 35 days, and obtaining a business license requires less than the world average of 218 days, but the entry cost of launching a business is quite high.

TRADE FREEDOM — 55.4

Kiribati's simple average tariff rate was 17.3 percent in 2007. Weak regulatory capacity, some import and export licensing, limited infrastructure, and significant geographic isolation add to the cost of trade. Ten points were deducted from Kiribati's trade freedom score to account for non-tariff barriers.

FISCAL FREEDOM — 42.2

Kiribati has relatively high taxes. The top income and corporate tax rates are 35 percent. In the most recent year, overall tax revenue, including revenue from fishing licenses, was equivalent to 69.7 percent of GDP.

GOVERNMENT SPENDING — 0

Total government expenditures, including consumption and transfer payments, are exceedingly high. In the most recent year, government spending equaled 119.4 percent of GDP. Budget management is poor. The Revenue Equalization Reserve Fund (an offshore investment fund) returns investment income equal to about 33 percent of GDP and continues to underwrite government recurrent expenditure, reducing the incentive to constrain spending.

MONETARY FREEDOM — 71.9

Inflation has been relatively high, averaging 8.2 percent between 2006 and 2008. After many years of minimal inflation (partly reflecting use of the Australian dollar as the domestic currency), surging prices for oil and other commodities increased inflationary pressure in 2008. The government maintains price controls on petroleum products and other basic commodities. Ten points were deducted from Kiribati's monetary freedom score to adjust for measures that distort domestic prices.

INVESTMENT FREEDOM — 25

Foreign investment is generally granted national treat-

ment. All foreign investment is screened and subject to various levels of approval, depending on the size of the proposal. Certain sectors are reserved for domestic activity. On average, it takes two to three months for a project to be approved, after which the government establishes criteria that the investor must fulfill with regard to employment, technology transfer, local content, and other requirements. Regulatory administration is ad hoc, limited, and non-transparent. Investment is limited by Kiribati's geographic isolation, limited infrastructure, and small markets. There are no controls on foreign exchange or capital transactions. Foreign investors may lease but not own land.

FINANCIAL FREEDOM — 30

Kiribati's small financial sector remains underdeveloped and dominated by banking. High credit costs and scarce access to financing severely impede entrepreneurial activity and development of the private sector. A large proportion of the population remains outside the formal banking system. The economy is burdened by a public sector that accounts for close to half of GDP, and state-directed lending to public enterprises remains considerable. A high level of non-performing loans, estimated at about one-third of total loans, continues to distress the financial system. There are two banks operating in Kiribati. The Bank of Kiribati, in which the government has 25 percent ownership, is the only commercial bank and has only four branches. The Development Bank of Kiribati generally lends to small businesses. Capital markets are underdeveloped and inefficient, offering a very limited range of financing options for the private sector.

PROPERTY RIGHTS — 30

The protection of movable property is secured by law and the courts. Land rights in cases of real property that is not owned by the government can be particularly complex and are subject to traditional land rights constraints. Non-citizens may not own land. The magistrates' courts have original jurisdiction in all cases involving land. Appeals of land cases are heard by the High Court.

FREEDOM FROM CORRUPTION — 31

Corruption is perceived as significant. Kiribati ranks 96th out of 179 countries in Transparency International's Corruption Perceptions Index for 2008. Laws providing criminal penalties for official corruption have not been implemented effectively, and government officials sometimes engage in corrupt practices with impunity. Nepotism based on tribal, church, and family ties is prevalent.

LABOR FREEDOM — 86.1

Kiribati's labor regulations are flexible. However, the formal labor market is not fully developed, and only a small share of the total labor force participates in the formal economy. The government is the major source of employment, providing jobs in public service and state-owned enterprises.

DEMOCRATIC PEOPLE'S REPUBLIC OF **KOREA**
(NORTH KOREA)

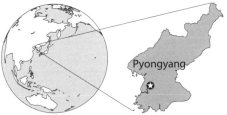

Pyongyang

World Rank: 179　　　　**Regional Rank: 41**

Economic Freedom Score

25　50　75

Least free 0 ⎯⎯⎯⎯ 100 Most free

1.0

North Korea's economic freedom score is 1.0, making its economy the least free in the 2010 *Index*. North Korea is ranked 41st out of 41 countries in the Asia–Pacific region.

North Korea scores some minimal points only in property rights and freedom from corruption. The Communist Party controls and commands almost every aspect of economic activity. Since the early 1990s, North Korea has replaced the doctrine of Marxism–Leninism with the late Kim Il-Sung's *juche* (self-reliance) as the official state ideology. The country's impoverished population is heavily dependent on government subsidies in housing and food rations even though the state-run rationing system has deteriorated significantly in recent years.

North Korea devotes a disproportionately large share of GDP to military spending, further exacerbating the country's already poor economic situation. Normal foreign trade is minimal, with China and South Korea being the most important trading partners. No courts are independent of political interference, and private property (particularly land) is strictly regulated by the state. Corruption is rampant but hard to distinguish from regular economic activity in a system in which arbitrary government control is the norm.

BACKGROUND: The Democratic People's Republic of Korea is an oppressed and closed society. Ever since the country's founding in 1948, its Communist rulers have denied citizens basic human rights and maintained ownership of all industry. The government imposes grossly ineffective agricultural and industrial policies that keep consumption at subsistence levels. Belligerent foreign policies and actions, including a quest to develop nuclear weapons in violation of U.N. resolutions, have led to international sanctions that reinforce North Korea's political and economic isolation. Pyongyang remains heavily reliant on economic support from China.

Country's Score Over Time

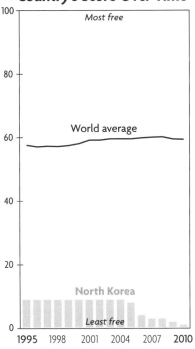

Quick Facts

Population: 23.9 million

GDP (nominal): $26.2 billion
　　　　(2008 estimate)
　　　　Growth in 2008 n/a
　　　　5-year compound
　　　　　annual growth n/a
　　　　Per capita n/a

Unemployment: n/a

Inflation (CPI): n/a

FDI Inflow: n/a

*2008 data unless otherwise noted
Data compiled as of September 2009*

How Do We Measure Economic Freedom?
See page 457 for an explanation of the methodology or visit the *Index* Web site at *heritage.org/index*.

NORTH KOREA'S TEN ECONOMIC FREEDOMS

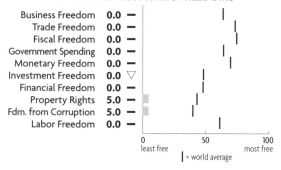

Business Freedom	0.0	
Trade Freedom	0.0	
Fiscal Freedom	0.0	
Government Spending	0.0	
Monetary Freedom	0.0	
Investment Freedom	0.0	
Financial Freedom	0.0	
Property Rights	5.0	
Fdm. from Corruption	5.0	
Labor Freedom	0.0	

0 least free — 50 — 100 most free
| = world average

BUSINESS FREEDOM — 0

The overall freedom to start, operate, and close a business is extremely restricted by North Korea's national regulatory environment. The state regulates the economy heavily through central planning. Economic reforms implemented in 2002 allegedly brought some changes at the enterprise and industrial levels, but entrepreneurial activity is still virtually impossible.

TRADE FREEDOM — 0

The government controls all imports and exports, and formal trade is minimal. North Korean trade statistics are limited and compiled from trading partners' data. Most trade is de facto aid, mainly from North Korea's two main trading partners, China and South Korea. Non-tariff barriers are significant. Inter-Korean trade remains constrained by North Korea's unwillingness to implement needed reform. Given the minimal level of trade, a score of zero was assigned.

FISCAL FREEDOM — 0

No data on income or corporate tax rates are available because no effective tax system is in place. The government plans and manages almost every part of the economy. Given the absence of published official macroeconomic data, such figures as are available with respect to North Korea's government revenues are suspect and outdated.

GOVERNMENT SPENDING — 0

The government owns virtually all property and sets production levels for most products, and state-owned industries account for nearly all GDP. The state directs all significant economic activity. Large military spending further drains scarce resources.

MONETARY FREEDOM — 0

North Korea stopped publishing economic statistics as long ago as the 1960s, when its rapid early growth began to slow. Price and wage reforms introduced in July 2002 consisted of reducing government subsidies and telling producers to charge prices that more closely reflect costs. Without matching supply-side measures to boost output, the result has been rampant inflation for many staple goods. Because of the ongoing crisis in agriculture, the government has banned sales of grain at markets and returned to rationing. Reports indicate that the effort to reassert state control and to control inflation has been largely ineffective. A score of zero was assigned.

INVESTMENT FREEDOM — 0

North Korea generally does not welcome foreign investment. A small number of projects may be approved by top levels of government, but the scale of these investments is also small. Numerous countries employ sanctions against North Korea, and ongoing political and security concerns make investment extremely hazardous. Internal laws do not allow for international dispute arbitration. North Korea allows limited foreign participation in the economy through special economic zones located at Rajin-Sonbong, Mount Kumgang, and Kaesong. Aside from these few economic zones where investment is approved on a case-by-case basis, foreign investment is prohibited.

FINANCIAL FREEDOM — 0

North Korea is a command-and-control economy with virtually no functioning financial sector. Access to financing is very limited and constrained by the country's failed economy. The central bank also serves as a commercial bank and had more than 200 local branches in 2007. The government provides most funding for industries and takes a percentage from enterprises. Foreign aid agencies have set up microcredit schemes to lend to farmers and small businesses. A rumored overhaul of the financial system to permit firms to borrow from banks instead of receiving state-directed capital has not materialized.

PROPERTY RIGHTS — 5

Property rights are not guaranteed. Almost all property, including nearly all real property, belongs to the state, and the judiciary is not independent. The government even controls all chattel property (domestically produced goods as well as all imports and exports).

FREEDOM FROM CORRUPTION — 5

After the mid-1990s economic collapse and subsequent famines, North Korea developed an immense informal market, especially in agricultural goods. Informal trading with China in currency and goods is active. There are many indicators of corruption in the government and security forces. Military and government officials reportedly divert food aid from international donors and demand bribes before distributing it.

LABOR FREEDOM — 0

As the main source of employment, the state determines wages. Since the 2002 economic reforms, factory managers have had limited autonomy to set wages and offer incentives, but highly restrictive government regulations hinder any employment and productivity growth.

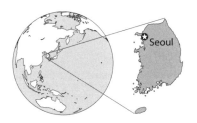
Seoul

REPUBLIC OF **KOREA**
(SOUTH KOREA)

Economic Freedom Score

Least free 0   100 Most free

69.9

S outh Korea's economic freedom score is 69.9, making its economy the 31st freest in the 2010 *Index*. Its overall score has increased by 1.8 points, reflecting improved scores in fiscal freedom, financial freedom, and trade freedom. South Korea is ranked 8th out of 41 countries in the Asia–Pacific region.

South Korea's export-oriented economy, which is one of Asia's most vibrant and successful, scores above the world average in nine of the 10 economic freedoms. It has long benefited from relative openness to global trade and investment, and South Korea has been pursuing additional trade agreements, including agreements with the United States, India, and the European Union. The overall regulatory environment has gradually become more efficient and transparent. Improving the efficiency of the tax system and making tax rates more competitive have been part of the government's reform agenda. Property rights and the rule of law are well maintained in a transparent manner.

The impact of the global financial turmoil on the banking sector has been relatively modest; monetary stability is relatively well maintained, and inflation is under control. South Korea's overall economic freedom is limited by lingering corruption and a low level of labor freedom. The labor market remains rigid despite some efforts by government to enhance flexibility.

BACKGROUND: South Korea is one of Asia's liveliest democracies and the world's 15th largest economy. In the years since South Korea's transition to democracy in 1988, the economy has been dominated to a significant extent by large conglomerates, or *chaebols*. The country has sophisticated electronics, telecommunications, automobile, and shipbuilding industries. President Lee Myung-bak, who took office in 2008 with a large electoral majority, vowed to liberalize the economy further through freer trade, deregulation, and the privatization of major industries, but he has been stymied by militant labor unions, fierce political opposition, and protectionism.

Country's Score Over Time

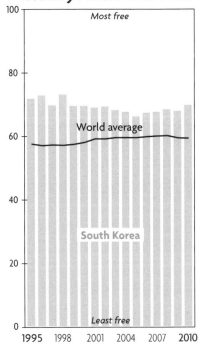

Quick Facts

Population: 48.6 million

GDP (PPP): $1.4 trillion
   2.2% growth in 2008
   4.1% 5-year compound
      annual growth
   $27,939 per capita

Unemployment: 3.2%

Inflation (CPI): 4.7%

FDI Inflow: $7.6 billion

2008 data unless otherwise noted
Data compiled as of September 2009

How Do We Measure Economic Freedom?
See page 457 for an explanation of the methodology or visit the *Index* Web site at *heritage.org/index.*

SOUTH KOREA'S TEN ECONOMIC FREEDOMS

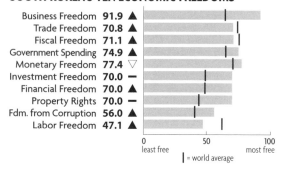

Business Freedom	91.9 ▲	
Trade Freedom	70.8 ▲	
Fiscal Freedom	71.1 ▲	
Government Spending	74.9 ▲	
Monetary Freedom	77.4 ▽	
Investment Freedom	70.0 —	
Financial Freedom	70.0 ▲	
Property Rights	70.0 —	
Fdm. from Corruption	56.0 ▲	
Labor Freedom	47.1 ▲	

0 least free   50   100 most free

| = world average

BUSINESS FREEDOM — *91.9*

The overall freedom to conduct a business is well protected under South Korea's regulatory environment. Starting a business takes an average of 14 days, compared to the world average of 35 days. Obtaining a business license requires much less than the world average of 18 procedures and 218 days. Closing a business is easy.

TRADE FREEDOM — *70.8*

South Korea's weighted average tariff rate was 7.1 percent in 2007. Some prohibitive tariffs, import and export restrictions, services market access barriers, import taxes, use of "adjustment" tariffs and taxes, burdensome and non-transparent standards and regulations, state trading, and subsidies add to the cost of trade. Fifteen points were deducted from South Korea's trade freedom score to account for non-tariff barriers.

FISCAL FREEDOM — *71.1*

The top income tax rate is 38.5 percent (35 percent plus a 10 percent resident surtax), and the top corporate tax rate has been reduced to 22 percent. Companies are also subject to a 10 percent resident surtax. Other taxes include a value-added tax (VAT), a capital acquisitions tax on certain items, and a property tax. In the most recent year, overall tax revenue as a percentage of GDP was 28.7 percent.

GOVERNMENT SPENDING — *74.9*

Total government expenditures, including consumption and transfer payments, are moderate. In the most recent year, government spending equaled 28.9 percent of GDP. Public debt is holding at about 30 percent of GDP but likely will rise as a result of two waves of stimulus spending during the recent recession.

MONETARY FREEDOM — *77.4*

Inflation has been moderate, averaging 3.9 percent between 2006 and 2008. Korean monetary policy has adjusted quickly to evolving international inflationary and deflationary pressures. The government can control prices on several products by emergency decree; can cap prices on key raw materials; and regulates or controls prices in certain sectors, including agriculture, telecommunications, other utilities, pharmaceuticals and medical services, and some energy products. Ten points were deducted from South Korea's monetary freedom score to account for policies that distort domestic prices.

INVESTMENT FREEDOM — *70*

The investment climate is increasingly open, but media, electric power, newspapers, fishing, power generation, airline transport, certain agricultural sectors, and a few other sectors remain restricted. Relevant ministries must approve investments in restricted sectors. Non-transparent and burdensome regulation, inflexible labor laws, and the lingering economic influence of large conglomerates undermine investment. Legal disputes can be complex, time-consuming, and expensive. Residents and non-residents may hold foreign exchange accounts. Payments, transfers, and repatriation of profits are subject to reporting requirements or restrictions on amounts for specified periods. Foreign individuals and corporations share the same rights as Koreans in purchasing and using land.

FINANCIAL FREEDOM — *70*

South Korea's modern financial sector has become more open and competitive, providing positive momentum for reforms in other sectors. Reforms have focused largely on improving transparency and efficiency and ending state-directed lending. Since the late 1990s, the government has succeeded in recapitalizing banks and non-bank financial institutions. Weak institutions have been closed or merged, and non-performing loans have decreased considerably. Foreign banks own majority stakes in major commercial banks, though foreign ownership remains restricted. The government has been selling its shares in private banks but retains some ownership positions. Capital markets are sophisticated and well developed. Despite considerable strain caused by the global financial crisis, the banking sector has weathered the financial turmoil relatively well, with government capital injections into the banking sector more modest than in other major countries. The Capital Market Consolidation Act, which removes about one-third of 300 financial regulations, came into force early in 2009.

PROPERTY RIGHTS — *70*

Private property is secure, and expropriation is highly unlikely, but the justice system can be inefficient and slow. The protection of intellectual property rights needs to be improved, as piracy of copyrighted material is significant.

FREEDOM FROM CORRUPTION — *56*

Corruption is perceived as present. South Korea ranks 40th out of 179 countries in Transparency International's Corruption Perceptions Index for 2008. Corruption is fostered by non-transparent rulemaking; exclusionary social, political, and business structures; and insufficient institutional checks and balances.

LABOR FREEDOM — *47.1*

Labor regulations are burdensome. The non-salary cost of employing a worker is moderate, but dismissing an employee is costly. Regulations on work hours are inflexible.

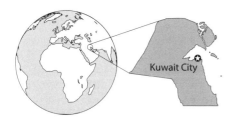

Kuwait City

KUWAIT

World Rank: 42   **Regional Rank: 3**

Kuwait's economic freedom score is 67.7, making its economy the 42nd freest in the 2010 *Index*. Its score is 2.1 points higher than last year, mainly because of improved scores in trade freedom and investment freedom. Kuwait is ranked 3rd out of 17 countries in the Middle East/North Africa region, and its overall score is well above the world and regional averages.

The Kuwaiti economy performs relatively well in many of the 10 components of economic freedom and significantly better than the world average in fiscal freedom and labor freedom. There is no income tax, and corporate taxes are more competitive since the 2008 reduction. Scores for investment freedom and financial freedom are about the world average.

Kuwait is a major energy producer, and high oil revenues have delayed privatization and other structural reforms that were intended to diversify the economy. Kuwait scores slightly below the world average in monetary freedom. The global financial turmoil necessitated a liquidity injection into the banking system, which is now relatively stabilized.

BACKGROUND: Kuwait, an oil-rich Arab constitutional monarchy, gained its independence from Britain in 1961. Occupied in 1990 by Iraq, it was liberated by a U.S.-led coalition in 1991. With an estimated 104 billion barrels of oil reserves, Kuwait controls roughly 10 percent of the world's oil supply. Oil accounts for nearly 50 percent of GDP and 95 percent of export revenues. The Al-Sabah dynasty has used state-owned oil revenues to build modern infrastructure and a cradle-to-grave welfare system for Kuwait's small population. Former Prime Minister Sabah al-Ahmad al-Jabr al-Sabah, chosen amir in January 2006, remains committed to cautious economic reform but faces opposition from Islamist and populist members of parliament. The May 2009 elections weakened Sunni Islamist parties, increased Shiite representation, and for the first time added four women to the 50-seat parliament.

Country's Score Over Time

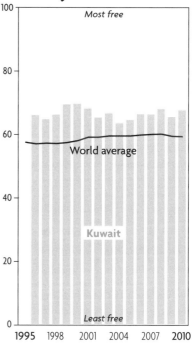

Quick Facts

Population: 3.4 million

GDP (PPP): $137.4 billion
2.5% growth in 2008
6.1% 5-year compound annual growth
$39,914 per capita

Unemployment: 5.7%

Inflation (CPI): 10.5%

FDI Inflow: $56 million

2008 data unless otherwise noted
Data compiled as of September 2009

How Do We Measure Economic Freedom?
See page 457 for an explanation of the methodology or visit the *Index* Web site at *heritage.org/index.*

KUWAIT'S TEN ECONOMIC FREEDOMS

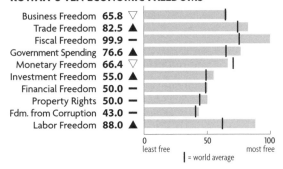

Business Freedom	65.8	▽
Trade Freedom	82.5	▲
Fiscal Freedom	99.9	—
Government Spending	76.6	▲
Monetary Freedom	66.4	▽
Investment Freedom	55.0	▲
Financial Freedom	50.0	—
Property Rights	50.0	—
Fdm. from Corruption	43.0	—
Labor Freedom	88.0	▲

0 least free — 50 — 100 most free
| = world average

BUSINESS FREEDOM — 65.8

The overall freedom to start, operate, and close a business is relatively well protected by Kuwait's regulatory environment. Starting a business takes 35 days, equal to the world average. Obtaining a business license takes slightly more than the world average of 18 procedures.

TRADE FREEDOM — 82.5

Kuwait's weighted average tariff rate was 3.7 percent in 2008. Some prohibitive tariffs, import restrictions, services market access barriers, import licensing requirements, local preference in government procurement, restrictive regulations and standards, and weak enforcement of intellectual property rights add to the cost of trade. Ten points were deducted from Kuwait's trade freedom score to account for non-tariff barriers.

FISCAL FREEDOM — 99.9

Kuwait does not tax individual or domestic business income. Foreign-owned firms and joint ventures are the only businesses that are subject to corporate income tax, which is now a flat 15 percent. There is no value-added tax (VAT). In the most recent year, overall tax revenue (mainly from duties on international trade and transactions) was 3.1 percent of GDP.

GOVERNMENT SPENDING — 76.6

Total government expenditures, including consumption and transfer payments, are moderate. In the most recent year, government spending equaled 27.9 percent of GDP. Planned privatizations are unlikely to occur given parliamentary opposition.

MONETARY FREEDOM — 66.4

Inflation has been relatively high, averaging 8.6 percent between 2006 and 2008. The U.S. dollar makes up much of the undisclosed, trade-weighted basket of currencies to which the dinar is pegged, owing to the predominance of dollar-denominated oil exports in the trade account. The government provides numerous subsidies and controls prices through state-owned utilities and enterprises, including telecommunications, ports, and transportation. Fifteen points were deducted from Kuwait's monetary freedom score to account for policies that distort domestic prices.

INVESTMENT FREEDOM — 55

Kuwait is open to foreign investment, but all proposals are screened and require government approval, and certain sectors are restricted to domestic entities. Licenses are required to establish new companies, but they can be time-consuming to acquire. Bureaucracy is often inefficient and non-transparent, and it can be biased in favor of domestic interests. Residents and non-residents may hold foreign exchange accounts, and there are no restrictions or controls on payments, transactions, transfers, or repatriation of profits. Non–Gulf Cooperation Council (GCC) citizens may not own land.

FINANCIAL FREEDOM — 50

Kuwait's financial system is relatively well developed and offers a full range of financial services for commercial transactions. There are seven commercial banks, six branches of foreign banks, three Islamic banks, and one specialized bank. The government intends to privatize its stakes in several commercial banks. Credit is generally allocated on market terms. The central bank has improved its supervision, ensuring fairer and more efficient credit distribution. Foreign banks may establish operations in Kuwait but are confined to a single branch. The global financial turmoil has put considerable pressure on the financial sector. In late 2008, with its loss on derivative transactions over $1 billion, the third-largest bank (Gulf Bank) was bailed out by the authorities, who took steps to guarantee customer deposits at local banks and implement a recapitalization plan. Defaulting on most of its $3 billion debt obligations, Kuwait's largest investment company was forced to undergo a debt restructuring.

PROPERTY RIGHTS — 50

The constitution provides for an independent judiciary, but the amir appoints all judges. The majority are non-citizens, and renewal of their appointments is subject to government approval. Foreign residents frequently claim that the courts favor Kuwaitis. Trials are lengthy. The Council of Ministers is considering patent and copyright legislation, and the government intends to implement proposed GCC-wide standards and trademark legislation, both of which would require parliamentary approval.

FREEDOM FROM CORRUPTION — 43

Corruption is perceived as significant. Kuwait ranks 65th out of 179 countries in Transparency International's Corruption Perceptions Index for 2008. The executive, legislative, and judicial branches are widely perceived as subject to corruption. In 2009, several investigations and trials involved current or former government officials accused of malfeasance. There have been no convictions for bribery since the end of the Gulf War in 1991.

LABOR FREEDOM — 88

Labor regulations are flexible. The non-salary cost of employing a worker is low, but dismissing an employee can be costly. There is no private-sector minimum wage. Restrictions on work hours can be rigid.

KYRGYZ REPUBLIC

Economic Freedom Score

25   50   75

Least
free   0   100   Most
free

61.3

World Rank: **80**	Regional Rank: **11**

The Kyrgyz Republic's economic freedom score is 61.3, making its economy the 80th freest in the 2010 *Index*. Its score is 0.5 point worse than last year, reflecting decreases in trade freedom and freedom from corruption. The Kyrgyz Republic is ranked 11th out of 41 countries in the Asia–Pacific region, and its overall score is slightly above the world average.

The Kyrgyz Republic's transition to greater economic freedom has progressed slowly. Some reforms have been implemented, but overall progress has been uneven. The country rates relatively well in business freedom, fiscal freedom, labor freedom, and government spending. The labor market is flexible; despite some remaining restrictions, implementation of a new labor code has helped to tailor employment to free-market conditions. Taxation has been simplified with a competitive personal and corporate flat rate of 10 percent. Government spending is also moderate. A new law governing internal audits of government agencies and institutions establishes a framework for conducting audits in line with international best practice.

The Kyrgyz Republic's property rights and freedom from corruption remain weak. Lax rule of law fosters pervasive corruption and insecure property rights, which jeopardize prospects for long-term economic growth and development.

BACKGROUND: President Kurmanbek Bakiyev's party won early parliamentary elections in December 2007, but political stability remains precarious because of rampant crime and religious extremism in the South. Ongoing concerns include a large external debt, heavy dependence on foreign aid, informal economic activity, and drug smuggling. GDP growth, buoyed by a strong recovery in gold production, was expected to fall to around 1 percent in 2009. In January 2009, Bakiyev announced the closure of the U.S. air base at Manas after Russia offered grants and loans of over $2 billion. Financial aid from Russia has helped the Kyrgyz Republic to offset some of the effects of the economic crisis.

Country's Score Over Time

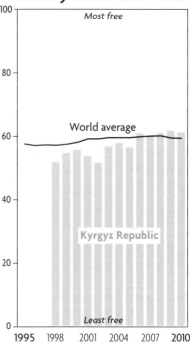

Quick Facts

Population: 5.3 million

GDP (PPP): $11.5 billion
7.7% growth in 2008
4.7% 5-year compound annual growth
$2,188 per capita

Unemployment: 8.1% (2007)

Inflation (CPI): 24.5%

FDI Inflow: $233.0 million

2008 data unless otherwise noted
Data compiled as of September 2009

How Do We Measure Economic Freedom?
See page 457 for an explanation of the methodology or visit the *Index* Web site at *heritage.org/index.*

KYRGYZ REPUBLIC'S TEN ECONOMIC FREEDOMS

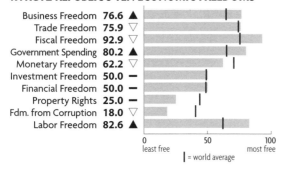

Business Freedom	76.6	▲
Trade Freedom	75.9	▽
Fiscal Freedom	92.9	▽
Government Spending	80.2	▲
Monetary Freedom	62.2	▽
Investment Freedom	50.0	—
Financial Freedom	50.0	—
Property Rights	25.0	—
Fdm. from Corruption	18.0	▽
Labor Freedom	82.6	▲

0 least free   50   100 most free

| = world average

BUSINESS FREEDOM — 76.6

The overall freedom to start, operate, and close a business is relatively well protected under the Kyrgyz Republic's regulatory environment. Starting a business takes an average of 11 days, compared to the world average of 35 days. Obtaining a business license requires less than the world average of 218 days.

TRADE FREEDOM — 75.9

The Kyrgyz Republic's weighted average tariff rate was 7 percent in 2008. Import bans and restrictions, import fees and taxes, export and import licensing requirements, complex regulations and standards, weak enforcement of intellectual property rights, and corrupt customs administration add to the cost of trade. Ten points were deducted from the Kyrgyz Republic's trade freedom score to account for non-tariff barriers.

FISCAL FREEDOM — 92.9

The Kyrgyz Republic has relatively low tax rates. The income and corporate tax rates are a flat 10 percent. As of January 2009, the value-added tax (VAT) rate was reduced from 20 percent to 12 percent. In the most recent year, overall tax revenue as a percentage of GDP was 22.6 percent.

GOVERNMENT SPENDING — 80.2

Total government expenditures, including consumption and transfer payments, are relatively low. In the most recent year, government spending equaled 25.7 percent of GDP.

MONETARY FREEDOM — 62.2

Inflation has been very high, averaging 19.3 percent between 2006 and 2008. Many price controls and subsidies have been eliminated, but the government regulates or influences prices through state-owned industries, including electricity, agriculture, telecommunications, water, and energy. Ten points were deducted from the Kyrgyz Republic's monetary freedom score to account for remaining price controls.

INVESTMENT FREEDOM — 50

Most of the economy is open to foreign investment, but rules and regulations are non-transparent and arbitrarily applied. Corruption remains a disincentive, red tape is burdensome, and contract enforcement is weak. The judi-

cial system is underdeveloped and lacks independence. Foreign investors lack the knowledge needed to work the system. Residents and non-residents may hold foreign exchange accounts. There are no restrictions on payments and transfers, but most capital transactions must be registered with the relevant government authority or are subject to controls. Foreign investors may lease but not purchase land.

FINANCIAL FREEDOM — 50

The Kyrgyz Republic has been trying to modernize and restructure its financial system. Financial intermediation has continued to increase, but high credit costs remain a barrier to entrepreneurial activity. Banking dominates the financial sector, and domestic credit provided by the banking sector amounted to about 12 percent of GDP in 2008. There are 21 banks, half of which are majority foreign-owned and account for more than 70 percent of total assets. Subsidiaries of Kazakhstan's banks have a large presence. There are no limits on foreign ownership of banks and microcredit institutions. The central bank has improved supervision and established minimum capital requirements, but the sector remains vulnerable to executive and legislative interference. Non-performing loans reached about 7 percent in early 2009. Capital markets are not fully developed, but there is a small stock exchange. In 2008, the parliament approved privatization of Aiyl Bank, one of the largest micro-finance institutions. A deposit insurance scheme came into effect in 2009.

PROPERTY RIGHTS — 25

Property right protections are slowly emerging, but the judicial system remains underdeveloped and lacks independence. Court actions can force the sale of property to enforce payments and other contractual obligations. Licensing, registration, and enforcement of contracts are prone to dispute. The Kyrgyz Republic is obligated to protect intellectual property rights as a member of the WTO. However, an estimated 98 percent of DVDs, CDs, and other audiovisual products sold are counterfeit.

FREEDOM FROM CORRUPTION — 18

Corruption is perceived as pervasive. The Kyrgyz Republic ranks 166th out of 179 countries in Transparency International's Corruption Perceptions Index for 2008, a decline from 2007. Corruption is endemic at all levels of society. Tax and customs agencies, law enforcement bodies, courts, and agencies controlling construction and the issuance of business licenses are notably corrupt. Thousands of cases of suspected official bribe-taking, negligence, fraud, embezzlement, and malfeasance have reportedly led to hundreds of arrests but no convictions.

LABOR FREEDOM — 82.6

Labor regulations are relatively flexible. The government has adopted a new labor code to further improve labor market flexibility. The non-salary cost of employing a worker is moderate, but restrictions on work hours remain rigid.

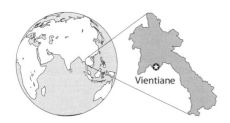

Vientiane

LAOS

Economic Freedom Score

Least free 0 — 25 — 50 — 75 — 100 Most free

51.1

World Rank: 138   **Regional Rank: 30**

Laos's economic freedom score is 51.1, making its economy the 138th freest in the 2010 *Index*. Its overall score has improved by 0.7 point, reflecting improved scores in five of the 10 economic freedoms. Laos is ranked 30th out of 41 countries in the Asia–Pacific region, and its overall score is below the world and regional averages.

The Laotian economy scores relatively well in fiscal freedom, government spending, and trade freedom. Although progress has been sluggish, the government has taken steps to modernize and reform the trade regime and management of public finance. Tariff barriers have been reduced, but significant non-tariff barriers remain. The government's responses to the economic slowdown, which have included suspension of a new value-added tax and improved expenditure management, have been consistent with reform efforts.

Many institutional challenges continue to have a negative effect on overall economic freedom and growth. The development of a more vibrant private sector is hindered by poor infrastructure, cumbersome regulations, and limited access to financing. The rule of law does not always hold against political influence, and corruption is rampant. Burdensome business regulations impede entrepreneurship, and regulatory as well as legal enforcement are in the hands of an opaque bureaucracy.

BACKGROUND: Laos is governed by one of the world's few remaining Communist regimes and is also one of Asia's poorest nations. Upon coming to power in 1975, the Communist government imposed a rigid socialist program that had a devastating impact on the economy. The government began to liberalize slowly in 1991, but with only limited success. The country remains highly dependent on international aid and suffers from high levels of corruption and weak rule of law. Basic human rights are still heavily restricted. In 1998, Laos began formal negotiations with the World Trade Organization with an eye to joining the WTO by 2010.

Country's Score Over Time

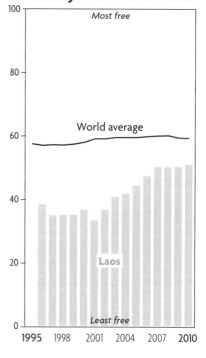

Quick Facts

Population: 6.2 million

GDP (PPP): $13.2 billion
7.5% growth in 2008
7.5% 5-year compound annual growth
$2,134 per capita

Unemployment: 2.4% (2005)

Inflation (CPI): 7.6%

FDI Inflow: $228 million

2008 data unless otherwise noted
Data compiled as of September 2009

How Do We Measure Economic Freedom?
See page 457 for an explanation of the methodology or visit the *Index* Web site at *heritage.org/index*.

LAOS'S TEN ECONOMIC FREEDOMS

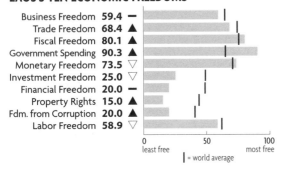

Business Freedom	59.4	▲
Trade Freedom	68.4	▲
Fiscal Freedom	80.1	▲
Government Spending	90.3	▲
Monetary Freedom	73.5	▽
Investment Freedom	25.0	▽
Financial Freedom	20.0	—
Property Rights	15.0	▲
Fdm. from Corruption	20.0	▲
Labor Freedom	58.9	▽

0 least free   50   100 most free

| = world average

BUSINESS FREEDOM — 59.4

The overall freedom to start, operate, and close a business is restricted by Laos's regulatory environment. Starting a business takes an average of 100 days, compared to the world average of 35 days. Obtaining a business license requires more than the world average of 18 procedures. Modern bankruptcy proceedings have not been fully developed.

TRADE FREEDOM — 68.4

Laos's weighted average tariff rate was 8.3 percent in 2007. There has been some liberalization, but prohibitive tariffs, import bans and restrictions, import taxes, restrictions on services market access, import licensing, corrupt and inefficient customs administration, and weak enforcement of intellectual property rights still add to the cost of trade. Fifteen points were deducted from Laos's trade freedom score to account for non-tariff barriers.

FISCAL FREEDOM — 80.1

Laos has a moderate income tax rate and a relatively high corporate tax rate. The top income tax rate is 25 percent, and the top corporate tax rate is 35 percent (20 percent for companies that fall under the Foreign Investment Law). Other taxes include a vehicle tax and a tax on insurance contracts. A value-added tax (VAT) introduced in January 2009 was suspended in March following pressure from the private sector. In the most recent year, overall tax revenue as a percentage of GDP was 12.0 percent.

GOVERNMENT SPENDING — 90.3

Total government expenditures, including consumption and transfer payments, are low. In the most recent year, government spending equaled 18.0 percent of GDP.

MONETARY FREEDOM — 73.5

Inflation has been relatively high, averaging 6.8 percent between 2006 and 2008, but has slowed in 2009, owing to a sharp decline in global prices for food and fuel. The government influences many prices through state-owned enterprises and utilities and sets the price for fuel products. Ten points were deducted from Laos's monetary freedom score to account for policies that distort domestic prices.

INVESTMENT FREEDOM — 25

Foreign investors may not engage in business activities that are deemed detrimental to national security, have a negative impact on the environment, or are regarded as harmful to health or national traditions. Foreign investors must submit project proposals for screening and approval by various levels of government. Investors must obtain a number of certificates, secure a license, and surmount other bureaucratic hurdles before gaining permission to operate. Arbitrary regulation, weak and inconsistent contract enforcement, and non-transparent bureaucracy inhibit investment. Residents and non-residents may hold foreign exchange accounts subject to restrictions and government approval. Some payments and transfers face quantitative restrictions or require indirect government approval. Foreign investors may lease but not own land.

FINANCIAL FREEDOM — 20

The financial system is underdeveloped and subject to heavy government involvement. High credit costs and scarce access to financing severely impede entrepreneurial activity and private-sector development. Much of the population remains outside the formal banking sector. Supervision and regulation are weak. Three state-owned banks dominate banking, accounting for more than 50 percent of assets. Activities of the 10 private and foreign banks are limited. A banking law passed in late 2006 permits foreign banks to set up branches in all provinces of Laos. The government directs credit allocation, and the central bank is not independent. Capital markets remain underdeveloped, but the government plans to open Laos's first stock market in 2010.

PROPERTY RIGHTS — 15

The judiciary is not independent, and judges can be bribed. Foreign investors are generally advised to seek arbitration outside of Laos, since the domestic arbitration authority cannot enforce its decisions. Foreign investors may not own land but may lease it with government permission. There is no copyright system. An intellectual property law drafted in 1996 with help from the World Intellectual Property Organization is still pending.

FREEDOM FROM CORRUPTION — 20

Corruption is perceived as rampant. Laos ranks 151st out of 179 countries in Transparency International's Corruption Perceptions Index for 2008, a slight improvement over 2007. Bribery of low-level officials to expedite business licenses and import permits is common, and there is growing anecdotal evidence of more pervasive corruption among higher-level officials within the executive and judicial branches.

LABOR FREEDOM — 58.9

Laos's labor regulations are relatively inflexible. The non-salary cost of employing a worker is low, but dismissing an employee can be costly and difficult. Changes in work hours can be challenged.

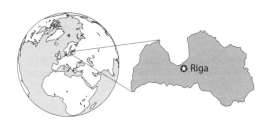

LATVIA

Economic Freedom Score

Least free 0   25   50   75   100   Most free

66.2

World Rank: **50**	Regional Rank: **23**

Latvia's economic freedom score is 66.2, making its economy the 50th freest in the 2010 *Index*. Its score has decreased by 0.4 point, reflecting reduced scores in five of the 10 economic freedoms. Latvia is ranked 23rd out of 43 countries in the Europe region, and its overall score is above the world average.

Latvia's transition to a market-oriented economy has been facilitated by trade liberalization and the adoption of a flat tax. The top income and corporate tax rates are competitive, and the transparency of business regulation promotes dynamic entrepreneurial activity. This institutional competitiveness is reflected in the country's relatively high scores in fiscal freedom, business freedom, and trade freedom.

Latvia faces growing fiscal deficits that are higher than 10 percent of GDP. Authorities aim to reduce the deficit through stronger fiscal management. A revised budget that drastically cut expenditure levels was approved in mid-2009, but the health minister resigned over cuts in health care. Inflation peaked at 17.9 percent in 2008, severely compromising monetary freedom, but the rate has fallen sharply since then. Corruption and money laundering remain significant problems.

BACKGROUND: Latvia regained its independence when the Soviet Union collapsed in 1991. It joined the European Union and NATO in 2004, and its political system has been generally stable despite regular changes of ruling coalitions. The government fell in February 2009 after the unrest caused by the global financial crisis, and Prime Minister Valdis Dombrovskis has headed a six-party center-right governing coalition since March 2009. The economy, including financial and transportation services, banking, electronics manufacturing, and dairy, had been developing quickly, and GDP grew by around 10 percent each year from 2004 to 2007. However, Latvia has been hit hard by the financial crisis and has been in deep recession.

Country's Score Over Time

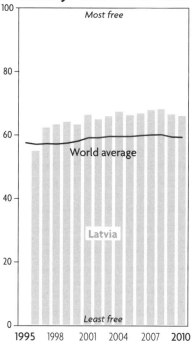

Quick Facts

Population: 2.3 million

GDP (PPP): $38.7 billion
−4.6% growth in 2008
6.8% 5-year compound annual growth
$17,100 per capita

Unemployment: 7.5%

Inflation (CPI): 15.3%

FDI Inflow: $1.4 billion

2008 data unless otherwise noted
Data compiled as of September 2009

How Do We Measure Economic Freedom?
See page 457 for an explanation of the methodology or visit the *Index* Web site at *heritage.org/index*.

LATVIA'S TEN ECONOMIC FREEDOMS

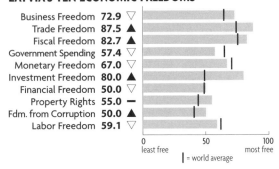

Business Freedom	**72.9** ▽	
Trade Freedom	**87.5** ▲	
Fiscal Freedom	**82.7** ▲	
Government Spending	**57.4** ▽	
Monetary Freedom	**67.0** ▽	
Investment Freedom	**80.0** ▲	
Financial Freedom	**50.0** ▽	
Property Rights	**55.0** —	
Fdm. from Corruption	**50.0** ▲	
Labor Freedom	**59.1** ▽	

0 least free — 50 — 100 most free

❙ = world average

BUSINESS FREEDOM — 72.9

The overall freedom to start, operate, and close a business is relatively well protected under Latvia's regulatory environment. Starting a business takes about half the world average of 35 days. Obtaining a business license takes less than the world average of 218 days. Closing a business is relatively straightforward.

TRADE FREEDOM — 87.5

Latvia's trade policy is the same as that of other members of the European Union. The common EU weighted average tariff rate was 1.3 percent in 2008. However, the EU has high or escalating tariffs for agricultural and manufacturing products, and its MFN tariff code is complex. Non-tariff barriers reflected in EU and Latvian policy include agricultural and manufacturing subsidies, quotas, import restrictions and bans for some goods and services, market access restrictions in some services sectors, non-transparent and restrictive regulations and standards, and inconsistent regulatory and customs administration among EU members. Ten points were deducted from Latvia's trade freedom score to account for non-tariff barriers.

FISCAL FREEDOM — 82.7

Latvia has a moderate income tax rate and a relatively low corporate tax rate. The income tax rate is a flat 23 percent, down from 25 percent, except for self-employed individuals, who are subject to a 15 percent rate. The corporate tax rate is 15 percent. Other taxes include a real estate tax, a value-added tax (VAT) increased in January 2009, and excise taxes increased in January and June 2009. In the most recent year, overall tax revenue as a percentage of GDP was 31.3 percent.

GOVERNMENT SPENDING — 57.4

Total government expenditures, including consumption and transfer payments, are relatively high. The budget deficit has been moderate. In the most recent year, government spending equaled 37.7 percent of GDP.

MONETARY FREEDOM — 67

High rates of inflation, averaging 13.2 percent between 2006 and 2008, have come down since mid-2008 when increases in oil and food prices came to an end. As a participant in the EU's Common Agricultural Policy, the government subsidizes agricultural production, distorting the prices of agricultural products. It also regulates rents, utility rates, transportation, and energy prices and influences prices through state-owned enterprises. Ten points were deducted from Latvia's monetary freedom score to account for policies that distort domestic prices.

INVESTMENT FREEDOM — 80

Foreign investors receive national treatment and may invest in most sectors. Except for acquisitions of former state enterprises through the privatization process, there are no performance requirements for a foreign investor to establish, maintain, or expand an investment. Bureaucracy can be non-transparent, and resolution of commercial disputes can be slow. Residents and non-residents may hold foreign exchange accounts. There are no restrictions or controls on payments, transactions, transfers, or repatriation of profits. Foreign investors may own land, subject to a number of restrictions.

FINANCIAL FREEDOM — 50

The banking sector dominates the financial system, accounting for more than 80 percent of the system's total assets. A unified capital and financial markets regulator has been in place since 2001. There were 21 commercial banks and four foreign bank branches as of mid-2008. Foreign banks receive domestic treatment. Efforts to combat money laundering have progressed slowly. The largest insurer is majority foreign-owned. Capital markets are not fully developed. The Riga Stock Exchange remains small. Latvia's financial system has been under stress in the face of the global financial crisis. The government nationalized the country's second largest bank, Parex Banka, at the end of 2008. In early 2009, the government introduced a bank-restructuring framework.

PROPERTY RIGHTS — 55

The Latvian constitution guarantees the right to private ownership. The judiciary is constitutionally independent, but court hearings and the enforcement of decisions are inefficient and subject to long delays. Some judges are not well trained. In an effort to meet EU and World Trade Organization requirements, Latvia has established a legal framework for the protection of intellectual property.

FREEDOM FROM CORRUPTION — 50

Corruption is perceived as significant. Latvia ranks 52nd out of 179 countries in Transparency International's Corruption Perceptions Index for 2008. Money laundering has been linked to tax evasion and to the proceeds from Russian organized crime.

LABOR FREEDOM — 59.1

Latvia's labor market regulations could be improved. The non-salary cost of employing a worker is high, and dismissing an employee can be difficult. Restrictions on work hours remain rigid.

Beirut

LEBANON

Economic Freedom Score

25   50   75

Least
free   0   100   Most
free

59.5

World Rank: **89**	Regional Rank: **9**

Lebanon's economic freedom score is 59.5, making its economy the 89th freest in the 2010 *Index*. Its score is 1.4 points higher than last year. Lebanon is ranked 9th out of 17 countries in the Middle East/North Africa region, and its overall score is about equal to the world average.

The Lebanese economy performs comparatively well in trade freedom and fiscal freedom. The financial sector is relatively well developed for the region, with an array of private banks and services. Lebanon has weathered the impact of the global economic turmoil, in part relying on the use of short-term fiscal adjustments. However, its long-term economic stability will depend on systematic reduction of public debt, which stands at about 160 percent of GDP.

Lebanon's overall entrepreneurial environment, hampered by political instability, remains unfavorable to private investment and productivity growth. Commercial regulations and bureaucratic red tape are burdensome. Property rights are severely undermined by an inefficient judiciary, and corruption is rampant.

BACKGROUND: Lebanon gained its independence from France in 1943 and was a trading and international banking center until its disastrous 1975–1990 civil war. Syria, which intervened ostensibly to halt the civil war, established hegemony over the country. In 2005, Syria was forced to withdraw its army after its government was implicated in the assassination of former Lebanese Prime Minister Rafiq Hariri. Prime Minister Fuad Siniora's economic reform efforts were set back by the Hezbollah-instigated conflict with Israel in 2006 and subsequently by tensions between the government and Hezbollah and other factions supported by Syria and Iran. A May 2008 agreement brokered by the government of Qatar installed Michel Suleiman, former head of the army, as president. Rafiq Hariri's son, Saad Hariri, was elected prime minister in June 2009.

Country's Score Over Time

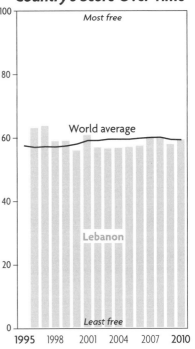

Quick Facts

Population: 4.1 million

GDP (PPP): $47.9 billion
8.0% growth in 2008
4.8% 5-year compound
annual growth
$11,570 per capita

Unemployment: 9.2% (2007)

Inflation (CPI): 10.8%

FDI Inflow: $3.6 billion

2008 data unless otherwise noted
Data compiled as of September 2009

How Do We Measure Economic Freedom?
See page 457 for an explanation of the methodology or visit the *Index* Web site at *heritage.org/index.*

LEBANON'S TEN ECONOMIC FREEDOMS

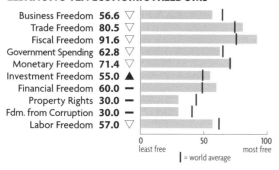

Business Freedom	56.6 ▽	
Trade Freedom	80.5 ▽	
Fiscal Freedom	91.6 ▽	
Government Spending	62.8 ▽	
Monetary Freedom	71.4 ▽	
Investment Freedom	55.0 ▲	
Financial Freedom	60.0 —	
Property Rights	30.0 —	
Fdm. from Corruption	30.0 —	
Labor Freedom	57.0 ▽	

0 least free   50   100 most free

▎ = world average

BUSINESS FREEDOM — 56.6

The overall freedom to establish and run a business is limited by Lebanon's regulatory environment. The cost of starting a business is high. Obtaining a business license takes about the same as the world average of 18 procedures and 218 days. Closing a business is a lengthy and costly process.

TRADE FREEDOM — 80.5

Lebanon's weighted average tariff rate was 4.8 percent in 2007. Import bans and restrictions, restrictive licensing rules, subsidies, burdensome sanitary and phytosanitary regulations, corrupt customs administration, and weak enforcement of intellectual property rights add to the cost of trade. Ten points were deducted from Lebanon's trade freedom score to account for non-tariff barriers.

FISCAL FREEDOM — 91.6

Lebanon has relatively low tax rates. The top income tax rate is 20 percent, and the corporate tax rate is 15 percent. Other taxes include a value-added tax (VAT), a transfer tax on real estate, and an inheritance tax of up to 45 percent. In the most recent year, tax revenue as a percentage of GDP was 14.8 percent.

GOVERNMENT SPENDING — 62.8

Total government expenditures, including consumption and transfer payments, are moderate. In the most recent year, government spending equaled 35.2 percent of GDP. The telecommunication sector remains in state hands despite plans for divestment. Privatization revenues, in conjunction with fiscal consolidation through changes in the VAT, could work to shrink the widening fiscal deficit.

MONETARY FREEDOM — 71.4

Inflation has been relatively high, averaging 8.7 percent between 2006 and 2008. The government influences prices through state-owned enterprises and subsidies and controls the prices of bread, petroleum derivatives, pharmaceuticals, and electricity. Ten points were deducted from Lebanon's monetary freedom score to account for policies that distort domestic prices.

INVESTMENT FREEDOM — 55

Foreign capital and domestic capital are legally equal, with a few exceptions. Foreign investors must register with the government, and foreign investment is restricted in the real estate, insurance, media, and banking sectors. The passage of several laws to promote investment has led to some progress, but red tape and corruption, arbitrary licensing decisions, dated legislation, an ineffectual judicial system, arbitrary and non-transparent interpretation of laws, political instability, and other security concerns continue to serve as impediments. Residents and non-residents may hold foreign exchange accounts, money market instruments, and derivatives. There are no restrictions on payments and transfers. Foreign investors may own land, subject to a number of restrictions.

FINANCIAL FREEDOM — 60

Lebanon's financial sector has undergone restructuring and consolidation, but overall progress has been slow in recent years. The five largest commercial banks account for roughly 60 percent of total banking assets. The government retains no ownership in any commercial banks, and competition among the private banks contributes to improving efficiency. Regulations are fairly transparent, and credit is allocated on market terms for both domestic and foreign businesses. The insurance sector is small, and regulations have been passed to tighten supervision and establish minimum capital requirements. Capital markets are relatively well developed. Bank regulations limit banks' exposure to structured financial products. Lebanon's banking sector has weathered the global financial turmoil relatively well and has maintained financial stability.

PROPERTY RIGHTS — 30

The judiciary is significantly influenced by the security services and the police. The government-appointed prosecuting magistrate exerts considerable influence over judges by, for example, recommending verdicts and sentences. Trials, particularly commercial cases, drag on for years. Although Lebanese law provides for some protection of intellectual property rights and the government continued to raid shops and warehouses that were storing or displaying pirated content in 2008, enforcement is generally weak.

FREEDOM FROM CORRUPTION — 30

Corruption is perceived as widespread and growing. Lebanon ranks 102nd out of 179 countries in Transparency International's Corruption Perceptions Index for 2008, down for the second year in a row. Corruption is more pervasive in government contracts (primarily in procurement and public works), taxation, and real estate registration than in private-sector deals. It is widely believed that investors routinely pay bribes to win government contracts, which are often awarded to companies close to powerful politicians.

LABOR FREEDOM — 57

Lebanon's labor regulations are relatively rigid. The non-salary cost of employing a worker remains high, and dismissing an employee is relatively expensive. Restrictions on work hours are moderate.

LESOTHO

Economic Freedom Score

48.1

25 · 50 · 75

Least free 0 · 100 Most free

World Rank: **155**　　　　Regional Rank: **34**

Lesotho's economic freedom score is 48.1, making its economy the 155th freest in the 2010 *Index*. Its score has decreased by 1.6 points from last year, reflecting deterioration in five of the 10 economic freedoms. Lesotho is ranked 34th out of 46 countries in the Sub-Saharan Africa region, and its overall score is below the world average.

Relatively sound macroeconomic management has enabled Lesotho to achieve annual economic expansion of around 4 percent over the past five years, but economic development remains fragile in the absence of a dynamic private sector. A tradition of direct government involvement in economic activity limits private-sector development, and privatization of agricultural parastatals has made little headway.

Lesotho continues to confront the challenge of improving competitiveness and promoting broad-based economic growth to reduce poverty. The poor quality of much basic infrastructure and the government's inefficiency in delivering public goods have been serious impediments to fostering more vibrant economic development. The overall entrepreneurial environment is hurt by weak property rights, limited access to finance, and bureaucratic red tape.

BACKGROUND: Lesotho became independent in 1966, but instability in the 1990s led to military intervention by South Africa and Botswana. An interim authority overhauled the government and oversaw elections in 2002. Lesotho is a constitutional monarchy. King Letsie III is ceremonial head of state, and Prime Minister Bethuel Pakalitha Mosisili is head of government and holds executive authority. Mosisili's party won a parliamentary majority in February 2007. Lesotho is surrounded by and economically integrated with South Africa. It sells water and electricity to South Africa, and many households depend on work in South African mines. Half of the population earns some income from agriculture or animal husbandry, but the agricultural sector accounted for only 15 percent of GDP in 2007. Lesotho's HIV/AIDS rate is one of the world's highest.

Country's Score Over Time

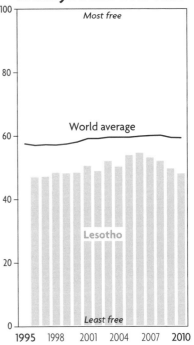

Quick Facts

Population: 2.0 million

GDP (PPP): $3.2 billion
3.9% growth in 2008
4.3% 5-year compound annual growth
$1,588 per capita

Unemployment: estimated to be over 20%

Inflation (CPI): 10.7%

FDI Inflow: $199 million

2008 data unless otherwise noted
Data compiled as of September 2009

How Do We Measure Economic Freedom?
See page 457 for an explanation of the methodology or visit the *Index* Web site at *heritage.org/index.*

LESOTHO'S TEN ECONOMIC FREEDOMS

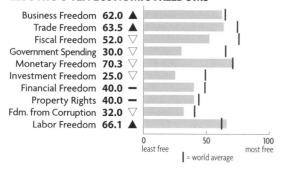

Business Freedom	62.0 ▲	
Trade Freedom	63.5 ▲	
Fiscal Freedom	52.0 ▽	
Government Spending	30.0 ▽	
Monetary Freedom	70.3 ▽	
Investment Freedom	25.0 ▽	
Financial Freedom	40.0 —	
Property Rights	40.0 —	
Fdm. from Corruption	32.0 ▽	
Labor Freedom	66.1 ▲	

0 least free   50   100 most free

| = world average

BUSINESS FREEDOM — 62

The overall freedom to establish and run a business is constrained by Lesotho's burdensome regulatory environment. Starting a business takes an average of 40 days, compared to the world average of 35 days. Obtaining a business license requires more than twice the world average of 218 days, and fees are high.

TRADE FREEDOM — 63.5

Lesotho's weighted average tariff rate was 13.3 percent in 2008. Import bans, controls and restrictions, import licensing, domestic preference in government procurement, some subsidies, and corruption add to the cost of trade. Ten points were deducted from Lesotho's trade freedom score to account for non-tariff barriers.

FISCAL FREEDOM — 52

Lesotho has a relatively high income tax and a moderate corporate tax. The top income tax rate is 35 percent, and the top corporate tax rate for companies other than those in manufacturing or farming is 25 percent; a 10 percent rate applies to all manufacturing and agricultural companies. Other taxes include a value-added tax (VAT) and a tax on dividends. In the most recent year, overall tax revenue as a percentage of GDP was 54.3 percent.

GOVERNMENT SPENDING — 30

Total government expenditures, including consumption and transfer payments, are high. In the most recent year, government spending equaled 48.3 percent of GDP. Lesotho has been running fiscal surpluses because of high revenues from textile manufacturing and diamond mining, but surpluses are shrinking as the government pursues a more expansionary fiscal policy.

MONETARY FREEDOM — 70.3

Inflation has been high, averaging 9.6 percent between 2006 and 2008. Annual inflation peaked at 12.1 percent in October 2008 but has subsequently fallen along with declines in the prices of food. Although many prices are freely determined in the market, the government influences prices through state-owned enterprises and utilities, especially in agriculture. Ten points were deducted from Lesotho's monetary freedom score to account for policies that distort domestic prices.

INVESTMENT FREEDOM — 25

Foreign investors generally receive national treatment. Ownership of small-scale retail and services businesses is restricted to domestic sources only. Lesotho's underdeveloped legal system, inadequate regulatory capacity, and non-transparent regulations inhibit investment. Residents and non-residents may hold foreign exchange accounts with some restrictions. Some payments and transfers are subject to prior government approval and limitations. Many capital transactions face restrictions or quantitative limits. Foreign investors may lease but not own land.

FINANCIAL FREEDOM — 40

Lesotho has a small and underdeveloped financial system that is closely tied to South Africa through the Common Monetary Area. Much of the population lacks adequate access to banking services. The high cost of credit hinders entrepreneurial activity and the development of a vibrant private sector. Lesotho's banking sector has three foreign-owned banks, and South African ownership of commercial banks is extensive. The central bank has promoted competition but with only limited success. Financial supervision remains insufficient. The insurance sector includes significant South African participation and one state-dominated company. Reflecting the lack of efficiency and depth in the financial system, capital markets remain rudimentary, and there is no stock exchange.

PROPERTY RIGHTS — 40

Private property is protected, and expropriation is unlikely. The judiciary is independent and has generally carried out its role effectively even during the years of military rule, but draconian internal security legislation gives considerable power to the police and restricts the right of assembly and some forms of industrial action. The government received international praise in 2006 for enacting a law to ensure the access of married women to property rights.

FREEDOM FROM CORRUPTION — 32

Corruption is perceived as significant. Lesotho ranks 92nd out of 179 countries in Transparency International's Corruption Perceptions Index for 2008. Corruption and lack of transparency remain major problems. Fallout continues from a scandal that began in the early 1990s and involved corrupt government officials and bribe-paying corporations engaged in constructing the multimillion-dollar, World Bank-funded Lesotho Highlands Water Scheme to transport water to South Africa.

LABOR FREEDOM — 66.1

Lesotho's labor regulations are relatively burdensome. The non-salary cost of employing a worker is low, and dismissing an employee is relatively easy. Restrictions on work hours remain rigid.

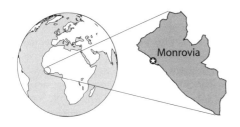
Monrovia

LIBERIA

Economic Freedom Score

25   50   75

Least free 0   100 Most free

46.2

Liberia's economic freedom score is 46.2, making its economy the world's 163rd freest in the 2010 *Index*. Its score has decreased by 1.9 points from last year, reflecting declines in four of the 10 economic freedoms. Liberia is ranked 40th out of 46 countries in the Sub-Saharan Africa region, and its overall score is below the world and regional averages.

In the aftermath of a decade-long civil conflict, much of Liberia's infrastructure remains in ruins, but some progress in economic recovery is occurring, supported by a substantial infusion of international development assistance.

Nevertheless, the Liberian economy faces a number of daunting challenges that include the absence of a dynamic private sector and a huge debt burden. Government expenditures are low, but misallocation remains a problem. Liberia's overall entrepreneurial environment remains unfavorable to private investment and productivity growth. Commercial regulations and bureaucratic red tape are burdensome, and the negative overall environment for business development keeps unemployment high. Property rights are severely undermined by an inefficient judiciary, and corruption is pervasive.

BACKGROUND: Founded by freed American and Caribbean slaves in 1820, Liberia is Africa's oldest republic and one of the world's poorest countries. In 1997, after an eight-year civil war, rebel leader Charles Taylor was elected president, but he was forced to resign in 2003. In 2005, Ellen Johnson Sirleaf became Africa's first democratically elected female president. U.N. bans on Liberia's exports of timber and diamonds ended in 2006 and 2007, and a U.N. peacekeeping operation remains in place. Unemployment and illiteracy are high, and instability, conflict, and international sanctions have destroyed most large businesses and driven out most foreign investors and enterprises. Rubber exports and the world's second-largest maritime registry generate major income, and private and public creditors are forgiving billions of dollars of loans to reduce a substantial public debt.

Country's Score Over Time

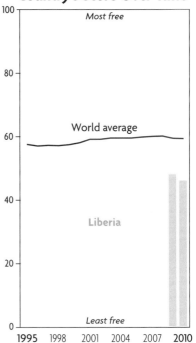

Quick Facts

Population: 3.8 million

GDP (PPP): $1.5 billion
7.1% growth in 2008
7.4% 5-year compound annual growth
$388 per capita

Unemployment: estimated to be over 20%

Inflation (CPI): 17.5%

FDI Inflow: $132 million (2007)

2008 data unless otherwise noted
Data compiled as of September 2009

How Do We Measure Economic Freedom?
See page 457 for an explanation of the methodology or visit the *Index* Web site at *heritage.org/index.*

LIBERIA'S TEN ECONOMIC FREEDOMS

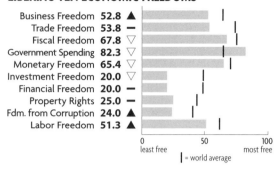

Business Freedom	52.8	▲
Trade Freedom	53.8	—
Fiscal Freedom	67.8	▽
Government Spending	82.3	▽
Monetary Freedom	65.4	▽
Investment Freedom	20.0	▽
Financial Freedom	20.0	—
Property Rights	25.0	—
Fdm. from Corruption	24.0	▲
Labor Freedom	51.3	▲

0 least free — 50 — 100 most free

| = world average

BUSINESS FREEDOM — 52.8

The overall freedom to establish and run a business is constrained by Liberia's regulatory environment. Starting a business takes an average of 20 days, compared to the world average of 35 days. Obtaining a business license takes more than the world average of 18 procedures. Regulations are sometimes inconsistent, and the entry cost of starting a business is high.

TRADE FREEDOM — 53.8

The International Monetary Fund estimates that Liberia's weighted average tariff rate was 15.6 percent in 2007. The government is trying to improve the trade regime, but some import bans and restrictions, inadequate trade capacity and infrastructure, licensing, minimal enforcement of intellectual property rights, and corruption add to the cost of trade. Fifteen points were deducted from Liberia's trade freedom score to account for non-tariff barriers.

FISCAL FREEDOM — 67.8

Liberia's tax rates are relatively high. The top income and corporate tax rates are 35 percent, which authorities plan to reduce to 25 percent. Other taxes include a property tax and a goods and services tax (GST). Import duties on rice, removed in 2008, remain suspended. In the most recent year, overall tax revenue as a percentage of GDP was 27.7 percent. Authorities have made efforts to eliminate discretionary tax exemptions that distorted total tax revenue.

GOVERNMENT SPENDING — 82.3

Total government expenditures, including consumption and transfer payments, are relatively low. In the most recent year, government spending equaled 24.3 percent of GDP. A rise in civil-service wages contributed to a big jump in expenditures. The government has tried to implement better budget preparation measures and regular fiscal reporting to improve fiscal governance, but more substantial reforms are needed to make spending more effective.

MONETARY FREEDOM — 65.4

Inflation has been high, averaging 15.1 percent between 2006 and 2008. Lower international oil and food prices have eased inflationary pressures in 2009. Ten points were deducted from Liberia's monetary freedom score to adjust for measures that distort domestic prices.

INVESTMENT FREEDOM — 20

As part of Liberia's reconstruction, much of the investment and commercial code is being reviewed. Older laws permit foreign investment but reserve a number of sectors for Liberian citizens, and investors must register with the government. Inadequate physical and administrative infrastructure, underdeveloped private markets, weak rule of law, and corruption inhibit investment. There are few restrictions on converting or transferring investment funds into foreign exchange, although the central bank regulates exchange transfers. Ownership of land is restricted to Liberian citizens.

FINANCIAL FREEDOM — 20

Liberia's underdeveloped financial system remains vulnerable to political and economic instability. The high cost of credit and scarce access to financing impede much-needed entrepreneurial activity and private-sector development. The financial sector is dominated by banking, but a large part of the population remains outside of the formal banking sector. The inefficient legal framework continues to deter financial intermediation across the country. With three new banks granted licenses in 2008, there are nine commercial banks operating in Liberia, most of which are foreign-owned. The only domestic bank is government-owned. Non-performing loans have been declining, but the overall quality of bank loans is still very poor. Liberia's capital markets remain poorly developed and unable to provide financing for businesses.

PROPERTY RIGHTS — 25

The archive of official records, including property deeds, was looted during the war, and disputes over real estate ownership are difficult to adjudicate. Conflicts between traditional and statutory land-tenure systems have not been reconciled. A lack of adequate facilities and salaries for judicial officers degrades enforcement of property rights. Judges sometimes decide cases in favor of the highest bidder. Holders of intellectual property rights have access to judicial redress, but enforcement is minimal.

FREEDOM FROM CORRUPTION — 24

Corruption is perceived as pervasive. Liberia ranks 138th out of 179 countries in Transparency International's Corruption Perceptions Index for 2008, an improvement over 2007. Corruption is systemic throughout the government due to a culture of impunity, although the president and other high-level government officials have publicly committed themselves to fighting it. Travelers may encounter officials who solicit bribes (often euphemistically referred to as "cold water" or "my Christmas").

LABOR FREEDOM — 51.3

Liberia's labor regulations are rigid. The non-salary cost of employing a worker is high, and dismissing an employee is relatively costly.

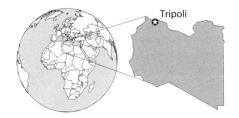
Tripoli

LIBYA

Economic Freedom Score

Least free 0   25   50   75   100   Most free

40.2

World Rank: 173   **Regional Rank: 17**

Libya's economic freedom score is 40.2, making its economy the 173rd freest in the 2010 *Index*. Its score has decreased by 3.3 points, reflecting declines in four of the 10 economic freedoms. Libya is ranked last out of 17 countries in the Middle East/North Africa region, and its overall score is well below the world and regional averages.

Libya's economic institutions remain poor and prevent dynamic entrepreneurial activity. Much-needed reforms in recent years have included the complete elimination of tariffs, but overall progress toward improving regulation and diversifying the economy has been marginal. The government remains the largest source of employment and dominates the energy sector.

The business and investment environments remain heavily encumbered by the strong state presence in many economic activities. The investment climate is uncertain, weakened by the risk of nationalization. Corruption is widespread, and fair adjudication of property rights is not guaranteed. Inefficient management of resource allocations results in market distortions and shortages of basic goods. Privatization, especially in banking, has been implemented slowly, and institutional resistance remains strong.

BACKGROUND: Oil and natural gas provide about 95 percent of Libya's export revenues and over half of GDP. Despite one of Africa's highest per capita incomes, the economy has been hurt by more than 30 years of socialist economic policies and international sanctions imposed after the 1989 Lockerbie airplane bombing. The United Nations lifted its sanctions in 2003 after Libya consented to a trial for the officials involved in the plot and agreed to compensate victims' families. The U.S. lifted most of its sanctions in 2004 after Muammar Qadhafi renounced weapons of mass destruction, and the Department of State removed Libya from its list of state sponsors of terrorism in 2006. Libya paid $1.5 billion to U.S. citizens in October 2008 as compensation for previous terrorist attacks.

Country's Score Over Time

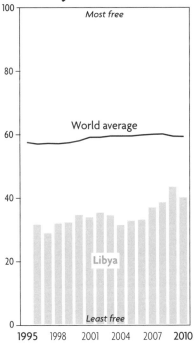

Quick Facts

Population: 6.3 million

GDP (PPP): $96.7 billion
7.0% growth in 2007
7.6% 5-year compound annual growth
$15,402 per capita

Unemployment: 30.0% (2004)

Inflation (CPI): 10.4%

FDI Inflow: $4.1 billion

2008 data unless otherwise noted
Data compiled as of September 2009

How Do We Measure Economic Freedom?
See page 457 for an explanation of the methodology or visit the *Index* Web site at *heritage.org/index*.

LIBYA'S TEN ECONOMIC FREEDOMS

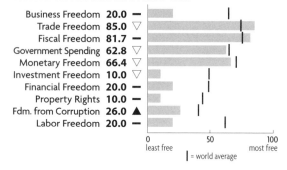

Business Freedom	20.0 —
Trade Freedom	85.0 ▽
Fiscal Freedom	81.7 —
Government Spending	62.8 ▽
Monetary Freedom	66.4 —
Investment Freedom	10.0 ▽
Financial Freedom	20.0 —
Property Rights	10.0 —
Fdm. from Corruption	26.0 ▲
Labor Freedom	20.0 —

0 least free   50   100 most free

| = world average

BUSINESS FREEDOM — 20

The overall freedom to start, operate, and close a business is significantly restricted by Libya's regulatory environment. Despite modest improvements in the business climate, Libya's bureaucracy remains one of the region's most burdensome.

TRADE FREEDOM — 85

Libya's weighted average tariff rate was 0 percent in 2006. In 2005, the Libyan Customs Administration cancelled duties on more than 3,500 product categories; however, a flat 4 percent "service fee" is levied on most imported products. Additional consumption and production taxes serve as a form of protection for local goods and companies. Import bans and restrictions, other import fees, non-transparent and discretionary regulation, aging infrastructure, state trade in petroleum products, subsidies, and customs corruption also add to the cost of trade. Fifteen points were deducted from Libya's trade freedom score to account for non-tariff barriers.

FISCAL FREEDOM — 81.7

The top tax rate on individual income is nominally 15 percent, but for incomes over 200,000 Libyan dinars, other taxes (such as those on commercial and industrial profits) may raise the top rate to 90 percent. The top corporate tax rate is 40 percent. Libya has no value-added tax (VAT) or inheritance tax. In the most recent year, overall tax revenue as a percentage of GDP was 2.9 percent.

GOVERNMENT SPENDING — 62.8

Total government expenditures, including consumption and transfer payments, are moderate. In the most recent year, government spending equaled 35.2 percent of GDP. Privatization has been slow, and the economy remains highly centralized and dominated by the energy sector.

MONETARY FREEDOM — 66.4

Inflation has been relatively high, averaging 8.6 percent between 2006 and 2008. Consumer prices have picked up sharply as the government has slowly relaxed some of its control of the domestic market. The government still determines most prices, either directly or through state-owned enterprises and utilities. Fifteen points were deducted from Libya's monetary freedom score to account for policies that distort domestic prices.

INVESTMENT FREEDOM — 10

Although foreign investment is generally welcome, it does not receive national treatment and is screened by the government. Foreign investors face additional regulatory requirements before projects can be approved. At least 35 percent of a non-Libyan business must be controlled by Libyan individuals or companies. Bureaucracy is non-transparent, complex, inefficient, and subject to political influence. Residents and non-residents may hold foreign currency accounts with prior approval. Repatriation and most capital transactions, including transactions involving capital, credit operations, and direct investment, are subject to controls, including approval requirements. Foreigners may not own land in most cases.

FINANCIAL FREEDOM — 20

Libya's highly centralized financial system remains subject to considerable state influence. The government, which nationalized all banks decades ago, recently eased banking laws to allow financial liberalization and privatization, but overall progress has been minimal. The banking sector is still dominated by four banks that are owned in full or majority-owned by the Central Bank of Libya. These four banks account for more than 90 percent of the sector's assets. The high cost of credit and limited access to financing impede private business development. Legislation passed in 2005 permits foreign banks to open branches.

PROPERTY RIGHTS — 10

The Libyan government eliminated all private property rights and most private businesses in 1978. The renting of property was declared illegal, and ownership of property was limited to a single dwelling per family, with all other properties being redistributed. The judiciary is not independent, the private practice of law is illegal, and all lawyers must be members of the Secretariat of Justice. There is little land ownership, and the government has the power to renationalize any property that has been privatized. Foreign companies are especially vulnerable, and the government has a history of expropriation. Trademark violations are widespread.

FREEDOM FROM CORRUPTION — 26

Corruption is perceived as widespread. Libya ranks 126th out of 179 countries in Transparency International's Corruption Perceptions Index for 2008. Government integrity is undermined by favoritism based on personal and family connections. The Qadhafi clan exercises near-total control of major government decisions.

LABOR FREEDOM — 20

Unemployment remains high, and the growing number of job seekers makes job creation a major priority. Libya's labor regulations are highly restrictive. The labor law specifies minimum wage rates, the number of work hours, night shift rules, and dismissal regulations.

Vaduz

LIECHTENSTEIN

World Rank: Not Graded   **Regional Rank: Not Graded**

Liechtenstein's economic freedom cannot be fully assessed in this edition of the *Index of Economic Freedom* because of the lack of complete data. The country will receive an economic freedom score and ranking in future editions as sufficient information becomes available.

Lichtenstein has long benefited from a well-diversified economic base. The country's overall entrepreneurial environment is strongly supported by a stable and efficient regulatory and legal framework. Liechtenstein's small economy is well integrated into the world economy and is open to global trade and investment.

Despite a lack of domestic natural resources and delayed industrialization, the country's structural and institutional advantages are notable. Political continuity and an efficient and predictable regulatory environment underpin vibrant entrepreneurial activity. The role of the state in economic activity has traditionally been kept low, and a low level of bureaucracy and a modern financial sector make Liechtenstein an attractive place in which to do business. The financial sector has benefited from the country's high political and social stability as well as its sound and transparent judicial system.

BACKGROUND: The tiny principality of Liechtenstein occupies about 60 square miles along the Rhine River between Switzerland and Austria. The small population (under 40,000) enjoys high living standards based on a vibrant free-enterprise economy with a usually flourishing financial sector. However, the world-wide financial crisis has provoked a sharp contraction in the banking sector. In May 2009, the Organisation for Economic Co-operation and Development removed all jurisdictions and principalities, including Liechtenstein, from its list of uncooperative tax havens. Liechtenstein's economy is closely linked with Switzerland, whose currency it shares, and the European Union. Liechtenstein is a member of the European Free Trade Association and joined the European Economic Area in 1995 to benefit from the EU's internal market.

Country's Score Over Time

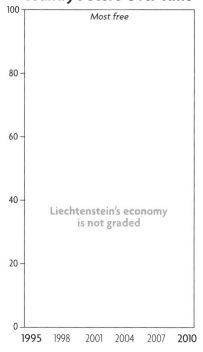

Liechtenstein's economy is not graded

Quick Facts

Population: 35,500

GDP (current): $4.2 billion
3.1% growth in 2007
5-year compound annual growth n/a
$118,040 per capita

Unemployment: 2.7%

Inflation (CPI): n/a

FDI Inflow: n/a

2008 data unless otherwise noted
Data compiled as of September 2009

How Do We Measure Economic Freedom?
See page 457 for an explanation of the methodology or visit the *Index* Web site at *heritage.org/index.*

BUSINESS FREEDOM — NOT GRADED

The overall freedom to conduct a business is relatively well protected under Liechtenstein's regulatory environment. Establishing a business is fairly easy. Administrative procedures are straightforward, and regulations affecting business are transparent and consistently applied.

TRADE FREEDOM — NOT GRADED

Liechtenstein's weighted average tariff rate was 0 percent in 2008. Import restrictions, services market access barriers, import taxes, import licensing, and restrictive sanitary and phytosanitary regulations add to the cost of trade, and high statutory tariffs or quotas block some agricultural trade altogether. If a score were being assigned, 10 points would have been deducted from Liechtenstein's trade freedom score to account for non-tariff barriers.

FISCAL FREEDOM — NOT GRADED

Historically a tax haven, Liechtenstein has a competitive tax system and imposes relatively low taxes on both nationals and non-nationals. Personal tax rates are low, even taking into account high municipality surtaxes. The top corporate tax rate is 15 percent, with an additional surcharge of up to 5 percent, bringing the top effective rate to 20 percent. Other taxes include a property tax, a withholding tax on interest, and a value-added tax (VAT).

GOVERNMENT SPENDING — NOT GRADED

Although the fiscal system lacks some transparency, government fiscal management seems to be sound. In recent years, the government has focused on reining in high social spending and increasing revenues to work toward a balanced budget.

MONETARY FREEDOM — NOT GRADED

Inflation is negligible. Liechtenstein participates in a customs union with Switzerland and uses the Swiss franc as its national currency. Government measures influence the prices of agricultural goods and pharmaceutical products, and the government influences prices through regulation, subsidies, and state-owned utilities. If Liechtenstein were being graded, 10 points would have been deducted from its monetary freedom score to account for policies that distort domestic prices.

INVESTMENT FREEDOM — NOT GRADED

Liechtenstein is generally open to foreign investment. Applications to establish a business require government approval. Certain activities are reserved for domestic companies, and certain business structures require resident nationals on their boards. Residents and non-residents may hold foreign exchange accounts. There are no restrictions on repatriation of profits, payments for invisible transactions, or current transfers. Real estate purchases by non-residents must be approved and may face some restrictions.

FINANCIAL FREEDOM — NOT GRADED

Liechtenstein has become a major financial center, particularly in private banking. Major financial services include private asset management, international asset structuring, investment funds, insurance, and reinsurance. Resident and non-resident clients enjoy equal access. Financial services account for 30 percent of GDP. The three largest banks together account for a market share of more than 60 percent. Banks, insurance companies, and trust companies are major sources of economic activity, representing around 14 percent of total employment. The Financial Market Authority, an independent and integrated authority, performs supervisory and regulatory functions. In March 2009, Liechtenstein agreed to conform to Organisation for Economic Co-operation and Development standards of fiscal transparency. The agreement effectively marked the end of the traditional bank secrecy upon which Liechtenstein's financial sector was built.

PROPERTY RIGHTS — NOT GRADED

The judiciary is independent, and contracts are secure. The principality has its own civil and penal codes, although courts composed of Liechtenstein, Swiss, and Austrian judges have jurisdiction over Liechtenstein cases in certain instances. Intellectual property laws are based on Switzerland's IPR protection regimes, which are among the best in the world for both foreign and domestic rights holders. Most foreigners have the same rights as Liechtenstein nationals when purchasing real property.

FREEDOM FROM CORRUPTION — NOT GRADED

Corruption is perceived as minimal. There were no reports of government corruption during the year. The government has made substantial progress in fighting money laundering; for example, new regulations require strict know-your-customer practices.

LABOR FREEDOM — NOT GRADED

Liechtenstein's labor market is dynamic, and unemployment has traditionally been very low. In recent years, labor market policies have focused on reducing youth unemployment. A new Labor Market Service was established in 2007 to facilitate job training programs and more efficient employment placements.

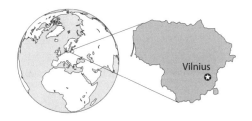

LITHUANIA

Economic Freedom Score

70.3

L ithuania's economic freedom score is 70.3, making its economy the 29th freest in the 2010 *Index*. Its overall score is 0.3 point higher than last year, reflecting improved scores in four of the 10 economic freedoms. Lithuania is ranked 15th out of 43 countries in the Europe region, and its overall score is well above the world and regional averages.

Economic and structural reforms have facilitated Lithuania's transition into a modern and flexible economy. Open to global trade and investment, Lithuania enjoys high degrees of business freedom, fiscal freedom, and financial freedom. The private sector accounts for about 80 percent of GDP and has driven steady economic growth at annual rates close to 7 percent over the past five years. That growth has come to a stop as a result of the global financial crisis, although Lithuania has weathered the turmoil better than some other countries have. Regulation is relatively transparent and efficient. The financial sector is advanced, regionally integrated, and subject to few intrusive restrictions.

Further growth in economic freedom in Lithuania will require strengthened management of public finance, better protection of property rights, and the elimination of corruption. The government has prioritized fiscal discipline and is striving for budgetary balance after years of fiscal deficits.

BACKGROUND: Lithuania, the largest of the Baltic States, regained its independence from the Soviet Union in 1991. It is a member of the European Union and NATO, having joined both in 2004. The Lithuanian economy has been one of the fastest-growing in Europe, with construction, financial services, and retail being particularly strong. More recently, however, the burst of the housing market bubble and the global banking crisis have had negative effects on the economy, provoking social unrest and public protests. Dalia Grybauskaite, a European Union budget commissioner and former finance minister, was elected president in May 2009.

Country's Score Over Time

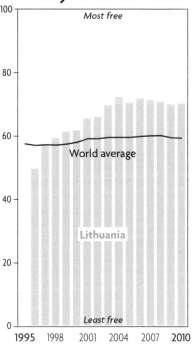

Quick Facts

Population: 3.4 million

GDP (PPP): $63.2 billion
    3.0% growth in 2008
    6.9% 5-year compound
       annual growth
    $18,824 per capita

Unemployment: 5.8%

Inflation (CPI): 11.1%

FDI Inflow: $1.8 billion

2008 data unless otherwise noted
Data compiled as of September 2009

How Do We Measure Economic Freedom?
See page 457 for an explanation of the methodology or visit the *Index* Web site at *heritage.org/index*.

LITHUANIA'S TEN ECONOMIC FREEDOMS

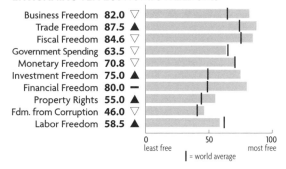

Business Freedom	82.0 ▽
Trade Freedom	87.5 ▲
Fiscal Freedom	84.6 ▽
Government Spending	63.5 ▽
Monetary Freedom	70.8 ▽
Investment Freedom	75.0 ▲
Financial Freedom	80.0 ▬
Property Rights	55.0 ▲
Fdm. from Corruption	46.0 ▽
Labor Freedom	58.5 ▲

0 least free   50   100 most free

❙ = world average

BUSINESS FREEDOM — 82

The overall freedom to start, operate, and close a business is well protected under Lithuania's efficient regulatory environment. Starting a business takes an average of 26 days, compared to the world average of 35 days. Obtaining a business license requires less than the world average of 18 procedures and 218 days. Closing a business is straightforward.

TRADE FREEDOM — 87.5

Lithuania's trade policy is the same as that of other members of the European Union. The common EU weighted average tariff rate was 1.3 percent in 2008. However, the EU has high or escalating tariffs for agricultural and manufacturing products, and its MFN tariff code is complex. Non-tariff barriers reflected in EU and Lithuanian policy include agricultural and manufacturing subsidies, quotas, import restrictions and bans for some goods and services, market access restrictions in some services sectors, non-transparent and restrictive regulations and standards, and inconsistent regulatory and customs administration among EU members. Biotechnology regulations exceed EU levels, and government procurement is non-transparent. Ten points were deducted from Lithuania's trade freedom score to account for non-tariff barriers.

FISCAL FREEDOM — 84.6

Lithuania's income tax rate is now 15 percent, down from 24 percent (with a 20 percent tax on redistributed profits), but the corporate tax rate has been raised to 20 percent from 15 percent. Other taxes include an inheritance tax and a value-added tax (VAT). In the most recent year, overall tax revenue as a percentage of GDP was 30.2 percent.

GOVERNMENT SPENDING — 63.5

Total government expenditures, including consumption and transfer payments, are moderate. In the most recent year, government spending equaled 34.9 percent of GDP. Expenditure targets set in the 2009 budget have not been met.

MONETARY FREEDOM — 70.8

Inflation has been high, averaging 9.2 percent between 2006 and 2008, but has fallen sharply in 2009. As a participant in the EU's Common Agricultural Policy, the government subsidizes agricultural production, distorting the prices of agricultural products. The government also regulates rents, electricity rates, and some energy prices and influences other prices through state-owned enterprises. Ten points were deducted from Lithuania's monetary freedom score to account for policies that distort domestic prices.

INVESTMENT FREEDOM — 75

Foreign capital and domestic capital are treated equally, and foreign investment is restricted in only a few sectors. Licenses and residency permits can be hard to obtain for foreign investors, and the regulatory bureaucracy can be non-transparent and subject to corruption. Residents may hold foreign exchange accounts. There are no controls or restrictions on repatriation of profits, current transfers, or payments. Some capital transactions must be registered with the central bank. The prohibition on foreign ownership of land for agriculture or logging is due to be phased out in 2011 in accordance with EU regulations.

FINANCIAL FREEDOM — 80

Lithuania's financial sector is well developed and competitive, offering a full range of financial services. Branch networks of Lithuanian commercial banks are well developed across the country, providing easy access to services. Lithuania's last state-owned bank was privatized in March 2002, and most commercial banks are now foreign-owned. Foreign firms dominate the insurance sector. Capital markets are well developed but small. Since late 2008, the banking system has experienced considerable credit contraction triggered by the global financial turmoil. Although the system remains relatively well capitalized, non-performing loans have become an increasing burden. The Financial Stability Law, which was passed in 2009, covers state guarantees for interbank lending, partial and full bank capitalization by the government, and asset acquisition.

PROPERTY RIGHTS — 55

Private property is protected against nationalization or requisition. Accession to the EU has encouraged judicial reform, including strengthened independence and streamlined proceedings to clear the backlog of criminal cases. Investors cite weak enforcement of contracts. Lithuania remains a transshipment point for pirated optical media products.

FREEDOM FROM CORRUPTION — 46

Corruption is perceived as significant. Lithuania ranks 58th out of 179 countries in Transparency International's Corruption Perceptions Index for 2008. Lithuania ratified the U.N. Convention Against Corruption in December 2006 but is not a signatory to the OECD Convention on Combating Bribery.

LABOR FREEDOM — 58.5

Lithuania's labor regulations are relatively rigid. The non-salary cost of employing a worker can be very high, but dismissing an employee is relatively easy. Restrictions on work hours are rigid.

LUXEMBOURG

Economic Freedom Score

Least free 0   100 Most free

75.4

L uxembourg's economic freedom score is 75.4, making its economy the 14th freest in the 2010 *Index*. Its overall score is slightly better than last year. Luxembourg is ranked 5th out of 43 countries in the Europe region.

Luxembourg, one of the leading global financial centers and a sophisticated service-dominated economy, has long benefited from a favorable climate for entrepreneurial activity and high levels of openness and flexibility. The judiciary, independent of politics and free of corruption, has demonstrated an exemplary ability to protect property rights. Institutional support for investment freedom, trade freedom, financial freedom, and business freedom is similarly strong.

Economic freedom is less well tended in other areas as measured in Luxembourg's fiscal freedom, government spending, and labor freedom scores. Personal tax rates remain high, although the corporate rate is relatively low. Government expenditures, while lower than in some other European Union countries, account for close to 40 percent of GDP. The government is undertaking gradual reforms to improve the management of public finance. A more flexible labor market is needed to promote employment growth. The minimum wage is one of the highest in the Organisation for Economic Co-operation and Development, and labor union membership stands at over 50 percent of all wage earners.

BACKGROUND: The Grand Duchy of Luxembourg is a small, stable, and wealthy country. A founding member of the European Union in 1957, it was also one of the founding members of the single European currency in 1999 and continues to play a primary role in promoting further European integration. Luxembourgers enjoy a high standard of living with one of the world's highest income levels. During the 20th century, Luxembourg evolved from an industrial economy into a mixed manufacturing and services economy that includes a very strong financial services industry. It has a skilled workforce and well-developed infrastructure.

Country's Score Over Time

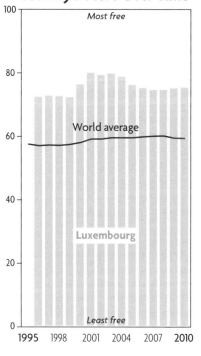

Quick Facts

Population: 0.5 million

GDP (PPP): $38.3 billion
–0.9% growth in 2007
4.4% 5-year compound annual growth
$78,599 per capita

Unemployment: 4.9%

Inflation (CPI): 3.4%

FDI Inflow: $3 billion

2008 data unless otherwise noted
Data compiled as of September 2009

How Do We Measure Economic Freedom?
See page 457 for an explanation of the methodology or visit the *Index* Web site at *heritage.org/index*.

LUXEMBOURG'S TEN ECONOMIC FREEDOMS

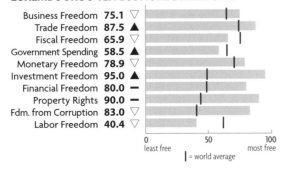

Business Freedom	75.1	▽
Trade Freedom	87.5	▲
Fiscal Freedom	65.9	▽
Government Spending	58.5	▲
Monetary Freedom	78.9	▽
Investment Freedom	95.0	▲
Financial Freedom	80.0	—
Property Rights	90.0	—
Fdm. from Corruption	83.0	▽
Labor Freedom	40.4	▽

0 least free   50   100 most free

| = world average

BUSINESS FREEDOM — 75.1

The overall freedom to start, operate, and close a business is relatively well protected under Luxembourg's regulatory environment. Starting a business takes 24 days, compared to the world average of 35 days. Obtaining a business license requires slightly less than the world average of 18 procedures and 218 days.

TRADE FREEDOM — 87.5

Luxembourg's trade policy is the same as that of other members of the European Union. The common EU weighted average tariff rate was 1.3 percent in 2008. However, the EU has high or escalating tariffs for agricultural and manufacturing products, and its MFN tariff code is complex. Non-tariff barriers reflected in EU and Luxembourg policy include agricultural and manufacturing subsidies, quotas, import restrictions and bans for some goods and services, market access restrictions in some services sectors, non-transparent and restrictive regulations and standards, and inconsistent regulatory and customs administration among EU members. Some biotechnology bans and services market barriers exceed the EU norm. Ten points were deducted from Luxembourg's trade freedom score to account for non-tariff barriers.

FISCAL FREEDOM — 65.9

Luxembourg has a relatively high income tax rate but a relatively low corporate tax rate. The top income tax rate is 39 percent (38 percent plus a 2.5 percent surcharge). The top corporate tax rate is 21.84 percent (21 percent plus a 4 percent employment fund contribution), but municipal business taxes ranging from 6 percent to 12 percent can raise the effective rate even higher. Other taxes include a value-added tax (VAT) and an inheritance tax. In the most recent year, overall tax revenue as a percentage of GDP was 37.6 percent.

GOVERNMENT SPENDING — 58.5

Total government expenditures, including consumption and transfer payments, are relatively high. In the most recent year, government spending equaled 37.2 percent of GDP. Public debt is low because of past fiscal surpluses, but a new fiscal stimulus package included both subsidies and tax exemptions.

MONETARY FREEDOM — 78.9

Luxembourg is a member of the euro zone. Inflation has been relatively low, averaging 3.1 percent between 2006 and 2008. As a participant in the EU's Common Agricultural Policy, the government subsidizes agricultural production, distorting the prices of agricultural products. The government also regulates electricity rates and some fuel prices and influences prices through state-owned enterprises. Ten points were deducted from Luxembourg's monetary freedom score to account for policies that distort domestic prices.

INVESTMENT FREEDOM — 95

Foreign and domestic businesses receive equal treatment. Investments in utilities or activities that directly affect national security are restricted. Bureaucratic procedures, including those for licenses and permits, are streamlined and transparent, and there is far less red tape than in larger European countries. Both residents and non-residents may hold foreign exchange accounts. There are no restrictions or barriers with respect to capital transactions, current transfers, repatriation of profits, purchase of real estate, or access to foreign exchange.

FINANCIAL FREEDOM — 80

Luxembourg is a global financial hub, and its sophisticated banking sector is well capitalized and competitive. Regulations are transparent and effective. Many of the world's leading banks have subsidiaries in Luxembourg. The one state-owned bank offers medium-term and long-term financing of investments by Luxembourg-based companies. The investment fund industry has been expanding rapidly. Capital markets are well developed, and trading on the Luxembourg Stock Exchange is very active. The financial system has been under stress because of the global financial crisis, and the government of Luxembourg joined several other European governments in bailing out two prominent banks.

PROPERTY RIGHTS — 90

Private property is well protected, and contracts are secure. Luxembourg adheres to key international agreements on intellectual property rights and protects patents, copyrights, trademarks, and trade secrets.

FREEDOM FROM CORRUPTION — 83

Corruption is perceived as minimal. Luxembourg ranks 11th out of 179 countries in Transparency International's Corruption Perceptions Index for 2008. Anti-corruption laws, regulations, and penalties are enforced impartially, and efforts to combat money laundering and the financing of terrorism are a priority.

LABOR FREEDOM — 40.4

Luxembourg's labor regulations are burdensome. Unemployment benefits are almost twice as high as those in neighboring countries. Restrictions on work hours remain rigid.

MACAU

World Rank: 20   **Regional Rank: 6**

Macau's economic freedom score is 72.5, making its economy the 20th freest in the 2010 *Index*. Its overall score has improved slightly since last year. Macau is ranked 6th out of 41 countries in the Asia–Pacific region, and its overall score is well above the world and regional averages.

Macau is an open and service-oriented economy. The services sector accounts for almost 90 percent of GDP and over 70 percent of total employment. Investment in resort and entertainment projects and related infrastructure has transformed the small economy into one of the world's leading gaming destinations.

As a free port, Macau has long benefited from global trade and investment. The overall entrepreneurial environment is efficient and streamlined, and property rights are relatively well respected. Foreign investors can conduct business on the same terms as nationals. Taxation is low and relatively efficient. Since opening up the gaming industry in 2002, Macau has attracted more foreign investment, spurring tourism and overall consumption. Other growth areas include finance, insurance, and real estate. Macau underwent a sharp decline in gambling revenue as a result of the global economic downturn, but growth has resumed since mid-2009.

BACKGROUND: Macau became a Special Administrative Region (SAR) of China in 1999. Like Hong Kong, also an SAR, it retains much of its historical political governance structure and economic system, although its chief executive is appointed by Beijing. Gambling revenues reportedly amounted to $13.7 billion in 2008, and direct taxes on gambling account for well over half of all government revenue. Manufacturing of textiles and garments, once the mainstay of the economy, has largely migrated to the Chinese mainland. Macau's economic fortunes are tied to those of China and Hong Kong, and its currency enjoys full convertibility with the Hong Kong dollar, which in turn is pegged to the U.S. dollar.

Country's Score Over Time

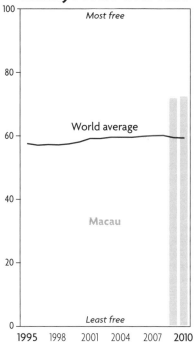

Quick Facts

Population: 0.5 million

GDP (PPP): $31.3 billion
     13.2% growth in 2008
     15.3 5-year compound
       annual growth
     $59,430 per capita

Unemployment: 3%

Inflation (CPI): 8.6%

FDI Inflow: $1.9 billion

2008 data unless otherwise noted
Data compiled as of September 2009

How Do We Measure Economic Freedom?
See page 457 for an explanation of the methodology or visit the *Index* Web site at *heritage.org/index.*

MACAU'S TEN ECONOMIC FREEDOMS

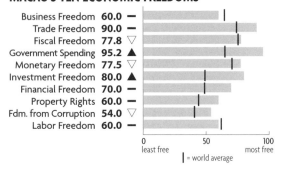

Business Freedom	60.0 —	
Trade Freedom	90.0 —	
Fiscal Freedom	77.8 ▽	
Government Spending	95.2 ▲	
Monetary Freedom	77.5 ▽	
Investment Freedom	80.0 ▲	
Financial Freedom	70.0 —	
Property Rights	60.0 —	
Fdm. from Corruption	54.0 ▽	
Labor Freedom	60.0 —	

0 — least free   50   100 — most free
| = world average

BUSINESS FREEDOM — *60*

Macau's overall regulatory environment is transparent and efficient. It takes three to four weeks to incorporate a company. License requirements vary by type of economic activity. General business activities such as retail, wholesale, and business consultancies do not require a license. A one-stop shop assists investors with company registrations and other relevant procedures.

TRADE FREEDOM — *90*

Macau's weighted average tariff rate was 0 percent in 2008. Some import restrictions, services market access restrictions, import taxes, restrictive food and energy labeling regulations, and problems with the enforcement of intellectual property rights add to the cost of trade. Ten points were deducted from Macau's trade freedom score to account for non-tariff barriers.

FISCAL FREEDOM — *77.8*

Except for the gambling industry, taxes in Macau are generally low. The top income and corporate tax rates are 12 percent. Gambling taxes accounted for over 82 percent of government revenue last year and act as the primary corporate tax. Gross casino revenues are subject to a 35 percent direct tax and an additional 4 percent social contribution tax, for an effective rate of 39 percent. In the most recent year, overall tax revenue as a percentage of GDP was 23.5 percent.

GOVERNMENT SPENDING — *95.2*

Total government expenditures, including consumption and transfer payments, are low. In the most recent year, government spending equaled 12.6 percent of GDP. Macau consistently runs fiscal surpluses, allowing it to respond easily to the global financial crisis with some adjustment assistance in the form of cash subsidies, tax relief, health care vouchers, and increases in public works investment.

MONETARY FREEDOM — *77.5*

Inflation has been moderate, averaging 7.6 percent between 2006 and 2008. Macau's currency is closely tied to the Hong Kong and U.S. dollars and backed by foreign-exchange reserves under the currency board system. No products are subject to price controls, but prices for bus fares, taxi fares, and such public utilities as water, electricity, telephone service, and the postal service are administered or monitored. Five points were deducted from Macau's monetary freedom score to adjust for measures that distort domestic prices.

INVESTMENT FREEDOM — *80*

Foreign investors generally may establish companies, branches, and representative offices but face a few restrictions in services markets. Regulations and bureaucracy are generally efficient and transparent. Profits, investment capital, earnings, loan repayments, lease payments, and capital gains can be freely converted and remitted. Land ownership is subject to restrictions.

FINANCIAL FREEDOM — *70*

Macau's small financial system functions without undue government influence. It employs less than 3 percent of the labor force, and banks account for about 98 percent of total assets. Credit is allocated on market terms, and sound regulation and supervision assure free flows of financial resources. Easy access to financing enhances private-sector activity. The Monetary Authority of Macau supervises the financial system. There are 28 banks, including 16 foreign bank branches. The Postal Savings Bank is the only banking institution wholly owned by the government. The non-bank financial sector has 11 life insurance companies and 13 non–life insurance companies. Macau has no stock exchange, but domestic firms may list in Hong Kong's stock markets.

PROPERTY RIGHTS — *60*

The legal system is based largely on Portuguese law. The territory has its own judicial system with a high court. Macau is a member of the World Intellectual Property Organization and has acceded to the Bern Convention for the Protection of Literary and Artistic Works. Patents and trademarks are registered. Copyright laws are TRIPS-compatible, and the government devotes considerable attention to enforcing intellectual property rights. It has made a particular effort against optical disc piracy and claims to have closed all illicit optical disc production lines. Piracy of television signals is rampant.

FREEDOM FROM CORRUPTION — *54*

Corruption is perceived as significant. Macau ranks 43rd out of 179 countries in Transparency International's Corruption Perceptions Index for 2008. The Commission Against Corruption has powers of arrest and detention, and a public outreach campaign has led to a significant increase in the number of complaints handled.

LABOR FREEDOM — *60*

Labor regulations are relatively flexible. The government sets minimum standards for the terms and conditions of employment. Severance payments range from seven to 20 days' salary per year of service. There is a minimum wage for public-sector cleaning and security services.

MACEDONIA

⊘ Skopje

Economic Freedom Score

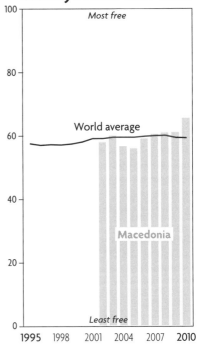

	50	
25		75

Least free 0   100 Most free

65.7

World Rank: 56   **Regional Rank: 26**

Macedonia's economic freedom score is 65.7, making its economy the 56th freest in the 2010 *Index*. Its overall score has increased 4.5 points from last year, reflecting a major improvement in labor freedom and smaller improvements in six other economic freedoms. Macedonia is ranked 26th out of 43 countries in the Europe region, and its overall score is above the world average.

Reforms in labor market flexibility and regulation of investment enabled Macedonia's economy to achieve one of the highest score improvements in the 2010 *Index*. Macedonia also enjoys high levels of trade freedom, fiscal freedom, and monetary freedom. Personal and corporate income tax rates are very competitive, and tax administration has been strengthened. Monetary stability is relatively well maintained. Macedonia is generally open to global trade, and the financial sector has weathered the global financial crisis relatively well.

Macedonia still lacks sufficient institutional support for property rights and the fight against corruption. The court system is prone to corruption, political interference, and inefficiency, and human trafficking and smuggling of drugs and weapons remain serious problems.

BACKGROUND: Since gaining its independence from the former Yugoslavia in 1991, the Republic of Macedonia has been politically and economically troubled. In 2001, the Ohrid Agreement prevented civil war by giving greater recognition to the Albanian minority within a unitary state. Macedonia still has high unemployment, weak economic growth, and significant informal economic activity. The elections that returned reform-minded Prime Minister Nikola Gruevski to power in June 2008 were criticized by international monitors; international observers agreed that the 2009 presidential and municipal elections marked a significant improvement. During the 2008 Bucharest summit, Greece blocked an invitation to Macedonia to join NATO because it believes that Macedonia's name does not appropriately acknowledge its Greek region. The dispute is expected to delay Macedonia's accession to the European Union as well.

Country's Score Over Time

Most free

World average

Macedonia

Least free

1995   1998   2001   2004   2007   **2010**

Quick Facts

Population: 2.0 million

GDP (PPP): $20.5 billion
4.9% growth in 2008
4.7% 5-year compound annual growth
$10,041 per capita

Unemployment: 33.5%

Inflation (CPI): 8.3%

FDI Inflow: $598 million

2008 data unless otherwise noted
Data compiled as of September 2009

How Do We Measure Economic Freedom?
See page 457 for an explanation of the methodology or visit the *Index* Web site at *heritage.org/index*.

MACEDONIA'S TEN ECONOMIC FREEDOMS

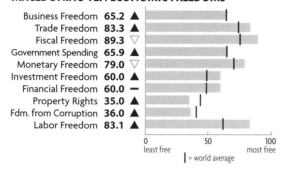

Business Freedom	65.2	▲
Trade Freedom	83.3	▲
Fiscal Freedom	89.3	▽
Government Spending	65.9	▲
Monetary Freedom	79.0	▽
Investment Freedom	60.0	▲
Financial Freedom	60.0	—
Property Rights	35.0	▲
Fdm. from Corruption	36.0	▲
Labor Freedom	83.1	▲

0 least free — 50 — 100 most free

| = world average

BUSINESS FREEDOM — 65.2

The overall freedom to establish and run a business in Macedonia has improved with recent regulatory reforms. Starting a business now takes an average of four days, compared to the world average of 35 days. Obtaining a business license is costly but takes less than the world average of 218 days.

TRADE FREEDOM — 83.3

Macedonia's weighted average tariff rate was 3.3 percent in 2008. Import taxes, some import restrictions, import licensing, non-transparent regulations and standards, and customs corruption add to the cost of trade. Ten points were deducted from Macedonia's trade freedom score to account for non-tariff barriers.

FISCAL FREEDOM — 89.3

Macedonia has low taxes. The individual income and corporate tax rates are a flat 10 percent. Other taxes include a value-added tax (VAT) and a property transfer tax. The capital gains tax was abolished effective January 1, 2009. In the most recent year, overall tax revenue as a percentage of GDP was 29.5 percent.

GOVERNMENT SPENDING — 65.9

Total government expenditures, including consumption and transfer payments, are moderate. In the most recent year, government spending equaled 33.7 percent of GDP. Some small and medium-size hydroelectric plants have been privatized, and the electricity sector remains an important target for further reform. Macedonia's expansionary fiscal stance in response to the global downturn is unique within the region, and pension and wage increases threaten future budget stability.

MONETARY FREEDOM — 79

Inflation has been moderately high, averaging 6.4 percent between 2006 and 2008, although the rate declined sharply in 2009. Most prices are determined in the market, but the government subsidizes agriculture and influences certain prices through state-owned enterprises and utilities, such as electricity. Five points were deducted from Macedonia's monetary freedom score to account for policies that distort domestic prices.

INVESTMENT FREEDOM — 60

Foreign and domestic investors receive equal treatment, and non-residents may invest in domestic firms with few exceptions. Despite reforms in the investment regime, the legal system and investment bureaucracy can be slow, inefficient, lacking in adequate resources, and subject to political pressures and corruption. Contract enforcement can be inconsistent. Residents and non-residents may hold foreign exchange accounts subject to approval and restrictions. Payments and transfers face few controls. Foreign investors are permitted land-use rights but not land ownership.

FINANCIAL FREEDOM — 60

Macedonia's financial sector is not fully developed, but it is growing as the country encourages private-sector development and foreign investment. Bank competition has increased, and the foreign presence in the financial system is substantial, accounting for more than 80 percent of total bank assets. The three largest banks account for about 70 percent of all deposits and loans. Banking intermediation is relatively low, but credit is allocated on market terms. Macedonia's 2007 Banking Law substantially enhanced the sector's legal and regulatory framework. Nonperforming loans have reduced by half, from more than 16 percent of total loans in 2004 to less than 8 percent in recent years. Capital markets are underdeveloped and unable to provide a full range of credit alternatives for businesses, but activity on the Macedonian Stock Exchange has grown, and the number of companies listed has increased.

PROPERTY RIGHTS — 35

Protection of property rights is weak. The judiciary is subject to executive influence. The lack of effective rule of law and the uncertainty of property rights, especially in registering real property and obtaining land titles, undermine investment and development. The government has taken some action to combat piracy of items like CDs, DVDs, and software, but many pirated items remain for sale.

FREEDOM FROM CORRUPTION — 36

Corruption is perceived as significant. Macedonia ranks 72nd out of 179 countries in Transparency International's Corruption Perceptions Index for 2008, an improvement for the second consecutive year. The law provides criminal penalties for official corruption; however, the government has not implemented the law effectively, and officials engage in corrupt practices with impunity. Corruption is found in all branches of government, especially the police and judicial system. Enforcement of laws against offenses like drug abuse, money laundering, and corrupt practices has been lackluster.

LABOR FREEDOM — 83.1

Macedonia's labor regulations have become more flexible. After years of chronic high unemployment, Macedonia has enacted major labor market reforms that include the use of fixed-term contracts and the easing of restrictions on work hours.

MADAGASCAR

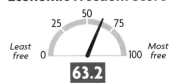

World Rank: 69   **Regional Rank: 3**

Economic Freedom Score

25   **50**   75

Least free 0   100 Most free

63.2

Madagascar's economic freedom score is 63.2, making its economy the 69th freest in the 2010 *Index*. Its score has increased by 1.1 points from last year, reflecting modest improvements in seven of the 10 economic freedoms. Madagascar is ranked 3rd out of 46 countries in the Sub-Saharan Africa region, and its overall score is above the world average.

Madagascar has implemented some notable reforms to enhance its entrepreneurial environment. Tax rates on individual and corporate income have been lowered, and the overall tax system has been simplified. Procedures for launching a business have been streamlined, and minimum capital requirements have been abolished.

Further economic development is hindered by a lack of institutional capacity and ongoing political instability that risks undermining much of the progress made in reducing poverty. Trade freedom suffered a setback with a rise in the average tariff rate. As in many other Sub-Saharan African nations, the judicial system is underdeveloped, and convoluted administrative procedures encourage corruption. Privatization has halted due to an unfavorable investment climate that has arisen from the political turmoil.

BACKGROUND: Both former President Didier Ratsiraka and opposition candidate Marc Ravalomanana claimed victory in the 2001 elections, and the resulting violence and economic disruption ended only when Ratsiraka fled into exile in 2002. Ravalomanana won a second term in 2006 but stepped down in March 2009 following a power struggle with the opposition. Opposition leader Andry Rajoelina seized power with military backing, declared himself President of the High Transitional Authority, and pledged to hold elections in 2010. Some donors have suspended aid, and both the African Union and the Southern African Development Community have suspended Madagascar's membership. Years of socialism and state planning have hindered economic growth in Madagascar, which depends heavily on agriculture and produces two-thirds of the world's vanilla exports. Infrastructure is poor, and bureaucracy is onerous.

Country's Score Over Time

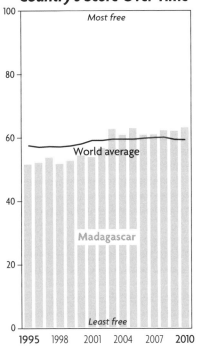

Quick Facts

Population: 19.1 million

GDP (PPP): $20.0 billion
6.9% growth in 2008
5.2% 5-year compound annual growth
$1,049 per capita

Unemployment: n/a

Inflation (CPI): 9.2%

FDI Inflow: $1.5 billion

2008 data unless otherwise noted
Data compiled as of September 2009

How Do We Measure Economic Freedom?
See page 457 for an explanation of the methodology or visit the *Index* Web site at *heritage.org/index.*

MADAGASCAR'S TEN ECONOMIC FREEDOMS

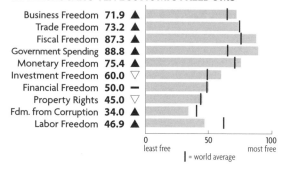

Business Freedom	71.9	▲
Trade Freedom	73.2	▲
Fiscal Freedom	87.3	▲
Government Spending	88.8	▲
Monetary Freedom	75.4	▲
Investment Freedom	60.0	▽
Financial Freedom	50.0	—
Property Rights	45.0	▽
Fdm. from Corruption	34.0	▲
Labor Freedom	46.9	▲

0 least free   50   100 most free
| = world average

BUSINESS FREEDOM — 71.9

The overall freedom to start, operate, and close a business is limited by Madagascar's regulatory environment. Starting a business takes seven days, compared to the world average of 35 days. Obtaining a business license requires less than the world average of 218 days and 18 procedures. Madagascar lacks modern and efficient bankruptcy procedures.

TRADE FREEDOM — 73.2

Madagascar's weighted average tariff rate was 8.4 percent in 2008. Some import and export bans and restrictions, import taxes, some import licensing, sanitary and phytosanitary regulations, inadequate infrastructure to support trade, some state trade, weak enforcement of intellectual property rights, and a customs process that is susceptible to corruption add to the cost of trade. Ten points were deducted from Madagascar's trade freedom score to account for non-tariff barriers.

FISCAL FREEDOM — 87.3

Madagascar has moderate tax rates. Both the top income tax rate and the top corporate tax rate are 24 percent, down from 30 percent. Other taxes include a value-added tax (VAT) and a capital gains tax. In the most recent year, overall tax revenue as a percentage of GDP was 10.9 percent.

GOVERNMENT SPENDING — 88.8

Total government expenditures, including consumption and transfer payments, are low. In the most recent year, government spending equaled 19.3 percent of GDP. Plans to transfer the struggling national water and power utility out of state hands have been put on hold indefinitely.

MONETARY FREEDOM — 75.4

Inflation has been high, averaging 9.6 percent between 2006 and 2008, but the rate declined in 2009. Most prices are determined in the market, but the government influences certain prices through state-owned enterprises and utilities such as electricity, although this influence is diminishing as privatization advances. Five points were deducted from Madagascar's monetary freedom score to account for policies that distort domestic prices.

INVESTMENT FREEDOM — 60

The government provides national treatment for foreign investment, but poor infrastructure, non-transparent regulation, a slow and complex commercial legal system, limited financing mechanisms, and political interference hinder investment levels overall. Residents and non-residents may open foreign exchange accounts, and there are no restrictions on payments or transfers. Foreign investors may own land, subject to a number of restrictions.

FINANCIAL FREEDOM — 50

Madagascar's underdeveloped financial sector is dominated by relatively well-capitalized banks. The government has been pursuing banking reform, and all of the major commercial banks are now partially privatized, often with French capital. There are five major commercial banks, and the central bank accounts for over one-third of financial-sector assets. The relatively high costs of financing and scarce access to credit are barriers to entrepreneurial activity. Less than 5 percent of the population has bank accounts or access to comprehensive financial services. An extensive network of savings and loan associations extends deposit functions more broadly. Non-performing loans have gradually declined to less than 10 percent of total loans. There is no stock market.

PROPERTY RIGHTS — 45

Secured interests in property are recognized but poorly enforced. Restrictions on land ownership by foreigners impede investment. A system of long-term leases of up to 99 years was established in 2008 to address the issue, but there have been long delays and few successes in the approval of land leases for foreigners. The judiciary is influenced by the executive and subject to corruption, and investors face a legal and judicial environment in which the enforcement of contracts cannot be guaranteed. Pirated copies of VHS movie tapes, music CDs, DVDs, and software are sold openly, and TV stations broadcast pirated copies of movies.

FREEDOM FROM CORRUPTION — 34

Corruption is perceived as widespread. Madagascar ranks 85th out of 179 countries in Transparency International's Corruption Perceptions Index for 2008. Complicated administrative procedures introduce delays and uncertainties and multiply the opportunities for corruption. Combating corruption is a stated priority of the government, and senior officials appear to be taking that effort seriously.

LABOR FREEDOM — 46.9

Labor regulations are restrictive. The non-salary cost of employing a worker is high, and dismissing an employee is not easy. Regulations on work hours remain rigid.

Lilongwe

MALAWI

Economic Freedom Score

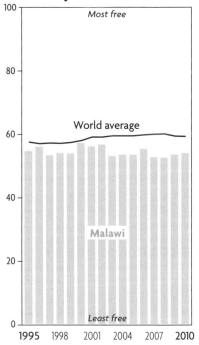

Least free 0   25   50   75   100 Most free

54.1

World Rank: **122**   Regional Rank: **22**

Malawi's economic freedom score is 54.1, making its economy the 122nd freest in the 2010 *Index*. Its score has increased 0.4 point from last year, primarily reflecting improved fiscal freedom. Malawi is ranked 22nd out of 46 countries in the Sub-Saharan Africa region, and its overall score is below the world average.

Malawi has achieved average economic growth of 7 percent over the past five years, but sustaining this growth will be challenging without institutional reform. The lack of equitable access to finance is a major constraint on private-sector development. Weak rule of law jeopardizes protection of property rights, and corruption is rampant. Monetary stability remains fragile, although government price distortions are not widespread.

Malawi ranks just below the world average in most areas of economic freedom. However, despite some lingering barriers, foreign investment is generally welcome. The small financial sector is relatively stable compared to others in the region. Malawi has taken steps to improve its regulatory framework in order to enhance its business environment and encourage a vibrant private sector, but progress has been slow.

BACKGROUND: After achieving its independence in 1964, Malawi became a one-party state that was ruled by Dr. Hastings Kamuzu Banda for 30 years. President Bingu wa Mutharika was elected in 2004 as the candidate of the ruling United Democratic Front. A year later, he threw the political system into chaos when he resigned from the UDF, accusing party leaders of impeding his anti-corruption efforts, and formed a new political party. Mutharika won reelection in May 2009 by a large margin. Malawi is one of Africa's most densely populated countries. Over 85 percent of the population depends on subsistence agriculture, and the agricultural sector accounts for over 35 percent of GDP and over 80 percent of exports. Tobacco, tea, and sugar are Malawi's most important exports.

Country's Score Over Time

Most free

World average

Malawi

Least free

1995   1998   2001   2004   2007   **2010**

Quick Facts

Population: 14.3 million

GDP (PPP): $11.9 billion
9.7% growth in 2008
7.1% 5-year compound annual growth
$837 per capita

Unemployment: n/a

Inflation (CPI): 8.7%

FDI Inflow: $37 million

2008 data unless otherwise noted
Data compiled as of September 2009

How Do We Measure Economic Freedom?
See page 457 for an explanation of the methodology or visit the *Index* Web site at *heritage.org/index.*

MALAWI'S TEN ECONOMIC FREEDOMS

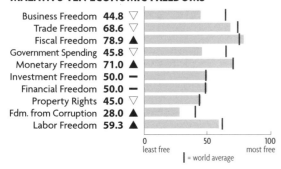

Business Freedom	44.8 ▽
Trade Freedom	68.6 ▽
Fiscal Freedom	78.9 ▲
Government Spending	45.8 ▽
Monetary Freedom	71.0 ▲
Investment Freedom	50.0 —
Financial Freedom	50.0 —
Property Rights	45.0 ▽
Fdm. from Corruption	28.0 ▲
Labor Freedom	59.3 ▲

0 least free   50   100 most free

| = world average

BUSINESS FREEDOM — 44.8

The overall freedom to start, operate, and close a business is restricted under Malawi's regulatory environment. The entry cost of starting a business is high, and obtaining a business license requires more than the world average of 18 procedures.

TRADE FREEDOM — 68.6

Malawi's weighted average tariff rate was 8.2 percent in 2008. Import and export restrictions, some services market access restrictions, import and export licensing requirements, import taxes, some discriminatory regulations, inadequate infrastructure, subsidies, and inefficient and corrupt customs administration add to the cost of trade. Fifteen points were deducted from Malawi's trade freedom score to account for non-tariff barriers.

FISCAL FREEDOM — 78.9

Malawi has moderate tax rates. The top income and corporate tax rates are 30 percent. Other taxes include a value-added tax (VAT) and an inheritance tax. In the most recent year, overall tax revenue as a percentage of GDP was 17.6 percent.

GOVERNMENT SPENDING — 45.8

Total government expenditures, including consumption and transfer payments, are high. In the most recent year, government spending equaled 42.5 percent of GDP. Efforts to engage in public–private partnerships as an alternative to privatization have fallen short. External grants sustain Malawi and have allowed authorities to expedite fiscal consolidation. Public financial management needs better mechanisms for monthly reporting. The run-up to May 2009 elections saw an increase in public-sector wages and food subsidies.

MONETARY FREEDOM — 71

Inflation has been high, averaging 9.0 percent between 2006 and 2008. Although most prices are determined in the market, the government influences certain prices through state-owned enterprises and utilities, such as electricity, transportation, water, and telecommunications; controls the prices of petroleum products and sugar; and uses subsidies to stabilize maize and fertilizer prices. Ten points were deducted from Malawi's monetary freedom score to account for policies that distort domestic prices.

INVESTMENT FREEDOM — 50

Foreign and domestic private investments are generally welcome in most sectors. There is no screening of foreign investment, although foreign and domestic investors are subject to licensing in certain sectors. While the government has implemented reforms and is moving forward with privatizations, red tape and poor infrastructure continue to impede investment. The legal system is slow, and contract enforcement can be uncertain. Non-residents may hold foreign exchange accounts, subject to restrictions and government approval. Because of shortages of foreign exchange, some payments and transfers face quantitative limits. Most capital transactions by residents require approval. Land ownership is subject to some restrictions.

FINANCIAL FREEDOM — 50

Malawi's developing financial sector remains small and dominated by banking. Ten commercial banks offer a variety of services and generally allocate credit on market terms. However, high credit costs and scarce access to financing hinder more vibrant business activity. Much lending goes to the government or subsidiaries, though a decline in state borrowing has led to greater competition. The two largest banks are the domestic National Bank of Malawi, which is 50 percent government-owned, and a subsidiary of a South African bank. Capital markets are not fully developed, and activity on the Malawi Stock Exchange remains very limited. In an attempt to enhance the financial sector's supervisory framework, the Reserve Bank of Malawi recently introduced amendments to the Banking Act and a Financial Services Bill.

PROPERTY RIGHTS — 45

Rights to property, both real and intellectual, are legally protected. There are reports of government intervention in some judicial cases and frequent allegations of bribery in civil and criminal cases. Court administration is weak, and due process can be very slow. Malawi adheres to international IPR treaties and agreements.

FREEDOM FROM CORRUPTION — 28

Corruption is perceived as widespread. Malawi ranks 115th out of 179 countries in Transparency International's Corruption Perceptions Index for 2008. Despite some progress, corruption is still seen as a major obstacle to doing business, and there have been allegations of serious problems in agencies handling customs, taxes, and procurement. The government says that the fight against corruption is a priority, but investigations and trials continue to move at a slow pace. In 2008, high-profile cases that were brought to trial included a former cabinet minister and the CEO of a utility company.

LABOR FREEDOM — 59.3

Malawi's labor regulations are burdensome. The non-salary cost of employing a worker is moderate, but laying off an employee is costly.

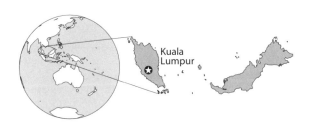
Kuala
Lumpur

MALAYSIA

Economic Freedom Score

25   50   75

Least free 0   100 Most free

64.8

M alaysia's economic freedom score is 64.8, making its economy the 59th freest in the 2010 *Index*. Its score is 0.2 point better than last year, reflecting improvements in four of the 10 economic freedoms. Malaysia is ranked 9th out of 41 countries in the Asia–Pacific region, and its overall score is above the world and regional averages.

Malaysia's ongoing reform measures have enhanced the overall entrepreneurial environment. The economy scores above the world average in eight of the 10 economic freedoms. The labor sector is relatively flexible, with simple employment procedures and no mandated minimum wage. The top income and corporate tax rates are moderate and have been reduced, and the overall tax burden is low as a percentage of GDP.

The financial sector has weathered the global financial crisis relatively well. Limits on foreign ownership in financial sub-sectors were eased, improving financial freedom, and numerous domestic equity requirements that restricted foreign investment were eliminated. Corruption and a judicial system that remains vulnerable to political influence remain significant challenges to economic freedom in Malaysia.

BACKGROUND: Malaysia, an ethnically and religiously diverse constitutional monarchy, became independent in 1957 and has been ruled since then by the United Malays National Organization. Huge electoral inroads made by the opposition coalition, led by the People's Justice Party, in March 2008 were due largely to popular dissatisfaction with pro-Malay affirmative action programs and widespread corruption. Malaysia has slowly liberalized its economy, but government ownership in such key sectors as banking, automobiles, and airlines remains high. Malaysia is a leading exporter of electronics and information technology products, and its industries range from agricultural goods to automobiles.

Country's Score Over Time

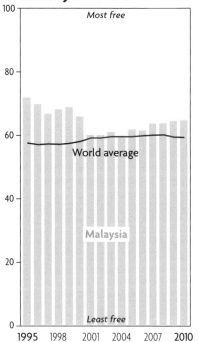

Quick Facts

Population: 27.0 million

GDP (PPP): $383.7 billion
4.6% growth in 2008
5.5% 5-year compound
annual growth
$14,215 per capita

Unemployment: 3.3%

Inflation (CPI): 5.4%

FDI Inflow: $8.1 billion

2008 data unless otherwise noted
Data compiled as of September 2009

How Do We Measure Economic Freedom?
See page 457 for an explanation of the methodology or visit the *Index* Web site at *heritage.org/index*.

MALAYSIA'S TEN ECONOMIC FREEDOMS

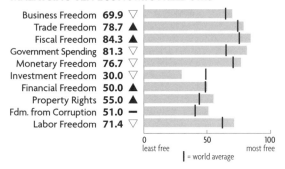

Business Freedom	69.9	▽
Trade Freedom	78.7	▲
Fiscal Freedom	84.3	▲
Government Spending	81.3	▽
Monetary Freedom	76.7	▽
Investment Freedom	30.0	▽
Financial Freedom	50.0	▲
Property Rights	55.0	▲
Fdm. from Corruption	51.0	—
Labor Freedom	71.4	▽

0 least free   50   100 most free

▌ = world average

BUSINESS FREEDOM — 69.9

The overall freedom to start, operate, and close a business is somewhat limited by Malaysia's regulatory environment. Starting a business takes an average of 11 days, compared to the world average of 35 days. Obtaining a business license takes more than the world average of 18 procedures and 218 days. Bankruptcy proceedings are relatively straightforward.

TRADE FREEDOM — 78.7

Malaysia's weighted average tariff rate was 3.1 percent in 2007. Some high tariffs, import and export taxes, import restrictions, high services market access barriers, import and export licensing, non-transparent regulations and standards, non-transparent government procurement, export subsidies, and weak protection of intellectual property rights add to the cost of trade. Fifteen points were deducted from Malaysia's trade freedom score to account for non-tariff barriers.

FISCAL FREEDOM — 84.3

Malaysia has moderate tax rates. The top individual income tax rate is 27 percent (non-residents are subject to a flat 28 percent tax). The corporate tax rate has been reduced to 25 percent from 26 percent. Other taxes include a capital gains tax and a vehicle tax. Under a single-tier tax system that became effective on January 1, 2008, dividend income is exempt from income tax. In the most recent year, overall tax revenue as a percentage of GDP was 14.8 percent.

GOVERNMENT SPENDING — 81.3

Total government expenditures, including consumption and transfer payments, are relatively low. In the most recent year, government spending equaled 25.0 percent of GDP.

MONETARY FREEDOM — 76.7

Inflation has been moderate, averaging 4.4 percent between 2006 and 2008. Most prices are determined in the market, but the government influences certain prices through state-owned enterprises; controls the prices of petroleum products, steel, cement, wheat flour, sugar, milk, bread, and chicken; and usually sets ceiling prices for a list of essential foods during major holidays. Ten points were deducted from Malaysia's monetary freedom score to account for policies that distort domestic prices.

INVESTMENT FREEDOM — 30

Foreign investment is welcome in certain sectors, and some domestic equity requirements have been eliminated. Certain kinds of investment are screened, though commercial operations can begin before approval. Resolving commercial disputes can be complex and time-consuming. Regulations are burdensome and non-transparent, and skilled labor is in short supply. Residents and non-residents may hold foreign exchange accounts, subject in many cases to government approval. Nearly all capital transactions are subject to restrictions or require government approval. Ownership of agricultural land is restricted to Malaysians.

FINANCIAL FREEDOM — 50

Supervision of banking has been strengthened, and non-performing loans have decreased to less than 5 percent. Mergers among local banks have been encouraged to increase overall competitiveness. There are 38 commercial banks, 20 of which are domestically owned. The central bank licenses and regulates banks. Islamic banking based on Sharia law accounted for around 17 percent of total banking assets in 2008. Foreign firms' overall participation in the financial sector remains restricted. Equity participation is limited to 30 percent for commercial banks, but in 2009, the central bank raised the foreign ownership limit concerning Islamic banks, investment banks, and insurance companies to 70 percent from the previous 49 percent. The financial system has withstood the global financial crisis relatively well, and banks remain generally well capitalized and liquid.

PROPERTY RIGHTS — 55

Private property is protected, but the judiciary is subject to political influence. Corporate lawsuits take over a year to file, and many contracts include a mandatory arbitration clause. Despite plans to ratify the World Intellectual Property Organization (WIPO) Copyright Treaty and the WIPO Performances and Phonograms Treaty, complaints about lax enforcement of intellectual property rights persist, and the manufacture and sale of counterfeit products have led to serious losses for producers of consumer products and pharmaceuticals.

FREEDOM FROM CORRUPTION — 51

Corruption is perceived as present. Malaysia ranks 47th out of 179 countries in Transparency International's Corruption Perceptions Index for 2008. The law provides criminal penalties for official corruption, but it has not been implemented effectively, and officials engage in corrupt practices with impunity. The media have reported numerous cases of alleged official corruption.

LABOR FREEDOM — 71.4

Labor regulations are relatively flexible. The non-salary cost of employing a worker is low, but dismissing an employee remains difficult and costly. There is no national minimum wage, and restrictions on work hours are flexible.

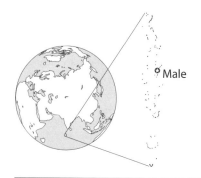

Male

MALDIVES

Economic Freedom Score

25   50   75

Least free 0   100 Most free

49.0

The Maldives' economic freedom score is 49.0, making its economy the 148th freest in the 2010 *Index*. Its score has decreased by 2.3 points from last year, reflecting declines in half of the 10 economic freedoms. The Maldives is ranked 34th out of 41 countries in the Asia–Pacific region, and its overall score is below the world and regional averages.

The Maldives scores above the world average in business freedom and fiscal freedom. The overall regulatory environment is streamlined and transparent. With no system of direct taxation, government revenue relies on import taxes, tourism taxes, and income generated by state-owned enterprises. The Maldives has undergone five years of steady economic growth, but continuing measures to enhance competitiveness will be vital as the economy becomes more integrated with global markets.

The Maldives' weaknesses include large government spending and widespread corruption. The government still plays a large role in the economy through state-owned enterprises, limiting and crowding out private-sector activity. Public ownership is widespread in every sector except tourism, and the public sector remains the largest source of employment, hiring over one-third of the labor force.

BACKGROUND: The Maldives has largely recovered from the devastation caused by the 2004 Asian tsunami. Tourism is the centerpiece of the economy, contributing 28 percent of GDP in 2007. Fishing employs about 11 percent of the labor force, and manufacturing provides less than 7 percent of GDP. The Maldives held its first multi-party presidential elections in October 2008. President Mohammed Nasheed was sworn into office on November 11, 2008, succeeding Maumoon Abdul Gayoom, who ruled the country for 30 years.

Country's Score Over Time

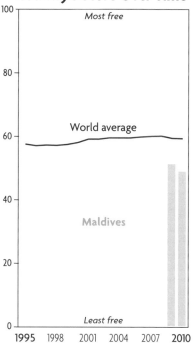

Quick Facts

Population: 0.3 million

GDP (PPP): $1.7 billion
   5.8% growth in 2008
   6.3% 5-year compound annual growth
   $5,504 per capita

Unemployment: 14.4% (2006)

Inflation (CPI): 12.3%

FDI Inflow: $15 million

2008 data unless otherwise noted
Data compiled as of September 2009

How Do We Measure Economic Freedom?
See page 457 for an explanation of the methodology or visit the *Index* Web site at *heritage.org/index.*

MALDIVES' TEN ECONOMIC FREEDOMS

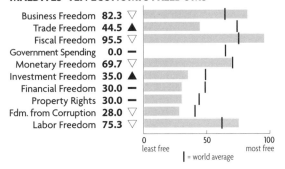

Business Freedom	82.3	▽
Trade Freedom	44.5	▲
Fiscal Freedom	95.5	▽
Government Spending	0.0	—
Monetary Freedom	69.7	▽
Investment Freedom	35.0	▲
Financial Freedom	30.0	—
Property Rights	30.0	—
Fdm. from Corruption	28.0	▽
Labor Freedom	75.3	▽

0 least free   50   100 most free

| = world average

BUSINESS FREEDOM — *82.3*

The Maldives' regulatory environment allows significant freedom to conduct a business. Starting a business takes only nine days, compared to the world average of 35 days. Obtaining a business license requires less than the world average of 18 procedures and 218 days.

TRADE FREEDOM — *44.5*

The Maldives' weighted average tariff rate was 20.3 percent in 2008. Import restrictions; import quotas on rice, flour, and sugar; import taxes and import licensing; inefficient customs administration; weak institutional capacity; weak enforcement of intellectual property rights; and corruption add to the cost of trade. Most imports are conducted through the government-owned State Trading Organization. Fifteen points were deducted from the Maldives' trade freedom score to account for non-tariff barriers.

FISCAL FREEDOM — *95.5*

The Maldives has neither a corporate tax nor a broad-based sales tax. Bank profits are subject to a profit tax. In the most recent year, overall tax revenue as a percentage of GDP was 21.1 percent. Revenues are collected from customs duties.

GOVERNMENT SPENDING — *0*

Total government expenditures, including consumption and transfer payments, are extremely high. In the most recent year, government spending equaled 66.9 percent of GDP. Expenditure levels skyrocketed after the 2004 tsunami, but most of the tsunami-related expenditures were financed by foreign aid. Moving forward, without dependable mechanisms for raising domestic revenue, the government will have to cut expenditures and better prioritize spending.

MONETARY FREEDOM — *69.7*

Inflation has been high, averaging 10.3 percent between 2006 and 2008. Privatization is progressing slowly, and the government continues to operate state-owned enterprises and to oversee prices through regulatory agencies. Ten points were deducted from the Maldives' monetary freedom score to adjust for measures that distort domestic prices.

INVESTMENT FREEDOM — *35*

While foreign investment in the Maldives is welcome in certain sectors, it is subject to individual agreements with the government that last for an initial period of five to 10 years for investments of less than $1 million. For larger projects, terms are negotiable. The government reviews all proposed investments before granting licenses. Foreign investors are required to pay annual royalty fees to the government. Bureaucracy can be non-transparent and prone to corruption. Dispute resolution can be non-transparent and burdensome. There are few restrictions on currency or capital transactions. There is little private land ownership. Foreign investors may lease but not own land.

FINANCIAL FREEDOM — *30*

The Maldives' shallow financial sector is dominated by banks. There is one partially state-owned domestic bank in addition to four branches of foreign banks. The Maldives Monetary Authority functions as a central bank and regulates banking activities. Short-term financing is widely available, and credit is generally allocated on market terms. However, the relatively high cost of credit and limited access to financial services hamper entrepreneurial activity and the development of a more vibrant private sector. In recent years, non-performing loans have dropped to under 3 percent of total loans. As part of the Maldives' ongoing efforts to enhance private-sector development, the government, which owns over half of the largest telecommunications company, has embarked on a mobile phone banking project with support from the World Bank. In a step toward strengthening liquidity management, an amendment to the Maldives Monetary Authority Act has reorganized the governing body of the central bank and separated management of the central bank and finance ministry.

PROPERTY RIGHTS — *30*

There is little private ownership of land. Land reform currently under consideration may result in more trade and private ownership of property. Foreign investors are not allowed to own land but can be granted lease rights. The Maldives lacks specific legislation to protect intellectual property rights and has not signed any related international agreements or conventions. The overall respect for and protection of property rights is weak.

FREEDOM FROM CORRUPTION — *28*

Corruption is perceived as widespread. The Maldives ranks 115th out of 179 countries in Transparency International's Corruption Perceptions Index for 2008, a significant drop from 2007. Corruption is a serious problem, and the new government has vowed to fight it. An Anti-Corruption Commission was created in December 2008.

LABOR FREEDOM — *75.3*

The Maldives' labor regulations are flexible. The non-salary cost of employing a worker is low, and dismissing an employee is not costly.

Bamako

MALI

25   50   75

Least   0   100   Most
free   free

55.6

| World Rank: **112** | Regional Rank: **17** |

M ali's economic freedom score is 55.6, making its economy the 112th freest in the 2010 *Index*. Its score is unchanged from last year. Mali is ranked 17th out of 46 countries in the Sub-Saharan Africa region, and its score is above the regional average.

Agriculture dominates economic activity in Mali and is the main source of economic growth. The sector provides over 70 percent of export income and employs more than one-third of the labor force. Mali's legal and regulatory framework is weak and does not facilitate either economic diversification or the development of a more vibrant formal private sector. An estimated 90 percent of private-sector activity takes place outside the formal economy.

Challenges to enhancing Mali's entrepreneurial environment are substantial. The investment climate remains inefficient, and business freedom is weak. Low scores in financial freedom, property rights, and freedom from corruption reflect serious institutional barriers to growth and economic development. Protection of property rights is undermined by the inefficient judiciary, which is subject to political interference. Corruption is widespread.

BACKGROUND: Mali was ruled as a one-party socialist state until a military coup in 1991. Multi-party democratic elections were held in 1992. Retired General Amadou Toumani Touré, who served as head of state during the transition to democracy in 1991 and 1992, won the 2002 election and was re-elected in 2007. Low-level conflict in northern Mali between the government and nomadic Tuareg tribes over land, cultural, and linguistic rights continues. Despite improved economic growth in recent years, Mali remains one of the world's poorest countries. Agriculture (mostly subsistence farming), livestock, and fishing occupy 70 percent of the population and accounted for about 33 percent of GDP in 2007. Cotton is a key export. Mining is growing, but mineral resources are generally underexploited, and infrastructure remains inadequate.

Country's Score Over Time

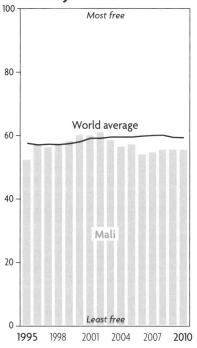

Quick Facts

Population: 12.7 million

GDP (PPP): $14.3 billion
5.0% growth in 2008
5.2% 5-year compound
annual growth
$1,128 per capita

Unemployment: estimated to be
over 10%

Inflation (CPI): 9.1%

FDI Inflow: $127 million

2008 data unless otherwise noted
Data compiled as of September 2009

How Do We Measure Economic Freedom?
See page 457 for an explanation of the methodology or visit the *Index* Web site at *heritage.org/index.*

MALI'S TEN ECONOMIC FREEDOMS

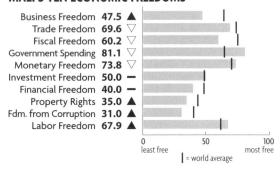

Business Freedom	47.5	▲
Trade Freedom	69.6	▽
Fiscal Freedom	60.2	▽
Government Spending	81.1	▽
Monetary Freedom	73.8	▽
Investment Freedom	50.0	—
Financial Freedom	40.0	—
Property Rights	35.0	▲
Fdm. from Corruption	31.0	▲
Labor Freedom	67.9	▲

0 least free   50   100 most free
| = world average

BUSINESS FREEDOM — 47.5

The overall freedom to establish and run a business is restricted by Mali's regulatory environment. Obtaining a business license requires less than the world average of 18 procedures and 218 days, but fees are high. The entry cost of starting a business remains very high.

TRADE FREEDOM — 69.6

Mali's weighted average tariff rate was 10.2 percent in 2008. Import and export restrictions, import licensing restrictions, some import taxes, inadequate infrastructure and trade capacity, state marketing of cotton, and inefficient customs implementation add to the cost of trade. Ten points were deducted from Mali's trade freedom score to account for non-tariff barriers.

FISCAL FREEDOM — 60.2

Mali has high tax rates. The top income tax rate is 50 percent, and the top corporate tax rate is 35 percent. Other taxes include a value-added tax (VAT) and an insurance tax. In the most recent year, overall tax revenue as a percentage of GDP was 16.1 percent.

GOVERNMENT SPENDING — 81.1

Total government expenditures, including consumption and transfer payments, are relatively low. In the most recent year, government spending equaled 25.1 percent of GDP. Primary targets for the next wave of privatizations are the national enterprises in telecommunications, banking, and cotton. Public financial management is improving.

MONETARY FREEDOM — 73.8

Inflation has been moderately high, averaging 6.6 percent between 2006 and 2008. Although most prices are determined in the market, the government influences certain prices through state-owned enterprises and utilities, such as telecommunications, and controls the price of fuel and cotton, which is one of the most important sectors of the economy. Ten points were deducted from Mali's monetary freedom score to account for policies that distort domestic prices.

INVESTMENT FREEDOM — 50

Foreign and domestic investments receive equal treatment, though both are screened by the government for approval.

Inconsistent enforcement of contracts, corruption in the commercial bureaucracy, poor infrastructure, and regional instability are deterrents to investment. Payments and transfers to some countries require government approval. Central bank rules require that all remittances go through its channels. Credit and loan operations and purchases of securities, derivatives, and other instruments may be subject to government authorization. Real estate purchases require special authorization.

FINANCIAL FREEDOM — 40

Mali has a small and underdeveloped financial sector. Financial intermediation remains low, and limited access to financing hampers entrepreneurial activity. Mali's inefficient legal framework is an impediment to enhancing the financial system. The country is a member of the West African Economic and Monetary Union, and the regional central bank governs financial institutions. There are over 10 commercial banks, including a development bank, an agricultural bank, and a housing bank. Only three commercial banks are fully private. Significant government ownership has hindered banking growth and has limited the range of services offered, although the foreign presence in the banking sector is considerable.

PROPERTY RIGHTS — 35

In theory, property rights are protected and the judiciary is constitutionally independent, but Mali's judicial system is considered notoriously inefficient and corrupt, with bribery and influence-peddling frequently encountered in the courts. The government has created a new agency, the Malian Center for the Promotion of Industrial Property, to implement the WTO's Trade-Related Aspects of Intellectual Property Rights (TRIPS) agreement. Mali also belongs to the African Property Rights Organization (OAPI).

FREEDOM FROM CORRUPTION — 31

Corruption is perceived as widespread. Mali ranks 96th out of 179 countries in Transparency International's Corruption Perceptions Index for 2008, an improvement from 2007. Corruption poses an obstacle to foreign direct investment. Government officials often solicit bribes in order to complete otherwise routine procedures. There are widely circulated reports of bribery in connection with large contracts and investment projects. Corruption appears to be most prevalent in government procurement and dispute settlement; it is not uncommon for government procurement agents to be paid a commission of 5 percent to 10 percent. Critics allege that senior government officials and major private and parastatal companies have engaged in widespread tax evasion and customs duty fraud.

LABOR FREEDOM — 67.9

Mali's labor regulations are relatively rigid. The non-salary cost of employing a worker is high, and the difficulty of laying off a worker creates a disincentive for additional hiring. Regulations on the number of work hours are not flexible.

MALTA

Economic Freedom Score

Least free 0   25   50   75   100   Most free

67.2

World Rank: 48   **Regional Rank: 22**

Malta's economic freedom score is 67.2, making its economy the 48th freest in the 2010 *Index*. Its score has increased by 1.1 points from last year, reflecting a large increase in investment freedom. Malta ranks 22nd out of 43 countries in the Europe region, and its overall score is just above the regional average.

Many aspects of business formation in Malta are relatively well organized and straightforward, and the overall entrepreneurial environment is flexible and dynamic. The judiciary is independent and fairly efficient, providing strong protection of property rights. The financial market is small but sound and open to foreign competition. The financial sector has weathered the global financial crisis relatively well.

Challenges to economic freedom in Malta include burdensome taxation, a high level of government spending, and rigid labor regulations. Total government expenditures remain high, accounting for more than 40 percent of GDP. The labor market remains hampered by rigid employment regulations that hinder growth in employment opportunities.

BACKGROUND: The Maltese economy depends on tourism, trade, and manufacturing. The country's well-trained workers, low labor costs, and membership in the European Union attract foreign investment, but the government also maintains a sprawling socialist bureaucracy, and the majority of spending is allocated to housing, education, and health care entitlements. Malta has made some moves toward liberalization of its economy since joining the European Union in 2004 and adopting the euro on January 1, 2008, and they have helped it to weather some of the fallout from the global economic crisis. However, weakness in tourism has sent the economy into recession. George Abela was elected president on April 4, 2009, and has singled out illegal immigration as a political cause.

Country's Score Over Time

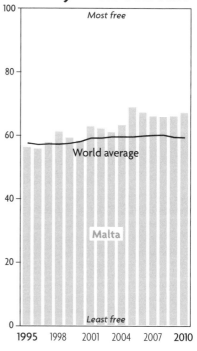

Quick Facts

Population: 413,000

GDP (PPP): $9.8 billion
1.6% growth in 2008
3.0% 5-year compound annual growth
$23,760 per capita

Unemployment: 5.9%

Inflation (CPI): 4.7%

FDI Inflow: $879 million

2008 data unless otherwise noted
Data compiled as of September 2009

How Do We Measure Economic Freedom?
See page 457 for an explanation of the methodology or visit the *Index* Web site at *heritage.org/index.*

MALTA'S TEN ECONOMIC FREEDOMS

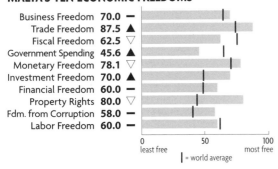

Business Freedom	70.0	—
Trade Freedom	87.5	▲
Fiscal Freedom	62.5	▽
Government Spending	45.6	▲
Monetary Freedom	78.1	▽
Investment Freedom	70.0	▲
Financial Freedom	60.0	—
Property Rights	80.0	▽
Fdm. from Corruption	58.0	—
Labor Freedom	60.0	—

0 least free   50   100 most free

| = world average

BUSINESS FREEDOM — 70

The overall freedom to start, operate, and close a business is relatively well protected under Malta's regulatory environment. Existing regulations are relatively straightforward and applied uniformly most of the time. Malta has adopted transparent and effective policies and regulations to foster competition.

TRADE FREEDOM — 87.5

Malta's trade policy is the same as that of other members of the European Union. The common EU weighted average tariff rate was 1.3 percent in 2008. However, the EU has high or escalating tariffs for agricultural and manufacturing products, and its MFN tariff code is complex. Non-tariff barriers reflected in EU and Maltese policy include agricultural and manufacturing subsidies, quotas, import restrictions and bans for some goods and services, market access restrictions in some services sectors, non-transparent and restrictive regulations and standards, and inconsistent regulatory and customs administration among EU members. Ten points were deducted from Malta's trade freedom score to account for non-tariff barriers.

FISCAL FREEDOM — 62.5

Malta has relatively high tax rates. Both the top income tax rate and the top corporate tax rate are 35 percent. Other taxes include a value-added tax (VAT) and a capital gains tax. In the most recent year, overall tax revenue as a percentage of GDP was 36.1 percent.

GOVERNMENT SPENDING — 45.6

Total government expenditures, including consumption and transfer payments, are high. In the most recent year, government spending equaled 42.6 percent of GDP. The government is significantly involved in the economy, subsidizes energy costs, and pledges to maintain free, universal health care without regard for fiscal concerns.

MONETARY FREEDOM — 78.1

Inflation has been moderate, averaging 3.5 percent between 2006 and 2008. As a participant in the EU's Common Agricultural Policy, the government subsidizes agricultural production, distorting the prices of agricultural products. The government also influences prices through state-owned enterprises, controls the prices of bread and milk,

and heavily subsidizes energy. Ten points were deducted from Malta's monetary freedom score to account for policies that distort domestic prices.

INVESTMENT FREEDOM — 70

Malta welcomes foreign investment, but the government examines all investments and carefully screens foreign proposals that are in direct competition with local business. Regulations are generally transparent, efficient, and consistently applied. Residents and non-residents may hold foreign exchange accounts, subject to reporting requirements. Maltese regulations and practices affecting remittances of investment capital and earnings have been improved as several foreign exchange controls were relaxed to conform to EU directives. Real estate purchases by non-residents require government approval.

FINANCIAL FREEDOM — 60

The financial sector has undergone transformation and restructuring and has expanded rapidly, with banking-sector assets equivalent to about five times the country's GDP. Supervision and regulation of the financial system have gradually become more transparent and consistent with international norms. Under a reform package that was passed in 2000 to induce more long-term foreign investment, many of the formerly state-owned banks have been privatized, and the presence of foreign banks is significant. Despite competition and diversification, the financial system still lacks effectively functioning capital markets. The stock exchange is small but active. Malta adopted the euro on January 1, 2008. The financial sector has withstood the global financial turmoil relatively well because of its limited exposure to structured financial instruments and its generally prudent lending practices.

PROPERTY RIGHTS — 80

Malta's judiciary is independent, both constitutionally and in practice. Property rights are protected, and expropriation is unlikely. Foreigners do not have full rights to buy property in Malta unless they obtain Maltese nationality. Malta has implemented the pertinent provisions of EU and WTO Trade-Related Aspects of Intellectual Property Rights (TRIPS) rules.

FREEDOM FROM CORRUPTION — 58

Corruption is perceived as present. Malta ranks 36th out of 179 countries in Transparency International's Corruption Perceptions Index for 2008. According to the Council of Europe's Group of States against Corruption (GRECO), Malta still lacks a comprehensive anti-corruption strategy, as well as appropriate institutions to implement and monitor anti-corruption activities.

LABOR FREEDOM — 60

Malta's labor regulations are relatively rigid. Labor relationships can be confrontational, and outdated and inefficient practices are persistent problems. The government mandates a minimum wage.

MAURITANIA

Economic Freedom Score

25   50   75

Least free   0   100   Most free

52.0

World Rank: 133   **Regional Rank: 26**

Mauritania's economic freedom score is 52.0, making its economy the 133rd freest in the 2010 *Index*. Its score has decreased by 1.9 points since last year, reflecting declines in four of the 10 economic freedoms. Mauritania is ranked 26th out of 46 countries in the Sub-Saharan Africa region, and its overall score is below the world and regional averages.

Years of political instability and poor governance, exacerbated by a coup in August 2008, have created a poor entrepreneurial environment in Mauritania. Business freedom has declined compared to other economies, and the weighted average tariff has increased, reducing trade freedom. Complex bureaucratic procedures and prescreening processes have reduced investment freedom.

Although the Mauritanian economy has expanded considerably from its limited productive base, it suffers from serious institutional weaknesses, and growth remains fragile. Court enforcement of property rights and labor regulations is subject to pervasive political interference. An underdeveloped financial sector hampers any dynamic activity by the private sector. Corruption and a lack of transparency increase uncertainty and risk.

BACKGROUND: A military junta ruled Mauritania from 1978 until 1992, when the first multi-party elections were held. President Maaouiya Ould Sid'Ahmed Taya won elections in 1992, 1997, and 2003. He was ousted in 2005, and a transitional government was appointed. Sidi Ould Cheikh Abdallahi was elected president in 2007 and overthrown in a bloodless coup in 2008. General Mohamed Ould Abdelaziz declared himself president of the Higher State Council that has ruled since then. Negotiations to establish a transitional government and hold elections are ongoing. Centuries of migration have produced a mixed population of Moors and Black Africans in which ethnic tensions have flared. Mauritania is predominantly desert and beset by drought, poor harvests, and unemployment. Mining and fishing dominate the economy. Oil production from offshore fields began in 2006.

Country's Score Over Time

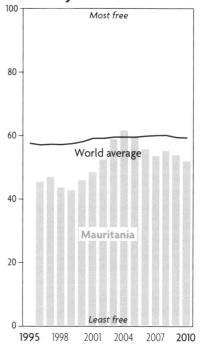

1995   1998   2001   2004   2007   2010

Quick Facts

Population: 3.0 million

GDP (PPP): $6.2 billion
2.2% growth in 2008
5.0% 5-year compound annual growth
$2,052 per capita

Unemployment: 30%

Inflation (CPI): 7.3%

FDI Inflow: $103 million

2008 data unless otherwise noted
Data compiled as of September 2009

How Do We Measure Economic Freedom?
See page 457 for an explanation of the methodology or visit the *Index* Web site at *heritage.org/index.*

MAURITANIA'S TEN ECONOMIC FREEDOMS

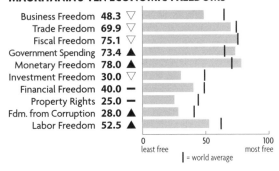

Business Freedom	48.3 ▽	
Trade Freedom	69.9 ▽	
Fiscal Freedom	75.1 ▽	
Government Spending	73.4 ▲	
Monetary Freedom	78.0 ▲	
Investment Freedom	30.0 ▽	
Financial Freedom	40.0 —	
Property Rights	25.0 —	
Fdm. from Corruption	28.0 ▲	
Labor Freedom	52.5 ▲	

0 50 100
least free   most free
| = world average

BUSINESS FREEDOM — 48.3

The overall freedom to establish and run a business is limited by Mauritania's regulatory environment. Despite an effort to streamline regulations, bureaucratic obstacles and delays remain. Starting a business takes about half the world average of 35 days, but the entry cost of launching a business is quite high. Obtaining a business license requires more than the world average of 18 procedures.

TRADE FREEDOM — 69.9

Mauritania's weighted average tariff rate was 10.1 percent in 2007. Import restrictions, import taxes, weak enforcement of intellectual property rights, inadequate infrastructure and trade capacity, and non-transparent customs administration add to the cost of trade. Ten points were deducted from Mauritania's trade freedom score to account for non-tariff barriers.

FISCAL FREEDOM — 75.1

Mauritania has a relatively high income tax rate and a moderate corporate tax rate. The top income tax rate is 40 percent, and the top corporate tax rate is 25 percent. Other taxes include a value-added tax (VAT) and a tax on insurance contracts. In the most recent year, overall tax revenue as a percentage of GDP was 16.4 percent.

GOVERNMENT SPENDING — 73.4

Total government expenditures, including consumption and transfer payments, are moderate. In the most recent year, government spending equaled 29.8 percent of GDP. Government intervention in the economy has increased. Expenditures on public investment and subsidies for the food-distribution program are high.

MONETARY FREEDOM — 78

Inflation has been relatively high, averaging 7.2 percent between 2006 and 2008. Most prices are determined in the market, but the government influences certain prices through state-owned enterprises and utilities, such as electricity. Although international prices for cereals and oil have fallen in 2009, the government has continued to subsidize food, electricity, and water. Five points were deducted from Mauritania's monetary freedom score to account for policies that distort domestic prices.

INVESTMENT FREEDOM — 30

Foreign investment is welcome in most sectors, and foreign and domestic investments are treated equally. Foreign investment is prescreened. Certain financial activity, mining and hydrocarbons, telecommunications, and utilities are subject to additional restrictions. Reforms have been implemented, but complicated and burdensome bureaucratic procedures, inadequate infrastructure, a lack of skilled labor, political uncertainty, corruption, and non-transparent legal, regulatory, and accounting systems inhibit investment. Residents and non-residents may hold foreign exchange accounts, but non-resident accounts are subject to some restrictions. Payments and transfers are subject to quantitative limits, bona fide tests, and prior approval in some cases.

FINANCIAL FREEDOM — 40

Mauritania's banking sector has undergone modernization and reform since 2007, but progress has been sluggish. Accounting for more than 80 percent of total assets, the banking sector dominates the financial system. There are 10 commercial banks, one of which is 50 percent government-owned. Foreign banks are new to the system; two French bank subsidiaries opened in 2006 and 2007. The banking sector is burdened by a high level of non-performing loans, which are estimated to be over 40 percent of total loans. Limited access to credit and the high costs of financing restrict more dynamic entrepreneurial activity. A new banking law enacted in 2007 has modestly enhanced competition and improved access to credit. Given the lack of depth and efficiency in the financial system, capital markets are virtually nonexistent, and there is no stock market.

PROPERTY RIGHTS — 25

Mauritania's judicial system is chaotic and corrupt. The judiciary is subject to influence from the executive. Poorly trained judges are intimidated by social, financial, tribal, and personal pressures. Mauritania signed and ratified the WTO's Trade-Related Aspects of Intellectual Property Rights (TRIPS) agreement in 1994 but has yet to implement it.

FREEDOM FROM CORRUPTION — 28

Corruption is perceived as widespread. Mauritania ranks 115th out of 179 countries in Transparency International's Corruption Perceptions Index for 2008. All levels of government and society are affected by corrupt practices. Affluent business groups and senior government officials reportedly receive favorable treatment with regard to taxes, special grants of land, and government procurement. Tax laws are routinely flouted. Widespread corruption weakens the government's ability to provide needed services.

LABOR FREEDOM — 52.5

Mauritania's labor regulations are restrictive. The non-salary cost of employing a worker is moderate, but laying off an employee is difficult. Restrictions on work hours are rigid.

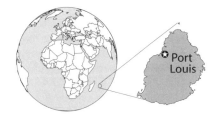
○ Port
Louis

MAURITIUS

Economic Freedom Score

25   50   75

Least   Most
free   0   100 free

76.3

World Rank: **12**	Regional Rank: **1**

Mauritius's economic freedom score is 76.3, making its economy the 12th freest in the 2010 *Index*. Its overall score is 2 points better than last year, reflecting major improvements in freedom from corruption and labor freedom. Mauritius is ranked 1st out of 46 countries in the Sub-Saharan African region, and its overall score is well above the world average.

Despite the global economic turmoil, Mauritius's economy has shown a considerable degree of resilience, and an environment already conducive to dynamic entrepreneurial activity has moved further toward economic freedom. The island's institutional advantages are noticeable. A transparent and well-defined investment code and legal system have made the foreign investment climate in Mauritius one of the best in the region. Taxation is competitive and efficient. The economy is increasingly diversified, with significant private-sector activity in sugar, tourism, economic processing zones, and financial services, particularly in offshore enterprises.

Although state monopolies exist, Mauritius has improved its management of public spending. The judiciary, independent of politics and relatively free of corruption, provides strong protection of property rights.

BACKGROUND: With a well-developed legal and commercial infrastructure and a tradition of entrepreneurship and representative government, Mauritius is one of the developing world's most successful democracies. It is also one of Sub-Saharan Africa's strongest economies and has one of the region's highest levels of per capita income. The government is trying to modernize the sugar and textile industries, which in the past were overly dependent on trade preferences, while promoting diversification into such areas as information and communications technology, financial and business services, seafood processing and exports, and free trade zones. Agriculture and industry have become less important to the economy, and services, especially tourism, accounted for over 72 percent of GDP. The government still owns utilities and controls imports of rice, flour, petroleum products, and cement.

Country's Score Over Time

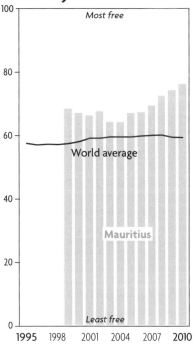

Quick Facts

Population: 1.3 million

GDP (PPP): $15.3 billion
5.3% growth in 2008
4.4% 5-year compound
annual growth
$12,079 per capita

Unemployment: 7.2%

Inflation (CPI): 8.8%

FDI Inflow: $383 million

2008 data unless otherwise noted
Data compiled as of September 2009

How Do We Measure Economic Freedom?
See page 457 for an explanation of the methodology or visit the *Index* Web site at *heritage.org/index.*

MAURITIUS'S TEN ECONOMIC FREEDOMS

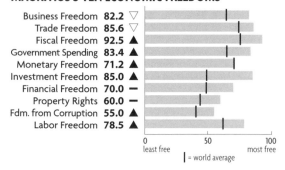

Business Freedom	82.2 ▽	
Trade Freedom	85.6 ▽	
Fiscal Freedom	92.5 ▲	
Government Spending	83.4 ▲	
Monetary Freedom	71.2 ▲	
Investment Freedom	85.0 ▲	
Financial Freedom	70.0 —	
Property Rights	60.0 —	
Fdm. from Corruption	55.0 ▲	
Labor Freedom	78.5 ▲	

0 least free   50   100 most free

▌ = world average

BUSINESS FREEDOM — 82.2

The overall freedom to start, operate, and close a business is relatively well protected under Mauritius's regulatory environment. Starting a business takes an average of six days, compared to the world average of 35 days. Obtaining a business license requires less than the world average of 218 days. Closing a business is easy.

TRADE FREEDOM — 85.6

Mauritius's weighted average tariff rate was 2.2 percent in 2008. The government has made considerable progress in liberalizing the trade regime, but some quotas, import restrictions, import and export permits, export-promotion programs, and weak enforcement of intellectual property rights add to the cost of trade. The government also controls imports of what it deems to be strategic products, including rice and wheat flour. Ten points were deducted from Mauritius's trade freedom score to account for non-tariff barriers.

FISCAL FREEDOM — 92.5

Mauritius has a very competitive tax regime. The income tax rate and the corporate tax rate are a flat 15 percent. Other taxes include a value-added tax (VAT) and a property tax. In the most recent year, overall tax revenue as a percentage of GDP was 17.4 percent.

GOVERNMENT SPENDING — 83.4

Total government expenditures, including consumption and transfer payments, are relatively low. In the most recent year, government spending equaled 23.5 percent of GDP. State-owned monopolies persist.

MONETARY FREEDOM — 71.2

Inflation has been high, averaging 8.9 percent between 2006 and 2008, but fell significantly in 2009. The government controls prices for a number of goods, including flour, sugar, milk, bread, rice, petroleum products, steel, cement, fertilizers, and pharmaceuticals; influences prices through state-owned enterprises and utilities; and subsidizes some agricultural and industrial production. Ten points were deducted from Mauritius's monetary freedom score to account for policies that distort domestic prices.

INVESTMENT FREEDOM — 85

Foreign and domestic investors are treated equally, and foreigners may control 100 percent of companies in most economic sectors. A transparent and well-defined foreign investment code makes Mauritius one of the best places in the region for foreign investment. The domestic legal system is generally non-discriminatory and transparent. Residents and non-residents may hold foreign exchange accounts. There are no controls on payments or transfers and few controls on capital transactions. Foreign nationals may acquire property subject to some restrictions.

FINANCIAL FREEDOM — 70

Mauritius's efficient financial sector has become more competitive, and its contribution to GDP has risen steadily. The banking sector consists of 19 commercial banks and 14 non-bank financial institutions. The four largest commercial banks account for around 70 percent of total assets. Several banks are still fully or partially owned by the government. Financial regulation is relatively solid and has become more efficient since the passage of the Bank of Mauritius Act 2004, which simplified the bank licensing structure. Distinctions between onshore and offshore banks have been eliminated. Capital markets are growing as Mauritius seeks to be a regional financial hub. With its banking sector not involved in sub-prime lending or exposed to other troubled assets, the Mauritian financial system has not suffered a liquidity problem during the global financial crisis.

PROPERTY RIGHTS — 60

The judiciary is independent, and trials are fair. The legal system is generally non-discriminatory and transparent. The highest court of appeal is the judicial committee of the Privy Council of England. Expropriation is unlikely. Trademark and patent laws comply with the WTO's Trade-Related Aspects of Intellectual Property Rights (TRIPS) agreement.

FREEDOM FROM CORRUPTION — 55

Mauritius ranks 41st out of 179 countries in Transparency International's Corruption Perceptions Index for 2008, an improvement over 2007. Mauritius is one of Africa's least corrupt countries. In 2002, the government adopted the Prevention of Corruption Act, which led to the setting up of an Independent Commission Against Corruption (ICAC) a few months later. The ICAC has the power to detect and investigate corruption and money-laundering offenses and can also confiscate the proceeds of corruption and money laundering. Corruption is not seen as an obstacle to foreign direct investment.

LABOR FREEDOM — 78.5

Mauritius's labor regulations are relatively flexible. The non-salary cost of employing a worker is low, but dismissing an employee can be relatively costly and difficult. Restrictions on work hours have become more flexible in recent years.

MEXICO

Economic Freedom Score

68.3

Mexico's economic freedom score is 68.3, making its economy the 41st freest in the 2010 *Index*. Its score has improved by 2.5 points since last year, reflecting modest improvements in five of the 10 economic freedoms. Mexico is ranked 3rd out of three countries in the North America region, but its score is well above the world average.

Mexico scores fairly well in business freedom, trade freedom, and fiscal freedom. Commercial operations are becoming more streamlined, and business formation is relatively efficient. Income and corporate tax rates are moderate, and the overall tax burden is low. The government's reform agenda has been extensive, but progress has been slow in improving expenditure efficiency and accountability and in promoting a more competitive and transparent financial sector. The government has attempted to limit monopoly power, and measures to reform the judiciary have been introduced.

Mexico's overall economic freedom remains limited by lingering institutional weaknesses that include considerable corruption and a rigid labor market. The judicial system is slow to resolve cases and vulnerable to corruption. The rule of law is undermined by drug cartels and kidnapping.

BACKGROUND: Mexico is a member of the North American Free Trade Agreement with Canada and the United States and in 1994 became the first Latin American member of the Organisation for Economic Co-operation and Development. The economy depends heavily on commercial relations with the United States and remittances from migrant workers in the U.S. Since the election of President Carlos Salinas in 1988, successive governments have adopted limited reforms and have begun to alter the corporatist economic model that defined Mexico since the revolution. President Felipe Calderon narrowly defeated populist Manuel Lopez Obrador in 2006 and has promised further liberalization, particularly in energy, but lacks a legislative majority. He also faces serious challenges fighting illegal drug trafficking.

Country's Score Over Time

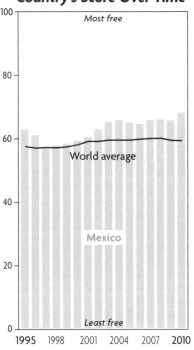

Quick Facts

Population: 106.4 million

GDP (PPP): $1.5 trillion
  1.8% growth in 2008
  3.2% 5-year compound
    annual growth
  $14,495 per capita

Unemployment: 4.0%

Inflation (CPI): 5.1%

FDI Inflow: $22 billion

2008 data unless otherwise noted
Data compiled as of September 2009

How Do We Measure Economic Freedom?
See page 457 for an explanation of the methodology or visit the *Index* Web site at *heritage.org/index.*

MEXICO'S TEN ECONOMIC FREEDOMS

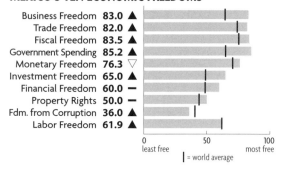

Business Freedom	83.0 ▲	
Trade Freedom	82.0 ▲	
Fiscal Freedom	83.5 ▲	
Government Spending	85.2 ▲	
Monetary Freedom	76.3 ▽	
Investment Freedom	65.0 ▲	
Financial Freedom	60.0 ▬	
Property Rights	50.0 ▬	
Fdm. from Corruption	36.0 ▲	
Labor Freedom	61.9 ▲	

0 least free   50   100 most free

| = world average

BUSINESS FREEDOM — 83

The overall freedom to start, operate, and close a business is protected under Mexico's regulatory environment. Starting a business takes an average of 13 days, compared to the world average of 35 days. Obtaining a business license requires less than the world average of 18 procedures and 218 days. Bankruptcy is relatively easy.

TRADE FREEDOM — 82

Mexico's weighted average tariff rate was 1.5 percent in 2008. Import restrictions; import taxes and fees; services market access barriers; import licensing and registration; restrictive standards and labeling rules; burdensome sanitary and phytosanitary regulations; non-transparent, complex, and inconsistent customs administration and valuation; various export-promotion programs; customs corruption; and weak enforcement of intellectual property rights add to the cost of trade. Fifteen points were deducted from Mexico's trade freedom score to account for non-tariff barriers.

FISCAL FREEDOM — 83.5

The top income and corporate tax rates are 28 percent. A 17 percent flat-rate business tax (known as the IETU) operates as an alternative to the corporate income tax for some companies. Other taxes include a value-added tax (VAT) and a real estate transfer tax. In the most recent year, overall tax revenue as a percentage of GDP was 9.0 percent.

GOVERNMENT SPENDING — 85.2

Total government expenditures, including consumption and transfer payments, are relatively low. In the most recent year, government spending equaled 22.2 percent of GDP. Privatization has progressed, but the energy and electricity industries remain government-controlled.

MONETARY FREEDOM — 76.3

Inflation has been moderate, averaging 4.7 percent between 2006 and 2008. A sharp decline in domestic demand reduced inflationary pressures in 2009. Although most prices are determined in the market, the government maintains suggested retail prices for medicines and influences prices through state-owned enterprises and utilities, including electricity and energy. Ten points were deducted from Mexico's monetary freedom score to account for policies that distort domestic prices.

INVESTMENT FREEDOM — 65

While Mexico generally welcomes foreign investment, a number of sectors are reserved for domestic or state interests or have restrictions capping the level of foreign ownership. About 95 percent of foreign investment does not require official approval. Reforms are ongoing; however, burdensome and non-transparent bureaucracy and a rigid labor code inhibit investment. Residents and non-residents may hold foreign exchange accounts. Most payments, transactions, and transfers are allowed without restriction. Foreign investment in some real estate is restricted.

FINANCIAL FREEDOM — 60

Mexico's financial sector has undergone considerable transformation and has become more competitive and stable. Government holdings in commercial banking have been significantly reduced, and foreign participation has grown rapidly over the past decade. Foreign institutions are prominent in the financial sector, holding about 75 percent of assets. Banks offer a wide range of services, but overall financial intermediation remains relatively low despite some increase in recent years. Six state-owned development banks provide financing to specific areas of the economy and influence credit. In late 2007, the Mexican Congress approved amendments to the Law of Credit Institutions that include creating a new limited banking license. The insurance sector is well developed, with five firms (three of which are foreign-owned) accounting for nearly 59 percent of policies. The impact of the global financial turmoil on the financial sector has been relatively modest. The banking system remains well capitalized.

PROPERTY RIGHTS — 50

The threat of expropriation is low. Contracts are generally upheld, but the courts are slow to resolve disputes and allegedly subject to corruption. Despite a legal framework for the enforcement of intellectual property rights, the prosecution of infringement cases is ineffective. Foreign real estate investors have found it difficult to secure enforcement of their property interests in state-level courts.

FREEDOM FROM CORRUPTION — 36

Corruption is perceived as significant. Mexico ranks 72nd out of 179 countries in Transparency International's Corruption Perceptions Index for 2008. Corruption has been pervasive for years, but President Calderon has committed his administration to fight against it at all levels of government—federal, state, and municipal. In 2008, Calderon launched Operación Limpieza, investigating and imprisoning corrupt government officials in enforcement agencies. The Secretariat of Public Administration has the lead on coordinating government anti-corruption policy.

LABOR FREEDOM — 61.9

Mexico's labor regulations are rigid. Reform remains stalled. The non-salary cost of employing a worker can be high, and laying off an employee is difficult.

MICRONESIA

Palikir

Economic Freedom Score

Least free 0   Most free 100

25   50   75

50.6

M icronesia's economic freedom score is 50.6, making its economy the 142nd freest in the 2010 *Index*. Its score has decreased by 1.1 points since last year. Micronesia is ranked 32nd out of 41 countries in the Asia–Pacific region, and its overall score is lower than the world and regional averages.

The Micronesian economy is heavily dependent on foreign aid, much of which comes as a result of a long-term compact with the United States. A substantial portion of economic activity is still concentrated in an outsized public sector, which is the largest source of employment. Government dominance reduces opportunities for private investment, and the state is not providing the institutional or physical infrastructure that is needed for an effective and efficient private sector. Fuelling corruption, Micronesia's legal framework remains inefficient and lacks transparency. Reform of the country's poorly performing tax regime has been delayed.

There are, however, a few bright spots. Average tariffs are low, and the economy is open to most imports. Inflation is well contained by the use of the U.S. dollar as the official currency, and tax rates are very low. Labor regulations do not constrain job growth.

BACKGROUND: Micronesia's population of approximately 100,000 is spread across a South Pacific archipelago containing more than 600 islands. Formerly administered by the United States as a U.N. Trust Territory, it became independent in 1986 and in that same year signed a Compact of Free Association with the United States. Under an amended compact, Micronesia receives $100 million annually from the U.S. in addition to $35 million in other U.S. government grants. As a result, the government sector employs more than half of Micronesia's workforce.

Country's Score Over Time

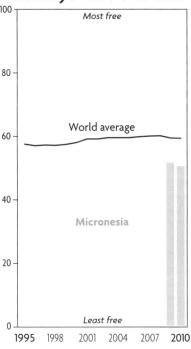

Quick Facts

Population: 0.1 million

GDP (PPP): $0.3 billion
  –1.0% growth in 2008
  –1.7% 5-year compound
    annual growth
  $2,830 per capita

Unemployment: estimated to be over 10%

Inflation (CPI): 5.0%

FDI Inflow: n/a

2008 data unless otherwise noted
Data compiled as of September 2009

How Do We Measure Economic Freedom?
See page 457 for an explanation of the methodology or visit the *Index* Web site at *heritage.org/index*.

MICRONESIA'S TEN ECONOMIC FREEDOMS

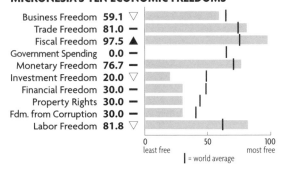

Business Freedom	59.1 ▽	
Trade Freedom	81.0 —	
Fiscal Freedom	97.5 ▲	
Government Spending	0.0 —	
Monetary Freedom	76.7 —	
Investment Freedom	20.0 ▽	
Financial Freedom	30.0 —	
Property Rights	30.0 —	
Fdm. from Corruption	30.0 —	
Labor Freedom	81.8 ▽	

0 least free   50   100 most free
| = world average

BUSINESS FREEDOM — *59.1*

The overall freedom to start, operate, and close a business is constrained by Micronesia's regulatory environment. Starting a business takes about half the world average of 35 days, but the entry cost is high. Closing a business is time-consuming and costly.

TRADE FREEDOM — *81*

Micronesia's simple average tariff rate was 4.5 percent in 2007. Some high tariffs, import restrictions, inadequate infrastructure, and underdeveloped markets add to the cost of trade. Ten points were deducted from Micronesia's trade freedom score to account for non-tariff barriers.

FISCAL FREEDOM — *97.5*

Micronesia's tax regime is poorly documented, and collection rates are low. National taxes include a wages and salary tax (10 percent at the highest level); a 3 percent gross revenue tax on businesses with turnover that exceeds $10,000 a year; and an excise tax on alcohol and tobacco products. Sales taxes are set and collected separately at the state level. In the most recent year, overall tax revenue as a percentage of GDP was only 11.7 percent.

GOVERNMENT SPENDING — *0*

Total government expenditures, including consumption and transfer payments, are extremely high. In the most recent year, government spending equaled 64.3 percent of GDP. Government and public enterprises account for nearly 40 percent of GDP and over 50 percent of paid employment.

MONETARY FREEDOM — *76.7*

Inflation has been moderate, averaging 4.4 percent between 2006 and 2008. The U.S. dollar is the official currency, and the government has few policy tools with which to affect inflation or interest rates. Ten points were deducted from Micronesia's monetary freedom score to adjust for measures that distort domestic prices.

INVESTMENT FREEDOM — *20*

The Foreign Investment Act of 1997 provides for non-discriminatory treatment of foreign investment, indicates the sectors in which foreign investment is not allowed, notes additional regulation for certain sectors, and sets out guarantees regarding expropriation. All foreign investment is prescreened. The states license and regulate all other sectors and may impose additional restrictions. Each of Micronesia's four states has a unique foreign investment regime and can counter national policy. Regulations are non-transparent and applied inconsistently, and enforcement of contracts is weak. There are no limitations on currency or capital transactions. Foreign investors may not own land but may lease it for short periods.

FINANCIAL FREEDOM — *30*

Micronesia's small financial system is hindered by a large government presence and is not developed enough to generate and support dynamic entrepreneurial activity. The formal private sector is small and constrained by ineffective regulation, high credit costs, and scarce access to financing. Much of the population remains outside of the formal banking sector. The financial sector is dominated by banking, which includes one state-owned development bank and two commercial banks, one of which is majority government-owned. State influence in allocating credit is substantial, and government-controlled or government-owned banks make a majority of all loans. Bank lending has been concentrated on state-owned enterprises in recent years.

PROPERTY RIGHTS — *30*

Foreign ownership of land is not permitted. Lease terms for real property are controlled at the state level and often limited to relatively short periods. Squatters, long-standing and multiple disputes over land ownership, and the absence of property records make leasing land extremely difficult, costly, and uncertain in some locales. Transfer of title sometimes occurs informally, and this causes a lack of accurate public pricing information. Most original land records in Chuuk State were destroyed in a fire; the other three states have functioning land offices. Copyrights are protected by statute, but there are no trademark, patent, or other intellectual property rights regulations in effect.

FREEDOM FROM CORRUPTION — *30*

Corruption in Micronesia is perceived as widespread. The level of corruption varies in each island state, with Chuuk perceived as the worst. Micronesia has laws prohibiting corruption, and there are penalties for corrupt acts. Bribery is punishable by imprisonment for not more than 10 years and disqualification from holding any government position. Micronesia has not signed or ratified the U.N. Convention on Corruption. Many government officials also own businesses.

LABOR FREEDOM — *81.8*

Micronesia's labor regulations are relatively flexible, but its formal labor market is not well developed. The non-salary cost of employing a worker is low, and dismissing an employee is fairly easy.

MOLDOVA

Economic Freedom Score

25 50 75

Least free 0   100 Most free

53.7

| World Rank: **125** | Regional Rank: **40** |

Moldova's economic freedom score is 53.7, making its economy the 125th freest in the 2010 *Index*. Its score has decreased by 1.2 points since last year, reflecting lower scores in five of the 10 economic freedoms. Moldova ranks 40th among 43 countries in the Europe region, and its overall score is below the world and regional averages.

Moldova scores just above the world average in trade freedom, business freedom, and fiscal freedom and has achieved relatively steady economic growth of 5 percent over the past three years. In recent years, the government has implemented measures to improve regulatory transparency and the overall entrepreneurial environment. Recent tax reforms have made the country's tax regime quite competitive.

Overall economic freedom remains constrained by a number of institutional shortcomings that impede economic dynamism within the private sector. Monetary stability, investment freedom, and freedom from corruption are weak. Foreign investment faces hurdles that range from bureaucratic inefficiency to outright restriction. There is significant corruption in most areas of the bureaucracy. Political instability has left fiscal policy fragmented. Strains on the budget are mounting.

BACKGROUND: Moldova became independent after the collapse of the Soviet Union in 1991 and continues to face a secessionist, Communist, and pro-Russian enclave in Transnistria. The reformed Communist Party, which enjoys a parliamentary majority, supports European integration and has not reversed market reforms instituted in the early 1990s. Agriculture remains central to the economy, and foodstuffs, wine, and animal and vegetable products are the main exports. Moldova is Europe's poorest country, and remittances account for one-third of GDP. The Communist Party won the April 2009 parliamentary election, but the results were disputed, and violent protests erupted. The Organization for Security and Cooperation in Europe concluded that violations during the elections did not affect the outcome.

Country's Score Over Time

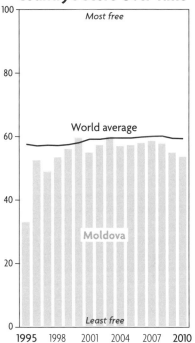

Quick Facts

Population: 3.6 million

GDP (PPP): $10.6 billion
7.2% growth in 2008
5.9% 5-year compound annual growth
$2,925 per capita

Unemployment: 2.1% (2007)

Inflation (CPI): 12.7%

FDI Inflow: $713 million

2008 data unless otherwise noted
Data compiled as of September 2009

How Do We Measure Economic Freedom?
See page 457 for an explanation of the methodology or visit the *Index* Web site at *heritage.org/index*.

MOLDOVA'S TEN ECONOMIC FREEDOMS

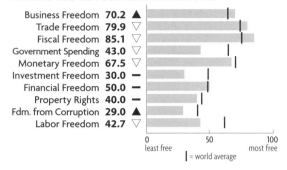

Business Freedom	70.2 ▲
Trade Freedom	79.9 ▽
Fiscal Freedom	85.1 ▽
Government Spending	43.0 ▽
Monetary Freedom	67.5 ▽
Investment Freedom	30.0 —
Financial Freedom	50.0 —
Property Rights	40.0 —
Fdm. from Corruption	29.0 ▲
Labor Freedom	42.7 ▽

0 least free — 50 — 100 most free

| = world average

BUSINESS FREEDOM — *70.2*

The overall freedom to conduct a business is relatively well protected under Moldova's regulatory environment. Starting a business takes an average of 10 days, compared to the world average of 35 days. However, obtaining a business license still requires more than the world average of 18 procedures and 218 days.

TRADE FREEDOM — *79.9*

Moldova's weighted average tariff rate was 2.5 percent in 2008. Import and export restrictions, import taxes and fees, burdensome regulations, non-transparent government procurement, weak enforcement of intellectual property rights, and an inefficient and non-transparent customs process that is prone to corruption add to the cost of trade. Fifteen points were deducted from Moldova's trade freedom score to account for non-tariff barriers.

FISCAL FREEDOM — *85.1*

Moldova's tax rates have been significantly reduced in recent years. The top income tax rate is 18 percent, and the corporate tax was eliminated as of January 2008. However, the tax regime remains complex, and businesses still have to file tax returns or be penalized. Other taxes include a value-added tax (VAT) and a capital acquisitions tax. In the most recent year, overall tax revenue as a percentage of GDP was 34.1 percent.

GOVERNMENT SPENDING — *43*

Total government expenditures, including consumption and transfer payments, are high. In the most recent year, government spending equaled 43.6 percent of GDP. The government is slowly revitalizing privatization and plans divestiture of MoldTelecom and a major state-owned bank.

MONETARY FREEDOM — *67.5*

Inflation has been high, averaging 12.6 percent between 2006 and 2008, but fell sharply in 2009 because of lower food and oil prices, relatively tight monetary policy, and falling domestic demand as the economy moved into recession. The government has phased out most price controls and many subsidies but still influences prices through numerous state-owned enterprises and utilities, including electricity and energy. Ten points were deducted from Moldova's monetary freedom score to account for policies that distort domestic prices.

INVESTMENT FREEDOM — *30*

Foreign capital and domestic capital are legally equal. Foreign investment is generally welcome, subject to some restrictions, and some sectors are reserved for state enterprises. There is no screening of investment. Regulatory administration can be non-transparent, burdensome, and inconsistent. Poor physical infrastructure and weak contract enforcement hinder investment. Government officials have been known to interfere in business decisions in favor of a privileged individual or to use governmental power to pressure businesses for personal or political gain. Legal disputes may not result in impartial rulings. Residents and non-residents may hold foreign exchange accounts. Some payments, capital transactions, and transfers require National Bank of Moldova approval. Non-Moldovans may not buy agricultural or forestry land.

FINANCIAL FREEDOM — *50*

Moldova's financial system has been undergoing restructuring and consolidation, and bank supervision and regulation are now more in line with international standards. New regulations are being implemented for non-banking financial sectors. Rapid credit growth has supported private-sector expansion, but long-term financing can still be a problem. The banking sector remains highly concentrated, and the top five of 16 commercial banks account for more than 50 percent of total assets. Foreign capital in banking has been increasing steadily. In July 2007, regulation in the non-bank financial sector was consolidated in a single National Commission for the Financial Markets. Capital markets remain underdeveloped.

PROPERTY RIGHTS — *40*

The judiciary has been improved but is subject to executive influence. Delayed salary payments make it difficult for judges to remain independent from outside influence and free from corruption. Moldova adheres to key international agreements on intellectual property rights and has a State Agency for Intellectual Property to protect copyrights, but IPR enforcement is sporadic.

FREEDOM FROM CORRUPTION — *29*

Corruption is perceived as widespread. Moldova ranks 109th out of 179 countries in Transparency International's Corruption Perceptions Index for 2008. The government is trying to adopt European anti-corruption and anti-crime standards and to participate in international cooperation and evaluation mechanisms. Corruption and bribery reportedly are serious problems for foreign investors. In 2007, Moldova ratified the United Nations Convention against Corruption.

LABOR FREEDOM — *42.7*

Moldova's labor regulations are rigid. The non-salary cost of employing a worker is high, and dismissing an employee is not easy. Restrictions on work hours remain rigid.

MONGOLIA

World Rank: 88   **Regional Rank: 15**

Economic Freedom Score

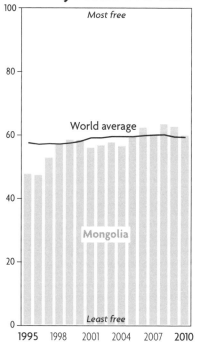

25   50   75

Least free 0   100 Most free

60.0

Mongolia's economic freedom score is 60.0, making its economy the 88th freest in the 2010 *Index*. Its overall score is 2.8 points lower than last year, reflecting reduced scores for monetary freedom, investment freedom, and government spending. Mongolia is ranked 15th out of 41 countries in the Asia–Pacific region, and its overall score is above the global and regional averages.

The Mongolian economy continues to benefit from relatively high levels of fiscal freedom, business freedom, and trade freedom, and the overall entrepreneurial environment supports private-sector development. The top income and corporate tax rates are competitive. Tariff barriers are moderate, although non-tariff restrictions undermine overall trade freedom. Commercial registration and licensing are efficient, and the flexibility of the labor market has increased.

Despite some progress in privatization, the government remains significantly involved in the economy and has passed legislation that reinforces its involvement in strategic sectors like mining. The government has tried to control the budget deficit, but government spending has been on the rise. The weak judicial system remains vulnerable to corruption.

BACKGROUND: Mongolia emerged from the shadow of the former Soviet Union with the adoption of a multi-party system and a new constitution in 1990. The electorate is split fairly evenly between the Communist Mongolian People's Revolutionary Party and the Democratic Party. Democratic Party candidate and former Prime Minister Tsakhiagiin Elbegdorj won the 2009 presidential election. Mongolia is a primary transportation conduit for trade between Russia and China, which together account for 40 percent of its foreign direct investment. Trade is tilted heavily toward China; two-way trade with China increased by 43 percent in 2007 to $2.08 billion, accounting for 52 percent of Mongolia's total trade. Livestock herding employs a majority of the population, but mining attracts the largest portion of foreign direct investment.

Country's Score Over Time

100

Most free

80

World average

60

40

Mongolia

20

Least free

0

1995   1998   2001   2004   2007   2010

Quick Facts

Population: 2.6 million

GDP (PPP): $9.4 billion
8.9% growth in 2008
8.7% 5-year compound
annual growth
$3,566 per capita

Unemployment: 2.8%

Inflation (CPI): 26.8%

FDI Inflow: $683 million

2008 data unless otherwise noted
Data compiled as of September 2009

How Do We Measure Economic Freedom?
See page 457 for an explanation of the methodology or visit the *Index* Web site at *heritage.org/index.*

MONGOLIA'S TEN ECONOMIC FREEDOMS

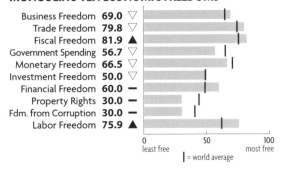

Business Freedom	69.0 ▽
Trade Freedom	79.8 ▽
Fiscal Freedom	81.9 ▲
Government Spending	56.7 ▽
Monetary Freedom	66.5 ▽
Investment Freedom	50.0 ▽
Financial Freedom	60.0 —
Property Rights	30.0 —
Fdm. from Corruption	30.0 —
Labor Freedom	75.9 ▲

0   50   100
least free   most free
❙ = world average

BUSINESS FREEDOM — 69

The overall freedom to conduct a business is relatively well protected under Mongolia's regulatory environment. Starting a business takes an average of 13 days, compared to the world average of 35 days. Obtaining a business license takes less than the world average of 218 days. Bankruptcy can be lengthy and burdensome.

TRADE FREEDOM — 79.8

Mongolia's weighted average tariff rate was 5.1 percent in 2008. Liberalization is progressing, but some import and export restrictions, restrictions in services markets, import and export taxes, weak enforcement of intellectual property rights, and inconsistent, inefficient, and corrupt customs implementation add to the cost of trade. Ten points were deducted from Mongolia's trade freedom score to account for non-tariff barriers.

FISCAL FREEDOM — 81.9

Mongolia has a low income tax rate and a moderate corporate tax rate. The individual income tax rate is a flat 10 percent, and the top corporate tax rate is 25 percent. Other taxes include a value-added tax (VAT), an excise tax on alcohol and vehicles, and a dividend tax. In the most recent year, overall tax revenue as a percentage of GDP was 33.0 percent.

GOVERNMENT SPENDING — 56.7

Total government expenditures, including consumption and transfer payments, are relatively high. In the most recent year, government spending equaled 38.0 percent of GDP.

MONETARY FREEDOM — 66.5

Inflation has jumped, averaging 20.2 percent between 2006 and 2008, but price increases moderated in 2009. Although most price controls and many subsidies have been phased out, the government influences prices through the public sector or through regulation, sometimes intervenes in the market to stabilize commodity prices, and still controls air fares and fuel prices. Five points were deducted from Mongolia's monetary freedom score to account for policies that distort domestic prices.

INVESTMENT FREEDOM — 50

Foreign capital and domestic capital are legally equal.

Investment is not screened. Foreign investment is subject to additional regulations or restrictions in activities involving petroleum extraction and strategic mineral deposits. The regulatory framework supporting investment is still developing, and regulations and investment-related laws are changed frequently. Rules may be inconsistently applied or misunderstood. Non-transparent bureaucracy can be prone to corruption, and contract enforcement is inconsistent. Residents and non-residents may hold foreign exchange accounts, subject to minimal restrictions. There are no restrictions on payments and transfers. Most credit and loan operations must be registered with the central bank. Foreign investors may lease but not own land.

FINANCIAL FREEDOM — 60

Restructuring of the banking sector has improved private-sector access to financing. The government imposes few restraints on the flow of capital, and foreign investors tap domestic capital markets freely. The banking sector's total assets are equivalent to over 80 percent of GDP. There are 16 private commercial banks, 10 of which are foreign-owned. State ownership of banks has been reduced. There are about 72 smaller, largely unregulated non-bank lending institutions. The government is refining insurance regulation. Capital markets are not fully developed. The stock market was set up to facilitate privatization of state-owned enterprises but now functions as a regular exchange. During the recent global financial turmoil, non-performing loans jumped to over 10 percent of the total in early 2009. The parliament approved a $389 million bailout package for troubled banks, and the fourth-largest bank has been taken over by the government.

PROPERTY RIGHTS — 30

The enforcement of laws protecting private property is weak. Judges generally do not respect contracts and regularly ignore their provisions in their rulings. The legal system does recognize the concept of collateralized assets. There is no mortgage law. Pirated optical media are readily available and subject to spotty enforcement.

FREEDOM FROM CORRUPTION — 30

Corruption is perceived as widespread. Mongolia ranks 102nd out of 179 countries in Transparency International's Corruption Perceptions Index for 2008. The law provides criminal penalties for official corruption, which is perceived to be a serious and continuing problem at all levels of government, particularly within the police, judiciary, and customs service. Corruption-related arrests and convictions are rare, and allegations of public-sector corruption include cases involving cabinet-level officials.

LABOR FREEDOM — 75.9

Mongolia's labor regulations are relatively flexible. The non-salary cost of employing a worker remains moderate, and dismissing an employee is costless. Regulations on work hours are not flexible.

MONTENEGRO

Economic Freedom Score

Least free 0 — 25 50 75 — 100 Most free

63.6

Montenegro's economic freedom score is 63.6, making its economy the 68th freest in the 2010 *Index*. Its score has improved by 5.4 points since last year, reflecting notable improvements in seven of the 10 economic freedoms. Montenegro ranks 32nd out of 43 countries in the Europe region, and its overall score is above the world average.

Sharply improved labor market flexibility and an improved regulatory environment for investment enabled Montenegro to score the largest increase in economic freedom in the 2010 *Index*. The country's flat tax has become more competitive due to recent tax cuts, and government spending has been held in check. Montenegro's ongoing transition to greater economic freedom facilitated impressive average economic growth of over 7 percent during the past five years.

Economic freedom in Montenegro still suffers from insufficient institutional support for property rights and the fight against corruption. The court system remains vulnerable to political interference and inefficiency. External debt has been growing, and government spending needs to be targeted more effectively.

BACKGROUND: The Republic of Montenegro officially declared its independence from Serbia on June 3, 2006, becoming independent for the first time in nearly a century. Montenegro is pursuing membership in the World Trade Organization, the European Union, and NATO. It formally requested talks to join the EU in December 2008, but widespread corruption and organized crime have generated opposition within EU member countries. Milo Djukanovic has served as prime minister or president almost continuously since 1991 and was elected prime minister most recently in January 2009. Having gradually pulled away from Serbia in the past decade, Montenegro introduced significant privatization and started using the German mark and then (despite not being a member of the euro zone) the euro as its legal tender. Ongoing problems include unemployment and the black market.

Country's Score Over Time

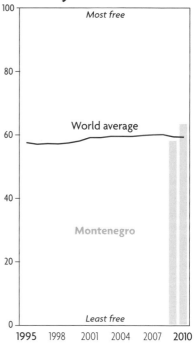

Quick Facts

Population: 0.6 million

GDP (PPP): $8.7 billion
7.1% growth in 2008
7.7% 5-year compound annual growth
$13,951 per capita

Unemployment: 14.7% (2007)

Inflation (CPI): 9.0%

FDI Inflow: $939 million

2008 data unless otherwise noted
Data compiled as of September 2009

How Do We Measure Economic Freedom?
See page 457 for an explanation of the methodology or visit the *Index* Web site at *heritage.org/index*.

MONTENEGRO'S TEN ECONOMIC FREEDOMS

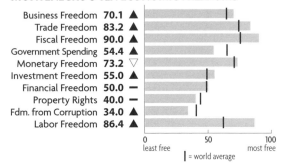

Business Freedom	70.1 ▲	
Trade Freedom	83.2 ▲	
Fiscal Freedom	90.0 ▲	
Government Spending	54.4 ▲	
Monetary Freedom	73.2 ▽	
Investment Freedom	55.0 ▲	
Financial Freedom	50.0 —	
Property Rights	40.0 ▌	
Fdm. from Corruption	34.0 ▲	
Labor Freedom	86.4 ▲	

0   50   100
least free   most free
▌ = world average

BUSINESS FREEDOM — 70.1

Starting a business takes an average of 13 days, compared to the world average of 35 days. Obtaining a business license takes slightly more than the world average of 18 procedures and 218 days. The application of regulations is sometimes inconsistent and non-transparent, and fees related to business start-up are high.

TRADE FREEDOM — 83.2

Montenegro's weighted average tariff rate was 3.4 percent in 2008. Progress has been made toward liberalizing the trade regime, but some high tariffs, import restrictions, weak implementation of non-transparent standards and regulations, weak enforcement of intellectual property rights, and corruption still add to the cost of trade. Ten points were deducted from Montenegro's trade freedom score to account for non-tariff barriers.

FISCAL FREEDOM — 90

Montenegro enjoys competitive flat tax rates. The flat individual income tax rate was reduced from 15 percent to 12 percent as of January 2009 and will be further reduced to 9 percent in 2010. The corporate tax rate is a flat 9 percent, levied at the state level. Other taxes include a value-added tax (VAT), an inheritance tax, and a property tax. In the most recent year, overall tax revenue as a percentage of GDP was 27.9 percent.

GOVERNMENT SPENDING — 54.4

Total government expenditures, including consumption and transfer payments, are relatively high. In the most recent year, government spending was estimated to be about 39.0 percent of GDP. Privatization has stalled, and necessary reforms have not been undertaken in the energy sector. The national aluminum plant has been partially renationalized.

MONETARY FREEDOM — 73.2

Inflation has been relatively high, averaging 7.0 percent between 2006 and 2008, but decelerated in 2009. State subsidies and price supports have been eliminated for most goods, and most prices are determined by market forces. However, the government influences a few prices through state-owned enterprises and regulates utility, energy, and transportation prices. Ten points were deducted from Montenegro's monetary freedom score to account for policies that distort domestic prices.

INVESTMENT FREEDOM — 55

Foreign capital and domestic capital are treated equally. Montenegro's Foreign Investment Law allows profit repatriation and guarantees against expropriation. However, the business, legal, and regulatory environment is still in transition, and bureaucracy can be non-transparent, burdensome, and prone to corruption. Implementation and enforcement of regulations and laws can be problematic. Residents and non-residents may hold foreign exchange accounts, and payments, capital transactions, and transfers are subject to few restrictions. Foreign investors can, based on reciprocity, acquire rights to real estate.

FINANCIAL FREEDOM — 50

Montenegro's financial sector, though small and underdeveloped, is becoming more competitive. Access to financing has gradually increased, and the banking sector includes 11 commercial banks, almost all with private ownership. The government privatized the last bank with direct majority state ownership in 2005. Foreign banks' participation and investment are significant. Despite growing competition, credit prices remain fairly high. The non-banking financial sector, including insurance and reinsurance, remains underdeveloped. Montenegro's securities sector is small but developing. In response to the global financial turmoil, the government introduced several measures that included a one year blanket deposit guarantee to slow down deposit withdrawals.

PROPERTY RIGHTS — 40

The constitution provides for an independent judiciary, but the system historically has been inefficient, and judges are poorly trained. Sales of pirated DVDs, CDs, and software and sales of counterfeit trademarked goods are fairly widespread.

FREEDOM FROM CORRUPTION — 34

Corruption is perceived as significant. Montenegro ranks 85th out of 179 countries in Transparency International's Corruption Perceptions Index for 2008. There is a widespread perception of government corruption, particularly in the executive and judicial branches and especially with regard to the privatization of state-owned firms. Conflict-of-interest legislation requiring the disclosure of government officials' salaries and property has not been fully implemented, and many officials refuse to comply. Organized crime, especially the smuggling of gasoline and cigarettes, is well established. In the past two years, Montenegro has implemented 16 of 24 compulsory anti-corruption recommendations adopted by the Council of Europe Group of States (GRECO).

LABOR FREEDOM — 86.4

Montenegro has taken steps to enhance labor market flexibility. A new labor law passed in mid-2008 reduces some of the rigidities, although the law still contains considerable employment protections that discourage more dynamic job creation.

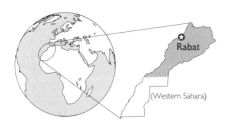

MOROCCO

World Rank: 91   **Regional Rank: 10**

Morocco's economic freedom score is 59.2, making its economy the 91st freest in the 2010 *Index*. Its score is 1.5 points better than last year, reflecting improvements in five of the 10 economic freedoms. Morocco is ranked 10th out of 17 countries in the Middle East/North Africa region, and its overall score is just below the world average.

Morocco's economic performance has been steady in recent years, sustained by reform measures focused on competitiveness and diversification of the productive base. Major structural reforms have been aimed at ensuring macroeconomic and financial stability and improving the overall entrepreneurial environment.

Morocco's economy benefits from relatively high levels of business freedom, monetary freedom, and investment freedom. Foreign and domestic investments receive equal treatment. The small but growing financial sector is fairly well developed for the region. Simplifying the tax regime and improving the transparency of fiscal management have been major parts of the government's reform agenda. Morocco scores less well in labor freedom, property rights, and freedom from corruption. The judiciary is inefficient and vulnerable to political interference. Labor market rigidity continues to discourage dynamic employment growth.

BACKGROUND: Morocco is a stable constitutional monarchy. King Mohammed VI has encouraged political and economic reform, expansion of civil rights, and elimination of corruption since coming to power in 1999. Morocco has the world's largest phosphate reserves, a large tourist industry, and a growing manufacturing sector, but agriculture accounts for about 20 percent of GDP and employs roughly 40 percent of the labor force. A free trade agreement with the United States took effect in January 2006. Economic growth slowed in 2007 as a result of the rising cost of energy imports and a drought that curtailed agricultural production and prompted increased imports of wheat, but the economy recovered to grow by almost 6 percent in 2008.

Country's Score Over Time

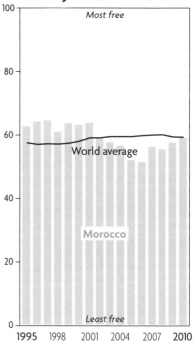

Quick Facts

Population: 31.2 million

GDP (PPP): $137.0 billion
5.8% growth in 2008
4.7% 5-year compound annual growth
$4,388 per capita

Unemployment: 10.0%

Inflation (CPI): 3.9%

FDI Inflow: $2.4 billion

2008 data unless otherwise noted
Data compiled as of September 2009

How Do We Measure Economic Freedom?
See page 457 for an explanation of the methodology or visit the *Index* Web site at *heritage.org/index*.

MOROCCO'S TEN ECONOMIC FREEDOMS

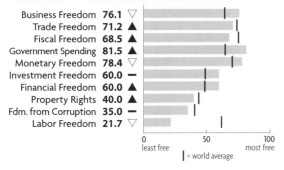

Business Freedom	76.1 ▽	
Trade Freedom	71.2 ▲	
Fiscal Freedom	68.5 ▲	
Government Spending	81.5 ▲	
Monetary Freedom	78.4 ▽	
Investment Freedom	60.0 —	
Financial Freedom	60.0 —	
Property Rights	40.0 ▲	
Fdm. from Corruption	35.0 —	
Labor Freedom	21.7 ▽	

0 least free   50   100 most free

| = world average

BUSINESS FREEDOM — 76.1

The overall freedom to start, operate, and close a business is relatively well protected under Morocco's regulatory environment. Starting a business takes less than half the world average of 35 days. Obtaining a business license takes less than the world average of 218 days. Bankruptcy is relatively easy and straightforward.

TRADE FREEDOM — 71.2

Morocco's weighted average tariff rate was 9.4 percent in 2008. Some prohibitive tariffs, import restrictions, import taxes, services market access barriers, restrictive biotechnology regulations, non-transparent and inconsistent customs valuation, export incentives, and corruption add to the cost of trade. Ten points were deducted from Morocco's trade freedom score to account for non-tariff barriers.

FISCAL FREEDOM — 68.5

Morocco's taxes are relatively high. The top income tax rate is 42 percent. The top corporate tax rate was reduced to 30 percent from 35 percent in 2008. Credit institutions and leasing companies are subject to a 37 percent rate. Other taxes include a value-added tax (VAT), a gift tax, and a property tax. In the most recent year, overall tax revenue as a percentage of GDP was 22.0 percent.

GOVERNMENT SPENDING — 81.5

Total government expenditures, including consumption and transfer payments, are relatively low. In the most recent year, government spending equaled 24.8 percent of GDP.

MONETARY FREEDOM — 78.4

Inflation has been moderate, averaging 3.4 percent between 2006 and 2008. Although price controls and subsidies are being phased out, the government influences prices through state-owned enterprises and utilities, including electricity; subsidizes fuel, health products, and educational supplies; and sets prices for staple commodities, including vegetable oil, sugar, flour, bread, and cereals. Ten points were deducted from Morocco's monetary freedom score to account for policies that distort domestic prices.

INVESTMENT FREEDOM — 60

Foreign and locally owned investments are treated equally, and 100 percent foreign ownership is allowed in most sectors. Investments exceeding 200 million MAD (USD 26 million) must be approved by a special ministerial committee chaired by the prime minister. No private foreign or domestic investment is permitted in sectors in which the state has a monopoly, such as phosphates, wholesale fruit and vegetable distribution, fish halls and slaughterhouses, and water and electricity supplies. The government has set up regional investment centers to decentralize and accelerate investment-related procedures, but red tape persists. Corruption and a non-transparent and inefficient legal system are additional deterrents. Residents and non-residents may hold foreign exchange accounts. Certain payments, transfers, and capital transactions require government approval. Foreign investors may not own agricultural land.

FINANCIAL FREEDOM — 60

Morocco's financial system is fairly well developed for the region, but credit costs are relatively high. Financial intermediation has increased, and almost 40 percent of the population has bank accounts and access to financial services. There are 16 banks, 11 of which are private. Six major banks account for more than 80 percent of total assets. The government still retains large shares in a number of banks. New legislation enhances the supervisory capacity of the central bank. Capital markets are relatively well developed, and there is an ongoing campaign to increase modernization and transparency. Morocco's Casablanca Stock Exchange is one of the few regional exchanges to impose no restrictions on foreign participation.

PROPERTY RIGHTS — 40

Private ownership is permitted in all but a few sectors that are reserved for the state, like phosphate mining. Apart from a few exceptions, private entities may freely establish, acquire, and dispose of interests in business enterprises. The judiciary is influenced by the king and is slow to deal with cases. It remains to be seen whether new laws protecting intellectual property rights will be enforced effectively. Counterfeit DVDs and CDs remain widely available throughout Morocco.

FREEDOM FROM CORRUPTION — 35

Corruption is perceived as significant. Morocco ranks 80th out of 179 countries in Transparency International's Corruption Perceptions Index for 2008. Despite laws and regulations to combat corruption, it remains a problem, in part because of low public-sector salaries. Corruption exists in the executive, legislative, and (especially) judicial branches of government. Comprehensive anti–money laundering legislation was passed in 2007, and a Financial Intelligence Unit was being set up in 2009.

LABOR FREEDOM — 21.7

Morocco's labor regulations are restrictive. The non-salary cost of employing a worker is high, and laying off an employee is difficult.

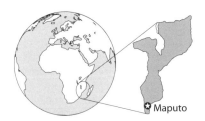

MOZAMBIQUE

Economic Freedom Score

| World Rank: **111** | Regional Rank: **16** |

56.0

Mozambique's economic freedom score is 56.0, making its economy the 111th freest in the 2010 *Index*. Its score has increased by 0.3 point since last year. Mozambique is ranked 16th out of 46 countries in the Sub-Saharan Africa region, and its overall score is below the world average but above the regional average.

Mozambique has made significant progress both in fostering accountability and transparency in the regulatory framework and in reforming public financial management. Private-sector involvement in the economy is substantial, although privatization of state-owned enterprises has slowed. Foreign capital and domestic capital are treated similarly in most cases, and overall trade liberalization has progressed despite lingering non-tariff barriers.

However, entrepreneurs still face substantial institutional challenges such as weak property rights, widespread corruption, and a poor business climate. Judicial enforcement is subject to corruption and the political whims of the executive. The inefficient regulatory environment is a burden on business formation, and many aspects of the labor market remain rigid.

BACKGROUND: After Mozambique became independent in 1975, the Front for the Liberation of Mozambique established a one-party socialist state. The ensuing 16-year civil war claimed an estimated one million lives. The reform process started by President Samora Machel in 1983 continued under Joaquim Chissano, who succeeded Machel in 1986, and continues under Armando Guebuza. Mozambique held its first democratic elections in 1994 and since then has been a model for development and post-war recovery. Economic growth has been generally strong since the mid-1990s, but the country remains poor and burdened by excessive regulation, state-sanctioned monopolies, and inefficient public services. Agriculture, fishing, and forestry employ roughly 80 percent of the population. The informal sector accounts for most employment. Major exports include aluminum, shrimp, and cash crops. HIV/AIDS is a serious problem.

Country's Score Over Time

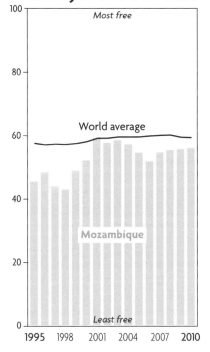

Quick Facts

Population: 21.8 million

GDP (PPP): $18.6 billion
6.5% growth in 2008
7.6% 5-year compound
annual growth
$855 per capita

Unemployment: n/a

Inflation (CPI): 10.3%

FDI Inflow: $587 million

2008 data unless otherwise noted
Data compiled as of September 2009

How Do We Measure Economic Freedom?
See page 457 for an explanation of the methodology or visit the *Index* Web site at *heritage.org/index*.

313

MOZAMBIQUE'S TEN ECONOMIC FREEDOMS

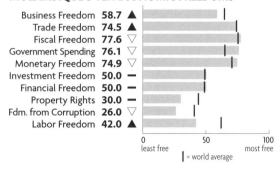

Business Freedom	58.7 ▲	
Trade Freedom	74.5 ▲	
Fiscal Freedom	77.6 ▽	
Government Spending	76.1 ▽	
Monetary Freedom	74.9 ▽	
Investment Freedom	50.0 —	
Financial Freedom	50.0 —	
Property Rights	30.0 —	
Fdm. from Corruption	26.0 ▽	
Labor Freedom	42.0 ▲	

0   50   100
least free   most free
| = world average

BUSINESS FREEDOM — 58.7

The overall freedom to start, operate, and close a business is restricted by Mozambique's regulatory environment. Starting a business takes an average of 26 days, compared to the world average of 35 days. Obtaining a business license takes more than the world average of 218 days, and fees are costly. Closing a business is burdensome.

TRADE FREEDOM — 74.5

Mozambique's weighted average tariff rate was 7.7 percent in 2007. Liberalization has progressed, but some import restrictions, import taxes and fees, import licensing and permits required for some goods, weak enforcement of intellectual property rights, time-consuming and bureaucratic customs clearance, and corruption still add to the cost of trade. Ten points were deducted from Mozambique's trade freedom score to account for non-tariff barriers.

FISCAL FREEDOM — 77.6

Mozambique has relatively high tax rates. The top income tax rate is 32 percent. The corporate tax rate is 32 percent except for income from agricultural or cattle breeding activities, both of which are subject to a 10 percent corporate tax. Other taxes include a value-added tax (VAT) and an inheritance tax. In the most recent year, overall tax revenue as a percentage of GDP was 14.0 percent.

GOVERNMENT SPENDING — 76.1

Total government expenditures, including consumption and transfer payments, are moderate. In the most recent year, government spending equaled 28.2 percent of GDP. Roughly 20 enterprises remain under state ownership. The national telecommunications and electricity companies are slated for the next round of privatizations. The 2009 budget lays the groundwork for public-sector wage reform, and social assistance constitutes roughly two-thirds of total expenditures.

MONETARY FREEDOM — 74.9

Inflation has been high, averaging 10.1 percent between 2006 and 2008, but has fallen sharply in 2009. The government influences prices through state-owned utilities, including electricity, telecommunications, ports, and transportation, and subsidizes passenger rail services. Five points were deducted from Mozambique's monetary freedom score to account for policies that distort domestic prices.

INVESTMENT FREEDOM — 50

Foreign capital and domestic capital are treated equally in most cases. Much of the economy is open to foreign investment, although certain sectors are subject to specific performance requirements. All foreign and domestic investment must be screened and approved. Bureaucracy can be burdensome, and the legal system is inefficient and antiquated. Additionally, regulations can be applied inconsistently, and the system is prone to corruption. The government must approve the employment of foreign workers. Mozambique allows repatriation of profits and retention of earned foreign exchange. Residents and non-residents may hold foreign exchange accounts. Payments and transfers are subject to maximum amounts, above which they must be approved by the central bank. All land is owned by the state.

FINANCIAL FREEDOM — 50

Mozambique's financial system has undergone a decade of restructuring. Dominated by banking, the small financial sector has been growing, and overall financial intermediation has deepened as banks' branch networks have expanded beyond the capital area. The 13 commercial banks are all majority foreign-owned, with Banco Internacional de Moçambique controlling over 40 percent of assets. The state retains shares in two large banks, but further privatization is under consideration. The small insurance sector is dominated by a state-owned insurance firm. Mozambique's financial sector is poorly integrated into global capital markets. Capital markets are very small, and the stock market mostly trades government debt.

PROPERTY RIGHTS — 30

Property rights are weakly protected, and the judiciary is corrupt. There is a severe shortage of qualified legal personnel, and the backlog of cases is substantial. Enforcement of contracts and legal redress through the courts cannot be assured. Most commercial disputes are settled privately. Pirated and counterfeit copies of audio and videotapes, CDs, DVDs, software, and other goods are sold in Mozambique.

FREEDOM FROM CORRUPTION — 26

Corruption is perceived as widespread. Mozambique ranks 126th out of 179 countries in Transparency International's Corruption Perceptions Index for 2008. Bribe-seeking by officials is endemic at every level. Conflicts of interest between senior officials' public roles and their private business interests are common and seldom investigated.

LABOR FREEDOM — 42

Mozambique's labor regulations are restrictive. The non-salary cost of employing a worker can be low, but the cost of laying off an employee is high. A recently passed labor law was intended to make the labor market more flexible but also increased overtime restrictions.

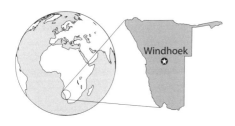

NAMIBIA

Economic Freedom Score

25   50   75

Least free   0   100   Most free

62.2

World Rank: **77**	Regional Rank: **6**

Namibia's economic freedom score is 62.2, making its economy the 77th freest in the 2010 *Index*. Its score has decreased by 0.2 point since last year, reflecting declines in five of the 10 economic freedoms. Namibia is ranked 6th out of 46 countries in the Sub-Saharan Africa region, and its overall score is above the world and regional averages.

The Namibian economy has been stable, with moderate growth averaging about 4 percent over the past five years. The overall regulatory environment is efficient and fairly straightforward. Tariff rates are average, but non-tariff barriers limit overall trade freedom.

With an average inflation rate close to 9 percent over the past three years, prices have been relatively unstable, and government measures distort domestic prices. Foreign and domestic investors are treated equally under the law, but foreign investors are encouraged to form partnerships with local companies. Scarce access to credit and banking services prevents people in rural areas from reaching their full economic potential. Property rights are jeopardized by the government's racially oriented land reform policy.

BACKGROUND: Namibia became officially independent in 1990 after years of fighting between South African troops and the South West Africa People's Organization. SWAPO leader Sam Nujoma, president from 1990 until 2005, was succeeded by SWAPO candidate Hifikepunye Pohamba. Namibia is rich in minerals, including uranium, diamonds, copper, gold, lead, and zinc. Parts of the economy are modern and well developed, but a majority of Namibians depend on subsistence agriculture and herding. Government pressure on white and foreign landowners to sell their property to the government with the objective of resettling "formerly disadvantaged" and landless Namibians has included selective expropriations. HIV/AIDS is a serious problem. State-owned enterprises operate in many key sectors. Namibia's economy is closely linked with that of South Africa, its major trading partner and former administering power.

Country's Score Over Time

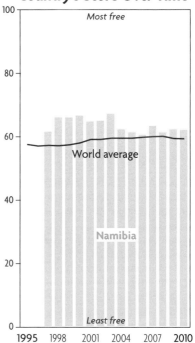

Quick Facts

Population: 2.1 million

GDP (PPP): $13.4 billion
  2.7% growth in 2008
  4.1% 5-year compound
    annual growth
  $6,343 per capita

Unemployment: 5%

Inflation (CPI): 10.3%

FDI Inflow: $746 million

2008 data unless otherwise noted
Data compiled as of September 2009

How Do We Measure Economic Freedom?
See page 457 for an explanation of the methodology or visit the *Index* Web site at *heritage.org/index*.

NAMIBIA'S TEN ECONOMIC FREEDOMS

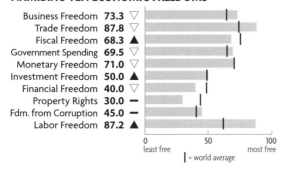

Business Freedom	73.3 ▽	
Trade Freedom	87.8 ▽	
Fiscal Freedom	68.3 ▲	
Government Spending	69.5 ▽	
Monetary Freedom	71.0 ▽	
Investment Freedom	50.0 ▲	
Financial Freedom	40.0 ▽	
Property Rights	30.0 —	
Fdm. from Corruption	45.0 —	
Labor Freedom	87.2 ▲	

0   50   100
least free   most free
| = world average

BUSINESS FREEDOM — 73.3

The overall freedom to start, operate, and close a business is relatively well protected under Namibia's regulatory environment. Starting a business takes an average of 66 days, compared to the world average of 35 days. Obtaining a business license takes less than the world average of 18 procedures and 218 days. Closing a business is relatively easy and not costly.

TRADE FREEDOM — 87.8

Namibia's weighted average tariff rate was 1.1 percent in 2008. The trade regime is relatively open, but import bans and restrictions, some services market access barriers, import licensing regulations, domestic preference in government procurement, corruption, and weak enforcement of intellectual property rights add to the cost of trade. Ten points were deducted from Namibia's trade freedom score to account for non-tariff barriers.

FISCAL FREEDOM — 68.3

Namibia has relatively high tax rates. Both the top income tax rate and the top corporate tax rate are 35 percent. Gas and oil extraction companies are subject to a special tax scheme, and diamond mining profits are subject to a surtax of 55 percent. There is also a value-added tax (VAT). In the most recent year, overall tax revenue as a percentage of GDP was 26.8 percent.

GOVERNMENT SPENDING — 69.5

Total government expenditures, including consumption and transfer payments, are moderate. In the most recent year, government spending equaled 31.9 percent of GDP.

MONETARY FREEDOM — 71

Inflation has been high, averaging 9.0 percent between 2006 and 2008. The government sets the prices of fuel products; influences prices through state-owned enterprises and utilities, including electricity, telecommunications, water, and transportation services; determines guideline prices for maize; and subsidizes agricultural production. Ten points were deducted from Namibia's monetary freedom score to account for policies that distort domestic prices.

INVESTMENT FREEDOM — 50

Namibian law provides for equal treatment of domestic and foreign investors and nondiscriminatory access to all sectors. There is no requirement for local participation in foreign investments, but the government actively encourages partnerships with historically disadvantaged Namibians. While Namibian companies are generally open to foreign investment, private domestic and foreign investments in state-owned enterprises are limited to joint partnerships. The administratively burdensome process of obtaining work permits for foreign employees is a hindrance to investment. Capital transactions, transfers, and payments are controlled. Residents and non-residents may hold foreign exchange accounts subject to restrictions and, in the case of residents, prior approval. Foreign investors can buy and own non-agricultural land.

FINANCIAL FREEDOM — 40

Namibia's financial sector is not fully developed. Financial intermediation remains uneven across the country, and scarce access to credit and banking services discourages entrepreneurial activity. The government owns the Agricultural Bank of Namibia, the Development Bank of Namibia, and the National Housing Enterprise and offers subsidized credits for subsistence farmers. Commercial banks are all at least partly foreign-owned. Namibia's non-bank financial sector has undergone modernization and reform. In 2008, amendments to the regulatory framework on pension fund and life insurance companies were introduced. The number of companies listed on the Namibian Stock Exchange has declined to less than 30 in recent years as a result of delistings and mergers.

PROPERTY RIGHTS — 30

The transfer of land owned by whites to landless blacks for resettlement is official policy, and the government has voiced concerns about the slow pace of land reform, raising fears that inadequately compensated expropriation could increase. The lack of qualified magistrates, other court officials, and private attorneys causes a serious backlog of property cases. Namibia lacks adequate mechanisms to address piracy and copyright violations.

FREEDOM FROM CORRUPTION — 45

Corruption is perceived as significant. Namibia ranks 61st out of 179 countries in Transparency International's Corruption Perceptions Index for 2008. Despite efforts by the Anti-Corruption Commission, Office of the Ombudsman, and Office of the Auditor General, public corruption remains a problem. Critics have charged that the Anti Corruption Commission interprets its mandate narrowly and focuses on minor cases, few of which are prosecuted.

LABOR FREEDOM — 87.2

Namibia's labor regulations are flexible. The non-salary cost of employing a worker is very low, and dismissing an employee is costless. Restrictions on work hours are moderately flexible.

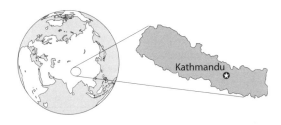

NEPAL

Economic Freedom Score

Least free 0 — 25 — 50 — 75 — 100 Most free

52.7

World Rank: **130**	Regional Rank: **28**

Nepal's economic freedom score is 52.7, making its economy the 130th freest in the 2010 *Index*. Its score is 0.5 point lower than last year, reflecting declines in five of the 10 economic freedoms. Nepal is ranked 28th out of 41 countries in the Asia–Pacific region, and its score is below the world and regional averages.

Nepal's economy is characterized by a combination of rapid population growth and inadequate economic growth that has led to widespread, chronic poverty. Overall, weak reform efforts have failed to stimulate broad-based economic growth. The state continues to hamper private-sector development, and political instability weakens the country's ability to implement economic reform or create a stable environment for development.

Although reforms in Nepal's trade regime are slowly having an effect, the average tariff rate remains high. Foreign investments must be approved or face licensing requirements. A lack of transparency, corruption, and a burdensome approval process impede much-needed private investment growth. Property rights are undermined by the inefficient judicial system, which is subject to substantial corruption and political influence.

BACKGROUND: The fall of the nine-month-old Maoist government in May 2009 has led to political uncertainty in Nepal. Maoist leader Pushpa Kamal Dahal resigned from the premiership following a dispute with Nepal's president over leadership of the army and the fate of some 20,000 Maoist fighters. A 22-party coalition led by Communist Party of Nepal (United Marxist Leninist) leader Madhav Kumar Nepal took power following the fall of the Maoist government but faces continual protests and weakening law and order. The Maoists, who fought a 10-year insurgency that left over 13,000 dead, signed a peace accord in 2006 that allowed for elections that they won in 2008. Economic development has largely stalled. Nepal attracts very little foreign direct investment, and its main industries are agriculture and services.

Country's Score Over Time

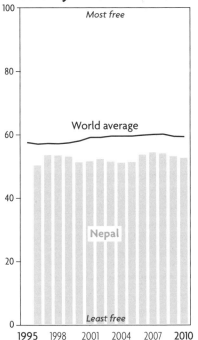

Quick Facts

Population: 28.6 million

GDP (PPP): $31.8 billion
5.3% growth in 2008
3.7% 5-year compound annual growth
$1,112 per capita

Unemployment: estimated to be over 20%

Inflation (CPI): 7.7%

FDI Inflow: $1 million

2008 data unless otherwise noted
Data compiled as of September 2009

How Do We Measure Economic Freedom?
See page 457 for an explanation of the methodology or visit the *Index* Web site at *heritage.org/index.*

NEPAL'S TEN ECONOMIC FREEDOMS

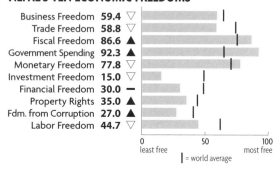

Business Freedom	59.4 ▽	
Trade Freedom	58.8 ▽	
Fiscal Freedom	86.6 ▲	
Government Spending	92.3 ▲	
Monetary Freedom	77.8 ▽	
Investment Freedom	15.0 ▽	
Financial Freedom	30.0 —	
Property Rights	35.0 ▲	
Fdm. from Corruption	27.0 ▲	
Labor Freedom	44.7 ▽	

0 least free   50   100 most free

| = world average

BUSINESS FREEDOM — 59.4

The overall freedom to start, operate, and close a business is limited under Nepal's regulatory environment. Starting a business takes an average of 31 days, compared to the world average of 35 days. Obtaining a business license takes almost twice the world average of 218 days. Bankruptcy proceedings are lengthy and complex.

TRADE FREEDOM — 58.8

Nepal's weighted average tariff rate was 13.1 percent in 2007. The government continues to implement reforms, but import bans, services market access barriers, import taxes, import and export licensing, non-transparent regulations, weak enforcement of intellectual property rights, inadequate infrastructure and trade capacity, and customs corruption add to the cost of trade. Fifteen points were deducted from Nepal's trade freedom score to account for non-tariff barriers.

FISCAL FREEDOM — 86.6

Nepal has moderate tax rates. Both the top income tax rate and the top corporate tax rate are 25 percent. Other taxes include a value-added tax (VAT) and a property tax. In the most recent year, overall tax revenue as a percentage of GDP was 9.6 percent.

GOVERNMENT SPENDING — 92.3

Total government expenditures, including consumption and transfer payments, are low. In the most recent year, government spending equaled 16.0 percent of GDP. The state oil company is a drain on the economy.

MONETARY FREEDOM — 77.8

Inflation has been moderately high, averaging 7.4 percent between 2006 and 2008. Although most price controls have been eliminated, the government regulates the prices of petroleum products and telecommunications services and subsidizes companies in strategic sectors. Five points were deducted from Nepal's monetary freedom score to account for policies that distort domestic prices.

INVESTMENT FREEDOM — 15

Nepal is generally open to investment in many sectors, but investments must be approved, and many face licensing requirements. Bureaucracy and regulatory administration are burdensome, non-transparent, inconsistently implemented, and inefficient. Political instability, pervasive corruption, and inadequate infrastructure and administrative capacity also inhibit investment. Residents may hold foreign exchange accounts in specific instances; most non-residents also may hold such accounts. Convertibility is difficult and not guaranteed. Most payments and transfers are subject to prior approval by the government. There are restrictions on most capital transactions, and all real estate transactions are subject to controls. Foreign investors may acquire real estate only for business use.

FINANCIAL FREEDOM — 30

Nepal's fragmented financial system is heavily influenced by the government. Financial supervision is insufficient, and anti-fraud efforts are lacking. Regulations are not transparent and fall short of international standards. The banking sector dominates the financial sector, and there are approximately 20 commercial banks operating in the country. The number of other financial intermediaries has increased in recent years, but the high cost of credit and limited access to financing still deter entrepreneurial activity. Nepal's government-owned banks represent more than 30 percent of total banking assets and account for more than half of total bank branches. The central bank has gradually phased out "priority sector" financing activities whereby banks must lend a certain amount to government-designated projects.

PROPERTY RIGHTS — 35

Nepal's judicial system suffers from corruption and inefficiency. Lower-level courts are vulnerable to political pressure, and bribery of judges and court staff is endemic. Weak protection of intellectual property rights has led to substantial levels of optical media copyright piracy.

FREEDOM FROM CORRUPTION — 27

Corruption is perceived as widespread. Nepal ranks 121st out of 179 countries in Transparency International's Corruption Perceptions Index for 2008. Foreign investors have identified corruption as an obstacle to maintaining and expanding direct investment, and there are frequent allegations of official corruption in the distribution of permits and approvals, the procurement of goods and services, and the awarding of contracts. The governmental Commission for the Investigation of the Abuse of Authority, mandated to investigate official acts of corruption, claimed a 75 percent success rate concerning corruption cases it filed, but some cases involving politicians were not filed or were defeated in court.

LABOR FREEDOM — 44.7

Nepal's labor regulations are restrictive. The non-salary cost of employing a worker is low, but laying off an employee is difficult.

THE NETHERLANDS

World Rank: **15**   Regional Rank: **6**

Economic Freedom Score

25   50   75

Least free   0   100   Most free

75.0

The Netherlands' economic freedom score is 75.0, making its economy the 15th freest in the 2010 *Index*. Its overall score is 2 points worse than last year due to considerable declines in business freedom, financial freedom, and labor freedom. The Netherlands is ranked 6th out of 43 countries in the Europe region, and its overall score is above the world and regional averages.

The Dutch economy is diversified and modern, with institutional strengths such as strong protection of property rights and an efficient legal framework. The entrepreneurial environment is generally facilitated by high levels of business freedom, trade freedom, monetary freedom, and investment freedom. The regulatory environment is efficient and transparent, and foreign investment is actively promoted. Monetary stability is well maintained, and the judiciary, independent of politics and free of corruption, has demonstrated an exemplary ability to protect property rights.

The Netherlands' overall economic freedom is restricted by a high level of government spending and the lack of fiscal competitiveness. Tax rates are high, and the overall tax regime is burdensome and complex. Efforts to reform welfare spending have been made to improve budget balance, but overall government spending remains high.

BACKGROUND: The Netherlands is a prosperous country that is heavily involved in international commerce, and its economy is sensitive to changes in international trade and the global economy. Rotterdam is one of the largest ports in the world. It is also by far Europe's largest port in terms of cargo tonnage. Despite the country's reputation as an open and modern economy, however, hours of operation for retail stores continue to be restricted. Assimilation of immigrant communities, especially a large Muslim population, has been problematic, and the right-wing Freedom Party of Geert Wilders placed second in the 2009 European elections.

Country's Score Over Time

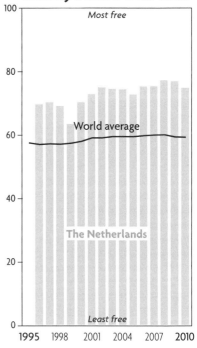

Quick Facts

Population: 16.4 million

GDP (PPP): $671.7 billion
2.1% growth in 2008
2.7% 5-year compound annual growth
$40,849 per capita

Unemployment: 2.8%

Inflation (CPI): 2.2%

FDI Inflow: –$3.5 billion

2008 data unless otherwise noted
Data compiled as of September 2009

How Do We Measure Economic Freedom?
See page 457 for an explanation of the methodology or visit the *Index* Web site at *heritage.org/index.*

319

THE NETHERLANDS' TEN ECONOMIC FREEDOMS

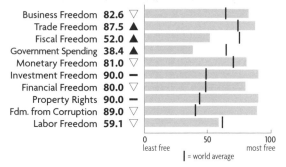

Business Freedom	82.6 ▽	
Trade Freedom	87.5 ▲	
Fiscal Freedom	52.0 ▲	
Government Spending	38.4 ▲	
Monetary Freedom	81.0 ▽	
Investment Freedom	90.0 ▬	
Financial Freedom	80.0 ▽	
Property Rights	90.0 ▬	
Fdm. from Corruption	89.0 ▽	
Labor Freedom	59.1 ▽	

0 least free   50   100 most free

| = world average

BUSINESS FREEDOM — 82.6

The overall freedom to start, operate, and close a business is protected under the Netherlands' regulatory environment. Starting a business takes an average of 10 days, compared to the world average of 35 days. Obtaining a business license takes about the world average of 18 procedures and 218 days.

TRADE FREEDOM — 87.5

The Netherlands' trade policy is the same as that of other members of the European Union. The common EU weighted average tariff rate was 1.3 percent in 2008. However, the EU has high or escalating tariffs for agricultural and manufacturing products, and its MFN tariff code is complex. Non-tariff barriers reflected in EU and Netherlands policy include agricultural and manufacturing subsidies, quotas, import restrictions and bans for some goods and services, market access restrictions in some services sectors, non-transparent and restrictive regulations and standards, and inconsistent regulatory and customs administration among EU members. Supplementary biotechnology and pharmaceuticals rules exceed EU policy, and enforcement of intellectual property rights can be problematic. Ten points were deducted from the Netherlands' trade freedom score to account for non-tariff barriers.

FISCAL FREEDOM — 52

The Netherlands has high income tax rates and moderate corporate tax rates. The top income tax rate is 52 percent, and the top corporate tax rate is 25.5 percent. Other taxes include a value-added tax (VAT), a property transfer tax, an inheritance tax, and environmental taxes. In the most recent year, overall tax revenue as a percentage of GDP was 38.0 percent.

GOVERNMENT SPENDING — 38.4

Total government expenditures, including consumption and transfer payments, are high. In the most recent year, government spending equaled 45.3 percent of GDP. State ownership persists in key sectors. Water and energy utilities are owned by local governments.

MONETARY FREEDOM — 81

The Netherlands is a member of the euro zone. Inflation has been low, averaging 2.0 percent between 2006 and 2008. As a participant in the EU's Common Agricultural Policy, the government subsidizes agricultural production, distorting the prices of agricultural products. The government also regulates energy prices, pharmaceutical prices, and housing rents. Ten points were deducted from the Netherlands' monetary freedom score to account for policies that distort domestic prices.

INVESTMENT FREEDOM — 90

Foreign investors receive national treatment, and 100 percent foreign ownership is allowed in areas where foreign investment is permitted. There is no pre-screening. Elaborate corporate protective measures may block acquisitions or takeovers by Dutch and foreign investors. Other regulations and restrictions in Dutch and EU policy can add to the cost of investment. There are no restrictions on or barriers to current transfers, repatriation of profits, purchase of real estate, or access to foreign exchange. Capital transactions are not restricted but are subject to reporting requirements.

FINANCIAL FREEDOM — 80

The Netherlands' financial system provides easy access to financing. Financial firms have an international reach and offer a variety of services. Three conglomerates account for about 75 percent of lending. There are few formal barriers to foreign banks, but foreign participation in retail banking is minimal because of intense competition and market saturation. The government guarantees loans for small to medium-size enterprises that lack sufficient collateral. Well-developed capital markets partner with other international exchanges. In October 2008, responding to the global financial turmoil, the government nationalized the Dutch parts of ABN Amro and Fortis Bank Netherlands. It also made capital injections into other large financial institutions.

PROPERTY RIGHTS — 90

Private property and contracts are secure, and the judiciary is sound. Citizens and foreigners purchasing real property receive equal treatment. Intellectual property rights are generally protected, but there is piracy of optical disc media by organized criminal organizations.

FREEDOM FROM CORRUPTION — 89

Corruption is perceived as minimal. The Netherlands ranks 7th out of 179 countries in Transparency International's Corruption Perceptions Index for 2008. Dutch law implementing the Organisation for Economic Co-operation and Development's 1997 Anti-Bribery Convention makes corruption by Dutch businessmen in landing foreign contracts a penal offense, and bribes are not deductible for corporate tax purposes. Low-level law enforcement corruption is not believed to be widespread or systemic.

LABOR FREEDOM — 59.1

The Netherlands' labor regulations are relatively rigid. The non-salary cost of employing a worker is high, and dismissing an employee is relatively costly and difficult. Restrictions on work hours are moderately flexible.

NEW ZEALAND

Wellington

Economic Freedom Score

Least free 0　　25　50　75　100　Most free

82.1

N ew Zealand's economic freedom score is 82.1, making its economy the 4th freest in the 2010 *Index*. Its score is 0.1 point better than last year, reflecting modest improvements in trade freedom and fiscal freedom. New Zealand is ranked 4th out of 41 countries in the Asia–Pacific region.

New Zealand continues to be a global leader in economic freedom, performing well on most of the components measured in the *Index*. The economy has an impressive record of market reforms and benefits from its openness to global trade and investment. The banking sector is characterized by sound regulations and prudent lending practices, and well-implemented structural reforms have allowed the New Zealand economy to weather the recent global financial and economic crisis relatively unscathed.

New Zealand's efficient legal and regulatory environment strongly supports entrepreneurial activity. Foreign and domestically owned businesses enjoy considerable flexibility in business formation and employment practices. Restrictions on foreign investment apply in only a few sectors. Facilitating the economy's overall competitiveness, the government has recently cut the corporate tax rate. Inflationary pressures have decreased, with monetary stability intact. New Zealand also boasts an efficient, independent judiciary that protects property rights, and the level of corruption is extraordinarily low.

BACKGROUND: New Zealand is a parliamentary democracy and one of the Asia–Pacific region's most prosperous countries. Far-reaching economic liberalization in the 1980s and 1990s largely deregulated the economy, which is powered mainly by its agricultural sector but also benefits from a strong manufacturing base and a thriving tourism industry. After 10 years of Labor Party–dominated governments, the National Party, led by Prime Minister John Key, returned to power in November 2008.

Country's Score Over Time

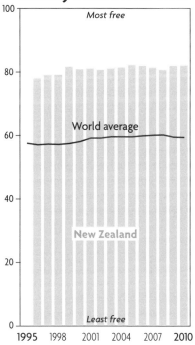

Quick Facts

Population: 4.3 million

GDP (PPP): $115.4 billion
　　　−1.6% growth in 2008
　　　2.0% 5-year compound
　　　　annual growth
　　　$27,029 per capita

Unemployment: 4.2%

Inflation (CPI): 4.0%

FDI Inflow: $2 billion

2008 data unless otherwise noted
Data compiled as of September 2009

How Do We Measure Economic Freedom?
See page 457 for an explanation of the methodology or visit the *Index* Web site at *heritage.org/index.*

NEW ZEALAND'S TEN ECONOMIC FREEDOMS

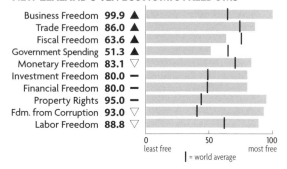

Business Freedom	99.9	▲
Trade Freedom	86.0	▲
Fiscal Freedom	63.6	▲
Government Spending	51.3	▲
Monetary Freedom	83.1	▽
Investment Freedom	80.0	—
Financial Freedom	80.0	—
Property Rights	95.0	—
Fdm. from Corruption	93.0	▽
Labor Freedom	88.8	▽

0 least free — 50 — 100 most free

| = world average

BUSINESS FREEDOM — 99.9

The overall freedom to start, operate, and close a business is strongly protected under New Zealand's regulatory environment. Starting a business is very easy and straightforward, taking only one day in comparison to the world average of 35 days. Obtaining a business license requires much less than the world average of 18 procedures and 218 days.

TRADE FREEDOM — 86

New Zealand's weighted average tariff rate was 2.0 percent in 2008. The trade regime is relatively open, but some import restrictions; services market access barriers; import taxes and fees; restrictive biotechnology, sanitary, and phytosanitary regulations; state trade in kiwi fruit; and issues involving the protection of intellectual property rights add to the cost of trade. Ten points were deducted from New Zealand's trade freedom score to account for non-tariff barriers.

FISCAL FREEDOM — 63.6

New Zealand has a relatively high income tax and a moderate corporate tax. The top income tax rate was reduced to 38 percent as of April 1, 2009, and is scheduled to be reduced further to 37 percent in April 2010. The flat corporate tax rate is 30 percent. Other taxes include a goods and services tax (GST) and a tax on interest. In the most recent year, overall tax revenue as a percentage of GDP was 36.0 percent.

GOVERNMENT SPENDING — 51.3

Total government expenditures, including consumption and transfer payments, are relatively high. In the most recent year, government spending equaled 40.3 percent of GDP. The state maintains significant stakes in the transportation, electricity, and telecommunications industries.

MONETARY FREEDOM — 83.1

Inflation has been relatively low, averaging 3.5 percent between 2006 and 2008. There are no official price controls, but the government regulates the prices of utilities and subsidizes pharmaceuticals. Five points were deducted from New Zealand's monetary freedom score to account for policies that distort domestic prices.

INVESTMENT FREEDOM — 80

New Zealand encourages foreign investment in most sectors. The government does not discriminate against foreign buyers, but it does limit foreign ownership in certain state-owned sectors. The New Zealand government's Overseas Investment Office screens foreign investments that exceed NZD100 million and represent 25 percent or more of the equity in a New Zealand enterprise. In general, regulations and bureaucracy are efficient and transparent, and contract enforcement is effective. There are no restrictions on current transfers, repatriation of profits, or access to foreign exchange. Land and real estate purchases are subject to government approval.

FINANCIAL FREEDOM — 80

New Zealand's financial sector is well developed and competitive, offering a full range of financing instruments for entrepreneurial activity. Regulation is efficient and transparent in accordance with international standards. Credit is allocated on market terms. The banking sector dominates the financial system, accounting for around 80 percent of the system's total assets. There are 16 banks registered in New Zealand. Foreign-owned banks account for approximately 90 percent of total assets, and the government fully owns Kiwibank, created in late 2002. Non-bank financial institutions may offer banking services, subject to normal restrictions. Capital markets are small but well developed, and stocks are traded actively. Insurance is lightly regulated, and foreign participation is high. Capital markets are open to foreign participation. The financial system has weathered the global financial turmoil relatively well; with very limited exposure to distressed assets, the banking sector remains well capitalized.

PROPERTY RIGHTS — 95

Private property is well protected. The judiciary is independent, and contracts are notably secure. Legislation has been proposed to bring the patent law into closer conformity with international standards by tightening the criteria for granting a patent. Manufacturers have expressed concern that parallel imports of "gray market" goods under New Zealand law will result in the importation of dated or unsuitable products.

FREEDOM FROM CORRUPTION — 93

Corruption is perceived as almost nonexistent. New Zealand is ranked 1st out of 179 countries in Transparency International's Corruption Perceptions Index for 2008; it has received this rank for two consecutive years. New Zealand is renowned for its efforts to ensure transparent, competitive, and corruption-free government procurement. Stiff penalties against bribing government officials or accepting bribes are strictly enforced.

LABOR FREEDOM — 88.8

New Zealand's labor regulations are flexible. The non-salary cost of employing a worker is low, and dismissing an employee is costless. Regulations on work hours are flexible.

NICARAGUA

World Rank: 98 **Regional Rank: 19**

Economic Freedom Score

Least free 0 — 25 — 50 — 75 — 100 Most free

58.3

Nicaragua's economic freedom score is 58.3, making its economy the 98th freest in the 2010 *Index*. Its overall score is 1.5 points worse than last year, reflecting declines in six of the 10 economic freedoms. Nicaragua is ranked 19th out of 29 countries in the South and Central America/Caribbean region, and its overall score is below the world average.

Nicaragua's trade liberalization has progressed, although moderately high non-tariff barriers still limit overall trade freedom. Tax administration has improved, and reforms to improve public finance management have gradually moved forward. Foreign investment is welcome, and foreign capital is accorded equal treatment, although certain restrictions still exist. The government has tried to enhance the economy's competitiveness and efficiency, but overall structural reforms have been sluggish, and privatization has all but stalled.

Other considerable challenges to Nicaragua's economic freedom include institutional weaknesses in strengthening property rights and combating corruption. The inefficient judicial system is inconsistent in contract enforcement and subject to political interference. Corruption is perceived as widespread and persistent.

BACKGROUND: Following a decade of Sandinista dictatorship, economic and political stability and respect for human rights improved under democratically elected governments from 1990 until 2006, when Sandinista leader Daniel Ortega returned to power with 38 percent of the vote. Despite claims that he has abandoned Marxism for "fair markets" and democracy, Ortega supports Venezuela's Hugo Chávez and Bolivia's Evo Morales and has been slow to restore confiscated properties to their rightful owners. Nearly half of the workforce is unemployed or underemployed. The Central America–Dominican Republic–United States Free Trade Agreement came into force in 2006, and the economy has diversified to include minerals and textiles. Electoral fraud in the November 2008 municipal elections and a crackdown on civil liberties led the U.S. to cancel part of its Millennium Challenge grant to Nicaragua.

Country's Score Over Time

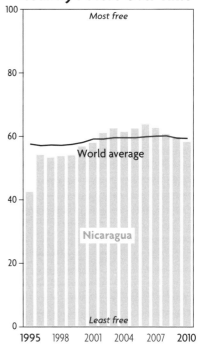

Quick Facts

Population: 5.7 million

GDP (PPP): $15.2 billion
3.5% growth in 2008
3.6% 5-year compound annual growth
$2,682 per capita

Unemployment: 5.6%

Inflation (CPI): 19.9%

FDI Inflow: $626 million

2008 data unless otherwise noted
Data compiled as of September 2009

How Do We Measure Economic Freedom?
See page 457 for an explanation of the methodology or visit the *Index* Web site at *heritage.org/index.*

NICARAGUA'S TEN ECONOMIC FREEDOMS

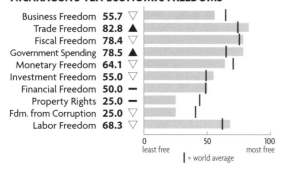

Business Freedom	55.7	▽
Trade Freedom	82.8	▲
Fiscal Freedom	78.4	▽
Government Spending	78.5	▲
Monetary Freedom	64.1	▽
Investment Freedom	55.0	▽
Financial Freedom	50.0	—
Property Rights	25.0	—
Fdm. from Corruption	25.0	▽
Labor Freedom	68.3	▽

0 least free   50   100 most free
▐ = world average

BUSINESS FREEDOM — 55.7

The overall freedom to start, operate, and close a business is limited under Nicaragua's regulatory environment. Starting a business takes an average of 39 days, compared to the world average of 35 days. Obtaining a business license requires about the world average of 18 procedures and 218 days, but the cost is high. Closing a business is relatively easy.

TRADE FREEDOM — 82.8

Nicaragua's weighted average tariff rate was 3.6 percent in 2007. The government has made progress in liberalizing the trade regime, but import restrictions, import taxes and fees, import licensing requirements for some goods, restrictive technical standards, weak enforcement of intellectual property rights, corruption, and delays in customs clearance add to the cost of trade. Ten points were deducted from Nicaragua's trade freedom score to account for non-tariff barriers.

FISCAL FREEDOM — 78.4

The top income and corporate tax rates are 30 percent. Other taxes include a value-added tax (VAT), a capital gains tax, and a property tax levied at the municipal level. During the most recent year, overall tax revenue as a percentage of GDP was 19.0 percent.

GOVERNMENT SPENDING — 78.5

Total government expenditures, including consumption and transfer payments, are relatively low. In the most recent year, government spending equaled 26.8 percent of GDP. Privatization has all but stalled.

MONETARY FREEDOM — 64.1

Inflation has been very high, averaging 16.8 percent between 2006 and 2008. Most price controls have been eliminated, but the government sets prices for pharmaceuticals, sugar, domestically produced soft drinks and cigarettes, and liquefied natural gas; regulates the retail price of butane gas and rates for electricity, energy, water, and telecommunications; and has a history of negotiating voluntary price restraints with domestic producers of important consumer goods. Ten points were deducted from Nicaragua's monetary freedom score to account for policies that distort domestic prices.

INVESTMENT FREEDOM — 55

Foreign investment is guaranteed equal treatment and allowed in most sectors. It is not screened and generally faces no performance requirements; however, the government has used the administration of regulations to introduce non-commercial concessions in contracts, and the labor code states that 75 percent of all employees (not including management posts) must be Nicaraguan. Commercial dispute resolution is burdensome, contract enforcement is weak, and property rights are poorly protected. Regulatory bureaucracy can be time-consuming and inconsistent. The law grants repatriation of capital and immediate remittance abroad of profits. Investors may hold foreign exchange accounts, but the process is cumbersome. There are no controls or restrictions on payments and transfers and very few restrictions on capital transactions. Investors may own property.

FINANCIAL FREEDOM — 50

Nicaragua's financial sector is concentrated in urban areas and not fully developed. Mergers and acquisitions have consolidated the banking system. The small banking sector is highly dollarized and has eight commercial banks that are majority private-owned and provide a limited but expanding range of financial services. The three largest banks account for about 70 percent of total assets. Insurance, once a state monopoly, is now open to private investors. A state-owned firm remains the largest insurer and controls the market. Capital markets are small, and the stock exchange trades primarily in government bonds, with only a small number of private companies listed.

PROPERTY RIGHTS — 25

Protection of property rights is weak. Contracts are not easily enforceable, and the judiciary is politicized and subject to corruption. Protection of intellectual property rights is almost nonexistent. Estimates of optical media piracy range from 70 percent of DVDs sold to almost 100 percent of music CDs sold. Weak land title registries and the many unresolved land expropriation cases from the 1980s seriously undermine real property interests.

FREEDOM FROM CORRUPTION — 25

Corruption is perceived as widespread. Nicaragua ranks 134th out of 179 countries in Transparency International's Corruption Perceptions Index for 2008. Nicaragua's legal environment is among the weakest in Latin America. Influence peddling in the judicial branch puts foreign investors at a sharp disadvantage in any litigation or dispute. Corruption and political deal-making, especially within the ruling Sandinista party, the National Police, and the judiciary, are viewed as pervasive.

LABOR FREEDOM — 68.3

Nicaragua's labor regulations are relatively flexible. The non-salary cost of employing a worker is moderate, and dismissing an employee is not costly. Regulations on work hours remain rigid.

NIGER

World Rank: 129   **Regional Rank: 24**

Niger's economic freedom score is 52.9, making its economy the 129th freest in the 2010 *Index*. Its score has decreased by 0.9 point since last year. Niger is ranked 24th out of 46 countries in the Sub-Saharan Africa region, and its overall score equals the regional average.

Niger scores above the world average on government spending and monetary freedom. Despite inflationary pressure, monetary stability has been relatively well maintained, and prices (except for petroleum products) are largely set by the market. The government has taken measures to improve the transparency and quality of its management of public finances, but results have been mixed. The average tariff rate has decreased, but non-tariff barriers limit overall trade freedom.

Economic freedom still faces considerable institutional challenges in Niger. The financial system is fractured and underdeveloped, and the limited availability of financial instruments and high cost of credit deter investment. The inefficient regulatory and legal environment constrains commercial operations and investment. Rigid labor regulations discourage employment growth. The judicial system remains vulnerable to corruption.

BACKGROUND: Niger had a single-party civilian government until a military coup in 1974. Civilian rule was restored in 1993 but overthrown again in 1996. A 1999 coup led to a transitional government and a new constitution. Mamadou Tandja won the presidency in 1999 and was re-elected in 2004. A Tuareg rebellion in northern Niger is a source of instability, but there have been no armed attacks since June 2008. Niger is one of the world's poorest countries. Despite substantial mineral resources, including gold and uranium, over 80 percent of the population depends on subsistence farming and herding. Most economic activity is informal, infrastructure is poor, and arid conditions and drought hinder food production. In 2008, China National Petroleum Corporation was granted the rights to explore and produce petroleum in northern Niger.

Country's Score Over Time

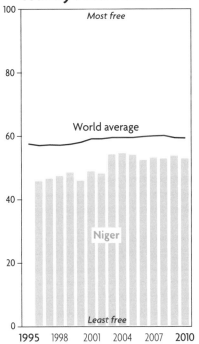

Quick Facts

Population: 14.7 million

GDP (PPP): 10.0 billion
9.5% growth in 2008
6.7% 5-year compound
annual growth
$684 per capita

Unemployment: n/a

Inflation (CPI): 11.3%

FDI Inflow: $147 million

2008 data unless otherwise noted
Data compiled as of September 2009

How Do We Measure Economic Freedom?
See page 457 for an explanation of the methodology or visit the *Index* Web site at *heritage.org/index.*

NIGER'S TEN ECONOMIC FREEDOMS

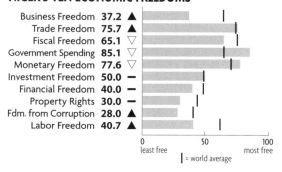

Business Freedom	37.2 ▲	
Trade Freedom	75.7 ▲	
Fiscal Freedom	65.1 ▽	
Government Spending	85.1 ▽	
Monetary Freedom	77.6 ▽	
Investment Freedom	50.0 —	
Financial Freedom	40.0 —	
Property Rights	30.0 —	
Fdm. from Corruption	28.0 ▲	
Labor Freedom	40.7 ▲	

0 50 100
least free   most free
| = world average

BUSINESS FREEDOM — 37.2

The overall freedom to start, operate, and close a business is significantly restricted under Niger's regulatory environment. The cost of launching a business is very high. Obtaining all necessary business licenses takes more than the global average of 218 days, and fees are high. Closing a business can be a lengthy process.

TRADE FREEDOM — 75.7

Niger's weighted average tariff rate was 7.1 percent in 2008. Some import restrictions, import taxes, import and export licensing, inefficient and non-transparent customs implementation and regulation, and widespread corruption add to the cost of trade. Ten points were deducted from Niger's trade freedom score to account for non-tariff barriers.

FISCAL FREEDOM — 65.1

Niger has a high income tax rate and a moderate corporate tax rate. The top income tax rate is 45 percent, and the top corporate tax rate is 35 percent, to be reduced to 30 percent by the end of 2009. Other taxes include a value-added tax (VAT), a tax on interest, and an insurance tax. The VAT and import taxes on food and fuel goods were suspended in 2008. In the most recent year, overall tax revenue as a percentage of GDP was 15.4 percent.

GOVERNMENT SPENDING — 85.1

Total government expenditures, including consumption and transfer payments, are relatively low. In the most recent year, government spending equaled 22.3 percent of GDP. In general, privatization has been stymied by the global financial downturn and the resulting lack of interested investors. The sale of a major telecommunications company and signing of petroleum exploration contracts with international partners increased non-tax revenue. Windfall petroleum revenues are being used for infrastructure investment projects.

MONETARY FREEDOM — 77.6

Inflation has been relatively high, averaging 7.5 percent between 2006 and 2008. With the exception of petroleum products, the market sets prices, but the government does influence prices through state-owned utilities. Five points were deducted from Niger's monetary freedom score to adjust for measures that distort domestic prices.

INVESTMENT FREEDOM — 50

Foreign capital and domestic capital are legally equal. Investment is not screened, and all sectors are open except for those deemed sensitive for national security purposes. Deterrents include underdeveloped markets, limited institutional capacity, inadequate infrastructure, corruption, and political instability. Residents may hold foreign exchange accounts subject to some restrictions. Non-residents may hold foreign exchange accounts with prior approval. Payments, capital transactions, and transfers to selected countries are subject to quantitative limits and approval. Real estate purchases by non-residents must be reported to the government. Land ownership requires government approval.

FINANCIAL FREEDOM — 40

Niger's underdeveloped financial system remains weak and fragmented, reflecting the small size of the formal economy. The number of available financial instruments is limited, and scarce access to financing hinders dynamic business activity. Bank credit to the private sector has been less than 10 percent of GDP. The Central Bank of West African States governs Niger's banking institutions and sets minimum reserve requirements. Credit is generally allocated on market terms, but the cost is high, and credit is usually extended only to large businesses. Four major commercial banks control about 90 percent of resources. The government holds shares in a number of financial institutions. Most capital market activity centers on the regional stock exchange in Côte d'Ivoire, which also has a very small branch in Niger.

PROPERTY RIGHTS — 30

Niger's judicial system is understaffed and subject to pressure from the executive. Corruption is fueled by low salaries and inadequate training programs. Despite a legal regime for the protection of intellectual property rights, the government lacks the capacity and resources to enforce copyright violations, and counterfeit CDs and videocassettes are readily available in most cities.

FREEDOM FROM CORRUPTION — 28

Corruption is perceived as pervasive. Niger ranks 115th out of 179 countries in Transparency International's Corruption Perceptions Index for 2008. Corruption in the executive and legislative branches is compounded by poorly financed, poorly trained law enforcement and weak administrative controls. Other major causes of corruption are low salaries; politicization of the public service; the influence of traditional kinship, ethnic, and family ties on decision-making; and a culture of impunity.

LABOR FREEDOM — 40.7

Niger's labor regulations are restrictive. The non-salary cost of employing a worker is high, and laying off an employee is difficult. Regulations on work hours are very rigid.

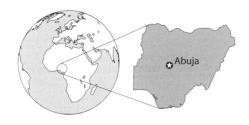

NIGERIA

Abuja

Economic Freedom Score

| World Rank: **106** | Regional Rank: **15** |

56.8

Nigeria's economic freedom score is 56.8, making its economy the 106th freest in the 2010 *Index*. Its score has improved by 1.7 points since last year, reflecting major improvements in trade freedom, investment freedom, and freedom from corruption. Nigeria is ranked 15th out of 46 countries in the Sub-Saharan Africa region, and its overall score is below the world average.

Nigeria has pursued structural reforms to diversify its productive base and stimulate more broad-based growth. These reforms have centered on enhancing management of public finance, improving the entrepreneurial environment, and expanding access to credit through banking and financial reforms. Progress has been mixed, and the economy remains heavily dependent on oil and gas. Public-sector reform has stalled.

Other lingering challenges impede private-sector development and growth of the non-energy sector, hampering long-term development and poverty reduction. The arbitrary application of regulations continues to hinder foreign investment. Nigeria's inefficient judiciary is prone to corruption, and contract enforcement is weak. Despite recent bank consolidations, the financial system remains relatively weak due to bureaucratic regulations and a cash-based economy.

BACKGROUND: Former General Olusegun Obasanjo, who oversaw a transition to civilian government in 1979, was elected president in 1999 and re-elected in 2003. His chosen successor, Umaru Yar'Adua, won a widely questioned election in 2007. Nigeria is Africa's leading oil producer, although violent attacks on and kidnappings of foreign oil workers in the Niger Delta impede oil production. Oil and gas accounted for about 18 percent of GDP, 90 percent of foreign exchange earnings, and 80 percent of government revenue in 2008. The informal economy is extensive, and a majority of the population, Africa's largest, is engaged in agriculture. Ethnic, regional, or religious violence has taken a heavy toll, most notably in the southeastern region of Biafra, and imposition of Islamic law in several states has aggravated religious tensions.

Country's Score Over Time

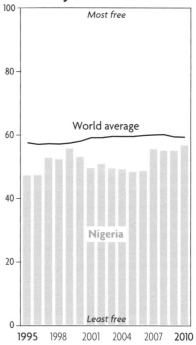

Quick Facts

Population: 151.3 million

GDP (PPP): $315.0 billion
5.3% growth in 2008
5.8% 5-year compound
annual growth
$2,082 per capita

Unemployment: 4.9% (2007)

Inflation (CPI): 11.2%

FDI Inflow: $20.3 billion

2008 data unless otherwise noted
Data compiled as of September 2009

How Do We Measure Economic Freedom?
See page 457 for an explanation of the methodology or visit the *Index* Web site at *heritage.org/index.*

NIGERIA'S TEN ECONOMIC FREEDOMS

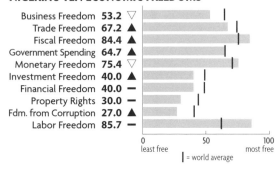

Business Freedom	53.2 ▽	
Trade Freedom	67.2 ▲	
Fiscal Freedom	84.4 ▲	
Government Spending	64.7 ▲	
Monetary Freedom	75.4 ▽	
Investment Freedom	40.0 ▲	
Financial Freedom	40.0 —	
Property Rights	30.0 —	
Fdm. from Corruption	27.0 ▲	
Labor Freedom	85.7 —	

0 least free   50   100 most free

| = world average

BUSINESS FREEDOM — 53.2

The overall freedom to start, operate, and close a business is limited under Nigeria's regulatory environment. Starting a business takes an average of 31 days, compared to the world average of 35 days. Obtaining a business license takes more than the world average of 218 days.

TRADE FREEDOM — 67.2

Nigeria's weighted average tariff rate was 8.9 percent in 2008. Trade liberalization has progressed, but prohibitive tariffs, import bans and restrictions, import fees, import and export taxes, arbitrary regulations, some export subsidies, weak enforcement of intellectual property rights, corruption, and inconsistent and non-transparent customs administration add to the cost of trade. Fifteen points were deducted from Nigeria's trade freedom score to account for non-tariff barriers.

FISCAL FREEDOM — 84.4

Nigeria has moderate tax rates. The top income tax rate is 25 percent, and the flat corporate tax rate is 30 percent. Oil and gas companies are subject to a special tax scheme. Other taxes include a value-added tax (VAT), a tax on interest, and a capital gains tax. Petroleum companies are subject to a profit tax of 85 percent rather than a corporate tax. In the most recent year, overall tax revenue as a percentage of GDP was 5.6 percent.

GOVERNMENT SPENDING — 64.7

Total government expenditures, including consumption and transfer payments, are moderate. In the most recent year, government spending equaled 34.3 percent of GDP. Government involvement in the economy is considerable. In September 2008, the privatization board outlined plans for more than 100 transactions, including the divestment of major gas and telecommunications companies. As of April 2009, no major divestments had been completed.

MONETARY FREEDOM — 75.4

Inflation has been high, averaging 9.6 percent between 2006 and 2008. With the exception of petroleum products, prices are set by the market. The government subsidizes agriculture and manufacturing; it also influences prices through state-owned enterprises and utilities. Five points were deducted from Nigeria's monetary freedom score to account for policies that distort domestic prices.

INVESTMENT FREEDOM — 40

Nigeria treats foreign and domestic investment equally under the law, and most sectors are open to investment. Investors in manufacturing may have to meet local content requirements, and foreign personnel are subject to quotas. Disincentives include inadequate infrastructure, arbitrary application of regulations, corruption, crime, security concerns, burdensome dispute resolution, and weak contract enforcement. Residents and non-residents may hold foreign exchange accounts. Some capital transactions are subject to documentation requirements and restrictions. Most payments and transfers must be conducted through banks. Acquiring and maintaining rights to real property can be difficult.

FINANCIAL FREEDOM — 40

Although Nigeria's financial system has undergone rapid transformation and consolidation, it remains weak and inefficient. The number of banks has declined from 89 to 24 as a result of a minimum capital decree. Restructuring has substantially reduced the number of non-performing loans. Banking development is still hindered by bureaucracy and a cash-based economy. Banks interact with a very limited portion of the population, and limited access to financing hampers entrepreneurial activity. The government owns six development banks and influences the allocation of credit. Capital markets are not fully developed, but the stock market is increasingly active. Financial stability has been sustained during the global financial turmoil, largely because of Nigeria's limited integration with the global financial system.

PROPERTY RIGHTS — 30

Nigeria's judiciary suffers from corruption, delays, insufficient funding, a severe lack of available court facilities, a lack of computerized systems for document processing, and unscheduled adjournments of court sessions because of power outages. One of the world's least efficient property registration systems makes acquiring and maintaining rights to real property difficult. Enforcement of copyrights, patents, and trademarks is weak.

FREEDOM FROM CORRUPTION — 27

Corruption is perceived as pervasive. Nigeria ranks 121st out of 179 countries in Transparency International's Corruption Perceptions Index for 2008, a significant improvement over 2007. Corruption is endemic at all levels of government and society, and the president, vice president, governors, and deputy governors are constitutionally immune from civil and criminal prosecution. Domestic and foreign observers recognize corruption as a serious obstacle to economic growth and poverty reduction.

LABOR FREEDOM — 85.7

Nigeria's labor regulations are relatively flexible. The non-salary cost of employing a worker is moderate, and dismissing an employee is relatively easy. Regulations on work hours are flexible.

NORWAY

World Rank: **37**	Regional Rank: **20**

Norway's economic freedom score is 69.4, making its econ-omy the 37th freest in the 2010 *Index*. Its overall score has decreased by 0.8 point since last year, reflecting declines in four of the 10 economic freedoms, including freedom from corruption. Norway is ranked 20th out of 43 countries in the Europe region, and its overall score is well above the world and regional averages.

Scoring fairly well in many of the 10 economic freedoms, the Norwegian economy enjoys vibrant entrepreneurial activ-ity and high levels of prosperity. The country has a strong tradition of openness to global trade and investment, and transparent and efficient regulations are applied evenly in most cases.

Norway's overall economic freedom is limited by the lack of fiscal competitiveness, the large presence of the gov-ernment in the economy, and labor market rigidity. The government has focused on containing expensive welfare programs in recent years, but government spending still remains more than one-third of GDP. The state still owns around 50 percent of all industries, including enterprises in manufacturing, telecommunications, hydroelectric power, and transportation. While the corporate tax rate is moder-ate, personal income taxes are very high, and the overall tax burden is considerable.

BACKGROUND: Norway is one of the world's most prosper-ous countries, and levels of productivity are high. Howev-er, its privatization agenda has stalled recently. Fisheries, metal, and oil are Norway's most important commodi-ties. The government continues to save a large portion of its oil revenues in investment funds outside of the country as insurance against depleting reserves. Norwegian voters have rejected membership in the European Union in two referenda. Instead, the country maintains close economic interaction with EU members under the European Economic Area agreement. Norway has been a member of NATO since 1949.

Country's Score Over Time

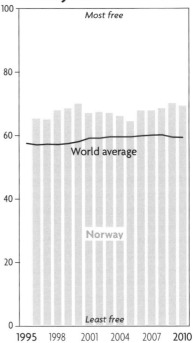

Quick Facts

Population: 4.8 million

GDP (PPP): $277.3 billion
2.0% growth in 2008
2.5% 5-year compound
annual growth
$58,138 per capita

Unemployment: 2.5%

Inflation (CPI): 3.8%

FDI Inflow: –$95 million

2008 data unless otherwise noted
Data compiled as of September 2009

How Do We Measure Economic Freedom?
See page 457 for an explanation of the methodology or visit the *Index* Web site at *heritage.org/index*.

NORWAY'S TEN ECONOMIC FREEDOMS

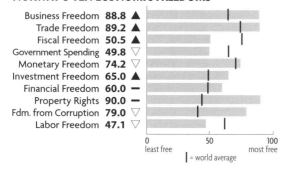

Business Freedom	88.8 ▲	
Trade Freedom	89.2 ▲	
Fiscal Freedom	50.5 ▲	
Government Spending	49.8 ▽	
Monetary Freedom	74.2 ▽	
Investment Freedom	65.0 ▲	
Financial Freedom	60.0 —	
Property Rights	90.0 —	
Fdm. from Corruption	79.0 ▽	
Labor Freedom	47.1 ▽	

0 least free   50   100 most free

| = world average

BUSINESS FREEDOM — 88.8

The overall freedom to start, operate, and close a business is strongly protected under Norway's regulatory environment. Starting a business takes an average of seven days, compared to the world average of 35 days. Obtaining a business license requires less than the world average of 18 procedures. Bankruptcy proceedings are relatively simple and straightforward.

TRADE FREEDOM — 89.2

Norway's weighted average tariff rate was 0.4 percent in 2008. Some import bans and quotas, restrictions in services markets, import licensing requirements, restrictive pharmaceutical and biotechnology policies, agriculture and manufacturing subsidies, and inconsistent enforcement of intellectual property rights add to the cost of trade. Ten points were deducted from Norway's trade freedom score to account for non-tariff barriers.

FISCAL FREEDOM — 50.5

Norway has a high income tax rate and a moderate corporate tax rate. The top income tax rate is 47.8 percent, and the flat corporate tax rate is 28 percent. Other taxes include a value-added tax (VAT), a tax on net wealth (reduced from a two-tiered system as of January 1, 2009), and a number of environmental taxes. Petroleum companies' profits are subject to a different tax scheme. In the most recent year, overall tax revenue as a percentage of GDP was 43.4 percent.

GOVERNMENT SPENDING — 49.8

Total government expenditures, including consumption and transfer payments, are relatively high. In the most recent year, government spending equaled 40.9 percent of GDP. The 2009 budget included some tax-relief measures for corporations as part of a larger stimulus package.

MONETARY FREEDOM — 74.2

Inflation has been low, averaging 2.9 percent between 2006 and 2008. The government regulates prices for agriculture products, sets maximum prices for pharmaceuticals, influences prices through state-owned enterprises and utilities, and subsidizes agriculture and manufacturing. Fifteen points were deducted from Norway's monetary freedom score to account for policies that distort domestic prices.

INVESTMENT FREEDOM — 65

Foreign and domestic investments are treated equally under the law, but regulations, standards, and practices often favor Norwegian, Scandinavian, and European Economic Area investors, and the government may screen investments to ensure that they are in the public interest. The state continues to play an important role in the economy and restricts investment in sectors in which it has a monopoly and sectors that are considered politically sensitive, such as fishing and maritime transport. Regulations and bureaucracy are generally transparent and efficient, but regulations can change suddenly. Residents and non-residents may hold foreign exchange accounts. There are no restrictions on payments, transfers, or repatriation of profits. Foreign investors may own land, subject to various restrictions.

FINANCIAL FREEDOM — 60

Supervision of Norway's well-developed financial system is prudent, and regulations are largely consistent with international norms. Credit is allocated on market terms, and banks offer a wide array of services. The government retains ownership of Norway's largest financial institution, which accounts for 40 percent of assets. Reluctance to allow foreign ownership of the domestic financial sector has eased, and the Ministry of Finance has eliminated remaining barriers to the establishment of branches by foreign financial institutions. The banking and insurance markets are highly integrated due to mergers between banks and insurance companies. Prudential lending practices and sound regulations made it possible for the banking sector to withstand the global financial turmoil, although there was a temporary liquidity crisis. In October 2008, the government bailed out the Norwegian operations of two Icelandic banks, Kaupthing and Glitnir.

PROPERTY RIGHTS — 90

Private property and contracts are secure, and the judiciary is sound. Norway adheres to key international agreements for the protection of intellectual property rights. Internet piracy and cable/satellite decoder and smart-card piracy have risen, and enforcement of IPR protection is spotty.

FREEDOM FROM CORRUPTION — 79

Corruption is perceived as present. Norway ranks 14th out of 179 countries in Transparency International's Corruption Perceptions Index for 2008. Corrupt activity by Norwegian or foreign officials is a criminal offense, and anti-corruption laws subject Norwegian nationals and companies that bribe officials in foreign countries to criminal penalties.

LABOR FREEDOM — 47.1

Norway's labor regulations are rigid. The non-salary cost of employing a worker is moderate, but dismissing an employee is relatively difficult and costly. Regulations on work hours are relatively rigid.

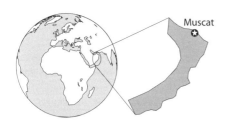
Muscat

OMAN

World Rank: **43**   Regional Rank: **4**

Economic Freedom Score

25   50   75

Least free 0   100 Most free

67.7

O man's economic freedom score is 67.7, making its economy the 43rd freest in the 2010 *Index*. Its score has improved by 0.7 point since last year, reflecting improvements in freedom from corruption and business freedom. Oman is ranked 4th out of 17 countries in the Middle East/North Africa region, and its overall score is above the world and regional averages.

Oman is a small, open economy in which the oil sector has been the most important engine of growth. The government has pursued reforms to diversify the country's productive base and stimulate broad-based economic development. There is no personal income tax, and corporate taxes are low. Foreign investment is welcome in many sectors, although the approval process can be burdensome. The impact of the global financial turmoil on the financial system has been slight.

Overall economic freedom in Oman remains constrained by the state's considerable involvement in the economy through public enterprises. High government spending is funded by a large state-owned energy sector. The judiciary is vulnerable to political influence.

BACKGROUND: Oman, an Arab monarchy, has been trying to modernize its oil-dominated economy without diluting the ruling al-Said family's power. It is a relatively small oil producer, and production has declined steadily since 2001, although this decline was offset by high oil prices in the mid-2000s. To promote economic diversification, the government seeks to expand exports of natural gas; to develop gas-based industries; and to encourage foreign investment in the petrochemical, electric power, telecommunications, and other industries. It also places a high priority on its policy of "Omanization" (the replacement of foreign workers with local staff) to reduce chronically high unemployment rates. Oman joined the World Trade Organization in 2000 and signed a free trade agreement with the United States in 2006.

Country's Score Over Time

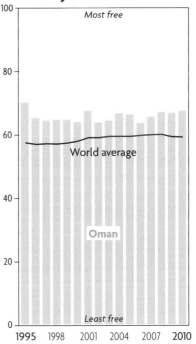

Quick Facts

Population: 2.8 million

GDP (PPP): $62.0 billion
6.4% growth in 2008
6.3% 5-year compound annual growth
$22,478 per capita

Unemployment: 15% (2004)

Inflation (CPI): 12.6%

FDI Inflow: $2.9 billion

2008 data unless otherwise noted
Data compiled as of September 2009

How Do We Measure Economic Freedom?
See page 457 for an explanation of the methodology or visit the *Index* Web site at *heritage.org/index*.

OMAN'S TEN ECONOMIC FREEDOMS

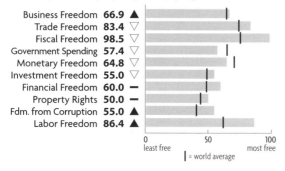

Business Freedom	66.9	▲
Trade Freedom	83.4	▽
Fiscal Freedom	98.5	▽
Government Spending	57.4	▽
Monetary Freedom	64.8	▽
Investment Freedom	55.0	▽
Financial Freedom	60.0	—
Property Rights	50.0	—
Fdm. from Corruption	55.0	▲
Labor Freedom	86.4	▲

0 least free   50   100 most free

| = world average

BUSINESS FREEDOM — 66.9

The overall freedom to conduct a business is limited under Oman's regulatory environment. Starting a business takes an average of 12 days, compared to the world average of 35 days. However, obtaining a business license takes more than the world average of 218 days, and costs are high. Bankruptcy proceedings are lengthy.

TRADE FREEDOM — 83.4

Oman's weighted average tariff rate was 3.3 percent in 2008. Some prohibitive tariffs, import bans and restrictions, import licensing requirements, non-transparent standards and regulations, local preference in government procurement, problems with protecting intellectual property rights, and subsidies add to the cost of trade. Ten points were deducted from Oman's trade freedom score to account for non-tariff barriers.

FISCAL FREEDOM — 98.5

Oman has low tax rates. There is no income tax on individuals, and the top corporate tax rate for most enterprises is 12 percent; foreign or unregistered companies are subject to a top corporate tax rate of 30 percent but are scheduled to fall under the 12 percent rate for domestic companies as of January 2010. Oil sales are subject to a special tax scheme. There is no consumption tax or value-added tax (VAT). In the most recent year, overall tax revenue as a percentage of GDP was 3.3 percent.

GOVERNMENT SPENDING — 57.4

Total government expenditures, including consumption and transfer payments, are relatively high. In the most recent year, government spending equaled 37.7 percent of GDP. Authorities are looking to increase the role of the private sector in telecommunications, water, and electricity.

MONETARY FREEDOM — 64.8

Inflation has been high, averaging 10.1 percent between 2006 and 2008. The government controls the prices of a range of core goods and services through an extensive subsidy system and influences prices through state-owned enterprises and utilities, including electricity and water. Fifteen points were deducted from Oman's monetary freedom score to account for policies that distort domestic prices.

INVESTMENT FREEDOM — 55

Foreign investment is allowed in many sectors, subject to government approval. The level of foreign ownership that is permitted varies with the level of capital committed. The "Omanization" requirement that only Omanis may work in specified occupational categories is an impediment to foreign investment. Regulations can be non-transparent and contradictory, and bureaucracy can be burdensome and time-consuming. Residents may hold foreign exchange accounts. There are no restrictions on capital repatriation, currency exchange, or transfer of dividends. Land ownership for foreigners is generally prohibited except in designated tourist areas and in industrial estates.

FINANCIAL FREEDOM — 60

Oman's financial sector, which is regulated by the Central Bank of Oman, has adopted new bank supervisory procedures in recent years. A 2000 banking law limited investments in foreign securities, raised capital requirements, and granted the central bank the authority to reject candidates for senior positions in commercial banks. Since then, several banks have merged. New regulations that focus on ensuring efficient management of banks were also promulgated. The banking sector has 17 commercial banks, 10 of which are foreign incorporated. Most credit is offered at market rates, but the government intervenes in credit markets through subsidized loans to promote investment. The Muscat Securities Market is very active and is open to foreign investors.

PROPERTY RIGHTS — 50

The threat of expropriation is low, but the judiciary is subject to political influence. Foreigners may hold title to homes inside specified tourism projects. Non–Gulf Cooperation Council nationals cannot own commercial real estate. Intellectual property laws on patents, copyrights, trademarks, industrial secrets, geographical indications, and integrated circuits are WTO-consistent, and enforcement has improved. Only the sultan, through royal decree, can amend the laws.

FREEDOM FROM CORRUPTION — 55

Corruption is perceived as present. Oman ranks 41st out of 179 countries in Transparency International's Corruption Perceptions Index for 2008, a decline from 2007. Although corruption is not considered a significant problem, several high-ranking government officials, including a member of the State Council, have been sentenced to between three and five years in prison for bribery, misuse of public office, and breach of trust in recent years.

LABOR FREEDOM — 86.4

Oman's labor regulations are relatively flexible. The non-salary cost of employing a worker is low, and dismissing an employee is not difficult. The labor laws enforce the "Omanization" policy that requires private-sector firms to meet quotas for hiring native Omani workers.

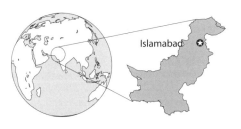
Islamabad

PAKISTAN

Economic Freedom Score

25   50   75

Least free 0   100 Most free

55.2

| World Rank: **117** | Regional Rank: **22** |

Pakistan's economic freedom score is 55.2, making its economy the 117th freest in the 2010 *Index*. Its score is 1.8 points lower than last year, mainly due to reductions in investment freedom and labor freedom. Pakistan is ranked 22nd out of 41 countries in the Asia–Pacific region, and its overall score is below the world and regional averages.

Pakistan has pursued reforms to improve its entrepreneurial environment and facilitate private-sector development. The financial sector has undergone modernization and restructuring and has weathered the global financial crisis relatively well. Yet Pakistan lags significantly behind other countries in the region.

Challenges to Pakistan's overall economic freedom include a wide range of institutional weaknesses. Trade freedom remains burdened by high tariffs and non-tariff barriers. The tax system is complex and inefficient, though reforms to cut tax rates, broaden the tax base, and increase transparency have been undertaken. The judicial system suffers from a serious case backlog and poor security. Considerable corruption taints the judiciary and civil service. Together with political instability, these shortcomings continue to undermine overall economic progress.

BACKGROUND: Pakistan, the world's second-largest Muslim-majority country, has alternated between unstable democratic government and military rule since becoming independent in 1947. It held largely successful democratic elections in February 2008 but continues to face terrorist attacks and an intensified insurgency along the border with Afghanistan. Former President Pervez Musharraf opened Pakistan somewhat to international trade and privatized state-run industries, but the economy is still heavily regulated, and property rights remain weak. Rising oil and food prices have led to a severe economic crunch. In November 2008, Pakistan received a two-year, $7.6 billion International Monetary Fund balance-of-payments support package to stabilize its economy and avoid default on debt payments. The military has received wide international backing for recent efforts to crack down on Taliban-backed militants in the Northwest.

Country's Score Over Time

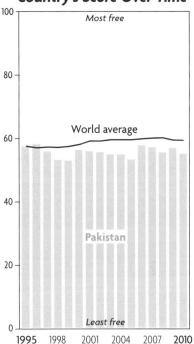

Quick Facts

Population: 166.0 million

GDP (PPP): $439.0 billion
6.0% growth in 2008
6.5% 5-year compound annual growth
$2,644 per capita

Unemployment: 7.4%

Inflation (CPI): 12.0%

FDI Inflow: $5.4 billion

2008 data unless otherwise noted
Data compiled as of September 2009

How Do We Measure Economic Freedom?
See page 457 for an explanation of the methodology or visit the *Index* Web site at *heritage.org/index.*

PAKISTAN'S TEN ECONOMIC FREEDOMS

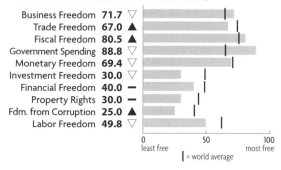

Business Freedom	71.7	▽
Trade Freedom	67.0	▲
Fiscal Freedom	80.5	▲
Government Spending	88.8	▽
Monetary Freedom	69.4	▽
Investment Freedom	30.0	▽
Financial Freedom	40.0	—
Property Rights	30.0	—
Fdm. from Corruption	25.0	▲
Labor Freedom	49.8	▽

0 least free — 50 — 100 most free

| = world average

BUSINESS FREEDOM — 71.7

The overall freedom to start, operate, and close a business is relatively well protected under Pakistan's regulatory environment. Starting a business takes an average of 20 days, compared to the world average of 35 days. Obtaining a business license takes about the world average of 18 procedures and 218 days, but costs are high. Closing a business is relatively easy and straightforward.

TRADE FREEDOM — 67

Pakistan's weighted average tariff rate was 9 percent in 2008. Liberalization has progressed, but import bans and restrictions, services market restrictions, import taxes, inconsistent and burdensome regulations, non-transparent government procurement, export subsidies, weak enforcement of intellectual property rights, and corruption add to the cost of trade. Fifteen points were deducted from Pakistan's trade freedom score to account for non-tariff barriers.

FISCAL FREEDOM — 80.5

Pakistan has moderate income tax rates and relatively high corporate tax rates. The top income tax rate is 25 percent, and the top corporate tax rate is 35 percent. Other taxes include a general sales tax (GST) and a property tax. The electricity tariff, scheduled to be revoked in mid-2009, remains in place. In the most recent year, overall tax revenue as a percentage of GDP was 10.2 percent.

GOVERNMENT SPENDING — 88.8

Total government expenditures, including consumption and transfer payments, are low. In the most recent year, government spending equaled 19.3 percent of GDP.

MONETARY FREEDOM — 69.4

Inflation has been high, averaging 10.6 percent between 2006 and 2008. The government controls pharmaceutical and fuel prices, subsidizes agriculture, and influences prices through state-owned enterprises and utilities, including electricity and water. Ten points were deducted from Pakistan's monetary freedom score to account for policies that distort domestic prices.

INVESTMENT FREEDOM — 30

Foreign investment receives national treatment, and foreign investors may own 100 percent of most businesses, except in certain sectors. Minimum initial investments are required in agriculture, infrastructure, and social services activities. Deterrents to investment include security threats, political instability, civil unrest, corruption, poor infrastructure, weak contract enforcement, inconsistent and arbitrary regulation, and a lack of coordination between the federal and regional governments. Restrictions on foreign exchange accounts include the need for government approval in some cases. Payments, transfers, and capital transactions may be subject to approval, quantitative limits, and other restrictions. Foreign investors may acquire real property.

FINANCIAL FREEDOM — 40

Pakistan's financial system has undergone restructuring. The state-dominated banking sector has gradually moved toward a more privately owned system as a result of consolidation, improved transparency, and modernization of the regulatory framework. Although a majority of the commercial banks are now in private hands, the sector remains concentrated and vulnerable to government influence. The government has a majority stake in the largest commercial bank and controls several specialized banks. Restrictions on the number of foreign bank branches have been removed, but the central bank must approve all new openings. Foreign investors are now allowed to hold up to 100 percent of the equity share of life and general insurance companies. However, competition remains limited by state domination, and a state-owned firm accounts for over 70 percent of the market. The impact of the global financial turmoil on banking has been relatively muted because of limited exposure to structured financial products. The banking sector remains well capitalized, but there have been some signs of asset quality deterioration. Non-performing loans had increased to over 10 percent of total loans in early 2009.

PROPERTY RIGHTS — 30

Pakistan's judiciary, separate by law from the executive, remains hampered by poor security for judges and witnesses, sentencing delays, a huge backlog of cases, and corruption. The government has taken steps to close down several pirate optical disc factories and has somewhat improved the enforcement of intellectual property rights.

FREEDOM FROM CORRUPTION — 25

Corruption is perceived as pervasive. Pakistan ranks 134th out of 179 countries in Transparency International's Corruption Perceptions Index for 2008. Corruption among executive and legislative branch officials is viewed as widespread. In September 2008, for the first time, the government appointed the leader of the political opposition as chairman of the National Accounts Committee, which oversees federal spending.

LABOR FREEDOM — 49.8

Pakistan's labor regulations are rigid. The non-salary cost of employing a worker is low, but laying off an employee is difficult.

Panama
City

PANAMA

Economic Freedom Score

25   50   75

Least   0   100   Most
free   free

64.8

Panama's economic freedom score is 64.8, making its economy the 60th freest in the 2010 *Index*. Its score has increased by 0.1 point since last year, reflecting notable improvements in property rights and freedom from corruption. Panama is ranked 13th out of 29 countries in the South and Central America/Caribbean region, and its overall score is above the world and regional averages.

The Panamanian government has pursued structural reforms to improve the entrepreneurial environment and enhance legal transparency. The economy has benefited from high levels of trade freedom and fiscal freedom, with average annual growth rates of over 9 percent over the past five years. Personal and corporate tax rates are moderate, and the overall tax burden is not high. Relatively prudent and sound public finance management has resulted in a high score for government spending, although public debt remains large.

Despite progress, Panama's overall economic freedom is limited by lingering institutional weaknesses. Despite reform efforts to reduce corruption, the judicial system remains vulnerable to political interference, burdened with backlogged cases, and lax in the enforcement of contracts.

BACKGROUND: Former businessman Ricardo Martinelli of the center-right Alliance for Change coalition was elected president in May 2009 and faces significant challenges in fighting money laundering, narcotics trafficking, and the illegal arms trade and in revitalizing a government-run education system that is not preparing Panama's youth for jobs in banking and the booming services sector, which accounts for 80 percent of the economy. Since 1999, Panama has been solely responsible for operating the Panama Canal and has converted U.S. bases in the former Canal Zone to commercial and tourism uses. The government is now constructing a third set of locks to modernize the canal. The U.S.–Panama Trade Promotion Agreement, if ratified by both governments, could provide a significant boost to economic growth and development.

Country's Score Over Time

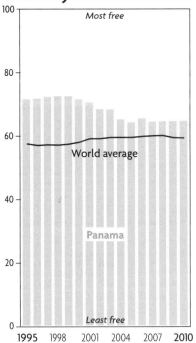

100   Most free

80

60   World average

40

Panama

20

0   Least free
1995   1998   2001   2004   2007   2010

Quick Facts

Population: 3.4 million

GDP (PPP): $42.4 billion
9.2% growth in 2007
9.1% 5-year compound
annual growth
$12,504 per capita

Unemployment: 5.6%

Inflation (CPI): 8.8%

FDI Inflow: $2.4 billion

2008 data unless otherwise noted
Data compiled as of September 2009

How Do We Measure Economic Freedom?
See page 457 for an explanation of the methodology or visit the *Index* Web site at *heritage.org/index.*

PANAMA'S TEN ECONOMIC FREEDOMS

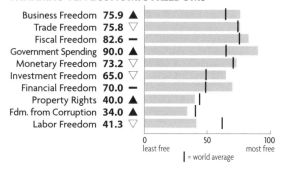

Business Freedom	75.9	▲
Trade Freedom	75.8	▽
Fiscal Freedom	82.6	—
Government Spending	90.0	▲
Monetary Freedom	73.2	▽
Investment Freedom	65.0	▽
Financial Freedom	70.0	—
Property Rights	40.0	▲
Fdm. from Corruption	34.0	▲
Labor Freedom	41.3	▽

0 least free   50   100 most free

| = world average

BUSINESS FREEDOM — 75.9

The overall freedom to start, operate, and close a business is relatively well protected under Panama's regulatory environment. Starting a business takes an average of 12 days, compared to the world average of 35 days. Obtaining a business license takes less than the world average of 218 days. Closing a business can be lengthy and costly.

TRADE FREEDOM — 75.8

Panama's weighted average tariff rate was 7.1 percent in 2008. Some import restrictions, services markets access restrictions, high tariffs on agriculture products, import taxes, import licensing or permit requirements, export subsidies, weak enforcement of intellectual property rights, and corruption add to the cost of trade. Ten points were deducted from Panama's trade freedom score to account for non-tariff barriers.

FISCAL FREEDOM — 82.6

Panama has moderate income and corporate tax rates. The top income tax rate is 27 percent. The corporate tax rate is 30 percent of net income or 1.401 percent of gross taxable income, whichever is greater. Other taxes include a value-added tax (VAT), a real estate tax, and a transfer tax. In the most recent year, overall tax revenue as a percentage of GDP was 10.7 percent.

GOVERNMENT SPENDING — 90

Total government expenditures, including consumption and transfer payments, are relatively low. In the most recent year, government spending equaled 18.3 percent of GDP. Increased spending on public investment and attempts to mitigate high food and fuel prices have driven up total expenditures.

MONETARY FREEDOM — 73.2

Inflation has increased, averaging 7.1 percent between 2006 and 2008. Panama uses the U.S. dollar as its currency. The government controls pharmaceutical and fuel prices, sets prices for a list of basic consumption items, and influences prices through state-owned enterprises and utilities, including electricity and water. Ten points were deducted from Panama's monetary freedom score to account for policies that distort domestic prices.

INVESTMENT FREEDOM — 65

Foreign investment receives national treatment in most sectors. The government limits foreign ownership in non-franchise retail and media and in other service sectors including medicine, law, and custom brokering. There is no government approval process, but investments must be registered. Some investment-related regulations are burdensome and non-transparent, and judicial processes can be cumbersome and arbitrary. Residents and non-residents may hold foreign exchange accounts. There are no restrictions or controls on payments, transactions, transfers, repatriation of profits, or capital transactions. Foreign investors may not purchase land within 10 kilometers of a national border or on an island. Domestic and foreign investors may lease but not own beaches or the shores of rivers or lakes.

FINANCIAL FREEDOM — 70

Panama is a regional financial hub providing a wide range of financial services, and banking is well developed and stable. There are 90 banks, and foreign banks account for more than 70 percent of total assets. Foreign and domestic banks are treated equally. The largest of the three state-owned banks controls about 10 percent of the market. There is no central bank; an independent Banking Superintendency oversees the financial sector. Regulations are largely in compliance with international standards. New legislation passed in 2008 aims to strengthen the supervisory framework for banks and includes stricter rules concerning money laundering. Panama has been removed from the OECD's tax haven and money-laundering blacklist. The government exercises little control over the allocation of credit, and domestic credit to the private sector has grown steadily. Capital markets are relatively sophisticated, although the stock market trades primarily in government debt.

PROPERTY RIGHTS — 40

Panama's judiciary is constitutionally independent but influenced by the executive. Backlogs and corruption are severe. Enforcement of copyrights and trademarks, though still inadequate, is improving. Special intellectual property courts hear commercial cases alleging infringement, but redress is slow.

FREEDOM FROM CORRUPTION — 34

Corruption is perceived as widespread. Panama ranks 85th out of 179 countries in Transparency International's Corruption Perceptions Index for 2008. Panama is a major drug-transit country. The general perception is that anti-corruption laws are not applied rigorously and that government enforcement bodies have lacked determination in prosecuting those who are accused of corruption, particularly in high-profile cases.

LABOR FREEDOM — 41.3

Panama's labor regulations are inflexible. The non-salary cost of employing a worker is high, and dismissing an employee is difficult. Regulations on work hours are rigid.

PAPUA NEW GUINEA

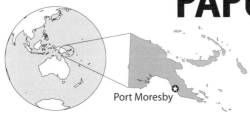

Port Moresby

Economic Freedom Score

Least free 0   100 Most free

25   50   75

53.5

Papua New Guinea's economic freedom score is 53.5, making its economy the 126th freest in the 2010 *Index*. Its score has decreased by 1.3 points from last year, mainly as a result of lower scores in monetary freedom and government spending. Papua New Guinea is ranked 25th out of 41 countries in the Asia–Pacific region, and its overall score is lower than the world and regional averages.

The Papua New Guinean economy scores relatively well in trade freedom, primarily because of low tariff barriers. The overall entrepreneurial environment has long suffered from macroeconomic instability, volatile economic growth, and low investment. Inconsistent government policies, weak property rights, poor infrastructure, lack of competition, and the dominant role of the state in the economy have contributed to the lack of economic development and widespread poverty across the country.

Private-sector growth has been minimal because of structural constraints. The government intrudes in many aspects of the economy through state ownership and regulation, raising the costs of conducting entrepreneurial activity and discouraging the development of a strong private sector. The lack of market competition has resulted in a number of highly inefficient state monopolies in key sectors of the economy.

BACKGROUND: Papua New Guinea is a democratic country with an extraordinarily diverse population of nearly 7 million people speaking hundreds of languages. The vast majority of its people depend on subsistence hunting or agriculture for their livelihood, and the formal economy is dominated by the mining of rich deposits of gold, copper, oil, and natural gas. Ongoing problems include corruption, election irregularities, weak governance, and crime.

Country's Score Over Time

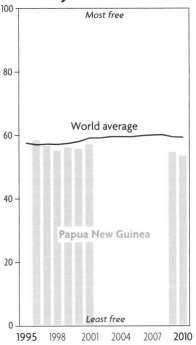

Quick Facts

Population: 6.4 million

GDP (PPP): $14.2 billion
5.8% growth in 2008
4.9% 5-year compound annual growth
$2,208 per capita

Unemployment: n/a

Inflation (CPI): 10.7%

FDI Inflow: –$30 million

2008 data unless otherwise noted
Data compiled as of September 2009

How Do We Measure Economic Freedom?
See page 457 for an explanation of the methodology or visit the *Index* Web site at *heritage.org/index*.

PAPUA NEW GUINEA'S TEN ECONOMIC FREEDOMS

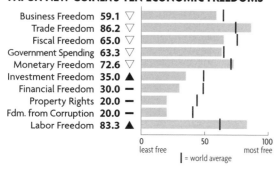

Business Freedom	59.1	▽
Trade Freedom	86.2	▽
Fiscal Freedom	65.0	▽
Government Spending	63.3	▽
Monetary Freedom	72.6	▽
Investment Freedom	35.0	▲
Financial Freedom	30.0	—
Property Rights	20.0	—
Fdm. from Corruption	20.0	—
Labor Freedom	83.3	▲

0 least free — 50 — 100 most free
| = world average

Certain sectors of the economy are reserved for domestic investors. Investment-related rules and regulations are non-transparent and burdensome. Foreign investors are expected to employ locals where the expertise is available and are encouraged to train locals to fill positions held by expatriates. Other deterrents to investment include weak enforcement of contracts, corruption, crime, inadequate infrastructure, and underdeveloped private markets. Foreign exchange and capital transactions face various documentation requirements and government approvals. Ninety-seven percent of land is communally owned, but foreign investors may lease land.

BUSINESS FREEDOM — 59.1

The overall freedom to start, operate, and close a business is constrained by Papua New Guinea's regulatory environment. Starting a business takes an average of 56 days, compared to the world average of 35 days. Obtaining a business license requires 24 procedures, compared to the world average of 18, and about the world average of 218 days.

TRADE FREEDOM — 86.2

Papua New Guinea's weighted average tariff rate was 1.9 percent in 2008. Some high tariffs, import and export bans and restrictions, import permits, import and export taxes, inefficient customs administration, limitations on trade infrastructure and capacity, and corruption add to the cost of trade. Ten points were deducted from Papua New Guinea's trade freedom score to account for non-tariff barriers.

FISCAL FREEDOM — 65

Papua New Guinea has high taxes. The top income tax rate is 42 percent, and the top corporate tax rate is 30 percent (48 percent for non-resident companies). Other taxes include a value-added tax (VAT), a tax on interest, and an excise tax on fuel. In the most recent year, overall tax revenue as a percentage of GDP was 28.9 percent.

GOVERNMENT SPENDING — 63.3

Total government expenditures, including consumption and transfer payments, are moderate. In the most recent year, government spending equaled 35.0 percent of GDP.

MONETARY FREEDOM — 72.6

Inflation has increased dramatically, averaging 7.6 percent between 2006 and 2008. Price controls are in effect for a number of consumer goods, mainly food products, although these are scheduled to be phased out. Ten points were deducted from Papua New Guinea's monetary freedom score to adjust for measures that distort domestic prices.

INVESTMENT FREEDOM — 35

Foreign investment is screened and requires government approval. Only foreign enterprises need to be certified, but all companies must be registered with the government.

FINANCIAL FREEDOM — 30

The financial system, dominated by banking, is not conducive to supporting investment and entrepreneurship. Although bank lending has expanded considerably in recent years, the system remains shallow and poorly developed. Financial intermediation varies across the country, and a large portion of the population does not use the formal banking sector. The high cost of financing and limited access to financial services impede development of the private sector. Papua New Guinea's commercial banking sector has five major banks that have become more competitive as a result of privatization and mergers. Bank South Pacific accounts for over 50 percent of the sector's total assets. Short-term financing dominates bank lending, and credit to the private sector accounts for about 20 percent of GDP. Capital markets remain underdeveloped.

PROPERTY RIGHTS — 20

Land is held communally, and traditional communities do not recognize a permanent transfer of ownership when land is sold. The laws have provisions for extensive rights for women in dealing with family, marriage, and property disputes, but women generally are still treated as inferiors. The idea of intellectual property rights is a fairly new concept in Papua New Guinea.

FREEDOM FROM CORRUPTION — 20

Corruption is perceived as pervasive. Papua New Guinea ranks 151st out of 179 countries in Transparency International's Corruption Perceptions Index for 2008. Corruption at all levels of government is a serious problem because of weak public institutions, lack of transparency, a lack of law and order, land tenure concerns that stifle investment, politicization of the bureaucracy, and the use of public resources to meet traditional clan obligations. Charges were filed in two cases of high-level corruption involving senior government officials in 2008, but at year's end, no investigation reports on either case had been released.

LABOR FREEDOM — 83.3

Papua New Guinea's labor regulations are flexible, but the formal labor market is not fully developed. The non-salary cost of employing a worker is low, and dismissing an employee is relatively straightforward.

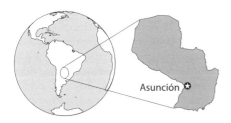

PARAGUAY

Economic Freedom Score

61.3

P araguay's economic freedom score is 61.3, making its economy the 81st freest in the 2010 *Index*. Its score has increased by 0.3 point from last year, reflecting a modest improvement in investment freedom. Paraguay is ranked 16th out of 29 countries in the South and Central America/Caribbean region, and its overall score is slightly above the world and regional averages.

Paraguay scores above the world average in six of the 10 economic freedoms. The average tariff barrier has been gradually lowered, but non-tariff barriers still limit overall trade freedom. Income and corporate tax rates are competitively low. The government has pursued a series of structural reforms to improve the entrepreneurial environment, but Paraguay still lags behind other countries in the region in terms of reform progress.

Overall economic freedom remains challenged by two significant institutional weaknesses that are critically in need of reform. Property rights are not strongly protected, and the judicial system remains weak and inefficient. Widespread corruption also poses a serious impediment to economic development.

BACKGROUND: Since the end of General Alfredo Stroessner's 35-year rule in 1989, Paraguayans have been working to implement durable democratic rule. Former Bishop Fernando Lugo, supported by the leftist Patriotic Alliance for Change coalition, was elected president in April 2008, ending more than 50 years of domination by the conservative Colorado Party. Lugo promised to support the indigenous population, redistribute land to the poor, and secure more revenue from the Itaipu Dam, a joint hydroelectric project with Brazil. Nearly half of all jobs are in agriculture, the major export earner. Unemployment is high, and more than one-third of Paraguayans live below the poverty line. Improved cooperation with neighboring countries and the United States has led to reduced smuggling and closer scrutiny of suspected Middle Eastern terrorist–supported groups in the tri-border area with Brazil and Argentina.

Country's Score Over Time

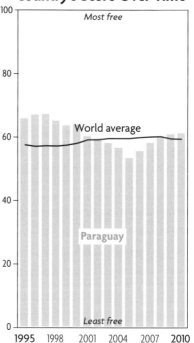

Quick Facts

Population: 6.2 million

GDP (PPP): $29.3 billion
5.8% growth in 2008
4.9% 5-year compound
annual growth
$4,709 per capita

Unemployment: 5.4%

Inflation (CPI): 10.2%

FDI Inflow: $320 million

2008 data unless otherwise noted
Data compiled as of September 2009

How Do We Measure Economic Freedom?
See page 457 for an explanation of the methodology or visit the *Index* Web site at *heritage.org/index.*

PARAGUAY'S TEN ECONOMIC FREEDOMS

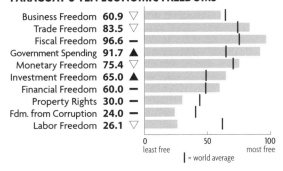

Business Freedom	60.9	▽
Trade Freedom	83.5	▽
Fiscal Freedom	96.6	—
Government Spending	91.7	▲
Monetary Freedom	75.4	▽
Investment Freedom	65.0	▲
Financial Freedom	60.0	—
Property Rights	30.0	—
Fdm. from Corruption	24.0	—
Labor Freedom	26.1	▽

0 least free   50   100 most free

| = world average

BUSINESS FREEDOM — *60.9*

The overall freedom to start, operate, and close a business is limited under Paraguay's regulatory environment. Starting a business takes an average of 35 days, which is consistent with the world average. Obtaining a business license takes more than the world average of 218 days. Closing a business can be a lengthy and difficult process.

TRADE FREEDOM — *83.5*

Paraguay's weighted average tariff rate was 3.3 percent in 2008. Some import bans and restrictions, import taxes and fees, burdensome labeling requirements, weak enforcement of intellectual property rights, and cumbersome and non-transparent customs procedures add to the cost of trade. Ten points were deducted from Paraguay's trade freedom score to account for non-tariff barriers.

FISCAL FREEDOM — *96.6*

Paraguay has low tax rates. Both the top income tax rate and the top corporate tax rate are 10 percent. Other taxes include a value-added tax (VAT) and a property tax. In the most recent year, overall tax revenue as a percentage of GDP was 11.7 percent. Tax administration is improving.

GOVERNMENT SPENDING — *91.7*

Total government expenditures, including consumption and transfer payments, are low. In the most recent year, government spending equaled 16.6 percent of GDP. Structural reforms are needed to strengthen the budgetary framework and improve the quality of public expenditures.

MONETARY FREEDOM — *75.4*

Inflation has been high, averaging 9.6 percent between 2006 and 2008. Most prices are set in the market, but the government controls the price of fuel and influences prices through state-owned enterprises and utilities, including electricity, telecommunications, transportation, and water. Five points were deducted from Paraguay's monetary freedom score to account for policies that distort domestic prices.

INVESTMENT FREEDOM — *65*

Paraguay guarantees equal treatment of foreign investors, and most sectors are open to private investment. The government maintains monopolies in oil and gas, cement, electricity, water, and basic and long-distance land-line telephone services. Deterrents to investment include an arbitrary and non-transparent judicial process, weak enforcement of contracts, corruption, and inadequate infrastructure. Residents and non-residents may hold foreign exchange accounts. Most payments, capital transactions, and transfers are permitted and subject to minimal restrictions or reporting requirements. Foreign investors may not purchase land within 50 kilometers of the borders.

FINANCIAL FREEDOM — *60*

Paraguay's financial sector has undergone restructuring and modernization following a period of instability that resulted in several domestic financial crises from 1995 to early 2000. Credit to the private sector has grown, and non-performing loans have gradually declined to less than 2 percent of total loans from over 10 percent in 2004. An inefficient legal framework remains a considerable impediment to the creation of a more dynamic financial sector. The adverse impact of the global financial turmoil on the financial system has been relatively minor. The banking sector consists of 13 banks, 14 savings and loan companies, and 24 foreign-exchange companies. The two largest banks are foreign-owned, and foreign banks account for around 30 percent of assets. Capital markets remain underdeveloped.

PROPERTY RIGHTS — *30*

Protection of property rights is extremely weak. Commercial and civil codes cover bankruptcy and give priority for claims first to employees, then to the state, and finally to private creditors. Acquiring title documents for land can take two years or more. Paraguay has increased the seizure and destruction of counterfeit and pirated goods. The government does not have a framework for safeguarding confidential data associated with regulatory approvals. As a result, some companies have decided not to market certain products, such as the latest pharmaceuticals, in Paraguay.

FREEDOM FROM CORRUPTION — *24*

Corruption is perceived as widespread. Paraguay ranks 138th out of 179 countries in Transparency International's Corruption Perceptions Index for 2008. Paraguay has a legacy of institutional corruption after decades of dictatorship. The multibillion-dollar contraband trade that occurs on the borders with Argentina and Brazil also facilitates money laundering. Weak institutions impede anti-corruption efforts. The slow pace of judicial reform and continued impunity are barriers to development.

LABOR FREEDOM — *26.1*

Paraguay's labor regulations are restrictive. The non-salary cost of employing a worker is moderate, but laying off an employee is difficult. Regulations on the number of work hours remain rigid.

PERU

Economic Freedom Score

Least free 0   100 Most free

67.6

Peru's economic freedom score is 67.6, making its economy the 45th freest in the 2010 *Index*. Its score is 3.0 points better than last year, reflecting notable improvements in trade freedom, investment freedom, and labor freedom. Peru is ranked 6th out of 29 countries in the South and Central America/Caribbean region, and its overall score is above the world and regional averages.

Peru has accelerated its progress toward greater economic freedom, achieving one of the 15 highest score improvements in the 2010 *Index*. The economy has recorded growth of over 8 percent annually over the past five years. Procedures for business formation have been streamlined, and labor regulations have become more flexible. Monetary stability is relatively well maintained, and the tariff barrier has been reduced, although non-tariff barriers still limit overall trade freedom.

Lingering challenges include weak protection of property rights under Peru's inefficient judicial system and a lack of institutional capacity to tackle corruption. Freedom from corruption is the only economic freedom component in which Peru scores considerably below the world average.

BACKGROUND: Peru has emerged from the political instability of the late 20th century. Former President Alberto Fujimori has been convicted and jailed for offenses during a decade of autocratic rule and a successful campaign against the Shining Path and other insurgents. President Alan Garcia, who served one term in the 1980s and was re-elected in 2006, has earned a reputation as the market-friendly regional alternative to Venezuela's Hugo Chávez by maintaining the trend toward economic liberalism, trade liberalization, and fiscal and monetary stability. Significant natural resources include gold, copper, and silver. More than 40 percent of Peru's people remain poor, but economic growth has improved and continues to run well above the Latin American average. A free trade agreement between Peru and the United States was ratified by both countries in 2007.

Country's Score Over Time

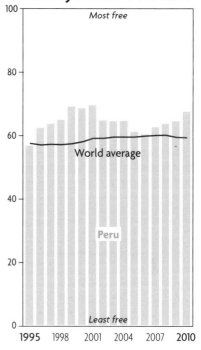

Quick Facts

Population: 28.8 million

GDP (PPP): $245.3 billion
9.8% growth in 2008
8.3% 5-year compound annual growth
$8,507 per capita

Unemployment: 8.1%

Inflation (CPI): 5.8%

FDI Inflow: $4.8 billion

2008 data unless otherwise noted
Data compiled as of September 2009

How Do We Measure Economic Freedom?
See page 457 for an explanation of the methodology or visit the *Index* Web site at *heritage.org/index*.

PERU'S TEN ECONOMIC FREEDOMS

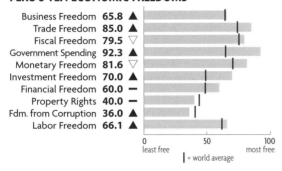

Business Freedom	65.8 ▲	
Trade Freedom	85.0 ▲	
Fiscal Freedom	79.5 ▽	
Government Spending	92.3 ▲	
Monetary Freedom	81.6 ▽	
Investment Freedom	70.0 ▲	
Financial Freedom	60.0 —	
Property Rights	40.0 —	
Fdm. from Corruption	36.0 ▲	
Labor Freedom	66.1 ▲	

0   50   100
least free   most free

| = world average

BUSINESS FREEDOM — 65.8

The overall freedom to start, operate, and close a business is moderately restricted under Peru's regulatory environment. Starting a business takes an average of 41 days, compared to the world average of 35 days. Obtaining a business license takes slightly less than the world average of 218 days. Closing a business can be a lengthy process.

TRADE FREEDOM — 85

Peru's weighted average tariff rate was 2.5 percent in 2008. Some import restrictions, services market access restrictions, export and import taxes, price bands for sensitive agricultural products, restrictive labeling, sanitary and phytosanitary regulations, domestic preference in government procurement, and improving but still weak enforcement of intellectual property rights add to the cost of trade. Ten points were deducted from Peru's trade freedom score to account for non-tariff barriers.

FISCAL FREEDOM — 79.5

Peru has moderate income tax rates. Both the flat income tax rate and the top corporate tax rate are 30 percent. Other taxes include a value-added tax (VAT), a property transfer tax, and a capital gains tax. Fuel subsidies were eliminated, but excise taxes on selected domestic fuel prices have been increased. In the most recent year, overall tax revenue as a percentage of GDP was 15.7 percent.

GOVERNMENT SPENDING — 92.3

Total government expenditures, including consumption and transfer payments, are low. In the most recent year, government spending equaled 16.0 percent of GDP. The government has restructured the privatization agency to focus on large enterprises. By 2008, public debt had been reduced to 25 percent of GDP.

MONETARY FREEDOM — 81.6

Inflation has been relatively low, averaging 4.5 percent between 2006 and 2008. Most prices are set in the market, but the government influences prices through regulation, state-owned enterprises, and utilities, and a special government fund is used to stabilize changes in fuel prices. Five points were deducted from Peru's monetary freedom score to account for policies that distort domestic prices.

INVESTMENT FREEDOM — 70

Peru provides national treatment to foreign investors, and there is no screening process. Investments in domestic and foreign banking and in defense-related industries require prior approval, and certain sectors are reserved for domestic investors. Other deterrents to investment include unpredictable and weak enforcement of contracts, non-transparent and burdensome bureaucracy, some restrictive labor regulations, and corruption. Residents and non-residents may hold foreign exchange accounts. There are no restrictions or controls on payments, transfers, or repatriation of profits. Capital transactions face minimal restrictions. Foreign investors may not acquire mines, lands, forests, waters, or fuel or energy sources within 50 kilometers of Peru's borders.

FINANCIAL FREEDOM — 60

Peru's financial sector continues to grow, becoming more competitive in providing a wide range of financial services for domestic business activity. The banking sector has undergone a transformation through consolidation and now has 15 commercial banks, four of which account for more than 80 percent of total loans. Foreign ownership is substantial, and two of Peru's largest commercial banks are majority foreign-owned. Credit to the private sector has increased steadily. The government has strengthened prudential standards and disclosure requirements. Credit is allocated on market terms. There is a small stock market. The impact of the global financial crisis on the banking sector has been minor. Banking remains well capitalized, and non-performing loans have decreased to less than 2 percent of the total.

PROPERTY RIGHTS — 40

The judicial system is slow to hear cases and issue decisions. Allegations of corruption and outside interference are common. Copyright piracy is extensive, and enforcement of intellectual property rights laws is inadequate. Peruvian law does not provide for protection of patents or protection from parallel imports.

FREEDOM FROM CORRUPTION — 36

Corruption is perceived as significant. Peru ranks 72nd out of 179 countries in Transparency International's Corruption Perceptions Index for 2008. Government corruption is viewed as pervasive. In October 2008, a kickback scandal involving a member of the ruling party and a foreign oil company led to the replacement of the prime minister, although investigators have not established that the prime minister was involved in the scandal.

LABOR FREEDOM — 66.1

Peru's labor regulations have become less rigid. The non-salary cost of employing a worker is now less burdensome as mandatory paid annual leave and severance payments have been reduced. Regulations on work hours remain relatively inflexible.

Manila

THE PHILIPPINES

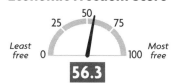

Economic Freedom Score

25   50   75

Least free 0   100 Most free

56.3

The Philippines has an economic freedom score of 56.3, making its economy the 109th freest in the 2010 *Index*. Its score is 0.4 point lower than last year, reflecting small reductions in monetary freedom and freedom from corruption. The Philippines ranks 20th out of 41 countries in the Asia–Pacific region, and its overall score is slightly below the world and regional averages.

The Philippines scores above the world average in half of the 10 economic freedoms. The government has pursued a series of structural reforms to improve the entrepreneurial environment and develop a stronger private sector that generates more dynamic job growth. Overall progress has been mixed, but some fiscal reforms have been accomplished. The top corporate tax rate has been reduced, and progress in privatization and fiscal prudence has helped to reduce the public debt. Improving tax administration remains a priority.

The Philippines is weak in business freedom, investment freedom, property rights, and freedom from corruption. The government imposes formal and non-formal barriers to foreign investment. Reflecting a lack of domestic economic dynamism, the Philippines still relies heavily on remittances from abroad. The judicial system remains weak and vulnerable to political influence.

BACKGROUND: The Philippines' diverse population, which speaks more than 80 languages and dialects, is spread over 7,000 islands in the Western Pacific Ocean. The country returned to democracy in 1986 after two decades of autocratic rule. President Gloria Arroyo took office in 2001 and since then has weathered multiple impeachment attempts. The government's failure to do anything substantial to liberalize the economy has set back efforts to attract much-needed foreign investment in basic industries and infrastructure, and the Philippines continues a long slide from being one of Asia's richest economies to being one of its poorest. The economy relies heavily on emigrants' remittances equivalent to about 10 percent of GDP.

Country's Score Over Time

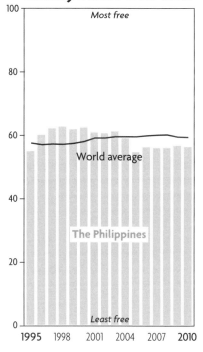

Most free

World average

The Philippines

Least free

1995   1998   2001   2004   2007   2010

Quick Facts

Population: 90.3 million

GDP (PPP): $317.1 billion
3.8% growth in 2008
5.5% 5-year compound annual growth
$3,510 per capita

Unemployment: 6.8%

Inflation (CPI): 9.3%

FDI Inflow: $1.5 billion

2008 data unless otherwise noted
Data compiled as of September 2009

How Do We Measure Economic Freedom?
See page 457 for an explanation of the methodology or visit the *Index* Web site at *heritage.org/index.*

THE PHILIPPINES' TEN ECONOMIC FREEDOMS

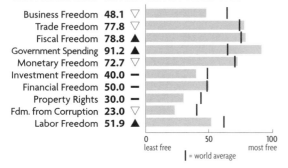

Business Freedom	48.1	▽
Trade Freedom	77.8	▽
Fiscal Freedom	78.8	▲
Government Spending	91.2	▲
Monetary Freedom	72.7	▽
Investment Freedom	40.0	—
Financial Freedom	50.0	—
Property Rights	30.0	—
Fdm. from Corruption	23.0	▽
Labor Freedom	51.9	▲

0 least free   50   100 most free

| = world average

BUSINESS FREEDOM — 48.1

The overall freedom to start, operate, and close a business is limited under the Philippines' regulatory environment. Starting a business takes an average of 52 days, compared to the world average of 35 days. Obtaining a business license takes less than the world average of 218 days. Closing a business can be a difficult and lengthy process.

TRADE FREEDOM — 77.8

The Philippines' weighted average tariff rate was 3.6 percent in 2007. Some high tariffs, import and export restrictions, quotas and tariff rate quotas, services market access barriers, import and export taxes, import licensing requirements, restrictive and non-transparent standards, labeling and other regulations, domestic bias in government procurement, inconsistent and non-transparent customs valuation and administration, export subsidies, widespread corruption, and weak protection of intellectual property rights add to the cost of trade. Fifteen points were deducted from the Philippines' trade freedom score to account for non-tariff barriers.

FISCAL FREEDOM — 78.8

The Philippines has relatively high tax rates. The top income tax rate is 32 percent. The top corporate tax rate is 30 percent, down from 35 percent as of January 1, 2009. Other taxes include a value-added tax (VAT), a real property tax, and an inheritance tax. In the most recent year, overall tax revenue as a percentage of GDP was 14.0 percent. Despite domestic political pressure, authorities did not repeal the VAT on petroleum products during the financial crisis.

GOVERNMENT SPENDING — 91.2

Total government expenditures, including consumption and transfer payments, are low. In the most recent year, government spending equaled 17.1 percent of GDP. Privatization of the power sector continues, with two more generating plants privatized in the past year.

MONETARY FREEDOM — 72.7

Inflation has been moderately high, averaging 7.4 percent between 2006 and 2008. The government influences prices through state-owned enterprises and utilities and controls the prices of electricity distribution, water, telecommuni-cations, and most transportation services. Price ceilings are usually imposed on basic commodities only in emergencies, and presidential authority to impose controls to check inflation or ease social tension is rarely exercised. Ten points were deducted from the Philippines' monetary freedom score to account for policies that distort domestic prices.

INVESTMENT FREEDOM — 40

Foreign investment is restricted in a number of sectors. All foreign investments are screened and must be registered with the government. Regulatory inconsistency and lack of transparency, corruption, and inadequate infrastructure hinder investment. Dispute resolution can be cumbersome and complex, and the enforcement of contracts is weak. Residents and non-residents may hold foreign exchange accounts. Payments, capital transactions, and transfers are subject to some restrictions, controls, quantitative limits, and authorizations. Foreign investors may lease but not own land.

FINANCIAL FREEDOM — 50

Banking dominates the growing financial sector, handling more than 90 percent of financial activity. In general, the financial system welcomes foreign competition, and capital standards and oversight have improved. Consolidation has progressed, and non-performing loans have gradually declined to less than 5 percent of total loans. The banking sector has 38 commercial banks, five of which dominate the sector. Two large state-owned banks account for about 15 percent of total assets. A small government Islamic bank serves Muslim citizens in the South. Credit is generally available at market terms, but banks are required to lend specified portions of their funds to preferred sectors. The non-bank financial sector remains small. Capital markets are centered on the Philippine Stock Exchange. The impact of the global financial crisis on banking has been relatively constrained because of the sector's very limited exposure to failed or distressed international financial institutions.

PROPERTY RIGHTS — 30

The judicial system is weak. Judges are nominally independent, but some are corrupt or have been appointed strictly for political reasons. Organized crime is a serious problem. Despite some progress, enforcement of intellectual property rights remains problematic.

FREEDOM FROM CORRUPTION — 23

Corruption is perceived as pervasive. The Philippines ranks 141st out of 179 countries in Transparency International's Corruption Perceptions Index for 2008, a decline from 2007. A culture of corruption is long-standing, and enforcement of anti-corruption laws is inconsistent.

LABOR FREEDOM — 51.9

Labor regulations in the Philippines are inflexible. The non-salary cost of employing a worker is low, but dismissing an employee is difficult.

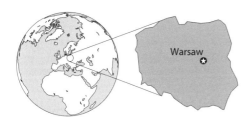

POLAND

Economic Freedom Score

25   50   75

Least   0   100   Most
free   free

63.2

World Rank: 71   **Regional Rank: 33**

Poland's economic freedom score is 63.2, making its economy the 71st freest in the 2010 *Index*. Its score has increased by 2.9 points from last year, reflecting notable improvements in five of the 10 economic freedoms. Poland is ranked 33rd out of 43 countries in the Europe region, and its overall score is above the world average.

The Polish government has continued to enhance its entrepreneurial environment, achieving one of the 15 highest score improvements in the 2010 *Index*. In response, the economy has recorded annual economic growth rates of around 5 percent over the past five years. Monetary stability is well maintained, and the financial sector has weathered the global financial turmoil relatively well. Tax rates have become more competitive with implementation of a flat corporate tax rate and a reduction in individual tax rates. Poland has also made progress in strengthening its legal framework and reducing levels of corruption.

Relatively high government spending holds down overall economic freedom in Poland. The pension system is a target for further reform, and efforts to limit expenditures and reverse rising fiscal deficits are being made. Property rights could be further improved, and the judicial system, though fairly reliable, is inefficient.

BACKGROUND: Poland's struggle for freedom from Soviet control ended with the Solidarity movement taking control of the parliament in 1989 and the presidency in the following year. In the 1990s, Poland had a favorable investment climate, achieved rapid real income growth, and joined the European Union and NATO. In August 2007, the pro-business, center-right Civic Platform (PO) party defeated the conservative Law and Justice party. The Polish People's Party has joined PO as its junior coalition partner. GDP growth in 2007 reached 6.5 percent, the fastest pace in a decade, but the global financial crisis led to a significant slowdown in 2009.

Country's Score Over Time

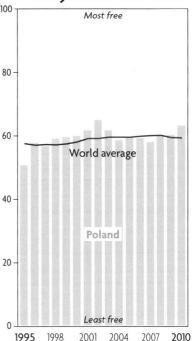

Quick Facts

Population: 38.1 million

GDP (PPP): $671.9 billion
4.8% growth in 2008
5.3% 5-year compound
annual growth
$17,625 per capita

Unemployment: 7.1%

Inflation (CPI): 4.2%

FDI Inflow: $16.5 billion

2008 data unless otherwise noted
Data compiled as of September 2009

How Do We Measure Economic Freedom?
See page 457 for an explanation of the methodology or visit the *Index* Web site at *heritage.org/index*.

POLAND'S TEN ECONOMIC FREEDOMS

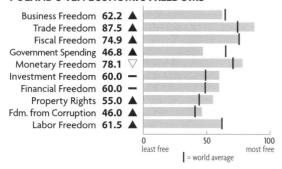

Business Freedom	62.2	▲
Trade Freedom	87.5	▲
Fiscal Freedom	74.9	▲
Government Spending	46.8	▲
Monetary Freedom	78.1	▽
Investment Freedom	60.0	—
Financial Freedom	60.0	—
Property Rights	55.0	▲
Fdm. from Corruption	46.0	▲
Labor Freedom	61.5	▲

0 least free — 50 — 100 most free
| = world average

BUSINESS FREEDOM — 62.2

The overall freedom to start, operate, and close a business is limited under Poland's regulatory environment. Starting a business takes an average of 32 days, compared to the world average of 35 days. Obtaining a business license requires more than the world average of 18 procedures and 218 days.

TRADE FREEDOM — 87.5

Poland's trade policy is the same as that of other members of the European Union. The common EU weighted average tariff rate was 1.3 percent in 2008. However, the EU has high or escalating tariffs for agricultural and manufacturing products, and its MFN tariff code is complex. Non-tariff barriers reflected in EU and Polish policy include agricultural and manufacturing subsidies, quotas, import restrictions and bans for some goods and services, market access restrictions in some services sectors, non-transparent and restrictive regulations and standards, and inconsistent regulatory and customs administration among EU members. Biotechnology restrictions and pharmaceuticals regulations exceed general EU policy, and the enforcement of intellectual property rights remains problematic. Ten points were deducted from Poland's trade freedom score to account for non-tariff barriers.

FISCAL FREEDOM — 74.9

Poland has a relatively high income tax rate and a relatively low corporate tax rate. The top income tax rate is 32 percent, down from 40 percent. The flat corporate tax rate is 19 percent. Other taxes include a value-added tax (VAT), an inheritance tax, and a transfer tax on items not subject to the VAT. In the most recent year, overall tax revenue as a percentage of GDP was 33.5 percent.

GOVERNMENT SPENDING — 46.8

Total government expenditures, including consumption and transfer payments, are relatively high. In the most recent year, government spending equaled 42.1 percent of GDP. Privatization has stalled.

MONETARY FREEDOM — 78.1

Inflation has been low, averaging 3.5 percent between 2006 and 2008. As a participant in the EU's Common Agricultural Policy, the government subsidizes agricultural production, distorting the prices of agricultural products. The government monitors utility rates and sets official prices for pharmaceutical and medical materials, taxi services, and any other goods or services deemed necessary for the proper functioning of the economy. Ten points were deducted from Poland's monetary freedom score to adjust for measures that distort domestic prices.

INVESTMENT FREEDOM — 60

Foreign capital and domestic capital are generally treated equally. The government does not screen investment and allows 100 percent foreign ownership in most sectors. All investors need government concessions, licenses, or permits to engage in certain activities including broadcasting, aviation, energy, weapons, mining, and private security services. Deterrents include regulatory unpredictability, administrative red tape, a slow court system, and numerous labor, health, safety, and environmental regulations. Residents and non-residents may hold foreign exchange accounts, subject to certain restrictions. Payments, transactions, and transfers over a specified amount must be conducted through a domestic bank. Capital transactions with non-EU nations may be subject to restrictions and government approval. Foreign ownership of land is subject to numerous restrictions and controls.

FINANCIAL FREEDOM — 60

Poland's financial system continues to grow. Credit is available on market terms, and foreign investors can access domestic financial markets. Banking competition has become intense. Commercial banks control nearly 90 percent of assets, and majority foreign-owned banks account for two-thirds of that amount. The government maintains majority control in two banks and provides low-interest loans to farmers and homeowners. Privatization of the state-controlled company that controls 50 percent of the insurance market has been slow. Capital markets have become more sophisticated, and the Warsaw Stock Exchange is expanding. The impact of the global financial turmoil has been relatively mild.

PROPERTY RIGHTS — 55

Property rights are moderately well protected. The legal system protects the acquisition and disposition of property. The judicial system is slow to resolve cases, and there can be unexpected changes in laws and regulations. Piracy of intellectual property continues despite government efforts to improve protection.

FREEDOM FROM CORRUPTION — 46

Corruption is perceived as significant. Poland ranks 58th out of 179 countries in Transparency International's Corruption Perceptions Index for 2008. The government has established a central office to combat corruption, which reportedly has declined as a result, especially in public procurement.

LABOR FREEDOM — 61.5

Labor regulations are relatively rigid. The non-salary cost of employing a worker is high, and dismissing an employee is difficult.

Lisbon

PORTUGAL

Economic Freedom Score

25   50   75

Least free   0   100   Most free

64.4

Portugal's economic freedom score is 64.4, making its economy the 62nd freest in the 2010 *Index*. Its score is 0.5 point lower than last year, with reductions in five of the 10 economic freedoms. Portugal is ranked 28th out of 43 countries in the Europe region, and its overall score is above the world average.

Reforms have modernized and diversified the Portuguese economy's productive base. The services sector is now the largest source of employment. Business formation is more efficient and streamlined. Consolidation and restructuring have increased efficiency in the financial sector, which weathered the global financial turmoil relatively well. The judiciary is independent and free of corruption, although resolution of cases is slower than the EU average.

Portugal's overall economic freedom remains limited by high government spending, low fiscal freedom, and a rigid labor market. Reforms in public finance administration are ongoing. The deficit had decreased to less than 3 percent of GDP but has been rising in recent years. The labor market is highly regulated.

BACKGROUND: In 1974, dictator Antonio de Oliveira Salazar was removed from power in a bloodless coup, and a parliamentary democracy was established after a brief period of instability. Portugal joined the European Union in 1986, liberalizing many parts of the economy and improving its infrastructure with the help of EU funds. However, it continues to suffer from public-sector inefficiency and a lack of private-sector confidence. Portugal's traditional comparative advantage in cheap labor has eroded since the accession of Central and Eastern European countries to the EU, and growth continues to lag behind that of the EU as a whole. Unemployment is high and growing. Increasing competitiveness remains a major objective for Socialist Party Prime Minister Jose Socrates, who came to power in 2005 and won re-election in 2009, though without the parliamentary majority he had enjoyed.

Country's Score Over Time

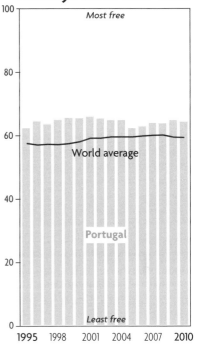

Quick Facts

Population: 10.6 million

GDP (PPP): $245.1 billion
0.0% growth in 2008
1.0% 5-year compound annual growth
$23,074 per capita

Unemployment: 7.7%

Inflation (CPI): 2.6%

FDI Inflow: $3.5 billion

2008 data unless otherwise noted
Data compiled as of September 2009

How Do We Measure Economic Freedom?
See page 457 for an explanation of the methodology or visit the *Index* Web site at *heritage.org/index*.

PORTUGAL'S TEN ECONOMIC FREEDOMS

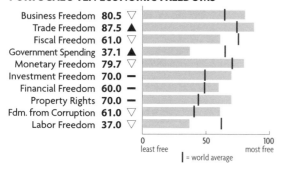

Business Freedom	80.5	▽
Trade Freedom	87.5	▲
Fiscal Freedom	61.0	▽
Government Spending	37.1	▲
Monetary Freedom	79.7	▽
Investment Freedom	70.0	—
Financial Freedom	60.0	—
Property Rights	70.0	—
Fdm. from Corruption	61.0	▽
Labor Freedom	37.0	▽

0   50   100
least free   most free
| = world average

BUSINESS FREEDOM — 80.5

The overall freedom to start, operate, and close a business is relatively well protected under Portugal's regulatory environment. Starting a business takes an average of six days, compared to the world average of 35 days. Obtaining a business license requires more than the world average of 18 procedures and 218 days.

TRADE FREEDOM — 87.5

Portugal's trade policy is the same as that of other members of the European Union. The common EU weighted average tariff rate was 1.3 percent in 2008. However, the EU has high or escalating tariffs for agricultural and manufacturing products, and its MFN tariff code is complex. Non-tariff barriers reflected in EU and Portuguese policy include agricultural and manufacturing subsidies, quotas, import restrictions and bans for some goods and services, market access restrictions in some services sectors, non-transparent and restrictive regulations and standards, and inconsistent regulatory and customs administration among EU members. Pharmaceutical regulations and non-transparent government procurement also add to the cost of trade. Ten points were deducted from Portugal's trade freedom score to account for non-tariff barriers.

FISCAL FREEDOM — 61

Portugal has a high income tax rate and a moderate corporate tax rate. The top income tax rate is 42 percent. The top corporate tax rate is 26.5 percent (a flat 25 percent plus a maximum 1.5 percent surtax). Other taxes include a value-added tax (VAT) and a property tax. In the most recent year, overall tax revenue as a percentage of GDP was 37.8 percent.

GOVERNMENT SPENDING — 37.1

Total government expenditures, including consumption and transfer payments, are high. In the most recent year, government spending equaled 45.8 percent of GDP.

MONETARY FREEDOM — 79.7

Portugal is a member of the euro zone. Inflation has been relatively low, averaging 2.6 percent between 2006 and 2008. As a participant in the EU's Common Agricultural Policy, the government subsidizes agricultural production, distorting the prices of agricultural products. The government also influences prices through state-owned enterpris-

es and utilities. Ten points were deducted from Portugal's monetary freedom score to account for measures that distort domestic prices.

INVESTMENT FREEDOM — 70

Foreigners may invest in almost all sectors that are open to private enterprise. Investments in defense, water management, telecommunications, railways, maritime transportation, and air transport require government approval. Private ownership in basic sanitation, international air transport, railways, ports, arms and weapons manufacture, and airports is limited to 49 percent. The government requires private firms to obtain permission to operate in a number of sectors (public service television, waste treatment), but grants it on a non-discriminatory basis. Dispute resolution can be cumbersome. Residents and non-residents may hold foreign exchange accounts. There are no restrictions on repatriation of profits, current transfers, payments for invisible transactions, or real estate transactions.

FINANCIAL FREEDOM — 60

Portugal's financial sector has undergone consolidation in recent years. The largest five bank groups account for about 80 percent of the sector's total assets. The country's largest bank, Caixa Geral de Depositos (CGD), is the only remaining government-controlled financial institution. Overall, the financial regulatory system is transparent and consistent with international norms. Credit is available on market terms, and the private sector enjoys access to a wide variety of credit instruments. The government influences the allocation of credit through a program designed to assist small and medium-size enterprises. Capital markets are small.

PROPERTY RIGHTS — 70

The judiciary is independent. The court system is slow and deliberate, and the number of years that it takes to resolve cases is well above the EU average. Portugal implements the WTO's Trade-Related Aspects of Intellectual Property Rights (TRIPS) agreement and European intellectual property protection standards and has increased the penalties for violators.

FREEDOM FROM CORRUPTION — 61

Corruption is perceived as present. Portugal ranks 32nd out of 179 countries in Transparency International's Corruption Perceptions Index for 2008. Foreign firms do not identify corruption as an obstacle to investment. Portugal has ratified the OECD Anti-Bribery Convention and has passed legislation to bring its criminal code into compliance with it. Tax evasion remains a problem for the government, which has implemented several initiatives to improve collection rates.

LABOR FREEDOM — 37

Portugal's labor regulations are inflexible. The non-salary cost of employing a worker is high, and dismissing an employee is difficult. Regulations on work hours are not flexible.

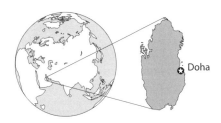

Doha

QATAR

Economic Freedom Score

Least free 0   100 Most free

69.0

Qatar's economic freedom score is 69.0, making its economy the 39th freest in the 2010 *Index*. Its score is 3.2 points better than last year, reflecting notable improvements in six of the 10 economic freedoms. Qatar is ranked 2nd out of 17 countries in the Middle East/North Africa region, and its overall score is above the world and regional averages.

The government of Qatar has pursued reforms to improve the entrepreneurial environment and broaden the economic base beyond oil and gas. Qatar scores above the world average in eight of the 10 economic freedoms, and its freedom from corruption score is over 20 points better than the world average. Qatari nationals pay no personal or corporate taxes, and the overall tax burden is low. The government has maintained a large current account surplus, and public spending is funded largely by oil revenues.

Notable challenges to overall economic freedom in Qatar remain in two areas. Investment is hindered by intrusive bureaucracy and a lack of transparency. Monetary stability is weak and adversely affected by lingering price controls.

BACKGROUND: Qatar has been ruled by the Al-Thani family since independence from Great Britain in 1971. Reforms promoted by Sheikh Hamad bin Khalifa al-Thani, who replaced his father in a bloodless coup in 1995, include universal suffrage, an independent judiciary, and more transparent government funding. Despite attempts to diversify, oil and gas account for about 85 percent of export revenues and more than 60 percent of GDP. Qatar has 15 billion barrels of oil and the world's third-largest natural gas reserves—about 15 percent of total world reserves. It has permitted extensive foreign investment in its natural gas industry and in 2007 became the world's largest exporter of liquefied natural gas. Qatar's immense energy reserves and small population have given it the world's second-highest per capita income.

Country's Score Over Time

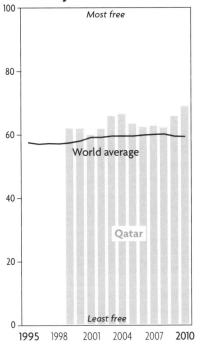

Quick Facts

Population: 1.1 million

GDP (PPP): $94.2 billion
16.4% growth in 2008
14% 5-year compound
annual growth
$85,868 per capita

Unemployment: 0.4%

Inflation (CPI): 15.0%

FDI Inflow: $6.7 billion

2008 data unless otherwise noted
Data compiled as of September 2009

How Do We Measure Economic Freedom?
See page 457 for an explanation of the methodology or visit the *Index* Web site at *heritage.org/index.*

349

QATAR'S TEN ECONOMIC FREEDOMS

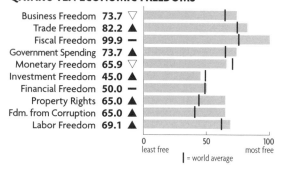

Business Freedom	73.7 ▽	
Trade Freedom	82.2 ▲	
Fiscal Freedom	99.9 —	
Government Spending	73.7 ▲	
Monetary Freedom	65.9 ▽	
Investment Freedom	45.0 ▲	
Financial Freedom	50.0 —	
Property Rights	65.0 ▲	
Fdm. from Corruption	65.0 ▲	
Labor Freedom	69.1 ▲	

0 least free   50   100 most free

| = world average

BUSINESS FREEDOM — 73.7

The overall freedom to start, operate, and close a business is relatively well protected under Qatar's regulatory environment. Starting a business takes six days, compared to the world average of 35 days. Obtaining a business license takes much less than the world average of 218 days, but costs are high.

TRADE FREEDOM — 82.2

Qatar's weighted average tariff rate was 3.9 percent in 2008. Some prohibitive tariffs, import restrictions and bans, services market access barriers, import licensing requirements, restrictive sanitary and phytosanitary regulations, and domestic preference in government procurement add to the cost of trade. Ten points were deducted from Qatar's trade freedom score to account for non-tariff barriers.

FISCAL FREEDOM — 99.9

Qatar imposes no income tax on individuals and no income tax on corporations that are wholly owned by Qatari nationals. The top corporate tax rate of 35 percent applies to foreign corporations operating in Qatar. Aside from customs duties, there are no other major taxes. In the most recent year, overall tax revenue as a percentage of GDP was 2.6 percent.

GOVERNMENT SPENDING — 73.7

Total government expenditures, including consumption and transfer payments, are moderate. In the most recent year, government spending equaled 29.6 percent of GDP. State involvement in the economy is still considerable despite some progress in privatization.

MONETARY FREEDOM — 65.9

Inflation has been very high, averaging 14.4 percent between 2006 and 2008. A record high rate of 15.1 percent annual average inflation in 2008 was followed by a sharp fall in the consumer price index in the first quarter of 2009. The government influences prices through regulation, subsidies, and numerous state-owned enterprises and utilities. Ten points were deducted from Qatar's monetary freedom score to account for policies that distort domestic prices.

INVESTMENT FREEDOM — 45

Foreign investment is limited to 49 percent of capital for most activities; however, upon special government approval, up to 100 percent ownership by foreign investors may be allowed in certain sectors, including agriculture, industry, health, education, tourism, energy, or mining. Some sectors are reserved for domestic investors or as a government monopoly. Foreign businesses must employ a local agent, and investment projects are screened. Implementing regulations may not be fully transparent. Residents and non-residents may hold foreign exchange accounts. There are no controls or restrictions on payments and transfers. Foreign investors may purchase residential land in certain areas.

FINANCIAL FREEDOM — 50

The Qatar Financial Center, which opened in 2005, has attracted major financial firms and is intended to rival other regional financial hubs. The government partially owns Qatar National Bank, which accounts for about 40 percent of total deposits and handles most of the government's business. The government must approve foreign investment in banking and insurance and has shares in two prominent insurers. Foreign banks hold less than 10 percent of the banking system's total assets. The Doha Securities Market has been opened to foreign investors, but holdings are restricted to 25 percent of the issued capital of nearly all listed companies. The government has put on hold its plan to set up a single regulatory authority to oversee all financial services.

PROPERTY RIGHTS — 65

Expropriation is unlikely, but the judiciary is subject to inefficiency and executive influence. The court system is slow, bureaucratic, and biased in favor of Qataris and the government. Foreigners are generally not allowed to own property. However, a law enacted in 2004 allows foreigners to own residential property in select projects. Successful prosecutions of violators of intellectual property rights have increased substantially.

FREEDOM FROM CORRUPTION — 65

Corruption is perceived as present. Qatar ranks 28th out of 179 countries in Transparency International's Corruption Perceptions Index for 2008, an improvement over 2007 and the highest ranking of any country in the Middle East. The law imposes penalties for bribery on public officials and those who attempt to influence them illegally. Officials are working to make government procurement more open and transparent. Qatar has ratified the U.N. Convention for Combating Corruption and has established a National Committee for Integrity and Transparency. There is no independent auditing body outside of the executive.

LABOR FREEDOM — 69.1

Qatar's labor force consists primarily of expatriate workers, and immigration and employment rules are flexible. The government does not mandate a minimum wage.

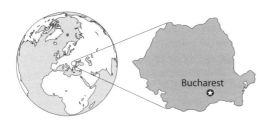

ROMANIA

Economic Freedom Score

Least free 0   25   50   75   100   Most free

64.2

World Rank: **63**   Regional Rank: **29**

Romania's economic freedom score is 64.2, making its economy the 63rd freest in the 2010 *Index*. Its score is 1.0 point better than last year, reflecting improvements in half of the 10 economic freedoms. Romania is ranked 29th out of 43 countries in the Europe region, and its overall score is higher than the world average.

The Romanian economy has continued its transition to greater economic freedom, achieving an average economic growth rate of over 6 percent over the past five years. The overall entrepreneurial framework has become more streamlined and efficient, and the tax regime is competitive with a flat rate of 16 percent for both individual and corporate taxes. Other recent structural reforms include privatization in the banking sector, a reduction in the public-sector wage bill, and tax administration reform.

Romania lags behind many other countries in the region, however, in terms of deeper structural reforms, facing ongoing institutional challenges to overall economic freedom as a result of widespread corruption and a rigid labor market that undermines dynamic job growth. Although Romania has made some progress in the fight against corruption, the judiciary remains vulnerable to political interference and inefficiency.

BACKGROUND: Romania has been a fast-growing member of the European Union and NATO, and the government has been implementing economic reforms that are consistent with the Maastricht criteria. The current ruling coalition is composed of the Democratic Liberal Party, the Social Democratic Party, and the Conservative Party. GDP reached 7.8 percent in 2008 but slowed significantly in 2009 as a result of the global economic crisis. Overall, macroeconomic improvements have spurred the growth of the middle class and have helped to reduce poverty. Parliamentary elections were scheduled for November 2009.

Country's Score Over Time

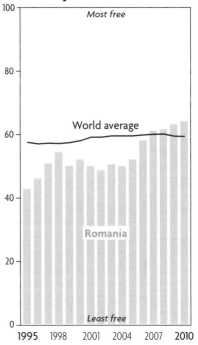

Quick Facts

Population: 21.5 million

GDP (PPP): $302.6 billion
9.2% growth in 2008
6.3% 5-year compound annual growth
$14,065 per capita

Unemployment: 5.8%

Inflation (CPI): 7.8%

FDI Inflow: $13.3 billion

2008 data unless otherwise noted
Data compiled as of September 2009

How Do We Measure Economic Freedom?
See page 457 for an explanation of the methodology or visit the *Index* Web site at *heritage.org/index*.

351

ROMANIA'S TEN ECONOMIC FREEDOMS

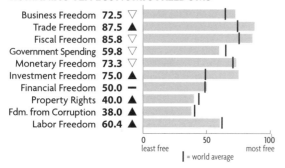

Business Freedom	72.5	▽
Trade Freedom	87.5	▲
Fiscal Freedom	85.8	▽
Government Spending	59.8	▽
Monetary Freedom	73.3	▽
Investment Freedom	75.0	▲
Financial Freedom	50.0	—
Property Rights	40.0	▲
Fdm. from Corruption	38.0	▲
Labor Freedom	60.4	▲

0 least free   50   100 most free

| = world average

BUSINESS FREEDOM — 72.5

The overall freedom to start, operate, and close a business is relatively well protected under Romania's regulatory environment. Starting a business takes 10 days, compared to the world average of 35 days. Obtaining a business license takes about the same as the world average of 18 procedures. Closing a business can be a lengthy process.

TRADE FREEDOM — 87.5

Romania's trade policy is the same as that of other members of the European Union. The common EU weighted average tariff rate was 1.3 percent in 2008. However, the EU has high or escalating tariffs for agricultural and manufacturing products, and its MFN tariff code is complex. Non-tariff barriers reflected in EU and Romanian policy include agricultural and manufacturing subsidies, quotas, import restrictions and bans for some goods and services, market access restrictions in some services sectors, non-transparent and restrictive regulations and standards, and inconsistent regulatory and customs administration among EU members. Restrictions on biotechnology and sanitary and phytosanitary regulations exceed EU policy, and corruption and the enforcement of intellectual property rights are problematic. Ten points were deducted from Romania's trade freedom score to account for non-tariff barriers.

FISCAL FREEDOM — 85.8

Romania has relatively low flat tax rates. Both the income tax rate and the corporate tax rate are 16 percent. Other taxes include a value-added tax (VAT) and a real property tax. In the most recent year, overall tax revenue as a percentage of GDP was 30.1 percent.

GOVERNMENT SPENDING — 59.8

Total government expenditures, including consumption and transfer payments, are moderately high and climbing. In the most recent year, government spending equaled 36.6 percent of GDP. Expenditures increased dramatically in the run-up to the elections in late 2008. Privatization of large-scale companies has been sluggish.

MONETARY FREEDOM — 73.3

Inflation has been moderately high, averaging 7.0 percent between 2006 and 2008. As a participant in the EU's Common Agricultural Policy, the government subsidizes agricultural production, distorting the prices of agricultural products. It also influences prices through regulation, subsidies, and state-owned enterprises and utilities. Ten points were deducted from Romania's monetary freedom score to account for policies that distort domestic prices.

INVESTMENT FREEDOM — 75

Foreign and domestic investments receive equal treatment under the law. Deterrents to investment include judicial and legislative unpredictability, frequent changes in the regulatory environment, and cumbersome and non-transparent bureaucracy. Residents and non-residents may hold foreign exchange accounts. Payments, capital transactions, and transfers face some reporting requirements and restrictions. EU citizens may own land, subject to reciprocity in their home countries, and foreign investors may purchase non-agricultural land for business use.

FINANCIAL FREEDOM — 50

Romania's financial supervision and regulation are largely consistent with international standards. Significant reforms since the late 1990s include the privatization of many state-owned banks. Banking is relatively sound and stable, with a satisfactory level of capitalization. Foreign-owned banks account for close to 90 percent of total assets. However, Romania's financial intermediation rate remains one of the lowest in the region. The state still owns the National Saving Bank, which accounts for around 4.5 percent of total assets. Capital markets are underdeveloped, and most trading involves government debt.

PROPERTY RIGHTS — 40

Investors have expressed concern about unpredictable changes in legislation and weak enforcement of contracts and laws. The judicial system suffers from corruption, inefficiency, and excessive workloads. Since the 2006 privatization of the Romanian Commercial Bank, Romania's mortgage market has been almost entirely private (the state-owned National Savings Bank also offers mortgage loans). Romania is a signatory to international conventions concerning intellectual property rights, but enforcement of legislation protecting patents, trademarks, and copyrights is very weak.

FREEDOM FROM CORRUPTION — 38

Corruption is perceived as widespread. Romania ranks 70th out of 179 countries in Transparency International's Corruption Perceptions Index for 2008. The government's Anticorruption Strategy, which includes enforcement of laws and procedures to combat money laundering and tax evasion, has had some success. Accession to the EU also spurred gains against corruption. Nevertheless, foreign investors complain of government and business corruption in the customs service, in municipal zoning offices, and among local financial authorities.

LABOR FREEDOM — 60.4

Romania's labor regulations are rigid. The non-salary cost of employing a worker is very high, and dismissing an employee is difficult. Regulations on work hours are not flexible.

RUSSIA

Economic Freedom Score

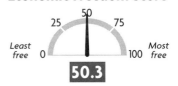

25 50 75

Least free 0   100 Most free

50.3

Russia's economic freedom score is 50.3, making its economy the 143rd freest in the 2010 *Index*. Its score is 0.5 point worse than last year, reflecting reduced scores in six of the 10 economic freedoms. Russia is ranked 41st out of 43 countries in the Europe region, and its overall score is below the world and regional averages.

The Russian economy scores above the world average only in fiscal freedom, in part because of a reduced corporate tax rate that became effective in January 2009. Economic growth has averaged better than 6 percent over the past five years, but overdependence on oil and gas increases the risk of a sudden loss of competitiveness.

State involvement in economic activity remains extensive. Non-tariff barriers significantly increase the cost of trade. Monetary stability is weak, and prices are heavily controlled and influenced by the government. Deterrents to foreign investment include bureaucratic inconsistency, corruption, and restrictions in lucrative sectors like energy. Corruption weakens the rule of law and increases the fragility of property rights.

BACKGROUND: The Russian Federation was formed in 1992 after the dissolution of the Soviet Union. Dmitry Medvedev won the presidential election in March 2008, but former President Vladimir Putin remains prime minister and de facto supreme leader. The state has reasserted its role in extractive industries and depends heavily on exports of natural resources, especially oil and natural gas. The global financial crisis, government involvement in the economy, and war with Georgia caused significant economic losses in 2008, and GDP was projected to contract by 6.5 percent in 2009. Russia has provided a joint loan program of $10 billion for countries in Eurasia and is a founding member of the Shanghai Cooperation Organization. Before joining the World Trade Organization, Russia wants a customs union with Belarus and Kazakhstan, as ratified by the Duma in October 2008.

Country's Score Over Time

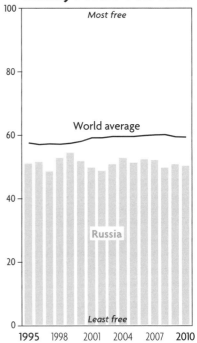

Quick Facts

Population: 141.8 million

GDP (PPP): $2.3 trillion
7.3% growth in 2008
6.9% 5-year compound
annual growth
$16,139 per capita

Unemployment: 6.4%

Inflation (CPI): 14.1%

FDI Inflow: $70.3 billion

2008 data unless otherwise noted
Data compiled as of September 2009

How Do We Measure Economic Freedom?
See page 457 for an explanation of the methodology or visit the *Index* Web site at *heritage.org/index.*

RUSSIA'S TEN ECONOMIC FREEDOMS

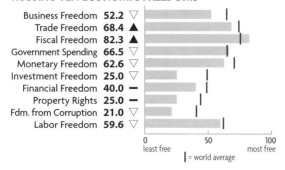

Business Freedom	52.2	▽
Trade Freedom	68.4	▲
Fiscal Freedom	82.3	▲
Government Spending	66.5	▽
Monetary Freedom	62.6	▽
Investment Freedom	25.0	▽
Financial Freedom	40.0	—
Property Rights	25.0	—
Fdm. from Corruption	21.0	▽
Labor Freedom	59.6	▽

0 least free — 50 — 100 most free

| = world average

BUSINESS FREEDOM — 52.2

The overall freedom to start, operate, and close a business is limited under Russia's regulatory environment. Bureaucratic obstacles are a particular problem for small businesses. Obtaining a business license takes much more than the world average of 18 procedures and 218 days. Bankruptcy proceedings can be lengthy and difficult.

TRADE FREEDOM — 68.4

Russia's weighted average tariff rate was 5.8 percent in 2008. Prohibitive tariffs; services market access barriers; import and export restrictions; discriminatory import and export taxes, charges, and fees; non-transparent regulations and standards; discriminatory licensing, registration, and certification; complex and non-transparent customs valuation; non-transparent and arbitrary customs administration; subsidies; corruption; and weak enforcement of intellectual property rights add to the cost of trade. Twenty points were deducted from Russia's trade freedom score to account for non-tariff barriers.

FISCAL FREEDOM — 82.3

Russia has relatively low taxes. The individual income tax rate is a flat 13 percent, and the top corporate tax rate is 20 percent, down from 24 percent as of January 1, 2009. Other taxes include a value-added tax (VAT) and a regional property tax. In the most recent year, overall tax revenue as a percentage of GDP was 34.6 percent.

GOVERNMENT SPENDING — 66.5

Total government expenditures, including consumption and transfer payments, are moderate. In the most recent year, government spending equaled 33.4 percent of GDP. The state maintains a strong presence in such key sectors as energy and mining.

MONETARY FREEDOM — 62.6

Inflation has been high, averaging 12.5 percent between 2006 and 2008. The government influences prices through regulation, extensive subsidies, and numerous state-owned enterprises and utilities. Fifteen points were deducted from Russia's monetary freedom score to account for policies that distort domestic prices.

INVESTMENT FREEDOM — 25

The 1999 Investment Law codifies the principle of national treatment for foreign investors; however, the law goes on to state that federal law may provide for a number of exceptions, including, where necessary, "the protection of the constitution, public morals and health, and the rights and lawful interest of other persons and the defense of the state." Thus, a large number of broadly defined exceptions give the Russian government considerable discretion in prohibiting or inhibiting foreign investment. Additionally, the government enacted the Strategic Sectors Law (SSL) in May 2008, introducing a list of 42 "strategic" sectors in which purchases of controlling interests by foreign investors must be pre-approved by the Russian government. Other deterrents to investment include inconsistent and burdensome government regulation, unreliable contract enforcement, inadequate infrastructure and financial capacity, and corruption. Residents and non-residents may hold foreign exchange accounts, subject to restrictions. Capital payments and transfers are also subject to restrictions. Foreign ownership of non-agricultural land that is not located near international borders is permitted.

FINANCIAL FREEDOM — 40

Russia's financial sector is not fully developed and is subject to government influence. Bank supervision and transparency are insufficient, although regulation was improved in 2006. The more than 1,000 licensed and registered banks are generally small and undercapitalized, but consolidation is underway. The banking sector is dominated by two state-owned banks that account for more than 30 percent of the sector's total assets. Capital markets are relatively small but growing and are dominated by energy companies. The global financial turmoil has placed increasing pressure on the financial sector.

PROPERTY RIGHTS — 25

Protection of private property is weak. The judicial system is unpredictable, corrupt, and unable to handle technically sophisticated cases. Contracts are difficult to enforce, and an ancient antipathy to them continues to impede Russian integration into the West. Mortgage lending remains in its initial stages. Violations of intellectual property rights continue to be a serious problem.

FREEDOM FROM CORRUPTION — 21

Corruption is perceived as pervasive. Russia ranks 147th out of 179 countries in Transparency International's Corruption Perceptions Index for 2008, a slight decline from 2007. Corruption is rampant, both in the number of instances and in the size of bribes sought. New anti-corruption legislation requires government employees and their families to declare their income and assets.

LABOR FREEDOM — 59.6

Russia's labor regulations are relatively rigid. The non-salary cost of employing a worker is high, and dismissing an employee is difficult. Regulations on the number of work hours are rigid.

RWANDA

Economic Freedom Score

Least free 0   25   50   75   100 Most free

59.1

World Rank: **93**	Regional Rank: **10**

Rwanda's economic freedom score is 59.1, making its economy the 93rd freest in the 2010 *Index*. Its score has increased by 4.9 points since last year, reflecting notable improvements in four of the 10 economic freedoms. Rwanda is ranked 10th out of 46 countries in the Sub-Saharan Africa region, and its overall score is slightly below the world average.

Rwanda has the fourth most improved economy in the 2010 *Index*. Structural reforms encourage entrepreneurial activity, and Rwanda scores relatively well in business freedom, fiscal freedom, government spending, and labor freedom. Personal and corporate tax rates are moderate. Of the 104 enterprises slated for privatization over the past decade, fewer than 15 remain state-owned.

Overall economic freedom is undermined by institutional weaknesses in investment freedom, financial freedom, property rights, and freedom from corruption. Although foreign investment is welcome, political instability is still a major deterrent. The government has tried to strengthen the financial sector, create infrastructure, and improve expenditure management. The judicial system lacks independence and capacity, and legal procedures are commonly subject to corruption.

BACKGROUND: Decades of ethnic tension culminated in 1994 with the genocidal slaughter of an estimated one million Tutsis and moderate Hutus. After Paul Kagame's Tutsi-led Rwandan Patriotic Front seized power, millions of Hutus fled to the Democratic Republic of Congo. Rwandan forces have entered the DRC repeatedly since the 1990s to confront Hutu militia. The most recent effort, in January 2009, was a joint operation with Congolese armed forces to eliminate an anti-Rwandan government militia. Kagame, who won a landslide victory in 2003 in the first presidential election since the genocide, has focused on political reconciliation and rebuilding Rwanda's shattered economy. Despite strong growth based on tourism and exports of coffee and tea, poverty remains widespread, and over 80 percent of Rwandans depend on subsistence agriculture supplemented by cash crops.

Country's Score Over Time

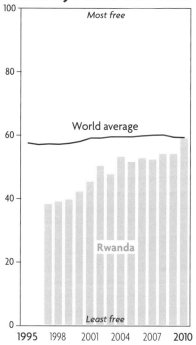

Quick Facts

Population: 9.7 million

GDP (PPP): $9.9 billion
11.2% growth in 2008
8.4% 5-year compound annual growth
$1,022 per capita

Unemployment: n/a

Inflation (CPI): 15.4%

FDI Inflow: $103 million

2008 data unless otherwise noted
Data compiled as of September 2009

How Do We Measure Economic Freedom?
See page 457 for an explanation of the methodology or visit the *Index* Web site at *heritage.org/index.*

RWANDA'S TEN ECONOMIC FREEDOMS

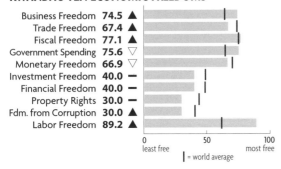

Business Freedom	74.5 ▲	
Trade Freedom	67.4 ▲	
Fiscal Freedom	77.1 ▲	
Government Spending	75.6 ▽	
Monetary Freedom	66.9 ▽	
Investment Freedom	40.0 —	
Financial Freedom	40.0 —	
Property Rights	30.0 —	
Fdm. from Corruption	30.0 ▲	
Labor Freedom	89.2 ▲	

0 least free   50   100 most free

| = world average

BUSINESS FREEDOM — 74.5

The overall freedom to start, operate, and close a business has considerably improved. Starting a business now takes an average of three days, compared to the world average of 35 days, but the entry cost of launching a business is high. Obtaining a business license takes less than the world average of 218 days and 18 procedures.

TRADE FREEDOM — 67.4

Rwanda's weighted average tariff rate was 11.3 percent in 2008. Liberalization of the trade regime has progressed, but some prohibitive tariffs, import restrictions, import taxes, import and export licensing, weak enforcement of intellectual property rights, complex and inefficient customs procedures, and corruption add to the cost of trade. Ten points were deducted from Rwanda's trade freedom score to account for non-tariff barriers.

FISCAL FREEDOM — 77.1

Rwanda has moderately high tax rates. The top income tax rate is 35 percent, and the top corporate tax rate is 30 percent. Other taxes include a value-added tax (VAT) and a property transfer tax. In the most recent year, overall tax revenue as a percentage of GDP was 13.0 percent.

GOVERNMENT SPENDING — 75.6

Total government expenditures, including consumption and transfer payments, are moderate. In the most recent year, government spending equaled 28.5 percent of GDP. Recent privatizations include cement and rice factories, banks, tea plantations, and a mining company.

MONETARY FREEDOM — 66.9

Inflation has been high, averaging 13.3 percent between 2006 and 2008. The government controls the prices of cement, electricity, water, telecommunications, petroleum, beer, and soft drinks and also influences prices through regulation and state-owned enterprises and utilities. Ten points were deducted from Rwanda's monetary freedom score to account for policies that distort domestic prices.

INVESTMENT FREEDOM — 40

Foreign investment is not subject to discriminatory treatment, and there are no restrictions on investment in any sector. Investment projects are subject to screening if investors are seeking government incentives. Rwanda's legal investment infrastructure is still being developed, and commercial courts began operations in May 2008. Bureaucracy can be cumbersome and prone to corruption. Residents and non-residents may hold foreign exchange accounts if they provide supporting documentation. Payments and transfers are subject to some authorizations, maximum allowances, and limits. Nearly all capital transactions require central bank approval. Land is owned by the state but may be leased by both foreign and local investors.

FINANCIAL FREEDOM — 40

The small but growing financial sector remains burdened by shortcomings in supervision, regulation, and oversight. The government reduced its involvement in banking in 2004 when it sold off two majority bank holdings, but it remains extensively involved and controls a significant portion of total assets. Non-performing loans stand at around 30 percent of total loans. The high costs of financing and limited access to credit remain serious challenges for entrepreneurs. About 14 percent of the adult population has bank accounts and access to financial services. There are eight commercial banks, the largest of which has a 50 percent stake controlled by the government. Capital markets are at an early stage of development, though there is a small stock exchange that was established in 2008.

PROPERTY RIGHTS — 30

Rwanda's judiciary is government-influenced and suffers from inefficiency, a lack of resources, and corruption. A land law passed in 2005 stipulates procedures for property registration, but no registries have been established. Despite adherence to key international agreements on intellectual property rights, sales of counterfeit goods and violations of pharmaceutical patents continue. A Registration Service Agency is designed to improve intellectual property rights by registering all commercial entities and facilitating business identification and branding.

FREEDOM FROM CORRUPTION — 30

Corruption is perceived as widespread. Rwanda ranks 102nd out of 179 countries in Transparency International's Corruption Perceptions Index for 2008, an improvement over 2007. The law provides criminal penalties for official corruption, and the government is implementing these laws with increasing effectiveness. The law does not provide for access to government information, and it remains difficult for citizens and foreigners, including journalists, to obtain access to government information.

LABOR FREEDOM — 89.2

Rwanda's labor regulations are now much more flexible. The non-salary cost of employing a worker is low, and dismissing an employee is easier. Regulations relating to the number of work hours are more flexible.

SAINT LUCIA

Economic Freedom Score

25   50   75

Least free 0   100 Most free

70.5

| World Rank: **25** | Regional Rank: **2** |

Saint Lucia's economic freedom score is 70.5, making its economy the 25th freest in the 2010 *Index*. Its score has increased by 1.7 points since last year, reflecting notable improvements in four of the 10 economic freedoms. Saint Lucia is ranked 2nd out of 29 countries in the South and Central America/Caribbean region, and its overall score is above the world average.

Saint Lucia scores above the world average in seven economic freedoms including business freedom, freedom from corruption, and monetary freedom. The entrepreneurial environment is efficient and transparent, and efforts to eliminate price controls have encouraged economic growth. The government implements penalties for corruption through the relatively efficient judicial system. The financial sector has weathered the global financial crisis, but the recession has hurt tourism.

Saint Lucia's trade freedom is limited by tariff and non-tariff barriers. Government spending is pushing public debt to over 65 percent of GDP. There is scope for further development and better regulation and supervision of the financial sector. Greater access to financing is crucial for private-sector development.

BACKGROUND: Saint Lucia is a two-party parliamentary democracy. Prime Minister Stephenson King of the business-friendly United Workers Party took office in 2007. Saint Lucia is a member of the Caribbean Community and Common Market and home to the Organization of Eastern Caribbean States. Its economy depends primarily on tourism, banana production, and light manufacturing. An educated workforce and improvements in roads, communications, water supply, sewerage, and port facilities have attracted foreign investment in tourism and in petroleum storage and transshipment. However, with the U.S., Canada, and Europe in recession, tourism declined by double digits in early 2009. Because of fluctuations in banana prices and possible World Trade Organization–imposed reductions in European Union trade preferences, the government is encouraging farmers to diversify into such crops as cocoa, mangos, and avocados.

Country's Score Over Time

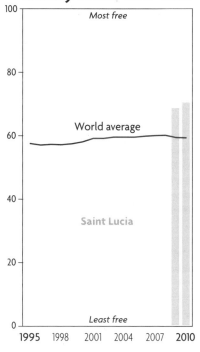

Quick Facts

Population: 0.2 million

GDP (PPP): $1.7 billion
2.3% growth in 2007
3.0% 5-year compound annual growth
$9,907 per capita

Unemployment: n/a

Inflation (CPI): 7.2%

FDI Inflow: $110 million

2008 data unless otherwise noted
Data compiled as of September 2009

How Do We Measure Economic Freedom?
See page 457 for an explanation of the methodology or visit the *Index* Web site at *heritage.org/index*.

SAINT LUCIA'S TEN ECONOMIC FREEDOMS

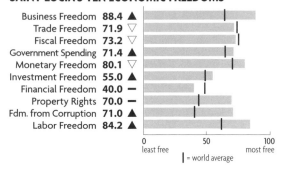

Business Freedom	88.4	▲
Trade Freedom	71.9	▽
Fiscal Freedom	73.2	▽
Government Spending	71.4	▲
Monetary Freedom	80.1	▽
Investment Freedom	55.0	▲
Financial Freedom	40.0	—
Property Rights	70.0	—
Fdm. from Corruption	71.0	▲
Labor Freedom	84.2	▲

0 least free   50   100 most free

| = world average

BUSINESS FREEDOM — 88.4

The overall freedom to start, operate, and close a business is well protected under Saint Lucia's regulatory environment. Starting a business takes an average of 14 days, compared to the world average of 35 days. Obtaining a business license requires nine procedures, compared to the world average of 18, and takes less than the world average of 218 days.

TRADE FREEDOM — 71.9

Saint Lucia's weighted average tariff rate was 9 percent in 2007. Some high tariffs, import bans and restrictions, import taxes, import fees, non-automatic import and export licensing, and limitations on trade capacity add to the cost of trade. Ten points were deducted from Saint Lucia's trade freedom score to account for non-tariff barriers.

FISCAL FREEDOM — 73.2

Saint Lucia's tax rates are moderately high. The top income tax rate is 30 percent, and the top corporate tax rate is 33.3 percent. Property sales and transfers are also subject to taxation. In the most recent year, overall tax revenue as a percentage of GDP was 26.0 percent. The government introduced a value-added tax (VAT) in 2009.

GOVERNMENT SPENDING — 71.4

Total government expenditures, including consumption and transfer payments, are moderate. In the most recent year, government spending equaled 30.9 percent of GDP.

MONETARY FREEDOM — 80.1

Inflation has been relatively low, averaging 5.5 percent between 2006 and 2008. Saint Lucia's currency is the Eastern Caribbean Dollar (EC$), a regional currency shared among members of the Eastern Caribbean Currency Union (ECCU). The Eastern Caribbean Central Bank (ECCB) issues the EC$, manages monetary policy, and regulates and supervises commercial banking activities in member countries. In 2003, the government began a comprehensive restructuring of the economy, including elimination of price controls and privatization of the state banana company. Five points were deducted from Saint Lucia's monetary freedom score to adjust for measures that distort domestic prices.

INVESTMENT FREEDOM — 55

In general, foreign and domestic firms are treated equally under the law, and many sectors are open to foreign investment. All investors must register with the government, and foreign investors must obtain a license to purchase land or shares in a company. A separate trade license must be obtained if more than 49 percent of the company's shares are held by foreign nationals or if the company is 100 percent foreign-owned. Licenses are renewed annually and are required for all foreign companies. National investment laws do not cover all aspects of commercial law, contract enforcement is problematic, and bureaucracy can be cumbersome. Foreign exchange and capital transactions are subject to a few restrictions and approvals.

FINANCIAL FREEDOM — 40

Saint Lucia's financial sector is small and not fully developed. There is a small offshore financial sector, and the banking sector is dominated by commercial banking. Saint Lucia is a member of the Eastern Caribbean Currency Union, which has a common central bank and currency. The financial services sector is also overseen by the government's Committee on Financial Services. A considerable portion of the population remains outside the formal banking sector, and limited access to financing remains a barrier to more dynamic business activity. Credit to the private sector has grown steadily. Non-performing loans have gradually declined since around 2003, although they edged up in 2008. The non-financial sector, led by insurance firms, has expanded rapidly. The global financial turmoil has not severely affected the financial system, but it did reveal weaknesses in the regulation of Saint Lucia's non-bank financial institutions, which are not subject to the same standards as banks and have engaged in riskier investment.

PROPERTY RIGHTS — 70

Saint Lucia has an efficient legal system based on British common law. The judiciary is independent and conducts generally fair public trials. Pirated copyrighted material is sold openly with no fear of arrest or prosecution.

FREEDOM FROM CORRUPTION — 71

Corruption is perceived as present. Saint Lucia ranks 21st out of 179 countries in Transparency International's Corruption Perceptions Index for 2008. The law provides criminal penalties for official corruption, and the government generally implements the law effectively.

LABOR FREEDOM — 84.2

Saint Lucia's labor regulations are flexible. The non-salary cost of employing a worker is low, and dismissing an employee is relatively easy.

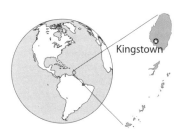

Kingstown

SAINT VINCENT AND THE GRENADINES

Economic Freedom Score

25   50   75

Least free 0   100 Most free

66.9

Saint Vincent and the Grenadines' economic freedom score is 66.9, making its economy the 49th freest in the 2010 *Index*. Its score has increased by 2.6 points since last year, reflecting improvements in five of the 10 economic freedoms. Saint Vincent and the Grenadines ranks 8th out of 29 countries in the South and Central America/Caribbean region, and its overall score is above the world average.

Economic reforms undertaken in recent years have helped Saint Vincent and the Grenadines to register one of the 15 highest increases in economic freedom in the 2010 *Index*. Reduced individual and corporate income tax rates have enhanced fiscal competitiveness, and business formation and investment procedures have become more streamlined and efficient.

In general, the judicial system is efficient. Punishments for official corruption are implemented effectively, although there is evidence that nepotism and corruption are prevalent in government contracting. Saint Vincent and the Grenadines scores poorly in financial freedom. Poor access to credit and the high costs of financing for entrepreneurial activity limit private-sector development and job growth.

BACKGROUND: Saint Vincent and the Grenadines is part of the British Commonwealth, and its judicial system, rooted in English common law, encourages stability. Banana production employs about 60 percent of the workforce and accounts for half of merchandise exports, leaving the economy vulnerable to price fluctuations and possible World Trade Organization–imposed reductions in European Union trade preferences. The global economic downturn has frustrated efforts to diversify the economy by promoting cruise-ship tourism. Saint Vincent and the Grenadines is a member of CARICOM and the Organization of Eastern Caribbean States, and many of its goods enter the United States duty-free under the U.S. Caribbean Basin Initiative. The government plans to join ALBA, a Venezuelan-led socialist trade alliance, and full membership could undermine regional economic integration under CARICOM's Single Market and Economy.

Country's Score Over Time

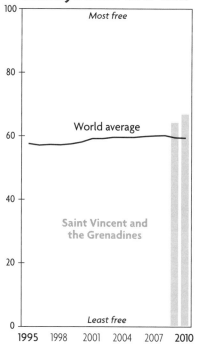

Quick Facts

Population: 0.1 million

GDP (PPP): $1.0 billion
1.0% growth in 2008
4.4% 5-year compound annual growth
$9,155 per capita

Unemployment: estimated to be over 10%

Inflation (CPI): 10.1%

FDI Inflow: $96 million

2008 data unless otherwise noted
Data compiled as of September 2009

How Do We Measure Economic Freedom?
See page 457 for an explanation of the methodology or visit the *Index* Web site at *heritage.org/index.*

ST. VINCENT & THE GRENADINES' TEN ECONOMIC FREEDOMS

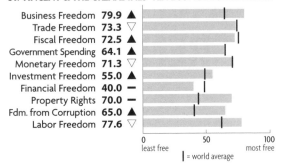

Business Freedom	79.9 ▲	
Trade Freedom	73.3 ▽	
Fiscal Freedom	72.5 ▲	
Government Spending	64.1 ▲	
Monetary Freedom	71.3 ▽	
Investment Freedom	55.0 ▲	
Financial Freedom	40.0 —	
Property Rights	70.0 —	
Fdm. from Corruption	65.0 ▲	
Labor Freedom	77.6 ▽	

0   50   100
least free   most free
❘ = world average

BUSINESS FREEDOM — 79.9

The overall freedom to start, operate, and close a business is relatively well protected under Saint Vincent and the Grenadines' regulatory environment. Starting a business takes an average of 11 days, compared to the world average of 35 days. Obtaining a business license takes less than the world average of 218 days.

TRADE FREEDOM — 73.3

Saint Vincent and the Grenadines' weighted average tariff rate was 8.4 percent in 2007. Some high tariffs, import bans and restrictions, import taxes, import fees, non-automatic import licensing, export-promotion programs, and limitations on trade capacity add to the cost of trade. Ten points were deducted from Saint Vincent and the Grenadines' trade freedom score to account for non-tariff barriers.

FISCAL FREEDOM — 72.5

Saint Vincent and the Grenadines introduced further tax reforms in 2009. The top income tax rate is 32.5 percent, down from 35 percent. The top corporate rate was also reduced to 32.5 percent. Other taxes include a property tax and a value-added tax (VAT), which has performed well since its introduction in May 2007. In the most recent year, overall tax revenue as a percentage of GDP was 25.3 percent.

GOVERNMENT SPENDING — 64.1

Total government expenditures, including consumption and transfer payments, are moderate. In the most recent year, government spending equaled 34.6 percent of GDP. Despite sustained spending on electricity subsidies, food price adjustments, and larger welfare and pension payments, total expenditure is declining slightly.

MONETARY FREEDOM — 71.3

Inflation has been relatively high, averaging 8.7 percent between 2006 and 2008. Saint Vincent and the Grenadines' currency is the Eastern Caribbean Dollar (EC$), a regional currency shared among members of the Eastern Caribbean Currency Union (ECCU). The Eastern Caribbean Central Bank (ECCB) issues the EC$, manages monetary policy, and regulates and supervises commercial banking activities in member countries. Ten points were deducted from Saint Vincent and the Grenadines' monetary free-

dom score to adjust for measures that distort domestic prices.

INVESTMENT FREEDOM — 55

In general, foreign investment is not subject to restrictions, and foreign investors receive national treatment. Foreigners must obtain a license to purchase land and shares or debentures in a company. Additional licensing may apply, depending on the activity. Foreign investment is screened if government incentives are being sought. Investment-related regulations and laws are complex and non-transparent. Joint ventures between foreign and national investors may repatriate profits equivalent to the extent of foreign ownership. Foreign firms are allowed to repatriate dividends abroad. Foreign exchange and capital transactions are subject to some restrictions and approvals.

FINANCIAL FREEDOM — 40

Saint Vincent and the Grenadines is a member of the Eastern Caribbean Currency Union, which has a common central bank and currency. All domestic commercial banks in Saint Vincent and the Grenadines are regulated by the Eastern Caribbean Central Bank. The financial sector is small and dominated by banking. Government influence in allocating credit is not substantial. There are six commercial banks, and the foreign presence (mainly subsidiaries of Canadian banks) is significant. Non-performing loans stand at around 4 percent of total loans. The financial-services sector plays an important role in the country's overall economic development strategy. The offshore financial sector is relatively small and concentrated. Capital markets are underdeveloped, and local entrepreneurs lack adequate access to a wide variety of financing instruments. Saint Vincent and the Grenadines' overall banking system remains sound and was not severely affected by the global financial turmoil.

PROPERTY RIGHTS — 70

Saint Vincent and the Grenadines' efficient judicial system is based on British common law. The judiciary is independent and conducts generally fair public trials. Pirated copyrighted material is sold openly with no fear of arrest or prosecution.

FREEDOM FROM CORRUPTION — 65

Corruption is perceived as present. Saint Vincent and the Grenadines ranks 28th out of 179 countries in Transparency International's Corruption Perceptions Index for 2008. The law provides criminal penalties for official corruption, but enforcement is not always effective. There is anecdotal evidence of corruption and nepotism in government contracting.

LABOR FREEDOM — 77.6

Saint Vincent and the Grenadines' labor regulations are relatively flexible. The non-salary cost of employing a worker is moderate, and dismissing an employee is relatively easy.

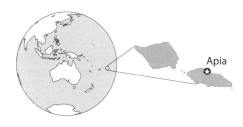

SAMOA

Economic Freedom Score

Least free 0   100 Most free

25   50   75

60.4

World Rank: 84   **Regional Rank: 13**

S amoa's economic freedom score is 60.4, making its economy the 84th freest in the 2010 *Index*. Its score has increased by 0.9 point since last year, reflecting improvements in business freedom and government spending. Samoa ranks 13th out of 41 countries in the Asia–Pacific region, and its overall score is above the world and regional averages.

The Samoan government has pursued economic reforms over the past decade, but overall progress has been mixed. The government still plays a substantial role in the economy, and regulations that increase the cost of doing business hamper entrepreneurial activity. The public sector accounts for more than 40 percent of GDP, crowding out private investment in some sectors. The government maintains ownership in a significant number of enterprises, some of which are safeguarded by monopoly privileges. The lack of formal employment opportunities and dynamic job growth remains a critical issue, particularly in light of the large presence of inefficient state-owned enterprises.

Despite some progress in streamlining business formation in recent years, government intrusiveness and lingering corruption create a poor investment climate and continue to undermine Samoa's overall economic freedom score. The lack of access to adequate financing impedes the growth of a stronger private sector.

BACKGROUND: Samoa is a small South Pacific archipelago with a population of less than 200,000. It is an electoral democracy but historically has been dominated politically by the Human Rights Protection Party. A political crisis over changing traffic laws to mandate driving on the left rather than the right, which had affected the makeup of parliament and risen to the Supreme Court, was resolved in September 2009 when the switch was made. The economy is based mostly on fishing, agriculture, and tourism. Remittances from Samoans working abroad account for about 24 percent of national income.

Country's Score Over Time

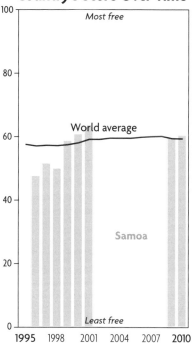

Quick Facts

Population: 0.2 million

GDP (PPP): $0.8 billion
—3.4% growth in 2008
4.6% 5-year compound annual growth
$4,485 per capita

Unemployment: n/a

Inflation (CPI): 7.1%

FDI Inflow: $6 million

2008 data unless otherwise noted
Data compiled as of September 2009

How Do We Measure Economic Freedom?
See page 457 for an explanation of the methodology or visit the *Index* Web site at *heritage.org/index.*

SAMOA'S TEN ECONOMIC FREEDOMS

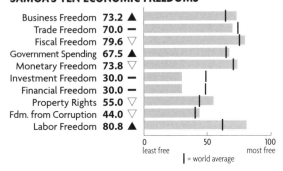

Business Freedom	73.2 ▲
Trade Freedom	70.0 —
Fiscal Freedom	79.6 ▽
Government Spending	67.5 ▲
Monetary Freedom	73.8 ▽
Investment Freedom	30.0 —
Financial Freedom	30.0 —
Property Rights	55.0 ▽
Fdm. from Corruption	44.0 ▽
Labor Freedom	80.8 ▲

0 least free — 50 — 100 most free
| = world average

BUSINESS FREEDOM — 73.2

The overall freedom to start, operate, and close a business is relatively well protected under Samoa's regulatory environment. Starting a business takes nine days, compared to the world average of 35 days. Obtaining a business license requires less than the world average of 218 days. Closing a business, however, is a lengthy and costly process.

TRADE FREEDOM — 70

Samoa's weighted average tariff rate was 10 percent in 2007. Some high tariffs, import restrictions, import taxes, import licensing and permit requirements, restrictive sanitary and phytosanitary measures, export-promotion schemes, and limitations in regulatory and trade capacity add to the cost of trade. Ten points were deducted from Samoa's trade freedom score to account for non-tariff barriers.

FISCAL FREEDOM — 79.6

Samoa's taxes are moderate. The top income and corporate tax rates are 27 percent. Other taxes include a recently increased value-added tax (VAT) and excise taxes. In the most recent year, overall tax revenue as a percentage of GDP was 24.1 percent.

GOVERNMENT SPENDING — 67.5

Total government expenditures, including consumption and transfer payments, are moderate. In the most recent year, government spending equaled 32.9 percent of GDP. Weak revenues and increased public spending have resulted in a poor fiscal position, and the government is grappling with spending prioritization as the deficit widens. Samoa is heavily reliant on development assistance.

MONETARY FREEDOM — 73.8

Inflation has been moderately high, averaging 6.5 percent between 2006 and 2008. The central bank maintains an exchange rate peg based on a basket of the currencies of Samoa's six main trading partners. The basket peg has kept the inflation rate relatively stable. Ten points were deducted from Samoa's monetary freedom score to adjust for measures that distort domestic prices.

INVESTMENT FREEDOM — 30

Foreign investment is generally welcome, but certain sectors of the economy are reserved for Samoan citizens. Investment is screened and subject to government approval. Underdeveloped private markets, non-transparent regulation, cumbersome and burdensome bureaucracy, difficulty in obtaining work permits for foreign labor, and inadequate infrastructure deter investment. Foreign exchange and capital transactions are subject to some restrictions and controls. Land ownership is restricted, and leases can be difficult to obtain.

FINANCIAL FREEDOM — 30

Samoa's small and underdeveloped financial sector is dominated by banking. Bank lending to the private sector has increased rapidly from 35 percent of GDP in 2004 to over 40 percent of GDP in recent years. Four commercial banks, two of which are foreign-owned, account for about 50 percent of total banking-sector assets. The offshore financial sector, first launched about two decades ago, plays an increasingly important role as a source of foreign exchange earnings, though it is still a minor contributor compared to remittances and tourism. A significant portion of the population remains outside the formal banking sector, and limited access to banking and financial services is a barrier to entrepreneurial activity. Reflecting the lack of financial efficiency and depth in Samoa, capital markets are poorly developed.

PROPERTY RIGHTS — 55

More than 80 percent of the land in Samoa is owned by extended families represented by their chiefs. Such land cannot be sold, and leases, even though legally possible, are difficult and expensive to arrange. These customary practices are seen as a major impediment to further tourism development and intensive agriculture. Samoa's efficient legal system is based on British common law. The judiciary is independent and conducts generally fair public trials.

FREEDOM FROM CORRUPTION — 44

Corruption is perceived as present. Samoa ranks 62nd out of 179 countries in Transparency International's Corruption Perceptions Index for 2008. The law provides criminal penalties for official corruption, and the government generally implements the law effectively. Penalties range from several months to several years of imprisonment if convicted. There have been isolated reports of government corruption, and the government bans reporting by the media on corruption cases.

LABOR FREEDOM — 80.8

Samoa's labor regulations are relatively flexible. The non-salary cost of employing a worker is moderate, and dismissing an employee is relatively easy. However, the formal labor market is not fully developed.

SÃO TOMÉ AND PRÍNCIPE

◆ São Tomé

World Rank: 149   **Regional Rank: 30**

Economic Freedom Score

25   50   75

Least free 0   100 Most free

48.8

São Tomé and Príncipe's economic freedom score is 48.8, making its economy the 149th freest in the 2010 *Index*. Its score has increased by 5.0 points from last year, reflecting notable improvements in trade freedom, fiscal freedom, government spending, and investment freedom. São Tomé and Principe is ranked 30th out of 46 countries in the Sub-Saharan Africa region, and its overall score remains below the world average.

São Tomé and Príncipe's economy has a narrow productive base and poor regulatory and legal frameworks. Heavy public debt and the large presence of the government in the economy have tended to crowd out private investment. The overall institutional environment, characterized by onerous bureaucracy, is not conducive to private-sector development. Corruption is considered pervasive.

In recent years, however, a number of reforms have been implemented. The corporate tax rate has been significantly reduced, and some progress has been made in achieving sounder management of public finance. The country's trade and investment regime has become more open and liberal, albeit at a slow pace. Through implementation of these reforms, São Tomé and Príncipe has achieved the second highest gain in economic freedom of any economy ranked in the 2010 *Index*.

BACKGROUND: The population of São Tomé and Príncipe, a two-island republic in the Gulf of Guinea, is heavily concentrated on São Tomé. International mediation in 2003 restored democratic governance after a week-long military coup. President Fradique de Menezes, first elected in 2001, was re-elected in 2006. Plantation agriculture, particularly cocoa and coffee, dominates the economy, although only about 15 percent of the workforce is engaged in agricultural activity. Cocoa represented 66 percent of exports in 2006. Offshore oil fields that São Tomé and Príncipe shares with Nigeria are thought to hold billions of barrels of oil but have not yet been exploited.

Country's Score Over Time

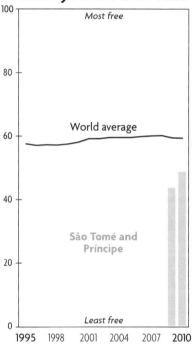

Most free

World average

São Tomé and Príncipe

Least free

1995 1998 2001 2004 2007 2010

Quick Facts

Population: 0.2 million

GDP (PPP): $0.3 billion
5.8% growth in 2008
6.0% 5-year compound annual growth
$1,738 per capita

Unemployment: n/a

Inflation (CPI): 26.1%

FDI Inflow: $33 million

2008 data unless otherwise noted
Data compiled as of September 2009

How Do We Measure Economic Freedom?
See page 457 for an explanation of the methodology or visit the *Index* Web site at *heritage.org/index*.

SÃO TOMÉ AND PRÍNCIPE'S TEN ECONOMIC FREEDOMS

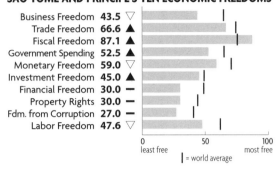

Business Freedom **43.5** ▽
Trade Freedom **66.6** ▲
Fiscal Freedom **87.1** ▲
Government Spending **52.5** ▲
Monetary Freedom **59.0** ▽
Investment Freedom **45.0** ▲
Financial Freedom **30.0** —
Property Rights **30.0** —
Fdm. from Corruption **27.0** —
Labor Freedom **47.6** ▽

0   50   100
least free   most free
| = world average

INVESTMENT FREEDOM — 45

Foreign and domestic firms are treated equally under the law, and nearly all sectors of the economy are open to some degree to foreign investment. Investment-related laws and regulations can be burdensome, and bureaucracy can be cumbersome and prone to corruption. Other deterrents to investment include lax regulatory enforcement, inadequate infrastructure, underdeveloped markets, security concerns, and political unrest. Foreign exchange and capital transactions are subject to some restrictions, approvals, and controls.

BUSINESS FREEDOM — 43.5

The overall freedom to start, operate, and close a business is constrained under São Tomé and Príncipe's regulatory environment. Starting a business takes an average of 144 days, compared to the world average of 35 days. The entry cost of launching a business is also high. Obtaining a business license takes more than the world average of 218 days.

TRADE FREEDOM — 66.6

São Tomé and Príncipe's weighted average tariff rate was 11.7 percent in 2007. Some high tariffs, services market access barriers, import restrictions, import taxes and fees, and limitations on regulatory and trade capacity add to the cost of trade. Ten points were deducted from São Tomé and Príncipe's trade freedom score to account for non-tariff barriers.

FISCAL FREEDOM — 87.1

São Tomé and Príncipe has implemented a significant tax reform package. A new tiered income tax scheme subjects five income brackets to rates ranging from 0 percent to a top rate of 20 percent. The top corporate tax was lowered to 25 percent from 45 percent. Taxpayer understanding of the changes is poor, and tax revenue could suffer in the coming year as a result. The reforms should boost compliance over time. In the most recent year, overall tax revenue as a percentage of GDP was 16.3 percent.

GOVERNMENT SPENDING — 52.5

Total government expenditures, including consumption and transfer payments, are relatively high. In the most recent year, government spending equaled 39.8 percent of GDP. Despite some improvements in recent years, poor control of public expenditures threatens fiscal stability. Transportation and telecommunication infrastructure is at least partially privatized (jointly held by the state and private entities), mostly as a result of the failures of national companies.

MONETARY FREEDOM — 59

Inflation has been extremely high, averaging 23.9 percent between 2006 and 2008. Ten points were deducted from São Tomé and Príncipe's monetary freedom score to adjust for measures that distort domestic prices.

FINANCIAL FREEDOM — 30

São Tomé and Príncipe's small and underdeveloped financial system is supervised by the central bank. Heavy external debt amounting to over 100 percent of GDP puts considerable pressure on the financial system. A large portion of the population lacks access to formal banking services. Although it is still dominated by one foreign government-owned bank, the banking system has undergone significant development in recent years as more private commercial banks have entered the sector. There are eight commercial banks, and the foreign presence in their ownership and management is considerable. In July 2007, an African banking group, Ecobank, also opened its first branch in São Tomé and Príncipe. Overall, domestic credit to the private sector remains limited and expensive, although it is available to both foreign and local investors without discrimination.

PROPERTY RIGHTS — 30

São Tomé and Príncipe's legal system is weak and subject to corruption. There is no separate commercial court system, and backlogs of civil cases cause long delays. International donor assistance projects aim to improve the judiciary by training staff and expanding physical capacity.

FREEDOM FROM CORRUPTION — 27

Corruption is perceived as widespread. São Tomé and Príncipe ranks 121st out of 179 countries in Transparency International's Corruption Perceptions Index for 2008. Corruption has been increasing and can involve bribery, embezzlement, and mismanagement of public funds. Analysts attribute the recent rise in corruption to low wages for government workers and officials, the absence of appropriate regulations, and the lack of strong leadership. Signs of corruption are particularly obvious during election campaigns, when voters receive money to favor certain candidates or political parties.

LABOR FREEDOM — 47.6

São Tomé and Príncipe's labor regulations are inflexible. The non-salary cost of employing a worker is high, and dismissing an employee is relatively costly.

SAUDI ARABIA

Economic Freedom Score

25 50 75

Least free 0   100 Most free

64.1

| World Rank: **65** | Regional Rank: **8** |

S audi Arabia's economic freedom score is 64.1, making its economy the 65th freest in the 2010 *Index*. Its score is 0.2 point lower than last year, reflecting modest declines in three of the 10 economic freedoms. Saudi Arabia is ranked 8th out of 17 countries in the Middle East/North Africa region, and its overall score is above the world average.

The Saudi Arabian economy performs well in trade freedom, fiscal freedom, and business freedom. The overall regulatory environment for business formation has become more streamlined and efficient. The tax regime is competitive, and the overall tax burden is low. Overall economic growth has slowed in recent years, but the impact of the recent global financial crisis on the banking sector has been relatively modest.

Saudi Arabia remains weak in monetary freedom, investment freedom, property rights, and freedom from corruption. The legal system remains vulnerable to political influence. Investment freedom is hampered by bureaucracy and a lack of transparency. Monetary stability is weak and continues to be adversely affected by lingering price controls.

BACKGROUND: Saudi Arabia, the largest Persian Gulf oil kingdom, has been ruled as an absolute monarchy by the Saud dynasty since 1932. It has roughly one-quarter of the world's oil reserves and, as the leading oil producer and exporter, plays a dominant role in the Organization of Petroleum Exporting Countries. Accession to the World Trade Organization in 2005 has led to gradual economic reform, and the government has sought to attract foreign investment and promote diversification. Efforts to integrate Saudi Arabia more fully into the world economy are opposed by Islamist extremists who have targeted Saudi oil facilities and foreign workers for terrorist attacks. In February 2009, King Abdullah, who has ruled since August 2005, reshuffled his cabinet, appointing several moderates (including the first female cabinet member) to important posts.

Country's Score Over Time

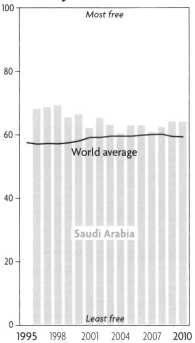

Quick Facts

Population: 24.6 million

GDP (PPP): $589.5 billion
4.2% growth in 2008
4.2% 5-year compound annual growth
$23,920 per capita

Unemployment: 11.8%

Inflation (CPI): 9.9%

FDI Inflow: $38.2 billion

2008 data unless otherwise noted
Data compiled as of September 2009

How Do We Measure Economic Freedom?
See page 457 for an explanation of the methodology or visit the *Index* Web site at *heritage.org/index*.

SAUDI ARABIA'S TEN ECONOMIC FREEDOMS

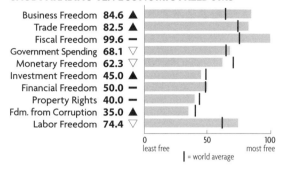

Business Freedom	84.6 ▲	
Trade Freedom	82.5 ▲	
Fiscal Freedom	99.6 —	
Government Spending	68.1 ▽	
Monetary Freedom	62.3 ▽	
Investment Freedom	45.0 ▲	
Financial Freedom	50.0 —	
Property Rights	40.0 —	
Fdm. from Corruption	35.0 ▲	
Labor Freedom	74.4 ▽	

0 least free   50   100 most free

▌ = world average

BUSINESS FREEDOM — 84.6

The overall freedom to start, operate, and close a business is well protected under Saudi Arabia's regulatory environment. Starting a business takes five days, compared to the world average of 35 days. Obtaining a business license takes about half of the world average of 218 days. Bankruptcy proceedings are relatively straightforward.

TRADE FREEDOM — 82.5

Saudi Arabia's weighted average tariff rate was 3.8 percent in 2008. Import bans and restrictions, export controls, services market access barriers, non-transparent and inconsistent standards implementation, domestic bias in government procurement, and weak protection of intellectual property rights add to the cost of trade. Ten points were deducted from Saudi Arabia's trade freedom score to account for non-tariff barriers.

FISCAL FREEDOM — 99.6

Saudi nationals or citizens of the Gulf Cooperation Council and corporations pay a 2.5 percent religious tax mandated by Islamic law rather than traditional income or corporate taxes. Foreign citizens are subject to a flat 20 percent income tax. Special tax regimes apply to natural gas and oil production. In the most recent year, overall tax revenue as a percentage of GDP was 5.6 percent.

GOVERNMENT SPENDING — 68.1

Total government expenditures, including consumption and transfer payments, are moderate. In the most recent year, government spending equaled 32.6 percent of GDP. State participation in the economy remains substantial. The state-owned mining company was privatized in 2008, and authorities are working to prepare the national airline for partial privatization.

MONETARY FREEDOM — 62.3

Inflation has been moderately high, averaging 7.8 percent between 2006 and 2008. The government influences prices through regulation, extensive subsidies, and state-owned enterprises and utilities. Twenty points were deducted from Saudi Arabia's monetary freedom score to account for policies that distort domestic prices.

INVESTMENT FREEDOM — 45

Foreign investment is generally welcome, but foreign investors must take local partners in certain sectors. All for-eign investors must be licensed by the General Investment Authority, and licenses for other projects may be required. Foreign investment is prohibited in 16 manufacturing and service sectors and sub-sectors. Dispute resolution is cumbersome, local hiring requirements are burdensome, and the licensing process is time-consuming. Residents may hold foreign exchange accounts; approval is required for non-residents. There are no controls or restrictions on foreign exchange transactions or capital payments and transfers. Foreign investors may acquire land for business use.

FINANCIAL FREEDOM — 50

Saudi Arabia's financial system has undergone gradual modernization and transformation. Regulatory, supervisory, and accounting standards are generally consistent with international norms. Foreign ownership of financial institutions is limited but growing. The government has eased licensing requirements for foreign investment in financial services and has raised the foreign equity ceiling in financial institutions to 60 percent. The government retains majority shares in the country's largest bank, the National Commercial Bank; holds minority shares in other domestically incorporated banks; and offers subsidized credit to preferred sectors. All insurance companies must be locally registered and must operate according to the cooperative insurance principle. Insurance has undergone some liberalization to allow greater competition from foreign insurers. Capital markets are relatively well developed, and the stock exchange is the region's largest.

PROPERTY RIGHTS — 40

Saudi courts do not necessarily enforce contracts efficiently. The court system is slow, non-transparent, and influenced by the ruling elite. Laws protecting intellectual property rights are being revised to comply with the WTO's Trade-Related Aspects of Intellectual Property Rights (TRIPS) agreement, but enforcement is weak and procedures are inconsistent. The International Intellectual Property Alliance announced in February 2009 that Saudi Arabia had the highest piracy levels of any country in the Gulf region. Legal and societal barriers constrain women from asserting their limited property rights.

FREEDOM FROM CORRUPTION — 35

Corruption is perceived as significant. Saudi Arabia ranks 80th out of 179 countries in Transparency International's Corruption Perceptions Index for 2008. The absence of transparency in government accounts and decision-making encourages a perception of corruption on the part of some members of the royal family and in the executive branch. Government procurement is an area of concern. Bribes, often disguised as "commissions," are reportedly commonplace.

LABOR FREEDOM — 74.4

Saudi Arabia's labor regulations are relatively flexible. The non-salary cost of employing a worker is low, and dismissing an employee is not burdensome. Regulations on work hours are relatively flexible.

SENEGAL

Economic Freedom Score

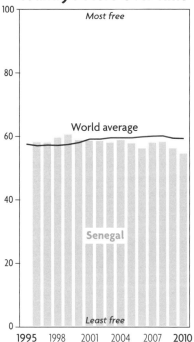

Least free 0 | 25 | 50 | 75 | 100 Most free

54.6

S enegal's economic freedom score is 54.6, making its economy the 119th freest in the 2010 *Index*. Its score has decreased by 1.7 points since last year, reflecting lowered scores in eight of the 10 economic freedoms, including freedom from corruption and property rights. Senegal is ranked 21st out of 46 countries in the Sub-Saharan Africa region, and its economic freedom score is below the world average.

Potential entrepreneurs confront a number of institutional challenges to economic freedom in Senegal. The overall regulatory and legal framework remains weak and is not conducive to developing a more dynamic private sector. The presence of the state in the economy is still considerable, despite major public-sector reforms since the early 2000s.

Senegal's investment regulations do not discriminate against foreign investors, but the regulatory environment can be burdensome for any investor. The financial sector is underdeveloped, and microfinance is playing an increasing role in providing access to credit. The inefficient judicial system lacks independence from the executive branch and remains vulnerable to corruption and bureaucracy.

BACKGROUND: Senegal became independent in 1960 and is one of the few African countries never to have experienced a coup. President Abdoulaye Wade, the first non-socialist to govern the country, was elected in 2000 and re-elected in 2007. Peace in the southern Casamance region has progressed fitfully since a 2004 accord between the government and rebel leaders, but sporadic fighting continues. Senegal serves as a regional gateway and business center and completely surrounds The Gambia. It has an arid climate in the North and a moist, tropical climate in the South. Agriculture and fishing occupy a majority of the population. Informal employment is common in both urban and rural areas. Senegal depends heavily on foreign assistance, which comprised over 20 percent of government spending in 2007.

Country's Score Over Time

Most free

World average

Senegal

Least free

1995 1998 2001 2004 2007 2010

Quick Facts

Population: 12.2 million

GDP (PPP): $21.6 billion
2.5% growth in 2008
3.8% 5-year compound annual growth
$1,772 per capita

Unemployment: 48.0% (2007)

Inflation (CPI): 5.8%

FDI Inflow: $706 million

2008 data unless otherwise noted
Data compiled as of September 2009

How Do We Measure Economic Freedom?
See page 457 for an explanation of the methodology or visit the *Index* Web site at *heritage.org/index*.

SENEGAL'S TEN ECONOMIC FREEDOMS

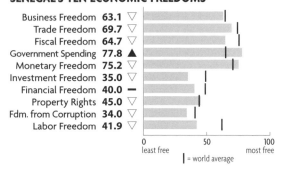

Business Freedom	63.1 ▽	
Trade Freedom	69.7 ▽	
Fiscal Freedom	64.7 ▽	
Government Spending	77.8 ▲	
Monetary Freedom	75.2 ▽	
Investment Freedom	35.0 ▽	
Financial Freedom	40.0 —	
Property Rights	45.0 ▽	
Fdm. from Corruption	34.0 ▽	
Labor Freedom	41.9 ▽	

0 least free   50   100 most free
| = world average

BUSINESS FREEDOM — 63.1

The overall freedom to start, operate, and close a business remains somewhat limited under Senegal's regulatory environment. Starting a business takes eight days, compared to the world average of 35 days. The entry cost of launching a business is high. Obtaining a business license takes about the world average of 18 procedures and 218 days.

TRADE FREEDOM — 69.7

Senegal's weighted average tariff rate was 10.1 percent in 2008. Import taxes and fees, non-transparent government procurement, inconsistent customs implementation, state import monopolies, weak enforcement of intellectual property rights, and corruption add to the cost of trade. Ten points were deducted from Senegal's trade freedom score to account for non-tariff barriers.

FISCAL FREEDOM — 64.7

Senegal has high income tax rates but moderate corporate tax rates. The top income tax rate is 50 percent, and the top corporate tax rate is 25 percent. Other taxes include a value-added tax (VAT) and a vehicle tax. In the most recent year, overall tax revenue as a percentage of GDP was 20.1 percent.

GOVERNMENT SPENDING — 77.8

Total government expenditures, including consumption and transfer payments, are relatively low. In the most recent year, government spending equaled 27.2 percent of GDP. The government has fully or partially privatized large state-owned enterprises, and food subsidies were suspended in 2009.

MONETARY FREEDOM — 75.2

Inflation has been moderate, averaging 5.5 percent between 2006 and 2008. Many prices are freely determined, but the government controls the prices of pharmaceuticals and medical services and influences prices across the economy through state-owned enterprises and utilities. Ten points were deducted from Senegal's monetary freedom score to account for policies that distort domestic prices.

INVESTMENT FREEDOM — 35

There is no legal discrimination against foreign investors, and 100 percent foreign ownership of businesses is permitted except in electricity, telecommunications, mining, and water. The government screens some proposed invest-

ments, mostly to verify compatibility with overall development goals. Businesses must be licensed and may need additional government approvals. Investment-related laws and regulations can be burdensome, and bureaucracy is cumbersome, non-transparent, and prone to corruption. Contract enforcement and dispute resolution can be arbitrary and non-transparent. Residents and non-residents may hold foreign exchange accounts. Foreign exchange transactions and capital transfers may be subject to restrictions, controls, and authorization.

FINANCIAL FREEDOM — 40

Senegal's financial system remains underdeveloped. Banking remains highly concentrated, with three banks holding two-thirds of deposits. Government ownership of banks has declined, and bank supervision has been strengthened. The government retains its shares in seven banks, including a majority share in the agricultural bank. Senegal is a member of the West African Economic and Monetary Union, and the Central Bank of West African States governs Senegal's financial institutions. The foreign presence is substantial, and branches and subsidiaries of foreign or regional banks play a relatively important role in financial intermediation. However, most lending is carried out with only a few borrowers, and most services are concentrated in the capital. The number of microfinance institutions, which provide financial services to small and medium-size companies, has grown.

PROPERTY RIGHTS — 45

The administration of property title and land registration procedures is uneven outside of urban areas. The government streamlined procedures for registering property and reduced associated costs in 2008 so that property can be registered within 18 days. The housing finance market is underdeveloped, and few long-term mortgage financing vehicles exist. Senegal lacks commercial courts staffed with trained judges, so decisions can be arbitrary and inconsistent. Despite an adequate legal and regulatory framework, enforcement of intellectual property rights is weak.

FREEDOM FROM CORRUPTION — 34

Corruption is perceived as significant. Senegal ranks 85th out of 179 countries in Transparency International's Corruption Perceptions Index for 2008. Corruption is an important obstacle to economic development and competitiveness. There are credible allegations of corruption in government procurement, dispute settlement, and regulatory and enforcement agencies. President Wade has made numerous pronouncements against corruption, but a significant gap persists between the rhetoric and its implementation. A new procurement code established in 2008 should reduce the number of projects that are sole-sourced or that receive exemptions from international tender procedures.

LABOR FREEDOM — 41.9

Senegal's labor regulations are restrictive. The non-salary cost of employing a worker is high, and dismissing an employee can be burdensome. Regulations on work hours are rigid.

SERBIA

Economic Freedom Score

Least free 0   25   50   75   100 Most free

56.9

Serbia's economic freedom score is 56.9, making its economy the 104th freest in the 2010 *Index*. Its score has increased by 0.3 point since last year, reflecting modest improvements in three of the 10 economic freedoms. Serbia is ranked 38th out of 43 countries in the Europe region, and its overall score is below the world average.

Structural reforms have helped Serbia to achieve macroeconomic stability and average annual growth of over 5 percent over the past five years. Individual and corporate income tax rates are competitively low, and business formation procedures have been made more efficient. The labor market is relatively flexible.

Large-scale privatization has proceeded slowly, and many state-owned assets remain unsold. Trade freedom is above the world average, but tariffs are higher than in most other European countries. Government expenditures are over 40 percent of GDP, and inconsistent rules and non-transparent regulations continue to hamper growth. Further reforms are needed to tackle bureaucracy, reduce corruption, and reform a weak judicial system that is vulnerable to political interference.

BACKGROUND: Following Montenegro's secession in May 2006, the National Assembly of Serbia declared Serbia the successor to the State Union of Serbia and Montenegro. Serbia began negotiations for a Stability and Association Agreement with the European Union in October 2005. Euro–Atlantic integration remains an aim of the government led by pro-Western President Boris Tadic. International confidence in Serbia grew following the arrest of wartime leader Radovan Karadzic, although Ratko Mladic remains at large, causing a significant roadblock to further EU negotiations. Following the failure of U.N.-sponsored talks on the status of Kosovo, the former province formally declared its independence on February 17, 2008. Serbia continues to maintain that this is illegal, and the issue has been referred to the International Court of Justice for an advisory opinion.

Country's Score Over Time

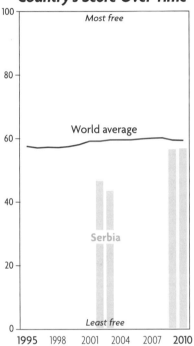

Quick Facts

Population: 7.4 million

GDP (PPP): $84.2 billion
5.6% growth in 2008
5.8% 5-year compound
annual growth
$11,456 per capita

Unemployment: 18.8% (2007)

Inflation (CPI): 11.7%

FDI Inflow: $3.1 billion

2008 data unless otherwise noted
Data compiled as of September 2009

How Do We Measure Economic Freedom?
See page 457 for an explanation of the methodology or visit the *Index* Web site at *heritage.org/index.*

SERBIA'S TEN ECONOMIC FREEDOMS

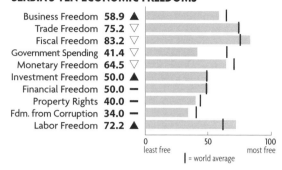

Business Freedom	58.9 ▲	
Trade Freedom	75.2 ▽	
Fiscal Freedom	83.2 ▽	
Government Spending	41.4 ▽	
Monetary Freedom	64.5 ▽	
Investment Freedom	50.0 ▲	
Financial Freedom	50.0 —	
Property Rights	40.0 —	
Fdm. from Corruption	34.0 —	
Labor Freedom	72.2 ▲	

0 least free   50   100 most free
| = world average

BUSINESS FREEDOM — 58.9

Overall business freedom remains constrained under Serbia's burdensome regulatory environment. Starting a business takes an average of 13 days, compared to the world average of 35 days. Obtaining a business license takes more than the world average of 18 procedures and 218 days, and costs are high. Enforcement of regulations can be inconsistent and non-transparent.

TRADE FREEDOM — 75.2

Serbia's simple average tariff rate was 7.4 percent in 2007. Some high tariffs, import restrictions and bans, import licensing and permits, non-transparent regulations and government procurement, and corruption add to the cost of trade. Ten points were deducted from Serbia's trade freedom score to account for non-tariff barriers.

FISCAL FREEDOM — 83.2

Serbia has competitive tax rates for individual and corporate income. The top individual income tax rate is 15 percent. Salaries are taxed at 12 percent, and other personal income (royalties, investment, and rent) can be taxed at up to 20 percent. The corporate tax rate is a flat 10 percent. Other taxes include a value-added tax (VAT), a property tax, and an inheritance tax. Excise taxes on tobacco and alcohol were increased in January 2009. In the most recent year, overall tax revenue as a percentage of GDP was 36.8 percent.

GOVERNMENT SPENDING — 41.4

Total government expenditures, including consumption and transfer payments, are high. In the most recent year, government spending was estimated to equal about 44.2 percent of GDP. The government plans to accelerate privatization of the national airline and telecommunications enterprises.

MONETARY FREEDOM — 64.5

Inflation has been high, averaging 10.5 percent between 2006 and 2008. The government can control the prices of certain basic products, including milk, bread, flour, and cooking oil; controls the prices of utilities, public transit, telecommunications services, and petroleum; and influences prices through numerous state-owned enterprises. Fifteen points were deducted from Serbia's monetary freedom score to account for policies that distort domestic prices.

INVESTMENT FREEDOM — 50

Serbian law provides for national treatment of foreign capital, and investment is not screened. Most sectors are open to foreign investment. Reforms have improved the investment environment, but ineffective competition policy, regulatory uncertainty, inadequate bureaucratic capacity, small private markets, and corruption are impediments. Residents and non-residents may hold foreign exchange accounts, subject to conditions. Payments, capital transactions, and transfers are subject to restrictions. Foreign and domestic entities may own real estate, and foreign investors may acquire concession rights on natural resources.

FINANCIAL FREEDOM — 50

Aggressive consolidation and privatization by the central bank since 2001 have helped to revive Serbia's banking sector, which now accounts for about 90 percent of financial-sector assets. The number of banks has plummeted as a result of the restructuring. There are now 34 banks, with 18 foreign banks accounting for more than 70 percent of the market. A wide range of credit instruments is available to the private sector, but the level of financial intermediation is relatively low. The insurance sector is dominated by state-owned insurers, although the government has announced its intention to privatize in this area. Capital markets are small but vigorous.

PROPERTY RIGHTS — 40

The Republic of Serbia's constitution creates an independent judiciary, but the system is corrupt and inefficient. Judges are poorly trained, underpaid, and difficult to dismiss for incompetence. Approximately 60 percent of all immovable property has been registered under an ongoing project. A register of movable goods has existed since 2005. Serbia now allows banks to issue mortgages on buildings that are under construction. The legal regime for protection of intellectual property rights has improved substantially, but enforcement is still insufficient.

FREEDOM FROM CORRUPTION — 34

Corruption is perceived as widespread. Serbia ranks 85th out of 179 countries in Transparency International's Corruption Perceptions Index for 2008. The authorities are inconsistent in condemning official corruption, and investigations are often politically motivated. Demands for bribes are expected at all stages of a business transaction. Organized criminal groups engage in money laundering. The Serbian Parliament has approved the creation of an Anti-Corruption Agency, which is scheduled to become fully operational in January 2010.

LABOR FREEDOM — 72.2

Serbia's labor regulations are relatively flexible. The non-salary cost of employing a worker is moderate, and dismissing an employee is not costly. Regulations on work hours are fairly flexible.

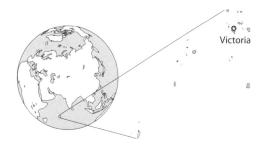

Victoria

SEYCHELLES

Economic Freedom Score

25   50   75

Least free   0   100   Most free

47.9

World Rank: **156**	Regional Rank: **35**

S eychelles' economic freedom score is 47.9, making its economy the 156th freest in the 2010 *Index*. Its score is almost unchanged from last year, with a severe decline in monetary freedom offsetting modest improvements in five of the 10 economic freedoms. Seychelles is ranked 35th among 46 countries in the Sub-Saharan Africa region, and its overall score is below the world average.

The Seychelles economy, with its services sector accounting for around 80 percent of GDP, was hit hard by the global economic slowdown. The impact was particularly severe on the tourism industry. The rate of growth has deteriorated, and public debt has risen to a level of over 150 percent of GDP.

Seychelles' entrepreneurial environment is challenging, characterized by an inefficient regulatory framework, poor access to financing, and the pervasive presence of the state in the economy. The inefficient public sector accounts for 40 percent of total employment. Trade and monetary freedom are undermined by distortions in prices, exchange rates, and interest rates.

BACKGROUND: The Seychelles People's Progressive Front has been the ruling party since 1977, when France Albert René seized power in a bloodless coup. After fending off several attempted coups, René ceded power to Vice President James Michel in 2004. Multi-party elections have proceeded smoothly since 1993, and Michel won election in his own right in 2006. The economy of the Seychelles, an archipelago in the Indian Ocean, relies heavily on tourism and fishing, and both industries are threatened by Somali piracy. Though per capita income is among the highest in the region, the economy's small size makes it vulnerable to external shocks. The government defaulted on its external debt in 2008, appealed to donors for debt relief, and entered into a comprehensive economic restructuring program under International Monetary Fund oversight.

Country's Score Over Time

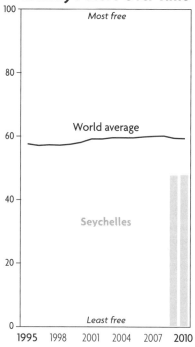

100 Most free

80

World average

60

40 Seychelles

20

0 Least free

1995 1998 2001 2004 2007 **2010**

Quick Facts

Population: 86,300

GDP (PPP): $1.9 billion
2.8% growth in 2008
5.7% 5-year compound annual growth
$21,530 per capita

Unemployment: 2.0% (2006)

Inflation (CPI): 37%

FDI Inflow: $364 million

2008 data unless otherwise noted
Data compiled as of September 2009

How Do We Measure Economic Freedom?
See page 457 for an explanation of the methodology or visit the *Index* Web site at *heritage.org/index*.

SEYCHELLES' TEN ECONOMIC FREEDOMS

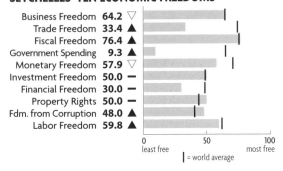

Business Freedom	64.2 ▽	
Trade Freedom	33.4 ▲	
Fiscal Freedom	76.4 ▲	
Government Spending	9.3 ▲	
Monetary Freedom	57.9 ▽	
Investment Freedom	50.0 —	
Financial Freedom	30.0 —	
Property Rights	50.0 —	
Fdm. from Corruption	48.0 ▲	
Labor Freedom	59.8 ▲	

0 least free   50   100 most free

| = world average

BUSINESS FREEDOM — *64.2*

The overall freedom to start, operate, and close a business is somewhat limited under Seychelles' regulatory environment. Starting a business takes about the world average of 35 days. Obtaining a business license requires less than the world average of 18 procedures and 218 days.

TRADE FREEDOM — *33.4*

Seychelles' weighted average tariff rate was 28.3 percent in 2007. The government is liberalizing its trade regime, but some high tariffs, import restrictions, import and export permit requirements, state import and export monopolies, burdensome and non-transparent regulations and standards, and inefficient and inconsistent customs administration add to the cost of trade. Ten points were deducted from Seychelles' trade freedom score to account for non-tariff barriers.

FISCAL FREEDOM — *76.4*

Seychelles' corporate tax rate is high, but there is no individual income tax. The top corporate tax rate is 40 percent. Other taxes include a goods and services tax (GST) and a vehicle tax. In the most recent year, overall tax revenue as a percentage of GDP was 27.6 percent. Progress in streamlining tax administration and broadening the tax base has been slow.

GOVERNMENT SPENDING — *9.3*

Total government expenditures, including consumption and transfer payments, are very high as a result of expenditures linked to recovery from the 2004 tsunami. In the most recent year, government spending equaled 55.0 percent of GDP. Privatization has been slow, but four state-owned enterprises were slated for privatization in 2009.

MONETARY FREEDOM — *57.9*

Inflation has been extremely high, averaging 25.7 percent between 2006 and 2008. Government mismanagement and excessive economic regulations, including a manipulated exchange rate, have resulted in foreign exchange shortages and a black-market currency exchange rate that is double the official rate. Ten points were deducted from Seychelles'

monetary freedom score to adjust for measures that distort domestic prices.

INVESTMENT FREEDOM — *50*

Although the government recognizes the need to reform Seychelles' investment environment, regulation and bureaucracy can be non-transparent and burdensome. Other deterrents to investment include inadequate infrastructure and underdeveloped private markets. Foreign workers may be employed only if no suitably qualified domestic labor is available. Foreign exchange and capital transactions are subject to restrictions and controls. Foreign investors may purchase land with approval from the government.

FINANCIAL FREEDOM — *30*

Seychelles' underdeveloped financial system remains weak. The banking sector consists of both state-owned and foreign financial institutions. The Seychelles Savings Bank is fully state-owned, and the state also has a majority stake in another commercial bank. The Development Bank of Seychelles is 55.5 percent controlled by the government. There are four other commercial banks in Seychelles, three of which are branches of foreign banks. There has been a delay in the government's plan to privatize the state-owned banks. A large part of the population lacks access to banking services, and limited lending to the private sector retards business development. The government recently implemented the Central Bank of Seychelles Act and the Financial Institutions Act to create a more independent central bank and strengthen the country's financial regulatory framework.

PROPERTY RIGHTS — *50*

Seychelles' judicial system is inefficient and subject to executive influence. Civil court cases take years to resolve. Changes in the law on property ownership were made recently, offering freehold title and residency rights to foreign owners and their immediate families in a bid to open the islands to more foreign investment.

FREEDOM FROM CORRUPTION — *48*

Corruption is perceived as widespread and as affecting all levels of government. Seychelles ranks 55th out of 179 countries in Transparency International's Corruption Perceptions Index for 2008. There are reports of rewards by the government to supporters of the ruling political party in the form of job assistance, land distribution, free building materials, and monetary payments.

LABOR FREEDOM — *59.8*

Seychelles' labor regulations are relatively inflexible. The non-salary cost of employing a worker is high, and dismissing an employee is relatively costly. The formal labor market is not fully developed.

SIERRA LEONE

World Rank: 157   **Regional Rank: 36**

Economic Freedom Score

25   50   75

Least free 0   100 Most free

47.9

Sierra Leone's economic freedom score is 47.9, making its economy the 157th freest in the 2010 *Index*. Its score remains almost the same as last year. Sierra Leone is ranked 36th out of 46 countries in the Sub-Saharan Africa region, and its overall score is below the global average.

Sierra Leone is still reconstructing in the aftermath of a decade-long civil conflict. Economic growth has been averaging about 6 percent over the past five years, but the challenges to maintaining growth momentum are considerable. The overall environment is not conducive to entrepreneurial activity, and the private sector faces significant constraints.

Mismanagement in public spending remains a serious problem and ultimately hurts implementation of necessary reforms. The protection of property rights is weak, and the judicial system lacks both independence and transparency. Legal proceedings are vulnerable to political interference and commonly subject to pervasive corruption. High tariffs and non-tariff barriers hinder trade.

BACKGROUND: Sierra Leone's civil war, which seriously damaged the country's infrastructure and economy, ended in 2002 with the help of African, British, and U.N. peacekeepers, but recovery has been fragile, the infrastructure remains deficient, and the people are still very poor. Ahmad Tejan Kabbah, elected president in 1996, was ousted in a coup, reinstated by Nigerian-led forces in 1998, and re-elected in 2002. Opposition candidate Ernest Bai Koroma was elected president in 2007 in the first peaceful transition of power from one party to another since Sierra Leone achieved its independence. Industry (primarily mining) accounted for about 25 percent of GDP in 2007. Diamonds are the primary export. Two-thirds of the population depends on subsistence agriculture, and agriculture accounted for an estimated 46 percent of the economy in 2007.

Country's Score Over Time

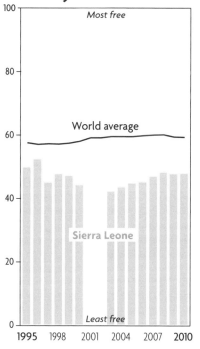

Quick Facts

Population: 5.6 million

GDP (PPP): $4.3 billion
5.1% growth in 2007
6.6% 5-year compound
annual growth
$766 per capita

Unemployment: n/a

Inflation (CPI): 14.8%

FDI Inflow: $30 million

2008 data unless otherwise noted
Data compiled as of September 2009

How Do We Measure Economic Freedom?
See page 457 for an explanation of the methodology or visit the *Index* Web site at *heritage.org/index*.

SIERRA LEONE'S TEN ECONOMIC FREEDOMS

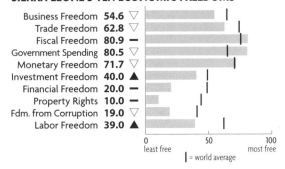

Business Freedom	54.6 ▽	
Trade Freedom	62.8 ▽	
Fiscal Freedom	80.9 —	
Government Spending	80.5 ▽	
Monetary Freedom	71.7 ▽	
Investment Freedom	40.0 ▲	
Financial Freedom	20.0 —	
Property Rights	10.0 —	
Fdm. from Corruption	19.0 ▽	
Labor Freedom	39.0 ▲	

0 least free   50   100 most free

| = world average

BUSINESS FREEDOM — 54.6

The overall freedom to start, operate, and close a business is restricted under Sierra Leone's regulatory environment. Starting a business takes an average of 12 days, compared to the world average of 35 days. Obtaining a business license takes more than the world average of 18 procedures and 218 days. Bankruptcy proceedings are fairly straightforward but costly.

TRADE FREEDOM — 62.8

Sierra Leone's simple average tariff rate was 13.6 percent in 2007. Liberalization of the trade regime is progressing, but import taxes and fees, non-transparent regulations, inefficient customs implementation and non-transparent customs valuation, inadequate infrastructure, and corruption add to the cost of trade. Ten points were deducted from Sierra Leone's trade freedom score to account for non-tariff barriers.

FISCAL FREEDOM — 80.9

Sierra Leone has moderate tax rates. Both the top income tax rate and the top corporate tax rate are 30 percent. There is also a tax on interest. In the most recent year, overall tax revenue as a percentage of GDP was 10.4 percent.

GOVERNMENT SPENDING — 80.5

Total government expenditures, including consumption and transfer payments, are relatively low. In the most recent year, government spending equaled 25.5 percent of GDP. Measures to widen the tax base and clamp down on expenditures are on the reform agenda, but weak control of public spending management remains a central problem. A goods and services tax (GST) was set to be enacted in September 2009.

MONETARY FREEDOM — 71.7

Inflation has been high, averaging 13.6 percent between 2006 and 2008. Most prices are freely set in the market, but the government influences prices through state-owned enterprises and utilities. Five points were deducted from Sierra Leone's monetary freedom score to account for policies that distort domestic prices.

INVESTMENT FREEDOM — 40

Foreign investment receives national treatment and is not screened, but it is restricted in certain sectors. All investors face licensing requirements and must register with the government. The judicial system is slow and prone to corruption. Weak regulatory enforcement, lack of administrative capacity, restrictive labor rules, licensing, weak contract enforcement, inadequate infrastructure, and corruption also deter investment. Residents and non-residents may hold foreign exchange accounts. Foreign exchange and capital transactions may be subject to some restrictions and certain approval requirements. Foreigners may lease but not own land.

FINANCIAL FREEDOM — 20

Sierra Leone's financial system was undermined by prolonged economic and political instability, and the recovery process has been rather sluggish. The banking sector has gradually expanded, with 13 commercial banks operating in the country. However, government-owned banks still account for a majority of banking assets, and the government's frequent bond auctions tend to crowd out credit to other markets. Non-performing loans have stayed at over 20 percent of total loans in recent years. A considerable portion of the population remains outside the formal banking sector, and scarce access to credit is a major impediment to vibrant business activity. Poor enforcement of contracts discourages lending, and corruption is endemic. A substantial shadow market in U.S. dollars hinders efforts to combat money laundering. The Sierra Leone stock exchange was launched in 2009.

PROPERTY RIGHTS — 10

Property is not secure. There is no land titling system, and judicial corruption is significant. Traditional tribal justice systems continue to serve as a supplement to the central government's judiciary, especially in rural areas. Optical discs and tapes of popular music and films are illegally copied and sold on a substantial scale.

FREEDOM FROM CORRUPTION — 19

Corruption is perceived as pervasive. Sierra Leone ranks 158th out of 179 countries in Transparency International's Corruption Perceptions Index for 2008, a drop from 2007. International companies cite corruption in all branches of government as an obstacle to investment. Bribes, kickbacks, extortion, and skimming on contracts and payments are common forms of corruption.

LABOR FREEDOM — 39

Sierra Leone's labor regulations are inflexible. The nonsalary cost of employing a worker is moderate, but the difficulty of firing workers is a significant disincentive to additional hiring.

SINGAPORE

World Rank: 2   **Regional Rank: 2**

S ingapore's economic freedom score is 86.1, making its economy the 2nd freest in the 2010 *Index*. Its score has declined by one point over the past year, due primarily to lower ratings in monetary freedom and investment freedom. Singapore is ranked 2nd out of 41 countries in the Asia–Pacific region, and its overall score remains significantly higher than the world average.

As a result of the global financial and economic turmoil, Singapore's economic growth has slowed significantly, achieving a rate of only about 1 percent in 2008 compared to an average of around 6 percent annually over the past five years. However, with strong fundamentals in place, the economy is likely to rebound quickly. The financial sector has shown considerable resilience, weathering the financial turmoil relatively well.

Flexibility and openness have been the foundation of Singapore's transformation into one of the most competitive and prosperous economies in the world. An efficient regulatory environment encourages vibrant entrepreneurial activity. Commercial operations are handled with transparency and speed, and corruption is perceived to be almost nonexistent. Singapore's very competitive tax regime and highly flexible labor market encourage investment, attracting global companies and enhancing innovation. Foreign and domestic investors are treated equally, and Singapore's legal system is efficient and highly protective of private property.

BACKGROUND: Singapore is a nominally democratic state that has been ruled by the People's Action Party (PAP) since 1965, when the country became independent. Certain rights, such as freedom of assembly and freedom of speech, remain restricted, but the PAP has also embraced economic liberalization and international trade. Singapore is one of the world's most prosperous nations. Its economy is dominated by services, but the country is also a major manufacturer of electronics and chemicals.

Country's Score Over Time

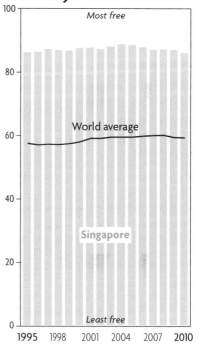

Quick Facts

Population: 4.8 million

GDP (PPP): $238.5 billion
1.1% growth in 2008
6.1% 5-year compound
annual growth
$49,284 per capita

Unemployment: 2.2%

Inflation (CPI): 6.5%

FDI Inflow: $22.7 billion

2008 data unless otherwise noted
Data compiled as of September 2009

How Do We Measure Economic Freedom?
See page 457 for an explanation of the methodology or visit the *Index* Web site at *heritage.org/index*.

SINGAPORE'S TEN ECONOMIC FREEDOMS

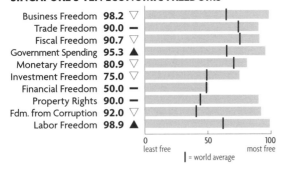

Business Freedom	98.2	▽
Trade Freedom	90.0	—
Fiscal Freedom	90.7	▽
Government Spending	95.3	▲
Monetary Freedom	80.9	▽
Investment Freedom	75.0	▽
Financial Freedom	50.0	—
Property Rights	90.0	—
Fdm. from Corruption	92.0	▽
Labor Freedom	98.9	▲

0 least free — 50 — 100 most free

| = world average

BUSINESS FREEDOM — 98.2

The overall freedom to conduct a business is well protected under Singapore's regulatory environment. Starting a business takes only three days, compared to the world average of 35 days. Obtaining a business license takes much less than the world average of 18 procedures and 218 days. Bankruptcy is straightforward.

TRADE FREEDOM — 90

Singapore's weighted average tariff rate was 0 percent in 2008, but import and export restrictions, services market barriers, import taxes, import and export licensing, burdensome sanitary and phytosanitary rules, problematic enforcement of intellectual property rights, and export incentive programs add to the cost of trade. Ten points were deducted from Singapore's trade freedom score to account for non-tariff barriers.

FISCAL FREEDOM — 90.7

Singapore has relatively low tax rates. The top income tax rate is 20 percent, and the top corporate tax rate is 18 percent. Other taxes include a value-added tax (VAT) and a property tax. In the most recent year, overall tax revenue as a percentage of GDP was 14.3 percent.

GOVERNMENT SPENDING — 95.3

Total government expenditures, including consumption and transfer payments, are low. In the most recent year, government spending equaled 12.5 percent of GDP. The state remains involved in the economy through Singapore's many government-linked companies. Plans to open state-owned energy and telecommunications enterprises to private investment have stalled.

MONETARY FREEDOM — 80.9

Inflation has been low, averaging 4.9 percent between 2006 and 2008. The government influences prices through regulation and state-supported enterprises and can impose controls as it deems necessary. Five points were deducted from Singapore's monetary freedom score to account for policies that distort domestic prices.

INVESTMENT FREEDOM — 75

Foreign and domestic businesses are treated equally, and nearly all sectors are open to 100 percent foreign ownership. Exceptions to the general openness to foreign invest-

ment are telecommunications, broadcasting, domestic news media, financial services, legal and other professional services, and property ownership. The government screens investments for incentive eligibility. Government-linked corporations play a dominant role in the economy. Residents and non-residents may hold foreign exchange accounts. There are no controls or requirements on current transfers, payments, or repatriation of profits. Foreign ownership of certain landed properties is subject to approval, but there are no restrictions on foreign ownership of industrial and commercial real estate.

FINANCIAL FREEDOM — 50

Singapore's modern financial sector is competitive. Bank consolidations have left three dominant banking groups. The largest is the government-controlled Development Bank of Singapore, which is publicly listed. The other two also have significant government-held minority shares. All three have remained relatively profitable throughout the global financial crisis but suffered write-downs of collateralized debt obligations linked to the U.S. sub-prime mortgage market. There were 116 commercial banks as of mid-2009; 110 were foreign. Barriers to foreign banks have been lowered, but the government seeks to maintain the domestic bank share of deposits above 50 percent, and the majority of domestic bank board members must be Singapore citizens and residents. Foreign banks are allocated to three categories: full-service, wholesale, and offshore. Foreign firms compete aggressively in insurance, fund management, and venture capital. With increasing ties with other Asian markets, Singapore's capital markets are well developed. In light of the recent global financial turmoil, the government has stepped in to guarantee all Singapore-dollar and foreign-currency deposits of individuals and non-bank customers in licensed banking institutions. The government has also implemented new programs such as the Bridging Loan Program and has extended existing programs to ensure liquidity in the markets.

PROPERTY RIGHTS — 90

The court system is efficient and protects private property. There is no expropriation, and contracts are secure. Singapore has one of Asia's strongest intellectual property rights regimes, and foreign and local entities may establish, operate, and dispose of their own enterprises.

FREEDOM FROM CORRUPTION — 92

Corruption is perceived as almost nonexistent. Singapore ranks 4th out of 179 countries in Transparency International's Corruption Perceptions Index for 2008. The government enforces strong anti-corruption laws. It is a crime for a citizen to bribe a foreign official or any other person, within or outside of Singapore.

LABOR FREEDOM — 98.9

Singapore's labor market is highly flexible. The non-salary cost of employing a worker is low, and dismissing an employee is not burdensome. Regulations related to work hours are very flexible.

SLOVAKIA

69.7

World Rank: **35**	Regional Rank: **18**

Slovakia's economic freedom score is 69.7, making its economy the 35th freest in the 2010 *Index*. Its score has increased by 0.3 point from last year, with a noticeable drop in labor freedom offset by small improvements in four other economic freedoms. Slovakia is ranked 18th out of 43 countries in the Europe region, and its overall score is higher than the world average.

Performing well in most of the 10 economic freedoms, Slovakia has recorded annual growth of around 8 percent for the past five years. Monetary stability has been maintained, taxes are competitive, and the entrepreneurial environment is increasingly conducive to private-sector development. Regulatory and legal frameworks are more transparent. Foreign investment is actively promoted and subject to few regulations in almost all areas. The financial sector is generally strong and has weathered the global financial turmoil relatively well.

Slovakia's overall economic freedom remains limited by two institutional weaknesses. The judicial system is inefficient and slow, and Slovakia scores relatively low in freedom from corruption, with only limited progress in recent years.

BACKGROUND: Slovakia became independent following its "Velvet Divorce" from the former Czechoslovakia in 1993. The reforms implemented by former Prime Minister Mikulas Dzurinda at that time have led to low labor costs, low taxes, and political stability, making Slovakia one of Europe's most attractive economies, especially for automobile and other manufacturing. Very high real GDP growth in 2007 was driven by strong domestic demand and net exports. Global weakness in 2008–2009 caused a significant slowdown. The cabinet of leftist Prime Minister Robert Fico is using interventionism to try to alleviate the effects of the financial crisis. The government is promoting highway construction, pressuring utilities to curb prices, providing loans for small and medium-size businesses, and according domestic suppliers preferential treatment. On January 1, 2009, Slovakia adopted the euro as its national currency.

Country's Score Over Time

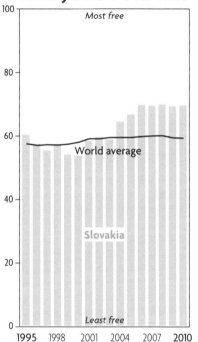

Quick Facts

Population: 5.4 million

GDP (PPP): $119.4 billion
6.4% growth in 2008
8.0% 5-year compound annual growth
$22,081 per capita

Unemployment: 9.5%

Inflation (CPI): 3.9%

FDI Inflow: $3.4 billion

2008 data unless otherwise noted
Data compiled as of September 2009

How Do We Measure Economic Freedom?
See page 457 for an explanation of the methodology or visit the *Index* Web site at *heritage.org/index.*

SLOVAKIA'S TEN ECONOMIC FREEDOMS

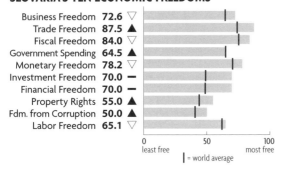

Business Freedom	72.6 ▽	
Trade Freedom	87.5 ▲	
Fiscal Freedom	84.0 ▽	
Government Spending	64.5 ▲	
Monetary Freedom	78.2 ▽	
Investment Freedom	70.0 —	
Financial Freedom	70.0 —	
Property Rights	55.0 ▲	
Fdm. from Corruption	50.0 ▲	
Labor Freedom	65.1 ▽	

0 least free — 50 — 100 most free
| = world average

BUSINESS FREEDOM — 72.6

The overall freedom to start, operate, and close a business is relatively well protected under Slovakia's regulatory environment. Starting a business takes an average of 16 days, compared to the world average of 35 days. Obtaining a business license takes less than the world average of 18 procedures but more than the world average of 218 days.

TRADE FREEDOM — 87.5

Slovakia's trade policy is the same as that of other members of the European Union. The common EU weighted average tariff rate was 1.3 percent in 2008. However, the EU has high or escalating tariffs for agricultural and manufacturing products, and its MFN tariff code is complex. Non-tariff barriers reflected in EU and Slovak policy include agricultural and manufacturing subsidies, quotas, import restrictions and bans for some goods and services, market access restrictions in some services sectors, non-transparent and restrictive regulations and standards, and inconsistent regulatory and customs administration among EU members. Pharmaceuticals regulation and non-transparent licensing procedures exceed general EU policy. Ten points were deducted from Slovakia's trade freedom score to account for non-tariff barriers.

FISCAL FREEDOM — 84

Slovakia's tax rates are relatively low. Both the income and corporate tax rates are a flat 19 percent. Other taxes include a value-added tax (VAT) and a property tax. In the most recent year, overall tax revenue as a percentage of GDP was 29.7 percent.

GOVERNMENT SPENDING — 64.5

Total government expenditures, including consumption and transfer payments, are moderate. In the most recent year, government spending equaled 34.4 percent of GDP.

MONETARY FREEDOM — 78.2

Inflation has been moderate, averaging 3.5 percent between 2006 and 2008. As a participant in the EU's Common Agricultural Policy, the government subsidizes agricultural production, distorting the prices of agricultural products. It also influences prices through regulations and state-owned enterprises and utilities. Ten points were deducted from Slovakia's monetary freedom score to account for policies that distort domestic prices.

INVESTMENT FREEDOM — 70

Foreign and domestic investments are treated equally under the law. There is no screening, and full foreign ownership is permitted in most sectors. The state owns railroad rights-of-way, postal services, water supplies, and forestry companies. Reforms have further streamlined and improved the transparency of investment rules, but bureaucratic efficiency could be improved. Dispute resolution through the judicial system can be slow, and corruption is a problem. Residents may establish foreign exchange accounts. There are very few controls on capital transactions. Non-residents from EU and OECD member countries may purchase land for business use.

FINANCIAL FREEDOM — 70

Most state-owned banks have been sold, and the presence of foreign banks is strong, with three foreign banks accounting for about 60 percent of total assets. Non-performing loans have declined to less than 5 percent of total loans. All financial service operations are regulated by the central bank. Interest rates have been liberalized, and credit limits have been abolished. The financial sector has become increasingly diversified as insurance and securities companies have grown. Capital markets remain relatively small and are not fully developed. With little exposure to the structured financial products that triggered the global financial turmoil, banking remains stable and well capitalized. Adoption of the euro proceeded smoothly in January 2009.

PROPERTY RIGHTS — 55

The judiciary is independent and comparatively effective, although decisions can take years and corruption remains significant. The courts recognize and enforce foreign judgments, subject to the same delays. Secured interests in property and contractual rights are recognized and enforced. The mortgage market is growing, and the recording system is reliable. Intellectual property rights are protected under Slovak law and in practice except for inadequate storage of proprietary data and improper registration of companies to produce generic drugs that are still under patent protection.

FREEDOM FROM CORRUPTION — 50

Corruption is perceived as significant. Slovakia ranks 52nd out of 179 countries in Transparency International's Corruption Perceptions Index for 2008. Legislative and executive branch corruption especially affects health care, the judiciary, and education. Slovakia is a signatory to the OECD Convention on Combating Bribery, and it is a criminal act to give or accept a bribe.

LABOR FREEDOM — 65.1

Slovakia's labor regulations are relatively flexible. The non-salary cost of employing a worker is moderate, and dismissing an employee is not costly. Regulations on work hours remain relatively rigid.

SLOVENIA

Ljubljana ✪

Economic Freedom Score

64.7

S lovenia's economic freedom score is 64.7, making its economy the 61st freest in the 2010 *Index*. Its score has increased by 1.8 points since last year, reflecting improvements in six of the 10 economic freedoms. Slovenia is ranked 27th out of 43 countries in the Europe region, and its overall score is well above the world average.

The transition of the Slovenian economy to greater economic freedom continues, facilitated by structural reforms and an increasingly vibrant private sector. The economy enjoys relatively high levels of business freedom, trade freedom, investment freedom, property rights, and freedom from corruption. Business regulations have become more straightforward and transparent, and recent reductions in the corporate tax rate have increased competitiveness. Foreign investment is encouraged, and the streamlining of investment rules has eliminated burdensome restrictions.

Weak scores in government spending and labor freedom hold down Slovenia's overall economic freedom. Government spending is more than 40 percent of GDP, and the privatization of state-controlled enterprises has been sluggish. Labor market reforms have also been delayed, hampering employment and productivity growth.

BACKGROUND: As the first entity to secede from the former Yugoslavia in 1991, Slovenia largely managed to avoid the bloody conflict that followed Croatia's secession. As a result, Slovenia's relatively strong economic infrastructure was left intact, and its economy became prosperous and stable, experiencing solid growth in recent years. However, the global recession has had a serious impact on Slovenian exports. Slovenia joined both the European Union and NATO in 2004 as part of a broader strategy of integration into the Euro–Atlantic community. It also adopted the euro as its currency on January 1, 2007, and chaired the European Union in 2008 and the Council of Europe in 2009.

Country's Score Over Time

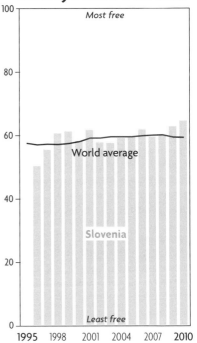

Quick Facts

Population: 2.0 million

GDP (PPP): $56.3 billion
   3.5% growth in 2008
   5.1% 5-year compound
      annual growth
   $27,605 per capita

Unemployment: 4.4%

Inflation (CPI): 5.7%

FDI Inflow: $1.8 billion

2008 data unless otherwise noted
Data compiled as of September 2009

How Do We Measure Economic Freedom?
See page 457 for an explanation of the methodology or visit the *Index* Web site at *heritage.org/index.*

SLOVENIA'S TEN ECONOMIC FREEDOMS

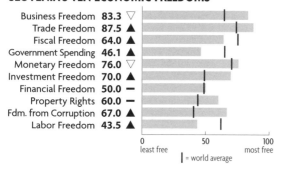

Business Freedom	83.3 ▽	
Trade Freedom	87.5 ▲	
Fiscal Freedom	64.0 ▲	
Government Spending	46.1 ▲	
Monetary Freedom	76.0 ▽	
Investment Freedom	70.0 ▲	
Financial Freedom	50.0 —	
Property Rights	60.0 —	
Fdm. from Corruption	67.0 ▲	
Labor Freedom	43.5 ▲	

0   50   100
least free   most free
| = world average

BUSINESS FREEDOM — 83.3

The overall freedom to start, operate, and close a business is relatively well protected under Slovenia's regulatory environment. Starting a business takes six days, compared to the world average of 35 days. Obtaining a business license takes less than the world average of 18 procedures and 218 days. Bankruptcy proceedings are fairly simple and straightforward.

TRADE FREEDOM — 87.5

Slovenia's trade policy is the same as that of other members of the European Union. The common EU weighted average tariff rate was 1.3 percent in 2008. However, the EU has high or escalating tariffs for agricultural and manufacturing products, and its MFN tariff code is complex. Non-tariff barriers reflected in EU and Slovenian policy include agricultural and manufacturing subsidies, quotas, import restrictions and bans for some goods and services, market access restrictions in some services sectors, non-transparent and restrictive regulations and standards, and inconsistent regulatory and customs administration among EU members. Pharmaceutical and government procurement regulations exceed general EU policy. Ten points were deducted from Slovenia's trade freedom score to account for non-tariff barriers.

FISCAL FREEDOM — 64

Slovenia has implemented another round of tax cuts. The top income tax rate is 41 percent. The corporate tax rate is now a flat 21 percent, down from 22 percent as of 2009, and is scheduled to be reduced further to 20 percent in 2010. Other taxes include a value-added tax (VAT), a property transfer tax, a special tax on insurance, and a sales tax on vehicles. The payroll tax was phased out in January 1, 2009. In the most recent year, overall tax revenue as a percentage of GDP was 38.4 percent.

GOVERNMENT SPENDING — 46.1

Total government expenditures, including consumption and transfer payments, are relatively high. In the most recent year, government spending equaled 42.4 percent of GDP. Privatization of state-controlled companies has slowed.

MONETARY FREEDOM — 76

Inflation has been moderate, averaging 4.9 percent between 2006 and 2008. As a participant in the EU's Common Agricultural Policy, the government subsidizes agricultural production, distorting the prices of agricultural products. It also controls the prices of pharmaceuticals, oil, electricity, natural gas, and railway transport and influences other prices through regulation and state-owned enterprises and utilities. Ten points were deducted from Slovenia's monetary freedom score to account for policies that distort domestic prices.

INVESTMENT FREEDOM — 70

Foreign investors receive national treatment, and all sectors are open to foreign investment with some restrictions. Investors seeking government incentives face job-creation requirements. Deterrents to investment include an incomplete commercial legal code, slowing privatization efforts, restrictive labor regulations, and burdensome bureaucracy. Residents and non-residents may hold foreign exchange accounts. There are some restrictions on foreign exchange or capital transactions, payments, and transfers. Foreign investors may acquire property.

FINANCIAL FREEDOM — 50

Despite the government's declared intentions, privatization of Slovenia's state-owned financial institutions has been rather slow. The three largest banks account for 50 percent of the sector's total assets. Established lending relationships are important in getting credit in Slovenia, and bank lending is biased toward existing big firms. Equity financing remains difficult for start-ups and smaller companies. Capital markets are relatively small and centered on the Ljubljana Stock Exchange. The impact of the global financial crisis on the banking sector has been relatively modest because of the sector's limited exposure to structured financial products and other toxic assets.

PROPERTY RIGHTS — 60

Private property rights are constitutionally guaranteed, but the courts are inadequately staffed and slow, and there are reports of corruption. Foreigners may own property. Comprehensive legislation to protect intellectual property reflects the World Trade Organization's Trade-Related Aspects of Intellectual Property Rights (TRIPS) agreement and various EU directives, but foreign investors complain about enforcement delays.

FREEDOM FROM CORRUPTION — 67

Corruption is perceived as present. Slovenia ranks 26th out of 179 countries in Transparency International's Corruption Perceptions Index for 2008. The number of cases of actual bribery is small and is generally limited to instances involving inspections and tax collection.

LABOR FREEDOM — 43.5

Slovenia's labor regulations are rigid. The non-salary cost of employing a worker is relatively high, and dismissing an employee is difficult. Regulations on work hours remain rigid.

SOLOMON ISLANDS

Honiara

World Rank: 170   Regional Rank: 38

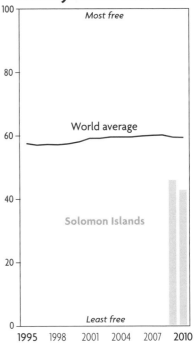

Economic Freedom Score

25 50 75

Least free 0   100 Most free

42.9

The Solomon Islands' economic freedom score is 42.9, making its economy the 170th freest in the 2010 *Index*. Its score has decreased by 3.1 points since last year, reflecting reduced scores in six of the 10 economic freedoms. The Solomon Islands is ranked 38th out of 41 countries in the Asia–Pacific region, and its overall score is well below the world average.

The Solomon Islands has a very narrow productive base and lacks basic institutional capacity essential to development of a strong private sector. The efficiency and overall quality of government services remain very poor. Reflecting the lack of economic dynamism, the agricultural sector continues to be the most important source of employment, although it accounts for less than 10 percent of GDP.

Despite recent economic growth, the economy of the Solomon Islands continues to face a number of serious challenges. Poor governance has played a significant role in ethnic conflicts and political instability. Regulations are inconsistent, and burdensome tariff and non-tariff barriers undermine overall trade freedom. A non-transparent and inefficient investment regime, combined with underdeveloped financial infrastructure, creates a hostile environment for investment growth. The judicial system, in addition to lacking independence and capacity, suffers from widespread corruption.

BACKGROUND: The Solomon Islands is a parliamentary democracy and one of Asia's poorest nations. Australia has intervened several times in recent years to defuse ethnic conflicts and stabilize the economy. Most of the islands' populations live in rural communities, and three-fourths of the workforce is engaged in subsistence farming and fishing. Economic growth depends largely on logging and exports of timber. Political tensions have subsided since 2008, and renewed foreign investment has led to strong economic growth.

Country's Score Over Time

Most free

World average

Solomon Islands

Least free

1995 1998 2001 2004 2007 2010

Quick Facts

Population: 0.5 million

GDP (PPP): $1.3 billion
7.4% growth in 2008
7.2% 5-year compound annual growth
$2,610 per capita

Unemployment: n/a

Inflation (CPI): 18.2%

FDI Inflow: $76 million

2008 data unless otherwise noted
Data compiled as of September 2009

How Do We Measure Economic Freedom?
See page 457 for an explanation of the methodology or visit the *Index* Web site at *heritage.org/index.*

SOLOMON ISLANDS' TEN ECONOMIC FREEDOMS

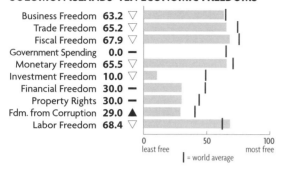

Business Freedom	63.2 ▽	
Trade Freedom	65.2 ▽	
Fiscal Freedom	67.9 ▽	
Government Spending	0.0 —	
Monetary Freedom	65.5 ▽	
Investment Freedom	10.0 ▽	
Financial Freedom	30.0 —	
Property Rights	30.0 —	
Fdm. from Corruption	29.0 ▲	
Labor Freedom	68.4 ▽	

0 least free   50   100 most free

| = world average

BUSINESS FREEDOM — 63.2

The overall freedom to start, operate, and close a business is limited under the Solomon Islands' regulatory environment. Starting a business takes an average of 57 days, compared to the world average of 35 days. Obtaining a business license takes less than the world average of 18 procedures and 218 days. Bankruptcy proceedings are fairly simple but costly.

TRADE FREEDOM — 65.2

The Solomon Islands' weighted average tariff rate was 12.4 percent in 2008. Some high tariffs, import restrictions, import and export taxes, import licensing, non-transparent sanitary and phytosanitary regulations, inefficient customs implementation and inconsistent customs valuation, problematic enforcement of intellectual property rights, and limitations on regulatory and trade capacity add to the cost of trade. Ten points were deducted from the Solomon Islands' trade freedom score to account for non-tariff barriers.

FISCAL FREEDOM — 67.9

The Solomon Islands has a relatively high income tax and a moderate corporate tax. The top income tax rate is 40 percent, and the top corporate tax rate is 30 percent. Non-resident companies are subject to a 35 percent tax rate. Other taxes include an excise tax on beer and tobacco, an insurance tax, and a property tax. In the most recent year, overall tax revenue as a percentage of GDP was 26.7 percent.

GOVERNMENT SPENDING — 0

Total government expenditures, including consumption and transfer payments, are extremely high. In the most recent year, government spending equaled 63.0 percent of GDP.

MONETARY FREEDOM — 65.5

Inflation has been high, averaging 15.0 percent between 2006 and 2008. The government controls the prices of petroleum products and influences prices through regulation and state-owned enterprises and utilities. Ten points were deducted from the Solomon Islands' monetary freedom score to adjust for measures that distort domestic prices.

INVESTMENT FREEDOM — 10

Investment is screened and requires government approval.

Several sectors are reserved for small-scale domestic investors. Investment-related laws can be non-transparent, and bureaucracy is burdensome and prone to corruption. Underdeveloped private markets, inadequate infrastructure, and political uncertainty also deter investment. Government approval is required for the importation of capital; repatriation of capital; transfer of profits, dividends, interest and royalties; borrowing of overseas funds; settlement of intercompany accounts; transfers overseas of the proceeds from sales of Solomon Islands assets; and direct investment overseas. Foreign investors may lease but not purchase land.

FINANCIAL FREEDOM — 30

The Solomon Islands' financial system is small and not fully developed. Banking dominates the financial sector, and limited access to credit constrains business development. The government has tried to ensure that banking services are available to the rural population. The three commercial banks are the key providers of financial intermediation for domestic and foreign clients. The National Bank of Solomon Islands was sold to the Bank of South Pacific of Papua New Guinea in 2007, and all three commercial banks are now branches of foreign banks. To encourage more Solomon Islanders to participate in entrepreneurial activity, the government reintroduced the Small Business Finance Scheme in 2007. Bank credits to the private sector have increased in recent years, growing by over 30 percent in 2008.

PROPERTY RIGHTS — 30

Land ownership is reserved for Solomon Islanders. Generally, land is still held on a family or village basis and may be handed down from the mother or father according to local custom. Islanders are reluctant to provide land for nontraditional economic undertakings, and there are continuous disputes over land ownership. Strengthening property rights is fundamental to improving development prospects. The protection of intellectual property rights is a relatively new concept in the Solomon Islands.

FREEDOM FROM CORRUPTION — 29

Corruption is perceived as widespread. The Solomon Islands ranks 109th out of 179 countries in Transparency International's Corruption Perceptions Index for 2008. The law provides criminal penalties for official corruption, but implementation has not been effective, and officials often engage in corrupt practices with impunity. The Regional Assistance Mission to the Solomon Islands, a multinational police-centered force organized by Australia, arrived in 2003 at the government's invitation to assist in restoring law and order and rebuilding the country's institutions.

LABOR FREEDOM — 68.4

The Solomon Islands' labor regulations are relatively flexible. The non-salary cost of employing a worker is moderate, and dismissing an employee is not costly. The formal labor market is not fully developed.

Pretoria

SOUTH AFRICA

Economic Freedom Score

25   50   75

Least
free   0   100   Most
free

62.8

S outh Africa's economic freedom score is 62.8, making its economy the 72nd freest in the 2010 *Index*. Its score is one point lower than last year, reflecting declines in five of the 10 economic freedoms. South Africa is ranked 4th out of 46 countries in the Sub-Saharan Africa region, and its overall score is higher than the world average.

South Africa's economy performs relatively well in trade freedom, business freedom, and government spending. Competitiveness and flexibility are encouraged by a sensible business regulatory environment. Continuing integration into global commerce has resulted in notable increases in productivity and economic expansion. Exchange controls have been liberalized, and the average tariff rate is now less than 5 percent.

Only eight state-owned enterprises remain, and government spending accounts for less than 30 percent of GDP. Monetary stability is relatively sound, but the government controls prices through regulation, state-owned enterprises, and support programs. The judicial system is slow, and race laws and unclear regulations hinder investment. The legal environment is relatively free from political interference and the threat of expropriation.

BACKGROUND: The transition from white minority rule to democratic, nonracial government culminated in 1994 with the election of Nelson Mandela as South Africa's first post-apartheid president. Thabo Mbeki succeeded Mandela in 1999 and was re-elected in 2004. Jacob Zuma was chosen president by the newly elected parliament in May 2009. South Africa is the economic hub of Sub-Saharan Africa and the world's largest producer and exporter of gold and platinum. Mining, services, manufacturing, and agriculture rival similar sectors in the developed world. However, poverty is widespread, and much of the population is poorly educated and lacks access to infrastructure and services. The government has sought to increase land ownership by black South Africans, and its affirmative-action mandates threaten private property rights. Crime, HIV/AIDS, and high unemployment are ongoing concerns.

Country's Score Over Time

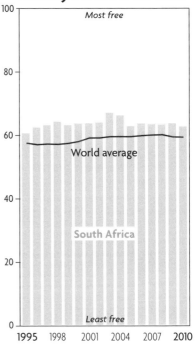

100   Most free

80

60   World average

South Africa

20

Least free
0
1995   1998   2001   2004   2007   2010

Quick Facts

Population: 48.7 million

GDP (PPP): $492.2 billion
3.1% growth in 2008
4.6% 5-year compound
annual growth
$10,109 per capita

Unemployment: 22.9%

Inflation (CPI): 11.5%

FDI Inflow: $9.0 billion

*2008 data unless otherwise noted
Data compiled as of September 2009*

How Do We Measure Economic Freedom?
See page 457 for an explanation of the methodology or visit the *Index* Web site at *heritage.org/index.*

SOUTH AFRICA'S TEN ECONOMIC FREEDOMS

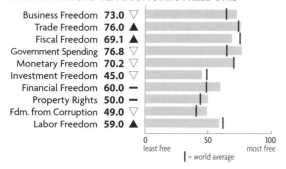

Business Freedom	73.0 ▽	
Trade Freedom	76.0 ▲	
Fiscal Freedom	69.1 ▲	
Government Spending	76.8 ▽	
Monetary Freedom	70.2 ▽	
Investment Freedom	45.0 ▽	
Financial Freedom	60.0 —	
Property Rights	50.0 —	
Fdm. from Corruption	49.0 ▽	
Labor Freedom	59.0 ▲	

0   50   100
least free   most free
| = world average

BUSINESS FREEDOM — 73

The overall freedom to start, operate, and close a business is relatively well protected under South Africa's regulatory environment. Starting a business takes 22 days, compared to the world average of 35 days. Obtaining a business license takes less than the world average of 18 procedures and 218 days. Closing a business is fairly simple and straightforward.

TRADE FREEDOM — 76

South Africa's weighted average tariff rate was 4.5 percent in 2008. Import and export restrictions, services market barriers, import and export permit requirements, burdensome technical standards, non-transparent government procurement procedures, burdensome regulations and inefficient bureaucracy, weak enforcement of intellectual property rights, inconsistent customs administration, and corruption add to the cost of trade. Fifteen points were deducted from South Africa's trade freedom score to account for non-tariff barriers.

FISCAL FREEDOM — 69.1

South Africa has a relatively high income tax rate and a moderate corporate tax rate. The top income tax rate is 40 percent, and the top corporate tax rate is 28 percent. Other taxes include a value-added tax (VAT), a property tax, a securities transfer tax, an inheritance tax, and a capital gains tax. In the most recent year, overall tax revenue as a percentage of GDP was 26.6 percent.

GOVERNMENT SPENDING — 76.8

Total government expenditures, including consumption and transfer payments, are relatively low. In the most recent year, government spending equaled 27.8 percent of GDP. The Department of Public Enterprises oversees eight major state-owned enterprises in the government-controlled diamond mining, telecommunications, defense, transportation, and utilities sectors.

MONETARY FREEDOM — 70.2

Inflation has been high, averaging 9.8 percent between 2006 and 2008. Prices are generally set by the market, but the government controls the prices of petroleum products, coal, paraffin, and utilities. Prices are also influenced through regulation, state-owned enterprises, and support programs. Ten points were deducted from South Africa's monetary freedom score to account for policies that distort domestic prices.

INVESTMENT FREEDOM — 45

Foreign and domestic investments are treated equally under the law, and foreign investment is permitted in most sectors. Non-transparent regulations, rigid labor laws, and crime are disincentives for investors. Residents and non-residents may establish foreign exchange accounts through authorized dealers, subject to government approval and quantity limits. Most purchases of foreign exchange, payments, capital transactions, and transfers are subject to restrictions, controls, and prior approval.

FINANCIAL FREEDOM — 60

South Africa's financial sector is large and accounts for 20 percent of GDP. Consolidation has reduced the number of domestic banks to 35; six are foreign-owned, and 15 are branches of foreign banks. Five large banks account for over 80 percent of operations. Under the Financial Services Charter, banks must have 25 percent black ownership by 2010, direct a portion of after-tax profits to specific projects, and employ a fair representation of disadvantaged individuals in management. Through development banks, the government dominates financing of medium-term and long-term lending. There are many microfinance institutions, and many credit operations of poorer South Africans are outside of formal banks. Capital markets are well developed and centered around the Johannesburg Securities Exchange, which is one of the world's 20 largest in terms of market capitalization. Due to its limited exposure to the high-risk securities or complex instruments that triggered the global financial turmoil, the overall banking system has not been severely affected.

PROPERTY RIGHTS — 50

The threat of expropriation is low. The judiciary is independent, and contracts are generally secure, but the courts are slow, understaffed, underfunded, and overburdened. Optical disc piracy is substantial, and end-use piracy is not a crime. The courts impose undue burdens and costs on rightsholders pursuing infringement cases. The Medicines Control Council is notoriously inefficient and tardy with approvals.

FREEDOM FROM CORRUPTION — 49

Corruption is perceived as significant. South Africa ranks 54th out of 179 countries in Transparency International's Corruption Perceptions Index for 2008, a decline from 2007. Official corruption, particularly in the police and the Department of Home Affairs, is viewed as widespread. Parliament voted to disband the South African Police Anti-Corruption Unit and the Directorate for Special Operations and fold its jurisdiction into the National Police in October 2008.

LABOR FREEDOM — 59

South Africa's labor regulations are inflexible. The non-salary cost of employing a worker is low, but dismissing an employee is difficult.

Madrid

SPAIN

World Rank: **36**   Regional Rank: **19**

Economic Freedom Score

25   50   75

Least free   0   100   Most free

69.6

Spain's economic freedom score is 69.6, making its economy the 36th freest in the 2010 *Index*. Its score is 0.5 point lower than last year, reflecting reduced scores in six of the 10 economic freedoms, including freedom from corruption. Spain is ranked 19th out of 43 countries in the Europe region, and its overall score is well above the world average.

The Spanish economy has benefited from fairly high levels of business freedom, trade freedom, investment freedom, financial freedom, and property rights. Procedures for business formation have become streamlined and efficient, and the overall entrepreneurial environment is conducive to vibrant private-sector development. Foreign investment is subject to few restrictions. Spain enjoys a modern and competitive financial system. Regulations are transparent, and domestic access to credit is good. The judicial system is independent of political interference.

Challenges to Spain's overall economic freedom remain in fiscal freedom, government spending, and labor freedom. Total government spending equals nearly 40 percent of GDP, and improving budget management would be a key reform. Wage growth has outpaced that in other European countries, home ownership has been heavily subsidized, and spending has been untargeted. The labor market remains rigid.

BACKGROUND: Spain, which has enjoyed democratic rule only since 1977, joined the European Community in 1986. Public security has been marred by the nearly 50-year terrorist campaign of the Basque separatist movement ETA, which has claimed more than 800 lives, including a politically motivated killing during the 2008 elections. Following years of economic reform and brisk growth under former Prime Minister José María Aznar, current Prime Minister José Luis Rodríguez Zapatero won office in the wake of the al-Qaeda massacre in Madrid in 2004 and was re-elected in 2008. The global economic crisis hit Spain hard in 2009, especially in the home-building sector.

Country's Score Over Time

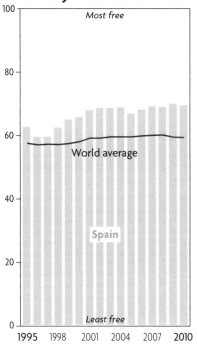

Most free

100

80

World average

60

40

Spain

20

Least free

0

1995   1998   2001   2004   2007   **2010**

Quick Facts

Population: 45.6 million

GDP (PPP): $1.5 trillion
1.2% growth in 2008
3.1% 5-year compound
annual growth
$31,954 per capita

Unemployment: 11.3%

Inflation (CPI): 4.1%

FDI Inflow: $65.5 billion

2008 data unless otherwise noted
Data compiled as of September 2009

How Do We Measure Economic Freedom?
See page 457 for an explanation of the methodology or visit the *Index* Web site at *heritage.org/index*.

SPAIN'S TEN ECONOMIC FREEDOMS

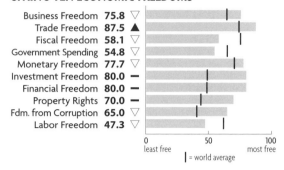

Business Freedom	75.8	▽
Trade Freedom	87.5	▲
Fiscal Freedom	58.1	▽
Government Spending	54.8	▽
Monetary Freedom	77.7	▽
Investment Freedom	80.0	—
Financial Freedom	80.0	—
Property Rights	70.0	—
Fdm. from Corruption	65.0	▽
Labor Freedom	47.3	▽

0 least free   50   100 most free

| = world average

BUSINESS FREEDOM — 75.8

The overall freedom to start, operate, and close a business is relatively well protected under Spain's regulatory environment. Starting a business takes 47 days, compared to the world average of 35 days. Obtaining a business license takes less than the world average of 18 procedures. Bankruptcy proceedings are fairly easy and straightforward.

TRADE FREEDOM — 87.5

Spain's trade policy is the same as that of other members of the European Union. The common EU weighted average tariff rate was 1.3 percent in 2008. However, the EU has high or escalating tariffs for agricultural and manufacturing products, and its MFN tariff code is complex. Non-tariff barriers reflected in EU and Spanish policy include agricultural and manufacturing subsidies, quotas, import restrictions and bans for some goods and services, market access restrictions in some services sectors, non-transparent and restrictive regulations and standards, and inconsistent regulatory and customs administration among EU members. Pharmaceutical and biotechnology regulations and services market access barriers exceed EU policy, and protection of intellectual property rights can be problematic. Ten points were deducted from Spain's trade freedom score to account for non-tariff barriers.

FISCAL FREEDOM — 58.1

Spain has a high income tax and a moderate corporate tax. The top income tax rate is 43 percent, and the top corporate tax rate is 30 percent. Other taxes include a value-added tax (VAT), a property tax, and a capital acquisitions tax. The wealth tax was abolished in 2009. In the most recent year, overall tax revenue as a percentage of GDP was 37.9 percent.

GOVERNMENT SPENDING — 54.8

Total government expenditures, including consumption and transfer payments, are relatively high. In the most recent year, government spending equaled 38.8 percent of GDP. A recent stimulus package equal to 1.1 percent of GDP provides for public works investment, support of the auto industry, and social assistance.

MONETARY FREEDOM — 77.7

Spain is a member of the euro zone. Inflation has been moderate, averaging 3.8 percent between 2006 and 2008. As a participant in the EU's Common Agricultural Policy, the government subsidizes agricultural production, distorting the prices of agricultural products. It also controls the prices of medicines and public transport and influences prices through regulation and state-owned enterprises and utilities. Ten points were deducted from Spain's monetary freedom score to account for policies that distort domestic prices.

INVESTMENT FREEDOM — 80

In general, foreign and domestic investments are treated equally under the law. Foreign investment of up to 100 percent of equity is permitted in most sectors. Bureaucratic procedures have been streamlined, and much red tape has been eliminated. There are no restrictions or controls on resident or non-resident foreign exchange accounts, capital movements, or repatriation of profits. The Bank of Spain requires reporting on most credit and lending activities.

FINANCIAL FREEDOM — 80

Spain's financial sector is well developed, providing a wide range of financing tools for entrepreneurial activity. The regulatory system is transparent and consistent with international norms. All commercial banks are privately owned, and credit is allocated on market terms. Four financial institutions dominate the banking system. The government provides subsidized financing for some activities. The non-bank financial sector remains small. Capital markets are well developed and open to foreign investors. Deterioration in asset quality that began in 2008 has resulted in a sharp increase in non-performing loans, which are now close to 4 percent of total loans.

PROPERTY RIGHTS — 70

The judiciary is independent in practice, but bureaucratic obstacles are significant. Contracts are secure, although enforcement is very slow. Patent, copyright, and trademark laws approximate or exceed EU levels of intellectual property protection. Enforcement actions (especially private-sector initiatives) using Spain's new IPR legal framework have greatly increased the criminal and civil actions against intellectual property pirates.

FREEDOM FROM CORRUPTION — 65

Corruption is perceived as minimal. Spain ranks 28th out of 163 countries in Transparency International's Corruption Perceptions Index for 2008. Giving or accepting a bribe is a crime, and bribes are not tax-deductible for corporations or individuals.

LABOR FREEDOM — 47.3

Spain's labor regulations are inflexible. The non-salary cost of employing a worker is high, and dismissing an employee is difficult. Regulations on work hours are rigid.

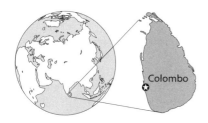

Colombo

SRI LANKA

Economic Freedom Score

25   50   75

Least free 0

Most free 100

54.6

World Rank: **120**	Regional Rank: **23**

Sri Lanka's economic freedom score is 54.6, making its economy the 120th freest in the 2010 *Index*. Its score is 1.4 points lower than last year, reflecting deterioration in four of the 10 economic freedoms. Sri Lanka is ranked 23rd out of 41 countries in the Asia–Pacific region, and its overall score is lower than the world average.

Reforms have been undertaken to enhance the efficiency of Sri Lanka's economy, but progress has been mixed. Sri Lanka scores relatively well in business freedom, government spending, and labor freedom. Business formation is relatively easy and streamlined. Government expenditures are still moderate, although political instability has driven up military expenditures and prevented the implementation of fiscal governance reforms.

Sri Lanka's trade freedom and fiscal freedom scores are moderate. The average tariff rate is not extremely high, but non-tariff barriers and corruption add to the costs of trade. Monetary freedom, investment freedom, financial freedom, property rights, and freedom from corruption are weak. The government generally welcomes foreign capital, but formal restrictions and the security situation discourage investment. Bureaucratic inefficiency and corruption affect many aspects of the economy. Court enforcement of property rights remains vulnerable to political interference.

BACKGROUND: In 2009, the government of President Mahinda Rajapakse defeated the terrorist Liberation Tigers of Tamil Eelam (LTTE) and eliminated its top leadership, ending a three-decade civil war that took the lives of some 70,000 people. The government's focus has now shifted to reconstruction and development of northern areas that for many years were controlled by the LTTE. More than 200,000 civilians displaced by the fighting are currently living in government-controlled camps. Bolstered mainly by agriculture, Sri Lanka's economy grew by 6 percent in 2008, down from 6.8 percent in 2007. Sri Lanka depends heavily on foreign assistance, and China has become a significant lender for infrastructure projects.

Country's Score Over Time

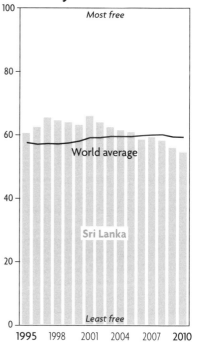

Quick Facts

Population: 20.2 million

GDP (PPP): $91.9 billion
6.0% growth in 2008
6.7% 5-year compound
annual growth
$4,560 per capita

Unemployment: 5.2%

Inflation (CPI): 22.6%

FDI Inflow: $752 million

2008 data unless otherwise noted
Data compiled as of September 2009

How Do We Measure Economic Freedom?
See page 457 for an explanation of the methodology or visit the *Index* Web site at *heritage.org/index.*

SRI LANKA'S TEN ECONOMIC FREEDOMS

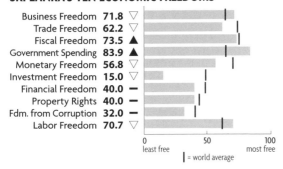

Business Freedom	71.8	▽
Trade Freedom	62.2	▽
Fiscal Freedom	73.5	▲
Government Spending	83.9	▲
Monetary Freedom	56.8	▽
Investment Freedom	15.0	▽
Financial Freedom	40.0	—
Property Rights	40.0	—
Fdm. from Corruption	32.0	—
Labor Freedom	70.7	▽

0 least free — 50 — 100 most free

| = world average

BUSINESS FREEDOM — 71.8

The overall freedom to start, operate, and close a business is relatively well protected under Sri Lanka's regulatory environment. Starting a business takes about the world average of 35 days. Obtaining a business license takes less than the world average of 218 days, but costs are high. Closing a business is relatively simple.

TRADE FREEDOM — 62.2

Sri Lanka's simple average tariff rate was 11.4 percent in 2007. Import bans and restrictions, services market barriers, import taxes, import fees, import licensing, restrictive standards and regulations, non-transparent government procurement, weak enforcement of intellectual property rights, export subsidies, and corruption add to the cost of trade. Fifteen points were deducted from Sri Lanka's trade freedom score to account for non-tariff barriers.

FISCAL FREEDOM — 73.5

Sri Lanka has relatively high tax rates. Both the top income tax rate and the top corporate tax rate are 35 percent. Corporations are also subject to the Social Responsibility Levy, a 1.5 percent surtax on taxable income. Other taxes include a value-added tax (VAT) and a stamp duty on the transfer of immovable property. In the most recent year, overall tax revenue as a percentage of GDP was 14.2 percent.

GOVERNMENT SPENDING — 83.9

Total government expenditures, including consumption and transfer payments, are relatively low. In the most recent year, government spending equaled 23.2 percent of GDP. No significant progress was made in privatization during the past year.

MONETARY FREEDOM — 56.8

Inflation has been very high, averaging 19.8 percent between 2006 and 2008. The government influences prices through regulations, state-owned enterprises, and subsidies for a wide array of goods. Fifteen points were deducted from Sri Lanka's monetary freedom score to account for policies that distort domestic prices.

INVESTMENT FREEDOM — 15

In general, foreign investment is welcome. The government allows 100 percent foreign ownership in certain sec-

tors and imposes ownership limits in others. Investment is screened and may need approval. Security concerns, inconsistent and non-transparent regulation, burdensome labor laws, inadequate infrastructure, and cumbersome bureaucracy are other impediments to investment. Outward direct investment must be approved by the government. Residents and non-residents may hold foreign exchange accounts subject to requirements, including government approval in some cases. Payments, capital transactions, and transfers are subject to reporting requirements, limits, or government approval. Private land ownership is limited to 50 acres per person. Foreign investors can purchase land, but there is a 100 percent tax on such transfers.

FINANCIAL FREEDOM — 40

Sri Lanka's financial system is growing but remains vulnerable to government influence. Banking dominates the financial sector, but high credit costs discourage more dynamic business activity. Regulations permit 100 percent foreign control of banks, insurance companies, and stockbrokerages. Regulations are largely consistent with international standards, but supervision and enforcement are insufficient. The banking sector, dominated by two state-owned banks, has 23 commercial banks, 12 of which are foreign. The two state banks, which have accumulated considerable bad debt, account for around 40 percent of total assets. The central bank is not fully independent. The government influences the allocation of credit and uses domestic financial resources to finance government borrowing. Capital markets are centered on the Colombo Stock Exchange, which is modern but relatively small.

PROPERTY RIGHTS — 40

The judiciary is influenced by other branches of government, and extensive delays lead investors most often to pursue out-of-court settlements. Intellectual property rights come under both criminal and civil jurisdiction. International recording, software development, motion picture, clothing, and consumer product companies claim that lack of IPR protection damages their businesses.

FREEDOM FROM CORRUPTION — 32

Corruption is perceived as widespread. Sri Lanka ranks 92nd out of 179 countries in Transparency International's Corruption Perceptions Index for 2008. Anti-corruption laws and regulations are unevenly enforced. The police and the judiciary are viewed as the most corrupt public institutions. Corruption in customs clearance enables wide-scale smuggling of certain consumer items. In 2008, the Supreme Court faulted a former President and the Secretary of the Treasury for wrongdoing in connection with the sale of two government properties. Both were fined, and the Secretary was removed from his position.

LABOR FREEDOM — 70.7

Sri Lanka's labor regulations are relatively flexible. The non-salary cost of employing a worker is moderate, but dismissing an employee is difficult.

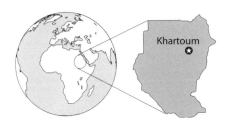

SUDAN

Economic Freedom Score

25   50   75

Least free   0 ——————— 100   Most free

World Rank: Not ranked   **Regional Rank:** Not ranked

The economy is not graded

Sudan's economic freedom is not graded because of the violence and political instability that have wracked the country in recent years. The last time Sudan was fully graded was in 2000, when it received a score of 47.2.

The entrepreneurial environment in Sudan is characterized by corruption and a lack of transparency in the enforcement of regulations. Outside of the oil sector, Sudan's economic growth is narrowly based and limited in reach. Despite recent progress in achieving some macroeconomic stability and market reforms, development of the non-oil sector remains stagnant. Most employment opportunities are still in the informal sector.

The average tariff rate is very high, and significant non-tariff barriers further impede trade. The state subsidizes a wide array of goods and influences prices through state-owned enterprises. Reforms are often slow or subject to frequent delays, and the government is riddled with corruption. Sudan is one of the world's 10 most corrupt nations.

BACKGROUND: A two-decade civil war between the Khartoum government in the North and the Sudan People's Liberation Movement/Army in the South claimed an estimated 1.5 million lives before ending in 2005. The South now has limited autonomy, and a referendum on independence is to be held by 2011. President Omar Hassan al-Bashir, in power since a 1989 military coup, was indicted by the International Criminal Court in 2009 for war crimes and crimes against humanity in Darfur, where more than 2 million people have been displaced and more than 200,000 killed. Tensions are high between Sudan and Chad, with each accusing the other of supporting anti-government rebels. Instability, poor infrastructure, mismanagement, and corruption hinder the economy. Significant oil production began in 2000, but most Sudanese remain engaged in agriculture.

Country's Score Over Time

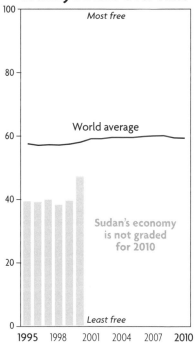

Sudan's economy is not graded for 2010

Quick Facts

Population: 41.3 million

GDP (PPP): $89.0 billion
8.3% growth in 2008
7.5% 5-year compound annual growth
$2,153 per capita

Unemployment: estimated to be over 10%

Inflation (CPI): 14.3%

FDI Inflow: $2.6 billion

2008 data unless otherwise noted
Data compiled as of September 2009

How Do We Measure Economic Freedom?
See page 457 for an explanation of the methodology or visit the *Index* Web site at *heritage.org/index*.

BUSINESS FREEDOM — NOT GRADED

Sudan's regulatory regime remains inconsistent, uneven, and non-transparent. Starting a business takes an average of 36 days, compared to the world average of 35 days. Obtaining a business license takes 271 days, compared to the world average of 218 days.

TRADE FREEDOM — NOT GRADED

Sudan's weighted average tariff rate was 11.4 percent in 2008. There has been some progress toward liberalizing the trade regime, but import restrictions, non-transparent regulations, discriminatory taxes, significant delays in customs clearance, inadequate infrastructure, and corruption add to the cost of trade. If Sudan were graded this year, 15 points would be deducted from its trade freedom score to account for non-tariff barriers.

FISCAL FREEDOM — NOT GRADED

Sudan has a low income tax rate but a relatively high corporate tax rate. The top income tax rate is 10 percent, and the top corporate tax rate is 35 percent. In the most recent year, overall tax revenue as a percentage of GDP was 7.0 percent.

GOVERNMENT SPENDING — NOT GRADED

Total government expenditures, including consumption and transfer payments, are relatively low. In the most recent year, government spending equaled 26.1 percent of GDP. The non-oil sector of the economy needs greater structural support. As oil revenues fall, Sudan's overall economic health and stability will rely on broadening of the tax base and better targeted spending.

MONETARY FREEDOM — NOT GRADED

Inflation has been high, averaging 12.1 percent between 2006 and 2008. The government influences prices through regulation, a wide range of subsidies, and state-owned enterprises and utilities, and petroleum products are subsidized and subject to price controls. If Sudan were graded this year, ten points would be deducted from its monetary freedom score to account for policies that distort domestic prices.

INVESTMENT FREEDOM — NOT GRADED

Officially, foreign and domestic investments are treated equally under the law. Foreign investment is restricted in certain sectors and requires government approval. Investment laws are non-transparent, and bureaucracy is cumbersome and prone to corruption. Political instability and inadequate infrastructure also discourage investment. All residents may hold foreign exchange accounts. Non-residents may hold foreign exchange accounts with government approval. Some restrictions and controls apply to all transactions involving capital market securities, money market instruments, credit operations, and outward direct investment.

FINANCIAL FREEDOM — NOT GRADED

Sudan's small financial system is underdeveloped and largely bound by Islamic financial principles, including a prohibition on charging interest. Supervision and regulation are weak. The banking sector is composed of completely or majority privately owned banks, and four new banks were licensed and came into operation in 2008. However, many banks suffer from the lack of efficient and accountable lending practices as well as from poor monitoring. A large portion of the population remains outside of the formal banking sector, and limited access to credit hinders businesses. The government continues to direct the allocation of credit, and non-performing loans are a problem. Capital markets are very small, consisting primarily of trade in bank shares on the Khartoum Stock Exchange.

PROPERTY RIGHTS — NOT GRADED

There is little respect for private property in Sudan, and the regime in Khartoum stands accused of genocide in Darfur and southern Sudan. The government influences the judiciary, and the military and civil authorities do not follow due process to protect private property. There have been numerous disputes between the government and various churches involving confiscated church property but no reports of court-ordered property restitution or compensation. Better protection of intellectual property rights would permit increased food production and food security through biotechnology applications.

FREEDOM FROM CORRUPTION — NOT GRADED

Corruption is perceived as rampant. Sudan ranks 173rd out of 179 countries in Transparency International's Corruption Perceptions Index for 2008. Relatives of high government officials often own companies that do business with the government and usually receive kickbacks for government business. Bribery of police is also a concern. There are no laws providing for public access to government information, and the government does not provide such access.

LABOR FREEDOM — NOT GRADED

The non-salary cost of employing a worker is moderate, but dismissing an employee is burdensome and costly. Regulations related to the number of work hours are somewhat flexible. Sudan's labor market remains underdeveloped, partly because of the country's lack of political stability.

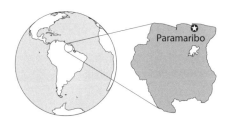

Paramaribo

SURINAME

Economic Freedom Score

25   50   75

Least   Most
free   0   100   free

52.5

| World Rank: **131** | Regional Rank: **22** |

S uriname's economic freedom score is 52.5, making its economy the 131st freest in the 2010 *Index*. Its score is 1.6 points lower than last year, reflecting reductions in five of the 10 economic freedoms. Suriname is ranked 22nd out of 29 countries in the South and Central America/Caribbean region, and its overall score is lower than the world and regional averages.

Suriname's annual economic growth has averaged around 5 percent over the past 5 years, and macroeconomic stability has improved. Average tariffs are slightly lower. Labor regulations are fairly flexible, but regulatory hurdles for starting a business are among the worst in the world.

Private-sector development has been hampered by the government's presence in the economy. The public sector employs over 60 percent of the labor force. Poor policy choices and the uncertainty generated by weak management of fiscal and monetary policy have increased the risks for entrepreneurs. Privatization has made little progress. Pervasive corruption is symptomatic of the weak rule of law, and there are no legal provisions for the protection of intellectual property.

BACKGROUND: Democracy was re-established in Suriname in 1991 after more than a decade of military rule. In 2005, incumbent President Ronald Venetiaan of the economic reform–oriented New Front Coalition defeated a strong challenge by former military dictator Desi Bouterse's National Democratic Party. The economy is dominated by exports of natural resources, especially alumina, oil, gold, nickel, lumber, and silver, as well as rice, bananas, shrimp, and fish. Prospects for the onshore oil industry are positive, and bauxite deposits are among the world's richest. Strong commodity prices encouraged GDP growth and higher tax revenues until the global economic downturn. Shortages of affordable energy inhibit industrial expansion, and protecting natural resources from illegal exploitation is difficult. Porous borders attract drug smugglers. Suriname remains one of South America's poorest and least-developed countries.

Country's Score Over Time

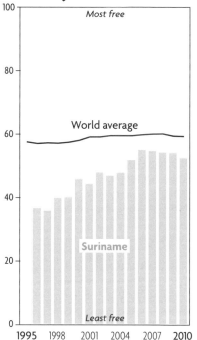

Quick Facts

Population: 0.5 million

GDP (PPP): $3.9 billion
7.0% growth in 2008
5.3% 5-year compound
annual growth
$7,506 per capita

Unemployment: 9.5% (2004)

Inflation (CPI): 14.6%

FDI Inflow: –$234 million

2008 data unless otherwise noted
Data compiled as of September 2009

How Do We Measure Economic Freedom?
See page 457 for an explanation of the methodology or visit the *Index* Web site at *heritage.org/index.*

SURINAME'S TEN ECONOMIC FREEDOMS

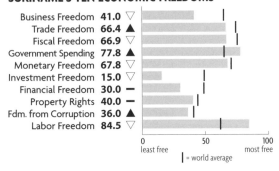

Business Freedom	41.0 ▽	
Trade Freedom	66.4 ▲	
Fiscal Freedom	66.9 ▽	
Government Spending	77.8 ▲	
Monetary Freedom	67.8 ▽	
Investment Freedom	15.0 ▽	
Financial Freedom	30.0 —	
Property Rights	40.0 —	
Fdm. from Corruption	36.0 ▲	
Labor Freedom	84.5 ▽	

0 least free   50   100 most free
| = world average

BUSINESS FREEDOM — 41

The overall freedom to start, operate, and close a business is very limited under Suriname's regulatory environment. Starting a business takes 694 days, compared to the world average of 35 days. Obtaining a business license takes much more than the world average of 218 days. Bankruptcy proceedings are difficult and often prolonged.

TRADE FREEDOM — 66.4

Suriname's weighted average tariff rate was 11.8 percent in 2007. The government has made progress toward liberalizing the trade regime, but import and export restrictions, import and export taxes, import fees, import and export licensing, and non-transparent regulations and standards add to the cost of trade. Ten points were deducted from Suriname's trade freedom score to account for non-tariff barriers.

FISCAL FREEDOM — 66.9

Suriname has relatively high tax rates. The top income tax rate is 38 percent, and the top corporate tax rate is 36 percent. Other taxes include a property tax, a tax on dividends, and an excise tax on tobacco and alcohol. In the most recent year, overall tax revenue as a percentage of GDP was 23.8 percent.

GOVERNMENT SPENDING — 77.8

Total government expenditures, including consumption and transfer payments, are relatively low. In the most recent year, government spending equaled 27.2 percent of GDP. Privatization has been slow and uneven. Direct state involvement in the economy through ownership or control remains considerable, and due to a lack of transparency, there is little information about the finances of existing state enterprises. The public sector is large and inefficient.

MONETARY FREEDOM — 67.8

Inflation had been high, averaging 12.3 percent between 2006 and 2008, but the rate dropped sharply in 2009. The government influences prices through regulations and state-owned enterprises and utilities, and prices of basic food items are controlled. Ten points were deducted from Suriname's monetary freedom score to account for policies that distort domestic prices.

INVESTMENT FREEDOM — 15

Foreign investors are not subjected to specifically discriminatory treatment, but investments are screened and approved by the government and may face political opposition. The oil sector is wholly state-owned. Investment regulation is conducted on a case-by-case basis. There are no limits on foreign ownership in a company. Labor laws are restrictive, the legal system is time-consuming, and the investment code and bureaucracy are non-transparent, burdensome, and prone to corruption. Residents and non-residents may hold foreign exchange accounts, subject to restrictions and approval. Payments, capital transactions, and transfers may be limited or require approval.

FINANCIAL FREEDOM — 30

Suriname's financial system remains underdeveloped and vulnerable to government influence. Financial regulations are antiquated, and supervision is poor. There are eight banks, three of which control more than 80 percent of deposits. The state owns a majority stake in two of the three major banks. The extension of credit has grown rapidly. Non-performing loans are about 12 percent of total loans and primarily affect small state-owned banks. The state also owns three minor commercial banks that are to be consolidated, with their bad loans assumed by the government. The non-banking financial sector, including insurance and pension funds, is small and underdeveloped. Capital markets offer only a narrow range of government and other securities.

PROPERTY RIGHTS — 40

Private property rights are not well protected. There is a severe shortage of judges, and dispute settlement can be extremely time-consuming. Although Suriname has signed key international intellectual property rights treaties, IPR protection is nonexistent in practice because it has not been incorporated into domestic law. Suriname is a member of the World Trade Organization but has not ratified the WTO's Trade-Related Aspects of Intellectual Property Rights (TRIPS) agreement.

FREEDOM FROM CORRUPTION — 36

Corruption is perceived as widespread. Suriname ranks 72nd out of 179 countries in Transparency International's Corruption Perceptions Index for 2008. Although some senior government officials take anti-corruption efforts seriously, cases of alleged corruption have involved the highest levels of the executive and legislative branches. A shortage of police personnel hampers investigations of fraud cases.

LABOR FREEDOM — 84.5

Suriname's labor regulations are fairly flexible. The non-salary cost of employing a worker is low, but dismissing an employee is difficult. There is no minimum wage. The formal labor market is not fully developed, and the public sector remains an important source of employment.

SWAZILAND

Mbabane

Economic Freedom Score

Least free 0   25   50   75   100 Most free

57.4

Swaziland's economic freedom score is 57.4, making its economy the 102nd freest in the 2010 *Index*. Its score is 1.7 points lower than last year, reflecting reduced scores in six of the 10 economic freedoms. Swaziland is ranked 14th out of 46 countries in the Sub-Saharan Africa region, and its overall score is below the world average.

Swaziland has lagged behind other economies in the region, averaging annual growth of only 2.8 percent over the past five years. Despite a fairly diversified economic base, inefficient regulatory and legal frameworks have held back investment and increases in productivity. Privatization is part of the government's reform agenda, but progress has been marginal.

There are many lingering constraints on the development of a more vibrant private sector. The most visible problems are related to poor public finance, administrative complexities, and the lack of respect for contracts. Bureaucratic inefficiency and corruption affect many aspects of the economy. Court enforcement of property rights is vulnerable to political interference.

BACKGROUND: Under the constitution, King Mswati III holds supreme executive, legislative, and judicial powers; in practice, authority is delegated to the prime minister, his cabinet, and traditional government structures. Swaziland is surrounded by South Africa to the west and Mozambique to the east. Its economy is closely linked to South Africa, the source of most imports and destination for most exports. Swaziland is part of the Southern African Customs Union (with Botswana, Lesotho, Namibia, and South Africa) and the Common Monetary Area (with Lesotho, Namibia, and South Africa). Much of the population depends on subsistence agriculture or herding. The soft-drink concentrate, textile, and cane sugar industries are the leading export earners and private-sector employers. Coal and diamonds are mined for export. Swaziland has one of the world's highest HIV/AIDS rates.

Country's Score Over Time

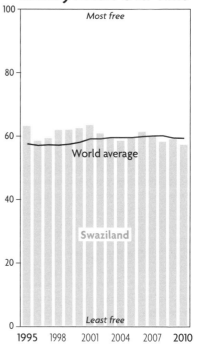

Quick Facts

Population: 1.2 million

GDP (PPP): $5.8 billion
    2.5% growth in 2008
    2.8% 5-year compound
    annual growth
    $4,928 per capita

Unemployment: estimated to be over 10%

Inflation (CPI): 13.1%

FDI Inflow: $10 million

2008 data unless otherwise noted
Data compiled as of September 2009

How Do We Measure Economic Freedom?
See page 457 for an explanation of the methodology or visit the *Index* Web site at *heritage.org/index.*

SWAZILAND'S TEN ECONOMIC FREEDOMS

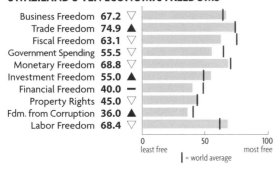

Business Freedom	67.2 ▽	
Trade Freedom	74.9 ▲	
Fiscal Freedom	63.1 ▽	
Government Spending	55.5 ▽	
Monetary Freedom	68.8 ▽	
Investment Freedom	55.0 ▲	
Financial Freedom	40.0 ▬	
Property Rights	45.0 ▽	
Fdm. from Corruption	36.0 ▲	
Labor Freedom	68.4 ▽	

0   50   100
least free   most free
❙ = world average

BUSINESS FREEDOM — 67.2

The overall freedom to start, operate, and close a business is constrained under Swaziland's regulatory environment. Starting a business takes an average of 61 days, compared to the world average of 35 days. Obtaining a business license takes less than the world average of 18 procedures and 218 days. Closing a business is fairly straightforward but costly.

TRADE FREEDOM — 74.9

Swaziland's weighted average tariff rate was 7.6 percent in 2008. Services market access barriers, select import permit requirements, import taxes, and weak enforcement of intellectual property rights add to the cost of trade. Ten points were deducted from Swaziland's trade freedom score to account for non-tariff barriers.

FISCAL FREEDOM — 63.1

Swaziland has moderately high tax rates. The top income tax rate is 33 percent, and the top corporate tax rate is 30 percent. Other taxes include a real estate tax and a fuel tax. In the most recent year, the overall tax burden was 41.2 percent of GDP.

GOVERNMENT SPENDING — 55.5

Total government expenditures, including consumption and transfer payments, are relatively high. In the most recent year, government spending equaled 38.5 percent of GDP. Implementation of the privatization agenda and meaningful reform of the inefficient civil service are undermined by a lack of political will. Better budget execution is a key goal.

MONETARY FREEDOM — 68.8

Inflation has been high, averaging 11.2 percent between 2006 and 2008. The government influences prices through regulations and numerous state-owned enterprises and utilities, and government-administered prices account for approximately 16 percent of the consumer price index. Ten points were deducted from Swaziland's monetary freedom score to account for policies that distort domestic prices.

INVESTMENT FREEDOM — 55

There are no formal policies or practices that discriminate against foreign investment, and companies can be 100 percent foreign-owned. Foreign investment faces minimal screening but is restricted in the telephone, water, and electricity sectors. Bureaucratic procedures are cumbersome, implementation of regulations is non-transparent and unpredictable, and obtaining work permits for foreign workers can be burdensome. With some restrictions, residents and non-residents may hold foreign exchange accounts. Payments and transfers are subject to quantitative limits and government approval in some cases. The central bank must approve inward capital transfers. Approximately 60 percent of land is held by the monarchy in trust for the people of Swaziland. Foreign investors may lease but not own land in most cases.

FINANCIAL FREEDOM — 40

Swaziland's financial sector is small but has been growing in recent years, driven mainly by the increasing number of non-bank financial institutions. Bank supervision is weak, and the sector remains subject to government influence. There are four commercial banks, three of which are foreign-controlled. The financial system is dominated by the non-bank financial sector, total assets of which are equivalent to around 55 percent of GDP. The sector has been expanding due to the liquidity surge triggered by the 2005 Retirement Fund Act, as well as insurance sector liberalization through the Insurance Act in 2005. Capital markets are small and centered on the Swaziland Stock Exchange, which remains largely inactive.

PROPERTY RIGHTS — 45

The judiciary suffers from inadequate training, low salaries, and a small budget. Delays are common, and the executive branch significantly influences decisions. Protection of patents, trademarks, and copyrights is inadequate. The government has acceded to the WTO's Trade-Related Aspects of Intellectual Property Rights (TRIPS) agreement but has not signed the World Intellectual Property Organization's Internet agreement.

FREEDOM FROM CORRUPTION — 36

Corruption is perceived as widespread. Swaziland ranks 72nd out of 179 countries in Transparency International's Corruption Perceptions Index for 2008, an improvement over 2007. Corruption is seen as significant in the executive and legislative branches of government, and efforts to combat it are viewed as insufficient. The Prevention of Corruption law came into effect in 2007 and there is an Anti-Corruption Unit, but the unit lacks sufficient financing, transport, and manpower. Credible reports indicate that unqualified businesses have won contracts because of their owners' relationships with government officials.

LABOR FREEDOM — 68.4

Swaziland's labor regulations are relatively flexible. The non-salary cost of employing a worker is low, but the cost of laying off a worker is high. The formal labor market is not fully developed.

○ Stockholm

SWEDEN

50
25   75

Least   0   100   Most
free   free

72.4

| World Rank: **21** | Regional Rank: **10** |

Sweden's economic freedom score is 72.4, making its economy the 21st freest in the 2010 *Index*. Its score has increased by 1.9 points since last year, reflecting improved scores in five of the 10 economic freedoms. Sweden is ranked 10th out of 43 countries in the Europe region, and its overall score is above the world and regional averages.

With its economy open to global trade and investment, Sweden scores well in trade freedom, investment freedom, monetary freedom, and financial freedom. The overall regulatory and legal environment, transparent and efficient, encourages robust entrepreneurial activity. Banking is guided by sensible regulations and prudent lending practices. Monetary stability is well maintained, with inflationary pressures under control. The judicial system, independent and free of corruption, provides strong protection of property rights.

However, Sweden's scores in fiscal freedom and government spending are among the lowest in the world. Although the corporate tax rate has been reduced and the wealth tax has been abolished, the overall tax burden remains large. The top income tax rate of 57 percent is one of the world's highest. Total government spending is more than half of GDP.

BACKGROUND: Sweden has enjoyed a buoyant economy since becoming a member of the European Union in 1995, although growth came to a halt in 2009 as a result of the international financial crisis. The economy relies heavily on international trade, mostly within Europe, and total trade accounts for more that 50 percent of GDP. Sweden rejected adoption of the euro by popular referendum in 2003. The Alliance for Sweden, a center-right coalition headed by Moderate Party leader Fredrik Reinfeldt, unseated the Social Democrat Party of Göran Persson in September 2006 with a pledge to sell state assets, increase growth, and reduce government debt. Sweden's principal exports include paper products, machinery and transport equipment, and chemicals.

Country's Score Over Time

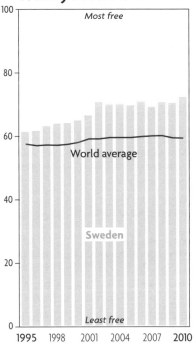

Most free

100

80

60   World average

40

Sweden

20

Least free

0

1995   1998   2001   2004   2007   2010

Quick Facts

Population: 9.2 million

GDP (PPP): $344.7 billion
　　　　　−0.2% growth in 2008
　　　　　2.5% 5-year compound
　　　　　　annual growth
　　　　　$37,383 per capita

Unemployment: 6.2%

Inflation (CPI): 3.3%

FDI Inflow: $43.7 billion

2008 data unless otherwise noted
Data compiled as of September 2009

How Do We Measure Economic Freedom?
See page 457 for an explanation of the methodology or visit the *Index* Web site at *heritage.org/index*.

395

SWEDEN'S TEN ECONOMIC FREEDOMS

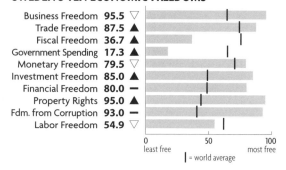

Business Freedom	95.5	▽
Trade Freedom	87.5	▲
Fiscal Freedom	36.7	▲
Government Spending	17.3	▲
Monetary Freedom	79.5	▽
Investment Freedom	85.0	▲
Financial Freedom	80.0	▬
Property Rights	95.0	▲
Fdm. from Corruption	93.0	▬
Labor Freedom	54.9	▽

0 least free — 50 — 100 most free
| = world average

BUSINESS FREEDOM — 95.5

The overall freedom to start, operate, and close a business is strongly protected under Sweden's regulatory environment. Starting a business takes 15 days, compared to the world average of 35 days. Obtaining a business license takes less than the world average of 18 procedures and 218 days. Bankruptcy proceedings are fairly easy and straightforward.

TRADE FREEDOM — 87.5

Sweden's trade policy is the same as that of other members of the European Union. The common EU weighted average tariff rate was 1.3 percent in 2008. However, the EU has high or escalating tariffs for agricultural and manufacturing products, and its MFN tariff code is complex. Non-tariff barriers reflected in EU and Swedish policy include agricultural and manufacturing subsidies, quotas, import restrictions and bans for some goods and services, market access restrictions in some services sectors, non-transparent and restrictive regulations and standards, and inconsistent regulatory and customs administration among EU members. Sanitary and phytosanitary regulations are burdensome, and enforcement of intellectual property rights is problematic. Ten points were deducted from Sweden's trade freedom score to account for non-tariff barriers.

FISCAL FREEDOM — 36.7

Sweden has a very burdensome income tax rate and a moderate corporate tax rate. The top income tax rate is effectively 57 percent, and the corporate tax rate is 26.3 percent, reduced from 28 percent as of January 1, 2009. Other taxes include a value-added tax (VAT), a property tax, and a capital gains tax. In the most recent year, overall tax revenue as a percentage of GDP was 48.9 percent.

GOVERNMENT SPENDING — 17.3

Total government expenditures, including consumption and transfer payments, are very high. In the most recent year, government spending equaled 52.5 percent of GDP. In response to the global crisis, Sweden undertook one of the largest fiscal stimulus programs in all of the European Union, estimated at 6.6 percent of GDP.

MONETARY FREEDOM — 79.5

Inflation has been low, averaging 2.7 percent between 2006 and 2008. As a participant in the EU's Common Agricultural Policy, the government subsidizes agricultural production, distorting the prices of agricultural products. Prices are generally set by the market, but oligopolies may hinder competition, and the government influences prices through regulations and state-owned enterprises and utilities. Ten points were deducted from Sweden's monetary freedom score to account for policies that distort domestic prices.

INVESTMENT FREEDOM — 85

Foreign companies may invest in most sectors in Sweden. Government monopolies are maintained in the retail sales of pharmaceuticals and alcoholic beverages. In general, investment laws and the bureaucracy are efficient. A complex network of permits and licenses applies to domestic and foreign firms, and labor and environmental regulations add to the cost of investment. Residents and non-residents may hold foreign exchange accounts. There are no controls on payments and transfers or repatriation of profits. The purchase of real estate by non-residents may require a permit.

FINANCIAL FREEDOM — 80

Regulation of the financial system is transparent and largely consistent with international norms. Banks offer a full range of financial services. Nearly all commercial banks are privately owned and operated, and credit is allocated on market terms. Foreign insurers are well represented in the insurance sector. The Stockholm Stock Exchange is modern, active, and open to domestic and foreign investors. Sweden's banking system has weathered the global financial crisis relatively well. No government takeovers of banks have occurred.

PROPERTY RIGHTS — 95

The judiciary is independent and fair. Contracts are respected, and Swedish law generally provides adequate protection for all property rights, including the right to intellectual property.

FREEDOM FROM CORRUPTION — 93

Corruption is perceived as almost nonexistent. Sweden tied with Denmark and New Zealand for 1st place out of 179 countries in Transparency International's Corruption Perceptions Index for 2008. Comprehensive laws on corruption are fully implemented, and Sweden has ratified the 1997 OECD Anti-bribery Convention. The constitution and law provide for public access to government information.

LABOR FREEDOM — 54.9

Sweden's labor regulations are rigid. The non-salary cost of employing a worker is high, and dismissing an employee is costly and burdensome.

SWITZERLAND

○ Bern

Economic Freedom Score

25　50　75

Least free 0 .... 100 Most free

81.1

| World Rank: **6** | Regional Rank: **2** |

Switzerland's economic freedom score is 81.1, making its economy the 6th freest in the 2010 *Index*. Its score has improved by 1.7 points since last year. Switzerland is ranked 2nd out of 43 countries in the Europe region, and its overall score is much higher than the world average.

The Swiss economy is diversified and modern, with high levels of prosperity and institutional strengths that include strong protection of property rights and an efficient legal framework. Openness to global trade and investment has enabled Switzerland to become one of the world's most competitive and flexible economies. Despite some stress in the financial system, Switzerland has emerged from the global economic turmoil relatively unscathed.

With an efficient and stable business climate, Switzerland has created a vibrant entrepreneurial environment. The average tariff rate is low, and commercial operations are aided by a flexible labor market and not overly burdened by regulation. Inflationary pressures are under control. Foreign investment is welcome, and screening applies to only a few sectors. Investors have access to adequate sources of credit. The judicial system, independent of political interference and free from corruption, enforces contracts reliably.

BACKGROUND: Switzerland, one of the world's richest and most investment-friendly destinations, is a multicultural society with four official languages. It has a long tradition of openness to the world yet jealously guards its independence and neutrality. The seat of the ill-fated League of Nations, Switzerland joined the United Nations only in 2002. Two referenda on membership in the European Union have failed by wide margins, and membership in the European Economic Area was rejected by referendum in 1992. Swiss–EU relations are based instead on an extensive range of bilateral technical agreements that are considered quite successful. Switzerland is an international banking center, but its economy also relies heavily on precision manufacturing, metals, pharmaceuticals, chemicals, and electronics.

Country's Score Over Time

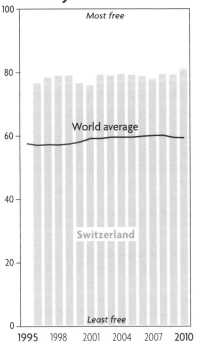

Quick Facts

Population: 7.6 million

GDP (PPP): $324.6 billion
1.6% growth in 2008
2.7% 5-year compound annual growth
$42,536 per capita

Unemployment: 3.5%

Inflation (CPI): 2.4%

FDI Inflow: $17.4 billion

2008 data unless otherwise noted
Data compiled as of September 2009

How Do We Measure Economic Freedom?
See page 457 for an explanation of the methodology or visit the *Index* Web site at *heritage.org/index*.

SWITZERLAND'S TEN ECONOMIC FREEDOMS

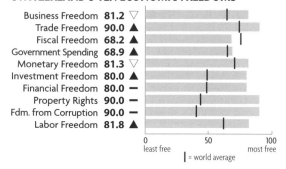

Business Freedom	81.2	▽
Trade Freedom	90.0	▲
Fiscal Freedom	68.2	▲
Government Spending	68.9	▲
Monetary Freedom	81.3	▽
Investment Freedom	80.0	▲
Financial Freedom	80.0	—
Property Rights	90.0	—
Fdm. from Corruption	90.0	—
Labor Freedom	81.8	▲

0 least free   50   100 most free
| = world average

BUSINESS FREEDOM — 81.2

The overall freedom to start, operate, and close a business is well protected under Switzerland's regulatory environment. Starting a business takes 20 days, compared to the world average of 35 days. Obtaining a business license takes less than the world average of 18 procedures and 218 days. Bankruptcy proceedings are relatively easy.

TRADE FREEDOM — 90

Switzerland's weighted average tariff rate was 0 percent in 2008. However, prohibitive agriculture tariffs and quotas block trade in some products altogether, and services market access barriers, import taxes, restrictive biotechnology regulations, and export subsidies add to the cost of trade. Ten points were deducted from Switzerland's trade freedom score to account for non-tariff barriers.

FISCAL FREEDOM — 68.2

Taxation is more burdensome at the cantonal levels than it is at the federal level. The top federal income tax rate is 11.5 percent, and the combined top income tax rate (federal and sub-federal) can be as high as 41.5 percent, though it is generally much lower. The top combined corporate tax rate can be as high as 24 percent. Other taxes include a value-added tax (VAT), a tax on securities and insurance premiums, and cantonal-level property taxes. In the most recent year, overall tax revenue as a percentage of GDP was 29.7 percent.

GOVERNMENT SPENDING — 68.9

Total government expenditures, including consumption and transfer payments, are moderate. In the most recent year, government spending equaled 32.2 percent of GDP. Direct government participation in the economy has been confined to such public services as post offices, railways, and defense.

MONETARY FREEDOM — 81.3

Inflation has been very low, averaging 1.9 percent between 2006 and 2008. Government measures influence the prices of agricultural goods and pharmaceutical products, and the government influences prices through regulation, sub-

sidies, and state-owned utilities. Ten points were deducted from Switzerland's monetary freedom score to account for policies that distort domestic prices.

INVESTMENT FREEDOM — 80

Foreign investment receives national treatment, and most sectors are open to private investment. Project screening applies in a few sectors. Joint stock companies must have a majority of resident Swiss nationals on their boards. Foreign investments are subject to review by the Competition Commission if the value of the investing firm's sales reaches certain levels. The investment code and its implementation are generally transparent and efficient, but this varies widely across cantons. Residents and non-residents may hold foreign exchange accounts. There are no restrictions on repatriation of profits or current transfers. Real estate purchases by non-residents must be approved by the canton in which the property is located.

FINANCIAL FREEDOM — 80

Switzerland is a leading financial center with highly developed and well-regulated institutions. Foreign and domestic investors have adequate access to capital and a wide variety of credit instruments. Mergers and acquisitions have reduced the number of banks, but there are still over 300 banks operating in the country. The two largest banking groups account for around 60 percent of the system's total assets. Credit is allocated on market terms. Insurance is well developed, and the state-owned postal service offers a variety of financial services. Capital markets are strong, and the stock exchange is one of Europe's largest. The global financial crisis hit the country's two major banks (UBS and Credit Suisse) hard. The government bailed out UBS in 2008 with asset purchases and a capital injection but sold off its stake in 2009.

PROPERTY RIGHTS — 90

The judiciary is independent, and contracts are secure. Switzerland has one of the world's best protection regimes for both foreign and domestic holders of intellectual property.

FREEDOM FROM CORRUPTION — 90

Corruption is perceived as almost nonexistent. Switzerland ranks 5th out of 179 countries in Transparency International's Corruption Perceptions Index for 2008. Corruption is not pervasive in any area of the economy, and enforcement against domestic corruption is effective. In 2007, the Federal Council approved the U.N. Convention Against Corruption, but ratification has not yet taken place.

LABOR FREEDOM — 81.8

Switzerland's labor regulations are relatively flexible. The non-salary cost of employing a worker is moderate, but dismissing an employee can be costly.

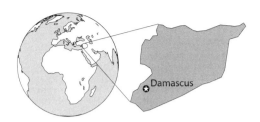

SYRIA

Economic Freedom Score

25   50   75

Least   Most
free   0   100   free

49.4

S yria's economic freedom score is 49.4, making its econo-my the 145th freest in the 2010 *Index*. Its score is 1.9 points lower than last year, reflecting reduced scores in five of the 10 economic freedoms, including freedom from corruption and property rights. Syria is ranked 15th out of 17 countries in the Middle East/North Africa region, and its overall score is lower than the regional average.

The Syrian economy, which has expanded at an average annual growth rate of more than 4 percent over the past five years, depends heavily on its oil sector, which provides half of government revenues and about two-thirds of export earnings. Diversification should be a top priority.

However, the overall entrepreneurial environment is ham-pered by significant institutional challenges. The regulato-ry and legal frameworks are deficient, and persistent state influence in most areas of the economy suppresses market competition. The judicial system is inefficient and remains vulnerable to political influence and widespread corruption. Average tariffs are high, keeping trade freedom far below the world average.

BACKGROUND: Syria has been ruled by the Assad regime since 1970, when Minister of Defense Hafez al-Assad seized power. His son Bashar, who succeeded him in 2000, has failed to deliver on promises to reform Syria's social-ist economy. Foreign investment has been constrained by government restrictions, U.S. economic sanctions, and Syr-ia's international isolation as a result of its involvement in the February 2005 assassination of former Lebanese Prime Minister Rafiq Hariri. Although the economy was helped by higher prices for Syria's declining oil exports in the mid-2000s, the Assad regime has been forced to undertake such belt-tightening measures as reducing subsidies on gasoline and other commodities. Syria's economy remains hobbled by a sluggish state bureaucracy, falling oil production, rising budget deficits, high unemployment, and inflation.

Country's Score Over Time

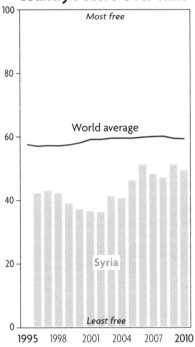

Quick Facts

Population: 21.2 million

GDP (PPP): $94.2 billion
5.2% growth in 2008
4.7% 5-year compound
annual growth
$4,440 per capita

Unemployment: 8.6%

Inflation (CPI): 14.5%

FDI Inflow: $2.1 billion

2008 data unless otherwise noted
Data compiled as of September 2009

How Do We Measure Economic Freedom?
See page 457 for an explanation of the methodology or visit the *Index* Web site at *heritage.org/index.*

SYRIA'S TEN ECONOMIC FREEDOMS

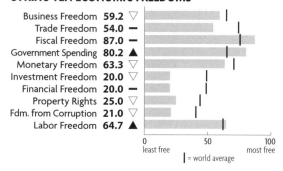

Business Freedom	59.2 ▽	
Trade Freedom	54.0 —	
Fiscal Freedom	87.0 —	
Government Spending	80.2 ▲	
Monetary Freedom	63.3 ▽	
Investment Freedom	20.0 ▽	
Financial Freedom	20.0 —	
Property Rights	25.0 ▽	
Fdm. from Corruption	21.0 ▽	
Labor Freedom	64.7 ▲	

0 least free   50   100 most free

| = world average

BUSINESS FREEDOM — 59.2

The overall freedom to start, operate, and close a business is constrained under Syria's regulatory environment. Starting a business takes about half of the world average of 35 days. Obtaining a business license requires slightly more than the world average of 18 procedures. Closing a business can be a lengthy and burdensome process.

TRADE FREEDOM — 54

Syria's weighted average tariff rate was 15.5 percent in 2002. Some prohibitive tariffs, import and export bans and restrictions, import taxes, import licensing, non-transparent trade regulations and government procurement, burdensome standards, inefficient customs administration, and corruption add to the cost of trade. Fifteen points were deducted from Syria's trade freedom score to account for non-tariff barriers.

FISCAL FREEDOM — 87

Syria has a relatively low income tax rate and a moderate corporate tax rate. The top income tax rate is 20 percent, and the top corporate tax rate is 28 percent. Other taxes include an estate tax and a property transfer tax. In the most recent year, overall tax revenue as a percentage of GDP was 10.8 percent. There is no value-added tax (VAT), but certain goods and services are subject to a consumption tax. The phasing out of fuel subsidies began in May 2008 and should be complete by 2010.

GOVERNMENT SPENDING — 80.2

Total government expenditures, including consumption and transfer payments, are relatively low. In the most recent year, government spending equaled 25.7 percent of GDP. The centralized, state-run economy is gradually opening. A private airline was launched in 2008. Public financial management needs improvement.

MONETARY FREEDOM — 63.3

Inflation has been high, averaging 11.7 percent between 2006 and 2008. The government controls prices for many goods, particularly in the agriculture sector; influences prices in other sectors through state-owned enterprises and utilities; and constrains private participation in manufacturing with input and output pricing limits. Fifteen points

were deducted from Syria's monetary freedom score to account for policies that distort domestic prices.

INVESTMENT FREEDOM — 20

Officially, foreign investment receives national treatment, and foreigners may own 100 percent of a company in certain sectors. Investment is screened. Arbitrary and non-transparent changes in investment law, burdensome bureaucracy, political instability, corruption, and the lack of an independent judiciary undermine investment. Most foreign exchange, capital transactions, and payments are subject to controls, government approval, or other restrictions. Repatriation of capital and profits is allowed, subject to some restrictions. Foreign investors may own land in connection with investments.

FINANCIAL FREEDOM — 20

There have been some considerable changes in Syria's financial sector. The government has opened the state-dominated banking sector. Since 2004, when the first private bank was licensed, the number of private banks has grown. Nine private banks are now in operation, including two Islamic banks. Total assets of these private banks represent 20 percent of total financial-system assets and are equivalent to about 13 percent of GDP. State-owned banks account for over 90 percent of private-sector lending, and the central bank is not independent. In 2005, the insurance sector was opened to private companies, breaking the monopoly previously enjoyed by the state-owned Syrian Insurance Company. Private insurance companies are allowed 100 percent foreign ownership. Despite these changes, Syria's financial system is still subject to heavy state influence. Regulations are cumbersome and unclear, and interest rates are set by the government. Capital markets are negligible and restricted to small amounts of government debt.

PROPERTY RIGHTS — 25

Protection of property rights is weak. Political connections and bribery influence court decisions. A law promulgated in 2007 permits foreigners to own or lease real property, but there is practically no legislation that protects intellectual property rights.

FREEDOM FROM CORRUPTION — 21

Corruption is perceived as widespread. Syria ranks 147th out of 179 countries in Transparency International's Corruption Perceptions Index for 2008, a decline for the second year in a row. Even members of the regime are said to be alarmed at the level of corruption in the legislative, judicial, and executive branches of government.

LABOR FREEDOM — 64.7

Syria's labor regulations are inflexible. The non-salary cost of employing a worker is moderate, but dismissing an employee is difficult.

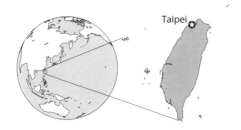

TAIWAN

Economic Freedom Score

70.4

Least free 0 — Most free 100

25 · 50 · 75

World Rank: 27   **Regional Rank: 7**

Taiwan's economic freedom score is 70.4, making its economy the 27th freest in the 2010 *Index*. Its score is 0.9 point higher than last year, primarily because of a notable improvement in business freedom. Taiwan is ranked 7th out of 41 economies in the Asia–Pacific region, and its overall score is higher than the world average.

The Taiwanese economy benefits from a well-developed legal and commercial infrastructure and a long tradition of entrepreneurship. Despite the recent economic contraction, the economy has achieved an average annual growth rate of close to 4 percent over the past five years. Small and medium-size enterprises continue to flourish in Taiwan's highly diversified economy.

Implementation of Company Act amendments in early 2009 eliminated minimum capital requirements and eased new business formation. Transparent and sound regulations facilitate an efficient investment climate. Tariffs are very low, and the government continues to improve the trade regime. Although the level of state involvement in the economy remains considerable, government spending is under control. Corruption and the rigid labor market continue to hold back Taiwan's overall economic freedom.

BACKGROUND: Taiwan, a dynamic multi-party democracy, is excluded from membership in the United Nations and other international organizations as a result of efforts from Beijing to pressure it into unification with China. In March 2008, former Taipei Mayor Ma Ying-jeou was elected president on a platform that promised a more open economic relationship with China. He has since moved to relax transportation and trade barriers with the mainland, although internal opposition to closer economic integration remains considerable because of fears that it will lead to ceding Taiwan's "unsettled" sovereignty to China. The move, however, seems to have attracted more foreign investment to the island. With a heavy emphasis on services, manufacturing, and high technology, Taiwan's modern, developed economy is one of the largest in Asia.

Country's Score Over Time

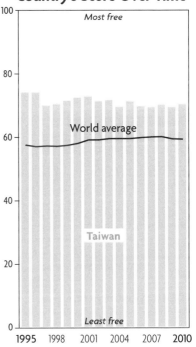

Quick Facts

Population: 23.0 million

GDP (PPP): $711 billion
0.1% growth in 2008
3.7% 5-year compound annual growth
$30,881 per capita

Unemployment: 4.1%

Inflation (CPI): 3.5%

FDI Inflow: $5.4 billion

2008 data unless otherwise noted
Data compiled as of September 2009

How Do We Measure Economic Freedom?
See page 457 for an explanation of the methodology or visit the *Index* Web site at *heritage.org/index.*

TAIWAN'S TEN ECONOMIC FREEDOMS

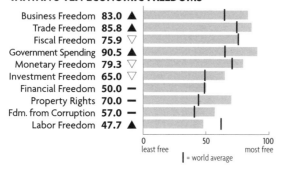

Business Freedom	83.0 ▲	
Trade Freedom	85.8 ▲	
Fiscal Freedom	75.9 ▽	
Government Spending	90.5 ▲	
Monetary Freedom	79.3 ▽	
Investment Freedom	65.0 ▽	
Financial Freedom	50.0 —	
Property Rights	70.0 —	
Fdm. from Corruption	57.0 —	
Labor Freedom	47.7 ▲	

0 least free   50   100 most free

| = world average

BUSINESS FREEDOM — 83

The overall freedom to conduct a business is well protected under Taiwan's regulatory environment. Starting a business takes an average of 23 days, compared to the world average of 35 days. Obtaining a business license requires less than the world average of 218 days. Bankruptcy proceedings are fairly easy and straightforward.

TRADE FREEDOM — 85.8

Taiwan's weighted average tariff rate was 2.1 percent in 2006. The government has been improving the trade regime, but some import and export bans and restrictions, services market access barriers, import taxes and fees, burdensome standards and certification requirements, restrictive pharmaceutical regulations, cumbersome sanitary and phytosanitary rules, state trade in rice, and weak enforcement of intellectual property rights add to the cost of trade. Ten points were deducted from Taiwan's trade freedom score to account for non-tariff barriers.

FISCAL FREEDOM — 75.9

Taiwan has a relatively high income tax rate and a moderate corporate tax rate. The top income tax rate is 40 percent, and the top corporate tax rate is 25 percent. A 10 percent surtax is applied to undistributed profits. Other taxes include a value-added tax (VAT), a property tax, and a stamp duty on insurance and employment contracts. In the most recent year, overall tax revenue as a percentage of GDP was 13.7 percent.

GOVERNMENT SPENDING — 90.5

Total government expenditures, including consumption and transfer payments, are low. In the most recent year, government spending equaled 17.8 percent of GDP. Privatization and deregulation have reduced the government's role in the economy, even in strategic sectors, but the state is still active in economic management.

MONETARY FREEDOM — 79.3

Inflation has been low, averaging 2.8 percent between 2006 and 2008. The government regulates the prices of pharmaceutical and medical products and influences prices through regulation, subsidies, and state-owned utilities. Ten points were deducted from Taiwan's monetary freedom score to account for policies that distort domestic prices.

INVESTMENT FREEDOM — 65

Foreign and domestic investments are equal under the law, and private investment is welcome in most sectors. However, foreign ownership is limited in certain sectors. Investment is screened, but approval time is usually short. Investment laws and bureaucracy are generally transparent and efficient. There are relatively few restrictions on converting or transferring direct investment funds. The remittance of capital invested in Taiwan must be reported to the government. Declared earnings, capital gains, dividends, royalties, management fees, and other returns on investments can be repatriated at any time. Large foreign exchange transactions may have to be conducted over time to prevent market disruptions. There are quantity restrictions on the level of total outbound investment. Investments in China are subject to additional restrictions.

FINANCIAL FREEDOM — 50

Taiwan's modern financial sector has become more competitive. Many restrictions on financial activities, particularly those of foreign financial institutions, have been reduced. A wide variety of financial instruments are available to foreign and domestic investors on market terms. Government-controlled banks dominate banking, accounting for about half of total assets. Two state-owned banks, Bank of Taiwan and the Central Trust of China, were merged to become the country's largest commercial bank in 2007. Foreign banks play a relatively small role, although their market share has increased to around 16 percent of total assets. Capital markets are sophisticated and developing, and the stock market is generally open to foreign participation.

PROPERTY RIGHTS — 70

Property rights are generally protected, and the judiciary enforces contracts, but the court system is very slow. Taiwan has passed several laws to improve enforcement of intellectual property rights, but criminals continue to sell pirated optical media, counterfeit pharmaceuticals, and counterfeit luxury goods. In July 2008, the government inaugurated an Intellectual Property Court to handle all new civil and administrative IPR litigation, as well as appeals on criminal cases.

FREEDOM FROM CORRUPTION — 57

Corruption is perceived as present. Taiwan ranks 39th out of 179 countries in Transparency International's Corruption Perceptions Index for 2008. Taiwan has implemented laws, regulations, and penalties to combat corruption. The Corruption Punishment Statute and the criminal code contain specific penalties for corrupt activities.

LABOR FREEDOM — 47.7

Taiwan's labor regulations are rigid. The non-salary cost of employing a worker is low, but dismissing an employee is relatively costly and burdensome. Regulations on work hours are not flexible.

TAJIKISTAN

World Rank: 128   **Regional Rank: 27**

Tajikistan's economic freedom score is 53.0, making its economy the 128th freest in the 2010 *Index*. Its score is 1.6 points lower than last year, reflecting reduced scores in eight of the 10 economic freedoms, including freedom from corruption, investment freedom, and property rights. Tajikistan is ranked 27th out of 41 countries in the Asia–Pacific region, and its overall score is lower than the world average.

Tajikistan has pursued reforms to foster sound macroeconomic management and improvement of the business climate, but progress has been marginal. Growth potential remains constrained by government interference, which has left the economy vulnerable in a changing political environment. Tajikistan continues to face many challenges that require rebuilding infrastructure, improving the entrepreneurial environment, and attracting foreign investment.

Despite some progress in privatizing small and medium-size public enterprises, the private sector is developing slowly. Dependence on remittances (estimated at over 45 percent of GDP) continues, reflecting the lack of domestic economic dynamism. Foreign investment is deterred by burdensome bureaucratic regulations and inconsistent administration. Tajikistan remains one of the world's most corrupt nations.

BACKGROUND: Tajikistan's transition to multi-party democracy has been problematic since the 1992–1997 civil war between Islamists and the ruling post-Communists. Parliamentary elections in February 2005 and President Imomali Rahmon's November 2006 re-election to a third seven-year term failed to meet international standards. Rahmon has limited political activity and tightened controls on civil society. Poverty remains pervasive, and remittances and drug production and trafficking are important sources of income. Major exports are aluminum (the price of which severely declined in 2008), cotton, and electricity from massive Soviet-era hydropower plants. A decline in remittances and the return of a large number of migrants could cause instability. Tajikistan is borrowing heavily from China to finance investments in energy infrastructure and requested support from the International Monetary Fund in 2009.

Country's Score Over Time

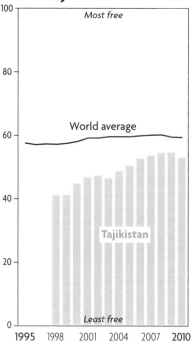

Quick Facts

Population: 6.8 million

GDP (PPP): $13.0 billion
7.9% growth in 2008
7.4% 5-year compound annual growth
$1,906 per capita

Unemployment: 2.4% (registered unemployed). If combined with underemployment, the rate would be much higher.

Inflation (CPI): 20.4%

FDI Inflow: $376 million

2008 data unless otherwise noted
Data compiled as of September 2009

How Do We Measure Economic Freedom?
See page 457 for an explanation of the methodology or visit the *Index* Web site at *heritage.org/index.*

TAJIKISTAN'S TEN ECONOMIC FREEDOMS

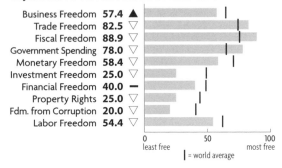

Business Freedom	57.4 ▲	
Trade Freedom	82.5 ▽	
Fiscal Freedom	88.9 ▽	
Government Spending	78.0 ▽	
Monetary Freedom	58.4 ▽	
Investment Freedom	25.0 ▽	
Financial Freedom	40.0 ▬	
Property Rights	25.0 ▽	
Fdm. from Corruption	20.0 ▽	
Labor Freedom	54.4 ▽	

0 least free — 50 — 100 most free
| = world average

BUSINESS FREEDOM — 57.4

The overall freedom to start, operate, and close a business is restricted under Tajikistan's regulatory environment. Starting a business takes an average of 25 days, compared to the world average of 35 days. Obtaining a business license requires more than the world average of 18 procedures, and costs are high. Closing a business is a protracted process.

TRADE FREEDOM — 82.5

Tajikistan's weighted average tariff rate was 3.8 percent in 2006. Some quotas, import bans and restrictions, non-transparent standards and other regulations, inadequate bureaucratic capacity, non-transparent and corrupt customs implementation, and weak enforcement of intellectual property rights add to the cost of trade. Ten points were deducted from Tajikistan's trade freedom score to account for non-tariff barriers.

FISCAL FREEDOM — 88.9

Tajikistan has competitive tax rates. The top income tax rate is 13 percent, and the top corporate tax rate is 25 percent. Other taxes include a value-added tax (VAT) and a tax on immovable property. In the most recent year, overall tax revenue as a percentage of GDP was 17.8 percent.

GOVERNMENT SPENDING — 78

Total government expenditures, including consumption and transfer payments, are relatively low. In the most recent year, government spending equaled 27.1 percent of GDP. State-owned enterprises are a drag on public finances. Despite employing 50 percent of the working population, the cotton sector accounts for only 4 percent of GDP and suffers from state interference and mismanagement.

MONETARY FREEDOM — 58.4

Inflation has been very high, averaging 17.7 percent between 2006 and 2008, but fell sharply in 2009. The government influences prices through regulation, subsidies, and numerous state-owned enterprises and utilities. Farmers are subject to state control of production and harvesting decisions, particularly in the cotton sector. Fifteen points were deducted from Tajikistan's monetary freedom score to account for policies that distort domestic prices.

INVESTMENT FREEDOM — 25

Both foreign and domestic investors face numerous barriers to investing in Tajikistan. All private investment is screened and requires government approval. Investment laws are inconsistently implemented, and the bureaucracy is non-transparent, burdensome, and prone to corruption. Contracts are weakly enforced, and infrastructure remains inadequate. Investors face ownership restrictions and cumbersome procedures with regard to tax and business registration. Remittance of profits abroad is allowed. Residents and non-residents may hold foreign exchange accounts. Foreign exchange and capital payments and transfers are subject to documentary requirements. All land is owned by the state, but land-use rights may be leased.

FINANCIAL FREEDOM — 40

Tajikistan's financial sector has undergone a gradual transformation that has led to increased transparency and improved supervision and regulation. Financial-sector assets have grown very rapidly in recent years, reaching around 40 percent of GDP. However, the banking sector's limited capacity to provide financial intermediation impedes the development of a more vibrant private sector. There are 11 private commercial banks, one of which is foreign-owned. The four largest banks, including one state-owned bank, control 80 percent of deposits. All banks except one are privately owned. Non-performing loans have been decreasing. The small non-banking financial sector includes several small insurance companies and one pension fund. Capital markets remain rudimentary, reflecting the lack of efficiency and depth in the financial system.

PROPERTY RIGHTS — 25

Protection of private property rights is weak. Judicial corruption is widespread, and the courts are sensitive to pressure from the government and paramilitary groups. Legal proceedings are not transparent, and a lack of respect for due process undermines the freedom of civil society. Tajikistan's weak enforcement regime lacks criminal penalties for violations of intellectual property rights.

FREEDOM FROM CORRUPTION — 20

Corruption is perceived as pervasive. Tajikistan ranks 151st out of 179 countries in Transparency International's Corruption Perceptions Index for 2008. Bribery and nepotism are endemic. Numerous observers have noted that power has become consolidated in the hands of a relatively small number of individuals. Anemic anti-corruption efforts from the Tajik government have proven ineffective, and some anti-corruption units are known to be particularly corrupt.

LABOR FREEDOM — 54.4

Tajikistan's labor regulations are inflexible. The non-salary cost of employing a worker is high, and dismissing an employee is difficult. Regulations on the number of work hours are not flexible.

2010 Index of Economic Freedom

TANZANIA

Economic Freedom Score

Least free 0   25   50   75   100   Most free

58.3

Tanzania's economic freedom score is 58.3, making its economy the 97th freest in the 2010 *Index*. Its score remains the same as last year. Tanzania is ranked 11th out of 46 countries in the Sub-Saharan Africa region, and its overall score is slightly lower than the world average.

Continuing reform has led to some progress in reducing poverty. Annual growth has averaged around 7 percent over the past five years, yielding improvements in various social and human development indicators. Tanzania has above-average scores in fiscal freedom, investment freedom, and government spending. Foreign and domestic investors receive equal treatment, although poor infrastructure, government control, and corruption remain deterrents. Government spending is moderate, and a relatively low level of debt has allowed the economy to undertake infrastructure projects without jeopardizing the stability of public finances.

Tanzania's tariff barrier has been reduced to less than 10 percent, but inefficient customs and other non-tariff barriers limit overall trade freedom. The judiciary is underdeveloped and vulnerable to the political whims of the executive. Corruption is pervasive despite ongoing reform efforts, and restoring the government's credibility remains critical.

BACKGROUND: The United Republic of Tanzania was formed in 1964 by the union of Tanganyika and Zanzibar, each of which had recently achieved independence. Zanzibar retains considerable local autonomy, including its own legislature and president. Tanzania's first president, Julius K. Nyerere, pursued socialist economic policies that severely constrained economic growth and development during his nearly 25 years in office. Under his successors, the historically state-led economy is becoming more market-based, but it remains hindered by poor infrastructure and the country's high rate of HIV/AIDS. Jakaya Kikwete, previously Tanzania's foreign minister, has served as president since winning election in December 2005. Tanzania remains very poor. Agriculture employs 80 percent of the population and accounted for over 40 percent of GDP in 2007.

Country's Score Over Time

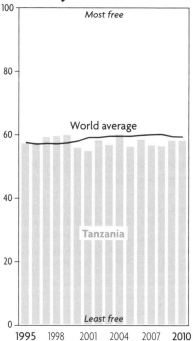

Quick Facts

Population: 42.5 million

GDP (PPP): $53.7 billion
7.5% growth in 2008
7.2% 5-year compound annual growth
$1,263 per capita

Unemployment: n/a

Inflation (CPI): 10.3%

FDI Inflow: $744 million

2008 data unless otherwise noted
Data compiled as of September 2009

How Do We Measure Economic Freedom?
See page 457 for an explanation of the methodology or visit the *Index* Web site at *heritage.org/index.*

TANZANIA'S TEN ECONOMIC FREEDOMS

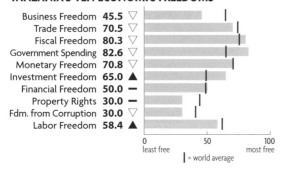

Business Freedom	45.5	▽
Trade Freedom	70.5	▽
Fiscal Freedom	80.3	▽
Government Spending	82.6	▽
Monetary Freedom	70.8	▽
Investment Freedom	65.0	▲
Financial Freedom	50.0	—
Property Rights	30.0	—
Fdm. from Corruption	30.0	▽
Labor Freedom	58.4	▲

0 least free   50   100 most free

| = world average

BUSINESS FREEDOM — 45.5

The overall freedom to conduct a business is seriously limited under Tanzania's regulatory environment. Starting a business takes an average of 29 days, compared to the world average of 35 days. Obtaining a business license takes more than the world average of 18 procedures and 218 days, and costs are high. Bankruptcy proceedings are fairly straightforward but relatively lengthy.

TRADE FREEDOM — 70.5

Tanzania's weighted average tariff rate was 9.7 percent in 2008. Some import and export restrictions, import taxes, import permit and licensing requirements, inefficient and slow customs administration, weak enforcement of intellectual property rights, and corruption add to the cost of trade. Ten points were deducted from Tanzania's trade freedom score to account for non-tariff barriers.

FISCAL FREEDOM — 80.3

Tanzania has moderate tax rates. Both the top income tax rate and the top corporate tax rate are 30 percent. Other taxes include a value-added tax (VAT), a transfer tax on motor vehicles, and a fuel levy on petroleum products. In the most recent year, overall tax revenue as a percentage of GDP was 13.0 percent.

GOVERNMENT SPENDING — 82.6

Total government expenditures, including consumption and transfer payments, are relatively low. After five years of growth, government spending in the most recent year equaled 24.1 percent of GDP. Privatization and restructuring of state-owned enterprises have progressed.

MONETARY FREEDOM — 70.8

Inflation has been high, averaging 9.2 percent between 2006 and 2008. The government influences prices through regulation, subsidies, and state-owned enterprises and utilities. Ten points were deducted from Tanzania's monetary freedom score to account for policies that distort domestic prices.

INVESTMENT FREEDOM — 65

Foreign and domestic investors receive equal treatment under the law in most sectors. There is no limit on foreign ownership in an enterprise, and investment is not screened. The Tourism Act of 2007 bars foreigners from engaging in some tourism-related businesses. Burdensome bureaucracy, inadequate infrastructure, and corruption are ongoing deterrents to investment. Enforcement of commercial law through the courts is difficult. Foreign exchange and capital transactions are permitted with few restrictions. Profits, dividends, and capital can be repatriated. The state owns all land, and investors may lease but not own land.

FINANCIAL FREEDOM — 50

Tanzania's financial system is relatively small but developing. Direct government influence has gradually diminished, and privatization is ongoing. Credit is allocated largely at market rates, and a range of commercial credit instruments are available to the private sector. There are minimal restrictions on foreign banks, which account for around 50 percent of the banking system's assets. More than 20 commercial banks are licensed and operating, and over 50 percent are foreign-affiliated. A controlling stake in the National Commercial Bank was sold to a foreign bank in 2001. The National Microfinance Bank was partially privatized in 2005, and further sales of the state's remaining 51 percent share have been planned. In 2008, the government implemented a leasing finance law in order to ease access to finance and facilitate the growth of leasing services. Pension funds, which remain poorly supervised, have been growing rapidly in recent years. Capital markets are rudimentary, reflecting the lack of efficiency and depth in the financial sector.

PROPERTY RIGHTS — 30

The legal system is slow and subject to corruption. A commercial court has been established to improve the resolution of commercial disputes. Recent reforms have been aimed at establishing a reliable system of transferable property rights. Legislation conforms to international intellectual property rights conventions, but violations are not seriously investigated, and courts lack experience and training in IPR issues.

FREEDOM FROM CORRUPTION — 30

Corruption is perceived as widespread. Tanzania ranks 102nd out of 179 countries in Transparency International's Corruption Perceptions Index for 2008. Despite improvements during the past decade, corruption remains pervasive throughout the government. The enforcement of laws, regulations, and penalties to combat corruption is largely ineffective. Areas where corruption persists include government procurement, privatization, taxation, ports, and customs clearance. The government launched a series of high-profile corruption prosecutions in late 2008.

LABOR FREEDOM — 58.4

Tanzania's labor regulations are restrictive. The non-salary cost of employing a worker is moderate, but dismissing an employee is difficult.

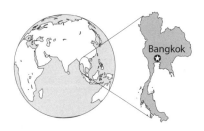

Bangkok

THAILAND

Economic Freedom Score

25   50   75

Least free 0   100 Most free

64.1

| World Rank: **66** | Regional Rank: **10** |

Thailand's economic freedom score is 64.1, making its economy the 66th freest in the 2010 *Index*. Its score is 1.1 points better than last year, reflecting improvements in five of the 10 economic freedoms, including freedom from corruption and investment freedom. Thailand is ranked 10th out of 41 countries in the Asia–Pacific region, and its overall score is higher than the world and regional averages.

The Thai economy has recorded relatively steady economic growth over the past five years, showing a moderate degree of resilience. The regulatory environment has gradually become more efficient and streamlined. Procedures for business formation are simple and transparent. The financial sector continues to strengthen and is more open to competition.

Challenges remain in monetary freedom, investment freedom, and freedom from corruption. The government directly subsidizes the prices of a number of staple goods. Inflation has fallen from highs in 2008, but the government has implemented expansionary monetary policy in response to the global financial crisis. Foreign investment is subject to a variety of severe restrictions, though they are not uniformly enforced. Corruption is significant but not as extensive as in many neighboring countries.

BACKGROUND: Thailand is a constitutional monarchy with a turbulent political history. Since 1932, the country has experienced 18 military coups d'etat. The government returned to democratic civilian control in December 2007 and, after a year of political turmoil, experienced a peaceful transfer of power to the political opposition. Demonstrations and protests have continued, however, and political instability is undoubtedly having a negative impact on economic growth. About 40 percent of the population is engaged in agriculture, but a thriving manufacturing sector, including the manufacture of such high-technology products as integrated circuits, contributes significantly to export-led growth.

Country's Score Over Time

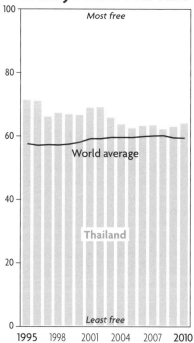

Quick Facts

Population: 67.4 million

GDP (PPP): $519.0 billion
2.6% growth in 2008
4.3% 5-year compound annual growth
$7,703 per capita

Unemployment: 1.4%

Inflation (CPI): 5.5%

FDI Inflow: $10.1 billion

*2008 data unless otherwise noted
Data compiled as of September 2009*

How Do We Measure Economic Freedom?
See page 457 for an explanation of the methodology or visit the *Index* Web site at *heritage.org/index*.

THAILAND'S TEN ECONOMIC FREEDOMS

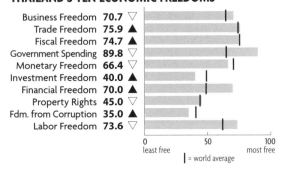

Business Freedom	70.7 ▽	
Trade Freedom	75.9 ▲	
Fiscal Freedom	74.7 ▲	
Government Spending	89.8 ▽	
Monetary Freedom	66.4 ▽	
Investment Freedom	40.0 ▲	
Financial Freedom	70.0 ▲	
Property Rights	45.0 ▽	
Fdm. from Corruption	35.0 ▲	
Labor Freedom	73.6 ▽	

0 least free   50   100 most free

| = world average

BUSINESS FREEDOM — 70.7

The overall freedom to start, operate, and close a business is relatively well protected under Thailand's regulatory environment. Starting a business takes an average of 32 days, compared to the world average of 35 days. Obtaining a business license takes less than the world average of 18 procedures and 218 days. Bankruptcy proceedings are fairly easy and straightforward.

TRADE FREEDOM — 75.9

Thailand's weighted average tariff rate was 4.6 percent in 2006. Prohibitive tariffs, some import bans and restrictions, services market access barriers, import taxes and fees, burdensome standards and import licensing requirements, restrictive sanitary and phytosanitary rules, non-transparent government procurement, non-transparent customs valuation, export subsidies, and weak enforcement of intellectual property rights add to the cost of trade. Fifteen points were deducted from Thailand's trade freedom score to account for non-tariff barriers.

FISCAL FREEDOM — 74.7

Thailand has a relatively high income tax and a moderate corporate tax. The top income tax rate is 37 percent, and the top corporate tax rate is 30 percent. Other taxes include a value-added tax (VAT) and a property tax. In the most recent year, overall tax revenue as a percentage of GDP was 16.2 percent.

GOVERNMENT SPENDING — 89.8

Total government expenditures, including consumption and transfer payments, are low. In the most recent year, government spending equaled 18.4 percent of GDP. Government intervention persists, and privatization has suffered several setbacks.

MONETARY FREEDOM — 66.4

Inflation has been relatively low, averaging 4.6 percent between 2006 and 2008. The government controls the prices of more than 200 products; can set price ceilings for basic goods and services; and influences prices through regulation, subsidies, and state-owned utilities. Twenty points were deducted from Thailand's monetary freedom score to account for policies that distort domestic prices.

INVESTMENT FREEDOM — 40

The government prohibits majority foreign ownership in most sectors and reserves certain professions for Thai nationals. Investment regulations are complex, investment laws are inconsistently enforced, and bureaucracy is non-transparent. Residents and non-residents may hold foreign exchange accounts, subject to some controls. Some foreign exchange transactions, repatriations, outward direct investments, and transactions involving capital market securities, bonds, debt securities, money market instruments, and short-term securities are regulated and face restrictions. Foreign investors may own land, subject to a number of restrictions.

FINANCIAL FREEDOM — 70

Thailand's financial system has undergone restructuring in recent years. The regulatory framework has been strengthened. Under the Financial Institutions Businesses Act, implemented in August 2008, the Bank of Thailand (BOT) and the Finance Ministry can ease restrictions on foreign ownership and the number of foreign directors in commercial banks. Foreign shareholders are now permitted to retain a 49 percent stake in financial institutions. Prior BOT approval is still required for foreign ownership between 25 percent and 49 percent. The law also gives the BOT the authority to allow foreign ownership above the 49 percent limit if such action is necessary to support financial stability. Credit is generally allocated on market terms. As of early 2009, there were 14 commercial banks, two of which are government-owned. Capital markets are relatively well developed. The stock exchange is active and open to foreign investors. The global financial turmoil's impact on the banking sector has been relatively muted.

PROPERTY RIGHTS — 45

Private property is generally protected, but the legal process is slow, and litigants, vested interests, or third parties can affect judgments through extralegal means. Despite a Central Intellectual Property and International Trade Court, piracy (especially of optical media) continues. The government can disclose trade secrets to protect any "public interest" not having commercial objectives, and there are concerns that approval-related data might not be protected against unfair commercial use.

FREEDOM FROM CORRUPTION — 35

Corruption is perceived as significant. Thailand ranks 80th out of 179 countries in Transparency International's Corruption Perceptions Index for 2008. Allegations of customs irregularities continue. The lack of administrative transparency is attributable to Thailand's complex hierarchical system of laws and regulations. The government is trying to make the evaluation of bids and awarding of contracts more transparent. Convictions of public officials on corruption-related charges are rare.

LABOR FREEDOM — 73.6

Thailand's labor regulations are relatively flexible. The non-salary cost of employing a worker is low, and dismissing an employee is not burdensome. Regulations on work hours are quite flexible.

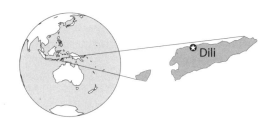

TIMOR-LESTE

World Rank: 164   **Regional Rank: 36**

Economic Freedom Score

25   50   75

Least free 0   100 Most free

45.8

Timor-Leste's economic freedom score is 45.8, making its economy the 164th freest in the 2010 *Index*. Its score has decreased by 4.7 points from last year, reflecting considerable declines in scores for freedom from corruption, investment freedom, and government spending. Timor-Leste is ranked 36th out of 41 countries in the Asia–Pacific region, and its overall score is well below the world and regional averages.

Timor-Leste has made some progress in economic reconstruction since achieving independence in 2002, but the economy continues to confront considerable institutional challenges, including weak public-sector and private-sector capacity and poor infrastructure.

The economy of Timor-Leste is dominated by government activity. Severe constraints in regulatory and legal frameworks, coupled with widespread corruption, impede the entrepreneurial environment. The country's overall business and investment climate suffers from poor regulatory capacity, volatility, and political instability. The general lack of institutional capacity has a particularly damaging effect on the protection of property rights.

BACKGROUND: Timor-Leste is one of the poorest countries in Asia. It gained its independence in 2002 after 25 years of sometimes brutal Indonesian occupation and two and a half years of administration by the United Nations. Since then, the government has struggled to pacify the country. Economic liberalization has mostly stalled, and the economy remains heavily dependent on foreign aid. Infrastructure is very poor, and corruption is rampant. Timor-Leste has relied heavily on considerable offshore petroleum revenues but remains primarily an agricultural economy. Timor-Leste's Petroleum Fund makes the country's national accounting unique. The fund, in which the government deposits all income from the oil sector, has grown in 2008 as a result of investments in U.S. government bonds. It is not counted as part of GDP but is reflected in government revenue figures.

Country's Score Over Time

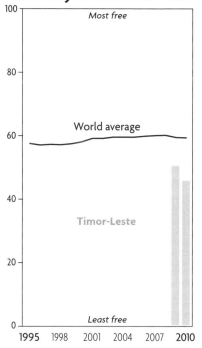

Quick Facts

Population: 1.1 million

GDP (PPP): $0.9 billion
13.2% growth in 2008
5.2% 5-year compound annual growth
$801 per capita

Unemployment: estimated to be over 10%

Inflation (CPI): 7.6%

FDI Inflow: n/a

2008 data unless otherwise noted
Data compiled as of September 2009

How Do We Measure Economic Freedom?
See page 457 for an explanation of the methodology or visit the *Index* Web site at *heritage.org/index*.

TIMOR-LESTE'S TEN ECONOMIC FREEDOMS

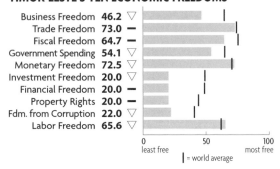

Business Freedom	46.2 ▽	
Trade Freedom	73.0 —	
Fiscal Freedom	64.7 —	
Government Spending	54.1 ▽	
Monetary Freedom	72.5 ▽	
Investment Freedom	20.0 ▽	
Financial Freedom	20.0 —	
Property Rights	20.0 —	
Fdm. from Corruption	22.0 ▽	
Labor Freedom	65.6 ▽	

0 least free   50   100 most free

| = world average

BUSINESS FREEDOM — 46.2

The overall freedom to start, operate, and close a business is constrained under Timor-Leste's burdensome regulatory environment. Starting a business takes an average of 83 days, compared to the world average of 35 days. Obtaining a business license requires 22 procedures, compared to the world average of 18. Minimum capital to start a business is quite high.

TRADE FREEDOM — 73

According to the International Monetary Fund, Timor-Leste's simple tariff rate was 6 percent in 2007. Import restrictions, import taxes and fees, some export taxes, import approval and licensing requirements, non-transparent regulations, inadequate infrastructure and trade capacity, and underdeveloped markets limit trade and increase costs. Fifteen points were deducted from Timor-Leste's trade freedom score to account for non-tariff barriers.

FISCAL FREEDOM — 64.7

Timor-Leste has low taxes. The top income and corporate tax rates are 10 percent. In the most recent year, overall tax revenue as a percentage of non-oil GDP was 133.9 percent, reflecting large tax revenues from petroleum projects in the Timor Sea.

GOVERNMENT SPENDING — 54.1

Total government expenditures, including consumption and transfer payments, are relatively high. In the most recent year, government spending jumped to 39.1 percent of non-oil GDP, reflecting growing social transfers and income supports including rice subsidies. The economy is relatively closed and was not significantly affected by the global downturn.

MONETARY FREEDOM — 72.5

Inflation has been relatively high, averaging 7.6 percent between 2006 and 2008. The economy operates under a U.S. dollar–based currency regime that, when combined with the monetary authority's lack of legal power to lend, has constrained the scope of monetary and exchange rate policies. Ten points were deducted from Timor-Leste's monetary freedom score to adjust for measures that distort domestic prices.

INVESTMENT FREEDOM — 20

Investment may be vetted by the government in any economic sector, but exploration, research, exploitation of oil and gas, and the extraction of mineral resources are governed by separate and additional regulations. Despite an investment and trade development organization intended to coordinate and monitor foreign investments and exports and to centralize the administrative procedures for authorizations, the investment environment is significantly limited by inadequate institutional capacity, complex licensing requirements, weak contract enforcement, underdeveloped markets, and internal instability. Foreign investors may lease but not own land.

FINANCIAL FREEDOM — 20

Timor-Leste's financial sector is at an early stage of development. Access to credit is very limited, though modest progress has been made in establishing an effective banking system. The banking sector consists of the monetary authority, three foreign-owned commercial banks, and a few specialized microfinance institutions. Bank deposits have increased, as have loans to individuals and construction projects. Banking services are used by less than 2 percent of the population. Poor credit assessment policies and difficulties in contract enforcement and loan recovery have contributed to an increase in non-performing loans, which remain a problem, with their ratio to total loans standing at around 28 percent.

PROPERTY RIGHTS — 20

A nascent legal system has been put in place, but the justice system remains among the weakest sectors of government, relying heavily on foreign assistance. Land titles from the Portuguese colonial period may conflict with competing claims from the Indonesian occupation and also with claims from squatters who may currently occupy the land. In some villages where traditional practices hold sway, women may not inherit or own property.

FREEDOM FROM CORRUPTION — 22

Corruption is perceived as widespread. Timor-Leste ranks 145th out of 179 countries in Transparency International's Corruption Perceptions Index for 2008, a significant drop from 2007. Official corruption, despite being subject to criminal penalties under the law, remains a serious problem. By law, the ombudsman's office is charged with leading national anti-corruption activities and has the authority to refer cases for prosecution. Cases investigated have included allegations of corruption involving both mid-level and senior government procurement officials. There are credible reports of petty corruption at the nation's port, and customs and border officials are suspected of facilitating the smuggling of gasoline, tobacco, and alcohol across the border from Indonesia.

LABOR FREEDOM — 65.6

Timor-Leste's employment regulations are relatively rigid. The non-salary cost of employing a worker is high, and dismissing an employee is relatively costly. The public sector accounts for around half the employment outside agriculture, and the formal labor market remains underdeveloped.

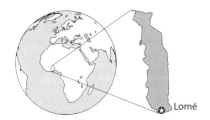

TOGO

Economic Freedom Score

47.1

Togo's economic freedom score is 47.1, making its economy the 161st freest in the 2010 *Index*. Its score is 1.5 points lower than last year, reflecting notable losses in trade freedom, monetary freedom, and investment freedom. Togo is ranked 39th out of 46 countries in the Sub-Saharan Africa region, and its overall score is well below the world and regional averages.

The Togolese government has undertaken a series of economic reforms in recent years, restructuring key sectors including banking, electricity, and transportation. The corporate tax rate, which had been one of the region's highest, was reduced to 33 percent in 2008.

Togo's competitiveness has nonetheless continued to suffer from a poor business environment and an undeveloped financial sector, both of which significantly handicap private-sector development. The country still depends to a large extent on foreign aid. Government spending is moderate, but improved public administration and privatization would stimulate broad-based economic growth. Foreign direct investment is allowed only in certain sectors, and regulatory and judicial systems lack transparency and are vulnerable to corruption and political interference.

BACKGROUND: In 2005, the military appointed Faure Gnassingbé to serve as president following the death of his father. Condemnation and sanctions by the Economic Community of West African States and the African Union, along with pressure from the international community, led Gnassingbé to step down. He won the subsequent 2005 election, which was widely viewed as flawed. The resulting political turmoil ended with legislative elections in 2007 that most observers viewed as free and fair. The next presidential election is scheduled for early 2010. Agriculture accounted for over 40 percent of GDP in 2006, and much of the population is engaged in subsistence agriculture. Principal exports include cement, cocoa, cotton, and phosphates. Services are also important, especially re-exports from the Lomé port facility to landlocked states in the region.

Country's Score Over Time

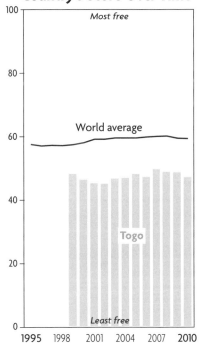

Quick Facts

Population: 6.5 million

GDP (PPP): $5.4 billion
1.1% growth in 2008
2.0% 5-year compound
annual growth
$829 per capita

Unemployment: n/a

Inflation (CPI): 8.4%

FDI Inflow: $68 million

2008 data unless otherwise noted
Data compiled as of September 2009

How Do We Measure Economic Freedom?
See page 457 for an explanation of the methodology or visit the *Index* Web site at *heritage.org/index.*

TOGO'S TEN ECONOMIC FREEDOMS

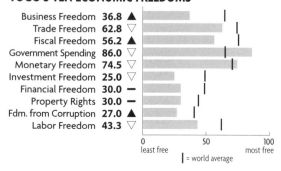

Business Freedom	36.8	▲
Trade Freedom	62.8	▽
Fiscal Freedom	56.2	▲
Government Spending	86.0	▽
Monetary Freedom	74.5	▽
Investment Freedom	25.0	▽
Financial Freedom	30.0	—
Property Rights	30.0	—
Fdm. from Corruption	27.0	▲
Labor Freedom	43.3	▽

0 least free   50   100 most free

❙ = world average

BUSINESS FREEDOM — 36.8

The overall freedom to conduct a business is seriously limited under Togo's regulatory environment. Starting a business takes an average of 75 days, compared to the world average of 35 days. Obtaining a business license takes longer than the world average of 218 days, and costs are high.

TRADE FREEDOM — 62.8

Togo's weighted average tariff rate was 13.6 percent in 2008. Some import restrictions, import taxes and fees, import permit requirements, export-promotion programs, inadequate infrastructure, and weak enforcement of intellectual property rights add to the cost of trade. Ten points were deducted from Togo's trade freedom score to account for non-tariff barriers.

FISCAL FREEDOM — 56.2

Togo has a high income tax rate and a relatively high corporate tax rate. The top income tax rate is 55 percent, and the top corporate tax rate is 33 percent, down from 37 percent as of January 1, 2009. Other taxes include a value-added tax (VAT), a property tax, and a vehicle tax. In the most recent year, overall tax revenue as a percentage of GDP was 16.4 percent. The government has scaled back tax exemptions to broaden the tax base.

GOVERNMENT SPENDING — 86

Total government expenditures, including consumption and transfer payments, are relatively low. In the most recent year, government spending equaled 21.6 percent of GDP. Togo relies heavily on donor aid, much of which is contingent on improvements in public management and privatization.

MONETARY FREEDOM — 74.5

Inflation has been relatively high, averaging 6.0 percent between 2006 and 2008, peaking at 15.8 percent in August 2008, and dropping sharply in 2009. The government controls the prices of petroleum products and influences prices through regulation and state-owned enterprises and utilities. Ten points were deducted from Togo's monetary freedom score to account for policies that distort domestic prices.

INVESTMENT FREEDOM — 25

Investment is permitted only in certain sectors and is screened on a case-by-case basis. Among other conditions for approval, at least 60 percent of the payroll must go to Togolese citizens. The lack of transparency and predictability in the regulatory and judicial systems inhibits investment. Residents and non-residents may hold foreign exchange accounts. Payments and transfers to certain countries are subject to authorization and quantitative limits in some cases. Capital transactions are subject to some controls or government approval. Purchases of real estate by non-residents for non-business purposes are subject to controls.

FINANCIAL FREEDOM — 30

The banking system is small and subject to strong government influence, with little foreign participation and weak product diversification. The system suffers from a lack of solvency and liquidity, and management is inadequate in major public financial companies and many banks. A substantial number of loans issued to state-controlled companies (more than 30 percent of total bank credits) are considered to be non-performing. The Central Bank of West African States governs Togo's financial institutions. Four of the eight commercial banks are state-controlled. Privatization of financial institutions has begun, but only one of the four state-owned banks has attracted private-sector interest.

PROPERTY RIGHTS — 30

The judicial system is subject to strong influence from the executive and does not provide independent protection of private property. Contracts are difficult to enforce. Ownership of physical property is frequently disputed because of poorly defined inheritance laws. Real and chattel property cases are further complicated by judicial non-transparency, which often favors domestic entities over foreign investors. Togo has a large informal market in pirated optical media, computer software, video and cassette recordings, and counterfeit beauty products.

FREEDOM FROM CORRUPTION — 27

Corruption is perceived as widespread. Togo ranks 121st out of 179 countries in Transparency International's Corruption Perceptions Index for 2008, a significant improvement over 2007. The executive and legislative branches are subject to corruption. Government procurement contracts and dispute settlements are subject to bribery. Bribery of private or government officials, while technically a crime, is generally expected.

LABOR FREEDOM — 43.3

Togo's labor regulations are restrictive. The non-salary cost of employing a worker is high, and dismissing an employee is difficult. Regulations on the number of work hours are rigid.

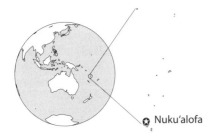

○ Nuku'alofa

TONGA

Economic Freedom Score

Least free 0   100 Most free

53.4

Tonga's economic freedom score is 53.4, making its economy the 127th freest in the 2010 *Index*. Its score has decreased by 0.7 point from last year, reflecting reduced scores in four of the 10 economic freedoms. Tonga is ranked 26th out of 41 countries in the Asia–Pacific region, and its overall score is below the world average.

Tonga's economy has expanded at a very slow rate. Over the past five years, growth has averaged just about 1 percent annually. Dominated by the public sector, the economy has long suffered from a lack of macroeconomic stability and the absence of a dynamic private sector to foster sustained economic growth and employment. Inefficient state-owned enterprises perpetuate low productivity, crowding out competition and investment from the private sector.

The economy of Tonga remains heavily dependent on overseas remittances, which account for more than 20 percent of GDP, outweighing income from tourism, agricultural exports, and other economic activities. The poor entrepreneurial environment has contributed significantly to a low level of economic dynamism despite a workforce that is considered the best educated among the Pacific Island nations. The government is the largest source of employment. Tonga's legal and regulatory framework remains weak, and opaque commercial regulations increase uncertainty and raise the overall cost of business activity. Protection of property rights is weak, and corruption remains a serious problem.

BACKGROUND: The Kingdom of Tonga is the South Pacific's last Polynesian monarchy. Some 100,000 people are spread across 48 of its 171 islands. Tonga has been independent since 1970, and its political life is dominated by the royal family, hereditary nobles, and a small number of other landholders. There are no political parties. More than half of Tonga's population lives abroad. Agriculture is the principal productive sector of the economy.

Country's Score Over Time

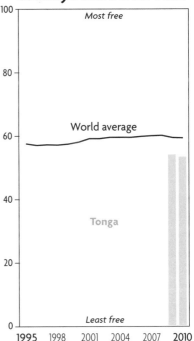

Quick Facts

Population: 0.1 million

GDP (PPP): $0.4 billion
1.2% growth in 2008
1.0% 5-year compound annual growth
$3,824 per capita

Unemployment: estimated to be over 10%

Inflation (CPI): 14.5%

FDI Inflow: $6 million

2008 data unless otherwise noted
Data compiled as of September 2009

How Do We Measure Economic Freedom?
See page 457 for an explanation of the methodology or visit the *Index* Web site at *heritage.org/index.*

413

TONGA'S TEN ECONOMIC FREEDOMS

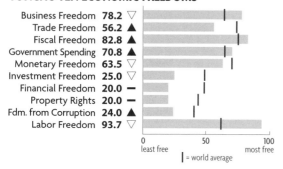

Business Freedom	78.2 ▽	
Trade Freedom	56.2 ▲	
Fiscal Freedom	82.8 ▲	
Government Spending	70.8 ▲	
Monetary Freedom	63.5 ▽	
Investment Freedom	25.0 ▽	
Financial Freedom	20.0 —	
Property Rights	20.0 —	
Fdm. from Corruption	24.0 ▲	
Labor Freedom	93.7 ▽	

0   50   100
least free   most free
| = world average

BUSINESS FREEDOM — 78.2

The overall freedom to start, operate, and close a business is respected under Tonga's regulatory environment. Starting a business takes an average of 25 days, compared to the world average of 35 days. Obtaining a business license requires less than the world average of 18 procedures. Closing a business is time-consuming and costly.

TRADE FREEDOM — 56.2

Tonga's weighted average tariff rate was 16.9 percent in 2006. Tonga has made progress in liberalizing its trade regime, but import restrictions, import taxes, import certification requirements, and inadequate infrastructure add to the cost of trade. Ten points were deducted from Tonga's trade freedom score to account for non-tariff barriers.

FISCAL FREEDOM — 82.8

A comprehensive tax reform package implemented in late 2007 resulted in consolidation of the corporate tax and simplification of the overall system. The top income tax rate is 10 percent, and the top corporate tax rate is 30 percent. Other taxes include a value-added tax (VAT) and a vehicle tax. In the most recent year, overall tax revenue as a percentage of GDP was 26.8 percent.

GOVERNMENT SPENDING — 70.8

Total government expenditures, including consumption and transfer payments, are moderate. In the most recent year, government spending equaled 31.2 percent of GDP. Steps have been taken to renationalize the private Shoreline power company.

MONETARY FREEDOM — 63.5

Inflation has been high, averaging 11.5 percent between 2006 and 2008. The government influences prices of petroleum products and other commodities through regulations. The ruling family and other Tongan nobles control other key prices through their ownership of most enterprises and utilities. Fifteen points were deducted from Tonga's monetary freedom score to adjust for measures that distort domestic prices.

INVESTMENT FREEDOM — 25

Involvement of foreign investors in certain sectors must be approved by the government. The government allows full ownership by a foreign investor in cases where manufacturing activities are using imported raw materials for export or the investments are too large for local investors; joint ventures are encouraged. Bureaucracy is generally transparent and efficient. The repatriation of funds, including dividends, profits, capital gains, interest on capital and loan repayment, and salaries, faces some restrictions. Land may be leased but not owned.

FINANCIAL FREEDOM — 20

Tonga's small financial sector remains underdeveloped and dominated by banking. It consists of two foreign-owned commercial banks, a locally incorporated commercial bank, and the government-owned Tonga Development Bank. The relatively high costs of credit and limited access to financing impede dynamic entrepreneurial activity. A considerable portion of the island's population is outside of the formal banking sector. Tonga's complex collateral system is inefficient and makes lending risky, particularly lending to small businesses. The National Reserve Bank of Tonga oversees banking, and the state-owned Tonga Development Bank finances many development projects. There are no capital markets.

PROPERTY RIGHTS — 20

Tonga has a fairly efficient legal system based on British common law. The judiciary is independent and conducts generally fair public trials, although all judges are appointed by the monarch. Property rights are uncertain. The constitution mandates that an 8.25-acre plot of communally owned land be given to each male at age 16, but there is not enough land available to fulfill that mandate for the rapidly growing population, and this is a source of dissension. Tonga has legislation protecting intellectual property rights, but enforcement of IPR laws is weak. A bill on enforcement and border measures has been endorsed by the cabinet and is under consideration. This legislation aligns Tonga's laws with its World Trade Organization obligations and contains stricter border controls for counterfeit products, which continue to be widely available on the local market.

FREEDOM FROM CORRUPTION — 24

Corruption is perceived as pervasive. Tonga ranks 138th out of 179 countries in Transparency International's Corruption Perceptions Index for 2008, a significant improvement over 2007. Although the law provides criminal penalties for official corruption, government officials sometimes engage in corrupt practices with impunity. Government preferences appear to benefit businesses associated with members of the royal family. An Office of the Anti-corruption Commissioner, charged with investigating official corruption, was established in 2008.

LABOR FREEDOM — 93.7

Tonga's labor regulations are flexible. The non-salary cost of employing a worker is low, and dismissing an employee is not costly. However, the formal labor market is not fully developed.

TRINIDAD AND TOBAGO

Port-of-Spain

World Rank: 55   **Regional Rank: 10**

Economic Freedom Score

25   50   75

Least free 0   100 Most free

65.7

Trinidad and Tobago's economic freedom score is 65.7, making its economy the 55th freest in the 2010 *Index*. Its score is 2.3 points lower than last year, with notable reductions in investment freedom and property rights. Trinidad and Tobago is ranked 10th out of 29 countries in the South and Central America/Caribbean region, and its overall score is higher than the world and regional averages.

Trinidad and Tobago has a sound macroeconomic framework and a long tradition of institutional stability. It scores relatively well in many of the 10 economic freedoms, and its economy has grown at an average rate of close to 7 percent over the past five years. The government has tried to diversify the economic base, and the country has evolved into a key financial center in the Caribbean region.

Nevertheless, overdependence on oil and gas hampers development of a more dynamic private sector. Non-oil productivity and job growth remain stifled by inefficient and non-transparent regulatory and legal frameworks. Approval of foreign investment can be subject to lengthy delays. The judiciary, though independent and competent, is weak in enforcing comprehensive laws protecting intellectual property rights. Corruption remains widespread.

BACKGROUND: Trinidad and Tobago, a parliamentary democracy and former British colony, gained its independence in 1962. Robust foreign investment since 1990 has made it the Western Hemisphere's largest supplier of liquefied natural gas and one of CARICOM's largest and most industrialized economies. The size of Trinidad and Tobago's economy has doubled since 2002, with the hydrocarbons sector accounting for more than 45 percent of GDP in 2008, although the rate of growth slowed substantially in 2009. In an attempt to introduce countercyclical fiscal policy, the government created the Heritage and Stabilization Fund in 2000 for revenue during periods when oil prices exceed the long-term average.

Country's Score Over Time

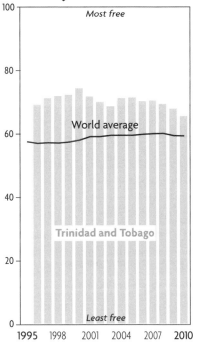

Quick Facts

Population: 1.3 million

GDP (PPP): $33.1 billion
3.4% growth in 2008
6.8% 5-year compound annual growth
$24,748 per capita

Unemployment: 5.5%

Inflation (CPI): 12.1%

FDI Inflow: $3.0 billion

2008 data unless otherwise noted
Data compiled as of September 2009

How Do We Measure Economic Freedom?
See page 457 for an explanation of the methodology or visit the *Index* Web site at *heritage.org/index.*

415

TRINIDAD & TOBAGO'S TEN ECONOMIC FREEDOMS

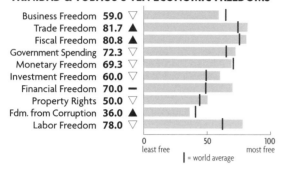

Business Freedom	**59.0** ▽
Trade Freedom	**81.7** ▲
Fiscal Freedom	**80.8** ▲
Government Spending	**72.3** ▽
Monetary Freedom	**69.3** ▽
Investment Freedom	**60.0** ▽
Financial Freedom	**70.0** —
Property Rights	**50.0** ▽
Fdm. from Corruption	**36.0** ▲
Labor Freedom	**78.0** ▽

0 least free   50   100 most free

| = world average

BUSINESS FREEDOM — 59

The overall freedom to conduct a business is limited under Trinidad and Tobago's regulatory environment. Starting a business takes an average of 43 days, compared to the world average of 35 days. Obtaining a business license takes slightly more than the world average of 18 procedures and 218 days. Bankruptcy proceedings are fairly easy and straightforward.

TRADE FREEDOM — 81.7

Trinidad and Tobago's weighted average tariff rate was 4.2 percent in 2008. Certain prohibitive tariffs, import restrictions, import taxes and fees, import and export licensing requirements, inefficient customs administration, and export-support programs add to the cost of trade. Ten points were deducted from Trinidad and Tobago's trade freedom score to account for non-tariff barriers.

FISCAL FREEDOM — 80.8

Trinidad and Tobago has moderate taxes. The top income tax rate and the standard corporate tax rate are 25 percent. Petroleum company profits are taxed up to 50 percent. Other taxes include a value-added tax (VAT) and a property tax. In the most recent year, overall tax revenue as a percentage of GDP was 25.9 percent.

GOVERNMENT SPENDING — 72.3

Total government expenditures, including consumption and transfer payments, are moderate. In the most recent year, government spending equaled 30.4 percent of GDP.

MONETARY FREEDOM — 69.3

Inflation has been high, averaging 10.7 percent between 2006 and 2008, but falling food prices, combined with weaker private and public consumption, lowered the rate significantly in 2009. The government retains price ceilings for a number of goods; controls prices for sugar, schoolbooks, and some pharmaceuticals; and influences prices through regulation, subsidies, and state-owned enterprises and utilities, including oil and gas. Ten points were deducted from Trinidad and Tobago's monetary freedom score to account for policies that distort domestic prices.

INVESTMENT FREEDOM — 60

Foreign investment receives national treatment but must be approved by the government. Certain projects must also be screened for their impact on the environment. Foreign investment in private business is not subject to limitations, but a license is needed to purchase more than 30 percent of a publicly held business. Investment approval can be non-transparent and subject to lengthy delays. Residents and non-residents may hold foreign exchange accounts. There are no restrictions or controls on payments, transactions, transfers, or repatriation of profits. Foreign ownership of land is restricted.

FINANCIAL FREEDOM — 70

The financial sector is relatively well developed and has been a catalyst for further economic growth. Financial services account for 9 percent of total employment, about 25 percent of non-energy GDP, and 70 percent of stock market capitalization. State influence in the sector is not substantial, and credit is allocated on market terms. Financial regulations and supervision are generally transparent and improving, and the level of non-performing loans has fallen below 2 percent. The Financial Institutions Act, enacted in 2008, focuses on modernizing the regulatory framework for banks, insurance companies, and other financial institutions. There are no restrictions on foreign banks or foreign borrowers, and all banks offer a wide range of services. There are six commercial banks, including one state-owned bank and several foreign banks. Insurance is dominated by a single large company. Capital markets are relatively well developed but small and centered on the stock exchange.

PROPERTY RIGHTS — 50

The judiciary is independent and fair, but cases are time-consuming, and the backlog is several years long. Legislation protecting intellectual property is among the hemisphere's most advanced, but enforcement is lax in some areas, particularly concerning copyright of music CDs and film DVDs. Prosecution for piracy is rare.

FREEDOM FROM CORRUPTION — 36

Corruption is perceived as widespread. Trinidad and Tobago ranks 72nd out of 179 countries in Transparency International's Corruption Perceptions Index for 2008. The law provides criminal penalties for official corruption, and the government generally implements the laws effectively. However, there is a widespread and growing public perception of corruption. The law requires that public officials disclose their assets, income, and liabilities, but many officials and candidates for public office are reluctant to comply.

LABOR FREEDOM — 78

Trinidad and Tobago's labor regulations are relatively flexible. The non-salary cost of employing a worker is low, but dismissing an employee can be relatively costly. Regulations on the number of work hours are flexible.

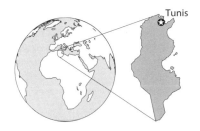
Tunis

TUNISIA

Economic Freedom Score

25   50   75

Least free 0   100 Most free

58.9

Tunisia's economic freedom score is 58.9, making its economy the 95th freest in the 2010 *Index*. Its score is one point higher than last year, reflecting improved scores in half of the 10 economic freedoms. Tunisia is ranked 12th out of 17 countries in the Middle East/North Africa region, and its overall score is just below the world average.

Tunisia has pursued structural reforms to maintain a prudent macroeconomic framework, liberalize domestic prices and controls, and reduce the public sector's role in economic activity. Regulation is more efficient and streamlined. Property rights are largely respected even though the executive branch is the supreme arbiter. Tunisia has been able to keep its fiscal deficits relatively low.

Despite these reforms, however, a number of institutional challenges remain to be addressed. Tunisia scores low in trade freedom and investment freedom. Excessively high tariffs, import restrictions, and licensing requirements limit trade freedom. Protectionist investment policies and cumbersome bureaucracy stifle a more stable inflow of foreign investment. The financial sector and judiciary are subject to political influence, and corruption remains significant.

BACKGROUND: Tunisia has charted a moderate, non-aligned foreign policy course since gaining its independence from France in 1956. It has had only two presidents in 50 years, and progress toward democracy and greater respect for human rights and civil liberties has been slow. Gradual economic reforms undertaken by President Zine al-Abidine Ben Ali since the early 1990s include privatization of state-owned firms, simplification of the tax code, and more prudent fiscal restraint. Ben Ali was re-elected for a 5th consecutive term in October 2009. Agricultural, mining, energy, tourism, and manufacturing are important industries. Tunisia's 1998 association agreement with the European Union, the first between the EU and a Maghreb country, has helped to create jobs and modernize the economy, which has also benefited from expanded trade and tourism.

Country's Score Over Time

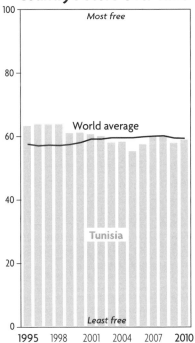

Most free

World average

Tunisia

Least free

1995 1998 2001 2004 2007 2010

Quick Facts

Population: 10.3 million

GDP (PPP): $82.6 billion
   5.1% growth in 2008
   5.1% 5-year compound
      annual growth
   $7,996 per capita

Unemployment: 14.1%

Inflation (CPI): 5.0%

FDI Inflow: $2.8 billion

2008 data unless otherwise noted
Data compiled as of September 2009

How Do We Measure Economic Freedom?
See page 457 for an explanation of the methodology or visit the *Index* Web site at *heritage.org/index.*

TUNISIA'S TEN ECONOMIC FREEDOMS

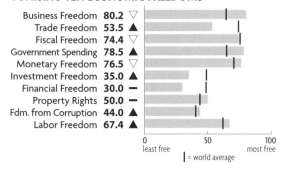

Business Freedom	80.2 ▽	
Trade Freedom	53.5 ▲	
Fiscal Freedom	74.4 ▽	
Government Spending	78.5 ▲	
Monetary Freedom	76.5 ▽	
Investment Freedom	35.0 ▲	
Financial Freedom	30.0 ▲	
Property Rights	50.0 ▬	
Fdm. from Corruption	44.0 ▲	
Labor Freedom	67.4 ▲	

0 least free   50   100 most free

| = world average

BUSINESS FREEDOM — 80.2

The overall freedom to start, operate, and close a business is relatively well protected under Tunisia's regulatory environment. Starting a business takes 11 days, compared to the world average of 35 days. Obtaining a business license takes much less than the world average of 218 days, but costs are fairly high. Bankruptcy proceedings are easy and straightforward.

TRADE FREEDOM — 53.5

Tunisia's weighted average tariff rate was 18.3 percent in 2006. Import restrictions, some prohibitively high tariffs, import taxes and fees, import licensing requirements, export-promotion programs, and inconsistent customs administration add to the cost of trade. Ten points were deducted from Tunisia's trade freedom score to account for non-tariff barriers.

FISCAL FREEDOM — 74.4

Tunisia has a relatively high income tax and a moderate corporate tax. The top income tax rate is 35 percent, and the top corporate tax rate is 30 percent. A special tax scheme applies to financial institutions and the hydrocarbons sector. Other taxes include a value-added tax (VAT), a property transfer tax, an inheritance tax, and a vehicle tax. In the most recent year, overall tax revenue as a percentage of GDP was 20.9 percent.

GOVERNMENT SPENDING — 78.5

Total government expenditures, including consumption and transfer payments, are relatively low. In the most recent year, government spending equaled 26.8 percent of GDP. The state-owned mobile and fixed-line telephone enterprise is slated for sale to a French telecommunications company.

MONETARY FREEDOM — 76.5

Inflation has been moderate, averaging 4.5 percent between 2006 and 2008. The government can set prices for subsidized goods and influences prices through regulation, subsidies, and state-owned utilities and enterprises. Ten points were deducted from Tunisia's monetary freedom score to account for policies that distort domestic prices.

INVESTMENT FREEDOM — 35

Tunisia restricts foreign investment in some sectors to min-imize the impact on domestic competitors. Foreign investment is screened. Investments in non-tourism onshore companies with a capital share larger than 49 percent require government authorization. In general, domestic trading can be carried out only by a company in which the majority of the share capital is held by Tunisians and management is Tunisian. Bureaucratic procedures are cumbersome and inconsistent, the ability to retain foreign labor is restricted, and the courts are susceptible to political pressure. Residents and non-residents may hold foreign exchange accounts, subject to restrictions and approval. There are some restrictions on capital transactions, payments, and transfers. Foreigners may not own agricultural land.

FINANCIAL FREEDOM — 30

Financial supervision and regulation have been brought up to international standards, but the financial sector remains underdeveloped. The government maintains control of the three largest banks. Despite some recent progress in reducing non-performing loans, they still account for over 15 percent of total loans. Five banks control around 70 percent of deposits. Over the past five years, the government has made progress in privatizing and consolidating a number of banks, but it remains the controlling shareholder in half of Tunisia's 20 banks. State-mandated lending and the legal difficulty of settling with debtors have hurt financial development. Capital markets are small and dominated by government securities. The stock exchange, which has been managed by the government-run Financial Market Council, has become more active with increased foreign participation and about 50 firms listed.

PROPERTY RIGHTS — 50

The executive branch is the supreme arbiter of events in the cabinet, government, judiciary, and military. Commercial cases take a long time to resolve, and legal procedures are complex. Tunisia's intellectual property rights law is designed to meet the WTO's Trade-Related Aspects of Intellectual Property Rights (TRIPS) minimum standards. Customs agents do not investigate copyright violations without a complaint by the copyright holder. Pirated print, audio, and video media products are sold openly. Illegal copying of software, CDs, and DVDs is widespread.

FREEDOM FROM CORRUPTION — 44

Corruption is perceived as significant. Tunisia ranks 62nd out of 179 countries in Transparency International's Corruption Perceptions Index for 2008. Corruption is less pervasive than in neighboring countries. Unfair practices and corruption among prospective local partners reportedly can delay or block specific investment proposals, and cronyism and influence peddling can affect investment decisions.

LABOR FREEDOM — 67.4

Tunisia's labor regulations are relatively rigid. The non-salary cost of employing a worker is high, and dismissing an employee is difficult.

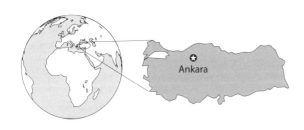

TURKEY

World Rank: 67   **Regional Rank: 31**

Turkey's economic freedom score is 63.8, making its economy the 67th freest in the 2010 *Index*. Its score is 2.2 points higher than last year, reflecting improved scores especially in investment freedom, freedom from corruption, and fiscal freedom. Turkey is ranked 31st out of 43 countries in the Europe region, and its overall score is higher than the world average.

Turkey has undertaken a series of reforms and accelerated its economic restructuring. The economy has recorded annual growth of about 5 percent over the past five years. The state's involvement in the economy remains considerable, but the private sector has grown more vibrant, and its role in economic development is increasing. The business environment has become more streamlined and efficient, albeit at a slow pace.

Turkey's overall economic freedom remains curtailed by lingering institutional weaknesses. Regulation and taxation, despite some improvements, remain burdensome and deter more dynamic entrepreneurial activity. The state still sets some prices and maintains state-owned enterprises. The labor market remains rigid. Property rights are usually enforced, but the judiciary is overburdened and slow. Corruption is perceived as significant.

BACKGROUND: Turkey is a secular state at the crossroads of Europe and the Middle East. With a constitution adopted in 1982 after a military coup, it is now a successful multi-party democracy. Prime Minister Recep Tayyip Erdogan has held office since 2003. The European Union agreed to accession talks in October 2005, but strong opposition from France, Germany, and Austria make Turkey's accession problematic. Turkey hopes to complete its implementation of the EU's body of law by 2014. Principal exports include foodstuffs, textiles, clothing, iron, and steel. Significant reforms are still needed to diversify and expand the economy, which is hampered by a high minimum wage. A two-decade conflict with a large Kurdish minority has cost an estimated 35,000 lives.

Country's Score Over Time

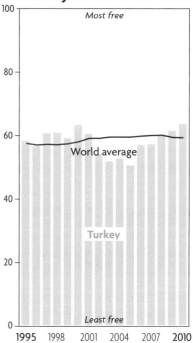

Quick Facts

Population: 73.9 million

GDP (PPP): $1.0 trillion
3.8% growth in 2008
5.2% 5-year compound annual growth
$13,920 per capita

Unemployment: 9.4%

Inflation (CPI): 10.4%

FDI Inflow: $18.2 billion

2008 data unless otherwise noted
Data compiled as of September 2009

How Do We Measure Economic Freedom?
See page 457 for an explanation of the methodology or visit the *Index* Web site at *heritage.org/index.*

TURKEY'S TEN ECONOMIC FREEDOMS

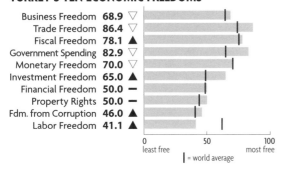

Business Freedom	68.9 ▽	
Trade Freedom	86.4 ▽	
Fiscal Freedom	78.1 ▲	
Government Spending	82.9 ▽	
Monetary Freedom	70.0 ▽	
Investment Freedom	65.0 ▲	
Financial Freedom	50.0 —	
Property Rights	50.0 —	
Fdm. from Corruption	46.0 ▲	
Labor Freedom	41.1 ▲	

0 least free   50   100 most free

| = world average

BUSINESS FREEDOM — 68.9

Turkey's regulatory environment has improved somewhat in recent years. Starting a business takes an average of six days, compared to the world average of 35 days. Obtaining a business license requires more than the global average of 18 procedures but less than the world average of 218 days, and costs are relatively low. Bankruptcy proceedings can be burdensome and lengthy.

TRADE FREEDOM — 86.4

Turkey's weighted average tariff rate was 1.8 percent in 2008. Some prohibitive tariffs for agriculture, import taxes, services market access barriers, restrictive import certification requirements for food and agriculture products, import licensing requirements, non-transparent and arbitrary standards and regulations, export-promotion programs, weak enforcement of intellectual property rights, and corruption add to the cost of trade. Ten points were deducted from Turkey's trade freedom score to account for non-tariff barriers.

FISCAL FREEDOM — 78.1

Turkey has a relatively high income tax rate and a relatively low corporate tax rate. The top income tax rate is 35 percent, and the top corporate tax rate is 20 percent. Manufacturing companies are exempt from corporate taxes. Other taxes include a value-added tax (VAT), a property tax, an environmental tax, and an inheritance tax. In the most recent year, overall tax revenue as a percentage of GDP was 23.7 percent.

GOVERNMENT SPENDING — 82.9

In the most recent year, Turkey's central government spending equaled 23.9 percent of GDP. Deregulation and privatization have somewhat increased the role of the private sector, but the energy and transportation sectors remain state-dominated. What remains of the public sector is bloated and inefficient.

MONETARY FREEDOM — 70

Inflation has been high, averaging 10.0 percent between 2006 and 2008. The government sets prices for many agricultural products and pharmaceuticals and influences prices through regulation, subsidies, and state-owned utilities and enterprises. Municipalities fix ceilings on the retail price of bread. Ten points were deducted from Turkey's monetary freedom score to account for policies that distort domestic prices.

INVESTMENT FREEDOM — 65

Foreign and domestic capital receive equal treatment under the law, but foreign investment is restricted in a number of sectors. Foreign investment is not screened. All investors face excessive bureaucracy, weaknesses in corporate governance, and frequent changes in the legal and regulatory environment. The judicial system is undergoing reforms, but procedures can still be time-consuming. Residents and non-residents may hold foreign exchange accounts. There are few restrictions on payments and transfers. Restrictions on purchases of real estate by foreigners are based on reciprocity and acreage.

FINANCIAL FREEDOM — 50

Turkey's financial sector has undergone a period of restructuring and transformation in recent years. Since the 2000–2001 financial crisis, the government has increased transparency, strengthened regulatory and accounting standards, and improved oversight. The banking sector dominates the financial system, with the five largest banks accounting for about 60 percent of total assets. As of late 2008, there were 33 commercial banks, three of which are government-owned and hold about 30 percent of total assets. Two of the 13 development banks are majority foreign-controlled. Reorganization of the state banks has been slow. There were 26 non-life and 26 life/pension insurance companies in late 2008; foreign companies are not broadly represented. Capital markets are relatively small and dominated by government securities.

PROPERTY RIGHTS — 50

Property rights are generally enforced, but the courts are overburdened and slow, and judges are not well trained for commercial cases. The judiciary is subject to government influence. The intellectual property rights regime has improved, but protection of confidential pharmaceutical test data is insufficient, and levels of piracy and counterfeiting of copyrighted and trademarked materials remain high.

FREEDOM FROM CORRUPTION — 46

Corruption is perceived as significant. Turkey ranks 58th out of 179 countries in Transparency International's Corruption Perceptions Index for 2008. An independent public procurement board has the power to void contracts. Bribery is outlawed, and some prosecutions of government officials for corruption have taken place, but enforcement is uneven. The judicial system is viewed as susceptible to external influence and somewhat biased against foreigners.

LABOR FREEDOM — 41.1

Turkey's labor regulations are inflexible. The non-salary cost of employing a worker is high, and dismissing an employee is difficult. The rigid labor market results in high unemployment and has contributed to the formation of a large informal sector.

TURKMENISTAN

World Rank: **171**   Regional Rank: **39**

Economic Freedom Score

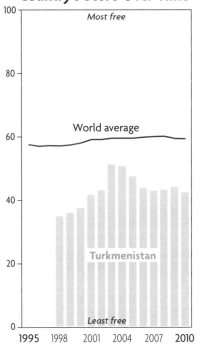

Least free 0   Most free 100

42.5

Turkmenistan's economic freedom score is 42.5, making its economy the 171st freest in the 2010 *Index*. Its score is 1.7 points lower than last year, reflecting reduced scores particularly in investment freedom and monetary freedom. Turkmenistan is ranked 39th out of 41 countries in the Asia–Pacific region, and its overall score is significantly lower than the world and regional averages.

Integration into the global economy has been slow. Turkmenistan's economy still depends heavily on energy, and the government controls most of the economy, making the transition to greater economic freedom marginal and unstable. The narrow economic base, together with government inefficiency and interference, has prevented the development of a robust private sector and slowed job growth.

The entrepreneurial environment is hampered by the lack of sound regulatory and legal frameworks. Regulation is opaque, enforcement is inconsistent, and cronyism is rampant. Foreign investors face a highly politicized and corrupt system. Financing is largely controlled by the government. Property rights are enforced intermittently, and corruption remains widespread.

BACKGROUND: Turkmenistan exports gas, oil, and petrochemicals, primarily to Russia and Iran, and most of its other gas exports are routed through Russia. President Gurbanguly Berdymukhammedov has been more receptive to the West than his predecessor, Saparmurad Niyazov (Turkmenbashi). He has hosted high-ranking Western officials, promised to reserve 10 billion cubic meters of gas for the European Union, attended the 2008 NATO summit in Bucharest, encouraged more foreign investment in hydrocarbons, allowed Internet access, pursued rapprochement with Azerbaijan, made overtures to Europe, and acted to diversify transportation routes. Construction of a major gas pipeline to China and possible participation in the proposed Nabucco pipeline indicate a policy shift. Turkmenistan's main agricultural product is cotton. The economic crisis has not significantly affected Turkmenistan, which in October 2008 established a stabilization fund to invest its oil and gas revenue surplus.

Country's Score Over Time

Quick Facts

Population: 5.0 million

GDP (PPP): $33.4 billion
9.8% growth in 2008
11.5% 5-year compound annual growth
$6,641 per capita

Unemployment: estimated to be over 20%

Inflation (CPI): 15.0%

FDI Inflow: $820 million

2008 data unless otherwise noted
Data compiled as of September 2009

How Do We Measure Economic Freedom?
See page 457 for an explanation of the methodology or visit the *Index* Web site at *heritage.org/index.*

TURKMENISTAN'S TEN ECONOMIC FREEDOMS

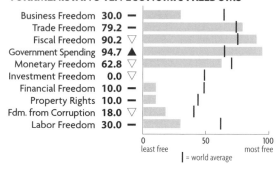

Business Freedom	30.0	—
Trade Freedom	79.2	—
Fiscal Freedom	90.2	▽
Government Spending	94.7	▲
Monetary Freedom	62.8	▽
Investment Freedom	0.0	▽
Financial Freedom	10.0	—
Property Rights	10.0	—
Fdm. from Corruption	18.0	▽
Labor Freedom	30.0	—

0 least free 50 100 most free

| = world average

BUSINESS FREEDOM — 30

The overall freedom to start, operate, and close a business is very limited under Turkmenistan's regulatory environment. The system is non-transparent, enforcement is inconsistent, and getting copies of laws and regulations is difficult. Personal relations with government officials often help to determine how and when regulations are applied.

TRADE FREEDOM — 79.2

Turkmenistan's weighted average tariff rate was 2.9 percent in 2002. Import and export bans and restrictions, some prohibitive duty rates for agricultural and food products, high import taxes and fees, services market access restrictions, cumbersome import and export contract registration requirements, import licensing, subsidies, and customs procedures that are bureaucratic, slow, and subject to corruption add to the cost of trade. Fifteen points were deducted from Turkmenistan's trade freedom score to account for non-tariff barriers.

FISCAL FREEDOM — 90.2

Turkmenistan has low tax rates. The top income tax rate is 10 percent, and the top corporate tax rate is 20 percent. Other taxes include a value-added tax (VAT) and an excise tax. Important gaps in the available data include figures for government finance. In the most recent year, overall tax revenue as a percentage of GDP was 21.8 percent.

GOVERNMENT SPENDING — 94.7

Total government expenditures, including consumption and transfer payments, are low. In the most recent year, government spending was 13.3 percent of GDP.

MONETARY FREEDOM — 62.8

Inflation has been high, averaging 12.3 percent between 2006 and 2008. Subsidies, price controls, and the free provision of utilities distort economic incentives. The government also influences prices through numerous state-owned utilities and enterprises. Fifteen points were deducted from Turkmenistan's monetary freedom score to account for policies that distort domestic prices.

INVESTMENT FREEDOM — 0

The government controls most of the economy and restricts foreign participation to a few sectors. The government chooses its investment partners selectively, and personal contact with high political officials is the best guarantor of approval. Other investors, foreign and domestic, face significant discrimination. The bureaucracy is non-transparent and politicized, and procedures are confusing and cumbersome. Inconsistent rule of law and high levels of corruption are strong disincentives to investment. Foreign exchange accounts require government approval, as do all payments and transfers. Capital transactions face restrictions and central bank approval in some cases. All land is owned by the state.

FINANCIAL FREEDOM — 10

Turkmenistan's financial system remains heavily government-influenced, and the flow of financial resources is severely restricted. Many banks are insolvent by international standards, and the financial sector is dominated by state-controlled institutions. Each of the six government-owned banks specializes in a specific sector such as agriculture, foreign trade, or mortgages. State-owned enterprises receive an estimated 90 percent of all loans, and the private sector's access to credit is very limited. The government directs credit allocation, often at subsidized rates. Most individuals hold their wealth in cash, preferably foreign currency. The central bank is not independent. Under new foreign exchange regulations introduced in 2008, the central bank can offer banks ready access to foreign exchange and permit commercial banks to establish correspondent bank accounts to support trade finance. There are no significant non-bank financial institutions, and the state-owned insurance company is the sole insurer. There is no private capital market.

PROPERTY RIGHTS — 10

The legal system does not enforce contracts and property rights effectively. Laws are poorly developed, and judicial employees and judges are poorly trained and open to bribery. All land is owned by the government, and other ownership rights are limited. Laws designed to protect intellectual property rights are implemented arbitrarily or not at all. Pirated copies of copyrighted and trademarked materials are widely available.

FREEDOM FROM CORRUPTION — 18

Corruption is perceived as pervasive. Turkmenistan ranks 166th out of 179 countries in Transparency International's Corruption Perceptions Index for 2008, a drop from 2007. All judges are appointed for five-year terms by the president without legislative review. The anti-corruption laws are ineffective. The non-transparency of the economic system and the existence of patronage networks fuel rampant corruption, especially in government procurement and performance requirements. There is a lack of accountability mechanisms, as well as fear of government reprisal.

LABOR FREEDOM — 30

Turkmenistan's employment regulations are very rigid. The government provides the majority of jobs. The formal labor market is not fully developed because there is no dynamic private sector.

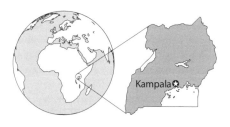

UGANDA

Economic Freedom Score

Least free 0   Most free 100

62.2

U ganda's economic freedom score is 62.2, making it the 76th freest economy in the 2010 *Index*. Its score is 1.3 points lower than last year, reflecting reduced scores in six of the 10 economic freedoms. Uganda is ranked 5th out of 46 countries in the Sub-Saharan Africa region, and its overall score is above the world average.

Uganda's economy has expanded at an average rate of close to 9 percent over the past five years. Services account for about half of GDP. Uganda has also made progress in diversifying its productive base, and the manufacturing sector has become more substantial.

Reforms have enhanced the entrepreneurial environment and fostered growth. Many state-owned enterprises have been privatized or divested. Price stability is largely restored, and the financial sector has become more open, although credit is still not easily available in rural areas. Tariff barriers have been eased, but non-tariff barriers still limit trade freedom. Corruption remains pervasive and is the most serious impediment to advancing Uganda's overall economic freedom.

BACKGROUND: Milton Obote led Uganda to independence in 1962, suspended the constitution in 1966, and was ousted in 1971 by Idi Amin Dada. When Tanzanian forces ousted Amin in 1979, Obote returned to power until being deposed by a military coup. Insurgent leader Yoweri Museveni took power in 1986. A multi-party government was established in 2005, and Museveni won a third term in 2006. The Lord's Resistance Army, forced out of Uganda, remains active in Sudan and the Democratic Republic of Congo and launched brutal attacks in late 2008 and early 2009. Despite market reforms and a decade of economic growth, Uganda remains poor and dependent on Kenya for access to international markets. Agriculture employs about 80 percent of the workforce but accounted for only about 30 percent of GDP in 2007.

Country's Score Over Time

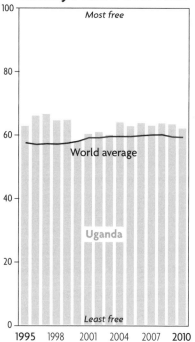

Quick Facts

Population: 31.7 million

GDP (PPP): $36.9 billion
9.5% growth in 2008
8.8% 5-year compound annual growth
$1,165 per capita

Unemployment: n/a

Inflation (CPI): 7.3%

FDI Inflow: $787 million

2008 data unless otherwise noted
Data compiled as of September 2009

How Do We Measure Economic Freedom?
See page 457 for an explanation of the methodology or visit the *Index* Web site at *heritage.org/index*.

UGANDA'S TEN ECONOMIC FREEDOMS

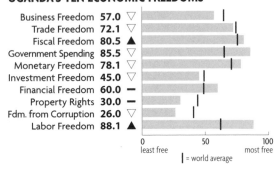

Business Freedom	57.0	▽
Trade Freedom	72.1	▽
Fiscal Freedom	80.5	▲
Government Spending	85.5	▽
Monetary Freedom	78.1	▽
Investment Freedom	45.0	▽
Financial Freedom	60.0	—
Property Rights	30.0	—
Fdm. from Corruption	26.0	▽
Labor Freedom	88.1	▲

0 least free   50   100 most free

▌ = world average

BUSINESS FREEDOM — 57

The overall freedom to start, operate, and close a business is limited under Uganda's regulatory environment. Starting a business takes an average of 25 days, compared to the world average of 35 days. Obtaining a business license takes less than the world average of 18 procedures and 218 days, but costs are high. Bankruptcy proceedings are fairly straightforward but costly.

TRADE FREEDOM — 72.1

Uganda's weighted average tariff rate was 8.9 percent in 2008. The government has made progress in liberalizing the trade regime, but import and export restrictions, some high tariffs, import and export taxes and fees, inefficient and non-transparent regulation and customs, export-promotion programs, weak enforcement of intellectual property rights, and corruption add to the cost of trade. Ten points were deducted from Uganda's trade freedom score to account for non-tariff barriers.

FISCAL FREEDOM — 80.5

Uganda has moderately high tax rates. The top income and corporate tax rates are 30 percent. Mining companies are subject to a special corporate tax rate of 45 percent. Other taxes include a value-added tax (VAT) and a property tax. In the most recent year, overall tax revenue as a percentage of GDP was 12.4 percent. Some minor tax cuts were introduced in the 2007–2008 budget to bring Uganda in line with other members of the East African Community.

GOVERNMENT SPENDING — 85.5

Total government expenditures, including consumption and transfer payments, are relatively low. In the most recent year, government spending equaled 22.0 percent of GDP.

MONETARY FREEDOM — 78.1

Inflation has been relatively high, averaging 7.1 percent between 2006 and 2008. The government influences prices through state-owned utilities and enterprises. Five points were deducted from Uganda's monetary freedom score to account for policies that distort domestic prices.

INVESTMENT FREEDOM — 45

Foreign investors do not receive equal treatment and may face a number of performance obligations as conditions for gaining business licenses. Foreign investment is allowed in most sectors, and foreign investors may form 100 percent foreign-owned companies. While some reforms have occurred and others are scheduled to revise and update the investment code, regulation and bureaucracy can be non-transparent, inconsistent, and subject to corruption. Dispute resolution can be lengthy and politicized, and infrastructure inadequate. Residents and non-residents may hold foreign exchange accounts. There are no restrictions or controls on payments, transactions, or transfers. A slow registry, complex regulations, and restrictions make land acquisition difficult or impossible.

FINANCIAL FREEDOM — 60

Uganda's small financial system is dominated by banking, which is relatively open to competition and subject to minimal government influence. Following the removal of the moratorium on new banks, there are now 22 banks and over 200 branches. Most banks are foreign-owned, and four account for about three-quarters of total assets. Bank lending to the private sector has grown by around 55 percent over the past two years. Access to financial services has gradually expanded across the country. The government has established a Microfinance Support Centre. The insurance sector is small, and the state-owned National Insurance Company is undergoing privatization. Capital markets are relatively small and underdeveloped, though more private companies are being listed on the stock exchange.

PROPERTY RIGHTS — 30

Uganda opened its first commercial court about seven years ago, but a shortage of judges and funding drives most commercial cases to outside arbitration or settlement. The judiciary suffers from corruption. Domestic private entities may own and dispose of property and other businesses. Foreign private entities share these rights, but there are restrictions on land ownership. Ugandan laws protect intellectual property in theory but rarely act as a deterrent to counterfeiters and pirates.

FREEDOM FROM CORRUPTION — 26

Corruption is perceived as widespread. Uganda ranks 126th out of 179 countries in Transparency International's Corruption Perceptions Index for 2008, a drop from 2007. The will to combat corruption at the highest levels of government has been questioned, and bureaucratic apathy and ignorance of rules within public organizations contribute to perceptions of corruption. Foreign businesses report some difficulties due to lack of transparency and possible collusion between competing business interests and government officials.

LABOR FREEDOM — 88.1

Uganda's labor regulations are flexible. The non-salary cost of employing a worker is low, and dismissing an employee is not difficult. Regulations on the number of work hours are relatively flexible.

UKRAINE

Economic Freedom Score

Ukraine's economic freedom score is 46.4, making its economy the 162nd freest in the 2010 *Index*. Its score is 2.4 points lower than last year, reflecting reduced scores in six of the 10 economic freedoms. Ukraine is ranked 43rd out of 43 countries in the Europe region, and its overall score is lower than the world average.

Ukraine has undertaken some significant structural reforms to strengthen its economic base and has achieved annual growth of 5 percent over the past five years. Positive steps have included implementation of competitive tax rates and membership in the World Trade Organization after a 14-year accession process.

In its transition to greater economic freedom, however, Ukraine lags behind other European countries, particularly in creating an entrepreneurial environment and eradicating corruption. Progress in privatization and attracting foreign investment has been slow. Regulatory and legal frameworks remain burdensome and inefficient. Bureaucratic hurdles make many commercial operations and business formation challenging. The judicial system lacks independence and capacity, and legal procedures are commonly subject to corruption.

BACKGROUND: Independent since the collapse of the Soviet Union in 1991, Ukraine has rich agricultural lands and significant natural resources and is an important route for oil and gas pipelines between Russia and Western Europe. In January 2009, Russia cut off gas supplies to Ukraine. A deal was reached, but relations remain tense. Because of political infighting between Prime Minister Yulia Tymoshenko and President Victor Yushchenko, promises of economic reform, better governance, and anti-corruption efforts made after the 2004 "Orange Revolution" remain unfulfilled. The recent economic crisis triggered a significant recession and an expected GDP contraction of 10 percent in 2009. A NATO Membership Action Plan is blocked by Russian, German, and French reservations. Ukraine has joined the World Trade Organization and the European Union's Eastern Partnership, but EU accession in the near term is unlikely.

Country's Score Over Time

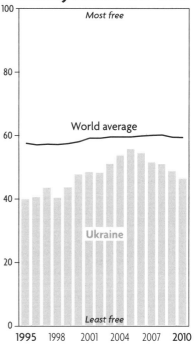

Quick Facts

Population: 46.3 million

GDP (PPP): $336.4 billion
2.1% growth in 2008
5.0% 5-year compound
annual growth
$7,271 per capita

Unemployment: 3%

Inflation (CPI): 25.2%

FDI Inflow: $10.7 billion

2008 data unless otherwise noted
Data compiled as of September 2009

How Do We Measure Economic Freedom?
See page 457 for an explanation of the methodology or visit the *Index* Web site at *heritage.org/index*.

UKRAINE'S TEN ECONOMIC FREEDOMS

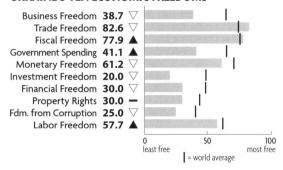

Business Freedom	38.7	▽
Trade Freedom	82.6	▽
Fiscal Freedom	77.9	▲
Government Spending	41.1	▲
Monetary Freedom	61.2	▽
Investment Freedom	20.0	▽
Financial Freedom	30.0	▽
Property Rights	30.0	—
Fdm. from Corruption	25.0	▽
Labor Freedom	57.7	▲

0 least free   50   100 most free

❚ = world average

BUSINESS FREEDOM — 38.7

The overall freedom to start, operate, and close a business is limited by Ukraine's regulatory environment. Starting a business takes 27 days, compared to the world average of 35 days. Obtaining a business license takes more than the world average of 18 procedures and 218 days, and costs are high. Bankruptcy is time-consuming and costly.

TRADE FREEDOM — 82.6

Ukraine's weighted average tariff rate was 3.7 percent in 2008. Ukraine is making progress in liberalizing its trade regime, but some export restrictions, services market access barriers, import taxes and fees, import licensing requirements, non-transparent government procurement, complex standards and certification regulations, burdensome customs procedures, and weak enforcement of intellectual property rights still add to the cost of trade. Ten points were deducted from Ukraine's trade freedom score to account for non-tariff barriers.

FISCAL FREEDOM — 77.9

Ukraine has relatively low tax rates. The top income tax rate is 15 percent, and the standard corporate tax rate is 25 percent. Insurance companies and agriculture profits are subject to special rates. Other taxes include a value-added tax (VAT), a property tax, and an inheritance tax. In the most recent year, overall tax revenue as a percentage of GDP was 36.9 percent.

GOVERNMENT SPENDING — 41.1

Total government expenditures, including consumption and transfer payments, are high. In the most recent year, government spending equaled 44.3 percent of GDP. Despite widespread privatization, the economy remains shackled by government intervention in the private sector.

MONETARY FREEDOM — 61.2

Inflation has been extremely high, averaging 20.7 percent between 2006 and 2008. The executive branch can set minimum prices for goods and services, and the government influences prices through regulation and state-owned enterprises and utilities. Ten points were deducted from Ukraine's monetary freedom score to account for policies that distort domestic prices.

INVESTMENT FREEDOM — 20

The laws provide equal treatment for foreign investors, but certain sectors are restricted or barred. Burdensome bureaucracy and regulations are the primary deterrents to investment. Contracts are not always upheld by the legal system, and privatization has slowed. Resident and non-resident foreign exchange accounts may be subject to restrictions and government approval. Payments and transfers are subject to various requirements and quantitative limits. Some capital transactions are subject to controls and licenses. Foreign investors may not own farmland.

FINANCIAL FREEDOM — 30

Ukraine's financial system remains weak and underdeveloped. Restructuring of banking has proceeded slowly, and the more than 150 small banks often suffer from insufficient capital. Two banks are state-owned, and the 10 largest banks account for over half of net assets. Since passage of amendments on banking activity in 2006 and accession to the World Trade Organization in May 2008, foreign banks and insurance companies have been permitted to open branch offices. Reflecting the lack of efficiency and depth in the financial system, the development of a domestic capital market is still at a rudimentary stage. A liquidity crisis and an increase in non-performing loans related to the global financial crisis have led to a large bailout package from the International Monetary Fund. The government has also taken controlling stakes in three of five banks in financial trouble and has been considering nationalization of the others.

PROPERTY RIGHTS — 30

Protection of property rights is weak. The judiciary is subject to executive branch and criminal pressure, and corruption is significant. Contracts are not well enforced, and expropriation is possible. Initiatives to develop a mortgage market have resulted in a strong increase in the number of mortgages and have laid the legislative and administrative groundwork for a functioning real estate market. Ukraine is a major transshipment point, storage location, and market for illegal optical media produced in Russia and elsewhere.

FREEDOM FROM CORRUPTION — 25

Corruption is perceived as widespread. Ukraine ranks 134th out of 179 countries in Transparency International's Corruption Perceptions Index for 2008, a drop from 2007. Corruption pervades all levels of society and government and all spheres of economic activity and is a major obstacle to foreign investment. Low public-sector salaries fuel corruption in local administrative bodies such as the highway police and tax administration, as well as in the education system.

LABOR FREEDOM — 57.7

Ukraine's labor regulations are relatively rigid. The non-salary cost of employing a worker is very high, and dismissing an employee is difficult.

UNITED ARAB EMIRATES

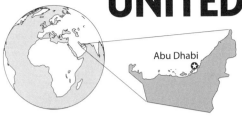

Abu Dhabi

Economic Freedom Score

25   50   75

Least free   0   100   Most free

67.3

The United Arab Emirates' economic freedom score is 67.3, making its economy the 46th freest in the 2010 *Index*. Its score is 2.6 points higher than last year, reflecting improved scores particularly in business freedom, investment freedom, and property rights. The UAE is ranked 6th out of 17 countries in the Middle East/North Africa region, and its overall score is higher than the world and regional averages.

A series of economic reforms has made the UAE the 14th most improved economy in the 2010 *Index*. Business formation has become more streamlined, and the overall entrepreneurial environment has been enhanced. The UAE has encouraged the development of a more dynamic private sector by eliminating minimum capital requirements and increasing the efficiency of the regulatory framework. The UAE aims to be a regional financial hub, and its banking sector has weathered the global financial turmoil with little disruption. The level of corruption is relatively low.

The UAE's overall economic freedom is curbed by weaknesses in the legal system and a burdensome investment framework. Foreign investment still confronts various restrictions, and the judicial system remains vulnerable to political influence.

BACKGROUND: The United Arab Emirates is a federation of seven Arab monarchies: Abu Dhabi, Ajman, Dubai, Fujairah, Ras Al-Khaimah, Sharjah, and Umm al-Qaiwain. Abu Dhabi accounts for about 90 percent of UAE oil production and takes a leading role in political and economic decision-making, but many economic policy decisions are made by the rulers of the individual emirates. Dubai has developed into the UAE's foremost center of finance, commerce, transportation, and tourism. The establishment of free trade zones that offer opportunities for 100 percent foreign ownership with zero taxation has attracted substantial foreign investment and helped to diversify the economy, but UAE nationals still rely heavily on the public sector for employment, subsidized services, and government handouts.

Country's Score Over Time

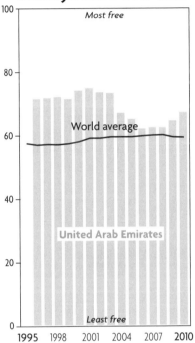

Quick Facts

Population: 4.7 million

GDP (PPP): $184 billion
7.4% growth in 2008
7.8% 5-year compound annual growth
$38,830 per capita

Unemployment: n/a

Inflation (CPI): 11.5%

FDI Inflow: $13.7 billion

2008 data unless otherwise noted
Data compiled as of September 2009

How Do We Measure Economic Freedom?
See page 457 for an explanation of the methodology or visit the *Index* Web site at *heritage.org/index.*

UNITED ARAB EMIRATES' TEN ECONOMIC FREEDOMS

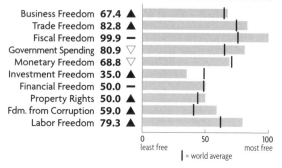

Business Freedom	67.4	▲
Trade Freedom	82.8	▲
Fiscal Freedom	99.9	—
Government Spending	80.9	▽
Monetary Freedom	68.8	▽
Investment Freedom	35.0	▲
Financial Freedom	50.0	—
Property Rights	50.0	▲
Fdm. from Corruption	59.0	▲
Labor Freedom	79.3	▲

0
least free
50
100
most free
| = world average

BUSINESS FREEDOM — 67.4

The overall freedom to start, operate, and close a business in the UAE has improved as a result of recent regulatory reforms. Starting a business takes less than half the world average of 35 days. Obtaining a business license takes much less than the world average of 218 days. Bankruptcy proceedings can be lengthy and burdensome.

TRADE FREEDOM — 82.8

The UAE's weighted average tariff rate was 3.6 percent in 2008. Import restrictions, services market access barriers, non-transparent standards, sanitary and phytosanitary regulations, and inconsistent government procurement and customs valuation add to the cost of trade. Only firms with a trade license may engage in importation, and only majority-owned UAE firms may obtain such a license (except for goods imported into free zones). Ten points were deducted from the UAE's trade freedom score to account for non-tariff barriers.

FISCAL FREEDOM — 99.9

The UAE has no income tax and no federal-level corporate tax, but there are different corporate tax rates for certain activities in some emirates. In general, foreign banks are taxed at 20 percent. Oil companies are taxed at 50 percent in Dubai and 55 percent in Abu Dhabi. There is no general sales tax, although a value-added tax (VAT) is planned. Property transfers are subject to taxation. In the most recent year, overall tax revenue as a percentage of GDP was 1.0 percent.

GOVERNMENT SPENDING — 80.9

Total government expenditures, including consumption and transfer payments, are relatively low. In the most recent year, government spending equaled 25.2 percent of GDP. The state remains significantly involved in the economy through regulation and state-owned enterprises. Salary increases and development spending are pushing up expenditures, and non-oil growth is declining slightly.

MONETARY FREEDOM — 68.8

Inflation has been high, averaging 11.2 percent between 2006 and 2008, but has fallen substantially since the beginning of 2009. The government influences prices through regulation, subsidies, and numerous state-owned enterprises and utilities, including oil, gas, electricity, and telecommunications. Ten points were deducted from the UAE's monetary freedom score to account for policies that distort domestic prices.

INVESTMENT FREEDOM — 35

Foreign investors do not receive national treatment. Except for companies in the free zones, at least 51 percent of a business must be owned by a UAE national, and projects must be managed by a UAE national or have a board of directors with a majority of UAE nationals. Company bylaws often prohibit foreign ownership. Distribution of goods must be conducted through an Emirati partner. Regulations are generally transparent. There are few controls or requirements on current transfers, access to foreign exchange, or repatriation of profits. Foreign investors face numerous restrictions or bans on land ownership.

FINANCIAL FREEDOM — 50

The UAE's modern financial sector has become more efficient and competitive in recent years. Financial supervision has been strengthened. Domestic banks offer a full range of services. Islamic banking is increasingly prominent, with seven Islamic banks operating in mid-2008. Six major banks account for 70 percent of total assets. Since 2003, when the central bank announced that it would resume giving licenses to foreign banks, several new foreign banks have established branches in the UAE. The banking sector currently consists of 50 banks, 35 of which are private. The 27 foreign banks have more than 100 branches around the country. State-owned banks have a strong presence in the financial sector. Fifteen state-owned banks account for more than 60 percent of the sector's total assets. Capital markets are relatively well developed, and the two stock markets have become more open to foreign investment.

PROPERTY RIGHTS — 50

The ruling families exercise considerable influence on the judiciary. All land in Abu Dhabi, largest of the seven emirates, is government-owned. Foreigners may buy and hold 99-year freehold interests in property in Dubai, and mortgages are available to them. The UAE leads the region in protecting intellectual property rights.

FREEDOM FROM CORRUPTION — 59

Corruption is perceived as present. The UAE ranks 35th out of 179 countries in Transparency International's Corruption Perceptions Index for 2008.

LABOR FREEDOM — 79.3

The UAE's employment regulations are relatively flexible. The non-salary cost of employing a worker is moderate, but dismissing an employee is relatively costly. Regulations on the number of work hours are not rigid. There is no minimum wage.

UNITED KINGDOM

Economic Freedom Score

Least free 0   25   50   75   100 Most free

76.5

The United Kingdom's economic freedom score is 76.5, making its economy the 11th freest in the 2010 *Index*. Its score is 2.5 points lower than last year, reflecting reduced scores particularly in freedom from corruption, financial freedom, and monetary freedom. The U.K. is ranked 4th out of 43 countries in the Europe region, and its overall score is much higher than the world average.

The U.K. has long benefited from openness to global trade and investment. Business formation is streamlined and efficient, and there is a long tradition of entrepreneurship. An independent and efficient judicial system enforces contracts and intellectual property rights.

The British economy has undergone far-reaching adjustments in reaction to the global financial and economic turmoil, and a dramatic expansion of state ownership has taken place since late 2008. The government has nationalized or seized considerable ownership in some of the major banks. Deterioration in public finances is worse than in other leading economies. Welfare benefits, the biggest component of government spending, have been rising. The government deficit is widening rapidly, and public debt has climbed to around 60 percent of GDP.

BACKGROUND: The United Kingdom is the world's fifth-largest economy. Following the market reforms instituted by Prime Minister Margaret Thatcher in the 1980s, Britain experienced steady economic growth, outpacing other large European Union economies throughout the 1990s. The Labour government of Tony Blair promoted a global economic outlook and made stability a priority. However, the government's size and spending have grown significantly under successive Labour governments, damaging Britain's competitive edge. Prime Minister Gordon Brown plunged Britain further into debt at the onset of the recent financial crisis with bank bailouts and stimulus packages. There was some minor reform of public services in the Blair years, but both the National Health Service and the British education system still need to be radically overhauled.

Country's Score Over Time

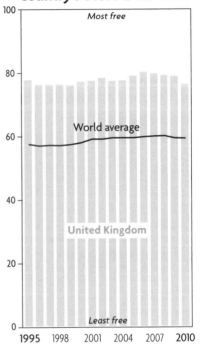

Quick Facts

Population: 61.4 million

GDP (PPP): $2.2 trillion
0.7% growth in 2008
2.2% 5-year compound annual growth
$35,445 per capita

Unemployment: 7.9%

Inflation (CPI): 3.6%

FDI Inflow: $96.9 billion

2008 data unless otherwise noted
Data compiled as of September 2009

How Do We Measure Economic Freedom?
See page 457 for an explanation of the methodology or visit the *Index* Web site at *heritage.org/index.*

UNITED KINGDOM'S TEN ECONOMIC FREEDOMS

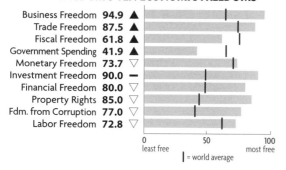

Business Freedom	94.9	▲
Trade Freedom	87.5	▲
Fiscal Freedom	61.8	▲
Government Spending	41.9	▲
Monetary Freedom	73.7	▽
Investment Freedom	90.0	—
Financial Freedom	80.0	▽
Property Rights	85.0	▽
Fdm. from Corruption	77.0	▽
Labor Freedom	72.8	▽

0 least free — 50 — 100 most free
| = world average

BUSINESS FREEDOM — 94.9

The overall freedom to start, operate, and close a business is strongly protected under the U.K.'s regulatory environment. Starting a business takes 13 days, compared to the world average of 35 days. Obtaining a business license takes less than the world average of 218 days and is not costly. Bankruptcy is easy and straightforward.

TRADE FREEDOM — 87.5

The U.K.'s trade policy is the same as that of other members of the European Union. The common EU weighted average tariff rate was 1.3 percent in 2008. However, the EU has high or escalating tariffs for agricultural and manufacturing products, and its MFN tariff code is complex. Non-tariff barriers reflected in EU and U.K. policy include agricultural and manufacturing subsidies, quotas, import restrictions and bans for some goods and services, market access restrictions in some services sectors, non-transparent and restrictive regulations and standards, and inconsistent regulatory and customs administration among EU members. Ten points were deducted from the U.K.'s trade freedom score to account for non-tariff barriers.

FISCAL FREEDOM — 61.8

The U.K. has a high income tax rate and a moderate corporate tax rate. The top income tax rate is 40 percent, and the top corporate tax rate is 28 percent. Profits from oil and gas extraction remain subject to a rate of 30 percent. Business and personal assets are subject to the same capital gains tax rate. Other taxes include a value-added tax (VAT) and an inheritance tax. In the most recent year, overall tax revenue as a percentage of GDP was 37.9 percent.

GOVERNMENT SPENDING — 41.9

Total government expenditures, including consumption and transfer payments, are high. Government spending has risen steadily since the 1990s and in the most recent year equaled 44.0 percent of GDP.

MONETARY FREEDOM — 73.7

Inflation has been moderate, averaging 3.2 percent between 2006 and 2008. As a participant in the EU's Common Agricultural Policy, the government subsidizes agricultural production, distorting the prices of agricultural products.

Prices are generally set by market forces, but pharmaceutical prices are capped, and the government influences prices through regulation and state-owned utilities. The government controls virtually all prices for health care services and rations treatment through its mandatory "single-payer" National Health Service. Fifteen points were deducted from the U.K.'s monetary freedom score to account for policies that distort domestic prices.

INVESTMENT FREEDOM — 90

Foreign investors receive the same treatment as domestic businesses, and there are few restrictions on foreign investment outside of a few service sectors. The government rarely blocks foreign acquisitions, but registered companies must have at least one U.K.-resident director. The investment code and bureaucracy are generally transparent and efficient. Residents and non-residents may hold foreign exchange accounts. Payments and proceeds on invisible transactions and current transfers are not subject to restrictions, and profits can be repatriated freely. Foreign investors may purchase land.

FINANCIAL FREEDOM — 80

The U.K.'s financial system is efficient and competitive. Supervision is prudent, regulations are transparent, and oversight is maintained by an independent institution. The insurance market is the world's second largest. Most large foreign insurers are represented, and many account for significant market shares. The London Stock Exchange, one of the world's largest, has strengthened its position after a merger with the Italian exchange. In response to the financial crisis, the Banking Act 2009 allows the government to take stakes in failing banks and includes a special liquidity scheme and an asset-protection scheme. The government has nationalized Northern Rock Bank and taken majority and minority stakes, respectively, in the Royal Bank of Scotland and Lloyds Banking Group.

PROPERTY RIGHTS — 85

Property rights are respected and enforced, and contracts are secure. The legal system protects intellectual property rights. Violations of IPR statutes are viewed as serious crimes that threaten the economy and consumers.

FREEDOM FROM CORRUPTION — 77

Corruption is perceived as minimal. The United Kingdom ranks 16th out of 179 countries in Transparency International's Corruption Perceptions Index for 2008, a decline from 2007. Bribery of domestic or foreign public officials is a criminal offense, and corrupt payments are not tax-deductible.

LABOR FREEDOM — 72.8

The United Kingdom's labor regulations are relatively flexible. The non-salary cost of employing a worker is moderate, and dismissing an employee is not burdensome. Regulations on work hours are not rigid.

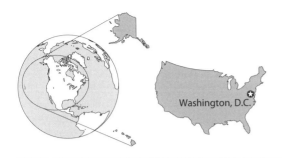

Washington, D.C.

UNITED STATES

Economic Freedom Score

25   50   75

Least free 0   100 Most free

78.0

The United States' economic freedom score is 78.0, making its economy the 8th freest in the 2010 *Index*. Its score is 2.7 points lower than last year, reflecting notable decreases in financial freedom, monetary freedom, and property rights. The United States has fallen to 2nd place out of three countries in the North America region.

The U.S. government's interventionist responses to the financial and economic crisis that began in 2008 have significantly undermined economic freedom and long-term prospects for economic growth. Economic freedom has declined in seven of the 10 categories measured in the *Index*.

Uncertainties caused by ongoing regulatory changes and politically influenced stimulus spending have discouraged entrepreneurship and job creation, slowing recovery. Leadership in free trade has been undercut by "Buy American" provisions in stimulus legislation and failure to pursue previously agreed free trade agreements with Panama, Colombia, and South Korea. Tax rates are increasingly uncompetitive, and massive stimulus spending is creating unprecedented deficits. Bailouts of financial and automotive firms have generated concerns about property rights.

BACKGROUND: The U.S. economy is the world's largest. Services account for more than 70 percent of economic activity, but the U.S. is also the world's largest producer of manufactured goods and fourth-largest producer of agricultural products. A federal form of government that reserves significant powers to states and localities has encouraged diverse economic policies and strategies. The national government's role in the economy, already expanding under President George W. Bush, has grown sharply under the Administration of President Barack Obama, who took office in January 2009. Economic growth, which collapsed in 2008, had resumed by the second half of 2009, but legislative proposals for large and expensive new government programs on health care and energy use (climate change) have increased prospects for significant economic disruptions and raised concerns about the long-term health of the economy.

Country's Score Over Time

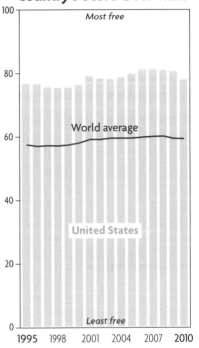

Quick Facts

Population: 304.1 million

GDP (PPP): $14.2 trillion
1.1% growth in 2008
2.2% 5-year compound annual growth
$46,716 per capita

Unemployment: 9.4% (as of May 2009)

Inflation (CPI): 3.8%

FDI Inflow: $316.1 billion

2008 data unless otherwise noted
Data compiled as of September 2009

How Do We Measure Economic Freedom?
See page 457 for an explanation of the methodology or visit the *Index* Web site at *heritage.org/index*.

UNITED STATES' TEN ECONOMIC FREEDOMS

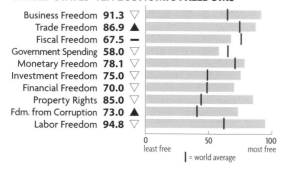

Business Freedom	91.3	▽
Trade Freedom	86.9	▲
Fiscal Freedom	67.5	—
Government Spending	58.0	▽
Monetary Freedom	78.1	▽
Investment Freedom	75.0	▽
Financial Freedom	70.0	▽
Property Rights	85.0	▽
Fdm. from Corruption	73.0	▲
Labor Freedom	94.8	▽

0 least free   50   100 most free

| = world average

BUSINESS FREEDOM — *91.3*

The overall freedom to start, operate, and close a business, regulated primarily at the state level, is still strongly protected. Starting a business takes six days, compared to the world average of 35 days. Obtaining a business license takes less than the world average of 218 days. Bankruptcy proceedings are very easy and straightforward.

TRADE FREEDOM — *86.9*

The weighted average U.S. tariff rate was 1.5 percent in 2008. Anti-dumping and countervailing duties, domestic preferences in government procurement, high out-of-quota tariffs, services market access restrictions, import licensing, restrictive labeling and standards, and export-promotion programs and subsidies add to the cost of trade. Ten points were deducted from the U.S. trade freedom score to account for non-tariff barriers.

FISCAL FREEDOM — *67.5*

U.S. tax rates are burdensome. The top income and corporate tax rates are 35 percent. Other taxes include an estate tax and excise taxes. Additional income, sales, and property taxes are assessed at the state and local levels. In the most recent year, overall tax revenue as a percentage of GDP was 28.3 percent.

GOVERNMENT SPENDING — *58*

Total government expenditures, including consumption and transfer payments, are relatively high and rising rapidly. In the most recent year, government spending equaled 37.4 percent of GDP. Spending increases totaled well over $1 trillion in 2009 alone, an increase of more than 20 percent over 2008. Stimulus spending set for the next three years is estimated to equal 5 percent of 2009 GDP.

MONETARY FREEDOM — *78.1*

Inflation has been relatively low, averaging 3.5 percent between 2006 and 2008. The Federal Reserve cut the interest rate on federal funds to near zero in December 2008, with low rates persisting through 2009. Price controls apply to some regulated monopolies; certain states and localities control residential rents; and the government influences prices through subsidies, particularly for the agricultural sector, dairy products, and some forms of transportation. Government interventions in housing, automotive, and financial markets have substantially increased price distortions. Ten

points were deducted from the U.S. monetary freedom score to account for policies that distort domestic prices.

INVESTMENT FREEDOM — *75*

Foreign and domestic enterprises are legally equal, and foreign investments face federal screening only if perceived as a potential threat to national security. Foreign investment in banking, mining, defense contracting, certain energy-related industries, fishing, shipping, communications, and aviation is restricted. Regulations are generally transparent; individual states may impose additional restrictions. There are few controls on currency transfers, access to foreign exchange, or repatriation of profits. Foreign investors may own most land, subject to some restrictions.

FINANCIAL FREEDOM — *70*

The U.S. financial sector has undergone drastic changes since the sub-prime mortgage crisis began in mid-2007, substantially reducing economic freedom. Mortgage guarantors Fannie Mae and Freddie Mac were placed in conservatorship. A number of prominent financial firms or banks have failed; government bailouts have kept others afloat; and the government has intruded on firms' management in unprecedented ways (for example, by setting caps on executive compensation). Despite the turmoil, the U.S. still has one of the world's most dynamic and developed financial markets. Foreign financial institutions and domestic banks are subject to the same restrictions. Foreign participation in equities and insurance is substantial. Concerns continue over the intrusive nature and cost of the 2002 Sarbanes–Oxley Act, which increased disclosure and internal control requirements to the detriment particularly of small firms.

PROPERTY RIGHTS — *85*

Property rights are guaranteed. Contracts are secure, and the judiciary is independent and of high quality. A well-developed licensing system protects patents, trademarks, and copyrights, and laws protecting intellectual property rights are strictly enforced. Government interventions in financial markets and the automotive sector have raised concerns about expropriation and violation of the contractual rights of shareholders and bondholders.

FREEDOM FROM CORRUPTION — *73*

Corruption is perceived as minimal. The U.S. ranks 18th out of 179 countries in Transparency International's Corruption Perceptions Index for 2008. The absence of transparency and accountability in the operations of the Troubled Asset Relief Program (TARP) and in other "bailout" programs managed by the Treasury and the Federal Reserve has increased concerns about the potential for government corruption.

LABOR FREEDOM — *94.8*

The United States' labor regulations are highly flexible. The non-salary cost of employing a worker is low, and dismissing an employee is not burdensome.

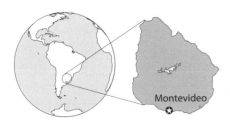

URUGUAY

U ruguay's economic freedom score is 69.8, making its economy the 33rd freest in the 2010 *Index*. Its score is 0.7 point higher than last year, due to improved scores in four of the 10 economic freedoms. Uruguay is ranked 4th out of 29 countries in the South and Central America/Caribbean region, and its overall score is significantly higher than the world average.

A series of structural reforms have facilitated annual economic growth averaging about 7 percent over the past five years. With its trade regime relatively open and monetary stability restored, Uruguay has managed to improve its entrepreneurial environment and reduce poverty. Recent reforms reduced the corporate tax to 25 percent and introduced an income tax with a top rate of 25 percent. The labor market is relatively flexible.

Uruguay's main structural vulnerabilities have been low levels of investment and productivity and weak public finance management. The state uses monopolies in certain sectors to control much of the economy. Inefficient regulatory and legal frameworks, coupled with an underdeveloped financial sector, undermine dynamic growth and development. The judiciary, while independent and relatively corruption-free, is subject to bureaucratic delays.

BACKGROUND: Uruguay has a large middle class, high GDP growth rates, and low levels of extreme poverty. The leftist Frente Amplio party won a majority in parliamentary elections in October 2009, and a presidential runoff was scheduled for late November. A founding member of MERCOSUR, Uruguay signed a Trade and Investment Framework Agreement with the United States in January 2007, but opposition from other MERCOSUR members and flagging U.S. support make pursuit of a free trade agreement difficult. The economy is based largely on beef and wool exports, but wood and software are gaining export market share. Historically, state involvement in the economy has been substantial. Further privatization is needed in telecommunications, energy, and public utilities.

Country's Score Over Time

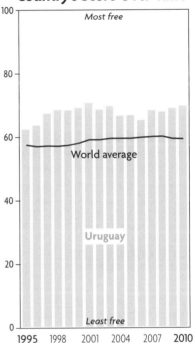

Quick Facts

Population: 3.3 million

GDP (PPP): $42.5 billion
　　8.9% growth in 2008
　　7.1% 5-year compound
　　　annual growth
　　$12,734 per capita

Unemployment: 7.6%

Inflation (CPI): 7.9%

FDI Inflow: $2.2 billion

2008 data unless otherwise noted
Data compiled as of September 2009

How Do We Measure Economic Freedom?
See page 457 for an explanation of the methodology or visit the *Index* Web site at *heritage.org/index.*

URUGUAY'S TEN ECONOMIC FREEDOMS

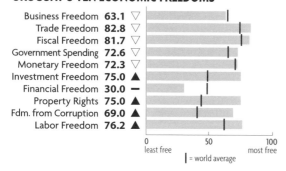

Business Freedom	63.1	▽
Trade Freedom	82.8	▽
Fiscal Freedom	81.7	▽
Government Spending	72.6	▽
Monetary Freedom	72.3	▽
Investment Freedom	75.0	▲
Financial Freedom	30.0	—
Property Rights	75.0	▲
Fdm. from Corruption	69.0	▲
Labor Freedom	76.2	▲

0 least free   50   100 most free

| = world average

BUSINESS FREEDOM — *63.1*

The overall freedom to start, operate, and close a business is limited under Uruguay's regulatory environment. Starting a business takes an average of 65 days, compared to the world average of 35 days. Obtaining a business license requires more than the world average of 18 procedures and 218 days. The process for closing a business is fairly easy and straightforward.

TRADE FREEDOM — *82.8*

Uruguay's weighted average tariff rate was 3.6 percent in 2008. Some import bans and restrictions, import taxes and fees, import registration requirements, import licensing requirements, and customs delays add to the cost of trade. Ten points were deducted from Uruguay's trade freedom score to account for non-tariff barriers.

FISCAL FREEDOM — *81.7*

Uruguay's tax rates have been moderate since the implementation of major tax reforms in July 2007. Corporate tax schemes were unified, and the top corporate tax rate is 25 percent. An income tax was implemented with a top rate of 25 percent. Other taxes include a value-added tax (VAT), a capital gains tax, a wealth tax, and a property transfer tax. In the most recent year, overall tax revenue as a percentage of GDP was 24.0 percent.

GOVERNMENT SPENDING — *72.6*

Total government expenditures, including consumption and transfer payments, are moderate. In the most recent year, government spending equaled 30.2 percent of GDP.

MONETARY FREEDOM — *72.3*

Inflation has been relatively high, averaging 7.8 percent between 2006 and 2008. Uruguay has eliminated most price controls, but the executive branch fixes prices of certain staples such as milk, and the government influences prices through regulation and/or ownership of numerous state-owned enterprises and utilities, including energy, petroleum products, and telecommunications. Ten points were deducted from Uruguay's monetary freedom score to account for policies that distort domestic prices.

INVESTMENT FREEDOM — *75*

In general, foreign capital and domestic capital are treated equally under the law. Foreign investors face few restrictions outside of state-monopoly sectors, and foreign investments are not subject to screening or approval requirements. The bureaucracy is generally transparent but can be cumbersome, especially in government tenders. Residents and non-residents may hold foreign exchange accounts. There are no restrictions or controls on payments, transactions, transfers, or repatriation of profits. Non-residents may purchase real estate.

FINANCIAL FREEDOM — *30*

Uruguay's small financial system, dominated by the banking sector, remains subject to considerable government influence. Banking accounts for more than 80 percent of the system's assets, and about 40 percent of bank assets are held by government-owned banks. The state-owned Banco de la República Oriental del Uruguay is the largest bank, and the state-owned Banco Hipotecario del Uruguay is the leading mortgage lender. The government-owned Banco de Seguros del Estadoize dominates the insurance sector, accounting for over half of the market. The economy is highly dollarized. There is limited bank credit available for small and medium enterprises. Capital markets are underdeveloped and concentrated in government debt. The two stock exchanges listed 26 firms in 2007, but trading remains largely inactive.

PROPERTY RIGHTS — *75*

Private property is generally secure, and expropriation is unlikely. Contracts are enforced, although the judiciary tends to be slow. The government has established a Settlement and Arbitration Center to improve investment relations. Regulations protecting copyrights appear to be working, but protection of confidential test data from unfair commercial use as required by the World Trade Organization's Trade-Related Aspects of Intellectual Property Rights (TRIPS) agreement remains inadequate. Aggressive anti-piracy campaigns have led to several successful prosecutions.

FREEDOM FROM CORRUPTION — *69*

Corruption is perceived as present. Uruguay ranks 23rd out of 179 countries in Transparency International's Corruption Perceptions Index for 2008. Although Uruguay has strong laws to prevent bribery and other corrupt practices, public surveys indicate a widespread perception of public-sector corruption. However, foreign firms have not identified corruption as an obstacle to investment.

LABOR FREEDOM — *76.2*

Uruguay's labor regulations are relatively flexible. The non-salary cost of employing a worker is low, and dismissing an employee is relatively easy. Regulations on the number of work hours are not flexible.

UZBEKISTAN

Economic Freedom Score

Least free 0   100 Most free

25   50   75

47.5

U zbekistan's economic freedom score is 47.5, making its economy the 158th freest in the 2010 *Index*. Its score is 3 points lower than last year, reflecting reduced scores in half of the 10 economic freedoms. Uzbekistan is ranked 35th out of 41 countries in the Asia–Pacific region, and its overall score is lower than the world average.

Economic reform is an unfinished process in Uzbekistan. The country scores poorly in most areas of economic freedom. The bright spot is fiscal freedom, where Uzbekistan scores relatively high because of a moderate income tax rate and a low corporate income tax rate. The overall entrepreneurial environment is inefficient and burdensome, and a weak legal framework undermines the development of a strong private sector.

State intervention remains considerable in many areas of the economy and continues to hold back long-run economic development. The courts are subject to political interference, and corruption is pervasive throughout the civil service.

BACKGROUND: President Islam Karimov, in power since the late 1980s, evicted the U.S. from the Karashi–Khanabad air base in 2005 but in 2008 allowed the U.S. and NATO limited use of an airfield and railroads to resupply military forces in Afghanistan. In October 2008, the European Union relaxed economic sanctions. In April 2009, the U.S. signed an agreement with Uzbekistan allowing shipment of nonlethal supplies to Afghanistan. Uzbekistan relies heavily on natural gas, oil, gold, and uranium exports, but cotton remains the main source of export revenues. Russian investment is growing in numerous sectors. GDP growth was 9 percent in 2008 according to official statistics, but the economy was negatively affected in 2009 both by declines in remittances and by falling prices and demand for Uzbekistan's major export commodities.

Country's Score Over Time

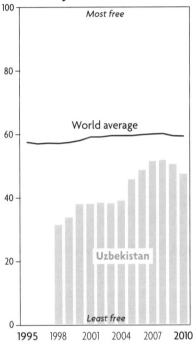

1995 1998 2001 2004 2007 **2010**

Quick Facts

Population: 27.3 million

GDP (PPP): $72.5 billion
9.0% growth in 2008
8.2% 5-year compound annual growth
$2,656 per capita

Unemployment: n/a

Inflation (CPI): 12.3%

FDI Inflow: $918 million

2008 data unless otherwise noted
Data compiled as of September 2009

How Do We Measure Economic Freedom?
See page 457 for an explanation of the methodology or visit the *Index* Web site at *heritage.org/index.*

UZBEKISTAN'S TEN ECONOMIC FREEDOMS

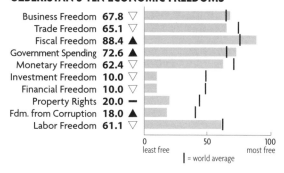

Business Freedom	67.8 ▽	
Trade Freedom	65.1 ▽	
Fiscal Freedom	88.4 ▲	
Government Spending	72.6 ▲	
Monetary Freedom	62.4 ▽	
Investment Freedom	10.0 ▽	
Financial Freedom	10.0 ▽	
Property Rights	20.0 ▽	
Fdm. from Corruption	18.0 ▲	
Labor Freedom	61.1 ▽	

0 least free   50   100 most free

| = world average

BUSINESS FREEDOM — 67.8

The overall freedom to start, operate, and close a business is limited under Uzbekistan's regulatory environment. Starting a business takes 15 days, compared to the world average of 35 days. Obtaining a business license takes more than the world average of 18 procedures and 218 days. Closing a business is a lengthy process.

TRADE FREEDOM — 65.1

Uzbekistan's weighted average tariff rate was 7.5 percent in 2008. Some high tariffs, services market access barriers, discriminatory import taxes and fees, non-transparent and burdensome standards and certification regulations, non-transparent government procurement, export subsidies, weak enforcement of intellectual property rights, corruption, and inefficient and cumbersome customs implementation add to the cost of trade. The government sometimes closes border posts to restrict trade. Twenty points were deducted from Uzbekistan's trade freedom score to account for non-tariff barriers.

FISCAL FREEDOM — 88.4

The top income tax rate is 25 percent, and the top corporate tax rate is 10 percent (15 percent for commercial banks). Other taxes include a value-added tax (VAT) and a property tax. In the most recent year, overall tax revenue as a percentage of GDP was 20.8 percent.

GOVERNMENT SPENDING — 72.6

Total government expenditures, including consumption and transfer payments, are moderate. In the most recent year, government spending equaled 30.2 percent of GDP. State intervention in the economy remains pervasive, hindering development of the private sector. Large state-owned enterprises have not been privatized. Uzbekistan's fiscal system lacks transparency, and there are large discrepancies in official statistics. Except for export revenues from Russia and Kazakhstan, Uzbekistan is relatively isolated from the global economy.

MONETARY FREEDOM — 62.4

Inflation has been high, averaging 12.8 percent between 2006 and 2008. Despite attempts to limit inflation by imposing price controls on basic foodstuffs and energy, inflation accelerated to 14 percent in 2008. The government influences prices through regulation, subsidies, and state-owned enterprises and utilities. It controls prices primarily by declaring companies or certain products national or regional monopolies, which automatically requires official review and approval of prices. Fifteen points were deducted from Uzbekistan's monetary freedom score to account for policies that distort domestic prices.

INVESTMENT FREEDOM — 10

Officially, foreign and domestic investments face equal treatment under the law. In general, numerous sectors are either reserved for the state or subject to limited-ownership restrictions and minimum capital requirements. In practice, investors face such barriers as cumbersome bureaucracy; the threat of expropriation; inconsistent, burdensome, and arbitrary regulation; weak contract enforcement; corruption; and political unrest and violence. Residents and non-residents may hold foreign exchange accounts, subject to some restrictions. Payments and transfers face quantitative limits and delays. Some capital transactions, including credit operations and real estate transactions, are subject to controls.

FINANCIAL FREEDOM — 10

Uzbekistan's undeveloped financial sector is subject to heavy government intervention. Along with the high costs of financing, the banking sector's limited capacity for financial intermediation remains a key barrier to development of the private sector. Banking is dominated by state-owned banks and lacks competition and transparency. Although the government has reduced the number of state-run banks in recent years, most of their assets have merely been transferred to smaller government-owned banks. Government-controlled banks support the government's economic priorities through subsidized loans offered to specific sectors. Foreign banks may operate only in a subsidiary status, and all routine banking operations require government permission. The insurance sector is minimal. Capital markets are virtually nonexistent, and the stock market is very small.

PROPERTY RIGHTS — 20

The government influences Uzbekistan's judiciary. Judicial procedures fall short of international standards, corruption is extensive, and expropriation is possible. There is no general system for registration of liens on chattel property. Pirated audiotapes, compact discs, videotapes, and other optical media are sold freely.

FREEDOM FROM CORRUPTION — 18

Corruption is perceived as pervasive. Uzbekistan ranks 166th out of 179 countries in Transparency International's Corruption Perceptions Index for 2008. Foreign-owned businesses view corruption as one of the largest obstacles to foreign direct investment. The law does not forbid government officials from acting as "consultants," a common method of extracting payment.

LABOR FREEDOM — 61.1

Uzbekistan's labor regulations are relatively rigid. The non-salary cost of employing a worker is high, but dismissing an employee is moderately easy. Regulations on the number of work hours remain rigid.

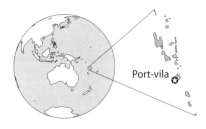

Port-vila

VANUATU

Economic Freedom Score

25   50   75

Least free   0   100   Most free

56.4

Vanuatu's economic freedom score is 56.4, making it the 108th freest economy in the 2010 *Index*. Its score has decreased by 2.0 points since last year, reflecting deterioration in six of the 10 economic freedoms, including investment freedom and trade freedom. Vanuatu is ranked 19th out of 41 countries in the Asia–Pacific region, and its overall score is below the world and regional averages.

Vanuatu has undertaken a number of reforms to strengthen its entrepreneurial framework and broaden its economic base. It scores well above the world average in fiscal freedom and monetary freedom. Tax rates are competitive, with a top personal income tax rate of 12.5 percent and no corporate taxes. Monetary stability is relatively well maintained. Vanuatu's small financial sector has undergone significant reforms in recent years to combat money laundering and inefficiency.

Despite some economic transformation and annual economic expansion of more than 6 percent over the past five years, Vanuatu faces significant constraints on long-term economic development. Most of the labor force works in the agriculture sector, which accounts for only 20 percent of GDP. State interference in the economy is pervasive, and inefficient state-owned enterprises crowd out private-sector investment. Corruption and a weak investment climate remain serious impediments to overall economic freedom.

BACKGROUND: The Republic of Vanuatu is composed of 83 islands spread over 4,500 square miles of the South Pacific. Formerly administered by a British–French condominium, it achieved independence in 1970. Today, it is an electoral democracy that remains divided between its English-speaking and French-speaking citizens. Vanuatu has largely avoided the political unrest experienced by several of its neighbors in the South Pacific. The economy is dominated by tourism and agriculture, and over 80 percent of the population is involved in farming. In the years since 2003, Vanuatu has experienced solid economic growth.

Country's Score Over Time

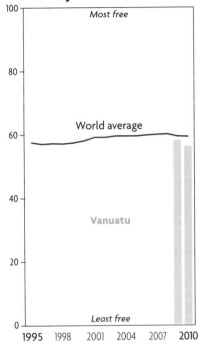

Quick Facts

Population: 0.2 million

GDP (PPP): $0.9 billion
6.6% growth in 2007
6.8% 5-year compound annual growth
$3,978 per capita

Unemployment: n/a

Inflation (CPI): 4.8%

FDI Inflow: $34 million

2008 data unless otherwise noted
Data compiled as of September 2009

How Do We Measure Economic Freedom?
See page 457 for an explanation of the methodology or visit the *Index* Web site at *heritage.org/index.*

VANUATU'S TEN ECONOMIC FREEDOMS

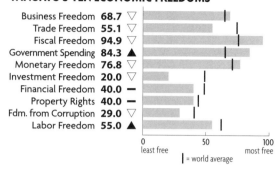

Business Freedom	68.7	▽
Trade Freedom	55.1	▽
Fiscal Freedom	94.9	▽
Government Spending	84.3	▲
Monetary Freedom	76.8	▽
Investment Freedom	20.0	▽
Financial Freedom	40.0	—
Property Rights	40.0	—
Fdm. from Corruption	29.0	▽
Labor Freedom	55.0	▲

0 least free   50   100 most free
▌ = world average

BUSINESS FREEDOM — 68.7

The overall freedom to start, operate, and close a business is constrained under Vanuatu's regulatory environment. Starting a business takes slightly more than the world average of 35 days, and the entry cost of launching a business is high. Obtaining a business license requires less than the world average of 18 procedures and 218 days. Bankruptcy is relatively time-consuming and costly.

TRADE FREEDOM — 55.1

Vanuatu's weighted average tariff rate was 15 percent in 2008. High tariffs, services market access restrictions, import taxes, import permit requirements, inadequate infrastructure and trade capacity, subsidies, underdeveloped private markets, and state participation in the marketing board for key agriculture exports add to the cost of trade. Fifteen points were deducted from Vanuatu's trade freedom score to account for non-tariff barriers.

FISCAL FREEDOM — 94.9

Vanuatu has low taxes. The top income tax rate is 12.5 percent. There is no corporate tax. Other taxes include a value-added tax (VAT) and import duties. In the most recent year, overall tax revenue as a percentage of GDP was 18.9 percent.

GOVERNMENT SPENDING — 84.3

Total government expenditures, including consumption and transfer payments, are relatively low. In the most recent year, government spending equaled 22.9 percent of GDP. Vanuatu's 24 state-owned enterprises are inefficient and in need of privatization.

MONETARY FREEDOM — 76.8

Inflation has been relatively low, averaging 4.3 percent between 2006 and 2008. Many of Vanuatu's state-owned enterprises are heavily subsidized, depleting budget resources and distorting price-setting mechanisms that would encourage private-sector development. Ten points were deducted from Vanuatu's monetary freedom score to adjust for measures that distort domestic prices.

INVESTMENT FREEDOM — 20

In general, foreign investors receive national treatment, but all foreign investment projects must be screened and approved, and certain sectors are reserved for domestic

investment. Foreign investors are generally subject to local hiring and training requirements. Barriers to private-sector development are significant and include inadequate infrastructure, a weak legal system, and a large state presence in the economy. Political unrest also adds to the cost of investment. Access to and use of foreign exchange may be subject to restrictions and approvals. Foreign investors may repatriate capital. Foreign investors may lease but not own land.

FINANCIAL FREEDOM — 40

Vanuatu's small financial sector has been transformed in recent years. Supervision has been strengthened, facilitating efforts to improve the country's reputation as a sound financial center. With a new commercial bank opening in 2007, Vanuatu now has four commercial banks, three of which are foreign-owned. The state-owned National Bank of Vanuatu has the largest branch network in the country. However, poor access to finance remains a serious impediment to private-sector development. Only 13 percent of the rural adult population has bank accounts, and without access to modern financial services, much of the population is unable to participate in the formal economy. Non-resident business activities dominate commercial banks' transaction services. Reflecting the lack of efficiency in the financial system, capital markets remain very rudimentary.

PROPERTY RIGHTS — 40

Vanuatu has a fairly efficient legal system based on British common law, but the judicial process is extremely slow. The constitution states that village or island courts, presided over by chiefs, should be established by parliament to deal with questions of customary law. Land disputes are a constant source of tension. All land is supposed to belong to traditional customary owners, except for public land. However, investors have acquired and subdivided large parcels of land, angering locals who have lost not only their control of the land, but in some cases direct access to the sea.

FREEDOM FROM CORRUPTION — 29

Corruption is perceived as widespread. Vanuatu ranks 109th out of 179 countries in Transparency International's Corruption Perceptions Index for 2008, a drop from 2007. The law provides criminal penalties for official corruption, but the government has not implemented the law effectively, and officials engage in corrupt practices with impunity. Recently, several high-ranking government officials were charged with forgery and theft in connection with a large-scale fraud scheme involving electoral development funds.

LABOR FREEDOM — 55

Vanuatu's labor regulations are relatively rigid. The non-salary cost of employing a worker is high, and dismissing an employee is moderately difficult. The agricultural sector remains the most important source of employment, and the formal labor market is not fully developed.

VENEZUELA

| World Rank: **174** | Regional Rank: **28** |

Economic Freedom Score

25   **50**   75

Least free 0   100 Most free

37.1

Venezuela's economic freedom score is 37.1, making its economy the 174th freest in the 2010 *Index*. Its score has decreased by 2.8 points since last year, reflecting deterioration in eight of the 10 economic freedoms. Venezuela is ranked 28th out of 29 countries in the South and Central America/Caribbean region, and its overall score is much lower than the world average.

Venezuela's government is increasingly interventionist, and overall economic freedom is severely limited by government regulations and controls. The state oil company, PDVSA, runs the petroleum sector. Government companies control electricity and important parts of the telecommunications and media sectors. Monetary stability is weak, and there are price controls on almost all goods and services. Corruption is rampant under an inefficient judicial system that is vulnerable to political influence.

The rule of law has been severely undermined by the government of Hugo Chávez. Contracts and property rights are poorly protected, and government expropriations have been on the rise. The government has nationalized cement and steel producers, some companies in milk and meat distribution, one of the country's largest private banks, numerous companies in oilfield services, and a processed rice plant owned by a U.S. company. These nationalizations and Venezuela's repressive entrepreneurial environment have sharply curtailed private investment.

BACKGROUND: Heading a government that has abandoned all but the trappings of democracy, President Hugo Chávez has positioned himself as the leader of Latin America's anti–free market forces and sought allies in China and Russia, as well as Iran and other rogue states. He has hobbled opponents, undermined speech and property rights, pursued a military buildup, and imposed foreign exchange controls. In 2009, education "reform" targeted religious educators and parochial school funding and reduced the autonomy of university administrations; a referendum removed term limits from the constitution. Venezuela has Latin America's highest inflation rates.

Country's Score Over Time

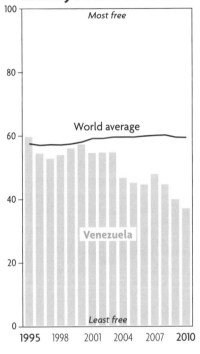

Quick Facts

Population: 27.9 million

GDP (PPP): $357.8 billion
4.8% growth in 2007
8.4% 5-year compound annual growth
$12,804 per capita

Unemployment: 7.4%

Inflation (CPI): 30.4%

FDI Inflow: $1.7 million

2008 data unless otherwise noted
Data compiled as of September 2009

How Do We Measure Economic Freedom?
See page 457 for an explanation of the methodology or visit the *Index* Web site at *heritage.org/index.*

VENEZUELA'S TEN ECONOMIC FREEDOMS

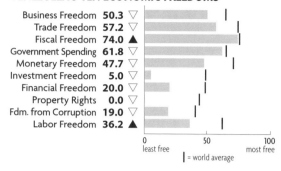

Business Freedom	50.3	▽
Trade Freedom	57.2	▽
Fiscal Freedom	74.0	▲
Government Spending	61.8	▽
Monetary Freedom	47.7	▽
Investment Freedom	5.0	▽
Financial Freedom	20.0	▽
Property Rights	0.0	▽
Fdm. from Corruption	19.0	▽
Labor Freedom	36.2	▲

0 least free — 50 — 100 most free

| = world average

BUSINESS FREEDOM — 50.3

The overall freedom to start, operate, and close a business is seriously restricted under Venezuela's regulatory environment. Starting a business takes 141 days, compared to the world average of 35 days. Obtaining a business license takes more than the world average of 218 days.

TRADE FREEDOM — 57.2

Venezuela's weighted average tariff rate was 11.4 percent in 2008. Import bans and restrictions, quotas, price bands for certain products, services market access barriers, import taxes and fees, import licensing requirements, non-transparent and discriminatory administration of tariff rate quotas, non-transparent government procurement, non-transparent standards and labeling regulations, export subsidies, inadequate access to foreign exchange, weak enforcement of intellectual property rights, and burdensome and inefficient customs implementation add to the cost of trade. Twenty points were deducted from Venezuela's trade freedom score to account for non-tariff barriers.

FISCAL FREEDOM — 74

Venezuela has burdensome tax rates. The top income and corporate tax rates are 34 percent. Certain oil companies, except those determined to be central to the "national interest," are subject to a 50 percent tax on net income. Other taxes include a value-added tax (VAT), a property tax, a financial transactions tax, and an inheritance tax. In the most recent year, overall tax revenue as a percentage of GDP was 17.0 percent. The VAT was raised from 9 percent to 12 percent on April 1, 2009.

GOVERNMENT SPENDING — 61.8

Total government expenditures, including consumption and transfer payments, are relatively high. In the most recent year, government spending equaled 35.7 percent of GDP.

MONETARY FREEDOM — 47.7

Inflation is nearly out of control, averaging 26.0 percent between 2006 and 2008. Real interest rates remain negative, giving depositors little incentive to save. The government controls almost all prices through regulation, subsidies, and numerous state-owned enterprises and utilities and uses a non-legislated system of guaranteed minimum prices to protect agricultural producers. Twenty points

were deducted from Venezuela's monetary freedom score to account for policies that distort domestic prices.

INVESTMENT FREEDOM — 5

Although the investment code generally provides equal treatment for foreign investment, the government restricts certain types of investment and investment in certain sectors. Investment laws and bureaucracy are non-transparent and burdensome, the legal system is slow and corrupt, and state domination of the economy is increasing. In 2008, the government expropriated key companies and assets in the cement, dairy, steel, and banking industries. It also revoked or refused to renew important concessions in the tourism industry and started the process of revoking mining concessions. The government controls foreign exchange and fixes the exchange rate. Repatriation of capital, dividends, or profits at the official rate requires authorization.

FINANCIAL FREEDOM — 20

Venezuela's financial system is subject to growing government control and has suffered recent takeovers and nationalizations. Assets are heavily concentrated in the six largest banks. Financial institutions are increasingly directed to provide credit in accordance with government requirements. Limits on profits are under consideration. The central bank's independence has deteriorated, and decisions are now controlled by the president. Assets held by foreign-owned banks in Venezuela have declined to under 25 percent of total banking assets. During the first half of 2009, the government took control of three banks and nationalized one bank amid concerns over their viability. Capital markets are small.

PROPERTY RIGHTS — 0

The judiciary is completely controlled by the executive, politically inconvenient contracts are abrogated, and the legal system discriminates against or in favor of investors from certain foreign countries. Pirated music, movies, and software are readily available. In the first months of 2009, the Chávez administration passed new laws to centralize control of ports, roads, and airports; nationalize major industries; and strip the opposition mayor of Greater Caracas of his authority and resources.

FREEDOM FROM CORRUPTION — 19

Corruption is perceived as rampant. Venezuela ranks 158th out of 179 countries in Transparency International's Corruption Perceptions Index for 2008. Government tenders are vulnerable because the process frequently lacks transparency. Critics allege that price and exchange controls, government and military officials' involvement in narcotics trafficking, and kickbacks on major weapons purchases are sources of corruption.

LABOR FREEDOM — 36.2

Venezuela's labor regulations are very inflexible. The non-salary cost of employing a worker is moderate, but dismissing an employee is difficult. Regulations on work hours remain inflexible.

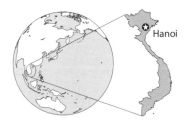

Hanoi

VIETNAM

World Rank: **144**	Regional Rank: **33**

Vietnam's economic freedom score is 49.8, making its economy the 144th freest in the 2010 *Index*. Its score has decreased by 1.2 points since last year, reflecting reduced scores in five of the 10 economic freedoms. Vietnam is ranked 33rd out of 41 countries in the Asia–Pacific region, and its overall score is lower than the world and regional averages.

Vietnam's gradual integration into global trade and investment systems has facilitated its transition to greater economic freedom and has built momentum for growth, which has averaged almost 8 percent over the past five years. The overall entrepreneurial environment has slowly become more efficient, encouraging the emergence of a more dynamic private sector. Reforms have included partial privatization of state-owned enterprises, liberalization of the trade regime, and increasing recognition of private property rights. A tax reform package that reduces rates for both individuals and corporations has been implemented.

Vietnam's overall economic freedom, however, is limited by several key institutional factors. The regulatory environment is not fully efficient and transparent. Investment is hindered by non-transparent bureaucracy and an unreliable legal system. State owned-enterprises still account for about 40 percent of GDP. The judiciary is weakened by widespread corruption, which inhibits the effective enforcement of contracts.

BACKGROUND: The Socialist Republic of Vietnam is a one-party authoritarian regime that has embarked on the path of economic liberalization only recently, starting with its doi moi reforms in 1986. In 2007, the country joined the World Trade Organization. Vietnam now boasts one of Southeast Asia's fastest-growing economies, which is driven primarily by tourism and exports. The government is slowly liberalizing key economic sectors, including financial institutions, but political repression and the lack of respect for basic human rights remain serious concerns.

Country's Score Over Time

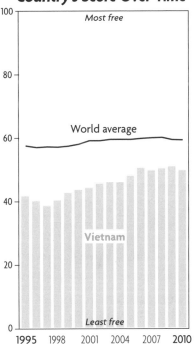

Most free

World average

Vietnam

Least free

1995   1998   2001   2004   2007   2010

Quick Facts

Population: 86.2 million

GDP (PPP): $240.1 billion
6.1% growth in 2008
7.8% 5-year compound
annual growth
$2,785 per capita

Unemployment: 2.4%

Inflation (CPI): 23.1%

FDI Inflow: $8.1 billion

2008 data unless otherwise noted
Data compiled as of September 2009

How Do We Measure Economic Freedom?
See page 457 for an explanation of the methodology or visit the *Index* Web site at *heritage.org/index.*

VIETNAM'S TEN ECONOMIC FREEDOMS

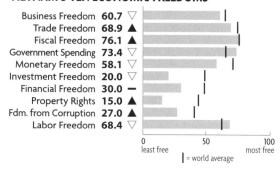

Business Freedom	60.7 ▽	
Trade Freedom	68.9 ▲	
Fiscal Freedom	76.1 ▲	
Government Spending	73.4 ▽	
Monetary Freedom	58.1 ▽	
Investment Freedom	20.0 ▽	
Financial Freedom	30.0 —	
Property Rights	15.0 ▲	
Fdm. from Corruption	27.0 ▲	
Labor Freedom	68.4 ▽	

0   50   100
least free   most free
| = world average

BUSINESS FREEDOM — 60.7

The overall freedom to start, operate, and close a business is limited under Vietnam's regulatory environment. Starting a business takes 50 days, compared to the world average of 35 days. Obtaining a business license takes less than the world average of 18 procedures and 218 days. Bankruptcy proceedings can be burdensome and lengthy.

TRADE FREEDOM — 68.9

Vietnam's weighted average tariff rate was 10.6 percent in 2007. The government continues to make progress toward liberalizing the trade regime, but some import bans and restrictions, services market access barriers, import taxes, import licensing requirements, non-transparent regulations, state trade in some commodities, weak enforcement of intellectual property rights, corruption, and customs inconsistencies add to the cost of trade. Ten points were deducted from Vietnam's trade freedom score to account for non-tariff barriers.

FISCAL FREEDOM — 76.1

Vietnam implemented tax reforms in January 2009. The top income tax rate was lowered from 40 percent to 35 percent, and the top corporate tax rate was reduced from 28 percent to 25 percent. Oil and gas are subject to a separate taxation scheme. Other taxes include a value-added tax (VAT) and a tax on the transfer of property. In the most recent year, overall tax revenue as a percentage of GDP was 23.2 percent.

GOVERNMENT SPENDING — 73.4

Total government expenditures, including consumption and transfer payments, are moderate. In the most recent year, government spending equaled 29.8 percent of GDP. Progress in privatization or restructuring of state-owned enterprises has been modest.

MONETARY FREEDOM — 58.1

Inflation has been very high, averaging 18.1 percent between 2006 and 2008. The government influences prices through regulation, subsidies, state-owned enterprises, banks, and utilities. Fifteen points were deducted from Vietnam's monetary freedom score to account for policies that distort domestic prices.

INVESTMENT FREEDOM — 20

All foreign investment projects must be screened and approved. Foreign investment is prohibited or subject to additional restrictions in certain sectors. Other deterrents include an unwieldy bureaucracy, non-transparent regulations, corruption, and an unreliable and cumbersome legal system. Frequent changes in the investment-related laws as the government continues to reform the investment regime cause inconsistent and non-transparent implementation of regulations. Residents and non-residents may hold foreign exchange accounts, subject to restrictions and some government approvals. Payments and transfers are subject to restrictions. Most transactions in money market and capital instruments, derivatives, commercial credits, and direct investments require government approval. All land is owned by the state.

FINANCIAL FREEDOM — 30

Despite reforms aimed at creating a more market-based system, the state remains heavily involved in Vietnam's underdeveloped financial sector. Lending by state banks is driven by government policy toward large state-owned enterprises, and interest rates may be subsidized. The four primary state-owned banks control most lending. Regulations, supervision, and transparency fall short of international standards, and the share of non-performing loans is estimated to be far higher than the reported rate of about 2 percent. Banking consists of a large number of small banks that are vulnerable to external shocks. In 2008, four foreign banks were permitted to launch fully owned subsidiaries. Capital markets are very small.

PROPERTY RIGHTS — 15

Only the rudiments of a system to protect property rights have been established. The judiciary is not independent, and corruption is common. Contracts are weakly enforced, and resolution of disputes can take years. All land belongs to the state, but the Land Law of 2003 allows foreign title holders to conduct real estate transactions, including mortgages. Foreign investors may lease land for (renewable) periods of 50 years, and up to 70 years in some poor areas. Starting in 2009, foreigners who meet certain criteria may own apartments. Infringement of intellectual property rights is widespread, and enforcement is problematic.

FREEDOM FROM CORRUPTION — 27

Corruption is perceived as widespread. Vietnam ranks 121st out of 179 countries in Transparency International's Corruption Perceptions Index for 2008. In December 2008, the government of Japan announced that it was suspending low-interest loans until Vietnam takes "meaningful" steps to eliminate corruption in public works programs.

LABOR FREEDOM — 68.4

Vietnam's labor regulations are relatively inflexible. The non-salary cost of employing a worker is moderate, but dismissing an employee is difficult. The government has increased the minimum wage in domestic and foreign-invested enterprises, partly to ease labor unrest.

YEMEN

Economic Freedom Score

25 50 75

Least free 0 100 Most free

54.4

World Rank: 121   **Regional Rank: 14**

Yemen's economic freedom score is 54.4, making its economy the 121st freest in the 2010 *Index*. Its score is 2.5 points lower than last year, reflecting deterioration in seven of the 10 economic freedoms. Yemen is ranked 14th out of 17 countries in the Middle East/North Africa region, and its overall score is lower than the world and regional averages.

The Yemeni economy is constrained by a limited productive base. Oil and agriculture still account for about 40 percent of GDP, rendering economic growth vulnerable to oil price fluctuations and other external shocks. Efforts to diversify the economic base have resulted in a growing services sector. The regulatory environment has also become more efficient and streamlined.

A series of reform measures, including reforms in public finance management and the legal framework, have been introduced, but many have not been fully implemented or face considerable delays. Pervasive government interference in the economy and an underdeveloped financial sector constrain the entrepreneurial environment and development of a more vibrant private sector. Widespread corruption remains the most serious impediment to Yemen's overall economic freedom.

BACKGROUND: Yemen is one of the poorest countries in the Arab world. Following the union between North and South Yemen in 1990, the central government's authority was challenged by a southern secessionist movement that was defeated in 1994. President Ali Abdallah Saleh, former president of North Yemen, continues to face intermittent challenges from unruly tribes and Islamic extremists who oppose his government's moderate foreign policy, cooperation with the United States in the war against terrorism, and efforts to modernize and reform Yemen both politically and economically. The government began an economic reform program in 2006 to strengthen the non-oil sectors and attract foreign investment, but declining oil production, terrorist attacks, clashes between Sunni and Shia Muslims, and kidnappings have undermined tourism and foreign investment.

Country's Score Over Time

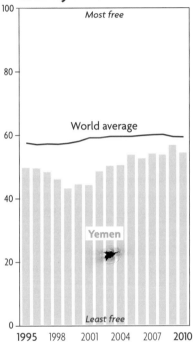

100 — Most free

80 —

World average

60 —

40 —

Yemen

20 —

0 — Least free

1995   1998   2001   2004   2007   **2010**

Quick Facts

Population: 23.1 million

GDP (PPP): $55.3 billion
3.9% growth in 2008
4.0% 5-year compound
annual growth
$2,400 per capita

Unemployment: 16.5%

Inflation (CPI): 19%

FDI Inflow: $463 million

2008 data unless otherwise noted
Data compiled as of September 2009

How Do We Measure Economic Freedom?
See page 457 for an explanation of the methodology or visit the *Index* Web site at *heritage.org/index*.

YEMEN'S TEN ECONOMIC FREEDOMS

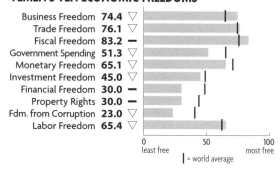

Business Freedom	**74.4**	▽
Trade Freedom	**76.1**	▽
Fiscal Freedom	**83.2**	—
Government Spending	**51.3**	▽
Monetary Freedom	**65.1**	▽
Investment Freedom	**45.0**	▽
Financial Freedom	**30.0**	—
Property Rights	**30.0**	—
Fdm. from Corruption	**23.0**	▽
Labor Freedom	**65.4**	▽

0 least free   50   100 most free

| = world average

BUSINESS FREEDOM — *74.4*

The overall freedom to start, operate, and close a business is relatively well protected under Yemen's regulatory environment. Starting a business takes an average of 12 days, compared to the world average of 35 days, although the entry cost of launching a business is high. Obtaining a business license takes less than the world average of 18 procedures and 218 days. Bankruptcy proceedings are relatively straightforward.

TRADE FREEDOM — *76.1*

Yemen's weighted average tariff rate was 6.9 percent in 2006. Some import bans and restrictions, import taxes, import licensing requirements, weak enforcement of intellectual property rights, inefficient customs administration, and corruption add to the cost of trade. Ten points were deducted from Yemen's trade freedom score to account for non-tariff barriers.

FISCAL FREEDOM — *83.2*

Yemen has a low income tax rate but a burdensome corporate tax rate. The top income tax rate is 20 percent, and the top corporate tax rate is 35 percent. Other taxes include a general sales tax (GST), a property tax, a fuel tax, and a religious tax on net wealth. In the most recent year, overall tax revenue as a percentage of GDP was 7.3 percent.

GOVERNMENT SPENDING — *51.3*

Total government expenditures, including consumption and transfer payments, are relatively high. In the most recent year, government spending equaled 40.3 percent of GDP. Low oil prices and fuel subsidies, combined with growing social expenditures have resulted in a widening fiscal deficit.

MONETARY FREEDOM — *65.1*

Inflation has been high, averaging 13.8 percent between 2006 and 2008, but fell sharply in 2009 as a result of a steep decline in the prices of foodstuffs and other commodities. The government controls the prices of pharmaceuticals and petroleum products and influences prices through regulation, subsidies, and state-owned enterprises and utilities. Ten points were deducted from Yemen's monetary freedom score to account for policies that distort domestic prices.

INVESTMENT FREEDOM — *45*

The government officially permits foreign investment in most sectors and grants equal treatment to domestic and foreign investors. Foreign investment in the oil, gas, and minerals sector is subject to production-sharing agreements. While the government has made progress toward improving the investment regime, investment-related laws and regulations can be non-transparent and inconsistently applied, and the state remains an important presence in the economy. Dispute resolution and contract enforcement are unreliable. Foreign exchange accounts are permitted. There are no restrictions on payments and transfers, and capital transactions are subject to few restrictions. Foreign investors may own land.

FINANCIAL FREEDOM — *30*

Yemen's small financial system remains underdeveloped and dominated by the state. Financial regulation is rudimentary. Credit to the private sector accounts for less than 10 percent of GDP, and the limited availability of financing precludes more vibrant entrepreneurial activity. Yemen's undercapitalized banking sector consists of about 17 banks, four of which are foreign-owned. The banking sector is inefficient and burdened with non-performing loans. The government has total ownership of the National Bank of Yemen and majority ownership of three other specialized banks. Commercial lending is limited to a small circle of clients, partly because of legal inability to collect overdue debts. The non-bank financial sector is small, capital markets are not developed, and there is no stock market. An improved bill to combat money laundering and the financing of terrorism was approved by the Yemeni Council of Ministers in late 2007 but was still pending in parliament in early 2009.

PROPERTY RIGHTS — *30*

The judiciary is subject to government pressure and corruption. Contracts are weakly enforced. Foreigners may own property, but foreign firms must operate through Yemeni agents. Protection of intellectual property rights is inadequate.

FREEDOM FROM CORRUPTION — *23*

Corruption is perceived as pervasive. Yemen ranks 141st out of 179 countries in Transparency International's Corruption Perceptions Index for 2008. The civil service is overstaffed, underpaid, and highly vulnerable to corruption. Illicit activities include soliciting and paying bribes to facilitate or obstruct projects, leveraging dispute settlements, skewing taxation and customs tariff augmentations, and engaging in family or tribal nepotism.

LABOR FREEDOM — *65.4*

Yemen's labor regulations are relatively flexible. The non-salary cost of employing a worker is low, but dismissing an employee can be burdensome.

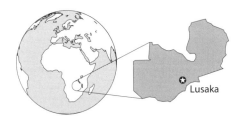

ZAMBIA

Economic Freedom Score

58.0

Zambia's economic freedom score is 58.0, making its economy the 100th freest in the 2010 *Index*. Its score has increased by 1.4 points, reflecting improved scores in four of the 10 economic freedoms, including a notable improvement in trade freedom. Zambia is ranked 12th out of 46 countries in the Sub-Saharan Africa region, and its overall score is below the world average.

Reform and relative macroeconomic stability have encouraged steady economic growth averaging about 6 percent over the past five years. Zambia's financial sector has benefited from reforms, including implementation of the Financial Sector Development Plan, and has weathered the global financial crisis relatively well. Management of public finance has been relatively sound, although the fiscal deficit has been on the rise more recently.

Progress in better governance, development of a more robust private sector, and diversification of the Zambian economy has been rather sluggish. Lingering institutional challenges include inefficient legal and regulatory frameworks, state influence, weak protection of property rights, and corruption. Corruption is widespread, and the judicial process is slow and ineffective.

BACKGROUND: Growing popular discontent led the government of Kenneth Kaunda, which had ruled since independence in 1964, to enact a new constitution instituting multi-party democracy in 1991. Frederick Chiluba was elected president and pursued economic reform, but his administration was dogged by allegations of corruption. Levy Mwanawasa, elected in 2001 and re-elected in 2006, made fighting corruption the centerpiece of his presidency. President Rupiah Banda won a narrow victory in October 2008. Zambia was the world's third-largest copper producer and a middle-income nation in the 1960s, but falling copper prices and mismanagement of state-owned mines led to steadily declining income from 1974 to 1990. Copper remains the biggest export, but mining contributes only about 5 percent of GDP. Subsistence agriculture is the main employer, and HIV/AIDS is a significant problem.

Country's Score Over Time

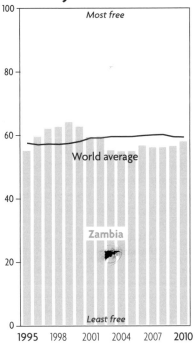

Quick Facts

Population: 12.6 million

GDP (PPP): $17.1 billion
6.0% growth in 2008
6.0% 5-year compound annual growth
$1,356 per capita

Unemployment: estimated to be over 20%

Inflation (CPI): 12.4%

FDI Inflow: $939 million

2008 data unless otherwise noted
Data compiled as of September 2009

How Do We Measure Economic Freedom?
See page 457 for an explanation of the methodology or visit the *Index* Web site at *heritage.org/index*.

ZAMBIA'S TEN ECONOMIC FREEDOMS

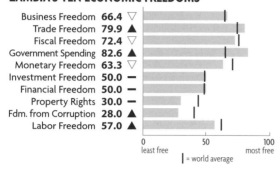

Business Freedom	66.4 ▽
Trade Freedom	79.9 ▲
Fiscal Freedom	72.4 ▽
Government Spending	82.6 ▲
Monetary Freedom	63.3 ▽
Investment Freedom	50.0 —
Financial Freedom	50.0 —
Property Rights	30.0 —
Fdm. from Corruption	28.0 ▲
Labor Freedom	57.0 ▲

0 least free   50   100 most free

| = world average

BUSINESS FREEDOM — 66.4

The overall freedom to start, operate, and close a business is restricted under Zambia's regulatory environment. Starting a business takes an average of 18 days, compared to the world average of 35 days. Obtaining a business license takes more than the world average of 218 days, and costs are high. Closing a business is relatively straightforward.

TRADE FREEDOM — 79.9

Zambia's weighted average tariff rate was 5 percent in 2008. Some import and export restrictions, services market access barriers, import taxes and fees, import and export permit and certification requirements, non-transparent standards, improving but still cumbersome customs implementation, and corruption add to the cost of trade. Ten points were deducted from Zambia's trade freedom score to account for non-tariff barriers.

FISCAL FREEDOM — 72.4

Zambia's tax rates are relatively high. Both the top income tax rate and the top corporate tax rate are 35 percent, with an array of special rates for banks, mining companies, and farmers. Other taxes include a value-added tax (VAT) and a property transfer tax. In the most recent year, overall tax revenue as a percentage of GDP was 17.5 percent. The windfall tax on mining introduced in April 2008 was removed in the 2009 budget.

GOVERNMENT SPENDING — 82.6

Total government expenditures, including consumption and transfer payments, are relatively low. In the most recent year, government spending equaled 24.1 percent of GDP. Despite ambitious reform schemes, progress on improving spending management and restructuring the public sector has been slow.

MONETARY FREEDOM — 63.3

Inflation has been high, averaging 11.7 percent between 2006 and 2008. The government subsidizes agricultural production inputs and influences prices through state-owned enterprises and utilities. Fifteen points were deducted from Zambia's monetary freedom score to account for policies that distort domestic prices.

INVESTMENT FREEDOM — 50

Foreign investors are granted national treatment. An investment board screens all investments for which incentives are requested. Investments in some sectors are subject to additional regulations and approvals. The retail sector is closed to foreigners. While the government has made progress on reforming the investment regime, bureaucracy can be slow, competition policy remains inadequate, contract enforcement can be weak, work permits can be difficult to obtain for foreign labor, and the dispute resolution process is burdensome. Corruption remains another important deterrent to investment. Residents and non-residents may hold foreign exchange accounts. There are no controls on payments, transfers, capital transactions, or repatriation of profits.

FINANCIAL FREEDOM — 50

Zambia has a relatively liberal and advanced banking regime. The financial system is dominated by a banking sector in which competition is increasing. There are 15 commercial banks, with two more foreign banks starting operation in 2008 and 2009. Bank supervision and regulation have improved. Financial intermediation and credit to the private sector remain low. The insurance market is open to competition. Though participation is increasing, capital markets remain very small. There are no restrictions on foreign investment in the stock exchange.

PROPERTY RIGHTS — 30

Zambia's judicial system suffers from inefficiency, government influence, and a lack of resources. Contract enforcement is weak, and courts are relatively inexperienced in commercial litigation. Despite constitutional and legal protections, customary law and practice place women in a subordinate status with respect to property, inheritance, and marriage. Trademark protection is adequate, but copyright protection is limited and does not cover computer applications. It takes at least four months to patent an item or process.

FREEDOM FROM CORRUPTION — 28

Corruption is perceived as widespread. Zambia ranks 115th out of 179 countries in Transparency International's Corruption Perceptions Index for 2008, an improvement over 2007. Controls on government funds and property are often weak, investigative units lack authority and personnel, and officials dealing with the public frequently demand illicit payments with impunity. The issuance of land titles has been singled out as particularly susceptible to corruption. The government has no clear policy for the disposal of confiscated assets, and a lack of transparency surrounds the liquidation of seized assets. The Anti-Corruption Commission investigates allegations of misconduct.

LABOR FREEDOM — 57

Zambia's labor regulations are rigid. The non-salary cost of employing a worker is low, but dismissing an employee is difficult.

Harare

ZIMBABWE

World Rank: **178**   Regional Rank: **46**

Zimbabwe's economic freedom score is 21.4, making its economy the 178th freest in the 2010 *Index*. Its score has decreased by 1.3 points from last year, reflecting notable declines in trade freedom, freedom from corruption, and investment freedom. Zimbabwe is ranked 46th out of 46 countries in the Sub-Saharan Africa region and is the world's second least economically free country.

The Zimbabwean economy performs poorly and is characterized by instability and volatility, both hallmarks of excessive government involvement. Economic policy is overly influenced by political considerations and state interference. The country's previously established economic infrastructure has crumbled under a tyrannical and oppressive regime. Zimbabwe's economic climate has become increasingly hostile to foreign investment. The financial system, which suffers from repeated crises, is failing.

Hyperinflation has crippled the national economy, severely undermining the country's economic potential. The government has used the Reserve Bank of Zimbabwe to finance deficit spending and to provide direct loans to state-owned enterprises. A corrupt and inefficient judicial system and general lack of transparency make entrepreneurial activity all but impossible.

BACKGROUND: When it became independent in 1965, Zimbabwe (then called Rhodesia) had a diversified economy, a well-developed infrastructure, and an advanced financial sector. The white minority eventually agreed to majority government, and Zimbabwe African National Union leader Robert Mugabe became prime minister in 1980 and president in 1987. In 2008, the ruling party lost its majority in parliament. Mugabe lost the 2008 presidential election but won the runoff when opposition leader Morgan Tsvangirai withdrew after widespread intimidation. Under a power-sharing agreement, Mugabe remains head of state, the cabinet, and the armed services. Mugabe's desperate attempts to retain power have included harsh political repression and economic mismanagement that has crippled agriculture, the mainstay of the economy. Zimbabwe is now one of Africa's poorest countries, and many Zimbabweans have fled.

Country's Score Over Time

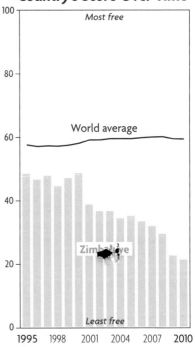

Quick Facts

Population: 11.7 million

GDP (PPP): $2.2 billion
−6.1% growth in 2007
−5.2% 5-year compound
annual growth
Per capita: $188

Unemployment: estimated to be over 20%

Inflation (CPI): 10,453.0%

FDI Inflow: $52 million

2007 data unless otherwise noted
Data compiled as of September 2009

How Do We Measure Economic Freedom?
See page 457 for an explanation of the methodology or visit the *Index* Web site at *heritage.org/index.*

ZIMBABWE'S TEN ECONOMIC FREEDOMS

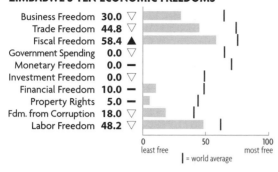

Business Freedom	30.0 ▽	
Trade Freedom	44.8 ▽	
Fiscal Freedom	58.4 ▲	
Government Spending	0.0 ▽	
Monetary Freedom	0.0 —	
Investment Freedom	0.0 ▽	
Financial Freedom	10.0 —	
Property Rights	5.0 —	
Fdm. from Corruption	18.0 ▽	
Labor Freedom	48.2 ▽	

0   50   100
least free   most free
| = world average

BUSINESS FREEDOM — 30

The overall freedom to start, operate, and close a business is seriously restricted under Zimbabwe's regulatory environment. Starting a business takes more than twice the world average of 35 days. Obtaining a business license takes much more than the world average of 218 days. Closing a business is relatively difficult and costly.

TRADE FREEDOM — 44.8

Zimbabwe's simple average tariff rate was 20.1 percent in 2007. Import bans and restrictions, services market access restrictions, import taxes, non-transparent regulations, government controls on exports and domestic trading of major agricultural commodities, inadequate access to foreign exchange, and customs inefficiency and corruption add to the cost of trade. Fifteen points were deducted from Zimbabwe's trade freedom score to account for non-tariff barriers.

FISCAL FREEDOM — 58.4

Zimbabwe has burdensome tax rates. The top income tax rate is 47.5 percent, and the top corporate tax rate is 30 percent. Other taxes include a 3 percent AIDS surcharge on all taxes, a value-added tax (VAT), and a capital gains tax. In the most recent year, overall tax revenue as a percentage of GDP was 31.7 percent.

GOVERNMENT SPENDING — 0

Total government expenditures, including consumption and transfer payments, are very high. In the most recent year, government spending equaled 97.8 percent of GDP.

MONETARY FREEDOM — 0

Inflation averaged 223.7 percent between 2006 and 2008. The government sets price ceilings for such essential commodities as agricultural seeds, bread, maize meal, sugar, beef, stock feeds, and fertilizer; controls the prices of basic goods and food staples; influences prices through subsidies and state-owned enterprises and utilities; and has begun to arrest traders for not complying with orders to cut prices on a range of products. If Zimbabwe had a positive monetary freedom score, 15 points would be deducted to account for policies that distort domestic prices.

INVESTMENT FREEDOM — 0

While hostile to most foreign investment, the government will consider investment up to 100 percent in high-priority projects with 51 percent indigenous ownership over time. Bureaucracy is non-transparent and corrupt, and the risk of expropriation, which is used to promote "indigenization," is high. The weak rule of law, restrictive labor rules, and inadequate foreign exchange significantly deter investment. Foreign exchange accounts are subject to government approval and restrictions. Payments and transfers are subject to government approval and numerous restrictions, and all outward capital transactions are controlled.

FINANCIAL FREEDOM — 10

Government intervention, inadequate supervision, and repeated crises have severely damaged Zimbabwe's financial system. In recent years, the financial sector has contracted significantly amid continuing uncertainty over economic policies and macroeconomic instability caused by the government. The government has used the Bank of Zimbabwe to finance deficit spending and direct loans to state-owned enterprises. Many banks suffer from a lack of liquidity, but the government has begun to tighten regulations and impose stricter capitalization requirements. The government also owns a savings bank and a development bank devoted to financing specific sectors. Political instability, the high cost of financing, and scarce access to credit have virtually destroyed the private sector.

PROPERTY RIGHTS — 5

The government's growing control of the economy puts many investments, particularly in real property, at risk. The U.N. estimates that the government's Operation Restore Order caused more than 700,000 persons to lose their homes, their means of livelihood, or both. Many of the confiscated properties had proper titles. The executive branch strongly influences the judiciary and openly challenges court outcomes. Corruption and expropriation are common.

FREEDOM FROM CORRUPTION — 18

Corruption is perceived as pervasive. Zimbabwe ranks 166th out of 179 countries in Transparency International's Corruption Perceptions Index for 2008, a decline from 2007. There is widespread corruption in government. The ongoing redistribution of expropriated commercial farms provides substantial opportunities for corruption. Top officials hand-pick multiple farms and register them in the names of family members to evade the official one-farm policy, and individuals aligned with top officials are allowed to seize land that is not designated for acquisition.

LABOR FREEDOM — 48.2

Zimbabwe's labor regulations are restrictive. The non-salary cost of employing a worker is high, and dismissing an employee is difficult. Regulations on the number of work hours are rigid.

Appendix

Index of Economic Freedom Scores, 1995–2010

Country	1995	1996	1997	1998	1999	2000	2001	2002	2003	2004	2005	2006	2007	2008	2009	2010
Afghanistan	n/a	n/a	n/a	n/a	n/a	n/a	n/a	n/a	n/a	n/a	n/a	n/a	n/a	n/a	n/a	n/a
Albania	49.7	53.8	54.8	53.9	53.4	53	56.6	56.8	56.8	58.5	57.8	60.3	61.4	62.4	63.7	66.0
Algeria	55.7	54.5	54.9	55.8	57.2	56.8	57.3	61.0	57.7	58.1	53.2	55.7	55.4	56.2	56.6	56.9
Angola	27.4	24.4	24.2	24.9	23.7	24.3	n/a	n/a	n/a	n/a	n/a	43.5	44.7	46.9	47.0	48.4
Argentina	68.0	74.7	73.3	70.9	70.6	70.0	68.6	65.7	56.3	53.9	51.7	53.4	54.0	54.2	52.3	51.2
Armenia	n/a	42.2	46.7	49.6	56.4	63.0	66.4	68.0	67.3	70.3	69.8	70.6	68.6	69.9	69.9	69.2
Australia	74.1	74.0	75.5	75.6	76.4	77.1	77.4	77.3	77.4	77.9	79.0	79.9	81.1	82.2	82.6	82.6
Austria	70.0	68.9	65.2	65.4	64.0	68.4	68.1	67.4	67.6	67.6	68.8	71.1	71.6	71.4	71.2	71.6
Azerbaijan	n/a	30.0	34.0	43.1	47.4	49.8	50.3	53.3	54.1	53.4	54.4	53.2	54.6	55.3	58.0	58.8
The Bahamas	71.8	74.0	74.5	74.5	74.7	73.9	74.8	74.4	73.5	72.1	72.6	72.3	72.0	71.1	70.3	67.3
Bahrain	76.2	76.4	76.1	75.6	75.2	75.7	75.9	75.6	76.3	75.1	71.2	71.6	71.2	72.2	74.8	76.3
Bangladesh	38.7	51.1	49.9	52.0	50.0	48.9	51.2	51.9	49.3	50.0	47.5	52.9	46.7	44.2	47.5	51.1
Barbados	62.9	62.3	64.5	67.9	66.7	69.5	71.5	73.6	71.3	69.4	70.1	71.9	70.0	71.3	71.5	68.3
Belarus	40.4	38.7	39.8	38.0	35.4	41.3	38.0	39.0	39.7	43.1	46.7	47.5	47.0	45.3	45.0	48.7
Belgium	n/a	66.0	64.6	64.7	62.9	63.5	63.8	67.6	68.1	68.7	69.0	71.8	72.5	71.7	72.1	70.1
Belize	62.9	61.6	64.3	59.1	60.7	63.3	65.9	65.6	63.5	62.8	64.5	64.7	63.3	63.0	63.0	61.5
Benin	n/a	54.5	61.3	61.7	60.6	61.5	60.1	57.3	54.9	54.6	52.3	54.0	55.1	55.2	55.4	55.4
Bhutan	n/a	n/a	n/a	n/a	n/a	n/a	n/a	n/a	n/a	n/a	n/a	n/a	n/a	n/a	57.7	57.0
Bolivia	56.8	65.2	65.1	68.8	65.6	65.0	68.0	65.1	64.3	64.5	58.4	57.8	54.2	53.1	53.6	49.4
Bosnia and Herzegovina	n/a	n/a	n/a	29.4	29.4	45.1	36.6	37.4	40.6	44.7	48.8	55.6	54.4	53.9	53.1	56.2
Botswana	56.8	61.6	59.1	62.8	62.9	65.8	66.8	66.2	68.6	69.9	69.3	68.8	68.1	68.2	69.7	70.3
Brazil	51.4	48.1	52.6	52.3	61.3	61.1	61.9	61.5	63.4	62.0	61.7	60.9	56.2	56.2	56.7	55.6
Bulgaria	50.0	48.6	47.6	45.7	46.2	47.3	51.9	57.1	57.0	59.2	62.3	64.1	62.7	63.7	64.6	62.3
Burkina Faso	n/a	49.4	54.0	54.5	55.0	55.7	56.7	58.8	58.9	58.0	56.6	55.8	55.1	55.7	59.5	59.4
Burma	n/a	45.1	45.4	45.7	46.4	47.9	46.1	45.5	44.9	43.6	40.5	40.0	41.0	39.5	37.7	36.7
Burundi	n/a	n/a	45.4	44.7	41.1	42.6	n/a	n/a	n/a	n/a	n/a	48.7	46.9	46.2	48.8	47.5
Cambodia	n/a	n/a	52.8	59.8	59.9	59.3	59.6	60.7	63.7	61.1	60.0	56.7	55.9	55.9	56.6	56.6

Index of Economic Freedom Scores, 1995–2010

Country	1995	1996	1997	1998	1999	2000	2001	2002	2003	2004	2005	2006	2007	2008	2009	2010
Cameroon	51.3	45.7	44.6	48.0	50.3	49.9	53.3	52.8	52.7	52.3	53.0	54.6	55.6	54.3	53.0	52.3
Canada	69.4	70.3	67.9	68.5	69.3	70.5	71.2	74.6	74.8	75.3	75.8	77.4	78.0	80.2	80.5	80.4
Cape Verde	n/a	49.7	47.7	48.0	50.7	51.9	56.3	57.6	56.1	58.1	57.8	58.6	56.5	57.9	61.3	61.8
Central African Republic	n/a	n/a	n/a	n/a	n/a	n/a	n/a	n/a	n/a	57.5	56.5	54.2	50.6	48.6	48.3	48.4
Chad	n/a	n/a	45.1	46.6	47.2	46.8	46.4	49.2	52.6	53.1	52.1	50.0	50.1	47.8	47.5	47.5
Chile	71.2	72.6	75.9	74.9	74.1	74.7	75.1	77.8	76.0	76.9	77.8	78.0	77.7	78.6	78.3	77.2
China, People's Republic of	52.0	51.3	51.7	53.1	54.8	56.4	52.6	52.8	52.6	52.5	53.7	53.6	52.0	53.1	53.2	51.0
Colombia	64.5	64.3	66.4	65.5	65.3	63.3	65.6	64.2	64.2	61.2	59.6	60.4	59.9	62.2	62.3	65.5
Comoros	n/a	n/a	n/a	n/a	n/a	n/a	n/a	n/a	n/a	n/a	n/a	n/a	n/a	n/a	43.3	44.9
Congo, Demo. Republic of	41.4	39.5	39.5	40.6	34.0	34.8	n/a	45.3	47.7	45.9	46.2	43.8	44.4	45.3	42.8	41.4
Congo, Republic of	n/a	40.3	42.2	33.8	41.6	40.6	44.3	45.3	47.7	45.9	46.2	43.8	44.4	45.3	45.4	43.2
Costa Rica	68.0	66.4	65.6	65.6	67.4	68.4	67.6	67.5	67.0	66.4	66.1	65.9	64.0	64.2	66.4	65.9
Côte d'Ivoire	53.4	49.9	50.5	51.3	51.7	50.2	54.8	57.3	56.7	57.8	56.6	56.2	54.9	53.9	55.0	54.1
Croatia	n/a	48.0	46.7	51.7	53.1	53.6	50.7	51.1	53.3	53.1	51.9	53.6	53.4	54.1	55.1	59.2
Cuba	27.8	27.8	27.8	28.2	29.7	31.3	31.6	32.4	35.1	34.4	35.5	29.3	28.6	27.5	27.9	26.7
Cyprus	n/a	67.7	67.9	68.2	67.8	67.2	71.0	73.0	73.3	74.1	71.9	71.8	71.7	71.3	70.8	70.9
Czech Republic	67.8	68.1	68.8	68.4	69.7	68.6	70.2	66.5	67.5	67.0	64.6	66.4	67.4	68.1	69.4	69.8
Denmark	n/a	67.3	67.5	67.5	68.1	68.3	68.3	71.1	73.2	72.4	75.3	75.4	77.0	79.2	79.6	77.9
Djibouti	n/a	n/a	54.5	55.9	57.1	55.1	58.3	57.8	55.7	55.6	55.2	53.2	52.4	51.2	51.3	51.1
Dominica	n/a	n/a	n/a	n/a	n/a	n/a	n/a	n/a	n/a	n/a	n/a	n/a	n/a	n/a	62.6	63.2
Dominican Republic	55.8	58.1	53.5	58.1	58.1	59.0	59.1	58.6	57.8	54.6	55.1	56.3	56.8	57.7	59.2	60.3
Ecuador	57.7	60.1	61.0	62.8	62.9	59.8	55.1	53.1	54.1	54.4	52.9	54.6	55.3	55.2	52.5	49.3
Egypt	45.7	52.0	54.5	55.8	58.0	51.7	51.5	54.1	55.3	55.5	55.8	53.2	54.4	58.5	58.0	59.0
El Salvador	69.1	70.1	70.5	70.2	75.1	76.3	73.0	73.0	71.5	71.2	71.5	69.6	68.9	68.5	69.8	69.9
Equatorial Guinea	n/a	n/a	n/a	n/a	45.1	45.6	47.9	46.4	53.1	53.3	53.3	51.5	53.2	51.6	51.3	48.6
Eritrea	n/a	n/a	n/a	n/a	n/a	n/a	n/a	n/a	n/a	n/a	n/a	n/a	n/a	n/a	38.5	35.3
Estonia	65.2	65.4	69.1	72.5	73.8	69.9	76.1	77.6	77.7	77.4	75.2	74.9	78.0	77.9	76.4	74.7

Index of Economic Freedom Scores, 1995–2010

Country	1995	1996	1997	1998	1999	2000	2001	2002	2003	2004	2005	2006	2007	2008	2009	2010
Ethiopia	42.6	45.9	48.1	49.2	46.7	50.2	48.9	49.8	48.8	54.5	51.1	50.9	53.6	52.5	53.0	51.2
Fiji	54.7	57.4	58.0	58.2	58.4	52.8	53.7	53.9	54.7	58.0	58.2	58.4	60.8	61.8	61.0	60.3
Finland	n/a	63.7	65.2	63.5	63.9	64.3	69.7	73.6	73.7	73.4	71.0	72.9	74.0	74.6	74.5	73.8
France	64.4	63.7	59.1	58.9	59.1	57.4	58.0	58.0	59.2	60.9	60.5	61.1	62.1	64.7	63.3	64.2
Gabon	57.5	55.7	58.8	59.2	60.5	58.2	55.0	58.0	58.7	57.1	54.8	56.1	54.8	54.2	55.0	55.4
The Gambia	n/a	n/a	52.9	53.4	52.1	52.7	56.6	57.7	56.3	55.3	56.5	57.3	57.7	56.9	55.8	55.1
Georgia	n/a	44.1	46.5	47.9	52.5	54.3	58.3	56.7	58.6	58.9	57.1	64.5	69.3	69.2	69.8	70.4
Germany	69.8	69.1	67.5	64.3	65.6	65.7	69.5	70.4	69.7	69.5	68.1	70.8	70.8	70.6	70.5	71.1
Ghana	55.6	57.7	56.7	57.0	59.4	58.1	58.0	57.2	58.2	59.1	56.5	55.6	57.6	57.0	58.1	60.2
Greece	61.2	60.5	59.6	60.6	61.0	61.0	63.4	59.1	58.8	59.1	59.0	60.1	58.7	60.6	60.8	62.7
Guatemala	62.0	63.7	65.7	65.8	66.2	64.3	65.1	62.3	62.3	59.6	59.5	59.1	60.5	59.8	59.4	61.0
Guinea	59.4	58.5	52.9	61.0	59.4	58.2	58.4	52.9	54.6	56.1	57.4	52.8	54.5	52.8	51.0	51.8
Guinea–Bissau	n/a	n/a	n/a	n/a	33.5	34.7	42.5	42.3	43.1	42.6	46.0	46.5	46.1	44.4	45.4	43.6
Guyana	45.7	50.1	53.2	52.7	53.3	52.4	53.3	54.3	50.3	53.0	56.5	56.6	53.7	48.8	48.4	48.4
Haiti	43.0	41.0	45.8	45.7	45.9	45.7	42.5	42.3	43.1	42.6	46.0	46.5	46.1	44.4	45.4	43.6
Honduras	57.0	56.6	56.0	56.2	56.7	57.6	57.0	58.7	60.4	55.3	55.3	57.4	59.1	58.9	58.7	58.3
Hong Kong	88.6	90.5	88.6	88.0	88.5	89.5	89.9	89.4	89.8	90.0	89.5	88.6	89.9	89.7	90.0	89.7
Hungary	55.2	56.8	55.3	56.9	59.6	64.4	65.6	64.5	63.0	62.7	63.5	65.0	64.8	67.6	66.8	66.1
Iceland	n/a	n/a	70.5	71.2	71.4	74.0	73.4	73.1	73.5	72.1	76.6	75.8	76.0	75.8	75.9	73.7
India	45.1	47.4	49.7	49.7	50.2	47.4	49.0	51.2	51.2	51.5	54.2	52.2	53.9	54.1	54.4	53.8
Indonesia	54.9	61.0	62.0	63.4	61.5	55.2	52.5	54.8	55.8	52.1	52.9	51.9	53.2	53.2	53.4	55.5
Iran	n/a	36.1	34.5	36.0	36.8	36.1	35.9	36.4	43.2	42.8	50.5	45.0	45.0	45.0	44.6	43.4
Iraq	n/a	17.2	17.2	17.2	17.2	17.2	17.2	15.6	n/a	n/a	n/a	n/a	n/a	n/a	n/a	n/a
Ireland	68.5	68.5	72.6	73.7	74.6	76.1	81.2	80.5	80.9	80.3	80.8	82.2	82.6	82.5	82.2	81.3
Israel	61.5	62.0	62.7	68.0	68.3	65.5	66.1	66.9	62.7	61.4	62.6	64.4	64.8	66.3	67.6	67.7
Italy	61.2	60.8	58.1	59.1	61.6	61.9	63.0	63.6	64.3	64.2	64.9	62.0	62.8	62.6	61.4	62.7
Jamaica	64.4	66.7	67.7	67.1	64.7	65.5	63.7	61.7	67.0	66.7	67.0	66.4	65.5	65.7	65.2	65.5

Index of Economic Freedom Scores, 1995–2010

Country	1995	1996	1997	1998	1999	2000	2001	2002	2003	2004	2005	2006	2007	2008	2009	2010
Japan	75.0	72.6	70.3	70.2	69.1	70.7	70.9	66.7	67.6	64.3	67.3	73.3	72.7	73.0	72.8	72.9
Jordan	62.7	60.8	63.6	66.8	67.4	67.5	68.3	66.2	65.3	66.1	66.7	63.7	64.5	64.1	65.4	66.1
Kazakhstan	n/a	n/a	n/a	41.7	47.3	50.4	51.8	52.4	52.3	49.7	53.9	60.2	59.6	61.1	60.1	61.0
Kenya	54.5	56.4	60.1	58.4	58.2	59.7	57.6	58.2	58.6	57.7	57.9	59.7	59.6	59.3	58.7	57.5
Kiribati	n/a	n/a	n/a	n/a	n/a	n/a	n/a	n/a	n/a	n/a	n/a	n/a	n/a	n/a	45.7	43.7
Korea, North	8.9	8.9	8.9	8.9	8.9	8.9	8.9	8.9	8.9	8.9	8.0	4.0	3.0	3.0	2.0	1.0
Korea, South	72.0	73.0	69.8	73.3	69.7	69.7	69.1	69.5	68.3	67.8	66.4	67.5	67.8	68.6	68.1	69.9
Kuwait	n/a	66.1	64.8	66.3	69.5	69.7	68.2	65.4	66.7	63.6	64.6	66.5	66.4	68.1	65.6	67.7
Kyrgyz Republic	n/a	n/a	n/a	51.8	54.8	55.7	53.7	51.7	56.8	58.0	56.6	61.0	60.2	61.1	61.8	61.3
Laos	n/a	38.5	35.1	35.2	35.2	36.8	33.5	36.8	41.0	42.0	44.4	47.5	50.3	50.3	50.4	51.1
Latvia	n/a	55.0	62.4	63.4	64.2	63.4	66.4	65.0	66.0	67.4	66.3	66.9	67.9	68.3	66.6	66.2
Lebanon	n/a	63.2	63.9	59.0	59.1	56.1	61.0	57.1	56.7	56.9	57.2	57.5	60.4	60.0	58.1	59.5
Lesotho	n/a	47.0	47.2	48.4	48.2	48.4	50.6	48.9	52.0	50.3	53.9	54.7	53.2	52.1	49.7	48.1
Liberia	n/a	n/a	n/a	n/a	n/a	n/a	n/a	n/a	n/a	n/a	n/a	n/a	n/a	n/a	48.1	46.2
Libya	n/a	31.7	28.9	32.0	32.3	34.7	34.0	35.4	34.6	31.5	32.8	33.2	37.0	38.7	43.5	40.2
Liechtenstein	n/a	n/a	n/a	n/a	n/a	n/a	n/a	n/a	n/a	n/a	n/a	n/a	n/a	n/a	n/a	n/a
Lithuania	n/a	49.7	57.3	59.4	61.5	61.9	65.5	66.1	69.7	72.4	70.5	71.8	71.5	70.9	70.0	70.3
Luxembourg	n/a	72.5	72.8	72.7	72.4	76.4	80.1	79.4	79.9	78.9	76.3	75.3	74.6	74.7	75.2	75.4
Macau	n/a	n/a	n/a	n/a	n/a	n/a	n/a	n/a	n/a	n/a	n/a	n/a	n/a	n/a	72.0	72.5
Macedonia	n/a	n/a	n/a	n/a	n/a	n/a	n/a	58.0	60.1	56.8	56.1	59.2	60.6	61.1	61.2	65.7
Madagascar	51.6	52.2	53.8	51.8	52.8	54.4	53.9	56.8	62.8	60.9	63.1	61.0	61.1	62.4	62.2	63.2
Malawi	54.7	56.2	53.4	54.1	54.0	57.4	56.2	56.9	53.2	53.6	53.6	55.4	52.9	52.7	53.7	54.1
Malaysia	71.9	69.9	66.8	68.2	68.9	66.0	60.2	60.1	61.1	59.9	61.9	61.6	63.8	63.9	64.6	64.8
Maldives	n/a	n/a	n/a	n/a	n/a	n/a	n/a	n/a	n/a	n/a	n/a	n/a	n/a	n/a	51.3	49.0
Mali	52.4	57.0	56.4	57.3	58.4	60.3	60.1	61.1	58.6	56.6	57.3	54.1	54.7	55.6	55.6	55.6
Malta	56.3	55.8	57.9	61.2	59.3	58.3	62.9	62.2	61.1	63.3	68.9	67.3	66.1	66.0	66.1	67.2
Mauritania	n/a	45.5	47.0	43.7	42.8	46.0	48.5	52.5	59.0	61.8	59.4	55.7	53.6	55.2	53.9	52.0

Index of Economic Freedom Scores, 1995–2010

Country	1995	1996	1997	1998	1999	2000	2001	2002	2003	2004	2005	2006	2007	2008	2009	2010
Mauritius	n/a	n/a	n/a	n/a	68.5	67.2	66.4	67.7	64.4	64.3	67.2	67.4	69.4	72.6	74.3	76.3
Mexico	63.1	61.2	57.1	57.9	58.5	59.3	60.6	63.0	65.3	66.0	65.2	64.7	66.0	66.2	65.8	68.3
Micronesia	n/a	n/a	n/a	n/a	n/a	n/a	n/a	n/a	n/a	n/a	n/a	n/a	n/a	n/a	51.7	50.6
Moldova	33.0	52.5	48.9	53.5	56.1	59.6	54.9	57.4	60.0	57.1	57.4	58.0	58.7	57.9	54.9	53.7
Mongolia	47.8	47.4	52.9	57.3	58.6	58.5	56.0	56.7	57.7	56.5	59.7	62.4	60.3	63.6	62.8	60.0
Montenegro	n/a	n/a	n/a	n/a	n/a	n/a	n/a	46.6*	43.5*	n/a	n/a	n/a	n/a	n/a	58.2	63.6
Morocco	62.8	64.3	64.7	61.1	63.8	63.2	63.9	59.0	57.8	56.7	52.2	51.5	56.4	55.6	57.7	59.2
Mozambique	45.5	48.4	44.0	43.0	48.9	52.2	59.2	57.7	58.6	57.2	54.6	51.9	54.7	55.4	55.7	56.0
Namibia	n/a	n/a	61.6	66.1	66.1	66.7	64.8	65.1	67.3	62.4	61.4	60.7	63.5	61.4	62.4	62.2
Nepal	n/a	50.3	53.6	53.5	53.1	51.3	51.6	52.3	51.5	51.2	51.4	53.7	54.4	54.1	53.2	52.7
The Netherlands	n/a	69.7	70.4	69.2	63.6	70.4	73.0	75.1	74.6	74.5	72.9	75.4	75.5	77.4	77.0	75.0
New Zealand	n/a	78.1	79.0	79.2	81.7	80.9	81.1	80.7	81.1	81.5	82.3	82.0	81.4	80.7	82.0	82.1
Nicaragua	42.5	54.1	53.3	53.8	54.0	56.9	58.0	61.1	62.6	61.4	62.5	63.8	62.7	60.8	59.8	58.3
Niger	n/a	45.8	46.6	47.5	48.6	45.9	48.9	48.2	54.2	54.6	54.1	52.5	53.2	52.9	53.8	52.9
Nigeria	47.3	47.4	52.8	52.3	55.7	53.1	49.6	50.9	49.5	49.2	48.4	48.7	55.6	55.1	55.1	56.8
Norway	n/a	65.4	65.1	68.0	68.6	70.1	67.1	67.4	67.2	66.2	64.5	67.9	67.9	68.6	70.2	69.4
Oman	70.2	65.4	64.5	64.9	64.9	64.1	67.7	64.0	64.6	66.9	66.5	63.7	65.8	67.3	67.0	67.7
Pakistan	57.6	58.4	56.0	53.2	53.0	56.4	56.0	55.8	55.0	54.9	53.3	57.9	57.2	55.6	57.0	55.2
Panama	71.6	71.8	72.4	72.6	72.6	71.6	70.6	68.5	68.4	65.3	64.3	65.6	64.6	64.7	64.7	64.8
Papua New Guinea	n/a	58.6	56.7	55.2	56.3	55.8	57.2	n/a	n/a	n/a	n/a	n/a	n/a	n/a	54.8	53.5
Paraguay	65.9	67.1	67.3	65.2	63.7	64.0	60.3	59.6	58.2	56.7	53.4	55.6	58.3	60.0	61.0	61.3
Peru	56.9	62.5	63.8	65.0	69.2	68.7	69.6	64.8	64.6	64.7	61.3	60.5	62.7	63.8	64.6	67.6
The Philippines,	55.0	60.2	62.2	62.8	61.9	62.5	60.9	60.7	61.3	59.1	54.7	56.3	56.0	56.0	56.8	56.3
Poland	50.7	57.8	56.8	59.2	59.6	60.0	61.8	65.0	61.8	58.7	59.6	59.3	58.1	60.3	60.3	63.2
Portugal	62.4	64.5	63.6	65.0	65.6	65.5	66.0	65.4	64.9	64.9	62.4	62.9	64.0	63.9	64.9	64.4
Qatar	n/a	n/a	n/a	n/a	62.0	62.0	60.0	61.9	65.9	66.5	63.5	62.4	62.9	62.2	65.8	69.0
Romania	42.9	46.2	50.8	54.4	50.1	52.1	50.0	48.7	50.6	50.0	52.1	58.2	61.2	61.7	63.2	64.2

Index of Economic Freedom Scores, 1995–2010

Country	1995	1996	1997	1998	1999	2000	2001	2002	2003	2004	2005	2006	2007	2008	2009	2010
Russia	51.1	51.6	48.6	52.8	54.5	51.8	49.8	48.7	50.8	52.8	51.3	52.4	52.2	49.8	50.8	50.3
Rwanda	n/a	n/a	38.3	39.1	39.8	42.3	45.4	50.4	47.8	53.3	51.7	52.8	52.4	54.2	54.2	59.1
Saint Lucia	n/a	n/a	n/a	n/a	n/a	n/a	n/a	n/a	n/a	n/a	n/a	n/a	n/a	n/a	68.8	70.5
Saint Vincent and the Grenadines	n/a	n/a	n/a	n/a	n/a	n/a	n/a	n/a	n/a	n/a	n/a	n/a	n/a	n/a	64.3	66.9
Samoa	n/a	47.6	51.5	49.9	58.7	60.8	63.1	n/a	n/a	n/a	n/a	n/a	n/a	n/a	59.5	60.4
São Tomé and Príncipe	n/a	n/a	n/a	n/a	n/a	n/a	n/a	n/a	n/a	n/a	n/a	n/a	n/a	n/a	43.8	48.8
Saudi Arabia	n/a	68.3	68.7	69.3	65.5	66.5	62.2	65.3	63.2	60.4	63.0	63.0	60.9	62.5	64.3	64.1
Senegal	60.4	58.2	58.1	59.7	60.6	58.9	58.7	58.6	58.1	58.9	57.9	56.2	58.1	58.3	56.3	54.6
Serbia	n/a	n/a	n/a	n/a	n/a	n/a	n/a	46.6*	43.5*	n/a	n/a	n/a	n/a	n/a	56.6	56.9
Seychelles	n/a	n/a	n/a	n/a	n/a	n/a	n/a	n/a	n/a	n/a	n/a	n/a	n/a	n/a	47.8	47.9
Sierra Leone	49.8	52.3	45.0	47.7	47.2	44.2	n/a	n/a	42.2	43.6	44.8	45.2	47.0	48.3	47.8	47.9
Singapore	86.3	86.5	87.3	87.0	86.9	87.7	87.8	87.4	88.2	88.9	88.6	88.0	87.1	87.3	87.1	86.1
Slovakia	60.4	57.6	55.5	57.5	54.2	53.8	58.5	59.8	59.0	64.6	66.8	69.8	69.6	70.0	69.4	69.7
Slovenia	n/a	50.4	55.6	60.7	61.3	58.3	61.8	57.8	57.7	59.2	59.6	61.9	59.6	60.2	62.9	64.7
Solomon Islands	n/a	n/a	n/a	n/a	n/a	n/a	n/a	n/a	n/a	n/a	n/a	n/a	n/a	n/a	46.0	42.9
South Africa	60.7	62.5	63.2	64.3	63.3	63.7	63.8	64.0	67.1	66.3	62.9	63.7	63.5	63.4	63.8	62.8
Spain	62.8	59.6	59.6	62.6	65.1	65.9	68.1	68.8	68.8	68.9	67.0	68.2	69.2	69.1	70.1	69.6
Sri Lanka	60.6	62.5	65.5	64.6	64.0	63.2	66.0	64.0	62.5	61.6	61.0	58.7	59.4	58.4	56.0	54.6
Sudan	39.4	39.2	39.9	38.3	39.6	47.2	n/a	n/a	n/a	n/a	n/a	n/a	n/a	n/a	n/a	n/a
Suriname	n/a	36.7	35.9	39.9	40.1	45.8	44.3	48.0	46.9	47.9	51.9	55.1	54.8	54.3	54.1	52.5
Swaziland	63.3	58.6	59.4	62.0	62.1	62.6	63.6	60.9	59.6	58.6	59.4	61.4	60.1	58.4	59.1	57.4
Sweden	61.4	61.8	63.3	64.0	64.2	65.1	66.6	70.8	70.0	70.1	69.8	70.9	69.3	70.8	70.5	72.4
Switzerland	n/a	76.8	78.6	79.0	79.1	76.8	76.0	79.3	79.0	79.5	79.3	78.9	78.0	79.5	79.4	81.1
Syria	n/a	42.3	43.0	42.2	39.0	37.2	36.6	36.3	41.3	40.6	46.3	51.2	48.3	47.2	51.3	49.4
Taiwan	74.2	74.1	70.0	70.4	71.5	72.5	72.8	71.3	71.7	69.6	71.3	69.7	69.4	70.3	69.5	70.4
Tajikistan	n/a	n/a	n/a	41.1	41.2	44.8	46.8	47.3	46.5	48.7	50.4	52.6	53.6	54.4	54.6	53.0

Index of Economic Freedom Scores, 1995–2010

Country	1995	1996	1997	1998	1999	2000	2001	2002	2003	2004	2005	2006	2007	2008	2009	2010
Tanzania	57.3	57.5	59.3	59.6	60.0	56.0	54.9	58.3	56.9	60.1	56.3	58.5	56.8	56.5	58.3	58.3
Thailand	71.3	71.0	66.1	67.3	66.9	66.6	68.9	69.1	65.8	63.7	62.5	63.3	63.5	62.3	63.0	64.1
Timor-Leste	n/a	n/a	n/a	n/a	n/a	n/a	n/a	n/a	n/a	n/a	n/a	n/a	n/a	n/a	50.5	45.8
Togo	n/a	n/a	n/a	n/a	48.2	46.4	45.3	45.2	46.8	47.0	48.2	47.3	49.7	48.9	48.7	47.1
Tonga	n/a	n/a	n/a	n/a	n/a	n/a	n/a	n/a	n/a	n/a	n/a	n/a	n/a	n/a	54.1	53.4
Trinidad and Tobago	n/a	69.2	71.3	72.0	72.4	74.5	71.8	70.1	68.8	71.3	71.5	70.4	70.6	69.5	68.0	65.7
Tunisia	63.4	63.9	63.8	63.9	61.1	61.3	60.8	60.2	58.1	58.4	55.4	57.5	60.3	60.1	58.0	58.9
Turkey	58.4	56.7	60.8	60.9	59.2	63.4	60.6	54.2	51.9	52.8	50.6	57.0	57.4	59.9	61.6	63.8
Turkmenistan	n/a	n/a	n/a	35.0	36.1	37.6	41.8	43.2	51.3	50.7	47.6	43.8	43.0	43.4	44.2	42.5
Uganda	62.9	66.2	66.6	64.7	64.8	58.2	60.4	61.0	60.1	64.1	62.9	63.9	63.1	63.8	63.5	62.2
Ukraine	39.9	40.6	43.5	40.4	43.7	47.8	48.5	48.2	51.1	53.7	55.8	54.4	51.5	51.0	48.8	46.4
United Arab Emirates	n/a	71.6	71.9	72.2	71.5	74.2	74.9	73.6	73.4	67.2	65.2	62.2	62.6	62.6	64.7	67.3
United Kingdom	77.9	76.4	76.4	76.5	76.2	77.3	77.6	78.5	77.5	77.7	79.2	80.4	79.9	79.4	79.0	76.5
United States	76.7	76.7	75.6	75.4	75.5	76.4	79.1	78.4	78.2	78.7	79.9	81.2	81.2	81.0	80.7	78.0
Uruguay	62.5	63.7	67.5	68.6	68.5	69.3	70.7	68.7	69.8	66.7	66.9	65.3	68.4	67.9	69.1	69.8
Uzbekistan	n/a	n/a	n/a	31.5	33.8	38.1	38.2	38.5	38.3	39.1	45.8	48.7	51.5	51.9	50.5	47.5
Vanuatu	n/a	n/a	n/a	n/a	n/a	n/a	n/a	n/a	n/a	n/a	n/a	n/a	n/a	n/a	58.4	56.4
Venezuela	59.8	54.5	52.8	54.0	56.1	57.4	54.6	54.7	54.8	46.7	45.2	44.6	47.9	44.7	39.9	37.1
Vietnam	41.7	40.2	38.6	40.4	42.7	43.7	44.3	45.6	46.2	46.1	48.1	50.5	49.8	50.4	51.0	49.8
Yemen	49.8	49.6	48.4	46.1	43.3	44.5	44.3	48.6	50.3	50.5	53.8	52.6	54.1	53.8	56.9	54.4
Zambia	55.1	59.6	62.1	62.7	64.2	62.8	59.5	59.6	55.3	54.9	55.0	56.8	56.2	56.2	56.6	58.0
Zimbabwe	48.5	46.7	48.0	44.6	47.2	48.7	38.8	36.7	36.7	34.4	35.2	33.5	32.0	29.5	22.7	21.4

* Note: Scores for "Serbia and Montenegro"

Methodology for the 10 Economic Freedoms

The *Index of Economic Freedom* is built upon analysis of 10 specific components of economic freedom, some of which are themselves composites of additional quantifiable measures. Each one of the 10 economic freedoms is graded using a scale from 0 to 100. The 10 component scores are equally weighted and averaged to get an overall economic freedom score for each country.

The following paragraphs provide detailed descriptions of the methodology used to determine the scores for each of the 10 components of economic freedom.

FREEDOM #1: BUSINESS FREEDOM

Business freedom is a quantitative measure of the ability to start, operate, and close a business that represents the overall burden of regulation as well as the efficiency of government in the regulatory process. The business freedom score for each country is a number between 0 and 100, with 100 equaling the freest business environment. The score is based on 10 factors, all weighted equally, using data from the World Bank's *Doing Business* study:

- Starting a business—procedures (number);
- Starting a business—time (days);
- Starting a business—cost (% of income per capita);
- Starting a business—minimum capital (% of income per capita);
- Obtaining a license—procedures (number);[1]
- Obtaining a license—time (days);
- Obtaining a license—cost (% of income per capita);
- Closing a business—time (years);

---

1. Obtaining a license indicates necessary procedures, time, and cost in getting construction permits.

- Closing a business—cost (% of estate); and
- Closing a business—recovery rate (cents on the dollar).[2]

Each of these raw factors is converted to a scale of 0 to 100, after which the average of the converted values is computed. The result represents the country's business freedom score. For example, even if a country requires the highest number of procedures for starting a business, which yields a score of zero in that factor, it could still receive a score as high as 90 based on scores in the other nine factors.

Canada, for instance, receives scores of 100 in nine of the 10 factors, the exception being the 14 licensing procedures required by the government, which equates to a score of 64.5 for that factor.

Each factor is converted to a scale of 0 to 100 using the following equation:

$$\text{Factor Score}_i = 50 \times \text{factor}_{average}/\text{factor}_i$$

which is based on the ratio of the country data for each factor relative to the world average, multiplied by 50. For example, on average worldwide, it takes 18.1 procedures to get necessary licenses. Canada's 14 licensing procedures is a factor value better than the average, resulting in a ratio of 1.29. That ratio multiplied by 50 equals the final factor score of 64.5.

For the eight countries that are not covered by the World Bank's *Doing Business* study, business freedom is scored by looking into business regulations based on qualitative information from reliable and internationally recognized sources.[3]

Sources. Unless otherwise noted, the *Index* relies on the following sources in determining business freedom scores, in order of priority: World Bank, *Doing Business 2010*; Economist Intelligence Unit, *Country Report*, *Country Commerce*, and *Country Profile*, 2007–2009; U.S. Department of Commerce, *Country Commercial Guide*, 2007–2009; and official government publications of each country.

FREEDOM #2: TRADE FREEDOM

Trade freedom is a composite measure of the absence of tariff and non-tariff barriers that affect imports and exports of goods and services. The trade freedom score is based on two inputs:

- The trade-weighted average tariff rate and
- Non-tariff barriers (NTBs).

Different imports entering a country can, and often do, face different tariffs. The weighted average tariff uses weights for each tariff based on the share of imports for each good. Weighted average tariffs are a purely quantitative measure and account for the basic calculation of the score using the following equation:

$$\text{Trade Freedom}_i = (((\text{Tariff}_{max}-\text{Tariff}_i)/(\text{Tariff}_{max}-\text{Tariff}_{min})) * 100) - \text{NTB}_i$$

where Trade Freedom$_i$ represents the trade freedom in country i, Tariff$_{max}$ and Tariff$_{min}$ represent the upper and lower bounds for tariff rates (%), and Tariff$_i$ represents the weighted average tariff rate (%) in country i. The minimum tariff is naturally zero percent, and the upper bound was set

---

2.   The recovery rate is a function of time and cost. However, the business freedom component uses all three subvariables to emphasize closing a business, starting a business, and dealing with licenses equally.

3.   Eight countries are not covered by the World Bank's *Doing Business* study: Barbados, Burma, Cuba, North Korea, Libya, Macao, Malta, and Turkmenistan. The methodology for business freedom dates to the 2006 *Index* because of the limited availability of quantitative data. For the 1995 through 2005 editions, we used a subjective assessment with a score of 1–5. Those earlier scores have been converted by means of a simple formula to make them comparable. Observations with the top score were converted to 100, the next best to 85, and so on. This conversion formula is different from the one used for other subjective factors, but it is unique because those other factors are not bridging to a new, data-driven methodology.

as 50 percent. An NTB penalty is then subtracted from the base score. The penalty of 5, 10, 15, or 20 points is assigned according to the following scale:

- **20**—NTBs are used extensively across many goods and services and/or act to effectively impede a significant amount of international trade.
- **15**—NTBs are widespread across many goods and services and/or act to impede a majority of potential international trade.
- **10**—NTBs are used to protect certain goods and services and impede some international trade.
- **5**—NTBs are uncommon, protecting few goods and services, and/or have very limited impact on international trade.
- **0**—NTBs are not used to limit international trade.

We determine the extent of NTBs in a country's trade policy regime using both qualitative and quantitative information. Restrictive rules that hinder trade vary widely, and their overlapping and shifting nature makes their complexity difficult to gauge. The categories of NTBs considered in our penalty include:

- **Quantity restrictions**—import quotas; export limitations; voluntary export restraints; import–export embargoes and bans; countertrade, etc.
- **Price restrictions**—antidumping duties; countervailing duties; border tax adjustments; variable levies/tariff rate quotas.
- **Regulatory restrictions**—licensing; domestic content and mixing requirements; sanitary and phytosanitary standards (SPSs); safety and industrial standards regulations; packaging, labeling, and trademark regulations; advertising and media regulations.
- **Investment restrictions**—exchange and other financial controls.
- **Customs restrictions**—advance deposit requirements; customs valuation procedures; customs classification procedures; customs clearance procedures.
- **Direct government intervention**—subsidies and other aid; government industrial policy and regional development measures; government-financed research and other technology policies; national taxes and social insurance; competition policies; immigration policies; government procurement policies; state trading, government monopolies, and exclusive franchises.

As an example, China received a trade freedom score of 72.2. China's weighted average tariff of 3.9 percent would have yielded a score by itself of 92.2, but the existence of significant NTBs in China reduced the score by 20 points.

Gathering data on tariffs to make a consistent cross-country comparison can be a challenging task. Unlike data on inflation, for instance, countries do not report their weighted average tariff rate or simple average tariff rate every year; in some cases, the most recent year for which a country reported its tariff data could have been as far back as 1999. To preserve consistency in grading the trade policy component, the *Index* uses the most recently reported weighted average tariff rate for a country from our primary source. If another reliable source reports more updated information on the country's tariff rate, this fact is noted, and the grading of this component may be reviewed if there is strong evidence that the most recently reported weighted average tariff rate is outdated.

The World Bank produces the most comprehensive and consistent information on weighted average applied tariff rates. When the weighted average applied tariff rate is not available, the *Index* uses the country's average applied tariff rate; and when the country's average applied tariff rate is not available, the weighted average or the simple average of most favored nation (MFN) tariff rates is used.[4] In the very few cases where data on duties and customs revenues are not available, data on international trade taxes or an estimated effective tariff rate are used instead. In all

---

4. MFN is now referred to as permanent normal trade relations (PNTR).

cases, an effort is made to clarify the type of data used and the different sources for those data in the corresponding write-up for the trade policy component.

Sources. Unless otherwise noted, the *Index* relies on the following sources to determine scores for trade policy, in order of priority: World Bank, *World Development Indicators 2009* and *Data on Trade and Import Barriers: Trends in Average Applied Tariff Rates in Developing and Industrial Countries, 1981–2007*; World Trade Organization, *Trade Policy Review*, 1995–2009; Office of the U.S. Trade Representative, *2009 National Trade Estimate Report on Foreign Trade Barriers*; World Bank, *Doing Business 2009* and *Doing Business 2010*; U.S. Department of Commerce, *Country Commercial Guide*, 2004–2009; Economist Intelligence Unit, *Country Report*, *Country Profile*, and *Country Commerce*, 2004–2009; and official government publications of each country.

FREEDOM #3: FISCAL FREEDOM

Fiscal freedom is a measure of the tax burden imposed by government. It includes both the direct tax burden in terms of the top tax rates on individual and corporate incomes and the overall amount of tax revenue as a percentage of GDP. Thus, the fiscal freedom component is composed of three quantitative factors:

- The top tax rate on individual income,
- The top tax rate on corporate income, and
- Total tax revenue as a percentage of GDP.

In scoring the fiscal freedom component, each of these numerical variables is weighted equally as one-third of the factor. This equal weighting allows a country to achieve a score as high as 67 based on two of the factors even if it receives a score of 0 on the third.

Fiscal freedom scores are calculated with a quadratic cost function to reflect the diminishing revenue returns from very high rates of taxation. The data for each factor are converted to a 100-point scale using the following equation:

$$\text{Fiscal Freedom}_{ij} = 100 - \alpha \times (\text{Factor}_{ij})^2$$

where Fiscal Freedom$_{ij}$ represents the fiscal freedom in country i for factor j; Factor$_{ij}$ represents the value (based on a scale of 0 to 100) in country i for factor j; and α is a coefficient set equal to 0.03. The minimum score for each factor is zero, which is not represented in the printed equation but was utilized because it means that no single high tax burden will make the other two factors irrelevant.

As an example, in the 2010 *Index*, Bulgaria has a flat rate of 10 percent for both individual and corporate tax rates, which yields a score of 97 for each of the two factors. Bulgaria's overall tax revenue as a portion of GDP is 34.2 percent, yielding a revenue factor score of 64.9. When the three factors are averaged together, Bulgaria's overall fiscal freedom score becomes 86.3.

Sources. Unless otherwise noted, the *Index* relies on the following sources for information on taxation, in order of priority: Deloitte, *International Tax and Business Guide Highlights*; International Monetary Fund, *Staff Country Report*, "Selected Issues and Statistical Appendix," and *Staff Country Report*, "Article IV Consultation," 2006–2009; PricewaterhouseCoopers, *Worldwide Tax Summaries*, 2007–2009; countries' investment agencies; other government authorities (embassy confirmations and/or the country's treasury or tax authority); and Economist Intelligence Unit, *Country Report*, *Country Profile*, *Country Commerce*, or *Country Finance*, 2007–2009.

For information on tax revenue as a percentage of GDP, the primary sources (in order of priority) were Organisation for Economic Co-operation and Development data; Eurostat, Government Finance Statistics data; African Development Bank and Organisation for Economic Co-operation and Development, *African Economic Outlook 2009*; International Monetary Fund, *Staff Country Report*, "Selected Issues and Statistical Appendix," and *Staff Country Report*, "Article IV Consultation," 2006–2009; Asian Development Bank, *Key Indicators of Developing Asian and Pacific Countries*

2008–2009; World Trade Organization, *Trade Policy Reviews*, 2008–2009; official government publications of each country; and individual contacts from government agencies and multinational organizations such as the IMF and World Bank.

FREEDOM #4: GOVERNMENT SPENDING

This component considers the level of government expenditures as a percentage of GDP. Government expenditures, including consumption and transfers, account for the entire score.

No attempt has been made to identify an ideal level of government expenditures. The ideal level will vary from country to country, depending on factors ranging from culture to geography to level of development. The methodology treats zero government spending as the benchmark, and underdeveloped countries with little government capacity may receive artificially high scores as a result. However, such governments, which can provide few if any public goods, will be penalized by lower scores on some of the other components of economic freedom (such as property rights and financial freedom).

The scale for scoring government spending is non-linear, which means that government spending that is close to zero is lightly penalized, while levels of government spending that exceed 30 percent of GDP receive much worse scores in a quadratic fashion (e.g., doubling spending yields four times less freedom), so that only really large governments receive very low scores.

The expenditure equation used is:

$$GE_i = 100 - \alpha \times (Expenditures_i)^2$$

where GE_i represents the government expenditure score in country i; Expenditures$_i$ represents the total amount of government spending at all levels as a portion of GDP (between 0 and 100); and α is a coefficient to control for variation among scores (set at 0.03). The minimum component score is zero.

In most cases, general government expenditure data include all levels of government such as federal, state, and local. In cases where general government spending data are not available, data on central government expenditure are used instead.

Sources. Unless otherwise noted, the *Index* relies on the following sources for information on government intervention in the economy, in order of priority: Organisation for Economic Co-operation and Development data; Eurostat data; African Development Bank and Organisation for Economic Co-operation and Development, *African Economic Outlook 2009*; International Monetary Fund, *Staff Country Report*, "Selected Issues and Statistical Appendix," and *Staff Country Report*, "Article IV Consultation," 2007–2009; Asian Development Bank, *Key Indicators of Developing Asian and Pacific Countries 2008–2009*; African Development Bank, *Selected Statistics on African Countries 2008*; official government publications of each country; and Economist Intelligence Unit, *Country Report and Country Profile*, 2007–2009.

FREEDOM #5: MONETARY FREEDOM

Monetary freedom combines a measure of price stability with an assessment of price controls. Both inflation and price controls distort market activity. Price stability without microeconomic intervention is the ideal state for the free market.

The score for the monetary freedom factor is based on two factors:
- The weighted average inflation rate for the most recent three years and
- Price controls.

The weighted average inflation rate for the most recent three years serves as the primary input into an equation that generates the base score for monetary freedom. The extent of price controls is then assessed as a penalty of up to 20 points subtracted from the base score. The two equations used to convert inflation rates into the monetary freedom score are:

$$\text{Weighted Avg. Inflation}_i = \theta_1 \times \text{Inflation}_{it} + \theta_2 \times \text{Inflation}_{it-1} + \theta_3 \times \text{Inflation}_{it-2}$$

$$\text{Monetary Freedom}_i = 100 - \alpha \times \sqrt{\text{Weighted Avg. Inflation}_i} - \text{PC penalty}_i$$

where θ_1 through θ_3 (thetas 1–3) represent three numbers that sum to 1 and are exponentially smaller in sequence (in this case, values of 0.665, 0.245, and 0.090, respectively); Inflation_{it} is the absolute value of the annual inflation rate in country i during year t as measured by the consumer price index; α represents a coefficient that stabilizes the variance of scores; and the price control (PC) penalty is an assigned value of 0–20 points based on the extent of price controls. The convex (square root) functional form was chosen to create separation among countries with low inflation rates. A concave functional form would essentially treat all hyperinflations as equally bad, whether they were 100 percent price increases annually or 100,000 percent, whereas the square root provides much more gradation. The α coefficient is set to equal 6.333, which converts a 10 percent inflation rate into a freedom score of 80.0 and a 2 percent inflation rate into a score of 91.0.

Sources. Unless otherwise noted, the *Index* relies on the following sources for data on monetary policy, in order of priority: International Monetary Fund, *International Financial Statistics Online*; International Monetary Fund, *World Economic Outlook Crisis and Recovery April 2009*; and Economist Intelligence Unit, *Country Report*, 2005–2009, *Country Profile*, 2005–2009, and official government publications of each country.

FREEDOM #6: INVESTMENT FREEDOM

In an economically free country, there would be no constraints on the flow of investment capital. Individuals and firms would be allowed to move their resources into and out of specific activities both internally and across the country's borders without restriction. Such an ideal country would receive a score of 100 on the investment freedom component of the *Index of Economic Freedom*.

In practice, most countries have a variety of restrictions on investment. Some have different rules for foreign and domestic investment; some restrict access to foreign exchange; some impose restrictions on payments, transfers, and capital transactions; in some, certain industries are closed to foreign investment. Moreover, labor regulations, corruption, red tape, weak infrastructure, and political and security conditions can also affect the freedom that investors have in a market.

The *Index* evaluates a variety of restrictions typically imposed on investment. Points, as indicated below, are deducted from the ideal score of 100 for each of the restrictions found in a country's investment regime. It is not necessary for a government to impose all of the listed restrictions at the maximum level to effectively eliminate investment freedom. Those few governments that impose so many restrictions that they total more than 100 points in deductions have had their scores set at zero.

Investment restrictions:

National treatment of foreign investment
- No national treatment, prescreening   25 points deducted
- Some national treatment, some prescreening   15 points deducted
- Some national treatment or prescreening   5 points deducted

Foreign investment code
- No transparency and burdensome bureaucracy   20 points deducted
- Inefficient policy implementation and bureaucracy   10 points deducted
- Some investment laws and practices are non-transparent or inefficiently implemented   5 points deducted

Restrictions on land ownership
- All real estate purchases restricted   15 points deducted
- No foreign purchases of real estate   10 points deducted
- Some restrictions on purchases of real estate   5 points deducted

Sectoral investment restrictions
- Multiple sectors restricted   20 points deducted
- Few sectors restricted   10 points deducted
- One or two sectors restricted   5 points deducted

Expropriation of investments without fair compensation
- Common with no legal recourse   25 points deducted
- Common with some legal recourse   15 points deducted
- Uncommon, but occurs   5 points deducted

Foreign exchange controls
- No access by foreigners or residents   25 points deducted
- Access available but heavily restricted   15 points deducted
- Access available with few restrictions   5 points deducted

Capital controls
- No repatriation of profits; all transactions require government approval   25 points deducted
- Inward and outward capital movements require approval and face some restrictions   15 points deducted
- Most transfers approved with some restrictions   5 points deducted

Up to an additional 20 points may be deducted for security problems, a lack of basic investment infrastructure, or other government policies that indirectly burden the investment process and limit investment freedom.

Sources. Unless otherwise noted, the *Index* relies on the following sources for data on capital flows and foreign investment, in order of priority: official government publications of each country; Economist Intelligence Unit, *Country Commerce, Country Profile*, and *Country Report*, 2005–2009; Office of the U.S. Trade Representative, *2009 National Trade Estimate Report on Foreign Trade Barriers*; and U.S. Department of Commerce, *Country Commercial Guide*, 2005–2009.

FREEDOM #7: FINANCIAL FREEDOM

Financial freedom is a measure of banking security as well as a measure of independence from government control. State ownership of banks and other financial institutions such as insurers and capital markets reduces competition and generally lowers the level of available services.

The *Index* scores this component by determining the extent of government regulation of financial services; the extent of state intervention in banks and other financial services; the difficulty of opening and operating financial services firms (for both domestic and foreign individuals); and government influence on the allocation of credit. This analysis is used to develop a description of the country's financial climate and assign an overall score on a scale of 0 to 100 through a comparison with the following standards:

- **100—Negligible government influence.** Independent central bank supervision and regulation of financial institutions are limited to enforcing contractual obligations and preventing fraud. Credit is allocated on market terms. The government does not own financial institutions. Financial institutions may engage in all types of financial services. Banks are free to issue competitive notes, extend credit and accept deposits, and conduct operations in foreign currencies. Foreign financial institutions operate freely and are treated the same as domestic institutions.

- **90—Minimal government influence.** Same as above with the following exceptions: Independent central bank supervision and regulation of financial institutions are minimal but may extend beyond enforcing contractual obligations and preventing fraud.
- **80—Nominal government influence.** Same as above with the following exceptions: Independent central bank supervision and regulation are straightforward and transparent but extend beyond enforcing contractual obligations and preventing fraud. Government ownership of financial institutions is a small share of overall sector assets. Financial institutions face almost no restrictions on their ability to offer financial services.
- **70—Limited government influence.** Same as above with the following exceptions: Credit allocation is slightly influenced by the government, and private allocation of credit faces almost no restrictions. Foreign financial institutions are subject to few restrictions.
- **60—Significant government influence.** Same as above with the following exceptions: The central bank is not fully independent, its supervision and regulation of financial institutions are somewhat burdensome, and its ability to enforce contracts and prevent fraud is insufficient. The government exercises active ownership and control of financial institutions with a significant share of overall sector assets. The ability of financial institutions to offer financial services is subject to some restrictions.
- **50—Considerable government influence.** Same as above with the following exceptions: Credit allocation is significantly influenced by the government, and private allocation of credit faces significant barriers. The ability of financial institutions to offer financial services is subject to significant restrictions. Foreign financial institutions are subject to some restrictions.
- **40—Strong government influence.** Same as above with the following exceptions: The central bank is subject to government influence, its supervision and regulation of financial institutions are heavy, and its ability to enforce contracts and prevent fraud is weak. The government exercises active ownership and control of financial institutions with a large minority share of overall sector assets.
- **30—Extensive government influence.** Same as above with the following exceptions: Credit allocation is extensively influenced by the government. The government owns or controls a majority of financial institutions or is in a dominant position. Financial institutions are heavily restricted, and bank formation faces significant barriers. Foreign financial institutions are subject to significant restrictions.
- **20—Heavy government influence.** Same as above with the following exceptions: The central bank is not independent, and its supervision and regulation of financial institutions are repressive. Foreign financial institutions are discouraged or highly constrained.
- **10—Near repressive.** Same as above with the following exceptions: Credit allocation is controlled by the government. Bank formation is restricted. Foreign financial institutions are prohibited.
- **0—Repressive.** Same as above with the following exceptions: Supervision and regulation are designed to prevent private financial institutions. Private financial institutions are prohibited.

Sources. Unless otherwise noted, the *Index* relies on the following sources for data on banking and finance, in order of priority: Economist Intelligence Unit, *Country Commerce, Country Finance, Country Profile,* and *Country Report,* 2007–2009; International Monetary Fund, *Staff Country Report,* "Selected Issues and Statistical Appendix," and *Staff Country Report,* "Article IV Consultation," 2007–2009; Organisation for Economic Co-operation and Development, *Economic Survey;* official government publications of each country; U.S. Department of Commerce, *Country Commercial*

Guide, 2007–2009; Office of the U.S. Trade Representative, *2009 National Trade Estimate Report on Foreign Trade Barriers*; U.S. Department of State, *Investment Climate Statements 2009*; World Bank, *World Development Indicators 2009*; and various news and magazine articles on banking and finance.

FREEDOM #8: PROPERTY RIGHTS

The property rights component is an assessment of the ability of individuals to accumulate private property, secured by clear laws that are fully enforced by the state. It measures the degree to which a country's laws protect private property rights and the degree to which its government enforces those laws. It also assesses the likelihood that private property will be expropriated and analyzes the independence of the judiciary, the existence of corruption within the judiciary, and the ability of individuals and businesses to enforce contracts. The more certain the legal protection of property, the higher a country's score; similarly, the greater the chances of government expropriation of property, the lower a country's score. Countries that fall between two categories may receive an intermediate score.

Each country is graded according to the following criteria:

- **100**—Private property is guaranteed by the government. The court system enforces contracts efficiently and quickly. The justice system punishes those who unlawfully confiscate private property. There is no corruption or expropriation.
- **90**—Private property is guaranteed by the government. The court system enforces contracts efficiently. The justice system punishes those who unlawfully confiscate private property. Corruption is nearly nonexistent, and expropriation is highly unlikely.
- **80**—Private property is guaranteed by the government. The court system enforces contracts efficiently but with some delays. Corruption is minimal, and expropriation is highly unlikely.
- **70**—Private property is guaranteed by the government. The court system is subject to delays and is lax in enforcing contracts. Corruption is possible but rare, and expropriation is unlikely.
- **60**—Enforcement of property rights is lax and subject to delays. Corruption is possible but rare, and the judiciary may be influenced by other branches of government. Expropriation is unlikely.
- **50**—The court system is inefficient and subject to delays. Corruption may be present, and the judiciary may be influenced by other branches of government. Expropriation is possible but rare.
- **40**—The court system is highly inefficient, and delays are so long that they deter the use of the court system. Corruption is present, and the judiciary is influenced by other branches of government. Expropriation is possible.
- **30**—Property ownership is weakly protected. The court system is highly inefficient. Corruption is extensive, and the judiciary is strongly influenced by other branches of government. Expropriation is possible.
- **20**—Private property is weakly protected. The court system is so inefficient and corrupt that outside settlement and arbitration is the norm. Property rights are difficult to enforce. Judicial corruption is extensive. Expropriation is common.
- **10**—Private property is rarely protected, and almost all property belongs to the state. The country is in such chaos (for example, because of ongoing war) that protection of property is almost impossible to enforce. The judiciary is so corrupt that property is not protected effectively. Expropriation is common.
- **0**—Private property is outlawed, and all property belongs to the state. People do not have the right to sue others and do not have access to the courts. Corruption is endemic.

Sources. Unless otherwise noted, the *Index* relies on the following sources for information on property rights, in order of priority: Economist Intelligence Unit, *Country Profile, Country Report*, and *Country Commerce*, 2005–2009; U.S. Department of Commerce, *Country Commercial Guide*, 2005–2009; and U.S. Department of State, *Country Reports on Human Rights Practices*, 2005–2009 and various news and magazine articles.

FREEDOM #9: FREEDOM FROM CORRUPTION

Corruption erodes economic freedom by introducing insecurity and uncertainty into economic relationships. The score for this component is derived primarily from Transparency International's Corruption Perceptions Index (CPI) for 2008, which measures the level of corruption in 180 countries.

The CPI is based on a 10-point scale in which a score of 10 indicates very little corruption and a score of 0 indicates a very corrupt government. In scoring freedom from corruption, the *Index* converts the raw CPI data to a scale of 0 to 100 by multiplying the CPI score by 10. For example, if a country's raw CPI data score is 5.5, its overall freedom from corruption score is 55.

For countries that are not covered in the CPI, the freedom from corruption score is determined by using the qualitative information from internationally recognized and reliable sources.[5] This procedure considers the extent to which corruption prevails in a country. The higher the level of corruption, the lower the level of overall economic freedom and the lower a country's score.

Sources. Unless otherwise noted, the *Index* relies on the following sources for information on corrupt market activities, in order of priority: Transparency International, *Corruption Perceptions Index*, 2008; U.S. Department of Commerce, *Country Commercial Guide*, 2005–2009; Economist Intelligence Unit, *Country Commerce, Country Profile*, and *Country Report*, 2005–2009; Office of the U.S. Trade Representative, *2009 National Trade Estimate Report on Foreign Trade Barriers*; and official government publications of each country.

FREEDOM #10: LABOR FREEDOM

The labor freedom component is a quantitative measure that looks into various aspects of the legal and regulatory framework of a country's labor market. It provides cross-country data on regulations concerning minimum wages; laws inhibiting layoffs; severance requirements; and measurable regulatory burdens on hiring, hours, and so on.

Six quantitative factors are equally weighted, with each counted as one-sixth of the labor freedom component:[6]

- Ratio of minimum wage to the average value added per worker,
- Hindrance to hiring additional workers,
- Rigidity of hours,
- Difficulty of firing redundant employees,
- Legally mandated notice period, and
- Mandatory severance pay.

Based on data from the World Bank's *Doing Business* study, these factors specifically examine labor regulations that affect "the hiring and redundancy of workers and the rigidity of working hours."[7]

5. Five countries are not covered by the 2008 CPI: the Bahamas, Fiji, Liechtenstein, Micronesia, and North Korea.

6. The labor freedom assessment in the 2009 *Index* expanded its factors to six from the four used in previous editions. This refinement was applied equally to past editions' labor freedom scores to maintain consistency. The method for labor freedom assessment dates to the 2005 *Index* because of the limited availability of the quantitative data.

7. For more detailed information on the data, see "Employing Workers" in World Bank, *Doing Business*, at *http://www.doingbusiness.org/MethodologySurveys/EmployingWorkers.aspx.*

In constructing the labor freedom score, each of the six factors is converted to a scale of 0 to100 based on the following equation:

$$\text{Factor Score}_i = 50 \times \text{factor}_{average}/\text{factor}_i$$

where country i data are calculated relative to the world average and then multiplied by 50. The six factor scores are then averaged for each country, yielding a labor freedom score.

The simple average of the converted values for the six factors is computed for the country's overall labor freedom score. For example, even if a country has the worst rigidity of hours in the world with a zero score for that factor, it could still get a score as high as 83.3 based on the other five factors.

For the eight countries that are not covered by the World Bank's *Doing Business* study, the labor freedom component is scored by looking into labor market flexibility based on qualitative information from other reliable and internationally recognized sources.[8]

Sources. Unless otherwise noted, the *Index* relies on the following sources for data on labor freedom, in order of priority: World Bank, *Doing Business 2010*; Economist Intelligence Unit, *Country Report, Country Commerce*, and *Country Profile*, 2006–2009; U.S. Department of Commerce, *Country Commercial Guide*, 2006–2009; and official government publications of each country.

ASSESSING OVERALL ECONOMIC FREEDOM

Equal Weight. In the *Index of Economic Freedom*, the 10 components of economic freedom are equally weighted so that the overall score will not be biased toward any one component or policy direction. It is clear that the 10 economic freedoms interact, but the exact mechanisms of this interaction are not easily definable. Is a minimum threshold for each one essential? Is it possible for one to maximize if others are minimized? Are they dependent or exclusive, complements or supplements?

These are valid questions, but they are beyond the scope of our fundamental mission. The purpose of the *Index* is to reflect the economic environment in every country surveyed in as balanced a way as possible. The *Index* has never been designed specifically to explain economic growth or any other dependent variable; that is ably done by empirical econometricians elsewhere. The raw data for each component are provided so that others can study and weight and integrate as they see fit.

Period of Study. For the current *Index of Economic Freedom*, scores are generally based on data for the period covering the second half of 2008 through the first half of 2009. To the extent possible, the information considered for each factor was current as of June 30, 2009. It is important to understand, however, that some component scores are based on historical information. For example, the monetary freedom component is a three-year weighted average rate of inflation from January 1, 2006, to December 31, 2008.

CONTINUITY AND CHANGE

With over a decade of experience measuring economic freedom in over a hundred nations annually, we have found that two issues regularly challenge our methodology.

The first challenge has to do with outdated data. Country data in the most up-to-date sources are often several years old. Also, countries often make policy changes during the year of grading. Sometimes the policy changes are not reflected in official data, and sometimes the changes are proposed but not made law, or made law but not enforced. Additionally, a country can experience a violent conflict or catastrophe that interrupts all efforts to measure the economy.

The second challenge is the balance between quality and consistency of the *Index* itself. The benefit, for comparison purposes, of methodological consistency from one year to the next must

8. See note 3.

be balanced against opportunities to incorporate new data and methods that improve the quality of the current year's scores.

Each time a change in methodology is implemented, we also attempt to make the scores continuous back to 1995. In this way, country performance is comparable from one year to the next.

Nevertheless, there are still some cases for which new data are not available going back to the first year, at least not in the same level of detail. There is a natural tension between the quality of the *Index* and the continuity of the *Index*. It would be easy to maintain perfect continuity if no changes were ever made, or vice versa, but we are committed to incorporating innovations into the methodology to optimize both the quality and continuity of the *Index* rather than simply maximizing one at the expense of the other.

Using the Most Currently Available Information. Analyzing economic freedom annually enables the *Index* to include the most recent information as it becomes available country by country. A cutoff date is used so that all countries are treated fairly. As described above, the period of study for the current year's *Index* considers all information as of the last day of June of the previous year (June 30, 2009). Any new legislative changes or policy actions effective after that date have no positive or negative impact.

Occasionally, because the *Index* is published several months after the cutoff date for evaluation, recent economic events cannot be factored into the scores. In the past, such occurrences have been uncommon and isolated to one region of the world. The Asian financial crisis, for example, erupted at the end of 1997 just as the 1998 *Index* was going to print. The policy changes in response to that crisis, therefore, were not considered in that year's scoring, but they were included in the next year's scores. Similarly, this year, government policies implemented since mid-2009 have not affected the rankings for 2010.

Major Works Cited

The 2010 *Index of Economic Freedom* relies on data from multiple sources to provide a picture of economic freedom in each country that is as comprehensive, impartial, and accurate as possible. The following sources provided the primary information for analyzing and scoring the 10 components of economic freedom. In addition, the authors and analysts used supporting documentation and information from various government agencies and sites on the Internet, news reports and journal articles, and official responses to inquiries. All statistical and other information received from government sources was verified with independent, internationally recognized sources.

African Development Bank, *Selected Statistics on African Countries 2008*, Macroeconomic Indicators, Table 32—Government Finances; available at *http://www.afdb.org/fileadmin/uploads/afdb/Documents/Publications/Selected_Statistics_African_Countries_2008_Volume_XXVII_01_Full_Report.pdf*.

African Development Bank and Organisation for Economic Co-operation and Development, *African Economic Outlook 2009*; available at *http://www.oecd.org/document/59/0,3343,en_2649_15162846_42689915_1_1_1_1,00.html* or *http://www.africaneconomicoutlook.org/en*.

Asian Development Bank, *Asian Development Outlook 2009: Rebalancing Asia's Growth*; available at *http://www.adb.org/Documents/Books/ADO/2009*.

————, *Key Indicators for Asia and the Pacific 2009*; available at *http://www.adb.org/documents/books/key_indicators/2009/default.asp*.

Country statistical agencies, central banks, and ministries of finance, economy, and trade; available at *http://unstats.un.org/unsd/methods/inter-natlinks/sd_natstat.asp*; *http://www.census.gov/aboutus/stat_int.html*; and *http://www.bis.org/cbanks.htm*.

Deloitte, International Tax and Business Guide, *Country Highlights*; available at *http://www.deloitte.com/view/en_PG/pg/insights-ideas/itbg/index.htm*.

———, direct correspondence with Country Office.

Economist Intelligence Unit, Ltd., *Country Commerce*, London, U.K., 2007–2009.

———, *Country Finance*, London, U.K., 2007–2009.

———, *Country Profile*, London, U.K., 2007–2008.

———, *Country Report*, London, U.K., 2007–2009.

European Bank for Reconstruction and Development, *Country Strategies*, 2007–2009; available at *http://www.ebrd.org/pubs/cs/country.htm*.

European Commission, Eurostat, *European Statistics*, 2009; available at *http://epp.eurostat.ec.europa.eu/portal/page/portal/statistics/themes*.

———, *Statistics in Focus: Tax Revenue in the European Union*, 2009; available at *http://epp.eurostat.ec.europa.eu/cache/ITY_OFFPUB/KS-SF-09-043/EN/KS-SF-09-043-EN.PDF*.

FedEx, International Resource Center, Country Profiles, 2009; available at *http://fedex.com/us/international/irc/profiles/?link=2*.

International Monetary Fund, *Annual Report on Exchange Arrangements and Exchange Restrictions, 2007*, Washington, D.C., September 2007.

———, *Article IV Consultation Staff Reports*, various countries, Washington, D.C., 2007–2009; available at *http://www.imf.org/external/ns/cs.aspx?id=51*.

———, *Country Information*; available at *http://www.imf.org/external/country/index.htm*.

———, *Regional Economic Outlook Reports, 2009*; available at *http://www.imf.org/external/pubs/ft/reo/reorepts.aspx*.

———, *Selected Issues and Statistical Appendix*, various countries, Washington, D.C., 2002–2008.

———, World Economic and Financial Surveys, World Economic Outlook Database, April 2009; available at *http://www.imf.org/external/pubs/ft/weo/2009/01/weodata/index.aspx*.

Low Tax Network, various countries; available at *http://www.lowtax.net*.

Organisation for Economic Co-operation and Development, *OECD Economic Outlook*, No. 85 (June 2009); available at *http://www.oecd.org/document/18/0,3343,en_2649_34109_20347538_1_1_1_1,00.html*.

———, *OECD Factbook 2009: Economic, Environmental and Social Statistics*; available at *http://lysander.sourceoecd.org/vl=2265723/cl=16/nw=1/rpsv/factbook2009/index.htm*.

———, *OECD Statistics Portal*; available at *http://www.oecd.org/statsportal/0,3352,en_2825_293 564_1_1_1_1_1,00.html*.

———, OECD Web site; available at *www.oecd.org/home*.

PricewaterhouseCoopers, *Worldwide Tax Summaries*, 2007–2009; available with registration at *http://www.taxsummaries.pwc.com/uk/wwts/wwts.nsf*.

Transparency International, *The Corruption Perceptions Index*, Berlin, Germany, 1999–2008; available at *http://www.transparency.org/policy_research/surveys_indices/cpi*.

UK Trade and Investment, Countries Listing; available at *https://www.uktradeinvest.gov.uk/ukti/appmanager/ukti/countries?_nfls=false&_nfpb=true&_pageLabel=countries_landing*.

———, "Inward FDI Flows, by Host Region and Economy, 1970–2007," Annex Table, in *World Investment Report, 2008*; available at *http://www.unctad.org/sections/dite_dir/docs/wir2008_inflows_en.xls*.

United States Central Intelligence Agency, *The World Factbook 2009*; available at *https://www.cia.gov/library/publications/the-world-factbook/index.html*.

United States Department of Commerce, *Country Commercial Guides*, Washington, D.C., 2005–2009; available at *http://www.buyusainfo.net/adsearch.cfm?search_type=int&loadnav=no*.

United States Department of State, *Country Reports on Human Rights Practices for 2008*, released by the Bureau of Democracy, Human Rights, and Labor, February 2009; available at *http://www.state.gov/g/drl/rls/hrrpt/2008*.

————, *Investment Climate Statements: 2007–2009*, released by the Bureau of Economic, Energy and Business Affairs; available at *http://www.state.gov/e/eeb/rls/othr/ics/2009/index.htm*.

United States Trade Representative, Office of the, *2009 National Trade Estimate Report on Foreign Trade Barriers*, Washington, D.C., 2009; available at *http://www.ustr.gov/about-us/press-office/reports-and-publications/2009/2009-national-trade-estimate-report-foreign-trad*.

World Bank, *World Bank World Development Indicators Online*, Washington, D.C., 2009; available by subscription at *http://publications.worldbank.org/WDI*.

————, *Country Briefs and Trade-at-a-Glance (TAAG) Tables*, Washington, D.C., 2008; available at *http://info.worldbank.org/etools/wti2008/docs/Brieftaags.htm*.

————, *Doing Business*, 2005–2010; available at *www.doingbusiness.org*.

World Trade Organization, *Trade Policy Reviews*, 1995–2009; available at *http://www.wto.org/english/tratop_e/tpr_e/tpr_e.htm*.